Principles of Microeconomics

SECOND EDITION

Principles of Microeconomics

SECOND EDITION

Roger Chisholm
Memphis State University

Marilu McCarty
Georgia Institute of Technology

Scott, Foresman and Company
Glenview, Illinois

Dallas, Texas Oakland, New Jersey Palo Alto, California
Tucker, Georgia London, England

Photograph Acknowledgments

Lawrence Klein: Courtesy Lawrence Klein.
Karl Marx: Brown Brothers.
William Stanley Jevons: BBC Hulton Picture Library.
Alfred Marshall: Historical Pictures Service, Inc., Chicago.
Thorstein Veblen: Brown Brothers.
Paul Sweezy: Courtesy *Monthly Review Press.*
Joan Robinson: Ramsey & Muspratt, Cambridge.
Andrew Carnegie: Brown Brothers.
John Kenneth Galbraith: Wide World.
George Stigler: Courtesy University of Chicago.
Lillian Gilbreth: United Press International.
Frank Knight: Courtesy University of Chicago.
Arthur Okun: Courtesy The Brookings Institute.
Kenneth Arrow: United Press International.

Library of Congress Cataloging in Publication Data

Chisholm, Roger K
Principles of microeconomics.

Also issued in a combined ed. with Principles of macroeconomics under title: Principles of economics.
Includes index.
1. Microeconomics. I. McCarty, Marilu Hurt, joint author. II. Title.
HB171.5C629 1981 330 80-26407
ISBN 0-673-15402-5

3 4 5 6—RRW—85 84 83 82

Preface

This text is intended for the one-semester principles of microeconomics course. Therefore, it is written for the student encountering economics for the first time. The "usual" subject matter of the first course is treated in a complete and detailed manner. However, this book is not an encyclopedia of economic topics or a grab bag offering far more than any instructor can cover. Fewer topics are covered but they are the core topics and they are explored in depth. Stressing a balance between economic theory and real-world examples, chapters are often a couple of pages longer than those found in other texts.

We have paid particular attention to the writing style and level. Chapters were reworked and polished many times to improve clarity and relevance. The terminology is that of the economist while the language is that of the economic journalist. Thus the writing style is like that found in *Business Week, The New York Times,* or *The Wall Street Journal.* The book speaks to today's students in a lively, colloquial fashion without emphasizing slang or adopting other overly cute devices. We hope that such language, besides facilitating learning, will convey the excitement of current economics.

An economics course should be, for most students, one of their most exciting and relevant courses. We believe this text will fulfill this goal.

The general organization of the text is fairly traditional. An introductory section of four chapters is followed by the microeconomic chapters.

SPECIAL FEATURES

Much effort was directed toward juxtaposing real-world examples and problems with economic theory and ideas. Three basic issues inserts were employed: Extended Examples, Viewpoints, and Economic Thinkers.

The Extended Examples are just what the title says; each explores a significant topic from the real world in greater depth and shows how it is an example of economic theory in action. In the chapter on monopoly, there is an Extended Example on monopoly in shopping malls. This example describes how exclusionary agreements are sometimes used to ensure profit for initial tenants in shopping malls.

The Viewpoints deal with economic controversies and with many of the unsolved economic problems of our times. Quite literally, the Viewpoints are taken from the headlines of newspapers and magazines. The Viewpoints enable students to apply the theory they have just learned. In fact, many of the Viewpoints challenge students to defend or disagree with the argument. The chapter on the government's role in the economy has a Viewpoint on the value-added tax; the issue of whether VAT is a better system than ours is discussed, with arguments for and against.

Our third issues insert is the Economic Thinkers, biographies of great economists. Actually, biographical data are limited to one or two paragraphs. Most of the biography deals with the important economic ideas contributed by that thinker. Some of our Economic Thinkers are Galbraith, Marx, Veblen, Marshall, Lawrence Klein, Kenneth Arrow, Joan Robinson—the list goes on and on.

The average length of these issues inserts is two text columns, or one full page. Thus these issues are not intended as diversions; they provide some real "meat" for students.

Other useful pedagogical tools are included. Each chapter starts with learning objectives. At the end of each chapter is a summary, a key words and phrases list, and questions for review. The key words and phrases are actually glossaries of all new terms in that chapter. In the interests of "pedagogical repetition," some terms appear in more than one glossary.

The Instructor's Manual provides suggestions for readings from popular magazines for both the students and teacher.

TOPICS OF NOTE

The chapters on consumer demand (Chapters 5–7) carefully develop fundamental concepts necessary for complete understanding of a wide range of economic principles. Marginal relationships, elasticity, and substitution and income effects receive extended verbal, mathematical, and graphical treatment. These and the following chapter on supply theory amplify fundamental concepts through application to current economic issues: productivity and government policies, expectations and incentives, taxes and subsidies.

Separate explorations of short- and long-run production theory (Chapters 8–9) give particular emphasis to the character and function of profit in making decisions. Important issues include corporate accountability, corporate democracy, efficient scale, innovation and adjustment to change, external economies and diseconomies, and price fluctuations in agriculture (the cobweb theorem).

Imperfect competition (Chapters 10–12) is critically examined as to its causes and consequences, with emphasis on considerations of equity and efficiency. The question of market power and regulation is explored in depth, along with the issues of price discrimination and social externalities. The treatment of theory is rigorous and the language is precise.

Chapters on resource employment and income distribution (Chapters 13–16) have been expanded and reorganized to focus separately on marginal productivity theory, work and labor resources, land and rent, capital employment and profits, and the problem of poverty. Modern production theory is integrated with the historical evolution of philosophies of and policies toward resource markets. Some significant issues have been added, including worker fringe benefits, labor-management cooperation to increase productivity, human capital investment, the diminishing supply of farmland, and the effects of discrimination in education.

The next to last part of the text (Chapters 17–19) takes an entirely new look at economic theory in a socio-political context. Market failure and public choice are discussed at some length. The actual results of market behavior are shown to differ significantly from the efficient and equitable results reached in theory. Proposed remedies from both ends of the political spectrum are examined in detail. Theory and policy considerations are then discussed fully in specific sectors of market failure: the health-care industry, energy, and environmental health and safety. Chapter 19 covers alternative economic systems, emphasizing socialist thought, the various roles of planning, and the ways in which all economic systems can be compared.

The two chapters on international economics (Chapters 20–21) stress basic theory and its application to current problems and policies. These chapters discuss changing terms of trade, the North-South dilemma, pressures for protection, responses to competition, and exporting technology.

ACKNOWLEDGMENTS

Naturally, such a major undertaking as writing a basic economics text leaves the authors in debt to many people. First there is the intellectual debt to many economists and other mentors, some of whom the authors have never met. Then there are the many students whose comments and complaints shape the authors' teaching of the course.

We would particularly like to thank the following professors who offered constructive comments on the manuscript:

Abraham Bertisch, Nassau C.C.
Donna Bialik, Indiana University—
Purdue University (Ft. Wayne)

Donald Coffin, Indiana University—
Purdue University (Indianapolis)
Loy Despain, Mesa Community College
Steven Erickson, Purdue University
Margaret Greenbaum, Northwestern University
James Johannes, Michigan State University
Robert Kenney, Miami-Dade C.C.
Margaret Moore, Franklin University
Athanasius Njoku, Benedict College
Pierce Nolan, El Paso C.C.
Rheyburn Nolan, Tyler Junior College
Sam Parigi, Lamar University
Stephen Renas, Wright State University
Dorothy Sanford, College of Notre Dame
Basil Zimmer, Central Michigan University

Author Chisholm would like to give special thanks to his wife, Jean, and his three daughters, Margaret, Janet, and Elizabeth, who have now endured the preparation of two editions of this book.

Roger K. Chisholm
Marilu H. McCarty

Contents

PART 1
An Introduction to Economics 1

1 What Is Economics? 2

What Economists Do 2
EXTENDED EXAMPLE The Economics of Housing 3
Economics as a Course of Study 4
Microeconomics and Macroeconomics
Economics as a Science 5
The Scientific Method / Economic Models / Positive and Normative Sciences / Try to Keep Cool / Some Traps to Avoid
ECONOMIC THINKERS The Model Builders 8
VIEWPOINT Economics and Politics 10
Criteria for Evaluating an Economic System 12
VIEWPOINT Reverse Discrimination? 13
Issues We Face 14
Summary 14
Key Words and Phrases 14
Questions for Review 15

APPENDIX
Using Graphs 16
Time-Series Graphs / Functional Graphs / Key Words and Phrases

2 The Economic Problem 19

Managing in a World of Scarcity 20
Kinds of Resources 20
Land / Labor / Capital / Entrepreneurship
Production Possibilities 22
Graphing Production / Opportunity Cost / The Law of Increasing Costs / Unemployment of Resources / Overemployment and Inflation / Changes in Production Possibilities
EXTENDED EXAMPLE Western Land Use Vs. Waste 24
VIEWPOINT The Opportunity Costs of R and D 28
Choosing Production 29
Specialization / Guns Vs. Butter / Private Vs. Public Consumption / Work Vs. Play
How Is the Choice Made? 31
The Four Questions
Types of Economic Systems 33
Traditional Economies / Command Economies / Market Economies
EXTENDED EXAMPLE To Work or Not to Work 33
ECONOMIC THINKER Karl Marx 35
Summary 37
Key Words and Phrases 37
Questions for Review 38

3 The Free Market: Supply and Demand 39

The Market: Some Dimensions 39

Beginnings: Adam Smith 40

Demand 41

Law of Demand / Graphing Demand / Changes in Demand / Changes in Demand Vs. Changes in Quantity Demanded

Supply 44

Law of Supply / Changes in Supply / Changes in Supply Vs. Changes in Quantity Supplied

Market Equilibrium 47

Changes in Supply and Demand / Expectations Can Make It So / The Search for Equilibrium

EXTENDED EXAMPLE Market for Commodities 50

Functions of the Price System 51

The Rationing Function / The Incentive Function / What Goods Will Be Produced / How Goods Will Be Produced / Who Will Get the Output / When Goods Will Be Enjoyed

The Market System: Pros and Cons 53

Advantages of the Market System / Disadvantages of the Market System

VIEWPOINT Should the Free Market Prevail? 54

Summary 55

Key Words and Phrases 55

Questions for Review 56

4 Government's Role in the Economy 58

Economic Functions of Government 59

Protect Private Property / Regulate Money / Allocate Public Goods and Services / Assess Social Costs / Regulate and Maintain Competition / Promote Economic Stability / Fight Poverty / Eliminate Discrimination

VIEWPOINT Government and the Free Market 63

Levels of Government 64

Government Outlays 65

State and Local Government / Federal Government

Government Taxation Policies 68

State and Local Government Taxation / Regressive Taxes and State and Local Government / Federal Government Taxation

Progressive Nature of Federal Income Taxes and State and Local Government 71

Advantages and Disadvantages of Progressive Taxes / Social Security Taxes

VIEWPOINT The Value-Added Tax 73

Evaluating Our Tax Structure 74

Summary 75

Key Words and Phrases 75

Questions for Review 76

PART 2
Consumer Behavior and Elasticity 77

5 Consumer Demand and Utility 78

The Demand for Goods and Services 79

Characteristics / Choice of Characteristics

The Utility of Goods and Services 80

Marginal Utility / Total Utility / Graphing Utility / Summing Up

Marginal Utility and Consumer Demand 83

The Demand Curve / Using Marginal Utility of Money to Plot Demand

VIEWPOINT Precision and Utility Analysis 84

EXTENDED EXAMPLE Marginal Utility and Income Taxes 86

Marginal Utility and Consumer's Surplus 88

Using Marginal Utility: Some Applications 89

ECONOMIC THINKER William Stanley Jevons 90

Summary 91

Key Words and Phrases 91

Questions for Review 91

APPENDIX
Another Explanation of Consumer Demand: Indifference Curves 92

A Consumer's Indifference Schedule / Graphing a Consumer's Indifference Schedule / Characteristics of Indifference Curves / The Consumer's Budget / Drawing the Consumer's Demand Curve / Changes in a Consumer's Income / Other Types of Indifference Curves / The Consumer's Budget and Substitutes or Complements / Some Applications of Indifference Curve Analysis

6 Measuring and Using Elasticity of Demand 101

The Demand Curve Again 102
The Substitution Effect / The Income Effect / The Influence of Income and Substitution Effects

Elasticity of Demand 103
The Interpretation of Elasticity / Special Kinds of Demand Curves

EXTENDED EXAMPLE Calculating Elasticity 104

Elasticity of Demand and a Firm's Revenue 107
Total Revenue / Marginal Revenue / Changing Elasticity to Increase Total Revenue / Revenue Problems in Agriculture

EXTENDED EXAMPLE Elasticity and Parking Fees 107

Elasticity of Demand: Some Special Features 111
What Determines Elasticity? / Income Elasticity of Demand / Cross Elasticity of Demand

EXTENDED EXAMPLE Monkey Business 112

EXTENDED EXAMPLE Loss Leaders in Retail Stores 114

EXTENDED EXAMPLE Cross Elasticity and the Law 116

Summary 115
Key Words and Phrases 116
Questions for Review 117

APPENDIX
Elasticity and Indifference Curves 118
Price Elasticity and the Price-Consumption Line / Income Elasticity and the Income-Consumption Line

7 Supply Elasticity and Government Policy 121

Supply Curves: A Review 121

Elasticity of Supply 122
Perfect Inelasticity / Infinite Elasticity / Elastic and Inelastic Supply Curves

EXTENDED EXAMPLE Calculating Elasticity of Supply 123

What Determines Elasticity of Supply? 124
Time / Technology / Expectations

EXTENDED EXAMPLE The Green Revolution 126

Market Equilibrium 127

Government in the Market 128
Elasticity and Taxes / Specific and Ad Valorem Taxes / Who Pays the Tax? / Taxes and Disincentives / Subsidies

EXTENDED EXAMPLE Taxes on Imports: The Case of Oil 132

When Government Sets Prices 133
Price Ceilings and Shortages / Price Floors and Surpluses / Price Fixing and Elasticity

VIEWPOINT Rent Control 134

Agriculture and Supply Elasticity 136

EXTENDED EXAMPLE Peanuts and Price Supports 137

EXTENDED EXAMPLE Trouble in Poland 139

Summary 138
Key Words and Phrases 140
Questions for Review 140

APPENDIX
Problems in Agriculture 141

PART 3
Costs of Production and Product Markets 147

8 Perfect Competition: Costs and Production Decisions in the Short Run 148

Businesses 148
The Business Hierarchy / Business Organization

VIEWPOINT Corporate Behavior 151

Perfect Competition 152
Four Basic Conditions / Putting the Conditions Together / Demand Curves in Perfect Competition

Measuring Costs of Production 154
Accounting Costs: The Bottom Line / Economic Costs: Efficient Resource Allocation / The Costs of College, Strawberries, and Other Things / Defining Profit

Resources in the Short Run 157

Production Decisions in the Short Run 157
Principle of Diminishing Marginal Product / Total, Marginal, and Average Product

EXTENDED EXAMPLE Decision Making at the Margin 158

Costs in the Short Run 161
Total Costs / Average or Unit Costs / Marginal Costs / Cost Data Summary

EXTENDED EXAMPLE Production Costs in the Food Industry 164

Profit Maximization in the Short Run 165
Costs, Revenue, and Profit / Average Cost and Average Revenue / Making Production Decisions at the Margin

Economic Profit and Short-Run Decisions 169
Measuring Economic Profit / Losses in the Short Run / Shut-Down Point in the Short Run / Equilibrium in the Short Run

ECONOMIC THINKER Alfred Marshall 171

Business Accounting 172
The Income and Expense Statement / The Balance Sheet

Summary 174
Key Words and Phrases 175
Questions for Review 176

APPENDIX
Isoquants and Isocosts 177
Isoquants / Isocosts

9 Perfect Competition: Costs and Production Decisions in the Long Run 182

Long-Run Competitive Equilibrium 183

Plant Size and the Long Run 185
Economies of Large Scale / Diseconomies of Large Scale / Plant Size and Optimum Scale / The Long-Run Planning Curve

EXTENDED EXAMPLE The Bicycle Boom 186

EXTENDED EXAMPLE The End of the Short Run 189

Profit Maximization in the Long Run 190
How Realistic Is This View of the Long Run? / Competitive Equilibrium: A Standard of Efficiency / What Determines the Number of Firms?

EXTENDED EXAMPLE Market Changes in the Long Run 191

EXTENDED EXAMPLE Sugar Elasticity and the Long Run 193

Industry Growth and Changing Costs 194
External Economies in the Very Long Run / External Diseconomies in the Very Long Run / Social Economies and Diseconomies / Internalizing Externalities

EXTENDED EXAMPLE Franchises and Ray Kroc's Burger Stand 195

Summary 199
Key Words and Phrases 200
Questions for Review 200

APPENDIX
The Cobweb Theorem of Agricultural Prices 201

10 Monopoly 204

Efficiency and Equity 204

Defining Monopoly 205
Characteristics of Monopoly / Methods of Monopoly

ECONOMIC THINKER Thorstein Veblen 207

EXTENDED EXAMPLE Monopoly in Dolls 209

Decision Making by the Monopolist 210
The Monopolist's Demand Curve / The Monopolist's Cost Curves / Economic Profit for the Monopolist / Elasticity Again / Price Discrimination

EXTENDED EXAMPLE Shopping Malls and Monopoly 213

VIEWPOINT Do Monopolies Really Maximize Economic Profits? 215

Shortcomings of Monopoly 217
Inefficiency of Monopoly / Inequities of Monopoly

ECONOMIC THINKER Paul Sweezy 218

Government and Monopolies 219
Government Regulation of Monopolies / Regulated Prices / Subsidies / Government Monopolies

EXTENDED EXAMPLE Price Discrimination by a Regulated Monopoly 220

VIEWPOINT Regulation or Strangulation? 222

VIEWPOINT The U.S. Postal Service 224

Summary 225
Key Words and Phrases 226
Questions for Review 226

11 Imperfect Competition: Monopolistic Competition and Oligopoly 227

Monopolistic Competition 228
Demand Curves in Monopolistic Competition / Costs in Monopolistic Competition / Long-Run Equilibrium in Monopolistic Competition

ECONOMIC THINKER Joan Robinson 229

EXTENDED EXAMPLE How to Be Successful in Monopolistic Competition 230

Shortcomings of Monopolistic Competition 232
Efficiency / Equity

EXTENDED EXAMPLE Monopolistic Competition in Ladies' Apparel 233

Oligopoly 234
Price and Output in Oligopoly / Duopoly / Price Rigidity and Kinked Demand Curves / Price Leadership / Mark-Up Pricing / Cartels / The Payoff Matrix / Other Approaches to Pricing

EXTENDED EXAMPLE Oligopoly in Chips? 235

EXTENDED EXAMPLE Concentration in the Aluminum Industry 238

EXTENDED EXAMPLE The Rent-a-Car War 240

Nonprice Competition 241
Advertising / Trademarks / Differentiated and Undifferentiated Oligopoly / Positioning

EXTENDED EXAMPLE Advertising as a Factor of Production 242

EXTENDED EXAMPLE How Sacred Is a Trademark? 244

Pros and Cons of Oligopoly 245
Efficiency / Equity

Summary 246
Key Words and Phrases 246
Questions for Review 246

12 Market Power and Public Policy 248

Our Contradictory Attitudes 248

The First Great Merger Movement 249
Horizontal Mergers / Vertical Mergers / Holding Companies

Antimerger Legislation 251
The Sherman Antitrust Act / The Clayton Antitrust Act / The Federal Trade Commission

EXTENDED EXAMPLE Giant of the Steel Industry 252

The Second Great Merger Movement 254
The Great Depression Antitrust Action / Post-World War II Antitrust Activity

EXTENDED EXAMPLE Menace at the Breakfast Table 255

The Third Great Merger Movement 257
Conglomerate Mergers / The Goliaths / Attacking the Conglomerates / The Changing Philosophy of Antitrust

EXTENDED EXAMPLE Merger Strategy in Japan 258

VIEWPOINT Antitrust in the Oil Industry 259

Regulation to Curb Market Power 261
The Interstate Commerce Commission / Inherent Weaknesses of Regulation

VIEWPOINT Advertising in the Professions 261

The Debate Over Bigness 263
Measuring Concentration / Trends in Concentration / Bigness Defended / Living with Bigness / Bigness Opposed

EXTENDED EXAMPLE The Little Engine That Could? 263

VIEWPOINT How Big Does a Company Have to Be? 266

ECONOMIC THINKER John Kenneth Galbraith 267

ECONOMIC THINKER George Stigler 269

Summary 270
Key Words and Phrases 271
Questions for Review 271

PART 4
Resource Markets 273

13 The Marginal Productivity Theory of Resource Allocation 274

Resource Allocation: The Background 274

The Theory of Marginal Productivity 276
Resource Demand in Perfect Competition / Marginal Revenue Product / Demand Curve for Resources

Market Demand for Resources 278
Determinants of Demand / Elasticity of Demand for Resources / Demand Under Imperfect Competition

EXTENDED EXAMPLE Trends in Productivity 280

Hiring Resources for Maximum Profit 283

Hiring More Than One Variable Resource

ECONOMIC THINKERS Frank and Lillian Gilbreth 283

Resource Supply 286

What Determines the Equilibrium Price of Resources? / Government Subsidies for Resource Development / Taxes to Discourage Resource Use

Earnings of Resource Suppliers 288

Determining Incomes / Marginal Revenue Productivity and Incomes / Changes in Resource Prices over Time / The Politics of Elasticity

Summary 291

Key Words and Phrases 292

Questions for Review 292

14 Employing Labor Resources: Unions, Work, and Wages 293

Labor Unions 294

A Brief History / Union Activity / Trends in Union Membership / Public Employee Unions / Labor Issues for the 1980s

EXTENDED EXAMPLE Labor/Management Cooperation to Increase Productivity 296

EXTENDED EXAMPLE COLAs and Inflation 299

EXTENDED EXAMPLE Fringe Benefits 300

The Market for Labor: Labor Supply 301

Work Vs. Leisure / Backward-Bending Supply Curves

Labor Demand and Equilibrium in the Labor Market 303

The Productivity of Labor / Wage Determination in Labor Markets

EXTENDED EXAMPLE Minimum Wage Laws 304

VIEWPOINT Worker Mobility Across Borders 306

EXTENDED EXAMPLE Efficiency in the Military 309

Summary 311

Key Words and Phrases 311

Questions for Review 312

15 Employing Land, Capital, and Entrepreneurial Resources 313

Land: The Theory of Rent 314

Alternative Uses for Land / A Tax on Land / The Rental Component of Wages

VIEWPOINT Speculating in Urban Land 315

EXTENDED EXAMPLE The Diminishing Supply of Farmland 318

Capital: The Theory of Interest 318

Saving and Investment / The Demand for Investment Funds: Capital Budgeting / Investments Lasting More Than One Year / Nominal and Real Interest Rates / Tax Credits / The Supply of Investment Funds: Savings / Financial Markets / Efficiency in Financial Markets

EXTENDED EXAMPLE Capital and Growth 326

Entrepreneurship: The Theory of Profit 327

Functions of Profit / Building Human Capital

EXTENDED EXAMPLE Profits 329

ECONOMIC THINKER Frank Knight 330

Resource Pricing and Income Distribution 331

Summary 332

Key Words and Phrases 332

Questions for Review 333

16 Poverty, Discrimination, and Public Assistance 334

Defining Poverty 334

Who Are the Poor? / Aiding the Poor / New Approaches

EXTENDED EXAMPLE Lyndon Johnson's War on Poverty 338

VIEWPOINT Can Poverty Be Abolished? 340

EXTENDED EXAMPLE An Island in Kentucky 341

Discrimination 344

Racial Discrimination / Sex Discrimination / Dual Markets / Government Policies Against Discrimination

EXTENDED EXAMPLE Women in the Labor Market 345

Inequality 347

Urban Poverty and Crisis 349
Urban Finance: Tax Revenues / Urban Finance: Expenditures / The Three E's / The Three E's and Urban Problems / The Cost of Poverty

ECONOMIC THINKER Arthur Okun 350

Summary 354
Key Words and Phrases 354
Questions for Review 355

PART 5
Market Failure: Problems and Responses 357

17 Market Failure and Public Choice 358

Decision Making in Perfect Competition 358

Why Markets Fail 360

Dealing with Market Failure 360
Welfare Economics / Public Choice Economics

ECONOMIC THINKER Kenneth Arrow 363

Measuring the Costs of Government Regulatory Policies 367
Direct Cost / Indirect Cost / Induced Cost

A Final Word 369

EXTENDED EXAMPLE Regulation Benefits 369

Summary 370
Key Words and Phrases 370
Questions for Review 370

18 Market Failure: Health Care, Energy, and Environmental Protection 371

The Health-Care Industry 371
Medicare and Medicaid / Market Supply / Proposed Government Programs / Market Incentive Programs

EXTENDED EXAMPLE The American Medical Association 374

Energy 377
Present Policies: Price Controls / Should We Decontrol Prices? / Backward-Bending Supply / Windfall-Profits Taxes / Alternative Energy Supplies / Some Energy Recommendations

EXTENDED EXAMPLE Health Hazards from Electric Power Generation 382

Environmental Health and Safety 384
Atmospheric Pollution / Water Pollution / Land Reclamation / Consumer Product Safety / Employee Health and Safety / Environmental Policies / Results of Environmental Policies

EXTENDED EXAMPLE Tanstaafl and the Environment 388

EXTENDED EXAMPLE The Economics of Georges Bank 389

Some Final Remarks on Trade-offs 390

Summary 390
Key Words and Phrases 391
Questions for Review 391

19 Alternative Economic Systems 393

The Role of Karl Marx 394
Direct and Indirect Labor / Constant and Variable Capital / Surplus Value / Alienation and Exploitation / The Eventual Decline of Capitalism / Marxism Updated

Basic Characteristics of Economic Systems 396
Ownership and Property Rights / Role of Labor / Degree of Centralization / Market Allocation or Economic Planning? / Incentives

Economic Planning 400
The Task of Planning / Setting Goals with the Material Balance Approach / Economic Accounting and Financial Planning / Planning Problems / Judging Economic Planning / Indicative Planning

The Soviet Economy 404
Labor / Agriculture / Growth / Prices and Taxes / Inflation / The Role of the Free Market / International Trade / The Future

EXTENDED EXAMPLE Work in the Factory 405

EXTENDED EXAMPLE Consuming and Selling in the Soviet Union 407

Yugoslavia 409
Industrial Organization / Labor / The Future

Summary 410
Key Words and Phrases 411
Questions for Review 412

PART 6
International Economics 413

20 International Trade 414

Beginnings of Trade 415

The Pure Theory of International Trade 415

Micro Aspects of International Trade 417
How Will International Trade Affect Price and Quantity? / What Are the Benefits of Specialization? / How Will International Trade Affect Incomes?

Macro Aspects of International Trade 419
National Income and Trade / The Foreign Trade Multiplier / Resource Allocation

Production Possibilities and Absolute Advantage 422
Comparing Productivity / The Principle of Absolute Advantage / Absolute Advantage of Individuals and Among Nations

Comparative Advantage 425
Opportunity Costs / Combined Production Possibilities / The Rate of Exchange on Traded Goods / Changing Terms of Trade and National Power

EXTENDED EXAMPLE Changing Terms of Trade 429

VIEWPOINT The North-South Dilemma 430

Summary 431
Key Words and Phrases 431
Questions for Review 431

21 International Commercial Policies and Institutions 433

Policies to Protect Domestic Industries 433
Tariffs / Other Barriers to Trade / Efforts to Eliminate Trade Restrictions / Trade and Long-Run Economic Growth

EXTENDED EXAMPLE Pressure for Protection 438

EXTENDED EXAMPLE Exporting Technology 441

EXTENDED EXAMPLE Responding to Import Competition 442

Institutions for International Cooperation 443
International Credit Organizations / Intraregional Trading Organizations

EXTENDED EXAMPLE Aid for Developing Nations 444

International Capital Movements 445
Eurodollars / Multinational Corporations

Summary 447
Key Words and Phrases 447
Questions for Review 447

Index 449

Principles of Microeconomics

SECOND EDITION

PART 1

An Introduction to Economics

1 What Is Economics?

2 The Economic Problem

3 The Free Market: Supply and Demand

4 Government's Role in the Economy

CHAPTER 1

What Is Economics?

Learning Objectives

Upon completion of this chapter, you should be able to

1. Define economics and indicate how it is related to (and different from) physical sciences and social sciences.
2. Explain why models are important and how economists use them.
3. Distinguish between a positive and a normative science.
4. Explain at least two types of "bad thinking" economists try to avoid.
5. Indicate the criteria economists use to evaluate an economic system.

Economics has been defined as the study of how human beings satisfy their material needs and wants. That isn't a complete definition, as we will see, but it will do for a beginning. We study economics for a number of reasons. Most of us want to know how we can live better next year than we live now. We want to know the types and numbers of jobs that will be available to us. We want to know how we can spend our incomes for the greatest satisfaction. Perhaps we also want to know what the needs of our business will be and how the business can best prepare to meet those needs.

As citizens we want to know how our community will grow and how we can contribute to and benefit from that growth. Our nation's growth and strength are important to us, too, as is the future of the human race. As voters we are concerned about our nation's economic policies: What policies will deal effectively with the problems of inflation, unemployment, and poverty? What taxes are appropriate, and how should the tax burden be shared? Should government spend more than it receives? Should we erect barriers to keep out foreign goods that compete with goods made here? Should we have a minimum wage law? These are only a few of the economic questions that concern us.

WHAT ECONOMISTS DO

Most of these questions are not new. In fact, for hundreds of years people have looked for answers to questions like these. *The study of economics developed to explore alternatives, to measure*

Extended Example The Economics of Housing

Economists are concerned with the social environment: how people live together and arrangements that can help them live better. Economists observe changes in the attitudes and habits of people and try to explain how these changes affect the economic life of the community. If a definite trend can be identified, the economist may project future problems and opportunities. Plans can be drawn up to deal with future possibilities, and predictions can be made about the outcome of various policies. We can better understand how economists affect our lives by examining just one part of the economy: the housing industry.

Everyone must have a place to live, so it is important that enough dwellings be produced. Nevertheless, most of us have a rather limited view of housing. We say to ourselves: "I have always lived in a house; all my friends for miles around have houses; when the time comes, I too will have a house." The future may indeed unfold in this manner. But ensuring that housing supply meets future demand by type and quantity is not always automatic. In fact, in the mid-1970s there was a shortage of houses and, in some areas, of apartments, too. What will happen in the housing industry tomorrow? Will there be enough housing to meet everyone's wants? How does the housing industry affect the rest of the economy?

Certain changes have been taking place in our social environment that will have a major impact on the housing industry in coming decades. One important change involves population growth. Changing trends in population growth will affect the number and kinds of new housing needed in the 1980s and 1990s. Back in the 1950s, the average couple produced 3.8 children. But the fast population growth of that period has now leveled off. Today we are approaching *zero population growth,* with only 1.8 children for the average couple of the 1970s.

The post–World War II baby boom from the late 1940s through the 1950s created a population "bulge" which moves along our age distribution and leads to abnormal demands for certain goods and services. For example, babies born in the 1950s are now forming households and wanting dwelling places of their own. Traditionally, young adults move first into apartments and then into moderately priced homes or condominiums. As they approach middle age, many are able to move into more expensive homes; finally, in old age, they move back into apartments, condominiums, or mobile homes. The age structure of our population at a particular time determines the kind of housing that will be in greatest demand. The bulge of young adults in the 1970s placed heavy demand on apartments, but by the 1980s this group began to want single-family homes. About 2.4 million houses will have to be built

the benefits and costs of policy choices. Almost every large corporation now has economists on its staff. Many of them work at analyzing prices and production costs. They study the way particular markets function and how workers, machines, and land combine to produce goods and services that people will buy. They try to predict the market for pickup trucks and subway trains, soybeans and electric power, fast foods and chocolate mousses. They are concerned with acquiring the resources needed for production and with using resources efficiently.

Governments employ economists to analyze these questions as well as broader issues. Government economists are often concerned with *aggregates,* or totals, such as total production, national income, and total employment in the entire nation. Some study how the monetary system and the tax structure affect national output and growth. Others try to predict the effects of alternative government spending policies on national income and prices and on job opportunities in the future.

Most economists specialize in particular fields. Economists in public finance deal with government budgets: tax revenues and spending appropriations. Monetary economists are concerned with the health of the banking system and its contribution to general economic health. Other economists specialize in international trade, labor relations, agricultural economics, or industrial organization. They may be asked to estimate the effects of higher oil prices, lower import tariffs, new labor laws, farm loans or subsidies, and proposed mergers of manufacturing firms.

Understanding how our economy works helps us plan better. Economic knowledge enables us to make the choices that will help us live better.

every year to meet the demand for single-family homes.

Other changes affect the number of total units needed. Rising incomes and growing numbers of "singles" mean that more individuals will want separate housing. Also, the energy crisis—with high heating and transportation costs—will probably lead to less demand for large, suburban homes and greater need for smaller dwellings near the center of town.

Growth in the homebuilding industry should provide job opportunities for new workers. Moreover, a growing housing industry will need materials and components from many other industries employing many workers. Suppliers of cement, lumber, roofing material, paint, and electrical and plumbing fixtures must prepare to satisfy demand. They must develop productive techniques and acquire machines needed for producing building materials. Other business firms will specialize in producing furniture, carpets, wallpaper, draperies, and appliances. They must pay close attention to new technology and to changing tastes.

Economists collect and interpret information to help individuals and business firms plan their policies for the future. Data gathered and interpreted by economists also help government plan policies to deal with changes in housing needs. If housing production is to continue smoothly, government must ensure ample credit for homebuyers. Government can direct its research and development funds toward more efficient forms of construction, helping to keep building costs down. Government can set policies for ensuring the best use of land and for conserving energy resources. Government may want to encourage rehabilitation of existing homes to meet the need for dwellings.

By the 1990s many of the "babies" of the 1950s will begin moving back into apartments and condominiums, and the homebuilding boom may slacken. Jobs in housing construction and related industries will be cut back. Economists can help government develop new programs to absorb the unemployed workers into new fields. A smooth transition into other employments will preserve workers' skills and maintain total production at a high level. Stable worker incomes will protect living standards for all workers and keep tax revenues flowing into government.

Consult the business section of your newspaper for information on the current status of housing. How do current costs, employment, and production compare with the recent past? What are analysts predicting for the future in the housing industry? How would economic distress in housing affect you, no matter what your job or your housing needs?

ECONOMICS AS A COURSE OF STUDY

In your college experience you will encounter three kinds of subjects: the arts and humanities, pure science, and applied science. In the *arts* we express our own feelings and develop our sensitivities to the world around us. In the *humanities* we describe events and eras of the past. Understanding the past enriches our lives and helps fix our place in the continuum of life on this planet.

Sciences go beyond mere description to explain why things behave as they do. Explanation requires careful experimenting and testing, as we will see. *Pure sciences* seek explanations to be able to expand understanding; the scientist is not concerned with whether the results of experiments will be immediately useful in a material way. *Applied sciences* seek answers to specific questions which affect the quality of life; the hope is that experiments will point to better ways of using the world's resources.

Economics has elements of both a pure and an applied science. The economist describes how our economic system works and explains why it behaves as it does. Then, in what is called *political economy*, the economist may go on to apply economic understanding to suggest ways for making the system work better. The final decision to apply economic understanding to real-world problems must often be made collectively by all the citizens of society.

Macroeconomics and Microeconomics

The subject matter of economics is divided into two parts: macroeconomics and microeconomics.

Macroeconomics deals with the economy as a whole. It talks of *aggregates* and looks at the combination of all market activities taken together. It is concerned with such questions as: What determines the total level of production? What determines total consumer spendable income? Should the federal government reduce taxes? How do the money supply and banking policies affect the economy? Some special problems studied in macroeconomics are inflation, unemployment, growth, and international finance.

Microeconomics is the study of activity in individual markets. Microeconomics is concerned with the actions of individual firms and households. It involves specific markets, such as those for diesel trucks, gypsum, typists, and golf clubs. The distribution of income and the allocation of resources are part of the study of microeconomics. Other issues examined in microeconomics are poverty, discrimination, monopoly, agricultural problems, big business and labor unions, and urban financial crises.

ECONOMICS AS A SCIENCE

A science attempts to understand, to explain, to discover. Some **physical sciences** are concerned with understanding physical or natural phenomena: physics, chemistry, biology, and geology. In their laboratories, physical and natural scientists conduct experiments which help them explain forces and relationships in our natural environment.

Social sciences are concerned with understanding forces and relationships in our social environment. Along with psychology, sociology, anthropology, history, and political science, economics is a social science. Like physical sciences, social sciences seek explanations of events that occur in the world around us.

The first step toward understanding our physical world is to gather and classify information describing a particular part of our environment. Much of this information is measurable. The biologist measures the effect of various nutrients on plant growth; the chemist measures the effect of temperature changes on the behavior of gases. Through repeated experiments, physical scientists gather and classify data describing the situations they are trying to understand. Then they use the data to explain the relationships within the system and to predict the effects of a change in conditions.

Economists work in much the same way as the physical scientists toward understanding our social environment. For instance, economists may be concerned with the effect of higher incomes on total spending in the United States. They may gather data showing that the average automobile assembly-line worker earns $15,000 per year after taxes. Of this total, $800 goes into a savings account and the remainder is spent. Economists can use the available data and observations of past behavior to predict the change in spending if workers bring home more income, say through a cost of living increase or through a reduction in tax rates.

You can see that numbers are very important in studying these relationships. Any time numbers are used, mathematical relationships are sure to follow. Like other scientists, economists do indeed employ the shorthand of mathematics to simplify and improve understanding.

Of course, economics is much more than the numbers and the unchanging facts of a physical science. Its subject matter is *social*—it studies *people*. Economics, like the other social sciences, deals with the relationships among people as they function in society. Sometimes, in fact, the "social" part weakens the "science" of economics. This may happen because people don't always behave in the same predictable patterns associated with a physical science. The human factor makes economic questions difficult to answer with certainty. Even worse, the social scientist is himself or herself a part of the problem being examined. The economist must be careful to eliminate personal preferences and prejudices and to examine the problem on its own merits.

The famous economist John Maynard Keynes called economics "the most difficult of the easy sciences." He meant that many of the ideas and facts of economics are simple. But clear-cut conclusions may be impossible.

The Scientific Method

Do you remember the story of the Greek scientist Archimedes? The King of Syracuse asked Archimedes whether his royal crown was really made of pure gold, as the maker claimed, or whether it was partly diluted with silver. Archimides was puzzled for an answer until one day, stepping into a bath, he noticed a relationship between the volume of his body and the quantity of water displaced from the tub. It occurred to him that he could find the answer to the king's question if he measured the amounts of water displaced by submerging (a) the crown, (b) an equal weight of gold, and (c) an equal weight of silver. If the crown were made entirely of gold, it would displace an amount of water equal to that displaced by the piece of gold. But if the crown were alloyed with silver, it would displace a greater amount of water. (Archimedes remembered that silver weighs less than gold per unit of volume. He reasoned that an equal weight of silver would require a greater volume, which in turn would displace more water.)

Archimedes was so excited by his discovery that he left the public bath, so the story goes, and ran home through the streets without his clothes, shouting, "Eureka, eureka" (I've found it, I've found it!).

Not everyone who runs naked through the streets (or streaks across a campus) has made a scientific discovery. The discoveries of science usually result from years of patient observation and gathering of data, followed by careful testing to make sure that the scientist's conclusion is valid.

Scientists refer to this process of analysis as the **scientific method.** The earliest use of the scientific method is associated with Francis Bacon in the seventeenth century. The scientific method requires the examiner to gather the important data describing the system under investigation. Data are classified and arranged to allow the examiner to explain the relationships and the forces at work within the system. The first tentative explanation of how a system works is called a *hypothesis.*

After stating a hypothesis, the examiner must conduct experiments to test the truth of the explanation. Experiments are conducted in laboratories where conditions not included in the hypothesis are controlled. For each experiment, the examiner makes a careful change in one of the conditions; temperature, air pressure, or humidity are examples of such variable conditions. The effect of each change is noted and compared with the expected effects. Unless the actual change conforms to the expected change, the proposed hypothesis must be rejected as unproven.

The examiner continues to propose new hypotheses until the results consistently conform to the proposed explanation. When a hypothesis is finally accepted, it can be stated as a **law** or **principle.** If you have studied one of the physical sciences, you know how carefully each hypothesis must be tested and how precisely each principle must be stated. Centuries of systematic study went into the principles that comprise our knowledge of physics and chemistry.

Like the King of Syracuse, most of us are perfectly happy to leave physics and chemistry to those who specialize in the field. Perhaps we would like to leave economics to the economists, too, but we can't. In our daily lives we are all involved in economics much of the time. The average family in the United States makes spending decisions involving thousands of dollars a year. Citizens vote for politicians who will spend hundreds of millions, even billions, of dollars. We will all pay taxes, too, and many of us will belong to unions that will bargain with our employers for our wages and working conditions. Some understanding of economics is helpful in making our personal decisions. And some understanding of how economists reason and make decisions will be helpful in evaluating proposals for national policy.

Economic Models

Examining the social environment is more complicated than examining the physical environment. In part, this is because the social scientist cannot use a laboratory for testing theories of human behavior. The economist's laboratory is the economic system itself. Experiments in the social laboratory would be costly and might unjustly affect the lives of many people. Moreover, experiments in the social laboratory could not be carried out under controlled conditions. Economists usually cannot isolate an entire community and test it for reactions to alternative policies. They can only rely on past observations of economic behavior to predict how people will respond to new policies.

Lacking social laboratories, economists test their theories through the use of **models.** Models are abstractions or simplified views of reality. They show relationships among selected phenomena occurring in our world; the selected phenomena are called *variables.* The purpose of the model is to enable the economist to analyze the effect of a change in a certain condition on the other variables in the model. To do this, the economist must first define the variables and state assumptions as to which variables are to be held constant in the model. Then he or she makes a controlled change in one of the variables and notes the possible effects on the others.

A model is a little like the diagram of a football play. In a football playbook players are represented by O's or X's. A plan is drawn up under the assumption that certain players will behave in certain predictable ways. Predicted movements by offensive players will be countered by planned defensive moves. Arrows show how the play should proceed. On the playing field the actions probably will not be exactly like the plans developed in the locker room. Too many unexpected events take place and change the outcome. The other team responds in unpredicted ways, new opportunities open up, or mistakes are made. But even when the play doesn't work as planned, the play as diagrammed is still useful.

Economic models relate to the real world in much the same fashion. The model will seldom give exactly the right answer. Even a mistake furnishes information to guide future analysts. Then, old models can be discarded in favor of more precise ones. Understanding how individual elements behave—the basic function of a model—helps economists understand the underlying logic of the economy.

Making predictions. Once the model is set up, a single change is made in one of the variables, and the total result is noted. The result allows the economist to predict how a similar change may affect the real social environment.

For instance, a model may be used to predict sales in the auto industry. It is assumed that growth in sales depends on such things as the age structure and income of the population, job security and the availability of credit, auto maintenance and fuel costs, availability of mass transit and imported cars. Sales depend also on prices, which in turn depend on union wage contracts, energy and material costs, taxes, and interest on borrowed funds. Prices may also depend on volume of autos produced; over a broad range of output, more autos can generally be produced at lower costs per auto.

A model may be drawn up to portray these conditions. But because a model is a simplified view of reality it must omit a variety of other market influences: technological breakthroughs that may affect production costs; new consumer attitudes that may affect spending; new legislation that may affect conditions of buying or selling. Omitting these other, unpredictable influences allows the observer to predict the effect of a single change: an improvement in credit terms, a rise in fuel costs, or a rise in the jobless rate.

If several economists study the same problem, they may arrive at different predictions. This happens when they build different assumptions about the behavior of economic variables into their models. They may make different assumptions about consumer response to price changes. They may have different evidence about producer response to changes in demand. Their statistics on past production costs may not correctly describe future conditions and changes.

All of this makes economic predictions uncertain. When predictions are wrong, it probably is not because the economist was careless or stupid. More likely, the problem is the complexity of the real world—which can hardly be reflected in a single experiment!

Ceteris paribus. In our model of the auto industry, we omitted all influences except the ones we were studying. Actually, the economist does not omit the other influences but assumes they are held temporarily constant or unchanging. We say that such a model is operating **ceteris paribus.** *Ceteris paribus* is a Latin phrase meaning "all other things remaining the same." The economist constructs models ceteris paribus to help approximate the controlled conditions of a scientific laboratory. Of course, this condition also reduces the realism of a model; it excludes some of the complexity of the real world.

Positive and Normative Sciences

Apart from their differences in subject matter, there is a second important difference between the physical sciences and the social sciences. Recall that scientific analysis generally leads to the formulation of a principle or law that explains the processes at work within a system. In the physical or natural sciences, principles

Economic Thinkers The Model Builders

Models are simplifications or abstractions of real-world complexities. They are set up to illustrate selected principles operating within an economy. There are models to predict auto sales and models to show the effect of changing prices on consumer purchases. Some economists have been particularly ambitious model builders. They have wanted a model of the whole national economy, predicting such things as the levels of total output, employment, and price inflation. Such a model could help us visualize how the whole economy works and enable us to predict future economic performance.

The first major model builders of a national economy were the **physiocrats.** These economic thinkers flourished in France during the eighteenth century. The physiocrats were so named because they believed that all systems evolve with a physical structure for operating most effectively in their respective environments. The human body, the economic and social system, even the universe have developed forms and patterns of behavior that adjust automatically to changes in environmental conditions. If economic systems themselves contain the means for adapting to change, then, said the physiocrats, government interference to respond to change would be unnecessary and ineffective.

The leading thinker of the physiocrats was, appropriately, a physician, Francois Quesnay. Quesnay summed up the beliefs of the physiocrats in his *tableau economique,* or "economic table." The table illustrated the interrelationships among all the groups in economic society: the consumers and producers of goods and services, the savers and investors of the nation's productive wealth, the receivers and spenders of the nation's income. The table resembled a physician's model in which incomes from production flow through the nation from buyer to seller to buyer again—stimulating industry and nourishing the economy like the circulation of the blood. Quesnay's table was the first attempt to visualize the performance of a complex economic system as a whole.

As useful as Quesnay's table was in showing how the whole economy works, his model was quite crude. The basic shortcoming of his model was its lack of precision. His model lacked the numbers and the mathematics necessary for calculating such precise values as level of total income or production. In fact, it wasn't until this century that we learned how to add up all the diverse things produced in the economy to determine the value of total production.

Jan Tinbergen was the first modern economist to construct a mathematical model of a national economy. He worked in Rotterdam, Netherlands, during the worldwide depression of the 1930s. He was particularly interested in models as tools for explaining and dealing with cycles in business activity.

Model building began in the United States after World War II with the work of Lawrence Klein, whose efforts over the past three decades earned him the Nobel Prize for Economics in 1980. While at the University of Pennsylvania's Wharton School, Klein investigated the many complex interrelationships among groups in the economy, which he expressed in fifty-one algebraic equations describing the effects on income and production of changes in any of fifty variables. The result was a mathematical model of the entire American economy—an *econometric model.*

Lawrence Klein's equations mix mathematical descriptions of past experience with intuition about future events. True, intuition requires detailed understanding of all dependent relationships and of all the political, psychological, and economic forces which influence them. The economist must break down each relationship and express mathematically all the significant factors that affect it: factors like government regulatory policies, political pressures, trends in tax revenues, credit policies, vacancy rates in housing, trends in business and consumer debt, quantity and age of consumer durable goods, shifts in consumer tastes, and the age and geographical distribution of population. Finally, the economist substitutes current economic data into the equations and programs a computer to solve the system of equations simultaneously. The result is a projection of the probable course of the national economy over future months and years.

A test of a model's validity is its ability to forecast and explain reality. Over the 1960s Lawrence Klein's econometric model performed well in predicting economic variables. It predicted the 1969–70 recession and the timing and dimensions of the recovery. But because a model is an abstraction from reality, it omits many details in order to focus on the major economic relationships. And in 1973 the Wharton model ran into the problem inherent in all abstractions from reality. It could not foresee the *external* shocks to the economy from higher fuel costs and higher worldwide food prices. There was nothing in past experience comparable to the massive shocks these events dealt our nation's economy.

This same problem is faced by other contempo-

Lawrence Klein

rary model builders: Otto Eckstein of Data Resources; Michael Evans, who founded Chase Econometrics, the model builders at the Massachusetts Institute of Technology; and others. All modern econometric models are limited *ceteris paribus*, by the conditions which the model assumes to be constant but which never are constant in the real world. The model builders must constantly work at revising their equations to reflect more correctly the changing conditions of the real world and to minimize the effects of assumptions made ceteris paribus.

In the 1970s, Professor Klein developed a larger model that links together the models of major countries. Klein's "Project Link" helps show how cycles in output and employment are transmitted among trading nations. The global model includes five thousand equations from thirteen Western industrialized nations, from socialist nations, and from developing nations.

All these models are imperfect. They are subject to the same criticism once made of physiocrats: Economic reality is too complex to be shown in a simple model. There are too many unforeseen and unpredictable forces that affect reality. Nevertheless, models represent a beginning effort toward more scientific analysis of the problems and policies that affect our economic health.

Devise a model to predict total sales of a hypothetical college bookstore for the month of September.

can be applied in useful ways to meet the needs of people. For instance, the principle of gas ignition under pressure is used to power the internal combustion engine. The principle of the growth of antibodies in the bloodstream is used to immunize people against disease.

In many of the social sciences, and especially in economics, applying principles often requires political decisions. Economists, speaking as social scientists, may propose and test economic hypotheses. They may state principles which explain the relationships among economic variables. They may even use their investigations to predict the results of alternative policies. When economists perform scientific investigations, we call this a *positive science.* However, when economists go beyond scientific investigation to suggest policies for curing specific economic ailments, we call this a *normative science.*

While a **positive science** examines *what is*, a **normative science** suggests *what ought to be.* Deciding what ought to be is not just an economic function but a political function to be decided by all the citizens. Most of our study of economics in this text, then, will be of positive economics. The emphasis will be on principles rather than on policy applications; these are the building blocks of any discipline.

Let's consider an example of this distinction. Income in the United States is distributed more equally now than in the early years of our industrialization, but there is still considerable inequality. Today the lowest one fifth of income earners in the United States receives only about one twentieth of total national income. What is the proper distribution of income? What income distribution is most desirable in terms of society's other goals? What other goals should be sacrificed in order to achieve the desired level of equality? The issue of the *proper* distribution of income is a normative one.

As positive scientists, economists would not give answers to such questions. Instead, they try to show the effects of alternative answers. For example, they may say that extreme income inequality will lead to a higher level of saving with greater investment in new productive capital. On the other hand, they may say that perfect equality will mean a higher level of consumer spending, with greater incentives to business productivity and growth. Which course should the nation pursue? How much inequality is proper? The questions are too com-

Viewpoint Economics and Politics

"I don't think any man worth a damn can be President of the U.S. unless he understands economics." The man who said that once wanted to be President, the late Senator from Minnesota, Hubert H. Humphrey.

Why is economics so important? It is difficult to name a national problem or issue that is not first of all an economic issue. Our domestic social problems of crime, poverty, illiteracy, and discrimination involve economic questions. Even problems of international relations are primarily conflicts over economic interests.

If economics is so important to our nation's strength, then it would seem that our political leaders would bend every effort toward solving these economic questions. Unfortunately, this is not so easy. It involves policymaking, and policymaking involves normative economics.

Political leaders differ in their approaches to normative questions. For example, Hubert Humphrey used his position in the Senate to support laws that would increase the role of government in solving economic problems. He sponsored a proposal to set up an economic planning board in Washington; representatives of business, labor, and consumers would meet with members of Congress to set long-term targets for the proper use of the nation's resources, to coordinate the activities of economic groups, and to suggest broad goals of government policy.

Whereas Humphrey looked to the federal government to solve economic questions, political leaders like Senator Barry Goldwater and President Ronald Reagan favor just the opposite approach. They fear the growing influence of Washington and want to return economic decision-making to the people themselves. One way to do this would be to eliminate federal economic programs and to allow local communities to decide whether or not to finance them with local tax revenues. Reagan's campaign for the 1976 presidential nomination involved proposals to abolish the federal role in welfare assistance, education, Medicaid, air-traffic control, postal subsidies, and some other services. Goldwater once proposed to make the Social Security program voluntary, so that individuals could plan their own retirement without federal intervention.

Our leaders differ also in their opinions on government regulation of business activities. Senator Edward Kennedy, for instance, is confident of the power of a strong national administration to direct the economic climate in which business operates. He objects to government regulation only when it is applied inconsistently or inefficiently. President Gerald Ford, on the other hand, recommended minimizing the role of government in business affairs. He opposed greater gov-

plicated to answer with economics alone.

As normative scientists, economists will differ on policy recommendations, in part because each emphasizes different *goals*. To some economists the goal of maximum individual liberty is more important than equality of income. They say that any interference at all with income distribution is an unacceptable interference with individual freedom. Other economists will say that maximum individual liberty is impossible if there is extreme inequality of incomes. To these, poverty prevents some American families from fully enjoying the rights of free people. Other goals might also mean the difference between a good life and deprivation for some of our nation's people. Price stability, job security, consumer protection, economic growth: Achieving all these goals together may not be possible. Economic growth may threaten price stability, consumer protection may threaten job security, and perfect economic freedom may threaten them all.

A normative economist arranges goals according to the priorities of the people for whom he or she speaks. The priorities of the economist representing the National Association of Manufacturers will differ from those of the economist representing the American Federation of Labor. Economists working for a firm or a group of firms in an industry will openly defend policies or goals of that firm or industry. Their goals might include maximum production, sales, and profits. Still others may defend the economic interests of labor unions, educators, environmentalists, or other nonprofit enterprises. Their goals might include better working conditions, a healthy environment, and improved social services. When economists are hired by government to evaluate policy alternatives, they will usually be given a set of goals on

ernment intervention in the private sector, so as to leave decision making power in the hands of consumers and businesses.

Why is it that intelligent and experienced leaders can disagree so completely on these important questions? Partly, the reason is that they begin with different convictions about the proper goals of our economic system. They set different priorities among the goals of growth, efficiency, and equality. They are tuned to different sets of information promising to achieve different objectives. And they attract followers who agree with their priorities and procedures.

The result of our democratic political system is a richly varied array of political opinion with ample opportunity for voters to express their individual economic preferences. Before you can develop your own preferences, however, it is important to expose yourself to a wide range of information. It is dangerous to speak too soon, before you understand all possibilities.

We think Senator Humphrey's statement should be expanded to "You can't be a good voter, and you won't understand the range of policy alternatives and the costs of these policies, until you have mastered the principles of economics!"

which to base their recommendations. All will use the methodology of economics to support their positions.

Some economists associate themselves with a political candidate or a political position. They give lectures and speeches outside the classroom, before audiences composed of people other than students. In so doing, they use their personal expertise and the prestige of their college or university to support and defend a particular solution to economic problems. They are engaging in *political economy.* The advocacy role uses the scientific methods of economics to achieve answers to questions in ways that favor the goals of one group or another. There is a proud tradition of such normative behavior in economics. Adam Smith, David Ricardo, Reverend Thomas Malthus, John Stuart Mill, and Karl Marx all engaged in the practice, which survives today.

Try to Keep Cool

In any science, there is no room for personal bias or prejudice. The scientific method requires the examiner to be cool and levelheaded. You will sometimes hear economists calmly discussing such questions as whether a *little* more unemployment must be tolerated to avoid *high* levels of inflation or whether a slowdown in military spending might be bad for employment. This does not mean that these economists are in favor of unemployment or militarism. It is their responsibility to examine every alternative that presents itself, calmly and objectively.

Personal bias is bad for scientific analysis because it blinds a person to the differences and distinctions that are the basis for intelligent understanding. Emotionally charged language should also be avoided, for much the same reason. A word that expresses our feelings may obscure or cover up reality. Those who dislike government-financed health insurance often call it *socialized medicine.* The term *socialized* conjures up an image of the all-powerful state. Those who favor higher taxes for the rich like to speak of *closing the tax loopholes.* They neglect to mention their own middle-class "loopholes," which they hope will stay open. Precision of language is important to any scientist and particularly to a social scientist.

Some Traps to Avoid

The failure of language is really a failure of thinking, since words are misused when thought is imprecise. There are other ways of failing to think.

One that is a danger in economics is the **fallacy of composition**—the assumption that what is true for a part will be true for the whole. If your pay doubles overnight, you will be twice as well off as before. But if everyone's pay were to double, probably no one would be any better off. Spending would rise so sharply that prices would also double. If you decide to save a larger portion of your earnings, you will probably be able to provide more security for your family. But if everyone should decide to save more, the sharp drop in spending would mean stacks of unsold goods. Business firms would have to cut back production and lay off workers, and the economic security of many people would be threatened.

The **false-cause fallacy** is another trap for students of economics. Because economic reality is so complex, the researcher must deal with a multitude of causes. In a controlled experiment, the scientist must keep all variables constant and then study the effects of a precise change in only one variable. This is not generally possible for the economist. Often, too many things are happening in the economy to separate specific cause-effect relationships. If poverty declines, is it a result of government programs to improve health and education or only a result of normal economic growth? Are rising prices the result of large corporations increasing their profits or of powerful labor unions increasing their wages? Is inflation the result of rising energy prices or of a rapidly growing money supply? It may be that there is not *one* cause but *several*. Economists must try to calculate how much importance to attach to each of them.

CRITERIA FOR EVALUATING AN ECONOMIC SYSTEM

As social scientists we must avoid these traps and apply rigid standards of objectivity to our economic analyses. We must be careful to avoid biases that would distort our conclusions. This is true when evaluating any economic system but especially when evaluating our own. We want to understand our system with all its strengths and all its weaknesses. Only through objective understanding will we be able to make effective judgments about the economic system that substantially affects our lives.

It will be helpful to establish a list of goals that an economic system should help achieve. Our goals will be the "performance criteria" by which our system can be judged and compared with others.

(1) *Productivity and growth.* Probably the first goals of an economic system would be improved productivity and growth. *Productivity* is a measure of average output produced per worker. Improved productivity means greater output per worker employed in agriculture or a manufacturing industry. Improved productivity also means growth in per capita income and rising per capita living standards. Our economic system provides strong incentives that encourage greater productivity and growth: Hard work and achievement are rewarded with higher incomes and social status.

(2) *Economic stability and security.* Two other related goals are economic stability and security. By *economic stability* we mean full employment and stable prices. By *security* we mean providing material necessities for people who can't work or earn enough to provide an adequate standard of living for themselves: the elderly, the sick, the poor, and the unemployed.

In our economic system, independent decision-making often leads to periods of instability: too rapid growth followed by painful cutbacks in production. Inflation (rising prices) and unemployment sometimes plague our system. Government control would probably improve the performance of the economy in terms of stability and security. But this alternative would mean a considerable loss of individual liberties.

(3) *Efficiency.* A necessary goal of any economic system is efficiency. We can define *efficiency* as the degree to which an economic system uses its resources to produce the maximum amount of wanted or needed goods. A perfectly efficient system would eliminate waste. Efficiency is thus closely related to productivity and growth. In fact, for a given level of resource use, increased productivity may not be possible without increased efficiency.

With regard to efficiency, our economic system performs very well indeed. The economic theory discussed in this text will show how decentralized decision-making can help bring about the most efficient use of our resources.

(4) *Personal freedom and equality.* Finally, we should include the goals of personal freedom and equality. Our economic system offers many opportunities for enhancing and developing the personal dignity and worth of every citizen. There is maximum freedom possible for pursuing personal goals and life-styles. Nevertheless, our goal of freedom may conflict with the goal of equality. If some individuals are free to succeed spectacularly, others must be free to fail drastically. Other economic systems probably offer greater equality but at the cost of personal freedom. Some systems, such as that of the Soviet Union, offer neither greater equality nor personal freedom.

Inequality may result not only from the inherent failures of our economic system but also from efforts to block the free exercise of individual rights and responsibilities. Discrimi-

Viewpoint **Reverse Discrimination?**

Title VII of the 1964 Civil Rights Act prohibits job discrimination on the basis of race, sex, religion, or national origin. But by itself a law cannot ensure equality. President Lyndon Johnson knew that when he signed the law and, soon after, the order establishing Affirmative Action. Affirmative Action is a federally directed program to help disadvantaged minorities compete more strongly for new opportunities.

In the beginning, Affirmative Action set goals to help guide employers and educators in providing jobs and educational programs for minorities. But what were intended to be flexible goals soon came to be seen as rigid quotas, strongly resisted by groups the so-called quotas appeared to exclude. In particular, white males have argued against what they feel to be "reverse discrimination"—unlawful under the 1964 law.

The first major legal case against minority preferences in education was that of a white male applicant to a California medical school. In the Bakke case, a white male charged he had been denied admission even though his test scores were higher than those of black applicants accepted into the program. The Supreme Court ruled in Bakke's favor but pointed out that race could be a factor in selecting applicants. This principle was more strongly spelled out in 1979 in the Weber case. This time a white male was excluded from a special job-training program which would have enabled him to gain a promotion. The Court ruled that a private firm may indeed establish a quota for blacks in a program designed to improve job skills and promotion potential of black employees.

The progress of Affirmative Action demonstrates the character of law in the United States. Law is not a fixed body of rules but a *process* by which citizens turn their beliefs into practice. In this case, the law recognized the need to establish new conditions for the fullest development of individual capabilities in our free society. It goes beyond applying fixed rules to ensure justice, beyond mere legislation to fulfill a moral obligation.

Affirmative Action programs have created tensions in our society and raised some questions. Their purpose was to change past patterns of neglect of minority education and job training. Improved worker skills and increased productive potential were expected to follow. This assumption ignored the possibility that resources used in Affirmative Action may not be the most efficient way to increase total output.

Despite these problems, our legal system appears to be saying that some costs must now be paid if we are to realize fully our national ideals in terms of productivity and growth, economic security, and personal equality.

How does this article illustrate the conflict of goals in our society? How does a society's level of development determine its priority of goals?

nation and laws limiting opportunity are barriers to equality that should not exist in an economic system.* Democratic processes provide the means for reducing inequalities like these while continuing to protect personal freedom.

Perfect equality is probably not desirable in our system or any other. A more appropriate goal is equity. *Equity* refers to fairness—fairness in the distribution of the goods and services an economic system produces and fairness in the distribution of the costs of production, too. Equity can only be defined according to one's own individual values and beliefs. What seems "fair" to some of us may seem grossly "unfair" to others.

Our economic system should be judged in terms of these performance criteria. Its strengths and weaknesses should be compared with the strengths and weaknesses of other systems. As long as its weaknesses represent a smaller cost than its benefits, most of us would hope to maintain the present system. We may use our understanding of goals and performance to help remedy some of the system's most troublesome defects.

*Although Constitutional amendments forbid certain forms of discrimination, some state and local laws continue to discriminate on the basis of race or sex.

ISSUES WE FACE

Because our economic system is not capable of achieving all goals, many problems remain. Unemployment and poverty stunt the lives of many citizens, large cities face crises of crime and decay, and economic growth has depleted many of our natural resources. Through our legislative procedures, we have asked government to place some restrictions on our individual freedom of choice and to use our resources toward correcting these kinds of problems.

You enjoy certain opportunities as a member of a free society, and you must accept certain responsibilities in return. You have a stake in our economic system. You must prepare yourself to propose answers to important economic questions, questions involving day-to-day problems and questions involving the health of our economic system in the years to come. How we answer these questions will determine whether there will be a job for you, how much you will earn, what you can buy in exchange for your earnings, and what kind of opportunities you can provide your children. The decisions we make as a nation will affect the quality of life in your community, the taxes you pay, the services you receive, and the health and safety necessary for growth. Moreover, all these choices will affect the world's use of resources and the level at which billions of people throughout the world will live for many generations to come.

All of this makes economics an important course of study for all citizens.

SUMMARY

This chapter has introduced you to the subject matter of economics and to the methods used in economic analysis. It describes how economics is similar to, yet different from, other branches of science. We study economics in order to understand the *hows* and *whys* of producing and using goods and services. The hope is that understanding will help us live and plan better—as individuals, as communities, and as a collection of nations.

The study of economics is divided into two parts: macroeconomics and microeconomics. Macroeconomics examines the operation of the economy as a whole; microeconomics examines how individual markets work.

We have seen how scientists approach a problem for analysis, and we have learned how economists apply the scientific method in their own field. One limitation of economic analysis is that we usually cannot make controlled laboratory experiments. However, there are ways of getting around this problem through the use of economic models, or simplified views of reality. Models help predict the outcome of various economic policy proposals.

Economics is both a positive science, examining *what is,* and a normative science, arguing *what ought to be. What ought to be* in economic policy often must be decided by the citizens of a society as a whole, through political processes. The economist, like any other scientist, must be careful not to inject bias or false thinking into the problem being examined. The fallacies of composition and false cause should also be avoided.

We can judge the performance of the market system and other economic systems by the following four basic criteria: (1) productivity and growth; (2) economic stability and security; (3) efficiency; and (4) personal freedom and equality.

Key Words and Phrases

ceteris paribus a Latin phrase meaning "everything else remaining the same"; describes assumption that all variables except the ones under investigation are temporarily held constant.

fallacy of composition the error in thinking that assumes what is true for the separate parts of a system must be true for the whole.

false-cause fallacy the error in thinking that assumes because one event follows another it must be a result of the first.

laws or principles tested explanations of why systems behave as they do

macroeconomics the study of how the economy works as a whole.

microeconomics the study of individual markets within an economic system.

model a simplified view of reality, useful for explaining economic relationships and for testing the effects of policy.

normative science an attempt to prescribe policy to improve a system.

performance criteria standards by which to judge an economic system.

physical science a science devoted to the study of the physical world; also called *natural science*.

positive science a discipline that describes and explains a system as it is.

scientific method a systematic procedure for investigating and explaining phenomena.

social science a science devoted to the study of people, their behavior, and their social institutions.

Questions for Review

1. Outline the steps you would take to investigate a problem in the natural sciences and one in economics. For example, what procedure would be useful for answering each of the following: (a) How are animal feeding habits affected by changes in weather? (b) How are personal expenditure patterns affected by changes in tax rates?
2. Explain the difference between positive and normative questions. Why is goal-setting important, and how are political considerations involved?
3. What performance criteria might be used in evaluating: (a) a track team; (b) a fast-food restaurant; (c) a history term paper?
4. Discuss the following statement: Precision of language is fundamental to economics.
5. Define: assumptions, equity, model.
6. Write a good definition for economics, using ordinary language.
7. Give an example of the fallacy of composition; of the fallacy of false cause.
8. Select an economic issue from current news. Discuss its political aspects. What are the alternative positions surrounding this issue?
9. Suppose the campus snack bar serves the following quantities during a typical week:

	Hot dogs	*Cheeseburgers*	*Milkshakes*
Monday	10	20	30
Tuesday	15	18	28
Wednesday	12	22	31
Thursday	12	20	29
Friday	15	25	35

The prices are Hot dogs, 50¢; Cheeseburgers, $1.00; and Milkshakes, 80¢. Try to draw up a model predicting total weekly sales revenue. What variables are included in your model? What assumptions are necessary for applying this model? What other information would you need to construct a model to predict weekly profits? Suppose the price of cheeseburgers changes. How would this affect your model?

Appendix

Using Graphs

Economists use graphs to illustrate economic models. A graph is a line drawing that expresses relationships between two values. Graphs are helpful because they summarize all relevant information in a simple and concise way. They can be interpreted at a glance and they avoid the need for lengthy explanations. The same information arranged in the form of a table would be much more difficult to interpret.

To illustrate the use of graphs, let us suppose you are conducting an experiment with a pair of dice. You throw the dice a hundred times and record the value on the dice each time. It is convenient to record your results on a table like Table 1. The first column shows the possible value of each throw: two through twelve. The second column shows the number of times each value appeared in your test. The table is difficult to interpret quickly. Plotting the data on a graph will help display the information more simply.

A graph is plotted on two axes, as shown in Figure 1. The *horizontal axis* represents the value of each throw. The scale is numbered from 2 to 12. The *vertical axis* represents the number of times each value appeared, from 0 to 20.

The value of 2 appeared 3 times in the test. To enter this result on the graph, move upward from 2 on the horizontal axis to 3 on the vertical and place your first point. Similarly, above 3 on the horizontal axis, place your second point at 5 occurrences. Continuing in this way, plot a series of points for each result in your experiment. Connecting the points produces a graph showing the number of occurrences of each value in your test.*

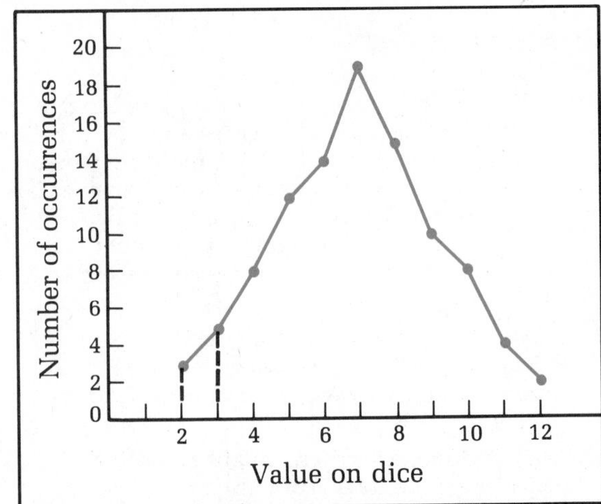

Figure 1 Graph of experiment with throws of dice. A quick glance reveals the pattern of results. Closer examination provides greater detail. There are no points associated with zero or one because those numbers can't occur when two dice are thrown.

Table 1 **Experiment with Throws of Dice**

Value of throw	Number of occurrences
2	3
3	5
4	8
5	12
6	14
7	19
8	15
9	10
10	8
11	4
12	2

What can we learn from the graph? The line reaches a peak at the value of 7, which occurred 19 times. (If you are a mathematician you understand why 7 was thrown more times than any other value.) The values 5, 6, and 8 occurred almost as often, but 2 and 12 occurred less frequently. The curve helps us interpret large amounts of statistical information at a glance.

*The line in Figure 1 is *continuous* (including information for an infinite number of very small possibilities) although the data are *discrete* (involving a definite number of precise possibilities). Displaying discrete data with a continuous line suggests some misleading information. The graph implies that the value $2\frac{1}{2}$ was thrown four times, although we know that occurrence is impossible. For most of the graphs in this text the data will be continuous: in thousands or billions or in terms of time. Thus, the value $2\frac{1}{2}$ might represent 2,500 labor hours or $2,500,000,000, and a point on a time line would represent, say, July of 1979.

We can learn detailed information by examining the graph more closely. For example, the value 11 occurred 4 times in one hundred throws, or 4 percent of the time.

In economics we will use graphs to illustrate economic variables. Graphs will help us see broad relationships at a glance; closer examination will provide specific information on particular quantities. Most graphs in economics are either time-series graphs or functional graphs.

Time-series graph. A graph that shows the value of a particular economic variable over time is called a **time-series graph.** For example, Figure 2 shows the average hourly pay of factory workers in the United States over recent years. We can see immediately that hourly pay rose fairly steadily, from $5.95 in January 1978 to $7.05 in March 1980. When we look more closely, we can also see that hourly pay slumped in mid-1978 when the economy seemed to be going into a recession. After a dip in early 1979, hourly earnings resumed their upward trend.

Figure 3 shows the average weekly pay of factory workers over the same time period. Weekly pay fluctuated more sharply. The fluctuations in weekly pay are the result of factory layoffs and variable work-hours per week.

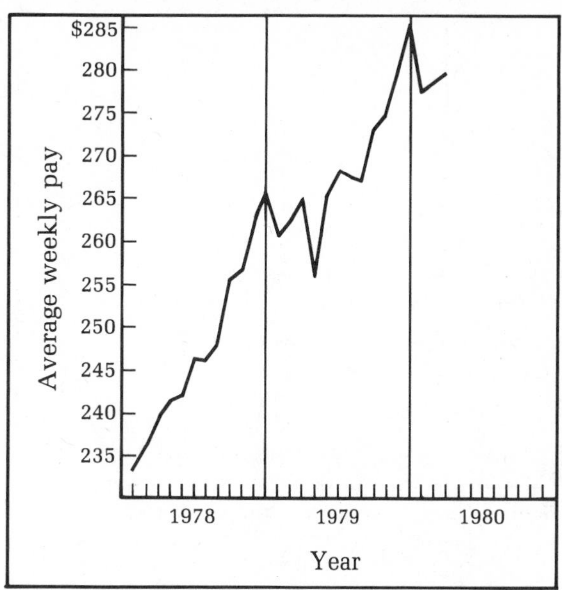

Figure 3 Time-series graph of average weekly pay for American factory workers over the same time period as in Figure 2. Though the trend is upward, progress is very uneven. This figure differs from Figure 2 because it includes weeks in which workers were laid off or worked overtime.

Functional graph. A graph that illustrates the relationship between two economic variables is called a **functional graph.** One of the variables is usually considered the **independent variable** and the other the **dependent variable.** A change in the independent variable (cause) is assumed to influence the value of the dependent variable (effect). This kind of relationship is called a *functional* relationship; we say that changes in the dependent variable are a **function** of changes in the independent variable.

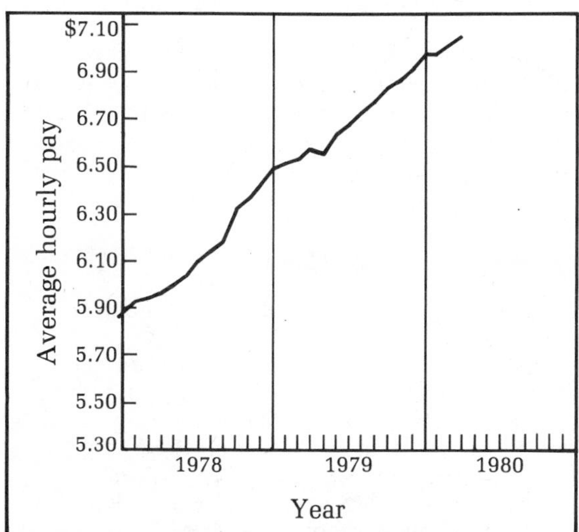

Figure 2 Time-series graph of average hourly pay for American factory workers over a three-year period. The overall trend is quickly seen to be upward, though a bit uneven.

Figure 4 shows a hypothetical relationship between the rate of interest on borrowed money and the quantity of business investment spending. In this graph the dependent variable, business investment spending, is shown on the horizontal axis. A functional relationship suggests that changes in interest rates (independent variable) will affect the quantity of business investment spending. A functional relationship may be drawn as a straight line (linear), or it may be curved. When the values are irregular, the function may have a jagged appearance.

The graph indicates that an interest rate of 10 percent will be associated with investment spending of $50 billion a year. But at interest rates of only 3 percent, investment spending would be $150 billion a year. Follow the dashed horizontal lines from 10 percent and 3 percent to

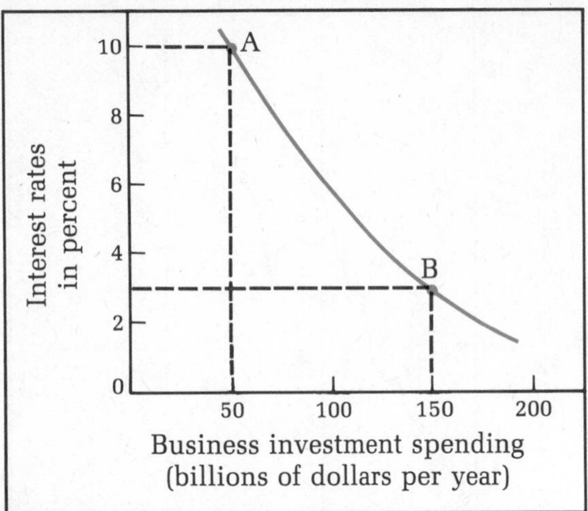

Figure 4 Functional graph of business investment spending as a function of interest. If investment spending is indeed a function of interest rates, then statistical data should help predict future investment spending.

points A and B. At point A business investment spending measures $50 billion on the horizontal axis. At point B business investment measures $150 billion. What interest rate would produce business investment spending of $100 billion per year?

The functional relationship of Figure 4 may be stated this way: Investment spending is a function of the rate of interest, or investment (I) equals a function of interest (i): $I = f(i)$.

The hypothetical relationship illustrated in Figure 4 is based on past observations and assumptions about business behavior. It suggests that high interest charges on borrowed money would discourage borrowing for new investment. High interest costs would reduce the expected profitability of investment, and business firms would be less inclined to invest. By the same reasoning, low interest charges might be expected to encourage greater investment spending. Low interest costs make new investment projects more profitable, and business firms would be more likely to invest.

If the assumed relationship between interest rates and investment spending conforms to reality, the economist can use it as a basis for evaluating alternative economic policies. A policy encouraging the banking system to reduce interest rates on bank loans, for instance, will be expected to cause investment spending to increase. The economist can then predict the effects of new investment spending on the level of total spending and income in the economy.

But remember what we said earlier about the fallacy of false cause. In reality, investment spending is not a simple function of the rate of interest. It depends also on changes in technology that make purchases of new equipment necessary. It depends on the level of consumer spending and on business expectations of future sales. It depends also on the stock of equipment goods already owned by business. In fact, investment spending appears to be strongly influenced by many other factors that cannot be included in a simple two-dimensional model—they were all put aside ceteris paribus. As a result, conclusions and policy recommendations based on this model must be made carefully.

Understanding a graph such as Figure 4 helps prevent the error of assuming that the factors held constant for drawing the curve actually remain constant for very long. The function shows the response of one variable, investment, to another variable, interest. If the rate of interest falls, investment will increase, ceteris paribus. In the graph, this would be shown as a movement from point *A* to point *B* along the line plotted.

Now suppose one of the conditions held ceteris paribus changes. For example, suppose population growth accelerates so that new homes, appliances, and household items are in great demand. Business firms attempt to satisfy their customers, with the result that a greater amount of investment is required at every interest rate. This might be shown (Figure 4b) as a movement of the function to the right.

Sketch a curve that illustrates the following relationships: (a) typical growth patterns of American males; (b) fuel consumption over a year in Minnesota; (c) the effect of telephone usage on a person's monthly bill; (d) the effect of family size on meals eaten out. Label axes and curves.

Key Words and Phrases

dependent variable a variable that is influenced by another.

function a mathematical relationship between two or more variables wherein changes in one are associated with changes in the other.

functional graph a graph that illustrates the relationship between two economic variables.

independent variable a variable whose behavior influences the behavior of another.

time series a series that shows changes in some economic variable over time.

time-series graph a graph that shows the value of a particular economic variable over time.

CHAPTER 2

The Economic Problem

Learning Objectives

Upon completion of this chapter, you should be able to

1. Explain the economic dilemma of scarcity.
2. List the four types of resources or inputs and give examples of each.
3. Explain what a production-possibilities curve is, distinguish between movement along the curve and movement of the curve, and draw such a curve if given the data.
4. Define *opportunity cost* and give examples of it.
5. Explain at least four different choices an economic system must make in using its productive resources.
6. Explain the four questions that every society must answer.
7. Indicate the three basic types of economic systems and explain how they differ.

As you read this, you may be wondering how you can arrange your time to finish this assignment, perform a chemistry experiment, write an English theme, solve some mathematical problems—and pick up your clothes at the laundry! You might enjoy spending a couple of hours at the student recreation center, but that may be farther down your list of priorities. There is so much to do and never enough *time*.

Or your concern may be with other types of needs. You may be wondering how you can make your allowance last out the week: How many dinners can you afford? Can you get a ride to the game or will you have to pay bus fare? Should you buy a Spanish workbook or a pair of gym shoes? Can you afford to get your clothes out of the laundry? There is so much you want and never enough *money*.

If you have experienced either of these situations, you will understand a fundamental problem of economics. The fundamental **economic problem** has two sides: *scarce resources* and *unlimited wants*. As individuals, as business firms, and as a nation our wants are greater than our ability to satisfy them. Indeed, every society now and in the past has faced this problem. There are never enough resources to produce all the goods and services a population (especially a growing population) wants.

In 1958 John Kenneth Galbraith published a book entitled *The Affluent Society*. He argued that modern Americans face problems quite different from those of our ancestors. Our forebears never had enough to go around, he said, but twentieth-century Americans live in a society rich enough to provide everyone with the basic requirements of life and much, much more. The phrase *affluent society* has now become a household term. We may not always *feel* affluent—there is always some bill waiting to be paid—but as a nation we think in terms of billions and trillions of dollars worth of goods and services. Nevertheless, with all our good fortune there are still many wants left unfulfilled. With all our affluence there is even a danger that we may lose sight of the basic economic problem: *the problem of scarcity*.

MANAGING IN A WORLD OF SCARCITY

Scarcity is not the same as poverty. Even the rich have to reckon with scarcity. The wealthy individual who can afford to give millions of dollars to a favorite charity or to endow a university with a building that will bear his or her name must still choose among benefactions. For most of us the problem of choice is far more urgent. We schedule our limited time so that each activity yields the greatest possible reward—hours for economics and chemistry and minutes for errands. We allocate our limited funds so that our expenditures yield the greatest possible usefulness—gym shoes and bus fare this week, but the laundry will have to wait.

As managers of enterprises, whether business firms or civic clubs, we organize our workers so that their available time and energy produce the greatest possible results. Organizing work for a class project must be done similarly. Students are willing to contribute their efforts toward school projects, but they try to use their resources effectively to produce the best result. Does the class need a parade float, a stage set, a vegetable garden? A few energetic students, some odds and ends, a little money, and a lot of imagination can do the job. There'll be costs, of course—skipped classes and missed meals. For students, both time and money are scarce. To use them in one way means giving up something else, so students try to use them carefully.

When asked to define their science, most economists say that economics is the study of making choices. Individuals must choose how to use their own resources for producing goods and services and how to use their incomes for consuming. Taken together, all individuals in a society must choose how to organize all their resources for producing the goods and services the people as a whole want most. Because resources are scarce and wants unlimited, choosing the best alternative is important. Choosing is the fundamental economic activity.

KINDS OF RESOURCES

Economic resources have value for us because they are useful for producing goods or providing services. Because they are scarce, they must be used carefully. Prices, which reflect the relative value of each resource and its relative scarcity, tend to discourage wasteful use. The rationing motive is an important part of our market system.

If a resource is so plentiful that it has no price, then we call it a **free good.** At one time our society considered many items to be free goods: air, water, sunshine, etc. But times change. There are some areas in this country where fresh air is no longer a free good. It is certainly not free in the depths of a mine or tunnel where it must be pumped in at some expense, or in a chemical plant where blowers must be operated to filter out pollution. In fact, industrial pollution threatens all our air and water, and keeping them clean involves costs. Sunlight is normally a free good—but not to Eskimos in their long, dark winters. (If they want to see the sunshine, they must buy an airline ticket south.) Bananas may be a free good to a Jamaican peasant, but they are certainly not free to a Manhattan worker.

Resources used to produce goods or services are called **factors of production.** They are classified in four basic groups: land, labor, capital, and entrepreneurship. In our market system all factors of production are paid a price for their contribution to total production.

Land

Land consists of all the original and irreplaceable resources of nature. Land includes both the fertile fields and pastures used in agriculture and the urban plots used for skyscrapers. Iron ore, virgin timber, granite, and other minerals are classified as land. The United States is rich in land resources, but even our land is limited. For each plot of land, we must choose the type of employment that contributes most toward filling our unlimited wants. We can have a parking lot or tennis courts, but not both, a strawberry patch or a strip mine, saw mills or a wildlife preserve. *Never both at the same time*—we must choose.

Labor

Labor is the purposeful work of human beings. Manual work and brainwork, creative work and routine work, are all classified as labor. Our labor force grows every year, and its quality improves with better health and education. Still, labor-hours must be used wisely to get the maximum benefits from this valuable resource. Even more importantly, today's labor-hours are available only today. If they are not used today, we sacrifice forever the goods and services they could have produced. Houses won't be built, autos repaired, or dental services performed. We won't have all the things we could have had. Human skills, unused during recession, represent a loss that is impossible to measure.

Capital

Capital consists of goods we have produced but that we keep aside and use to produce other goods and services. **Capital goods** are distinguished from **consumer goods,** which we can use directly. Tools and machines, transportation and communication networks, buildings, and irrigation facilities are capital goods. They continue to produce goods and services in the future. If we are to have capital goods, we must first save. Farmers save a portion of their grain crop to use for seed in the next planting season. Their seed grain is a capital good which allows them to produce more in the future.

Education (including all types of training in useful skills) may be thought of as **human capital.** To build human capital requires that we sacrifice something today for goods in the future. Like the farmers who give up grain, students give up jobs—and their families give up trips to Disneyland—all for the opportunity to develop a stock of capital. Human capital is an important basis for the growing productivity of U.S. workers.

The word *capital* is sometimes also used to mean a supply of money, as in **financial capital,** but this is not what we mean when we speak of capital as a factor of production. Financial capital is savings which are provided to business firms for construction of capital goods. This is the way savers give up something today for the sake of greater production in the future.

Entrepreneurship

The fourth factor of production is more difficult to define, but it is perhaps the most important of all in the market system. This resource is the ability to organize the other resources into a creative combination for the purpose of production. Economists use a word of French origin for the person who performs this function: the *entrepreneur.* Entrepreneurship implies more than simply managing an ongoing enterprise. That can be done by routine. **Entrepreneurship** requires *initiative* and *willingness to take the risks* involved in doing something new. A person who leaves a comfortable job to go into business is functioning as an entrepreneur on a small scale. Entrepreneurs are exceptional people—outside the usual mold. They don't do things in the usual way; if they did they would not be entrepreneurs. They are the pathbreakers, the creators, the Andrew Carnegies, Henry Fords, and Edwin Lands. The American spirit of individual enterprise encourages the development of entrepreneurial talent.

In years past, the entrepreneurial role was played mostly by individuals who began their own businesses, gathering the resources and organizing production to carry out a new idea. But times have changed. Performing these same functions in a complex modern economy may be too difficult for a single individual. In fact, many new ideas are now carried out by large corporations in which entrepreneurial functions may be divided among many individuals: risk-taking stockholders, an imaginative board of directors, and creative company executives. This arrangement has the advantage that persons are required to perform only those specific functions they do best. There may also be the disadvantage that no single individual has total responsibility for the actions of the corporation.

PRODUCTION POSSIBILITIES

We have seen that the economic problem requires us to choose among unlimited wants. Each of us must choose whether to buy stereo equipment or a trip to the beach, or whether we should save for some purchase in the future. Sometimes our decisions are made unconsciously, but the result reflects our own individual goals. We draw up a list of wants according to priorities. Then, we allocate our budgets to achieve the greatest benefits. We realize that any choice we make requires a sacrifice of something else; so we choose carefully.

A society, like a person, must choose its priorities within the limits of its resources. A community must choose whether to build a new school or to enlarge the old one, to pay off old debts or to reduce taxes, to hire more police officers or more fire fighters. Our national government collects many billions of dollars in taxes. Still, it must choose: education for toddlers or for space scientists, research into missile guidance systems or cancer prevention, new highways or mass transit systems.

What are our alternatives and how do we choose? This is part of the subject matter of economics.

We can begin with a simple model. The variables in our model are the community's existing quantity of productive resources and the goods and services it can produce. A fundamental assumption for our model is that technology is fixed ceteris paribus. Moreover the character of many resources is fixed, so that they are suitable for only one type of production. With the most efficient use of its limited resources and technology, the community can produce a certain quantity of goods and services.

For this simple model we will divide all goods and services into two groups. This is because we can illustrate production of two types of goods and services on a two-dimensional sheet of paper. If it were convenient to illustrate three-dimensionally, we could divide all goods and services into three groups, or even more. It will be useful to name our two groups *corn* and *autos*. For these purposes, corn represents agricultural products and autos represent manufactured goods. We will use our resources and technology efficiently to maximize total output of corn and autos.

We could have named our groups Whatzits and Whozits, or we could have classified everything from A to M in the first group and everything from N to Z in the second. It doesn't matter. What is important is to recognize that the community's resources and technology limit us to some particular total level of production of both groups.

Table 1 **Production Possibilities per Year**

	Corn (in tons)	Autos
Combination 1	10,000	0
Combination 2	9,000	1,000
Combination 3	7,000	2,000
Combination 4	4,000	3,000
Combination 5	0	4,000

Now suppose that, using all our resources—land, labor, capital, and entrepreneurship—to produce corn, we can harvest 10,000 tons a year. This would leave us with zero auto production. On the other hand, using all our resources to produce autos, we can make 4000 autos a year. Again, this would mean the sacrifice of all corn. Our resources are limited.

But there are other alternatives; we have several **production possibilities.** If our community divides its factors of production between corn and autos, we can produce various combinations of both, as shown in Table 1. If we are willing to *give up* 1000 tons of corn by shifting farm labor into auto factories, we can *produce* 1000 autos. If we give up 2000 *more* tons of corn, we could have 1000 *more* autos, for a total of 7000 tons of corn and 2000 autos. How much *more* corn must we give up to produce 1000 *more* autos?

Graphing Production

Now let us plot all possible combinations of corn and autos on a graph, as in Figure 1. The vertical axis shows corn, measured in thousands of tons. The horizontal axis shows autos, measured in thousands of units. Point A represents the community's decision to specialize completely in corn; point *B*, a decision to specialize completely in autos. In between are various other choices.

Everything *to the right* of our curve is beyond our system's current production capabilities. Point C is a combination of corn and autos that is outside the community's possibilities. Our resources and technology do not enable us to produce 8000 tons of corn and 7000 autos at the same time. Everything *to the left* of our curve reflects underemployment of our resources. Point *D* is an example. To produce only 3000 tons of corn and 2000 autos would mean sacrificing part of the community's possible output. We would not be using our scarce resources efficiently to produce goods we need.

Figure 1 is called a **production-possibilities curve.** It shows the existing possibilities and limitations of the community. It illustrates the problem of scarcity and the need to make choices. For any community, the curve may change over time as technology changes or as new supplies of resources become available; but at any point in time it is fixed. If the community is to get the maximum benefit from its limited resources, it will produce a combination of corn and autos that lies somewhere *on* the production-possibilities curve. It cannot now go beyond the curve to *C*, and it should not, in its own interest, operate inside the curve at *D*.

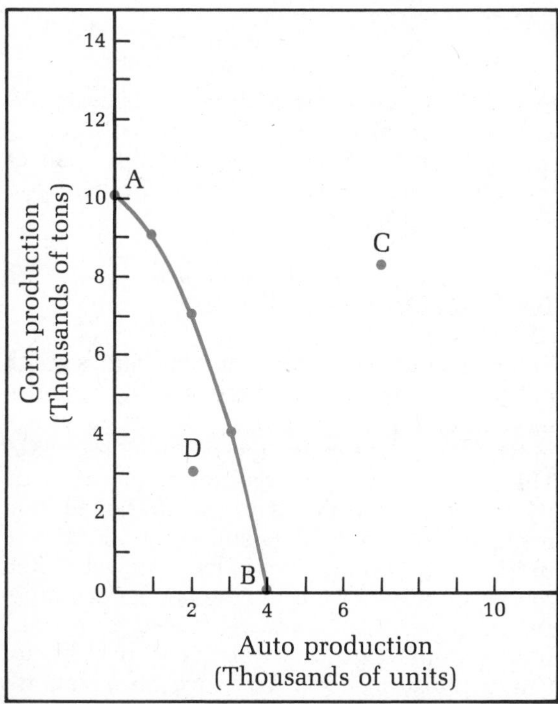

Figure 1 Production possibilities with increasing costs. To move along the curve from *A* to *B* requires larger sacrifices of corn for each gain in autos.

Opportunity Cost

The production-possibilities curve illustrates the need to make choices. As we move along the curve, we choose among alternative combinations of corn and autos. For any combination chosen, other possibilities must be sacrificed. More corn means fewer autos; more autos mean less corn.

This can be said another way. If we are presently producing 10,000 tons of corn and zero autos, the *cost* of producing 1000 autos would be 1000 tons of corn (since the community would have to reduce corn production from 10,000 tons to 9000). Economists refer to the value of a *forgone* opportunity as **opportunity cost.** Thus, for the opportunity of producing 1000 autos, we would pay 1000 tons of corn, or an opportunity cost of one ton for each auto. The opportunity cost of the second 1000 autos is 2000 tons of corn, or two tons per auto. What is the opportunity cost of producing the next 1000 autos? What is the opportunity cost per auto? What is the opportunity cost of the last 1000? What is the opportunity cost per auto?

We all encounter opportunity costs when we make choices. The diligent student of economics sacrifices the opportunity to read a novel or to play soccer. The buyer of a new stereo tape sacrifices the opportunity to buy a pair of gloves. The school that builds a gym may sacrifice the opportunity to equip a laboratory. A nation that produces guns may feed its children poorly.

Making choices based on opportunity costs. Before we can make choices, we must understand all our alternatives. We arrange our wants according to priorities. At the top of the list are our most urgent wants. To sacrifice these would involve large opportunity costs. Farther down the list are wants of lower priority and therefore smaller opportunity cost. Most of us make our decisions so that we hold opportunity costs to a minimum. For every possible alternative, we calculate the opportunity cost of all the goods and services we must give up. Then we compare alternatives and select the one with the smallest opportunity cost. In this way we can enjoy the goods we want most with the smallest personal sacrifice.

You followed this procedure, perhaps unconsciously, when you decided to attend college. You compared the opportunity costs of a

Extended Example Western Land Use Vs. Waste

We have defined land as "the original and irreplaceable resources of nature," and that is literally true. We cannot replace land, although we can sometimes move it around so as to use it better. (The land which was built out into Lake Michigan and on which part of Northwestern University sits is an example.) Regrettably, we can also destroy land, losing its value for future generations—perhaps forever.

It is difficult to think of Western prairies as fragile, but ecologists say it is. Some of the earliest explorers of the American West urged that the land not be settled at all. To break up the grasslands, they said, would leave the dry soil exposed to erosion. Despite these warnings, settlers moved in; cattle ranchers turned their livestock out onto the range; miners opened the ground to the wind. As the land was depleted, settlers moved on to damage more hundreds of acres. By the 1930s, dust storms were bringing Western soil as far east as Washington, D.C.

Something had to be done. The Bureau of Land Management was established in 1946, but its powers were limited. Western entrepreneurs resisted government efforts to restrain freedom of enterprise. Cattle continued to trample down valuable grasses, destroying the root systems and leaving the soil to waste. Dr. Jack D. Johnson at the University of Arizona estimated that Arizona, New Mexico, and west Texas turn $1 billion of fertile land into useless desert each year.

A stronger law was passed in 1976 but the controversy between environmentalists and ranchers continues. Movements to reduce land use for cattle raising raise threats of beef shortages with higher prices to consumers. Programs to fence off portions of the land for reseeding are costly to the taxpayers and involve government intervention into private business. The livelihood of hundreds of cattle raisers is at stake.

Use a hypothetical production-possibilities curve to diagram the tradeoff between our concern for the Western environment and our need for products of Western lands. How does the tradeoff change over time? On what basis should the decision be made to forgo beef for the sake of prairie land? Cite other recent examples of this kind of choice.

college education with the opportunity costs of immediate entry into the work force.

The opportunity costs of college are greater than just your tuition; your tuition fees and the interest they would earn in some other use are just one of several opportunity costs. For each year you spend in college you sacrifice the opportunity to earn income in some useful work. You probably sacrifice some personal freedoms if you remain financially dependent. Your total opportunity costs include all the activities you could have enjoyed had you not chosen to remain a student.

But look at the other side of this decision. The important costs of taking a job immediately may not come due until years in the future. Beginning work early in life may mean the sacrifice of opportunities to develop skills for greater long-range productivity and higher income in the future. It may lead to routine work without the challenging experiences that make life interesting.

You may add personal examples of other costs associated with each of these two alternatives. You are willing to pay the tuition costs and to forgo current income and personal freedom for four years, because the opportunity costs of the second alternative are greater. So here you are—at college!

The Law of Increasing Costs

Refer again to the production-possibilities graph in Figure 1. Have you noticed that the opportunity cost of producing autos increases as we move along the production-possibilities curve? This is a result of the assumptions we made when we drew it. We assumed, first of all, that resources are not equally suited for all types of production. Certain types of land are well suited for agriculture but too remote for manufacture; certain types of labor are well suited for specialized manufacture but relatively useless for heavy physical work. To move all a nation's resources into one type of production would eventually mean smaller gains and higher costs. Secondly, we assumed that some of the community's resources are fixed in quantity and use. The quantity of agricultural land is fixed and suitable only for raising corn. The quantities of factories and machinery are fixed and suitable only for making autos. Certain other resources can be used to produce either output. Some types of labor, for example, can be sent either into the cornfields or into the factories.

Now look again at Figure 1. To move from specialization in corn at point *A* requires that workers be taken from agriculture and employed in auto production. At first, moving workers into factories, moving down the production-possibilities curve, may allow factories to operate more efficiently. More autos can be built with a small opportunity cost in corn production. However, as more workers move into the factories, each additional worker has less machinery to work with and becomes less productive. Fewer additional autos are produced. Meanwhile, as the factories fill up, fewer workers are left to till the fields. Corn production falls by larger amounts as more workers leave corn production. The opportunity cost of producing each additional auto rises as more and more resources are shifted from farms to factories.

The changing pattern of opportunity costs is called the **law of increasing costs:** Opportunity costs change because the *proportion* of resources used changes. Total specialization in corn requires an excessive use of labor on a fixed quantity of land. At first, shifting labor into auto production improves the proportion of labor to land in corn production, and the opportunity cost for each additional auto is low. Continuing to shift labor, however, worsens the proportion of labor in corn and in auto production, and unit costs per auto increase.

Something like this is usually the case in the real world, and that is why the law of increasing costs is important. If it were not for increasing costs, the production-possibilities curve would be a straight line: The cost of producing another auto would not increase but stay the same in terms of amounts of corn forgone. Table 2 shows combinations of corn and autos for which the cost of producing more autos is constant at two tons of corn per auto. Figure 2 is the graph of production possibilities under conditions of constant costs.

In the real world, the tradeoff between producing autos and corn will generally obey the law of increasing costs. Only if techniques of producing the two goods are quite similar would the production-possibilities curve be a straight line. For example, the production-possibilities curve for producing either soybeans or corn would be close to a straight line. The proportions of land, labor, capital, and entrepreneurship used are roughly the same for producing soybeans as for producing corn. Thus the move from producing one good to another can be accomplished without loss of productivity.

Table 2 **Production Possibilities per Year**

	Corn (in tons)	Autos
Combination 1	8,000	0
Combination 2	6,000	1,000
Combination 3	4,000	2,000
Combination 4	2,000	3,000
Combination 5	0	4,000

Unemployment of Resources

In our discussion of production possibilities we assumed that the resources of the community were being fully and efficiently employed. But it

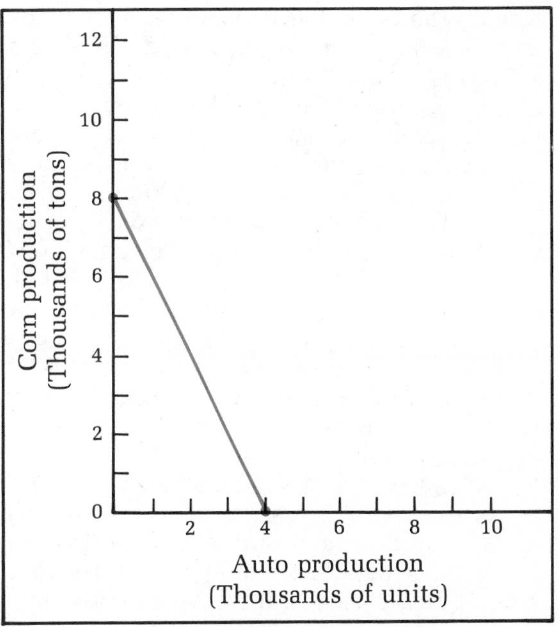

Figure 2 Production possibilities with constant costs. Movement along the curve requires equal sacrifices of corn for each gain in autos.

sometimes happens that a society is very far from the full and efficient use of its resources. This would be shown by placing a point somewhere inside the production-possibilities curve, say at *D* in Figure 1. If a society is at *D*, it can move in several different directions toward the curve by employing idle resources in any of various combinations.

The United States was inside its production-possibilities curve during the recession of 1974–75. Unemployment exceeded 8 percent of the labor force, or more than 7.5 million workers. As a result, we failed to produce about $200 billion worth of goods and services these workers could have produced. The most severe example of unemployment in this century was the Great Depression of the 1930s when the leading industrial countries of the Western world were all inside their production-possibilities curves. Not only was there 25 percent unemployed labor, but capital and land lay unused, too. The problem was not solved until the beginning of World War II, when all resources were employed to meet the added demand for production of military goods.

Overemployment and Inflation

At other times we have tried to produce outside our production-possibilities curve. The most recent example of this situation was the "Guns and Butter" dilemma that faced the United States in the late 1960s.

To illustrate this we will name our production possibilities *military goods* and *civilian goods.* On Figure 3 the horizontal axis measures units of military production: military equipment and military services. The vertical axis measures units of civilian production: consumer goods and services and capital goods. In 1965 the United States was operating very close to our production-possibilities curve, say at *A*. But in that year we began our heavy military build up in Vietnam. Our government began to spend heavily for planes and equipment, pilots, and infantry for the war.

Increased military production involved an opportunity cost. To use our scarce resources in military production meant foregone opportunities in the production of automobiles, television sets, and new houses. If we were to have more "guns," to move from *a* to *b*, we would have to give up some "butter," move from *d* to *c*.

President Johnson's economic advisers reminded him of this. They recommended that

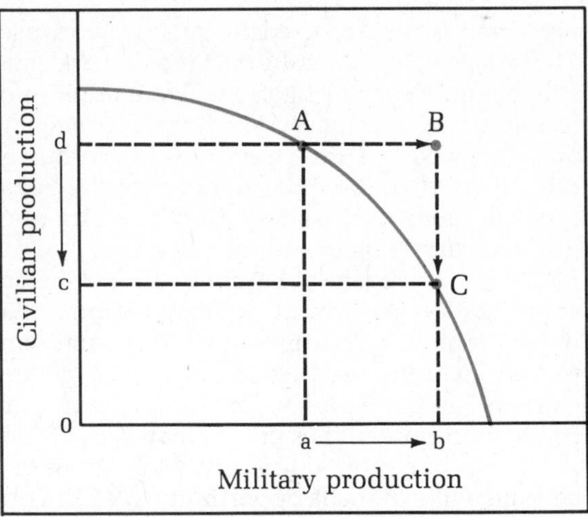

Figure 3 The attempt to produce beyond production possibilities. The quantity *ab* represents the increase in military production. The quantity *cd* represents the necessary decline in civilian production.

consumers be forced to reduce their spending for civilian goods so that resources could move into military production. How could this be accomplished? The answer was through higher taxes. But this answer was unacceptable to the President and to Congress. The war was unpopular and taxes were unpopular. Congress and the President were concerned about the reaction of citizens, and taxes were not immediately increased.

As a result, civilian spending continued at high levels while military spending rose higher and higher. The economy attempted to move from *A* to *B*, but *B* was beyond our production possibilities.

So, as more military goods were produced, civilian production had to fall to *C*. How was this accomplished without a tax increase? The heavy spending led to rising prices as civilian producers and government bid against each other for the existing quantity of scarce resources. With higher prices, the purchasing power of incomes fell. The nation experienced *price inflation.* Higher prices acted as a tax on incomes, reducing the spending power of families and cutting down purchases of civilian goods.

Changes in Production Possibilities

As we have seen, our nation's production possibilities are limited at any given point in time. In the long run, however, production possibilities can change—up or down. More frequently, production possibilities increase. Economic growth can be defined as an increase in production possibilities. There are two major factors affecting production possibilities: resource supplies and technological advance. Changing either one of these will affect our overall possibilities. Let's examine each in more detail.

Resource supplies. What if the resources available to the economy increase? We assumed that our hypothetical community's supplies of land, capital, labor, and entrepreneurship were fixed. But, in time, population growth will add to the labor supply. Moreover, through exploration, additional natural resources will be discovered, and better education and health care will improve human capital. The effect on production possibilities is to move the curve outward, as in Figure 4.

Depletion of resources will have the opposite effect. Unless new resources are developed, or technological change is great enough to offset the depletion of resources, the production-possibilities curve will shift to the left, as in Figure 5. A smaller stock of resources limits a nation to lower total production.

The Industrial Revolution that began in the eighteenth century was based largely on energy produced by burning coal. Since then, much of the cheap coal supply of leading industrial countries has been depleted. However, we found important new energy sources in oil, natural gas, and hydroelectric power to help us grow in the first three quarters of the twentieth century. Now the oil and natural gas are running out and becoming more expensive. Will atomic or solar energy replace them in the future? The search goes on.

An important source of growth in the United States has been an increase in capital

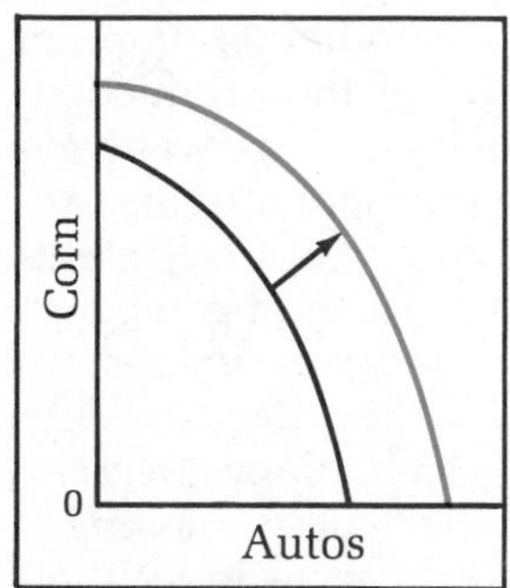

Figure 4 Expanding production possibilities.

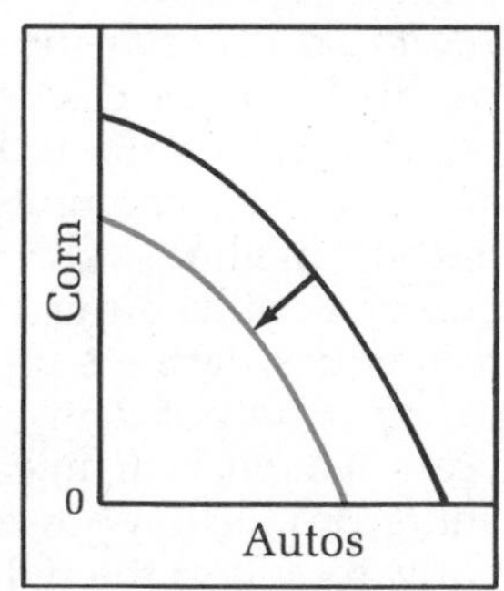

Figure 5 Declining production possibilities.

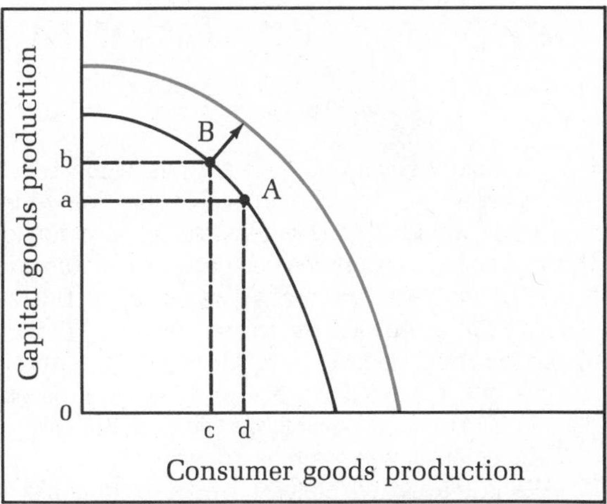

Figure 6 Increasing production possibilities through investments in capital goods. To produce *ab* more capital goods, the economy must give up *cd* consumer goods. But more capital resources will eventually move production possibilities further to the right.

resources. Capital investment requires choices, and the choices involve opportunity costs. Again the production-possibilities curve is useful. This time let us list all goods and services for *current* consumption on one axis; on the other axis we will list all capital goods for use in *future* production. On Figure 6 the horizontal axis represents production of food and clothing, medicine and schoolbooks, autos and stereos, and all other consumer goods and services. The vertical axis represents production of drill presses and lathes, welding torches and assembly lines, power plants and blast furnaces. Capital goods like these do not provide consumer goods in the current period, but they enable us to produce more in the future.

If we are currently producing *Oa* of capital goods and *Od* of consumer goods, our production possibilities can be represented by *A*. If, in the interests of economic growth in the future, we increase the production of capital goods to *b*, the production-possibilities curve dictates that we will have to decrease production of consumer goods to meet *b* at *B;* we will have to decrease production from *d* to *c*. For the period of time represented by this model, living standards of the community will be lower than they would have been had all production been in consumer goods. But the accumulation of capital goods increases the community's stock of productive resources.

Growth in production possibilities depends

Viewpoint The Opportunity Costs of R and D

There's a story about a famous scientist who worked months on a new invention only to decide finally that the design wouldn't work and should be abandoned. The inventor's assistant was bemoaning the hours and hours of work in what he saw as a wasted effort. But the scientist corrected him by saying, "But our experiments have not failed. We have succeeded in eliminating one of the ways that won't work. Now let us get busy to eliminate others until we find one that will!"

The scientist was Thomas Edison.

We in the United States have been fortunate in having the creative skills and a free business environment which have permitted invention to flourish. We have enjoyed bountiful resources and a favorable climate for producing the goods we need for life. In short, our environment and economic system have provided the material necessities of life and an economic surplus to do with as we wanted. As a result we have been able to direct resources toward scientific advance, enabling us to achieve even greater growth in output.

Our fortunate advantages have not been available to many primitive economies where scarcity is a life-and-death matter. In such nations every action must focus on survival alone. The people cannot afford the luxury of failure; thus they cannot enjoy the fruits of success.

Although we have been fortunate in the wider range of opportunities available to choose among, we must not assume that we will always have these advantages. The fortunate circumstances we now enjoy are partly the result of choices made many years ago. Throughout our history, American leaders in business and government have chosen to allocate a part of our productive resources toward research and development of new goods and services. These decisions helped push out the frontier of production possibilities, widening the range of choices open to new generations.

Research can be classified in two ways: *Basic research* aims at increasing knowledge; *applied research* seeks practical uses for new knowledge. *Development* involves putting new knowledge to use in real production. R and D is costly and time consuming, using resources which might otherwise be used for producing goods and services. Almost $50 billion, was spent for R and D in 1979, more than half provided by the federal government. Most basic research is actually carried out in universities, under contract to industry or government. Applied research and devel-

significantly on increasing a nation's stock of capital. To use scarce resources for the production of capital goods, the population must be willing (and able) to give up the opportunity to produce some consumer goods. This is possible only if the people can afford the sacrifice. In many parts of the world, production possibilities are so low that any sacrifice at all would lead to severe hardships and even starvation. Prospects for economic development are slim—or zero.

Many nations have five-year plans for allocating resources toward production of capital goods. India, some Eastern European countries, and some developing nations are examples. The United States, with its production decisions made individually by many consumers and business firms, allocates a smaller percentage of resources to capital goods than centrally controlled economies. Consequently, this has reduced our growth rate below that of the Soviet Union and some other countries. The basis of the Soviet five-year plan is to deny consumers as much as possible now in order to devote more resources toward catching up with the United States. The Soviets plan at that point to change goals; then, they expect, their citizens will be able to enjoy as many consumer goods as Americans do.

Technological advance. Another assumption we made in our discussion of the production-possibilities curve was that technology was fixed and that the community could not alter its production methods. Over time, of course, methods of production can change. Using modern techniques, farmers produce many times more corn per unit of land today than they did fifty years ago. Such changes in technology affect the entire production-possibilities curve, moving it outward and to the right. Advances in technology are necessary for a society to grow and

opment are carried out primarily by private industry.

The goals of R and D have changed over recent decades, from defense in the 1950s and space in the 1960s to health, energy, and the environment in the 1970s. Recessions have slowed the growth of R and D expenditures, and environmental and safety regulations have made industry cautious about new products and processes. To avoid the risk of costly failures, many firms have turned their research efforts toward new ways of marketing old products, rather than breaking new paths. If the slow growth of R and D continues, the pace of American technological development may slow as well. Failure to develop new technologies will impair our international competitiveness, slow economic growth, and reduce the number of new jobs available for our growing labor force.

What considerations enter a firm's decision to invest in R and D? What considerations are influenced by government? What industries do you suppose are the largest investors in R and D? Cite examples of results of R and D expenditures in recent product development. How might R and D decisions in a market economy differ from those in a command economy? How might they be similar?

become more productive, to produce more goods with each unit of resources.

Technological advance involves research, invention, and development, or *innovation* (adapting present knowledge to new uses); it may mean the addition of, or improved operation of, physical equipment. Technological advance also includes improved organization of production. Better techniques of management, incentive systems to motivate workers, and a healthy environment for enterprise can help increase production possibilities.

CHOOSING PRODUCTION

The model of the production-possibilities curve shows the limits of production capabilities. Within these limits the community must choose a particular combination of output. Any given choice imposes an opportunity cost in things the community must give up. This means the economy must choose carefully.

Specialization

In primitive societies, individuals and groups produce all the goods and services they need for existence. Such societies are *self-sufficient*. Self-sufficiency is necessary when there are few opportunities for trade. Modern, industrialized nations have the advantage of *specialization*. **Specialization** means that individuals produce a single type of good or service. Few individuals produce all the goods—food, housing, tools, etc.—needed for their existence; they specialize and trade for the things they need. When people specialize, they gain skill in producing their certain good, which enables them to produce more. The wide range of consumer products, from autos and movies to mopeds and discos, is possible only with specialization.

Specialization also means we can't live in isolation. We must exchange the goods or services we produce for those produced by others. Specialization inevitably involves exchange and trade. Not only do we trade with people in our own community, but different areas within our nation tend to specialize and trade—Detroit specializes in autos, the Carolinas in tobacco, Chicago in electrical goods and candy, Hollywood in movies, etc. And, finally, nations tend to specialize and engage in international trade.

If an entire country specializes in a few types of production, that nation will have to depend on trade to exchange its specialties for some of the other goods it needs. A trading nation will produce certain goods most appropriate to its unique endowments of fixed resources and labor; it will export these goods in return for goods it can obtain more cheaply abroad. For example, Denmark's resources are suitable for agricultural production, and Denmark chooses a point on its production-possibilities curve nearer the agricultural axis. Then, Denmark sells large quantities of bacon to England in return for England's manufactures. England in turn concentrates much of its productive effort on manufactured goods for export. If England tried to produce all the food it needed, it would have to sacrifice manufactured goods, and the opportunity cost would be high. If Denmark were to increase manufactures, it

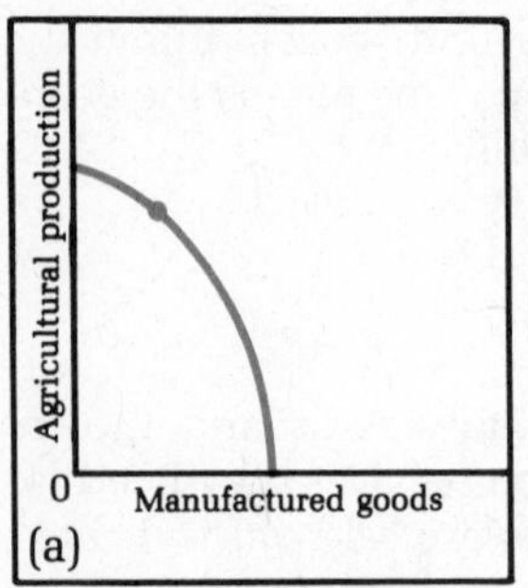

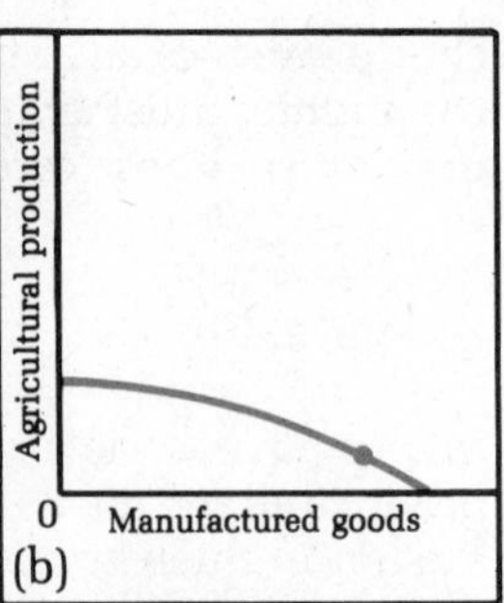

Figure 7 Hypothetical production possibilities for (a) Denmark and (b) England. Nations that specialize depend on trade to provide many goods they need. The dot on each curve shows the combinations of goods produced in Denmark and England.

would have to take resources from the low-cost production of agricultural exports and use them in the high-cost production of automobiles and television sets. Specialization and trade help both countries enjoy more goods and services, keeping opportunity costs low.

The hypothetical production-possibilities curves for England and Denmark are shown in Figure 7. For Denmark to increase production of manufactured goods, it would have to sacrifice large quantities of agricultural products. For England to produce agricultural products would mean great sacrifice of manufactured goods.

Guns Vs. Butter

Many countries are forced to choose between production of military equipment ("guns") and civilian goods ("butter"). If a nation is threatened by enemies, it may choose guns over butter, as shown in Figure 8. During World War II the United States turned its assembly lines to the production of tanks instead of automobiles, airfields instead of school buildings, and bombs instead of home appliances.

Citizens willingly made the sacrifices because they knew that military production was necessary for their security. They reduced their consumption of meat, bought fewer pairs of shoes, and drove their automobiles only when necessary. Scarce items were rationed, and saving was encouraged. A democratic society depends on the cooperation of its citizens in times of crisis.

One important basis for the prosperity of Germany and Japan today is that they were defeated in World War II. For some years they were not allowed to spend very much on military production and used their resources to build steel mills, shipyards, and modern manufacturing plants. Their living standards are probably higher than they would have been if they had won the war.

Private Vs. Public Consumption

Societies must also choose between producing **private goods,** goods and services for private use, or **public goods,** goods and services for public use. Public goods include public health and recreation facilities, public education, police and fire protection, social service programs, and defense. The more of its resources a society devotes to production of public goods and services, the fewer private goods it can enjoy. Figure 9 illustrates this choice.

An example of the results of the choice between public and private goods is the experience of Great Britain. Great Britain was in the forefront of the Industrial Revolution in the nineteenth century and experienced strong growth in production. Profitable growth enabled British entrepreneurs to accumulate savings for capital investment. Gradually, however, national prosperity and the increasing political power of working people appeared to change British priorities. During the twentieth century, more and more resources were chan-

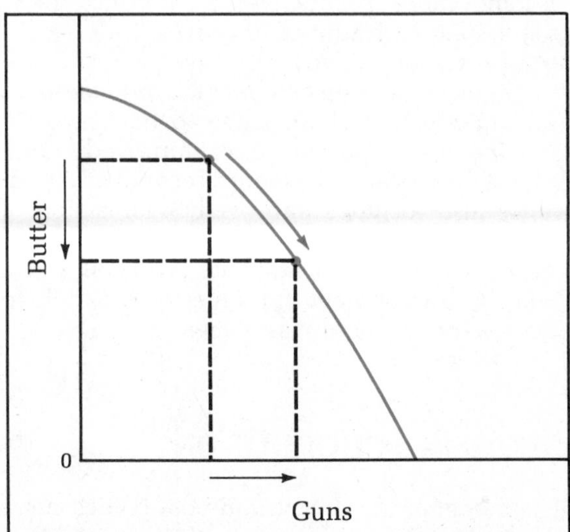

Figure 8 Producing more guns requires a sacrifice of butter.

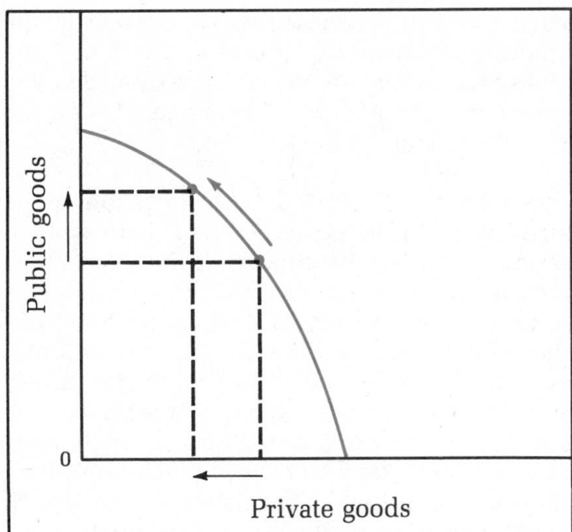

Figure 9 Producing more public goods requires a sacrifice of private goods.

neled to public services provided by government. In the decade 1965–75 the portion of Britain's output devoted to public spending rose from 45 percent to 60 percent. In the meantime, other nations were developing technologically, and their productive capacities grew to surpass those of Great Britain.

In 1979 British voters became concerned about their country's direction. They elected a government which promised to cut spending for social programs and return some government-owned industries to the private sector. They hope that private initiative will bring new life to the British economy.

Communities in the United States have chosen to use tax revenues for expenditure on public goods and services. Citizens who pay taxes have less income remaining to spend for private goods. Most of us make the sacrifice willingly, but we would like to see our tax money spent wisely.

In China, Russia, and some Eastern European countries most workers are employed by government. Government limits the production of private goods and chooses to allocate productive resources toward the public sector.

Work Vs. Play

There is another choice available to prosperous economies. The society may use some of its resources to "produce" *leisure.* As resources are freed from any production at all, the community sacrifices some goods and services they might have produced. The opportunity cost of lazing in the shade is the cabinet you might have built.

Figure 10 illustrates the opportunity cost of leisure. If many people enjoy the simple life, their desire for goods and services may be very small. The economic decision to work or to enjoy leisure is often a cultural one; certain nations at some point in time may place a higher premium on leisure than on work. For example, the British are renowned for "doing without" or preferring leisure, while the Japanese would rather work, producing and enjoying more goods and services.

HOW IS THE CHOICE MADE?

Societies don't always make their production decisions by conscious choice. How decisions are made depends on the fundamental ideology and institutions that have developed in the community. These cultural differences affect business incentives to invest, consumer plans to save, government economic policies, and private financial decisions. Many developing countries do not depend on the independent actions of private individuals. As we have seen, they

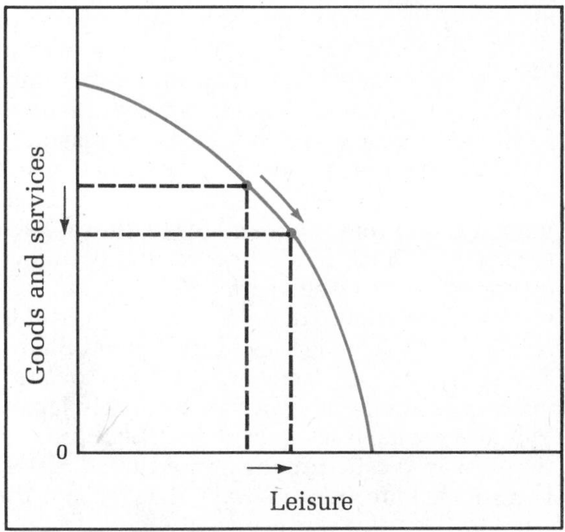

Figure 10 Enjoying more leisure requires a sacrifice of goods and services.

draw up plans for economic growth under the direction of central authority.

The Four Questions

In making its decisions every community or society must answer four basic questions: *What* is to be produced? *How* is it to be produced? *For whom* is it to be produced? *When* can the community enjoy the fruits of its productive resources?

What? No society can produce everything that all its citizens might want and in the quantities they want. We might all like to live in twenty-room houses with swimming pools and a car for every member of the family, but this is not possible. Somehow the society must decide whether to build twenty-room houses or cluster townhouses, swimming pools or cars, schools or airports, stereos or drill presses, parks or theaters. And it must decide how many resources can be freed from productive work to enjoy leisure. The answers a community gives to the question *What* will determine the quality of life in our society, now and for generations to come.

How? Almost everything can be produced in more than one way. Houses once were made of mud and still are in some countries. In our country they were once made of brick, but real brick houses are rarely built nowadays.* In many areas, it is more economical to build houses of plywood and shingles or with a thin veneer of brick on the outside. Many products that once were made of metal or wood are now made of synthetic chemical compounds called plastics.

Communities are endowed with particular combinations of resources which help determine the way they build and make things. Each community must decide how to use its unique combination of resources in the most efficient way. An abundance of land area would lead to *land-intensive* farming—as in the United States. An abundance of labor would lead to *labor-intensive* farming and manufacture—as in Japan. Plentiful capital leads to *capital-intensive* production—as in West Germany or the United States. If resources are used in ways that are not the most efficient, then society is poorer by the amount of extra output that is given up. The answers a society gives to the question *How* will determine the quantity of resources it is able to pass on to coming generations.

For whom? The third basic question to be answered is how society is to divide what it produces among its citizens. Some consumers receive more than others. Some producers receive more than others. Physicians, for example, usually receive more than farmers or teachers. The system by which society divides its output depends on the value it places on the contribution of each. In the Soviet Union poets and ballerinas tend to receive much more than they would in the United States. In the United States we reward business executives, rock stars, and quarterbacks. The answers society gives to the question *For whom* will provide the incentives for production in the future.

When? An even more difficult question may be the choice between "jam today" and "jam tomorrow." An economy must choose whether to produce consumer goods for use this year or to produce capital goods in order to be more productive in the next. In some very poor nations the second choice may not be possible: All available resources may be needed just to produce the food and supplies to keep people alive. In more prosperous economies, people may decide to sacrifice production of some consumer goods for the sake of future production. When resources are shifted away from consumer-goods industries into the production of capital goods, living standards will be temporarily reduced.

A nation with many students does this. Students use their energies to develop skills for use in future production. They train as designers, engineers, chemists, managers, and teachers. In the meantime their living standards are relatively low, and total production of consumer goods is less than it might be otherwise.

The United States encourages production of capital goods by providing tax advantages to business investors. Moreover, our highly developed system of banks and other financial institutions helps channel the funds of savers into investment in capital goods. As a result, we have accumulated productive capital, and our production-possibilities curve has continued to shift to the right.

*Except in the Southwest, where materials are plentiful and cheap.

Extended Example To Work or Not to Work?

"Perpetual holiday is a good working definition of hell." Do you believe that? George Bernard Shaw did.* In the quote above, he was referring to our need to be needed, to be a part of a productive system and to earn rewards from our contribution to production. Lately, some social analysts have suggested that these sentiments are disappearing, that the "work ethic" of the past has been replaced by the "me generation" of the 1970s. If this is true, the possible consequences should be of interest to future generations.

In terms of numbers, certainly more people are working—or want to work—than ever before. Not only are more people working but a larger fraction of the population considers itself a part of the work force: 63.6 percent in 1978, up from 55.7 percent forty years ago. New workers may not be as productive as experienced workers, but the fault may not lie entirely with a decline in the "work ethic." One reason may be the sheer numbers of new workers. The "baby boom" of the 1950s has flooded the labor market, making it doubtful that many workers may ever achieve their employment aspirations. They may have simply accepted the limits to their success in work and shifted their attention to other types of life satisfaction. Moreover, with more members of the family now working, it becomes less necessary for any single worker to increase his or her productivity.

The increase in the working population has also changed the ratio of labor to capital equipment in much of American industry. More workers per machine often mean lower output per worker. In addition, many of today's new workers work in service occupations where measuring the value of output is especially difficult.

The 1970s experienced a decline in population growth, so that by the 1990s there will be a scarcity of new workers and a reversal of today's productivity problems. The scarcity of workers will put a premium on skills and encourage a drive for achievement. Salary and promotion incentives will be high. In the 1990s the abundance of capital equipment relative to workers should enhance labor productivity and increase its rewards.

There will always be those who just don't want to work. But most of us would probably react like Shaw to a life of continual leisure. Whether we choose to work or not may depend on the motivations and opportunities our society offers us.

What elements of American society encourage work and what elements discourage it?

*G. B. Shaw is responsible for some of the most entertaining works in Western literature, including the play on which the musical "My Fair Lady" was based.

Other means of accomplishing the same result are used in the Soviet Union. Led by Josef Stalin, the Soviet Union began its first five-year plan in 1928. With enormous sacrifice and hardship the USSR built up its industrial capacity, which helped it withstand the German invasion in World War II. Since the war it has continued its five-year plans and is now in its eleventh (1981–85).

TYPES OF ECONOMIC SYSTEMS

As we have already seen, societies and communities usually do not answer these questions by conscious choice. Nobody comes to your door and says, "I'm a poll taker. How many cars do you think we ought to produce this year?" But every society does have a system for working out the answers.

Traditional Economies

In simpler economies of the distant past, decisions were based on a **traditional economic system.** Even today, some societies answer the four questions (What? How? For whom? When?) as they have done for generations. Potters produce cook pots, Carpenters build dwellings, Hunters and Farmers provide food, and Tanners prepare hides for clothing. This is the origin of many of our family names; Shepherd, Carter, Miller, Smith, and Taylor are other examples.

In primitive societies, following tradition is necessary because there is only a slim margin between life and death. One bad harvest or disastrous winter can bring ruin. Survival depends on keeping to the ways which proved successful in the past. There is very little **economic surplus** with which to experiment. As a result, there may be few opportunities for economic growth and development. The only hope for such societies may be loans and grants from wealthier nations. Food aid, for example, can provide a surplus which will free some of a country's own resources for the production of capital goods. Construction of industrial capital by foreign firms may also increase productivity and provide the basis for independent growth.

Command Economies

In some areas of the world, a favorable climate or fertile land has helped production grow beyond the amount necessary for survival. Then the choice of what to produce becomes more complex. A prosperous community can choose to use its resources for new types of production. For example, a forward-looking community can decide to build capital equipment for economic growth: factories, machinery, roads, bridges. Or an aggressive community can decide to produce military equipment: walls and fortresses to protect it from attack, vehicles and guns to invade other areas. Or communities like those of Renaissance Italy can produce luxurious palaces and formal gardens for the ruling class, jewelry and ceremonial robes for priests, or great public buildings and stadiums to celebrate national power.

In such societies the basic economic decisions have often been made by a central authority: a king, a dictator, or a central planning board. We call this a **command economic system.** Command economies tend to develop where it is acceptable to control the use of resources for the sake of an important goal. To leave production decisions in the hands of many independent individuals may conflict with the national objective. We have seen that in the Soviet Union the objective is to build an industrial base for increasing production in the future. To reach this goal a central planning board was set up to make most production decisions.

There are elements of command in other nations where the goal may be capital accumulation, military power, or a luxurious life-style for the controlling elite. A command economy may operate efficiently to channel resources toward the national goal. But whatever the goal, a command economy necessarily interferes with the liberties of its citizens. Loss of individual freedoms is one of the costs of a command economy.

Today there are two basic economic systems that rely at least partly on command: communism and socialism.*

Communism. **Communism** consists of government ownership of property and the means of production; hand in hand with this centralized economic power is a political dictatorship. In communist nations the government decides what is to be produced. Quotas are set on how many bicycles, radios, autos, washing machines, pairs of pants, etc., are to be produced. Examples of communist nations are the Soviet Union, China, Cuba, Albania, Poland, Hungary, and the other Eastern European countries. However, in some of these countries, especially those of Eastern Europe, many small businesses and farms are privately owned.

Socialism. Socialism is not as easily defined as communism since it is a word that has become "stretched" in different directions. To followers of Marxist terminology, socialism exists in nations such as the Soviet Union and its Eastern European allies. Such a definition of socialism allows neither economic democracy nor political democracy.

To many people in Western Europe and North America, socialism does not require the loss of political democracy. Under this definition, Sweden, Denmark, and Great Britain are examples of socialism. Sometimes this variation is called *democratic socialism*.

We can note one feature common to any definition of socialism and will use it for our definition. **Socialism** is an economic system where government owns the means of production but not property. Strictly speaking, this means all forms of production. However, we will note that the real world has no country that fits exactly any common definition of communism, socialism, or capitalism. Therefore, we will classify countries like Great Britain and Sweden as

*Actual conditions in communistic and socialist economies differ significantly from the ideal societies described by Karl Marx.

Economic Thinker **Karl Marx**

Karl Marx (1818–83) was born in Germany and grew up during the time when the Industrial Revolution was reshaping society. The European population was booming and urban slums were growing. It was a time when philosophers were examining the social world around them for explanations of why social systems developed as they did. As a young man, Marx became interested in political conflict and began his career as a political journalist. Then, he began to weave his observations about conflict into a major theory of historical change.

Marx's view of history was based on the belief that history moves in stages. History moves from one stage to a higher one because of conflict between competing groups. In each stage, one particular class in society exercises the greatest power. But a new class develops, with interests which clash with those of the dominant class. Finally, the new class would become powerful enough to overturn the old and set itself up as the newly dominant power. Of course, it would soon be subject to challenge by a still newer class seeking power in *its* own interest. Furthermore, the relative economic positions of classes in any one stage of history would determine all the basic arrangements of society: the legal and political arrangements and even the religion, the social traditions, and the cultural arrangements. According to Marx, all this was inevitable.

What was the basis by which any class gained power in any particular stage? In Marx's view the basis for control was ownership of the means of production. The groups in society who controlled the means of pro-

socialist, since many of the major means of production—steel mills, shipyards, railroads, airlines, health care—are owned and operated by the government. These socialist countries have obvious elements of command, since government sets output or determines the size of these industries.

Market Economies

Citizens of other democratic societies are allowed greater influence in making economic decisions. Where resources are available for ample production, societies may choose the **market economic system** to answer the four questions: *What, How, For whom,* and *When* are decided in the market, where many buyers and sellers compete for their own advantage.

Although no poll taker comes to your door, you do vote your preference for goods and services through the dollars you spend in the market. Nowadays we see many more small cars on the roads than a few years ago. Nobody made a formal decision to produce more small cars and fewer large ones. It happened because millions of individual car buyers changed their minds about automobiles, and producers were forced to respond.

In free markets buyers express their preferences by their dollar expenditures. These expenditures answer the question *What*.

ducing and exchanging goods and services would hold the reins of power.

Marx was able to show how previous history had moved through various economic stages. The first stage in modern civilization was feudalism. Under feudalism the means of production were controlled by the landed aristocracy. Ownership of land enabled the nobles of Europe to hold the peasant class in servitude, dependent on landowners for their security and for their means to life. But a new class developed to undermine the power of the feudal lords. The beginnings of trade opened the way for merchants and capitalists to assert their control through commerce and industry in the new towns. The power of the lords was then broken as the peasants flocked to the towns to take jobs in factories.

Under capitalism, ownership of the means of production enabled capitalists to drive a hard bargain with workers. Exploitation of the working class permitted factory owners to accumulate even greater wealth and power. A challenge to that power was sure to come. Marx predicted that the "propertyless proletariat" (the workers) would rise up in violent revolution and overthrow the dominant capitalist class. The revolution would come in a nation where capitalism had developed to the fullest. There, industry would have become increasingly monopolized by a few large firms. Their monopoly would have enabled them to force wages down and to collect high profits. Misery and unemployment among the working class would finally bring on massive uprisings and the workers would take over the means of production.

There would be two more stages of economic development: socialism and communism. Under socialism the nation's means of production would be owned and controlled by the state. During the transition period to the highest stage, there would be a "dictatorship of the proletariat." All classes other than the working class would be suppressed. Finally, under communism, the workers themselves would own the means of production "in common" and operate them democratically in the interests of all the people. Goods and services would be distributed to all according to their needs. There would be no need for social classes, and eventually government, too, would wither away.

Throughout Marxist theory there is little regard for the power of intellect or free will to affect important events. A society's technical-economic structure or stage is, according to Marx, its most dominant trait. This is both a serious weakness of Marxist theory and a real contribution to historical thinking. The idea that human relationships are strongly influenced by the technology and economic development of their age was a new one and has had a major impact on subsequent historical analysis.

For millions of the world's people who live in poverty and despair, Marxism seems to offer hope and salvation. The almost religious fervor of Marx's writings promises a life of plenty with peace and harmony among all workers. The reality has been different in the nations which claim to follow Marx. Productivity is often low, inequality among classes persists, and personal freedoms are suppressed.

Sellers compete to satisfy buyers by offering the most desired goods at the lowest possible price. They try to use the most efficient technology and the lowest-cost resources available. This response to consumer demand answers the question *How.*

Goods and services are divided among people according to their incomes. Incomes are based on the contribution of each to production. We each receive goods equal in value to the resources we contribute. This division of goods is the market's answer to *For whom.*

Individuals freely make the decision whether to produce for now or later. Savers and investors sacrifice present purchases for the expectation of having more later. Thus private incentives answer the question *When.*

Capitalism. Like the word *socialism, capitalism* is a term that resists easy, clear definition. *Capitalism* is often used interchangeably with *market economy* or *free markets,* but, strictly speaking, capitalism entails much more. We can define our term by its properties. **Capitalism** is an economic system characterized by the following: (1) private ownership of capital or the means of production; (2) free enterprise, the ability to start or dissolve any business; (3) free and competitive markets for producing goods and services; and (4) freedom of choice for people to buy what they please and to work where they wish. This definition is sometimes known as *pure capitalism*. No nation in the world fits this description completely, though the United States probably comes closest.

Mixed economy and mixed capitalism. Although the United States is mainly a market economy, we retain some elements of tradition in many communities and a degree of command. We do not leave every decision to individual choice in free markets, and we recognize that certain goods and services must be provided outside the market system. Individual buyers and sellers will not be able to arrange for the production of such things as roads and bridges, educational opportunities for all, equipment for national defense, and public buildings. We authorize government to take care of these needs.

We limit the working of the market in other ways: by prohibiting the sale of certain drugs; by restricting gambling and pornography; by regulating certain business practices that are considered monopolistic or undesirable; and by taxing higher incomes more than lower incomes in order to distribute income from production more equally. This means that our economy is actually a *mixed economy*—primarily a market economy but with some elements of command and tradition.

The United States economy is more accurately described as *mixed capitalism*. All four of the characteristics of capitalism are modified, frequently by government. Not everything is privately owned, since our government owns railroad passenger service, research laboratories, and the postal system. Although free enterprise generally exists, government does regulate some businesses and may even help prevent a business from going bankrupt (as with Chrysler in the early 1980s).

Free markets are also subject to interference from individuals or groups. Groups with monopoly power may restrict the free flow of goods to market and raise their prices. Advertising may guide consumer choice toward particular goods. Labor unions might succeed in keeping employment levels artificially high by enforcing restrictions in hiring.

In the next chapter we will begin to show how individual buyers and sellers participate in answering the four important economic questions.

SUMMARY

In this chapter we have explored the basic economic problem that every society faces. At any single point in time, a society has limited quantities of resources and a fixed level of technology. Its existing resources enable it to produce some total quantity of goods and services—its production possibilities. On the other hand, the wants of its people are unlimited.

Economic resources are called *factors of production* and are classified as land, labor, capital, and entrepreneurship. Because productive resources are scarce, we must choose carefully how we will use them. Within the limits of production possibilities, any community may choose among alternative combinations of goods and services: military equipment or civilian goods; consumer goods or capital goods; private goods or public goods; more goods or more leisure. Each choice involves an opportunity cost of alternative goods and services given up. Opportunity costs increase as a society moves more resources into the production of certain goods or services and out of production of others. This is because of the fixed character of many resources available for production.

Production possibilities depend on a nation's stock of resources and its available technology. Growth in either of these enables a nation to produce more. Capital is also an important resource for growth, but producing capital requires an opportunity cost of consumer goods not produced.

Deciding how to use productive resources requires answers to four questions: What? How? For whom? When? Some communities make these decisions by tradition or through the command of a ruling party. Some democratic societies decide through the market system.

Key Words and Phrases

capital goods goods produced for use in producing other goods.

capitalism an economic system in which the means of production are owned and operated by individual owners, or capitalists.

command economic system a system in which the questions *What, How, For whom,* and *When* are goods produced are answered by a central authority.

communism an economic system in which the means of production and property are owned and operated by the state; in addition, the state is a political dictatorship.
constant costs a condition in which expanding output causes no change in the additional costs of producing each unit.
consumer goods goods which are used directly by final consumers.
economic problem a situation in which resources are limited, relative to the wants of the people.
economic surplus those goods, services, and resources available after minimum requirements for existence are provided for the people.
entrepreneurship creative activity to combine and use other resources or factors of production.
factors of production land, labor, capital, and entrepreneurship which are used to produce goods and services.
financial capital money savings which can be used to purchase capital goods.
free goods resources which have no economic value (price) because they are in unlimited supply.
human capital the developed and refined skills of people.
labor purposeful activity of human beings.
land the original and irreplaceable resources of nature.
law of increasing costs when output of a good is increased relative to the production of another good, unit costs tend to increase; opportunity costs tend to increase, the more we produce of a good.
market economic system a system in which the questions *What, How, For whom,* and *When* are goods produced are answered through independent decisions of the people.
mixed economic system a system in which there are elements of tradition, command, and the market.
opportunity cost the sacrifice of some good or service given up because of a decision to acquire some other good or service.
private goods goods and services which are consumed by individuals.
production possibilities various combinations of goods and services which can be produced with a nation's available resources and technology.
production-possibilities curve a graph showing the maximum quantities of goods and services which can be produced with available resources and technology.
public goods goods and services which are consumed by the community as a whole.
socialism an economic system in which the means of production are owned and operated by the state.
specialization concentrating skills in one type of production alone.
traditional economic system a system in which the questions *What, How, For whom,* and *When* are goods produced are answered in the same way from generation to generation.

Questions for Review

1. What are the opportunity costs of becoming a concert violinist? How is a violinist compensated for incurring the costs?
2. How is the law of increasing costs involved in a hamburger stand? a chain of hamburger stands?
3. Draw up a schedule of production possibilities for a hypothetical economy. Classify output as public goods and private goods. Make certain your data confirm the law of increasing costs. Plot your data on a graph and show that additional costs do increase as the economy approaches total specialization.
4. Explain how a nation's goals influence the selection of a point on its production-possibilities curve. Select examples from current news. How have modern transportation and communication affected goal selection in many countries?
5. What are the opportunity costs of unemployed resources?
6. Assume the nation is at full employment and government decides to increase expenditures for programs to provide education and health care for low-income families. What results would you predict: in the immediate period? over the long term?
7. What is the cost to a city of preserving a historic building in the center of town?
8. "You can't have your cake and eat it too." Explain.
9. How does communism differ from socialism? from capitalism?
10. What conditions were held ceteris paribus for drawing the production-possibilities curve for Figure 1?

CHAPTER 3

The Free Market: Supply and Demand

Learning Objectives

Upon completion of this chapter, you should be able to:

1. Define the law of demand, explain why it's true, graph a demand schedule, and give four reasons why a demand curve might change.
2. Define the law of supply, explain why it's true, graph a supply schedule, and give four reasons why a supply curve might change.
3. Define market equilibrium, explain why it occurs, and explain what may prevent it from occurring.
4. Explain the functions of a market or price system.
5. Indicate the advantages of a market system, as well as its shortcomings.
6. Distinguish between microeconomics and macroeconomics.

Sam had been in business for years. He manufactured a beverage known in the mountains as White Lightning, and at his peak he turned out twelve thousand gallons a week. His distribution costs were low, and he had no advertising expenses. His price of $4 a gallon brought him a handsome profit. But times change, even in the hills of North Carolina, and things began to happen to Sam's business.

First, his production costs rose. The prices of sugar, rye flour, corn meal, yeast, and coal kept chasing each other upward like dogs going after a raccoon. Then his equipment began to wear out. Sam's capital goods included a 280-gallon cooker, a 150-gallon barrel, two 55-gallon barrels, 60 feet of copper coil, mash boxes, and a 150-gallon coal boiler. The cost of replacing this equipment almost doubled.

After he raised his price to $6 a gallon, Sam discovered that some of his old customers no longer came around. In fact, many of them weren't there anymore. They'd moved out of the hills into town and were earning enough to buy legal whiskey instead of moonshine. To cover all his expenses, Sam figured he would have to raise his price to $8 a gallon—but most of his remaining customers couldn't afford that price.

It wasn't the "revenooers" who put Sam out of business—it was the market.

THE MARKET: SOME DIMENSIONS

We saw in Chapter 2 that the market is a basic institution of American society. The market decides such questions as *what* will be produced, *how* it will be produced, *for whom* society will divide the total product, and *when* goods can be enjoyed. Actually, there are many markets. There is a market for automobiles, a market for labor, a market for corn whiskey, and so on. Some markets are concentrated in particular places, like the farmers' markets that we see in many cities during the summer. Other markets are worldwide—the market for grain and the market for motion picture films. A market may be centralized in a particular building, like the stock market, even though buyers and sellers are scattered everywhere.

Economists use the term free or perfectly competitive **market** to mean, in Alfred Marshall's words, "the whole of any region in which buyers and sellers are in such free intercourse with one another that the prices of the same goods tend to equality easily and quickly." The market for automobiles has now become practically worldwide. An auto company in Detroit has to think about its competitors in Germany and Japan and elsewhere when it designs and prices its cars; otherwise it may find its customers drifting away like the customers of Sam the moonshiner.

BEGINNINGS: ADAM SMITH

The first modern scholar to study the market was Adam Smith. Adam Smith was a respected professor and scholar during the early years of the Industrial Revolution in England. At that time, European economies operated under the economic principles of **mercantilism.** The goal of a mercantilist system was to increase national wealth through favorable trading relationships with other nations. To the mercantilist this meant more exports than imports. By developing its industry and agriculture, a nation could trade its own goods for the gold and raw materials of other nations. In order to ensure production of the correct goods for trade, government made many of the production decisions in a mercantile system.

In 1776, the year of the American Declaration of Independence, Smith published his great work, *An Inquiry into the Nature and Causes of the Wealth of Nations.* In this book Adam Smith described a new economic system that was beginning to take hold in the democratic nations of the West. This new form of economy was one in which people were free to decide for themselves what they would produce and how they would spend their incomes. Individual consumers who were free to express their preferences in free markets, producers who were free to seek profits by providing goods and services—these were the participants in free markets. The independent choices of individual buyers and sellers would bring about the best results for the community without the need for government regulation of production. The community would prosper and grow as if an **"invisible hand"** were guiding it.

Smith's "invisible hand" is one of the most famous phrases in all of economic literature. It describes how competition in free markets guides production in ways that increase well-being for all people. In a system of free markets, producers compete against each other to sell more goods. Each tries to produce at lowest cost, and prices are forced down. If certain goods are scarce, buyers offer high prices, drawing more producers into industries where the need is greatest. "It is not from the benevolence of the butcher, the brewer, or the baker that we expect our dinner," said Adam Smith, "but from their regard to their own interest. We address ourselves not to their humanity but to their self-love, and never talk to them of our own necessities but of their advantage." Such a system is known as a **market economy.**

From its beginning, the United States made most economic decisions through the free market system. It is appropriate that a nation built on freedom of choice in its political life would also provide freedom of choice in its economic life. Our political democracy is based on the idea that each voter helps determine government policy. Our **economic democracy** rests on the principle that each dollar spent helps determine the goods and services that are to be produced. In a free market, consumers determine what and how much is to be produced by the way they spend their dollars.

The market system has been very successful in developing the American economy. More goods have been produced through the market system than through any other system. Nowhere else have average incomes been consistently higher. Over the years our economy has grown to meet the wants of our people.

Production in the market system may occasionally include unpopular or unnecessary goods and services, of course. Edsel automobiles, palm readings, pet rocks, pornography, and medical quackery are some examples. And production may fall short in needed areas: low-cost housing, long-lasting appliances and clothing, tasty and nutritious food, and quality television entertainment. But this is the nature of the market system. Production in the market system is directed mainly by what consumers are willing and able to pay for rather than by what someone decides is "good for" them.

Adam Smith recognized that the ideal results of the market system did not always exist in the real world. And we recognize some of the weaknesses of the market system: job insecurity and inequality of incomes. But we recognize its strengths as well: incentives to greater productivity and growth, efficiency in the allocation of resources, and personal freedom to choose one's own life-style.

DEMAND

Under the market system the question of what will be produced is decided largely by consumers. By **consumers** we mean persons or households who buy goods and services. When they buy, they are, in effect, voting for the kinds of goods and services they prefer. If they prefer smaller cars that use less gasoline, then the message goes to auto companies to respond to this or face the consequences—loss of profits.

Law of Demand

The basic principle underlying consumer preference is called the law of demand. The **law of demand** states that consumers normally choose to buy fewer units of a good at high prices and more units at low prices. The quantity of a good that a particular consumer would buy at various prices can be shown in a **schedule of demand.**

Table 1 shows demand schedules for the Smith and Jones families. Each schedule indicates the quantity of ski weekends that the Smith or Jones family would buy per season at various prices. At this point, it is impossible to tell which of all the quantities shown each family will actually buy and the price that will actually be paid. A demand schedule shows what each *would* buy, depending on what price is charged. The data in Table 1 refer to a particular period of time in which all other factors that affect demand do not change. Such factors as consumer tastes, income, and expectations are assumed constant for now. Later we will see what happens when any one of these factors changes.

Table 1 **Demand for Ski Weekend Accommodations**

Price	Quantity		
	Smith family	Jones family	Market demand
$100	0	4	10,000
80	4	6	20,000
70	10	8	30,000
60	18	10	40,000
50	20	12	50,000

The Smiths are avid skiers. If the price is $50 per weekend, they would buy twenty weekends per year for a total expenditure of $1000. Their demand would decline, however, if prices were higher: At $100 they apparently would prefer to spend their money on something else. The Joneses are less enthusiastic about skiing often but like to ski at least a few weekends per season. At a price of $100, when the Smiths would be turned off, the Joneses would still be in the market for four weekends.

The "market," of course, includes many families besides the Smiths and the Joneses. Some consumers would demand more ski weekends than others at a given price; some consumers would buy at a much higher price than others. The total market demand at each price is shown in the third column of Table 1.

The demand schedule in Table 1 describes consumer intentions over a short period of time during which certain assumptions are made ceteris paribus. Factors that might affect demand are assumed to remain constant: consumer *tastes*, consumer *incomes*, the *number* of consumers, prices of *other goods*, and *expectations* of prices and incomes.

Graphing Demand

The market for a consumer good or service can be illustrated by a graph. Figure 1 is drawn from the information given in Table 1. The quantity of ski accommodations is shown on the horizontal axis. Price is shown on the vertical axis. Each column under "Quantity" in Table 1 is projected onto a separate graph. The quantities for the families in Table 1 appear as points on the graphs in Figure 1. Connecting these points

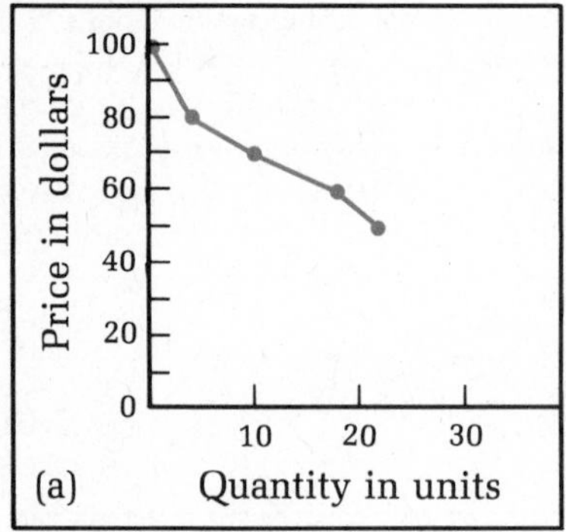

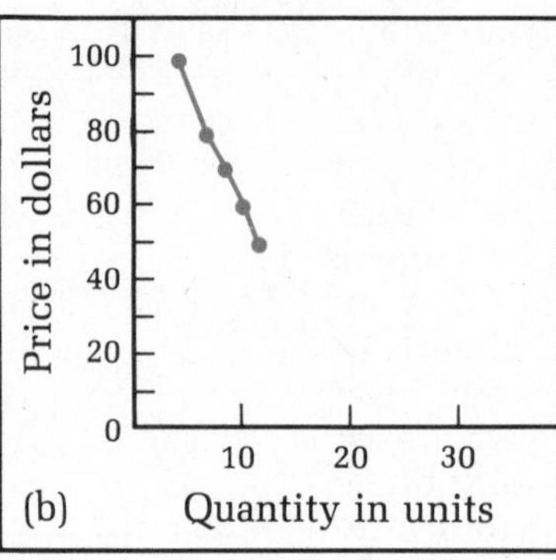

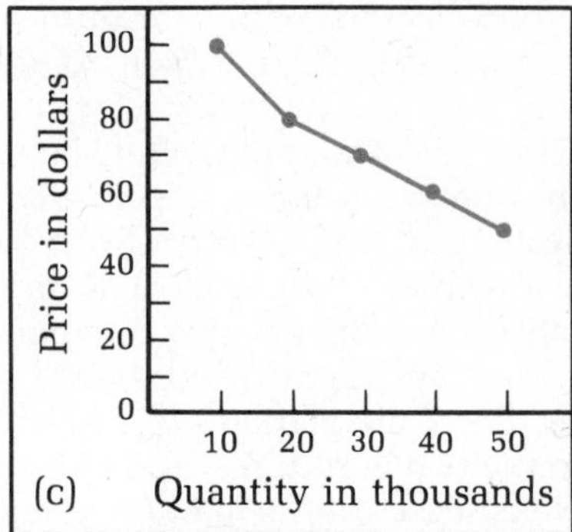

Figure 1 Demand curves for ski weekend accommodations for (a) the Smith family, (b) the Jones family, and (c) total market demand.

with a line produces what is known as a **demand curve.** (The more points that are plotted and connected, the smoother the curve will be. If we could plot an infinite number of points, the curve would be absolutely smooth, with no straight segments.) Using this procedure, the separate behaviors of the Smith and Jones families can be translated into demand curves (a) and (b). There will be as many individual demand curves as there are consumers.

The Smith curve is flatter than the Jones curve because the Smiths are more responsive to changes in price: If price should fall from $70 to $50, the Smiths would buy twice as many ski weekends, while the Joneses would buy only half again as many. If we add all the quantities which would be bought at each price, we obtain the market demand curve in Figure 1c. The shape of this curve is quite different from the shapes of the Smith and Jones curves. The shape of the market demand curve depends on the shape and position of all individual demand curves. If price falls from $70 to $50, total quantity demanded would increase by two thirds.

Notice that all three demand curves slope downward. This characteristic is true of all normal demand curves. The downward slope is a graphical interpretation of the law of demand: At lower prices, more will be demanded than at higher prices (all other factors constant).

Changes in Demand

The demand curves in Figure 1 show the relationship between price and quantity for a particular period of time. All other factors which might influence demand are held constant in order to observe the effects of price alone. Consumers' tastes and incomes, numbers of consumers, prices of other goods, and expectations are set aside ceteris paribus. A change in any of these factors will change the demand for a particular product. An entirely new demand curve must be constructed to show the new quantity that will be bought at every price.

Tastes. Everyone who follows clothing fashions knows that a dress or coat that sold well last year may not find favor at all this year. People still buy clothing, of course, but tastes change. Just why tastes change isn't always clear. Sometimes the public seems to fall in love with plaid trousers, Toyota cars, and ragtime and out of love with Beatle records and button-down shirt collars. Producers who are sensitive to the public mood can profit from changes in tastes, either by making a product to suit a new taste or by altering an existing product in a suitable way.

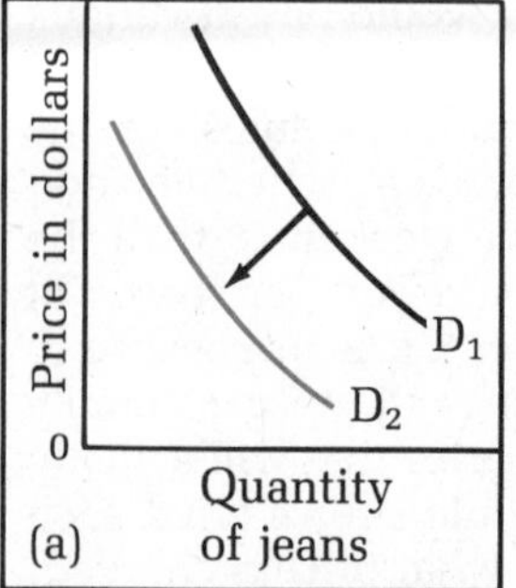

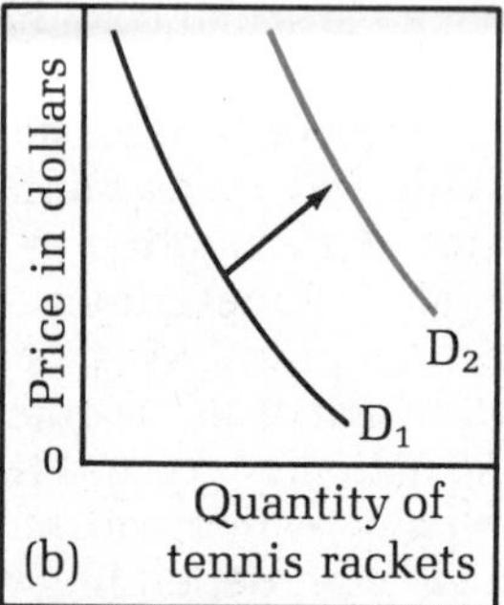

Figure 2 (a) A change in tastes reduces the quantity of studded jeans consumers would buy at every price. (b) Higher incomes increase the quantity of tennis rackets consumers would buy at every price.

For example, the popularity of blue jeans with a worn look led many manufacturers to incorporate blue denim in the design of other consumer goods.

When tastes change, demand curves shift to show the different quantities consumers would buy at every price level. Figure 2a shows how a specific change in consumer tastes—people don't care for studded jeans anymore—has decreased demand, *D*, shifting the demand curve to the left.

Incomes. Changes in incomes also affect demand curves. When people earn higher incomes, they are likely to buy more of certain types of goods, particularly items they haven't been able to afford before. We might expect enthusiastic skiers to plan more ski weekends at every price. They will also buy more restaurant meals and perhaps a second car. On the other hand, they may buy less chicken or cabbage because they will prefer to spend their money on steaks or other high-priced foods.

Whenever large numbers of people experience increases in income, it is safe to predict that sales of luxury goods will increase while sales of less-preferred goods will decrease. Economists distinguish between *superior goods,* whose purchases increase more than proportionately to income, from *inferior goods,* whose purchases increase less than proportionately. Demand curves will shift to show the new quantities which will be bought at every price. Figure 2b shows how rising incomes have affected demand for tennis rackets. For many people, recreational activities are superior; therefore, demand has increased and the demand curve has shifted to the right.

Prices of related goods. Demand for one good may be affected by a change in the price of another good. We would expect that the demand for pork would be affected by beef prices, since people tend to eat more pork when beef becomes expensive and less pork when beef becomes affordable again. Similarly, an increase in the price of postage stamps is likely to increase the demand for long-distance telephone calls as people turn to calling instead of writing. These are called **substitute goods;** one may be replaced by the other. An increase in the price of a good will increase the demand for its substitute. Figure 3a shows how rising coffee prices have affected demand for tea.

Some goods, on the other hand, go together, like ham and eggs or skis and ski jackets; these are called **complementary goods.** An increase in the price of a good is likely to be accompanied by a decrease in demand for its complement. In the United States we have seen that a steep increase in the price of gasoline reduces the demand for autos that burn a lot of fuel. Figure 3b shows how low turkey prices affect demand for cranberries.

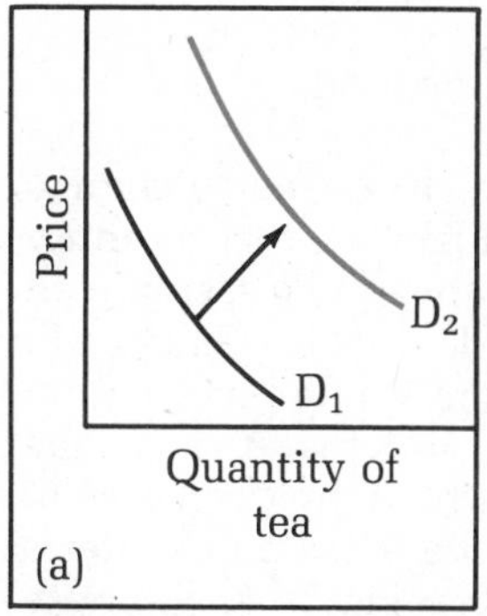

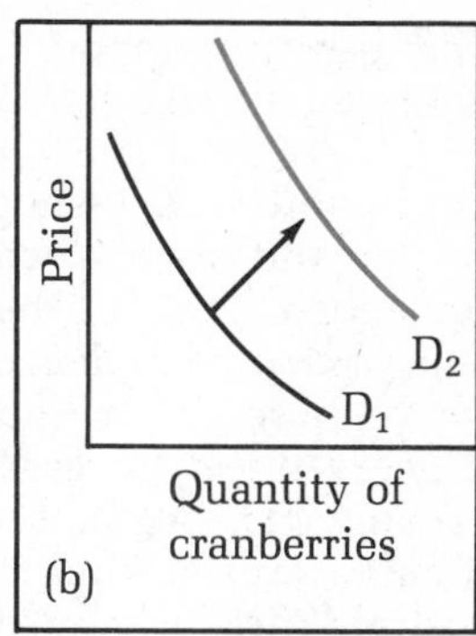

Figure 3 (a) An increase in the price of coffee increases demand for its substitute, tea. (b) A lower price for turkey increases demand for its complement, cranberries.

Number of buyers. An increase in the number of customers will ordinarily increase demand for a product. Such an increase may result from larger families or from improvements in transporting the goods to a greater number of customers. Foreign trade is an important source of a shift in demand. Increased exports of a good shift demand to the right, and U.S. farmers are able to satisfy demand for food.

Expectations. Finally, if consumers expect their incomes to increase in the near future, they are more likely to buy expensive items than if they expect their incomes to decline. Much installment buying of consumer durables, such as clothes dryers and TV sets, is done because consumers expect to make payments out of future income. Or if consumers expect the prices of these goods to rise, they may be induced to buy them sooner than they had planned. If consumers expect shortages of a good to develop there may be panic buying; the resulting demand may be so great that the good may indeed become scarce. Conversely, if people are afraid of losing their jobs, they are likely to postpone many purchases. Fear of the future was an important factor in the drop in sales of many consumer goods in the 1980 recession.

Changes in Demand Vs. Changes in Quantity Demanded

It is important to distinguish between a change in demand and a change in the quantity demanded. Each of the above five factors can cause a **change in demand**—that is, a change in any of these factors leads to a different quantity at every price. Increases in demand cause the demand curve to shift to the right; decreases in demand cause a shift to the left. You can demonstrate this for yourself in Figure 1. Suppose a crisp, new snowfall encourages more skiers to enter the market so that the number of ski weekends demanded at each price doubles.

The prices have not changed so skiers already in the market are not changing their behavior and buying either more or fewer accommodations (they are not moving along their demand curves). There are simply more people demanding accommodations at all price levels. The demand curve will shift to the right.

A **change in quantity demanded** occurs when *price changes* but other factors remain the same. For example, going back to Figure 1 again, if the price of ski weekends should fall from $70 to $60, quantity demanded would increase from 30,000 to 40,000. If price should rise from $70 to $80, quantity demanded would fall from 30,000 to 20,000. Both are changes in quantity demanded. For changes in quantity demanded, the curve remains the same; moving along the curve leads to a new quantity at the new price.

Here are some examples from recent events showing the difference:

1. The number of teenagers in the population increases, and the demand for soft drinks increases. Larger quantities would be bought at every price. This is a *change in demand;* as demand increases, market demand curves shift to the right.

2. Falling incomes as a result of the 1980 recession forced people to postpone purchases of new household appliances. Smaller quantities were bought at every price. This is a *change in demand;* as demand falls, market demand curves shift to the left.

3. Higher prices for oil *reduce quantity demanded* as buyers move up their demand curves. Higher prices increase the costs of producing synthetic fibers, and clothing firms look to cotton as a substitute. There is a *change in demand* for cotton at all price levels—market demand increases.

4. Higher prices for feed grains cause farmers to reduce the quantity used to fatten cattle and hogs. This is a *change in quantity demanded.* Farmers feed their livestock soybeans instead, and demand curves for soybeans shift to the right. This is a *change in demand.*

5. Lower prices for stereo equipment lead to larger sales. This is a *change in quantity demanded* as consumers move down their demand curves. Owners of new stereos buy more records, and record demand increases. This is a *change in demand* for records.

Note that changes in quantity demanded depend on how readily buyers respond to price change. Some goods must be bought no matter how high the price, and some will not be bought in larger quantities whatever the price.

SUPPLY

Now it's time to look at the other side of the market. We have described the behavior of buyers over a short period of time and the reasons for their decisions. For every buyer, of course, there has to be a seller. Sellers decide what to put on the market and how much they will make available at any given price during a particular period of time.

Law of Supply

The principle underlying sellers' decisions is called the law of supply. **The law of supply** states that sellers normally choose to provide smaller quantities of a good at low prices and larger quantities at high prices. The reason is simple. For any short period of time, some resources used in production are fixed in amount. A producer's fixed plant and equipment are designed to produce a certain amount of output over some limited range. To push quantity beyond this range is inefficient, involving higher production costs for each additional unit. If suppliers are to be persuaded to produce more, they must be offered a higher price. Then, the higher price can be used to bid productive resources away from their current use for producing larger quantities of the desired good.

On the other hand, in most markets for goods and services, a small quantity may be sold at lower prices. Given a supplier's existing fixed resources, the additional cost of producing a

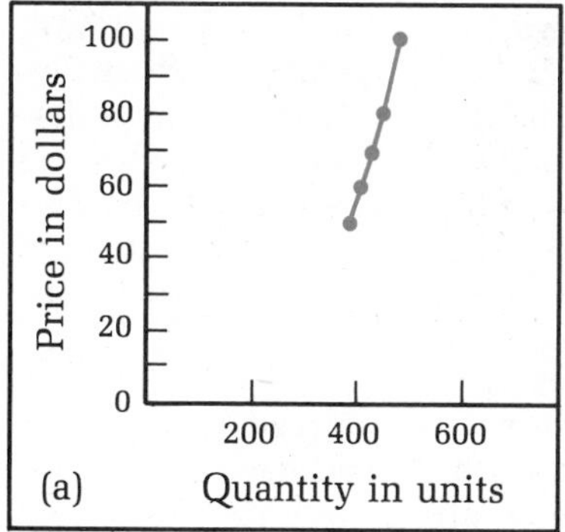

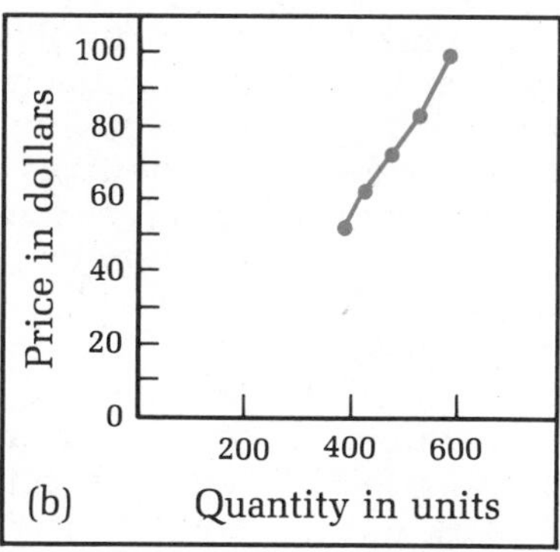

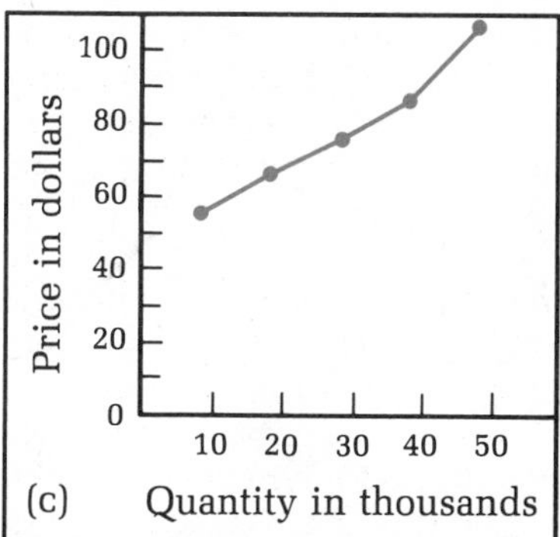

Figure 4 Supply curves for ski weekend accommodations for (a) Wonderland, (b) Alpine, and (c) total market supply.

small quantity is not very much. Few additional resources have to be bid away from alternative employments, and price need not be as high.

The behavior of sellers can be depicted in **supply schedules** that correspond to the demand schedules of buyers. Table 2 shows supply schedules for two ski resorts at Snowy Mountain: Wonderland and Alpine. The schedules indicate the quantities of ski accommodations that would be provided per season at various prices. Again, it is impossible to tell precisely the quantity each firm will actually supply. A supply schedule shows what each *would* supply, depending on price.

The supply schedule in Table 2 describes intentions over a short period of time during which certain assumptions are made ceteris paribus. Certain factors that may influence supply are assumed to remain constant: the costs of resources used in production, prices of other products firms could be selling, expectations of costs and prices, and the number of suppliers.

Note that if prices are low, Wonderland and Alpine each would provide 400 weekend accommodations. At higher prices, both would manage to find ways of accommodating more people. They would open sooner in the fall and remain open longer in the spring. They would rearrange some facilities to house more people and hire more personnel to operate their restaurant and entertainment services. But all this would be costly and would be possible only at higher prices. Wonderland appears to be more limited in its ability to vary supply if price changes. Alpine's facilities are more flexible.

Table 2 **Supply of Ski Weekend Accommodations**

Price	Quantity		
	Wonderland	Alpine	Market supply
$100	500	600	50,000
80	490	550	40,000
70	475	500	30,000
60	450	450	20,000
50	400	400	10,000

The final column in Table 2 shows the total quantities of accommodations of all ski resorts that would be supplied at various prices during the period. Figure 4 is drawn from Table 2 and shows the supply curves of Wonderland and Alpine together with the market supply curve. Just as with demand, a **supply curve** plots quantity along the horizontal axis and price along the vertical axis. In general, *supply curves slope upward*. This is because larger quantities will be supplied only at higher prices during the short period of time for which the curve is drawn.

Changes in Supply

Our supply schedule shows the relationship between quantity and price during a particular period of time. We have assumed that other things remain the same. In time, other things may not remain the same; the supply curve may shift to the right or to the left. It will shift to the right if supply increases—that is, if more ski accommodations become available at every price. It will shift to the left if fewer accommodations are available at every price.

A **change in supply** may be the result of changes in costs of production, changes in the prices of other goods, changes in suppliers' expectations about prices, and changes in the number of suppliers. Let's discuss each of these changes in supply, using some familiar examples.

Changes in costs of production. Over a longer period of time, costs of supplying a good or service may fall because of technological improvements or because the prices of resources used in production have fallen. Solar heating for ski lodges might reduce operating costs and move the supply curve to the right. Cheaper chemical fertilizer would have the same effect on supply curves for wheat and soybeans. A striking example of how a new technology has affected supply is the development of miniature electronic circuits. Miniature circuits have made it possible to produce inexpensive calculators that can be carried in a pocket. Over time supply curves shifted to the right as the new technology became available to many firms.

Increases in production costs cause supply curves to shift to the left. When energy prices rose sharply in 1979, the supply curve for most industrial products moved leftward. Wage changes are also an important part of production costs for many goods and services. If wage costs increase, then every unit produced must sell for a higher price, and supply curves move leftward. Rising prices for new housing are due in part to much higher wages demanded by construction workers and higher costs for lumber, materials, and financing.

Prices of other products. Most producers are able to make more than one product. They will naturally want to produce the combination of products that is most profitable for them. If the price of soybeans rises, Illinois farmers may switch some of their land out of corn and into soybeans. The result is a decrease in the supply of corn. Many shopping centers used to have bowling alleys. As ice skating began to be popular, owners shifted their facilities from bowling to skating. Supply curves for bowling games shifted to the left, and supply curves for hockey games shifted to the right.

Expectations. Supply will change if the price of a good or service hasn't risen yet but is expected to in the future: Suppliers' expectations will cause supply to change. For example, farmers may keep some of their soybeans from the last harvest stored in a silo in the hope of getting more for their crop later on. Businesses are deeply involved in expectations. They borrow funds and invest in equipment or raw materials on the basis of expected future prices. In the early 1970s many builders invested heavily in vacation homes, and supply curves shifted to the right. The builders expected to earn substantial profits from rising prices of housing. Unfortunately, the recession of 1973–75 cut into their markets. Many firms were forced out of business and projects were abandoned. Expectations of hard times ahead will probably hold down the supply of new vacation homes into the 1980s.

Number of producers. In Figure 4, if ski weekends are selling at $70, market supply would be 30,000. But suppose the number of ski resorts doubles as many new firms take advantage of expected profitability. If this happens, market supply will be 60,000 weekends at the same price of $70. The supply curve will have shifted to the right. This is not very likely to happen on such a large scale in any industry, but when we make an assumption ceteris paribus we are assuming that it doesn't happen at all.

Foreign trade is an important source of a shift in supply. Increased imports of a good cause supply curves to shift to the right. American consumers can choose among a wider variety of goods supplied by foreign producers.

Changes in Supply Vs. Changes in Quantity Supplied

All of the above changes involve factors we hold constant when drawing a supply curve. A **change in supply** is a result of a change in one of these factors. When one of these factors changes, the entire supply schedule changes, and we must draw a new supply curve. When supply changes, the supply curve shifts either to the left or right.

Any one supply curve shows the quantities that would be supplied at every price during a short period of time when other factors are held constant. A change in price brings on a **change in quantity supplied.** If the price of ski weekends rises from $70 to $80, quantity supplied will increase by 10,000 units. If price falls from $70 to $60, quantity supplied will fall by 10,000 units. A change in price leads to a change in quantity supplied. The curve remains the same when quantity supplied changes.

MARKET EQUILIBRIUM

You're probably not accustomed to hearing the word *supply* used without any mention of *demand*. The two words seem to go together; in fact, economists usually speak of them in the same breath. That is because interaction of supply and demand is what determines the actual price at which a good will be sold and the actual quantity that will change hands. In Table 3 we have combined the market demand schedule for ski weekends (from Table 1) and the market supply schedule for ski weekends (from Table 2). The table may seem to be just a collection of numbers, but if you examine it closely you will find that it gives precise answers to the questions: How many ski weekends will people actually buy? What price will they actually pay?

Begin by setting price at $100. Checking the supply column, we can see that 50,000 units would be offered for sale at $100. However, if we look at the demand column we find that only 10,000 units would be purchased at $100. At a price of $100 there is a **surplus** of 40,000 units. This obviously won't satisfy sellers, who could find more customers if they reduce price. If they come down to $80, they could sell 20,000 units. They would still be left with a surplus, however, so it would pay to reduce price another notch to $70. At this price, they could sell 30,000 units. The surplus has disappeared: At this price, customers are willing to buy all 30,000 units.

We can see the interaction more easily in Figure 5. Figure 5 is a graph of the demand and supply schedules in Table 3. If price is set at $100, there is a surplus: Quantity supplied is greater than quantity demanded. This is shown as the horizontal distance between the demand and supply curves at a price of $100. In the adjustments that follow, sellers try to dispose of their surplus by reducing price; they move down their supply curves. Buyers are willing to buy larger quantities as price falls; they move down their demand curves. Finally, a price is reached that *just clears the market:* Quantity supplied is equal to quantity demanded. At this point we say that the market is *in equilibrium*. **Market equilibrium** occurs where quantity supplied equals quantity demanded.

Table 3 **Demand for and Supply of Ski Weekend Accommodations**

Price	Quantity demanded	Quantity supplied	Market condition
$100	10,000	50,000	Surplus 40,000
80	20,000	40,000	Surplus 20,000
70	30,000	30,000	Equilibrium
60	40,000	20,000	Shortage 20,000
50	50,000	10,000	Shortage 40,000

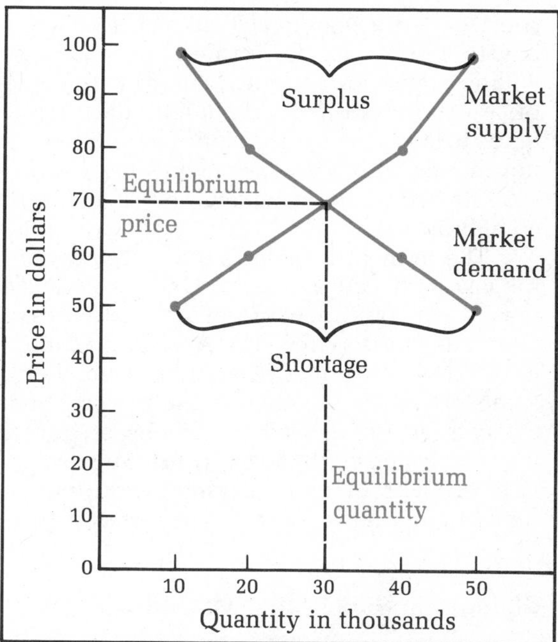

Figure 5 Market equilibrium for ski accommodations occurs at the intersection of supply and demand. Equilibrium price is $70 and equilibrium quantity is 30,000 units.

The same result, market equilibrium, follows if we begin at the other end of the supply-demand schedules and set a price of only $50. At that price, would-be skiers are willing to buy 50,000 ski weekends, but only 10,000 will be supplied. This time there is a **shortage** of 40,000 units, shown on the graph as the distance between quantity demanded and quantity supplied at a price of $50. Adjustments follow. Buyers compete with each other for what is available by bidding up the price; they move up their demand curves. Sellers are willing to provide larger quantities at higher prices; they move up their supply curves. Finally, a higher price is reached which just clears the market. We have again reached equilibrium: At a price of $70, quantity demanded is equal to quantity supplied.

The price at which quantity demanded is equal to quantity supplied is called **equilibrium price.** Only at equilibrium is there no surplus or shortage. At a price of $70 all skiers willing to pay this price will be satisfied. All businesses willing to provide accommodations at the going price will be satisfied. At equilibrium the price tends to stay where it is as long as conditions do not change. This is because all buyers and sellers are satisfied to go on buying and selling at the equilibrium price.

The term *price system* is often used synonymously with *market economy.* Under a **price system,** supply and demand determine prices for all goods and services. The American economy is referred to as a price system, even though some prices are set outside the market. Some markets are influenced by actions of government or actions of business firms. Such actions interfere with the free operation of supply and demand and make markets "imperfect."

Changes in Supply and Demand

Equilibrium may not last very long in any market. Conditions may change and set forces in motion that disturb it. Buyers and sellers will adjust to the new conditions, moving toward a new equilibrium price.

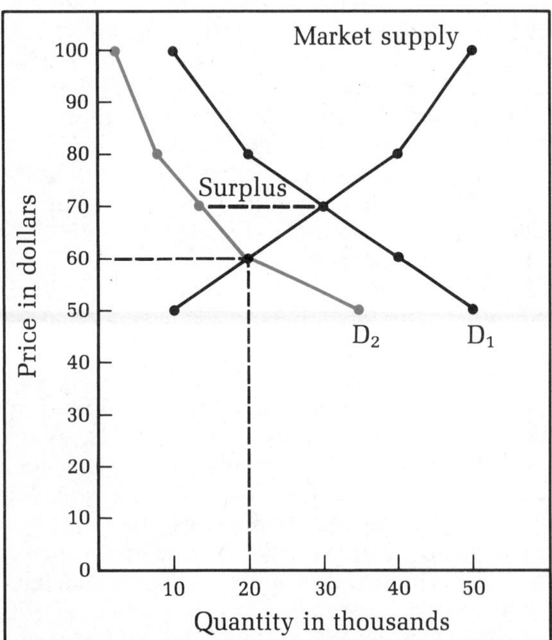

Figure 6 A decrease in demand causes a surplus at the old equilibrium price. Price falls to a new equilibrium at $60.

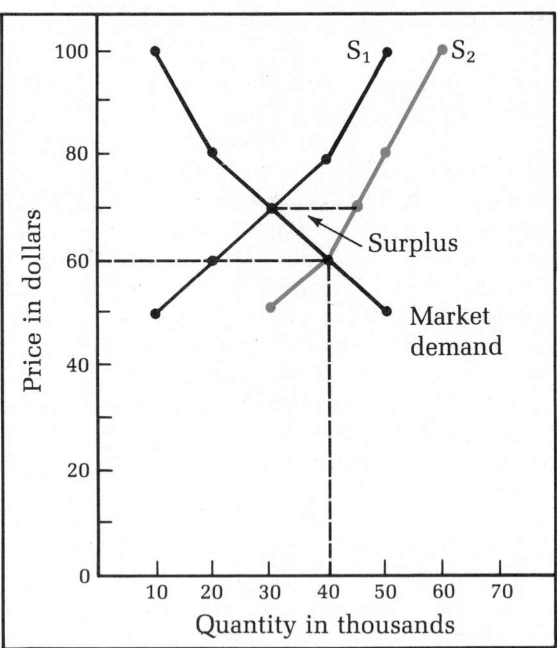

Figure 7 An increase in supply causes a surplus at the old equilibrium price. Price falls to a new equilibrium at $60.

Recall all the demand and supply factors we held ceteris paribus. Changes in any of those factors will cause a shift in one or both curves and a change in equilibrium price.

One possibility is a change in consumer tastes. Suppose the conviction grows among skiers that skiing is dangerous. Perhaps they have seen too many injured skiers brought down from the slopes by sled. Demand schedules fall, and the market demand curve shifts to the left. In Figure 6 demand shifts from D_1 to D_2. At the old equilibrium price of $70, supply now exceeds demand. Recreation firms will reduce their prices in an effort to retain customers. They move down their supply curves. When price has fallen to $60, the market will be in equilibrium again. At this price, only 20,000 weekend accommodations will be sold instead of the 30,000 at the previous equilibrium price.

Now let's assume that a change occurs in the number of firms supplying the services. A building boom makes more overnight lodgings available for skiers. The supply curve shifts to the right. In Figure 7 supply shifts from S_1 to S_2. At the old equilibrium price, supply now exceeds demand. Firms will reduce their prices to capture more customers. As prices fall, buyers will move down their demand curves and buy larger quantities. When prices have fallen to $60, the market will be in equilibrium again. Forty thousand weekend accommodations will be sold.

Graphical analysis is useful because it helps us see changes in market equilibrium almost at a glance. We can see the effect of an increase in demand when supply remains the same. If the demand curve shifts to the right and the supply curve remains the same, equilibrium price, and quantity, will rise. We cannot predict how high prices will rise without knowing the shape of the supply and demand curves. Still it is very useful to know that the general effect of an increase in demand is to increase both equilibrium price and quantity supplied. The general effect of a decrease in demand is just the opposite: if supply remains the same, equilibrium price and quantity demanded will fall.

The effects of supply changes are simple to work out. If supply increases and demand remains the same, equilibrium price will fall but quantity will increase. If supply falls and demand remains the same, equilibrium price will rise and quantity will fall.

When both supply and demand change at the same time, the effects are even more difficult to predict precisely. The changes in price and quantity will depend on the relative sizes of the shifts in the curves. Use graphical analysis to determine the effects of shifts of various sizes. Can you summarize your results in terms of general principles? Figure 8 illustrates a number of recent shifts in market supply and demand. Interpret each in terms of change in price and quantity.

Expectations Can Make It So

We have suggested that buyer and seller expectations are important for determining demand and supply. If buyers expect prices to fall, they will postpone their purchases and demand curves will shift to the left. Expectations of falling prices can also cause an increase in supply. Sellers offer more goods on the market for what they can get before price falls, and supply curves shift to the right. What is the result? Prices fall as expected!

On the other hand, expectations of rising prices can cause an increase in demand as buyers begin to stock up on a good. Expectations of rising prices can cause a reduction in supply as sellers hold their stocks off the market. What is the result? Prices rise as expected!

In economics it is interesting that the expectations of buyers and sellers often come true. If they expect prices to rise and if they behave as if prices will rise, prices *do rise*.

The Search for Equilibrium

Market equilibrium is neat and clearly defined on paper. In the real world it may be a different story. In the real world paribus (everything else)

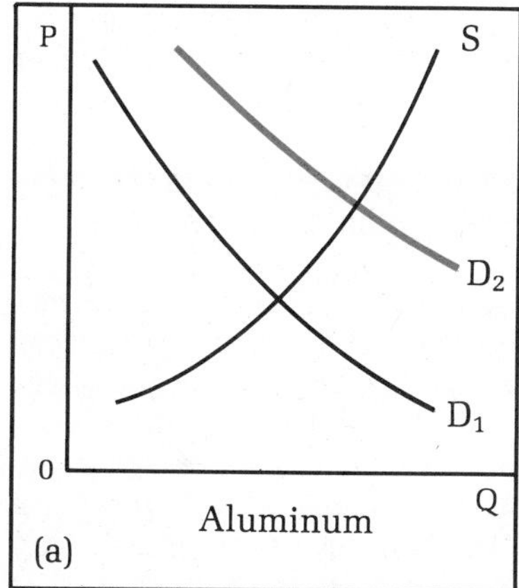

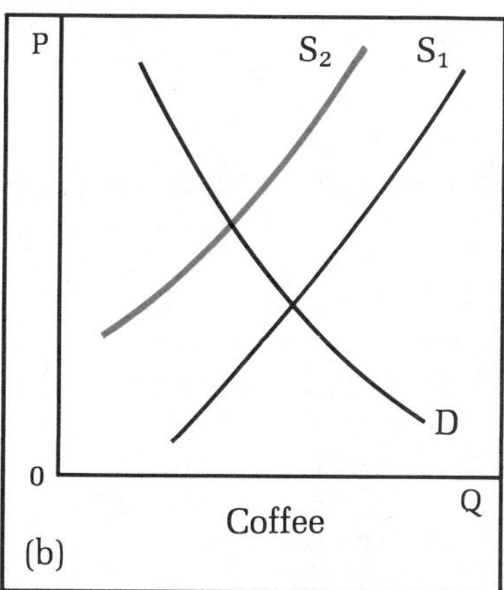

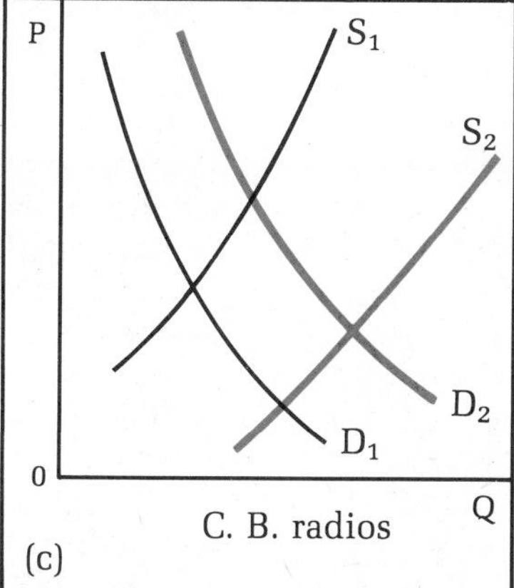

Figure 8 Effects on equilibrium price of: (a) an increase in demand; (b) a decrease in supply; (c) a simultaneous increase in both demand and supply. P stands for price, and Q stands for quantity.

Extended Example Markets for Commodities

Most of us are more interested in ski lodge rates than in prices of, say, soybeans, copper, or chemical fertilizers. However, we can't really afford to ignore what happens to the prices of those raw commodities which go into the production costs of the goods and services we want. Raw material prices change frequently, moving both up and down, as a result of supply and demand factors; by contrast, prices of manufactures are relatively more stable since large firms and powerful labor unions can maintain price levels in spite of market changes. Because many raw commodities are produced by small-scale enterprises throughout the world and because the products are fairly uniform, there is little market power to affect prices.

Changes in commodity prices cause similar changes in prices of consumer goods and services. Increasing population and rising incomes have increased world demand for raw commodities. Moreover, the drive for industrial development in many newly developing nations is pushing commodity demand curves to the right. Supply has not increased as fast. Crop failures in many parts of the world and government restrictions on planting and extraction in the United States have been partly responsible. High energy and labor costs have reduced productivity in the mining and forest industries, keeping supplies low.

The United States produces major portions of important agricultural commodities: soybeans, corn, wheat, rice, tobacco, and cotton. But we are seriously dependent on sources in other nations for many minerals necessary for U.S. industry. Manganese, cobalt, graphite, chromium, aluminum, platinum, tin, nickel, mercury, and zinc are examples. Some analysts worry that foreign suppliers may follow the lead of OPEC and limit mineral production so as to increase prices. This is unlikely, since mineral-producing nations are neither as close geographically nor as similar politically as the OPEC nations. Moreover, higher prices for many of these materials would lead to greater recovery efforts and possibly to development of synthetic substitutes.

What can be done to prevent a surge in commodity inflation? One approach is to encourage investment in improved production: tax credits to business, low-interest loans for equipment expenditures, and grants for research and development to improve productivity. Another would be to remove restrictions on agricultural production, keeping food costs down to offset expected price increases for other commodities.

For OPEC nations a price rise meant higher earnings on sales of oil. Do higher prices always mean greater revenues? If your answer is "No," explain your reasoning. Use supply and demand drawings to illustrate the behavior of commodity prices.

is generally not ceteris (fixed). Conditions are constantly changing, causing demand and supply curves to shift back and forth. Information may not be quickly transmitted among markets so that there are shortages in some and surpluses in others. By the time all adjustments have taken place, conditions may have changed again and markets will begin to move toward another new equilibrium. In short, markets are *dynamic;* few markets ever reach and maintain a static equilibrium like the one we have shown. The principles are still true, however. Understanding a static economy enables us to analyze ceteris paribus the adjustments of the real-world, dynamic economy.

Remember that a model is only a simplified version of reality. It does not truly reflect all conditions in the real world. It reflects only how people *would* behave when most of the determinants of behavior are held constant. It assumes people are free to behave according to their own interests without government intervention and without the influence of powerful firms. Market imperfections may sometimes prevent a market from behaving as we have shown. Still, understanding how perfect markets *would work* helps us analyze and evaluate imperfect markets.

Price rigidity. One source of market imperfections is **price rigidity,** or *sticky prices.* Prices don't always respond quickly to changing market conditions, especially in the downward direction. *Minimum wage laws, union contracts,* and *monopoly power* on the part of producing firms can prevent prices from dropping—even when the existence of a surplus dictates that they should drop. The result may be prolonged periods of *disequilibrium.*

Shortages and surpluses. Often shortages or surpluses persist and prevent equilibrium. Large retailers search for equilibrium when they order gift items for the Christmas buying season. Their market researchers study buying habits of past years. They assess the mood of the public and try to predict demand for bicycles, fur coats, electric shavers, and stuffed toys. Nevertheless, even the most scientific forecasts will leave many stores with a surplus of some gift items and a scarcity of others.

Figure 9 illustrates the market for an unpopular item, say recordings of "Jingle Bells" by a Latvian rock group. Equilibrium price for the records would have been $1 each, but price is rigid downward. Why? The retailer has set a price of $5 and will not sell any records below that price. At the established price there is a surplus of 200 units (and the store's buyer is probably out of a job). After the gift-buying season the retailer will announce a Clearance Sale and sell the entire stock for $1 each or even less.

The opposite situation can be just as frustrating. A popular Christmas gift one year was an electronic game played on an ordinary television set. Figure 10 illustrates larger than expected demand. At the advertised price of $100, ten thousand more games could have been sold. Many customers went away angry, and salespeople were annoyed about the shortage. When prices are widely publicized in advance, it is impractical to increase price to a level that would "clear the market." The result is that markets cannot reach equilibrium. Surpluses and shortages are more serious when they affect the well-being of many people.

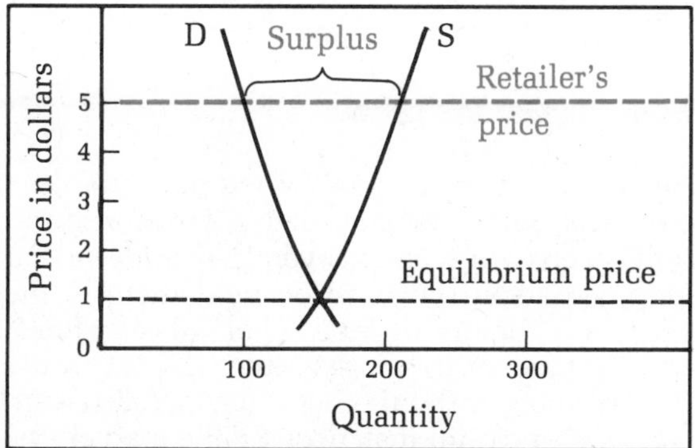

Figure 9 The market for "Jingle Bells" records. The established retail price is above equilibrium price, and a surplus persists.

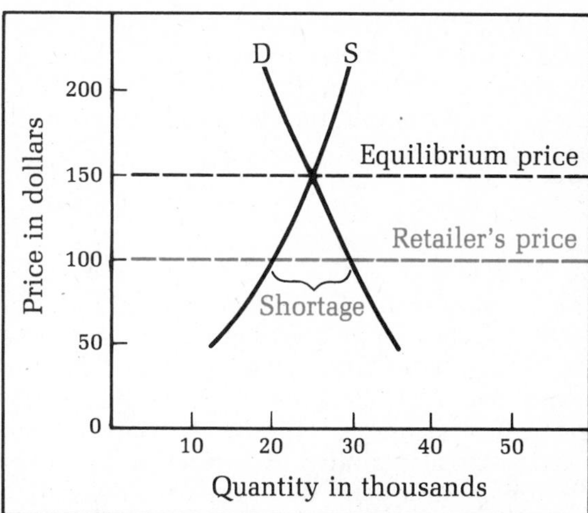

Figure 10 The market for electronic television games. The established retail price is below equilibrium price, and a shortage persists.

Government action in the market. For some goods, government may set a low price, with the intent to protect the interests of low- and middle-income consumers. The market for natural gas is an example. In 1954 the Federal Power Commission established a maximum price on natural gas. With price below equilibrium, demand came to exceed supply, and shortages developed.

For some goods, government may set a high price, with the intent to protect the interests of sellers. The market for certain types of unskilled labor is an example. Congress has passed a minimum wage law that sets a minimum price on hourly workers. With price above equilibrium, supply came to exceed demand and a surplus developed.

FUNCTIONS OF THE PRICE SYSTEM

Earlier we explored the interaction of supply and demand in a particular market—the market for ski weekends. We've seen that price and quantity tend to move toward equilibrium so that the amount sellers are willing to supply is equal to the amount customers are willing to buy. If some sellers find the price too low to be worth their while, they withdraw from that particular market and go elsewhere. If some buyers find price too high for their pocketbooks, they are free to spend their money on something else or not to spend it at all. Prices perform two functions: (1) a **rationing function** and (2) an **incentive function.**

The Rationing Function

Prices ration out the available goods and services among buyers according to the amounts each buyer wants and is able to pay for. If Harry wants lots of ski trips, he can have them. Others, whose desire is less urgent, will buy less. Skiers may also arrange their time so that they go during the week when prices are lower than on weekends. In this way the price differential between weekdays and weekends encourages a more balanced use of resources.

The Incentive Function

Prices also provide an incentive for firms to produce more. Where demand is great, prices will rise, encouraging firms already in the industry to produce more and drawing new firms into the industry. Where demand is falling, prices will normally fall, too. Firms will cut back their production, releasing resources for use in other industries where demand is greater.

Firms are buyers as well as sellers. They buy materials and supplies from other firms, behaving exactly as private individuals do in deciding what to buy and how much. If a certain material can be substituted for another at a saving, a firm will buy the low-cost resource in order to compete with other firms.

The economy is tied together by millions of these interactions, linking producers with one another and with consumers, linking one product with other products, and linking every market with other markets. It is this interrelatedness that we mean when we speak of the market system. Adam Smith described how individual buyers and sellers in a free market would send and receive signals by means of prices. Prices were the means of communicating society's needs. Prices helped ensure flexible adjustment to changing conditions of demand and supply. It is through the free market system that our economy answers the four basic economic questions:

What Goods Will Be Produced

What do American consumers want? Our wants are changing all the time. Forty years ago we had no television industry. When the first sets were introduced, consumers were willing to pay high prices for this new "toy." Resources flowed toward the television industry to take advantage of the profits to be made. New stars and new shows were born, and many established performers were drawn from the movies and radio broadcasting into TV. As television expanded, consumers spent less for other forms of entertainment. Movie theaters began to lose money, and many went out of business. Many popular magazines found it difficult to compete with television and eventually had to stop publication. Through it all, consumers expressed their preferences by the prices they were willing to pay. Owners of economic resources responded by moving resources into the types of production people wanted.

How Goods Will Be Produced

What resources will be used in production? Most goods can be produced in different ways, depending on the relative prices of the resources involved. The most plentiful resources have lower prices and are used in abundance. Less plentiful resources are used more sparingly. Plentiful supplies of petroleum enabled manufacturers to substitute plastics for wood in making many goods. New technologies permitted substitution of mechanical devices for scarce labor resources.

Who Will Get the Output

Nearly everybody owns a TV set. But some own color sets, some own polished oak consoles, and some even own screens several feet wide so that Johnny Carson seems to be right there in the bedroom. Each of us buys what we can afford, and for most of us a large-screen TV set would require going without other things we also want (ski weekends, for instance). So the market system rations these TV sets to consumers whose incomes permit a wider range of choices.

When Goods Will Be Enjoyed

Most of us prefer enjoyment today to enjoyment in the future. We require some incentive if we are to sacrifice our share of the good life for the sake of greater productivity in the future. The promise of gain is an important motivation for building the capital that helps us all live better. Shopkeepers save from current income to purchase facilities for meeting customers' needs; manufacturers save to modernize and expand their machinery; families save to invest in homes or condominiums; others save and make their funds available for capital investment through banks and savings and loan associations. Without a central authority for planning production, the market system guides resources into the kinds of investment that satisfy our needs far into the future.

THE MARKET SYSTEM: PROS AND CONS

We don't live in an ideal society. Every day our newspapers tell of crime, corruption, and poverty. We hear that our air and water are polluted. We see that some people seem to have plenty of income and others not enough.

In describing the way the price system works to guide free markets, we don't want to claim too much. Every economist will agree that our society can stand a lot of improving.

Advantages of the Market System

The great advantage of the market system is the "invisible hand," which turns the private individual's self-seeking into the greatest good for the greatest number. Prices serve as signals to guide production in the ways we want. In command economies most production decisions are made by a central planning board and by political leaders. Production may not reflect the wishes of the people, and producer incentives may be low. Some command economies have proposed combining central planning with some limited use of the market system. That would take part of the responsibility from planning authorities and allow some questions to be answered by individual buyers and sellers. Hungary and Yugoslavia are now experimenting with "market socialism."

When it works, the market system is efficient because it channels resources to the places where they are in greatest demand—where they can be most productive and yield the highest returns to their owners. In fact, the market system is probably the *most efficient system* for producing the largest quantity of goods.

The price system also increases freedom, particularly economic freedom, since it leaves decision-making to individuals rather than to central authorities.

Disadvantages of the Market System

Critics of the market system say that there is a big difference between the ideal and the reality. One of the greatest shortcomings of the market system is *unequal distribution* of income and resources. Strong and capable people are able to use the system more effectively than the weak; many of the rich grow richer, and many of the poor stay poor. Some of the inequalities of society are even magnified through the price system: People with more money get more education and better jobs, which enable them to earn still more money and to pass their advantages on to their children. Similarly, big companies have advantages over little companies and can sometimes drive their small competitors out of business.

This is a way of saying that the market system is far from ideal. There are frictions and obstacles that prevent it from working as smoothly as it seems in theory. Sometimes barriers interfere with the free flow of resources to where they are needed. There are barriers of bigness and barriers of ignorance, as well as a natural human reluctance to change.

Another failing of the market system is that it makes society as a whole pay some of the costs of private producers. The factory that pours out smoke and pollutes the atmosphere creates a social burden for which it doesn't pay. These are called *social costs,* which the community pays in terms of illnesses and clean-up costs. Moreover, when left to itself the market system may fail to produce items that yield benefits to the community as a whole. Private construction firms may produce too little low-cost housing in favor of luxury apartments where

Viewpoint Should the Free Market Prevail?

If the market system is such a good way of organizing the economy, perhaps we should let it operate more freely than we do. That is the opinion of some economists, including Milton Friedman of the Hoover Institute.

Friedman is one of the country's most respected economists and a Nobel Prize winner. The role of government, according to Friedman, should be only to maintain peace and security so that individuals can enjoy life, liberty, and the pursuit of happiness. On almost every question of public policy, Friedman asks: Would this matter be better handled if it were left to the workings of the market? More often than not, his answer is yes. He believes so strongly in the free market system that he even favors abolishing public schools and letting people spend their tax savings on private schools of their own choice. Many economists disagree with him, but they still appreciate the care and precision of his analyses and the consistency of his conclusions.

In Friedman's view, government intervention leads to the misuse of resources. A case in point involves federal compensation for people who have suffered property damage in floods. Friedman maintains that the federal government should stop reimbursing flood victims for loss of property. These are his reasons:

(1) In a free housing market, people choose their residence after taking everything into consideration, including the danger of being washed out in a flood. Safe locations are in greater demand, and their prices are higher than unsafe locations. Greater concentrations of people develop in these safe areas.

(2) Fewer people will settle in unsafe places. Those who do will pay a lower price. The amount they save may later be used to repair flood damage.

(3) If government assumes the risks and compensates property owners directly for flood damage, more people will find the lower price of unsafe land attractive. They will move into cheap and unsafe areas. When a flood occurs, the damage will be greater than it would have been otherwise.

(4) The result is a misallocation of resources: using land for purposes for which it is unfit. Once government starts to intervene, it may find reasons for intervening further—perhaps requiring people to adjust their living patterns in accordance with government policies on resource use.

What do you think of Professor Friedman's argument? Does it fit the actual circumstances of most flood victims? How might Friedman react to aid to victims of Mt. St. Helens? What arguments might be posed against his proposal for abolishing public schools?

profitability is high; some wealthy individuals enjoy private benefits, but middle-income families may suffer. In both cases, market prices fail to reflect the true costs of producing the good or service.

Fortunately, we have ways of correcting the most unpleasant results of the free market. Citizens of democratic societies can use their influence as voters to affect government economic policy. We vote for policies which ensure at least a minimum standard of living to all people. Through public health and education we assist poor families to improve their lives. We provide opportunities for job counseling and training and financial aid to help unemployed workers move to new jobs.

One purpose of our income tax and estate tax laws is to limit the size of fortunes that can be earned and passed on. And our antitrust laws foster competition and limit the power of large enterprises in order to protect the small operator. When ecological disaster threatens, other laws protect communities against the worst results of industrial activity: the pollution, the noise, and the destroyed landscapes.

Our tax revenues are used to provide benefits that the price system overlooks. We subsidize mass transit; we provide parks and recreation centers; and we subsidize cultural activities for the enjoyment of the entire community. Moreover, we give government the power to prevent certain types of production which we believe to be harmful.

This text has described our market system as a *mixed economy*. We depend primarily on the market, but we modify the results through government action within our democratic processes. We admire the efficiency and the flexibility of the market. We admire the way the "invisible hand" helps make very efficient decisions for us. But we worry about the problems of inequality and social justice.

These topics are of such vital concern to all of us that we will return to them again and again in the text. As you develop further skills in economic principles, you may be able to analyze more complicated aspects of a market economy.

SUMMARY

The market system helps us answer the fundamental questions *what* to produce, *how* to produce it, *who* is to enjoy the goods and services produced, and *when* should goods and services be consumed.

Adam Smith was the first economist to describe how the market system works. Smith pointed out how free markets link self-interest with the common interest through an "invisible hand."

Consumers express their preferences for goods and services through their demand schedules. A demand curve illustrates the quantities that would be demanded at every price over a particular period of time. The law of demand states that consumers normally choose to buy fewer units of a good at high prices and more units at low prices. On a graph, this means demand curves are generally downward sloping.

Other factors, such as tastes, incomes, prices of related goods, number of buyers, and price expectations, must be held constant when drawing a demand curve. Changes in these factors may lead to a change in demand, causing the demand curve to shift.

Sellers show their selling plans for goods and services through their supply schedules. A supply curve illustrates the quantities that would be supplied at every price over a particular period of time. The law of supply states that sellers normally choose to provide smaller quantities of a good at low prices and larger quantities at high prices. On a graph, supply curves are generally upward sloping.

Other factors, such as costs of production, prices of related goods, price expectations, and number of suppliers, must be held constant when drawing a supply curve. Changes in these other factors may lead to a change in supply, causing the supply curve to shift.

The actual prices and quantities sold depend on the interaction of demand and supply. Market equilibrium occurs at the price at which the quantity consumers want to buy is just equal to the quantity sellers want to supply. At equilibrium there is no surplus or shortage, and all buyers and sellers are satisfied. Changes in other factors will cause changes in market equilibrium. The market may not reach equilibrium if other factors continue to change or if prices are not allowed to change. Occasionally government intervenes to limit price changes.

Prices help ration goods among those whose desire is greatest and who have the means to buy. Prices also provide the incentive for producers to expand output or to cut back.

Efficiency is the greatest strength of the market system. Its greatest weakness is probably a degree of inequality in the distribution of market benefits and costs. We have developed government economic policies to remedy some of the major shortcomings of our market system.

Key Words and Phrases

change in demand a shift of the entire demand curve in response to some change other than price in the market.

change in quantity demanded a movement along a demand curve in response to a change in price.

change in quantity supplied a movement along a supply curve in response to a change in price.

change in supply a shift of the entire supply curve in response to some change other than price in the market.

complementary good a good which is ordinarily used together with another.

consumers buyers of finished goods and services.

demand curve a graph which shows the relationship between quantity demanded and price for a good during a particular time period.

disequilibrium a condition in which some forces act to prevent the market from reaching equilibrium.

economic democracy system in which dollars spent in the market "vote" for what and how much is to be produced.

equilibrium price the price at which the market reaches equilibrium.

incentive function advantage of the price system in which producers are encouraged to produce the goods people want most, as reflected by price.

invisible hand the guidance of competition in free markets that directs a nation's output of goods and services and its distribution among income earners.

law of demand over any single time period, consumers tend to buy more of a particular good if its price is low than if its price is high.

law of supply over any single time period sellers tend to produce more of a good if its price is high than if its price is low.

market an area over which buyers and sellers communicate their purchase and production decisions such that price tends to reach the same level throughout; we may speak of a specific market for some good or of all markets taken together.

market economy an economy which depends on free choice in the production and distribution of output.

market demand the sum of individual demands; the total quantity of a good or service which will be bought at various prices during a single time period.

market equilibrium a condition in which quantity demanded is equal to quantity supplied; there is no tendency for price to change (all other factors held constant).

market supply the total quantity of a good or service which will be supplied at various prices during a single time period.

mercantilism an economic system aimed at increasing national wealth through favorable trading relationships.

price rigidity a tendency for price to remain constant in spite of the existence of a surplus or shortage.

price system a market system where supply and demand are free to determine equilibrium prices for all goods and services.

rationing function advantage of the price system in which scarce goods and services are distributed among various uses according to the urgency of wants, as reflected by willingness and ability to pay the price.

schedule of demand data that show the quantity of a good consumers will buy at various prices over a single time period.

schedule of supply data which show the quantity of a good sellers will supply at various prices.

shortage supply less than demand; occurs when price is lower than equilibrium.

substitute good a good which is easily used in place of another.

supply curve a graph which shows the relationship between quantity supplied and price for a good during a particular time period.

surplus supply greater than demand; occurs when price is higher than equilibrium.

Questions for Review

1. What determines the "dollar votes" an individual casts in the market place? How does the distribution of "votes" affect a nation's position on its production-possibilities curve?
2. Distinguish clearly between a change in demand and a change in quantity demanded. Give examples of both from recent news.
3. Indicate whether each of the following is an example of a change in supply or a change in quantity supplied: (a) lack of snow in the Midwest reduces groundwater and impairs winter wheat production; (b) removal of embargo against Cuba allows sugar shipments to reach the United States; (c) shortage of coffee leads many consumers to switch to tea, and the price of tea rises; (d) slowing rate of population growth causes firms to cut back production of baby foods.
4. How would a government program to purchase food grains affect market demand? Show how changes in government purchases could be used to maintain a stable price in the face of harvests which fluctuate from year to year. Might government sales from accumulated stocks also be useful at some times? Illustrate graphically.
5. Define: market equilibrium, equilibrium price, and price system.
6. Equilibrium is not always reached in our economy. What factors may prevent equilibrium?
7. Explain the two functions of prices: the rationing function and the incentive function.
8. Consumer boycotts are often arranged as a means of forcing price reductions for certain items in scarce supply. Sugar, beef, and coffee are recent examples of boycotted goods. Explain how boycotts may sometimes have the opposite effect from the one intended.
9. High gasoline prices during the summer of 1979 were blamed for a fall in the price of Maine lobsters. Why? Are gasoline and lobsters substitutes or complements? Illustrate graphically.

10. Make lists of consumer goods and services which are (1) complements of gasoline and (2) substitutes for gasoline. Predict future changes in their equilibrium prices and quantities on the basis of recent trends in gasoline prices.
11. Look for current examples of how government intervenes in markets with the aim of correcting some of the disadvantages of the market system. What goals (from Chapter 1) are emphasized and what goals are sacrificed?
12. Demonstrate graphically why movie tickets cost more at night than in the afternoon. Then demonstrate why tomatoes cost less in summer than winter. Why does the price of firewood rise *before* the weather turns cold?
13. Use a series of graphs to illustrate the effects of government's antismoking campaign on tobacco markets.
14. List as many markets as you can think of which have been affected by the "running" craze.
15. Do lower equilibrium prices increase or decrease total sales revenue? Explain your answer and illustrate graphically.

CHAPTER 4

Government's Role in the Economy

Learning Objectives

Upon completion of this chapter, you should be able to:

1. Identify and explain at least seven economic functions of government.
2. Distinguish and compare the economic roles of the federal, state, and local governments.
3. Indicate the principal outlays by the federal government and by the state and local governments.
4. Identify the chief sources of taxation for each level of government.
5. Discuss each tax in terms of its being progressive or regressive.

Remember the story of Robinson Crusoe? He was the shipwrecked adventurer who washed ashore on a deserted Caribbean island. Through intelligence and hard work, Crusoe fashioned his little island into a virtual economic paradise. He did it almost entirely alone: No one told him when to work, what crops to grow, or how to grow them. Crusoe did as he pleased, when he pleased, with only Nature to obey. Crusoe was an economically and socially free individual.

Economic theory generally assumes that individual buyers and sellers in the marketplace act as freely as Crusoe did on his island. For example, economic theory assumes that when you buy a car, you do so because *you* want to. The salesperson sells to you because *she* wants to. No one forces you to buy or her to sell. Economic theory assumes that *all* buyers and sellers act out their economic desires with virtually complete freedom of choice.

Yet this is a most unrealistic assumption. Unlike Robinson Crusoe, we are members of a society. As such, we cannot act—economically or any other way—with complete freedom. As a famous Supreme Court Justice put it: "One man's freedom to swing his fist ends where another man's nose begins." The truth is that in society one individual's actions may often affect a neighbor. This is all the more so as populations increase and distances between nations and peoples diminish. A tension arises between individual freedom and social responsibility. To regulate this tension we need a powerful force. This force is government.

Government is really no more than a set of rules and the power to see that the rules are obeyed. The rules and power differ among societies and over the centuries. Sometimes kings hold all the power. Sometimes elite committees do. In societies such as ours, power is placed in the hands of voters, who in turn elect representatives to wield the power.

By eliminating, changing, or creating laws, government plays a major role in the functioning of our economy. Sometimes the influence is sharply focused, as when the federal government spends billions of dollars to fight a war. Sometimes the influence is more diffused, as when Congress passes laws to regulate working conditions in factories or to restrain environmental pollution.

ECONOMIC FUNCTIONS OF GOVERNMENT

This chapter will examine a number of government's important economic functions. We shall examine some of the things government does and describe how it collects the revenues to carry out its responsibilities. Because government plays an important part in the economy's performance, and because our economic lives affect our social, cultural, and political lives, understanding government's economic functions is especially important.

Protect Private Property

Our political and economic system rests fundamentally upon the institution of private property. This is an important ingredient of economic freedom. Unless individuals own and control resources, they cannot choose between buying and selling or between producing and consuming. If you don't own your bank account, you cannot choose to purchase a car. If the car dealer does not own the car, she cannot choose to sell the car to you.

Therefore, one of the most important economic functions of government in our system is to protect property. Government protects individual citizens' property against other citizens who might wish to take it for themselves. You can readily see the importance of this protection. Imagine, for example, how difficult it would be to produce and consume goods and services if bandits and looters were free to steal and destroy. Time and energy which could be used to produce goods would instead be wasted in combating robbers and looters.

Property rights are a fundamental and necessary part of any and *all* economic systems. Our system differs from that of the communist and socialist countries in our greater emphasis on *private property* and *personal freedom* as opposed to *communal property* and *social responsibility*.

In simple societies it is clear what property is. Pigs and horses, beads and lumps of gold—such things comprise personal property in primitive tribes. In complex societies of today property is often symbolized by contracts. **Contracts** are agreements to perform certain activities and to pay specific amounts. The agreement to buy a car is often a contract. You agree to pay monthly installments; the seller agrees to deliver the car. If either of you violates the terms of the contract, the deal is off.

Laws ensuring the sanctity of contracts are fundamentally laws to protect property. If both parties agree to terminate the contract, then a satisfactory arrangement must be worked out to protect the interests of both parties. For example, divorce proceedings are terminations of marriage contracts. Lawyers argue to a judge how property of the couple should be divided, and how future commitments are to be met. Neither side may be completely satisfied with the judge's final ruling, but a neutral arbitrator is surely preferable to a more violent resolution of the issue. Once the ruling is made, both parties can turn their minds away from wrangling and toward more constructive activity.

Protection of property extends to transactions even where there is no formal contract. During this century our government has moved to protect property in ways that surely would have seemed strange to earlier generations. Let us discuss a few examples.

Product safety. The most fundamental form of private property is, after all, the human body. Protecting human life against reckless actions of others has also become more complex in today's economy. In the early 1900s the meat-packing industry in this country was free to produce virtually any kind of meat products it wanted to, in any way it pleased. But when investigators discovered that the quality of the products and the production conditions behind them were harmful to the consuming public, government began regulating the meat-packing industry. A regulatory agency was set up to establish product standards and to require that producers clearly state on each product exactly what it contains. Today this governmental body is known as the *Food and Drug Administration* (FDA). It is responsible for protecting the public against potentially harmful foodstuffs and drugs.

More recent examples of government regulation by the FDA are the ban on cyclamates in diet soft drinks and the ban on thalidomide in tranquilizers. Both chemicals were found to be potentially harmful. The individual consumer, however, could not have discovered the danger until it was too late.

There are products other than food and drugs that can be harmful to consumers. Other federal agencies were established to supplement the actions of the FDA; the Consumer Products Safety Commission, the Environmental Protection Agency, and the Occupational Safety and Health Administration are examples. Defective wiring in Christmas tree lights, flammable baby clothing, and unsafe working conditions are just a few of the many areas that come under the review of government agencies.

False advertising. A second example of the need for government regulation concerns false advertising. When a zealous manufacturer claims a product is something it really is not, and a consumer purchases the product, then the consumer has suffered a loss of property. Another governmental agency, the *Federal Trade Commission* (FTC), is charged with making sure that advertisers tell the consuming public the truth about the products they sell.

A famous recent case involved advertisements from trade schools. The schools were said to be making false claims about the jobs their graduates could expect to find. In order to protect potential students, the FTC closed down some schools and required others to give the true picture of their graduates' employment opportunities.

When government interferes in such cases as food and drug production and truth in advertising, the industries involved may lobby against the new rules. They argue that they are free under the Constitution to do and say what they please.

Sometimes they have a point. But as society becomes more complex and as technology improves, individual buyers become generally less qualified to evaluate the products they buy. How can an average consumer judge the effects on the body of cyclamates in soft drinks? How can factory workers be sure the factory's fire escape will work in case of a fire? How can you be sure the water you drink does not contain toxic particles and gases?

Of course, the average consumer often cannot judge. Therefore, governmental agencies—from the Federal Trade Commission to local building inspectors and water commissioners—are established to protect the property of citizens.

Regulate Money

Governments also have tried to *standardize* their nation's money and have established money symbols that people will accept. Money serves as a standard of value, as a medium of exchange, and as a store of value. Government guarantees to citizens that the money in circulation is not counterfeit, and so can be used without fear of fraud. In addition, government decides how much money is to be supplied to the economy and how the supply is to grow or shrink. By regulating the supply, government helps maintain the value of money and thus its acceptability in exchange. The entire history and philosophy of money are indeed complex, and they form an important part of macroeconomics. One thing is obvious: Government's responsibility to maintain a healthy monetary system is fundamental to our nation's productivity and growth. The regulation of money is one of government's most important economic functions.

Allocate Public Goods and Services

Thus far we have spoken of two basic economic functions of government: protection of property and regulation of money. Once these responsibilities are carried out, you might expect that individual buyers and sellers, acting freely in the marketplace, could carry out the task of producing and allocating the goods and services a modern economy needs.

But this is not quite so. There are two categories of goods and services: private goods and services and public goods and services. The difference is the result of an important fact about consumption: Consumption of some goods and services is exclusive, while consumption of others is nonexclusive. **Private goods and services** are usually "exclusive in consumption"; that is, they benefit only their possessor or owner. **Public goods and services** are usually "nonexclusive in consumption"; they benefit many. For this reason they are sometimes called *social goods and services.* This is an important concept and can best be understood through an example.

Suppose you buy a car. The benefits of ownership come to you, exclusively. *You* get the benefits, not your next-door neighbor. Your car is exclusive in consumption. Similarly if you buy a hockey ticket, stereo system, or trip to Mexico, the benefits of the purchase are enjoyed by you. You are willing to pay the price of these items because you are ensured **exclusivity** in consumption. As a result, pricing and production of these goods and services are determined in the market. The intersections of many private demand curves with market supply curves determine market equilibrium.

However, some goods and services are nonexclusive. Suppose you are a sailor and live by a harbor. There is a shoal outside your harbor, around which you must sail if you are to avoid running aground. The shoal is difficult to see at high tide. To remind yourself where it is, you spend your own money and time to build a marker above it. Now you can sail in at day's end, see the marker, and avoid the shoal. You get the benefits of your investment in the marker.

But the benefits are *not* yours exclusively. Soon other sailors realize the importance of *your* marker and use it to navigate their own boats. *They* get the benefits, too, even though *you* made the purchase. You cannot stop them from seeing the marker, so you cannot keep the marker's benefits to yourself, exclusively. There is **nonexclusivity** in consumption of the marker. It is shared socially. Your marker is a private good, but it might just as well be considered a public good since so many share in its benefits.

The pricing of private goods is a job handled by the marketplace. Buyers and sellers of cars meet and individually agree on a price for cars. You pay the price; you get the benefits. But herein lies the problem of public goods. The whole society enjoys the benefits, and no single individual may want (or be able) to bear the costs. Go back to the example of the marker. One expenditure—yours—provided benefits for all sailors. They got a good deal: Their safety for your money with no expenditure on their part. On the other hand, you paid for everyone. In many instances, the benefits to a single individual may not be great enough to justify the cost of providing the public good. This is where government enters the picture. When goods and services are nonexclusive in consumption, the total benefits to society justify spreading the cost over all citizens. No single individual may take the responsibility for providing goods and services to be enjoyed by many others. All may simply step aside and wait for others to act, with the result that important social needs are not met.

Another problem involves the proper price that should be placed on public goods and the proper quantity that should be produced. Since no citizen can be excluded from enjoying the benefits, there are no individual demand curves to locate equilibrium price and quantity.

In brief, the marketplace cannot determine the price or output of public goods. If the market cannot, who can? The answer, of course, is government.

Through our elected representatives we decide on the goods and services we would like to consume as a community. If a local community decides a new water-treatment plant is needed, local officials tax the entire community to pay for the plant. If the nation decides collectively that national defense goods and services are necessary, Congress taxes all of us to provide the armies and weapons we need. You can think of any number of public goods and services, from fire and police protection to port facilities and city streets. And you can see the price you pay for them when you pay your taxes.

Spending for public goods and services is the way society allocates resources toward the public sector. Through democratic processes we agree to refrain from private consumption by the amount of taxes we pay. Then we agree that these tax revenues will be used for public, not private, consumption. The nation moves along its production-possibilities curve toward greater production for the public sector and less production for the private sector.

Assess Social Costs

Public goods and services are those whose *benefits* are nonexclusive in consumption. Government takes over production and pricing decisions for these goods and services. *Costs* of goods and services are sometimes nonexclusive, too, and it is government's responsibility to regulate these costs.

Most economic costs are paid exclusively by private firms. Suppliers of raw materials, electric power, machines, and labor, for example, must be paid incomes at least as high as their opportunity cost. Individual firms pay for each input they use, and in this way compensate for the use of the community's scarce resources.

However, some firms use resources that are not exchanged in resource markets. Goods that private firms are not required to buy are often called "free goods." Some free goods are fresh air, sunshine, and attractive natural surroundings. When a private firm uses one of these resources—a river to carry away the factory's garbage—that firm is not required to pay for the resource. The community suffers a loss of its resources for which it is not compensated.

The portion of production costs for which the community is not compensated is called **social cost.** Social costs are nonexclusive. No citizen can avoid bearing the cost of foul air and water, destroyed landscapes, and industrial noise. Every citizen must absorb these costs whether or not he or she bought the good or service involved.

Many seaside communities have firsthand experience with social costs. When oil tankers use faulty equipment to unload cargo, the result may be a messy oil spill. The polluted shores are a cost borne by all the sailors and swimmers and all the businesses in the area. Some of the costs of transporting oil, in other words, are nonexclusive.

It is government's responsibility to deal with nonexclusive costs. It generally does so in either of two ways. First, government can simply require private firms to pay for the use of the free good. For example, if a manufacturing firm plans to locate a plant in a community, the local government may establish a fee for the air and water that will be used in the production process. Or government may set up legal standards which require the firm to clean up the air and water after use in production. This may mean additional investment in antipollution equipment. Either way, the firm must include social costs in total production costs. The firm can then pass these higher costs along to consumers of the final output. All the costs of production are then exclusive. They are paid by the users of the product only.

The second way is for government to tax goods and services whose production creates social costs. The tax is added to the price of the offending good or service. Buyers pay the tax and government uses the tax revenue to correct the pollution problem. Again the costs are exclusive to those who buy the product.

Whichever method government uses, the important point to remember is that some form of government intervention is necessary to solve the problem of social costs. Because the costs are social, the private marketplace cannot be relied upon to do the job.

Regulate and Maintain Competition

Government is charged with regulating or policing some activities when operation in the private marketplace has had unsatisfactory results. An example of this is the stock market. For many years, stock markets were unregulated. But when the Great Crash of 1929 exposed the effects of fraud and unrestrained speculation, Congress passed legislation providing for regulation of the securities industry. Today, the *Securities and Exchange Commission* (SEC) has broad responsibility to see that the nation's stock markets function smoothly, without fraud or deceit.

Another economic role of government is to ensure competitive markets. If you study market structures later in microeconomics, you will find that monopoly firms tend to produce less output and charge higher prices than competitive firms. In the late nineteenth century in this country, several huge monopolies or "trusts" came under attack from economic reformers. These attacks led to important antitrust legislation. Under antitrust laws, the Justice Department has the responsibility to ensure that no single firm can control pricing and production decisions. If there is proof of monopolistic activity, government can step in and punish the offenders.

Promote Economic Stability

Another broad responsibility of government is to promote stability in the nation's economic activity. The history of production in the market system shows times of great prosperity, with high employment and rising output and incomes. At other times, depressions like the Great Depression of the 1930s have brought widespread suffering. As governments come to understand the workings of national economies, they develop policies to regulate the level of economic activity. The Employment Act of 1946 obligates the federal government to do what it can to maintain reasonably full employment and stable production.

Fight Poverty

Government has also assumed responsibility for individual economic security. It provides welfare payments, food stamps, public housing, low-cost legal aid, and the like, to poor families. Government increased its role in the fight against poverty in the 1960s when President Johnson launched the "War on Poverty." The record shows, unfortunately, that we have not been completely successful in eliminating poverty. However, the many income supplements and outright grants have lessened the burden of poverty for millions and have moved many above the poverty line.

Eliminate Discrimination

Finally, there is the matter of discrimination. Most of us accept the principle that citizens should not suffer discrimination because of their religion, race, sex, or age. Nonetheless, you need only look into your own life or the lives of friends to discover that discrimination does exist. Women generally find it difficult to get the same jobs—at the same pay—as men. Blacks may get less desirable jobs—at lower pay—than whites. The elderly are too often denied jobs even when they can perform them well.

To guarantee equal opportunity for all citizens in the economy, government has been

Viewpoint Government and the Free Market

Unless you've been driving a car for a long time, you've probably never heard of a "Henry J" or a "Studebaker." Makers of these cars eventually were unable to compete in the nation's vigorous auto industry and finally went out of business. This is the way it sometimes is in a free market system—or the way it used to be.

In 1979 Chrysler Corporation supplied less than a tenth of the U.S. auto market, down from a fourth in 1946 when Chrysler was second in the market. Its low volume made new safety and environmental changes costly. The firm expected to lose almost a billion dollars during the year.

Chrysler's management appealed to the federal government for help: at least $1 billion in advances to be added to future corporate tax payments. Other corporations had received help from government in the past. In 1971 Lockheed Aircraft Corporation received government guarantees for $250 million in bank loans to enable it to survive cost overruns on defense production. Many small businesses receive low-interest loans from quasi-government agencies to encourage industrial development and to provide jobs. When the national interest seems to justify it, some sort of government aid may be extended to private business.

Is this true for Chrysler? Certainly the 150,000 employees of Chrysler and the 350,000 more suppliers whose jobs depend on Chrysler think so. And the individual stockholders, banks, and pension funds which have financial interests in the firm think so. Moreover, persons who fear bigness and monopoly power would like to see healthy domestic competition for General Motors and Ford.

There is another side, of course. True believers in free markets see financial problems as a signal that a firm is not performing efficiently: Its product is not popular with consumers; its production costs are too high; its policymakers have been guilty of poor management. For these, to aid a struggling firm would be to perpetuate a misallocation of valuable productive resources. Investors should accept the loss which is a necessary risk in any investment strategy. For government to protect a badly run enterprise will only weaken the U.S. economy and slow economic growth, with the likelihood that much more money will eventually follow the initial $1 billion.

Late in 1979, the Secretary of the Treasury agreed to ask Congress to guarantee loans of $1.5 billion if Chrysler could raise another $2 billion itself. Chrysler's labor union, stockholders, and bankers were asked to cooperate by making certain sacrifices: lower wage gains, lower dividends, lower interest payments, and longer terms on existing loans.

Discuss the dilemma policymakers face in defining the national interest in cases like this. How do government guaranteed loans differ from government loans? What would be the consequences of default? What future problems does this case imply?

Table 1 **Summary of Economic Functions of Government**

Protect property
Ensure product safety
Prevent false advertising
Regulate money
Allocate public goods and services
Bear or assess social costs
Regulate and maintain competition
Promote economic stability
Fight poverty
Eliminate discrimination

called upon to fight discrimination. This role took on much greater importance in the 1960s, and statistics now indicate that more women and minority groups are finding employment and salary opportunities comparable to those of white males. Although the discrimination picture has brightened in recent years, work remains to be done. One statistic: In 1979 the unemployment rate for adult men was 4.1 percent; for adult women, 5.7 percent; for whites, the rate was 5.1 percent; for nonwhites, 11.3 percent. These figures suggest that economic discrimination may still exist. How far we want government to go to achieve absolute economic equality is a part of normative economics.

LEVELS OF GOVERNMENT

Undeniably, government has many important economic functions. To accomplish these tasks and to support a basically democratic philosophy, government's responsibilities in the United States are distributed among a variety of levels of government. In general, Americans have avoided placing too many responsibilities in the hands of the central government. We have preferred instead to decentralize authority, placing responsibilities in the hands of local governments whenever possible. We believe that local citizens and their elected officials are capable of making many important decisions and of directing important activities for themselves. Still, we recognize the need for a strong central government to protect the interests of all.

For these reasons we have a wide variety of governments. The biggest and most powerful is the federal government. The next level is the state, followed by local government. Local government usually includes towns and cities, school districts, and, in many regions of our nation, the county or township.

The relationship between federal and state governments is never entirely tranquil. Some of their separate responsibilities are stated in the U.S. Constitution. Others have been assumed by one or the other as the need arises. Local governments are regulated by their own state governments and state constitutions in carrying out these responsibilities. Because intergovernmental relationships are flexible, various levels of governments are continually threatened by the loss of power to other levels. Moreover, whenever local governments look to the federal government for economic aid, the federal government can impose its will on the localities.

A clear example of this is the program called **revenue sharing.** In the late 1960s, Congress decided that the federal government would disperse some federal tax revenues to local governments. However, certain grants would be distributed only to local governments that met required standards relating to employment, welfare, and educational practices. Federal funds were not, for example, available to school districts where racial discrimination was permitted. Thus, through its control of billions of dollars in revenue-sharing funds, the federal government reduced the independence of local levels of government.

It is difficult to say with certainty how the balance of power is shifting between federal, state, and local governments. One interesting statistic is that the number of federal government employees increased only 35 percent between 1950 and 1979, from 2 million to 2.7 million. But state and local government employment *more than tripled,* rising from 4 million employees in 1950 to 12.7 million by 1979. Figure 1 shows the growth in state and local spending relative to total government spending and to all public and private spending in the United States since 1950. The chart shows little significant increase in federal government spending as a share of total spending since the 1950s, while state and local spending was increasing sharply: Over the period shown, federal spending rose by a multiple of nine and state and local spending rose by a multiple of twenty-eight.

These figures do not necessarily mean that state and local governments have wrested power away from Washington, since some forms of power cannot be measured in terms of expenditures. In fact, a good argument can be given for just the opposite case. But the figures do show

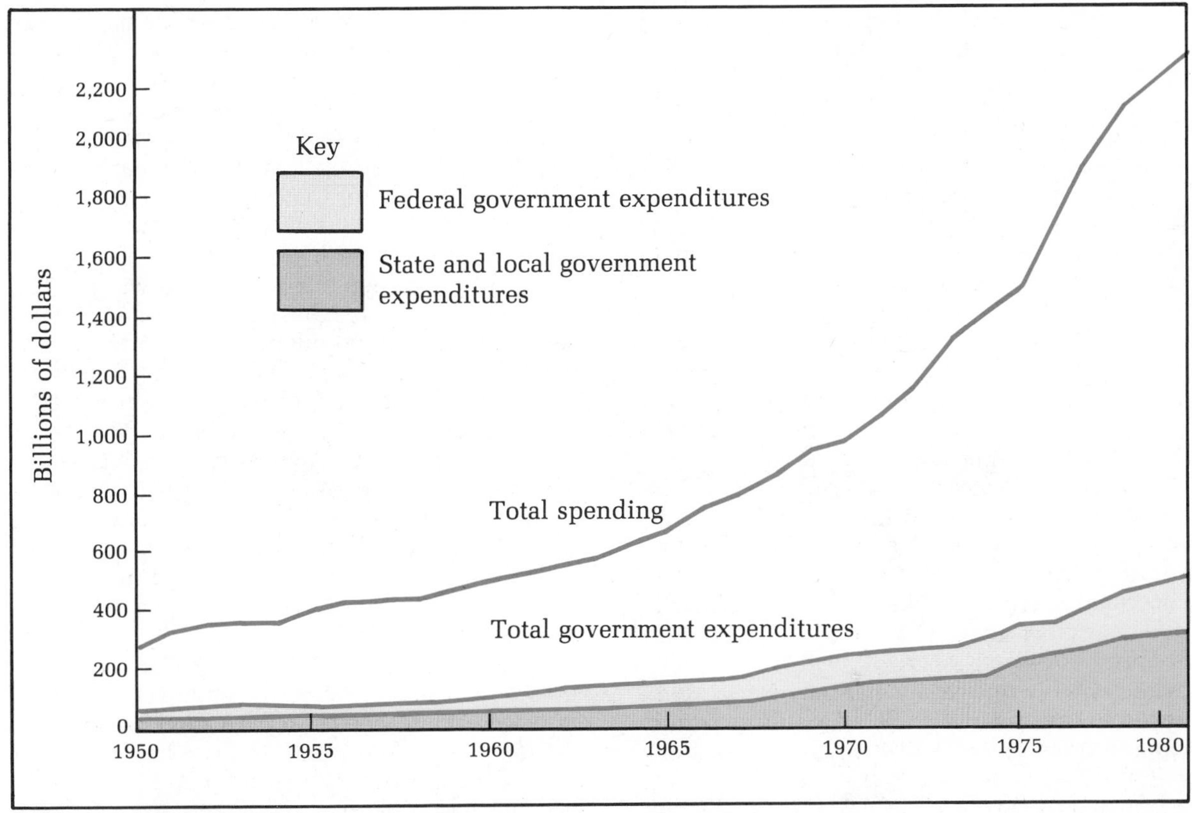

Figure 1 Federal spending and state and local spending in relation to total spending (by consumers, firms, and government) and total government. Total spending in the decade 1965–75 rose faster than either federal or state and local government spending. (Figures obtained from *Economic Report of the President.*)

that a major growth sector has been state and local government. Even so, as financially troubled states and cities look increasingly to the federal government for help, it is safe to bet that the federal government will continue to use its power to influence state and local government.

GOVERNMENT OUTLAYS

State and Local Government

Economists generally lump state and local governments together because the services they offer tend to overlap. Costs of schools, highways, and hospitals, for example, are often shared between state and local authorities. Cities provide local school systems, street cleaning and maintenance, fire and police protection for city residents, water and sewage facilities, parks, and libraries. Counties also provide these services for county residents not served by city governments. In some parts of the United States, townships are important suppliers of some services, particularly education. And there may be broader units of government organized to provide particular goods and services over several counties and including more than one city. Examples are school districts, park districts, and rural water and fire protection districts.

State governments provide a wider range of goods and services. The reason is simply that the state's jurisdiction extends over all the state's residents. Among the services provided by state governments are agricultural research and information, public colleges and universities, natural resource development, vocational training, treatment for alcoholism and mental disorders, and professional and auto licensing.

In addition, state governments may provide local governments with supplemental funds for health, education, and welfare programs. Generally, states will give such assistance in order to standardize the quality of services statewide. If one county has very poor schools, for example, the state may wish to assist that county and bring its educational quality up to par with other counties. Often, the wealthier counties subsidize such programs by paying higher taxes into state treasuries.

State and local governments are major spenders in the economy. In 1979, for example, these two levels of government combined spent $467.1 billion for goods and services. The federal government spent just $166 billion, with most of these purchases going for national defense. The largest single state and local government expenditure was for education, which consumed about 37 percent of the total. Welfare payments constituted 13 percent of state and local expenditures, and highways consumed 8 percent.

State and local government purchases exceeded federal spending for fourteen of the fifteen years between 1964 and 1980. They constitute about 65 percent of total government purchases and some 13 percent of all spending for goods and services. In 1940, by contrast, they accounted for just 8 percent of total spending. Whether state and local financial crises experienced in the mid-1970s will slow this growth in expenditures in the future remains to be seen.

Federal Government

Let us now turn from the decentralized governmental units to the central government. Basically there are two uses for its spending: *Purchases* of goods and services and *income-support payments*, also known as *transfer payments*.

Federal purchases. In order to carry out its various responsibilities to the nation's citizens, the federal government must purchase many billions of dollars worth of goods and services. Total purchases for 1979 were about $166.0 billion. Of that, $117.7 billion was spent on national defense; $11.1 billion was provided for international affairs and research and development involving science, space, and energy. Completing the federal government's shopping list were expenditures for agricultural and natural resource development, commerce and transportation, community development, housing, education, and health.

Historians will look upon the first three quarters of this century as a time when government activity in the economy mushroomed. Total federal purchases have risen from just 1 percent of total spending in 1929 to more than 7 percent in 1979. Percentages were higher in war years: 42 percent in 1944, 16 percent in 1953, and 11 percent in 1968. The recent history of U.S. government purchases is shown in Figure 2.

Why has federal spending expanded in recent years? The development of an active international role for the United States has been a major factor; spending for war and international affairs reflects this historical change. Other causes have been our nation's growing affluence and public demands for more and better services. As our population has shifted from rural farm to urban and suburban living, demand for government services has increased. You may be able to live like Robinson Crusoe if you reside on an isolated farm, but not when you move to a congested city! Finally, changes in age distribution within the total population have stimulated demand for government services. Advances in health care mean more children survive, so more schools and playgrounds are demanded. At the other end of the spectrum, people live longer, past the time when it is possible for them to be fully employed. Providing for their needs has further increased demand for public goods and services.

In a word, society has progressed: We have become more civilized and more affluent. We provide for this increase in civilization by funneling more of our earnings to government for purchasing public goods and services. The famous Supreme Court justice Oliver Wendell Holmes put it this way: "Taxes are the price we pay for civilization."

Transfer payments. The largest group of federal outlays is *transfer payments*. **Transfer payments** are grants provided, without an exchange in goods and services, to individuals who qualify under certain government programs. Retired persons receive transfer payments in the form of Social Security checks. Unemployed persons receive transfer payments as unemployment and/or disability insurance payments. Welfare, veterans' benefits, and other income-support payments are all examples of federal transfer payments.

The growth in transfer payments has been remarkable. In 1949 they were about 20 percent of total government outlays. By 1979 they were almost 50 percent. In fiscal year 1979 more than thirty-three million people received $104.5 billion from the federal government in the form of Social Security benefits. Medicare, medicaid, and other health programs provided $45.1 bil-

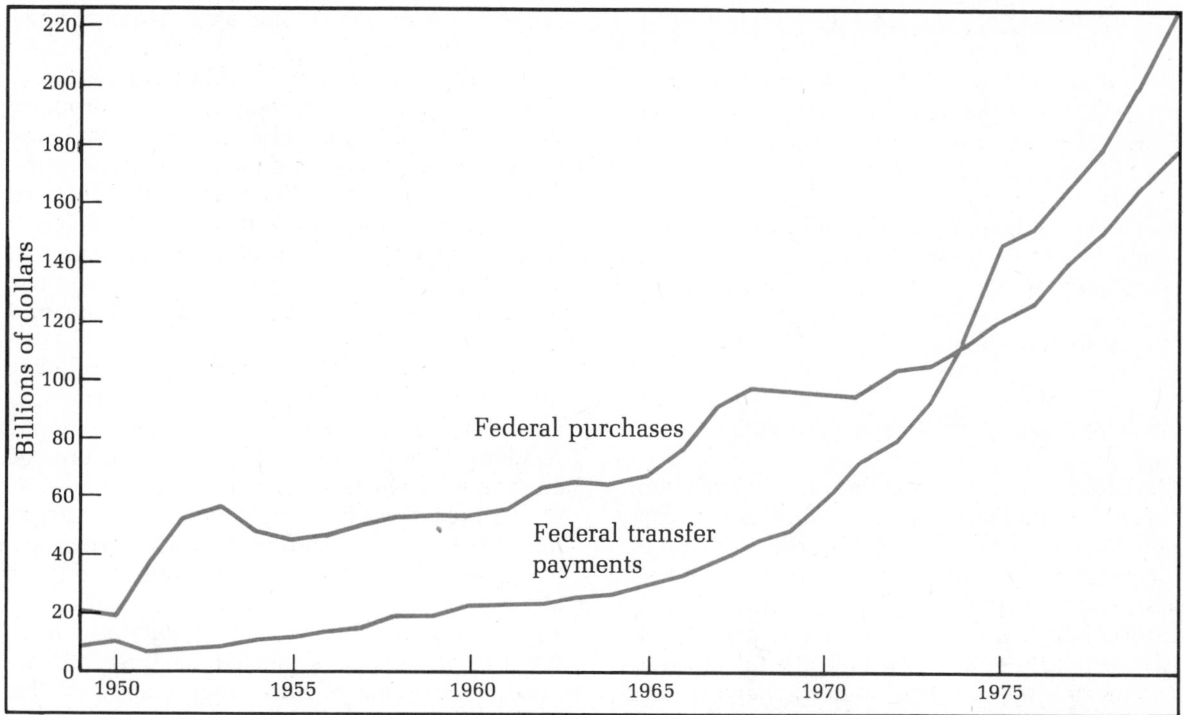

Figure 2 Recent trends in federal government (1) purchases of goods and services, and (2) transfer payments. Sharpest increases in purchases were in the early 1950s during the Korean war and in the mid-1960s during the Viet Nam war. Transfer payments have increased dramatically since the late 1960s. (Figures obtained from the *Economic Report of the President.*)

lion in aid. Another $22.9 billion paid for public assistance, food stamps, and family allowances. Payments for unemployment compensation were $11.8 billion in 1979. Interest on the public debt—the money the government borrows to meet its obligations—is also a transfer payment. Because the debt has grown and because interest rates have increased in recent years, interest payments were almost $55 billion in 1979. Figure 2 illustrates the sharp increase in U.S. government transfer payments since 1949.

Almost all American citizens receive help from one or more government programs. Millions receive aid under the programs listed above. Others receive benefits from federally subsidized housing, small business loans, college student loans, crop loans or GI benefits.

Not only do transfer payments significantly ease citizens' burdens, but they also help stabilize total spending. If private spending declines sharply, unemployment usually increases. Then transfer payments to individuals increase, helping keep incomes fairly stable. On the other hand, if private spending and income rise, the unemployed are rehired, and unemployment compensation stops. In both cases, the result is to help stabilize incomes and to moderate changes in the level of economic activity. For this reason, transfer payments are often referred to as **automatic stabilizers.**

By now you are aware that in economics (as everywhere else) even the best programs have their drawbacks. Transfer payments are no exception. Some income-support payments may reduce the incentive to work. Transfer payments generally are not taxable. Thus in some low-paid occupations an individual's after-tax income from work may not be much greater than the tax-free income he or she would receive from transfer payments. It is important not to overemphasize this problem, however. The work disincentive is probably rather small simply because the transfer payments are generally small. Moreoever, the drudgery and humiliation involved in accepting public charity are themselves significant incentives to find a job. If the disincentive problem proves serious, one solution might be to limit future income-support payments to those physically unable to work and to provide government-sponsored employment to those who cannot find private sector employment.

GOVERNMENT TAXATION POLICIES

Now that you know some of the things various levels of government do for citizens, you may be wondering *how* they do it. From where, you should ask, come the funds?

Of course, the answer is taxes (and, to a lesser extent, borrowing, a concern of macroeconomics). All levels of government levy taxes on the citizens within their jurisdiction to provide those citizens with the public goods and services they want to consume.

State and Local Government Taxation

State and local governments collect a variety of taxes. Their major source of revenue is the **property tax;** it provides about one fourth of state and local revenues. Property taxes must be paid on residential, commercial, and industrial property. The homeowner pays the property tax directly. The apartment dweller pays the tax indirectly, through the rent the landlord charges. And consumers pay a good share of industry's property taxes, as business firms build these taxes into the selling prices of their goods and services.

Secondly, there are **sales taxes** on the price paid for a good or service. Sales taxes are generally levied by state governments, and for a good reason: The sales tax should be uniform throughout the state in order to discourage shoppers from going from town to town to avoid paying. Even though uniformity is desirable, it is not always achieved. In many parts of New York state, for example, the sales tax is 4 percent. But in New York City, the rate is 8 percent. Why? Because the state levies a 4 percent sales tax and the city an additional 4 percent sales tax of its own. Knowing this, it will come as no surprise to you that not many new cars are sold in Manhattan.

As a group (with many variations from the average), states collected some one fourth of their revenues from sales taxes in recent years.

Two important additional forms of taxes are **personal and corporate income taxes.** These are taxes levied against individuals' incomes and against corporate profits (that is, what remains after all other costs have been paid). In the case of individual income taxes, the rate generally increases as the size of a worker's income increases (although many states levy uniform rates). For corporations the rate is usually a fixed percentage of profits.

Only about 10 percent of state and local revenues come from personal and corporate income taxes. The reason is that high income-tax rates tend to discourage individuals and businesses from moving into an area. After all, who wants to pay more taxes if it can be avoided? Most states would like to encourage productive individuals and firms to move within their boundaries, so they avoid levying high income taxes.

A few cities have income taxes, too. But that doesn't mean only city dwellers pay the tax. New York City, among others, has levied a nonresident income tax which taxes the income of anyone who works in the city—no matter that the worker may *live* in New Jersey. The reasoning is that many suburban dwellers earn their living in the city and so should contribute to its upkeep.

Yet another one fourth of state and local revenue comes from the federal government. Federal aid to states was rather small until the 1950s, when the federal government began to provide grants for education, social services, and highway construction. Then in 1972 the federal government began its *revenue-sharing program* to state and local governments. The amount of funds provided is based on a formula measuring the size of populations and the urgency of need in various localities. The aim is to distribute federal tax revenues among states according to need rather than according to income. It was hoped that federal tax moneys would enable poorer state and local governments to raise the quality of their social programs in accordance with local needs. The alternative was for the federal government to take over the job entirely. See Table 2 for a summary of state and local receipts.

Regressive Taxes and State and Local Government

Taxes can be described as either *proportional*, *regressive*, or *progressive* in their effects. A **proportional tax** collects an equal percentage of income from all who pay the tax. A **progressive tax** collects a higher percentage of income from high-income families than from low-income families. A **regressive tax,** by contrast, collects a smaller share of a wealthy family's income than

Table 2 **Receipts and Outlays of State and Local Governments (1978)**

Receipts	Billions of dollars	Percentage of total	Outlays	Billions of dollars	Percentage of total
Property taxes	19.0	8%	Education	87.7	36%
Income taxes	43.1	17%	Highways	23.2	9%
Sales, excise, and misc. taxes	64.8	25%	Public welfare	40.2	16%
All other	67.3	26%	All other	95.7	39%
Aid from federal government	60.4	24%			
Total receipts	254.6	100%	Total outlays	247.8	100%

of a poor family's income. The federal Social Security tax is probably the most regressive tax. However, the majority of regressive taxes are imposed by state and local governments. Sales taxes are regressive. So are property taxes.

Take an example. Suppose a low-income family earns $12,000 a year and lives in a $36,000 house. A wealthy family earns $100,000 and lives in a $200,000 house. The low-income family lives in a house worth more relative to its income than does the wealthy family. Now suppose the first family pays property taxes of $1000; the second family pays $6000 in property taxes. Why is the tax regressive?

To answer this, compare the amount of tax with each family's income. For the low-income family, the property tax bill is 1000/12,000 = 8.4 percent of income. For the second family, the percentage is 6000/100,000 = 6 percent of income. The regressive tax imposes a higher *percentage* tax burden on low-income than on high-income families. The property tax tends to be regressive because: (1) ownership of real property does not generally increase proportionately with earnings, and (2) tax assessments do not always increase proportionately with property values.

Sales taxes are usually regressive, too. You might well ask, "If both rich and poor pay the same percent, how can the tax be regressive?" If the $12,000-year family spends $10,000 on taxable items, and the sales tax is 4 percent, then the tax bill will be $10,000 × .04 = $400; this is 400/12,000 = 3.3 percent of the family's income. If the $100,000-year family spends $50,000 for taxable items, its tax bill will be $50,000 × .04 = $2000, or 2000/100,000 = 2 percent of income. Sales taxes are regressive because low-income families generally must spend a greater percentage of income on taxed items like food,* clothing, fuel, etc., than do high-income families, who purchase more services and save more of their incomes.

Some state sales taxes are less regressive than others because they exempt food and medicine from the tax. The regressive nature of state and local taxes is also offset somewhat by providing more benefits to poorer than to wealthier families. For example, police and fire protection are often required in greater amounts in poor sections of towns; there may be more violence there. Also, health services are provided to poor families more often than to wealthy ones. Suffice it to say that calculating the true regressivity of taxes is a complicated task when *benefits received* are considered.

Federal Government Taxation

If you don't like paying taxes in a particular state or city, you have the option of moving to another. But this option does not apply to federal taxes. If you move from New York to Los Angeles, you will pay the same federal tax in your new setting as you did in your old, assuming your income remains the same. (True, you could leave the country, but that is a rather unlikely choice for most of us.) This illustrates an important aspect of federal tax policies: The federal government can use any tax it requires to raise the revenues it needs; it need not fear massive avoidance by people leaving its jurisdiction. The federal government's only tax concern is that very high, "confiscatory" taxation might stifle incentives to produce and therefore might

*Some states exempt food and medicine from sales taxes.

Table 3 **Receipts and Outlays of the Federal Government, 1980 (estimated)**

Receipts	Billions of dollars	Percentage of total	Outlays	Billions of dollars	Percentage of Total
Personal income taxes	236.4	43%	Purchases of goods and services	178.2	33%
Corporate income taxes	78.2	15	Total transfer payments	282.1	52
Excise taxes and other indirect taxes	30.4	6	Aid to state and local governments	78.9	15
Social Security taxes	168.8	31			
New borrowing	25.4	5			
Total receipts	539.2	100%	Total outlays	539.2	100%

reduce the economy's total output of goods and services.

Politicians know that the public dislikes taxes. As a famous seventeenth-century French economist advised the tax collectors: "The art of taxation involves plucking the goose . . . to get the most feathers with the least hissing."

To extract the most revenues with the least hissing from taxpayers, the federal government relies heavily on income taxes. Federal income taxes are certainly large, and the "hissing" is reduced by withholding payments from salaries (rather than requiring one large lump payment). Personal income taxes yielded about $190 billion in 1979; corporate income taxes yielded another $62.5 billion or so. Beyond these two income taxes, contributions for social insurance (Social Security taxes and unemployment compensation taxes) constituted almost $109 billion. Other federal taxes include *excise taxes, gift taxes, estate taxes, gasoline taxes,* and *customs duties.* Since you may pay some of these taxes, we will describe each briefly; then, we will consider income taxes and social payments at length. Table 3 summarizes federal government receipts.

Excise taxes. **Excise taxes** are levied on specific goods and services that are generally considered luxuries. Occasionally, an excise tax is levied in order to discourage consumption of some commodity, such as liquor or cigarettes. In other cases, an excise tax is applied against items purchased by only a few taxpayers, so as to minimize public opposition. An example of this is the 10 percent excise tax on most jewelry items.

Gift taxes. **Gift taxes** are levied against gifts to individuals when the gift is $3000 or more in a single year. Rates range from 2¼ percent on small gifts to almost 50 percent on large gifts. Gift taxes discourage wealthy families from passing along wealth to following generations without paying estate taxes at death.

Estate taxes. **Estate taxes** are levied against the assets of a person who dies. Again, the purpose is to restrain wealthy families from passing all their wealth along to following generations. Without gift and estate taxes it might be easier for the rich to get richer and the poor, poorer. Part of an individual's estate may be passed on to the surviving spouse. As much as half the estate is then exempt from taxes. Tax rates on the remaining value range from 3 percent for an estate of less than $5000, to 32.5 percent on $1 million and 60.9 percent on $10 million.

Gasoline taxes. Next time you fill up your tank, look at the price schedule on the pump. There you will see that several cents of each gallon's price is a federal gasoline tax. (In addition, most states—and some cities and counties—charge a tax on gasoline.) Most of these federal tax collections flow into highway trust funds, on the assumption that motorists should pay for the construction and repair of the nation's highways. The gasoline tax is an example of a user tax; bridge tolls are another. **User taxes** are collected so that persons who benefit from a particular public service pay the cost.

Customs duties. Many goods and services are cheaper in other countries than in ours. To discourage massive imports of such goods, the government requires importers and American travelers to pay **customs duties,** called *tariffs,* on the items they bring back into this country when these items exceed a certain total value. Therefore, if you go to Switzerland and purchase some fine wristwatches, be prepared to hand the customs inspector a tax to get your purchases across the U.S. border. Very little revenue is received from imports, since the high rate acts to keep the goods out of the country. Export taxes are forbidden by the Constitution.

PROGRESSIVE NATURE OF FEDERAL INCOME TAXES

As we said above, the federal government relies heavily upon income taxes, both personal and corporate. One important feature of federal income taxes is that they are progressive. Remember that progressive taxes are those which collect a higher percent of taxes from high-income families than from low-income families.

Here is how the federal income tax works.

The taxpayer is allowed **exemptions** from income for each member of the household. In 1980 the value of each exemption was $1000. A family could reduce its income for tax purposes by $1000 times the number of persons.

Next, the taxpayer may deduct certain allowable expenses. These include state and local taxes, interest payments on loans, donations to charitable organizations, some health and medical expenses, and some expenses incurred in carrying on business. Allowable expenses may be itemized precisely or the taxpayer may use the standard deduction of $3400.

Note that deductions represent a nonfiscal aspect of government's influence in the economy. For example, home owners may deduct mortgage interest, since government believes home owners make good citizens. Working parents are allowed to deduct some of the costs of providing for school-aged children because government believes education should be subsidized. Other goals of government may be attained by raising or lowering certain deductions.

When deductions are subtracted, the result is the family's taxable income. Table 4 is the tax rate schedule for married taxpayers filing joint tax returns. Column (1) indicates income brackets for computing tax. Column (2) lists the first term in a taxpayer's tax computation. Column (3) lists the tax rates which apply to each income bracket. A standard deduction of $3400 has already been considered for assigning tax rates. The taxpayer's tax computation includes the amount in Column (2) plus the fraction (3) of income earned in that income bracket.

The tax rate in Column (3) is called the **marginal tax rate.** It is the rate applied to additional dollars of income. Note that the first one thousand dollars of a family's taxable income is taxed at the rate of 14 percent. The next one thousand dollars is taxed at the rate of 16 percent. The one-hundredth thousand dollars is taxed at the rate of 59 percent. The highest marginal tax rate

Table 4 **1979 Tax-Rate Schedule Y Married Taxpayers Filing Joint Tax Returns**

Tax brackets	Tax computation		
(1)	(2) *Pay this amount*	(3) *Plus this fraction*	(4) *of the amount over*
3,400– 5,500	0	14%	3,400
5,500– 7,600	294	16%	5,500
7,600– 11,900	630	18%	7,600
11,900– 16,000	1,404	21%	11,900
16,000– 20,200	2,265	24%	16,000
20,200– 24,600	3,273	28%	20,200
24,600– 29,900	4,505	32%	24,600
29,900– 35,200	6,201	37%	29,900
35,200– 45,800	8,162	43%	35,200
45,800– 60,000	12,720	49%	45,800
60,000– 85,600	19,678	54%	60,000
85,600–109,400	33,502	59%	85,600
109,400–162,400	47,544	64%	109,400
162,400–215,400	81,464	68%	162,400
215,400– +	116,504	70%	215,400

is 70 percent, applied to incomes greater than $215,400. This means that a family earning $215,400 in taxable income is allowed to keep only thirty cents of the last dollar earned.

To illustrate the use of the tax-rate schedule, let us consider two families earning $16,000 and $100,000 a year, respectively. Both families have four members and are entitled to four exemptions of $1000 each. The appropriate income for computing tax is $16,000 − $4000 = $12,000 for the first family and $100,000 − $4000 = $96,000 for the second. Look in the table for the bracket which includes $12,000. Total tax is $1,404 plus 21 percent of the difference between income and $11,900: total tax = 1404 + .21(12,000 − 11,900) = 1404 + 21 = $1425. The first term, $1404, is the sum of taxes due on all previous tax brackets: 14 percent of the difference between $5500 and $3400, plus 16 percent of the difference between $7600 and $5500, plus 18 percent of the difference between $11,900 and $7600. The tax rate on the last addition to income is this family's marginal tax rate, 21 percent.

The second family is in a higher tax bracket with a marginal tax rate of 59 percent. This family pays tax of 33,502 + .59(96,000 − 85,600) = 33,502 + 6136 = $39,638. Because its marginal tax rate is higher, the second family pays a higher fraction of its income in taxes than the first: 39,638/100,000 = 39.6 percent versus 1,425/16,000 = 8.9 percent. This is an important result of the progressive tax system.

Of course, in the real world of taxpaying, tax avoiding,* and taxshifting, progressivity works somewhat differently. The Internal Revenue Code is full of ways for wealthier families to reduce their tax bite. They can employ tax accountants and lawyers to advise them on legal deductions from taxable income. And then they can deduct the costs of these accountants and lawyers. Opportunities for reducing tax bills are often called *tax loopholes* by crusading politicians, but reserve your judgment when you hear this phrase. Some loopholes can benefit you, too. For example, if you are a home owner, you can deduct your mortgage interest payments from taxable income and reduce your own tax bill. The apartment dweller may call your tax break a loophole. You may prefer to call it "encouraging private home ownership."

*There is a difference between tax *avoidance* and tax *evasion*. Tax avoidance is using legal means to reduce the tax bill (taking advantage of all possible deductions).

Disadvantages and Advantages of Progressive Taxes

The reason the tax code has loopholes is that there is a serious potential problem with progressive taxes. The problem is that high tax rates may be a disincentive to do worthwhile things. For example, many corporations depend on the sale of stocks to provide funds for expansion and modernization. Growth in production and creation of new jobs require firms to use savings from many small savers. However, if much of the gain to be made from purchasing stocks were to be taxed away through a very progressive income-tax schedule, chances are people wouldn't buy them. To overcome this problem, the tax code states that no matter what your income level, *capital gains* on sales of securities held nine months or longer are to be taxed at only 40 percent of your regular rate. A **capital gain** is the money earned by the sale of an asset; it is the difference between purchase price and selling price. **Dividends,** which are the income earned from *holding* stocks, are considered part of personal income and are taxed as such.

There are many other examples of loopholes in the tax code meant to overcome the problem of tax disincentives. Contributions to religious, educational, or scientific organizations are tax deductible. Tax credits are also available to business firms when they make capital investments or employ welfare recipients in job-training programs.

The progressive tax performs an important function aside from its role as a successful revenue raiser. This second function is to help provide greater stability in the level of total spending, output, employment, and prices. In a free economy like ours, independent decisions may sometimes cause economic instability as buyers abruptly change their spending plans. A progressive tax structure helps cushion the effects of sudden changes in spending and helps correct problems of inflation or unemployment.

Suppose buyers decide to speed up their spending for consumer goods and services and investment goods. Incomes increase and production expands, pushing against the limits of our productive capacity and creating inflationary pressures. But as incomes increase, families move into higher tax brackets and pay higher marginal tax rates. Unemployed workers are hired and become taxpayers, too. As a result, tax revenues increase faster than incomes. Larger

Viewpoint The Value-Added Tax

You won't meet many people who like paying taxes. Most of us think we pay too much and that others—somehow—get by without paying their share. Since we must pay, we want to make certain that our taxes are used efficiently, that worthwhile programs are carried out without waste and with a minimum of bureaucratic ineptitude. We expect public officials to be accountable for their actions in administering our money.

Americans paid an average of $3436 in taxes to state, local, and federal governments in 1979. Total taxes paid amounted to less than a third of the value of national output, and it was less than taxes paid in any other major nation except Greece, Japan, and Spain.

Most European tax revenues come from the *Value Added Tax* (VAT). The VAT is actually a nationwide sales tax, but instead of the consumer paying a percentage of the purchase price, say 15 percent on a $10,000 automobile, manufacturers pay a 15 percent tax on the value added to the auto at each stage of production. The final price to the buyer, $11,500, can be the same either way, but with the VAT the tax is hidden in the purchase price. Taxpayers don't receive a tax bill from their government and may be less likely to complain.

VAT has some other advantages. The Value Added Tax applies only to consumer goods, giving some encouragement to saving for investment in capital goods. Revenue from VAT remains fairly stable during business cycles, whereas income-tax revenue tends to fluctuate as incomes change. (Remember, however, that fluctuating income-tax revenue is an important automatic stabilizer for economic activity.) Some members of Congress have recommended replacing Social Security taxes with VAT in the U.S. This would reduce employment costs for business firms and increase take-home pay for workers. The VAT on goods intended for export would be refunded to the producer by government; the saving would be passed on to the customer as lower prices. U.S. manufacturers would be able to sell abroad at lower prices than they currently can. This practice is followed in most European countries to encourage their exports.

Critics point out that the VAT is a regressive tax. Low-income persons spend a greater portion of their income on taxed items and have a heavier relative tax burden than high-income persons, who spend a greater fraction of their incomes on services and save more. Tax credits could be designed to overcome this problem.

A major criticism of VAT is that it could be inflationary, at least in the short run, if government raises all prices immediately by the amount of the tax.

Show how VAT collects the same tax on a $10,000 auto as a sales tax does. Who pays the tax in either case?

tax payments drain from incomes, limiting the rise in spending and reducing inflationary pressures.*

Progressive taxes also help cushion a sudden drop in spending. If consumers and business firms decide to spend less, income and production will fall. Some workers will lose their jobs and unemployment will increase. But as incomes fall, families will move into lower tax brackets; unemployed workers will pay no income tax at all. This time the tax drain from income will fall faster than income falls. Lower tax bills will enable families to maintain spending at almost a normal level, limiting the drop in production and moderating the decline in employment. Like transfer payments, progressive income taxes are often referred to as automatic stabilizers.

*This feature of progressive taxes became a major problem in 1979 and 1980. Taxpayers complained that their inflated incomes had not grown in terms of real purchasing power. Yet, they moved into higher tax brackets and were required to pay higher taxes.

Social Security Taxes

After personal and corporate income taxes, the second major source of federal tax revenue is contributions to Social Security. Social Security legislation was passed in the 1930s as a means of providing disability and retirement benefits for workers and their dependents. Employed persons pay 6.13 percent of their earnings up to $25,900 (1980) to the Social Security Trust Fund. The tax is deducted from paychecks by employers, who contribute another 6.13 percent. Each year 33 million widows, dependents, and retired people receive income-support payments from Social Security.

In recent years Social Security has become a "pay-as-you-go" revenue plan. This means that tax revenues collected from workers currently in the work force are paid directly to the nation's Social Security recipients. In other words, working sons and daughters pay the benefits to their retired parents (and even grandparents) as the government deducts Social Security taxes from the workers' paychecks. This pay-as-you-go nature of Social Security may soon become a major problem.

The problem is that the number of old people relative to younger workers is expected to increase dramatically within the next seventy-five years. This means that workers in coming decades will be forced to shoulder an increasing burden of Social Security benefits. Already, the money paid into the system is barely enough to cover present benefits.

One solution to the problem would be to increase the tax rate, but that is hardly politically popular. Since the Social Security tax is regressive, this would mean that poor workers would pay a larger share of the tax. Another would be to supplement the Social Security system with income-tax revenues. But that would remove the appearance that workers are paying for their retirement through deductions from their own paychecks. This appearance was judged to be very important when Social Security legislation was passed in the late 1930s.

Another more immediate problem with Social Security taxes is that they are regressive. Although the same tax rate, 6.13 percent, is charged to all workers, it is applied against only the first $25,900 of income. There is no tax charged on the amount of earnings over this $25,900 ceiling. Income from sources other than work is not taxed at all.

To see how this is regressive, consider again the $12,000-year and the $100,000-year families. If we assume the entire income is earned by one member of the family, their taxes are as follows:

	$12,000	$100,000
6.13% of first $25,900	$735.60	$1587.67
Tax as % of income	$735.60/12,000 = 6.13%	$1587.67/100,000 = 1.59%

As in the case of all regressive taxes, the *relative* tax burden is greater on the low-income family even though the *absolute* tax bill is lower. Because Social Security taxes are regressive, they do not function as automatic stabilizers, and they remain fairly constant even when total income increases.

EVALUATING OUR TAX STRUCTURE

We have shown that state and local governments raise funds primarily through regressive property and sales taxes. Federal tax revenues are collected primarily from progressive income taxes. The effect of all taxes taken together is less regressive and less progressive than either would be alone.

Recall that a tax which takes the same percentage of income at every income level is called a proportional tax. Over a wide range of earnings, the total effect of all state, local, and federal taxes is roughly proportional. In fact, in the 1970s families earning between $4000 and $25,000 paid about 32 percent of their income in taxes. The percentage paid was different at the low and the high extremes of income. Families earning less than $4000 generally paid a higher percentage in taxes, as much as 50 percent at very low incomes. For this reason, it is said that our tax structure is regressive for incomes less than $4000. Families earning more than $25,000 also paid a higher percentage, again as much as 50 percent at very high incomes. This makes our tax structure progressive for earned incomes greater than $25,000.

The actual effect of particular taxes is difficult to measure. This is because taxes are often shifted from the person who actually pays the tax to another party. For instance, a retailer pays taxes, but the revenue for taxes is collected by increasing the price of the good or service produced. Landlords pay taxes, but they collect the revenues in rents their tenants pay. Employers pay taxes but they acquire the revenue by reducing the wages paid to employees. The actual burden of taxes depends on tax incidence. **Tax incidence** refers to who actually pays the tax, who actually gives up purchasing power. It is possible to estimate the incidence of taxes, but not precisely.

You may not enjoy paying taxes. But before you grumble too much or too loudly, make sure you grumble about the correct thing: net taxes.

We are concerned about net taxes because many families receive **negative taxes,** or transfer payments. **Net taxes** are the amount of actual taxes a family *pays* minus the transfer payments the family *receives.* The net tax structure reflects the true tax burden of families at various income levels.

Families at low-income levels generally pay low taxes and receive more transfer benefits. As a result, their net tax rate is very low and may even be negative. Families at high-income levels generally pay high taxes and receive fewer transfer benefits. Their net tax rate is much closer to their actual tax rate. The effect of transfer payments is to make our net tax structure much more progressive than the actual tax structure.

SUMMARY

While economic theory often assumes a world of completely free economic agents, we know that this is not the case in the real twentieth-century world. Governments impose rules and regulations that restrain our actions and play an important role in economic activity.

One important economic function of government is to protect property. Laws regarding contracts, safety standards, and product labeling aim at fulfilling this responsibility. Government must also provide a modern, functioning monetary system conducive to stable economic growth and development. In addition, the private marketplace cannot be relied upon to allocate public goods and services and social costs properly because both are nonexclusive. Government must play a role in their production and allocation, too. Finally, government encourages a competitive marketplace, promotes economic stability, fights poverty, and prohibits discrimination.

State and local governments provide basic services such as fire and police protection, sanitation, and education. Revenues are often shared within a state to equalize the quality of public goods and services statewide. All together, state and local government purchases amount to more than one half of all government purchases.

Federal government purchases of goods and services include defense spending and community services. Federal spending for social services has increased dramatically in this century because the age mix of the population has changed. Also, we expect more and better civilization as our economy grows and prospers.

Transfer payments are more than one half of all federal outlays. They provide income support payments, health and nutrition benefits, and many other services. There are few Americans who do not benefit from some transfer-payment program. Transfer payments, like progressive income taxes, help stabilize total spending during times of rising or falling incomes.

Local governments raise most of their revenues through property taxes. State governments raise the majority of their revenues through sales taxes. Many states and some cities also use income taxes, though rates are generally low. About 25 percent of state and local government revenues come from federal revenue sharing programs. State and local taxes are generally regressive.

The major sources of revenue for the federal government are personal and corporate income taxes. The income tax is progressive. After exemptions and deductions, high-income families usually pay a higher marginal tax rate than low-income families do. Highly progressive taxes may stifle incentives to perform valuable services. However, progressive taxes do help stabilize total spending during periods of rising or falling incomes. And they provide increasing revenues as the economy grows. The Social Security tax is regressive. Social Security revenues do not vary much with income, so this tax is not a good stabilizer.

The total tax burden tends to be regressive at low levels of income, proportional over a wide range of middle incomes, and progressive at higher levels. However, examination of net taxes shows our entire tax structure to be slightly progressive.

Key Words and Phrases

automatic stabilizers tax payments and transfer payments which work automatically to moderate changes in consumers' incomes and total spending.

capital gain the gain from the sale of a capital asset for a higher price than its total cost.

contract an agreement to perform certain acts and to pay certain amounts.

customs duties taxes levied on goods brought into a nation from abroad.

deductions reductions in taxable income based on certain allowable expenses.
estate taxes taxes levied on bequests of property.
excise taxes taxes levied on particular items generally considered luxuries.
exclusivity the opportunity to enjoy goods and services individually and to pay the costs individually.
exemptions reductions in taxable income based on the number of persons supported by the income and their need for support.
gift taxes taxes levied on gifts of property of more than $3000 in one year.
marginal tax rate the percentage tax levied on additional dollars of income; in a progressive income tax system the marginal tax rate increases.
money anything that serves society as a medium of exchange; today governments are responsible for issuing money and for controlling its supply.
negative taxes reverse taxes or transfer payments.
net taxes taxes paid less transfer payments received from government; figured as percentage of income.
nonexclusivity the inability to restrict the use of goods or services or their costs to a single individual or group.
personal and corporate income taxes taxes levied on the incomes of individuals and corporations.
private goods and services goods and services which are exclusive, restricted to the use of a single individual or group.
progressive tax a tax which is a higher percentage for high-income persons than for low-income persons.
property taxes taxes levied on the value of real and personal property.
proportional tax a tax which is the same percentage for high-income persons as for low-income persons.
public goods and services goods and services which are nonexclusive, enjoyed by the community as a whole.
regressive tax a tax which is a higher percentage for low-income persons than for high-income persons.
revenue sharing a system of intergovernmental transfer of funds, generally from the federal government to state and local governments.
sales taxes taxes levied on the price of a good or service and paid at the time of purchase.
social costs costs in resource use which are imposed on the community as a whole; pollution is the most common social cost.
tax incidence measurement of who actually gives up purchasing power when a tax is levied.
transfer payments payments from government for which no good or service is provided in exchange; welfare, unemployment benefits, and Medicare are transfer payments.
user taxes taxes collected from the persons who use a public service; the costs of public services, such as highways, are paid by those who use them, as through gasoline taxes.

Questions for Review

1. What have been the trends in public goods and services relative to private goods and services in the United States? What does this imply about the role of government in our national life? What other circumstances have contributed to these trends?
2. Name and explain the economic functions of government. Give examples of each.
3. With respect to the role of government in future years, what do you see as potential reasons for greater government influence? What are the opportunities and dangers of this course? What alternatives are there to increased government?
4. Explain the concept of revenue sharing, showing how it attempts to resolve the conflict between centralization and decentralization of authority. Do you think revenue sharing is necessary?
5. Outline the primary sources of and uses for funds in (1) the federal government and (2) state and local governments.
6. Distinguish between government expenditures and transfers.
7. Define regressive tax and progressive tax and give advantages and disadvantages of each. Under what circumstances does a tax serve as an automatic stabilizer?
8. Explain how the Social Security tax works. What problem confronts Social Security?
9. Define: incidence of a tax, net tax, exclusivity, and nonexclusivity.
10. Use the Social Security information in this chapter to compute taxes for one worker earning $25,000 and for another earning $75,000. Demonstrate how the tax is regressive.
11. Explain how our tax system can be regressive, proportional, and progressive at different incomes.
12. Discuss the advantages and disadvantages of collecting a tax on capital gains. What would be the likely effect on stock prices of no capital gains tax at all? How might the capital gains tax be unfair to investors? Should small savers be given the same type of exemption as small stockholders?

PART 2

Consumer Behavior And Elasticity

5 Consumer Demand and Utility

6 Measuring and Using Elasticity of Demand

7 Supply Elasticity and Government Policy

CHAPTER 5

Consumer Demand and Utility

Learning Objectives

Upon completion of this chapter, you should be able to:

1. Explain what all consumers choose in their purchases.
2. Understand and apply the ideas of marginal decision-making and declining marginal utility.
3. Distinguish between total and marginal utility, both verbally and graphically.
4. Explain and apply the equal marginal utility principle.
5. Plot rough demand curves from a consumer's marginal utility of money.
6. Explain and graph consumer's surplus for any item.

"Let your fingers do the walking through the Yellow Pages," runs the advertising slogan. Most of us do just that, once we have decided what we want to buy. Knowing what we want must come first. How do we decide?

Economists have a theory of how we do this. It is called the *theory of consumer choice*. The theory is important because it helps explain how individuals express their preferences in free markets. The decisions of millions of consumers, made in thousands of stores and shops, must somehow influence production of all the goods and services we want.

If we look closely, we find common patterns in the way consumers make their choices. These patterns apply to fur coats and beer, dental care and hockey tickets, copper tubing and laboratory technicians. The principles that explain consumer choice are fundamental to the competitive market system. It is consumer choice that guides the decisions of producers on *what* is to be produced, *how* production is to be carried out, *for whom* output is to be provided, and *when* goods can be enjoyed. Without knowing it, consumers send signals to producers of the goods and services they buy (or don't buy), telling them how to allocate scarce resources among different productive uses.

Suppose this were not so. If there were no competitive market, decisions would have to be made in some other way. In a centrally planned economy, for example, a planning board has to draw up a list of priorities to replace the market. The plan specifies how much of what kinds of goods to produce, for whom to produce the goods, how to combine resources in production, and when to produce the goods. Everything has to be planned so that the right inputs arrive at the right place at the right time. The process is enormously complicated, as you might imagine. In a free market system these decisions are made independently by producers and distributors in response to the signals of consumers.

Of course, the market system isn't quite as simple as we've made it sound. Because of the time required to produce some things, production has to be planned in advance. This may lead to overproduction or underproduction of some items. A real-estate developer may build fifty $100,000 houses only to find that not all of them can be sold at that price. Or a farmer may plant apple trees and discover several years later that there are too many apples. Sometimes a producer may introduce an entirely new good or service in the hope of eventually persuading people to buy it. In all these cases the initial decision is made by the producer. But it is up to the consumer to demonstrate whether it was the right decision.

In the chapters that follow we will describe the behavior of consumers in free markets and present the theory that explains their behavior. Later we will look at the market system as a whole and explore some proposals for making the system work better. But in this chapter let's look more closely at how consumers choose the things they buy.

THE DEMAND FOR GOODS AND SERVICES

Let's suppose we decide to buy a hamburger. We go to the Golden Arch or the Jolly King and ask for a Super Deluxe Cheeseburger with everything. While we're waiting for our order to be filled, we reflect on what we've done. We find that we've already made a number of choices. We've chosen to buy a hamburger—not just any hamburger but a Jolly King burger. Furthermore, we've selected their biggest, with melted cheese and mustard and onions and relish. If the chef were to bring us a plain hamburger, we'd be highly annoyed, even though the plain hamburger would satisfy our hunger just as well. But we didn't ask for something to satisfy our hunger; we asked for a very specific combination of *characteristics.*

If we pursue this a little further, we'll see that in many of our purchases what we are really buying is a bundle of properties or qualities. For instance, we don't buy bread, we buy raisin bread, thin-sliced rye bread without caraway seeds, or Mrs. Porter's cracked wheat bread with molasses. We all want different combinations of qualities, of course. Because we want different qualities, we may react quite differently to the same thing. Status seekers may be willing to pay the high price to buy a Rolls Royce. Others, who are able to pay the price, may refuse to buy a Rolls because they feel that seeking status through owning a car is ridiculous.

Characteristics

Not every possible property of a good or service is necessarily relevant to a decision to buy it. A bottle of fine wine probably has certain disinfectant qualities, but a consumer seldom considers this while choosing fine wines. A lawyer may be a champion handball player, but this has nothing to do with the legal service rendered. It is not necessary to consider all properties—only those which affect the consumer's decision. The collections of properties that may possibly affect a particular consumer choice are called **characteristics.**

Some goods or services may have only a single characteristic. For example, the several brands of aspirin tablets basically all have one characteristic: they provide five grains of acetylsalicylic acid, which works to kill pain. One function of advertising is to make the consumers believe that a particular firm's product has some *other* valuable characteristic. The fact that consumers do buy expensive name-brand aspirins proves how well advertising adds *salable characteristics*.

Choice of Characteristics

The decision to buy a good is the result of choosing a particular combination of characteristics. Choosing proceeds in two steps. First a consumer evaluates the kinds and amounts of characteristics provided by various goods and services. Then, the consumer decides whether to buy one collection of characteristics or another. Generally the characteristics themselves can be objectively measured, but a consumer's reaction to characteristics is highly individualistic. For example, one brand of stereo speakers might be more suitable for listening to rock music while another might be better for classical music. A consumer must choose the desired characteristic for his or her own purposes.

Since most goods and services contain a bundle of characteristics, consumers buy a certain good or service because it has the particular mix of characteristics desired. Presumably consumers will try to obtain as much as possible of each characteristic they desire. They will be limited by their incomes, of course, unless they use some of their accumulated savings or go into debt. No two consumers will try to consume precisely the same bundle of characteristics, but they will try to consume as much of the desired characteristics as their incomes allow.

The first step, then, is to choose a collection of goods which contain the characteristics desired. The second is to obtain as much of the characteristics as possible within a person's limited income and accumulated wealth or ability to borrow. (Of course, spending one's stock of savings or spending by going into debt reduces the ability to consume in the future.)

THE UTILITY OF GOODS AND SERVICES

We buy goods and services because we enjoy the particular characteristics they provide. Characteristics are desirable because they fulfill our basic wants or because they provide enrichment to life.

Economists compare the desirability of various goods and services by comparing their utility. **Utility** is a measure of the satisfaction obtained from a purchase. All consumers are alike in one respect: They try to obtain as much utility or satisfaction as they can from the goods and services available to them.

The utility of owning an item involves more than its usefulness. Some of the things we buy are not strictly useful in the sense that they are not absolutely necessary for life. They provide satisfaction of another sort, and the satisfaction is different for different owners. *Utility is a very subjective matter, varying with the individual.* But we can say—and this is true of everyone—that the amount of added utility we get from anything tends to diminish as the amount of the good or service we have increases.

Economists have developed a theory of consumer choice based on *diminishing marginal utility.* The total quantity of food and clothing we have provides some total quantity of utility. But if we have plenty of food and clothing for a particular period of time, the additional utility we get from having one more can of beans or another T-shirt will be small. Likewise the total amount of recreational activity we enjoy provides some total amount of utility. But again, over a particular period of time even the most enthusiastic TV viewer or ice fisher will eventually grow tired of the activity.

Notice the emphasis here is on each *additional* consumption of a good. Economists have a word to describe the increment, or most recent addition, to a quantity: **marginal.** A marginal purchase is the last purchase, or the additional purchase within some period of time. "Marginal" differs from "total," which is the sum of all amounts within some time period.

Unfortunately for the purpose of our theory, utility cannot be measured. An individual can say, "I would prefer to have a new jacket rather than a third chair for my apartment." But economists can't say just how badly the individual wants the new jacket. There is no real unit of measure to describe the satisfaction consumers gain from the things they buy. For now, we will ignore this problem and proceed as if it were possible to measure utility. We will assign values to each purchase as if each buyer's utility were known and measurable.

Marginal Utility

Tables 1 and 2 are marginal utility schedules for a Miss Jones and a Mr. Smith. The tables show the quantities of additional satisfaction each gets from owning additional opera tickets and additional stereo tapes during a particular period of time. The quantities of satisfaction are measured in *utils.* Of course, *the util is imaginary;* there are no instruments for measuring utils. We couldn't say, for example, that we get twenty utils from eating a porterhouse steak but only one util from brussel sprouts. We use this imaginary measure because it is useful in constructing our theory of consumer choice. Remember that although the unit of measurement is imaginary, the satisfaction derived from consumption is not imaginary. The tables of consumer preferences that

Table 1 **Marginal Utility Associated with Purchases of Opera Tickets (one season)**

	Miss Jones	Mr. Smith
1*st* purchase	10 utils	10 utils
2*nd* purchase	9 utils	5 utils
3*rd* purchase	8 utils	0 utils
4*th* purchase	7 utils	−5 utils
5*th* purchase	6 utils	−10 utils

Table 2 **Marginal Utility Associated with Purchases of Stereo Tapes (one year)**

	Miss Jones	Mr. Smith
1*st* purchase	12 utils	10 utils
2*nd* purchase	8 utils	8 utils
3*rd* purchase	4 utils	6 utils
4*th* purchase	0 utils	4 utils
5*th* purchase	0 utils	2 utils

we construct using utils are models of the way each consumer makes choices.

As Table 1 shows, Miss Jones receives ten utils from owning her first opera ticket and nine *additional* utils from the second. Mr. Smith is as enthusiastic as Miss Jones about his first visit to the opera, but his enthusiasm starts to wane after that. His interest in a third visit is zero, and he would have to be dragged kicking and screaming to a fourth performance.

Now look at Table 2. It shows that Miss Jones attaches a high degree of utility to the purchase of her first stereo tape but considerably less to the purchase of additional tapes. Mr. Smith, on the other hand, keeps getting satisfaction from additional tapes, though in lesser amounts.

Tables 1 and 2 show the *marginal utility* obtained from opera tickets and stereo tapes. **Marginal utility** is the utility gained from owning or consuming an *additional* unit of a good or service during a particular period of time—paintings, apples, autos, pet rocks, or what you will. It is important to remember that marginal utility refers to the utility resulting from an additional unit of consumption. For Miss Jones, the fourth opera ticket *adds* seven utils to her utility, while for Mr. Smith the fourth opera ticket actually *decreases* utility by five utils.

In general, we can say that marginal utility declines as more units of a particular good or service are consumed within the time period. That is, each good or service provides **diminishing marginal utility.** Almost all the pleasures of life seem to diminish as we indulge them.

Total Utility

Marginal utility declines—but what about total utility? We define **total utility** as the sum of the utility provided by all the units of a good or service that we have purchased within the time period. As long as marginal utility is positive, total utility increases with each additional purchase. It increases more and more slowly, of course, because each new purchase adds less utility than the previous purchases. At some level of purchase, marginal utility may become negative. When this happens, further purchases will cause total utility to decline. This must be true for everything we purchase, because sooner or later a large amount of anything gets to be a nuisance. The most avid moviegoer would find it inconvenient to visit the theater ten times a day. The most ardent collector of antique autos will eventually run out of space for storing them.

Tables 3 and 4 show the amounts of total utility that Miss Jones and Mr. Smith get from their purchases of opera tickets and stereo tapes. Total utility is calculated by adding the marginal utility associated with each purchase within the

Table 3 **Total Utility Associated with Purchases of Opera Tickets (one season)**

	Miss Jones	Mr. Smith
1*st* purchase	10 utils	10 utils
2*nd* purchase	19 utils	15 utils
3*rd* purchase	27 utils	15 utils
4*th* purchase	34 utils	10 utils
5*th* purchase	40 utils	0 utils

Table 4 **Total Utility Associated with Purchases of Stereo Tapes (one year)**

	Miss Jones	Mr. Smith
1*st* purchase	12 utils	10 utils
2*nd* purchase	20 utils	18 utils
3*rd* purchase	24 utils	24 utils
4*th* purchase	24 utils	28 utils
5*th* purchase	24 utils	30 utils

time period. Compare Tables 3 and 4 with Tables 1 and 2 to see that this is true. For Miss Jones, total utility increases with each purchase of opera tickets over the range shown. It increases by smaller and smaller amounts, however, because marginal utility diminishes with each purchase. For Mr. Smith, the total utility of opera tickets reaches a peak very soon and then stops rising. Total utility starts declining when his marginal utility becomes negative (on the fourth purchase). This is because the suffering that Mr. Smith must endure when he attends the fourth opera offsets the pleasure he got from the first two. For Mr. Smith, four operas provide less total utility than two or three.

Graphing Utility

It is easy to see the relationship between marginal and total utility if we use graphs. The utility data for opera tickets for Miss Jones and Mr. Smith are graphed in Figures 1 and 2. The points for marginal utility are plotted *between* the numbers on the horizontal axis because utility, the satisfaction derived from the opera, increases (or decreases) *during* the process of adding another unit.

Figure 1 shows Miss Jones' marginal and total utility curves for opera tickets during the current season. Notice that the line of total utility (TU) continues to rise over the entire range. But the line of marginal utility (MU) declines. This suggests that eventually the marginal utility of opera tickets may become zero even for Miss Jones, and that her total utility curve may reach a peak. In other words, at some point, further visits to the opera during a single season may provide no additional satisfaction even for so avid a fan as Miss Jones. Mr. Smith, you remember, reaches that point early in the season. His total utility curve (Figure 2a) looks like the roof of the Astrodome, and his marginal utility curve (Figure 2b) slopes steeply downward.

Summing Up

Let's sum up what we have learned about utility curves thus far. First, we have noted that marginal utility tends to decline as additional units are consumed during a single time period. Eventually, for most goods and services, marginal utility will fall to zero and may even become negative.

Total utility can be calculated by adding the marginal utilities of each unit purchased. Total utility for three units is represented by the height of the curve at point 3 in Figure 1a. It is the sum of the marginal utilities of the first three units shown in Figure 1b. As long as marginal utility is positive, the purchase of another unit *increases* total utility. When marginal utility starts to decline, but still is positive, total utility will continue to increase but by smaller amounts. We say then that the total utility curve increases at a decreasing rate.

At some point, marginal utility may become zero. Adding another unit during a particular time period adds nothing to total utility. Then the total utility curve levels off. Should marginal utility become negative, total utility will start to decline: The purchase of another unit *decreases* total utility. Total utility may remain positive, but each additional unit purchased pulls the curve down a little more.

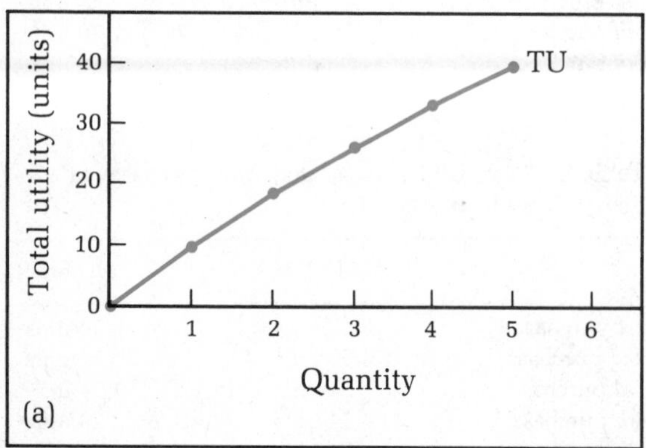

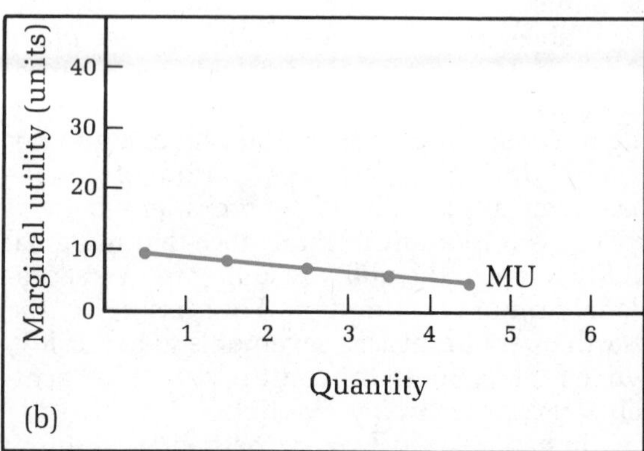

Figure 1 Utility data for Miss Jones' opera purchases: (a) total utility; (b) marginal utility.

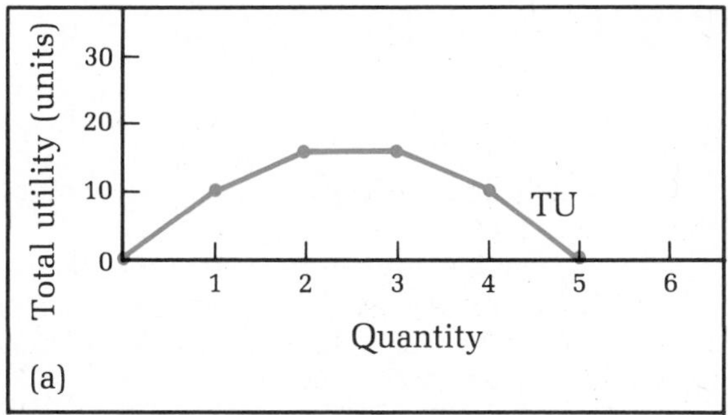

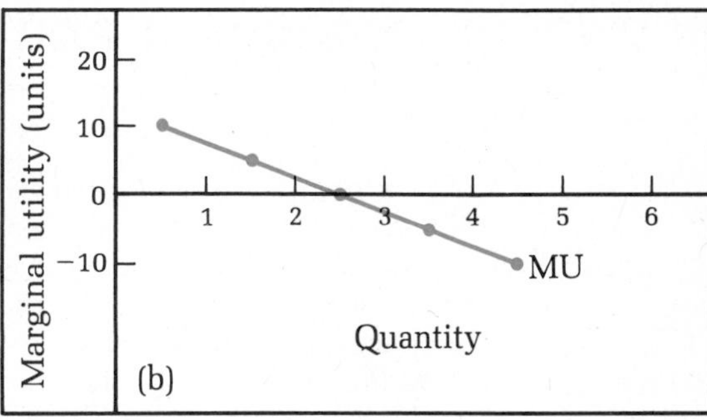

Figure 2 Utility data for Mr. Smith's opera purchases: (a) total utility; (b) marginal utility.

MARGINAL UTILITY AND CONSUMER DEMAND

Thus far, our discussion of marginal utility has omitted an important factor involved in consumer choice. Before we can calculate consumer demand we must know something about prices and about what consumers have to spend.

As a consumer you may imagine a multitude of marginal utility curves associated with the things you buy. There is a curve for automobiles, motorcycles, and bicycles; for coats, shoes, and shirts; for steaks, cans of soup, and pizzas. Over any particular time period the additional utility associated with owning an automobile may be much greater than that to be gained from another pizza. Yet you buy a pizza rather than an automobile. Why? Your choice depends on prices and on your budget.

Table 5 shows hypothetical marginal utility schedules for autos, shirts, and pizzas for a particular time period. Marginal utility (MU) is measured in utils as before. The price (P) of each item is listed also. Including prices enables us to measure the marginal utility gained per dollar spent on any one of the items. The third column in each schedule shows the marginal utility per dollar of each purchase: MU/P = utils per dollar of expenditure. The subscripts indicate the specific purchase.

We can see from Table 5 that the purchase of an automobile would add substantial utility. However, because the price of autos is high, the value of marginal utility per dollar spent (MU/P) is very low. For the first auto purchase it is only one util, while for the first shirt it is 2 utils and for the first pizza, 5 utils.

Consumers normally plan their expenditures so as to achieve what they believe to be the greatest marginal utility per dollar of expenditure. For the consumer in Table 5, the most desired expenditure would be for a pizza. This is because pizzas offer the greatest marginal utility per dollar of expenditure—greater than the consumer could obtain from shirts or autos. Notice that this is the case for this consumer's second pizza as well; MU/P is 4 utils compared to only 2 for the first purchase of a shirt or 1 for an auto. Even a third pizza would be preferred to shirts and autos in this consumer's utility schedule.

Table 5 **Hypothetical Marginal Utilities per Dollar of Expenditures (over one month)**

	Autos			Shirts			Pizzas		
	MU_a	P_a	MU_a/P_a	MU_s	P_s	MU_s/P_s	MU_P	P_P	MU_P/P_P
1*st* purchase	100	$100	1	50	$25	2	25	$5	5
2*nd* purchase	50	100	0.5	40	25	1.6	20	5	4
3*rd* purchase	−100	100	−1	25	25	1	15	5	3
4*th* purchase	−200	100	−2	10	25	0.4	10	5	2
5*th* purchase	−500	100	−5	0	25	0	5	5	1
6*th* purchase	−1000	100	−10	−5	25	−0.2	0	5	0
7*th* purchase	−2000	100	−20	−10	25	−0.4	−10	5	−2
8*th* purchase	−3000	100	−30	−15	25	−0.6	−20	5	−4

Viewpoint Precision and Utility Analysis

Marginal utility analysis is a way of comparing benefits with costs. Most of us are accustomed to making these comparisons among goods when we allocate our budgets (though we don't call the comparisons marginal utility analysis). For instance, we unconsciously compare the utility gained from additional purchases of articles of clothing. A Permapress shirt does not require ironing and it remains crisp and fresh throughout a day's wearing. Furthermore, price comparisons often favor Permapress clothing over cotton or wool. This is because Permapress fabric is made from fibers produced synthetically from petroleum. Until 1973, relatively low-cost Arab oil helped keep petroleum prices low and reduced the cost of producing synthetic fibers for clothing. We might purchase a Permapress shirt for $10, whereas a shirt made of cotton fiber might sell for $20.

The result of our comparison would appear as follows:

$$\frac{\text{Marginal utility}}{\text{Price}_{pp}} > \frac{\text{Marginal utility}}{\text{Price}_{cot}}$$

where pp stands for Permapress and cot for cotton. According to the equal marginal utility principle, the consumer would increase purchases of Permapress shirts until the MU/P is equal for all purchases. In this fashion, society would gain the greatest amount of utility from all shirt purchases. Right?

Wrong. Biologist Barry Commoner suggests that we should look more closely at the costs involved in producing these two items. To produce fibers for cloth requires the use of energy. Production of cotton fibers uses energy from the sun, converting the chemical content of air and water to long strings of molecules in a form of congealed solar energy.

On the other hand, production of synthetic fibers uses energy to heat petroleum, to break it apart, and to combine it again into long strings of molecules. The raw materials are oil and natural gas, with natural gas used to provide the necessary heat. The chemical industry now accounts for about 7 percent of the nation's annual fuel consumption. When we Americans indulge our preference for Permapress over cotton shirts we are encouraging the use of nonrenewable resources (oil and gas) rather than of a constantly renewable one (sunlight). Moreover, we are expelling heat energy to the environment and creating pollution in the process.

How can we include these considerations in our MU/P comparison? How can we adjust our strictly economic calculations to include all these secondary costs? First we must make sure we have correctly evaluated the utility of the Permapress shirt: the comfort

The consumer is said to be in equilibrium when purchases within a single time period are arranged so that the marginal utilities per dollar spent are equal for every item. This is called the **equal marginal utility principle.** It can be stated in symbols as

$$\frac{MU_a}{P_a} = \frac{MU_s}{P_s} = \frac{MU_p}{P_p} = \ldots = \frac{MU_z}{P_z}.$$

That is, the marginal utility per dollar of expenditure on autos equals that for shirts, pizzas, and so on for all goods. When the consumer has chosen correctly, all the goods in the particular collection purchased should yield the same marginal utility per dollar.

To see why, consider how a consumer moves toward equilibrium. Suppose, for instance, that the purchase of the next pizza would yield more MU/P than the next purchase of a shirt. The consumer would increase total utility by purchasing more pizzas and fewer shirts. But as more pizzas are bought, the marginal utility of further purchases of pizzas would decline. The consumer would continue purchasing more pizzas relative to shirts until MU_p/P_p is finally equal to MU_s/P_s. At this point the consumer is in equilibrium, purchasing shirts and pizzas in the correct proportions for achieving maximum total utility.

But this isn't the whole story. The condition that the MU/P's be equal for all goods and services only tells us what *proportions* of products will be consumed. But there are several possible combinations. So we also want to know precisely *how much* of each item is consumed. A wealthy person may consume a larger collection of all goods than a person of modest means. The *relative* amounts in each consumer's collection are determined by personal preferences, as

and appearance of the fabric, the durability of the garment, and, of course, the increased leisure for the laundry-person. Next we must include in costs the *total* cost of the shirt. To the purchase price we should add any additional cost of environmental pollution and the replacement cost of the energy used in production. To develop replacements for a nonrenewable resource will require substantial investment in new research and technology. Including all secondary costs might yield an entirely different relationship:

$$\frac{MU}{\text{Full cost}_{pp}} < \frac{MU}{\text{Full cost}_{cot}}$$

In this case, the equal marginal utility principle dictates the purchase of a cotton shirt.

When the economy as a whole allocates its spending according to *full* costs and benefits, the result may be greater conservation of our nonrenewable resources. Thus the tools of economic analysis are useful not only for evaluating strictly economic alternatives. They are equally suitable for the many complex questions we must consider when we establish priorities for using our scarce resources.

How would you evaluate proposals for building a new highway to the center of the city versus an improved mass transit system?

expressed in the ratios mentioned above. The wealthy person will have a larger budget to spend, however, and may therefore purchase a larger total collection. To determine the quantities bought, we need to know the size of the consumer's budget.

In our example shown in Table 5, the consumer will begin by purchasing three pizzas. This is because the third pizza yields more marginal utility per dollar of expenditure than a single purchase of shirts or autos. But if the consumer's budget permits, the next purchase will be one shirt. With a more substantial budget, after acquiring a number of pizzas and shirts, the consumer may reach a level at which the purchase of an auto is possible.

With a budget of $45 per time period, the consumer in Table 5 would choose one shirt and four pizzas, receiving an equal marginal utility per dollar of 2 for the fourth pizza and for the first shirt: $MU_s/P_s = MU_p/P_p = 2$. Total utility would be 120 utils (the sum of the marginal utilities of four pizzas and one shirt). This is the maximum amount of utility the consumer can get with a budget of $45.

Suppose the consumer's budget is $200 per time period. Looking at Table 5 we see that the consumer maximizes utility with a purchase of one auto ($100), three shirts ($75), and five pizzas ($25). Marginal utility per dollar is equal for all items:

$$\frac{100}{\$100} = \frac{25}{\$25} = \frac{5}{\$5} = 1.$$

Total utility is calculated thus:

auto (100)	= 100 utils
shirts (50 + 40 + 25)	= 115 utils
pizzas (25 + 20 + 15 + 10 + 5)	= 75 utils .
	290 utils

This is the maximum utility possible with a budget of $200.

The Demand Curve

We have been able to determine the quantity of each item purchased because we knew the prices of all the goods, the amount the consumer could spend, and the consumer's preferences among goods (marginal utility schedule). Recalling the earlier discussion of supply and demand (Chapter 3), we can think of each quantity purchased as a single point on the consumer's demand curve for that item. That is, given a certain budget, the point on the curve is the quantity of pizzas, shirts, or autos the consumer will buy at a particular price during a particular period of time. Now let us suppose prices change.

Suppose, for instance, that the price of owning an automobile falls to $25 in a given time period. There will be a change in the marginal utility per dollar (MU/P) for autos. As P_a falls to $25, MU_a/P_a rises—100/$25 = 4. Consumers will adjust their purchases to conform to the new MU_a/P_a. In short, within consumers' budget limitations, they will tend to purchase more autos until MU_a/P_a is again equal to MU_s/P_s and MU_p/P_p.

The price change has enabled us to plot a second point on the consumer demand curve for

Extended Example Marginal Utility and Income Taxes

Government policymakers consider marginal utility when they establish income-tax rates. Most income-tax rates are *progressive*—that is, they are proportionately greater for higher incomes. One reason has to do with differences among taxpayers in their own $MU_\$$.

Figure 3 presents marginal utility curves for money for our friends Miss Jones and Mr. Smith. The curves are based on the assumption that the marginal utility of money diminishes in much the same way as the marginal utility of goods. Miss Jones earns an income of $200 per week and Mr. Smith earns $150. If we assume that the marginal utility of money diminishes equally for both taxpayers, then the 200th dollar received by Miss Jones yields less utility than the 150th dollar received by Mr. Smith. Miss Jones achieves total utility equal to the entire area under her marginal utility curve, up to an income of $200. Similarly, Mr. Smith receives total utility equal to the area under his marginal utility curve, up to an income of $150. Total utility for the community is the sum of the utilities enjoyed by Miss Jones, Mr. Smith, and all the other citizens.

Now, suppose government imposes an income tax. It plans to collect revenues averaging $10 per taxpayer per week. How should the tax bill be shared?

First, consider what happens when the tax bill is shared equally by all taxpayers. Miss Jones and Mr. Smith each pay $10, making their disposable incomes $190 and $140, respectively. Total utility of each is reduced by the appropriate area under each marginal utility curve. But the payment of $10 involves a smaller sacrifice for Miss Jones than for Mr. Smith, as indicated by the heights of the two areas. Under our assumptions, citizens with higher incomes lose less utility than citizens with lower incomes because of the diminishing marginal utility of money.

If we want to impose more nearly equal sacrifices upon Miss Jones and Mr. Smith, we would tax them differently. Suppose tax rates are set so that Miss Jones must pay $15 per week and Mr. Smith only $5. The $15 tax for Miss Jones would reduce her after-tax income to $185. Total utility would be less than with the $10 tax, by the shaded area in Figure 3a. But the $5 tax for Mr. Smith would bring his disposable income to $145. As a result, his total utility would be greater than if he paid the $10 tax, by the shaded area under his MU curve (see Figure 3b). The loss to Mr. Smith would not be greater than the loss to Miss Jones under this system of taxation, because his MU is higher at this level of income than Miss Jones'. Thus the extra sacrifice imposed on Miss Jones would be less than the satisfaction gained by Mr. Smith. His greater spendable income would add more to his total utility than her loss would subtract from hers.

Supporters of progressive taxation argue that total utility within the whole community, total community welfare, increases when higher income earners bear a larger portion of the tax burden. Their argument rests upon the assumption that all citizens have the same marginal utility schedules for money. Equal $MU_\$$

autos. A lower price for automobiles is associated with larger MU/P and larger quantities purchased. A higher price would produce the opposite result. If the price of autos should rise, MU_a/P_a would fall and consumers would buy fewer autos.

In this way it is possible to construct an entire demand schedule. Within their individual budget limitations, consumers will allocate their spending so as to achieve maximum total utility. *Higher-priced items will generally be associated with relatively low MU/P,* and smaller quantities of them will be purchased. *Lower-priced items will generally be associated with higher MU/P,* and larger quantities of them will be purchased. By plotting the quantities of an item that would be purchased at different prices, derived from a utility schedule like those in Table 5, we can obtain a consumer's demand schedule.

Using Marginal Utility Of Money to Plot Demand

We have seen that consumers' selections of goods and services vary according to the marginal utility they provide. But our money wealth can also be said to have marginal utility. When

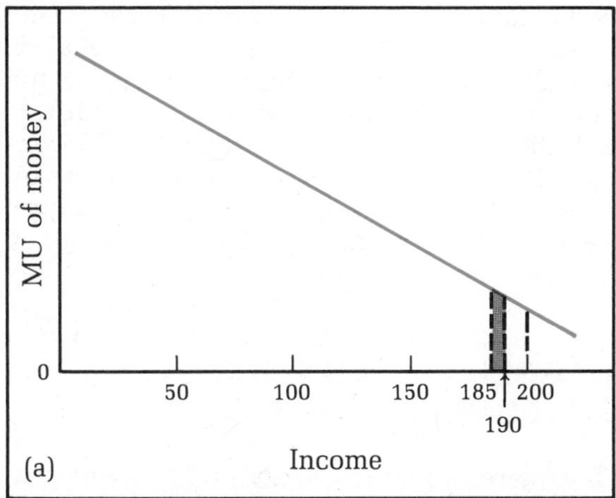

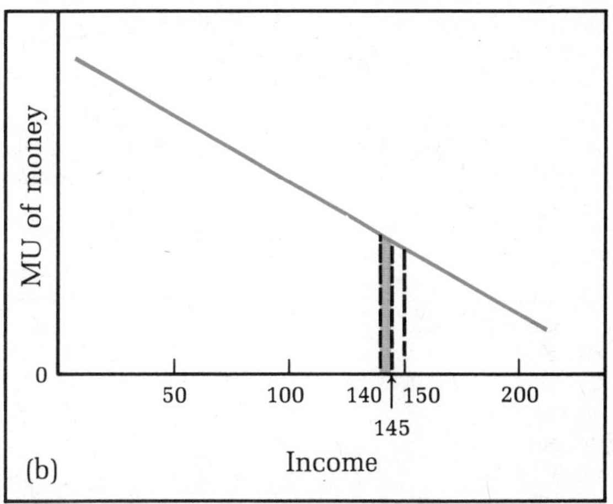

Figure 3 Marginal utility of income for (a) Miss Jones and (b) Mr. Smith. Areas between the dotted lines show lost utility due to taxes. Notice that the area between $190 and $200 for Miss Jones is smaller than the area between $140 and $150 for Mr. Smith. The assumption of equal marginal utility of income supports arguments in favor of progressive income taxes.

schedules would mean that all citizens have the same needs for money and things that money can buy. Critics of this argument say, "How do you know? It may be that individuals differ in their enjoyment of goods and services. Miss Jones may require a weekly trip to the opera to keep her happy, while Mr. Smith may obtain his satisfaction by sleeping ten hours a day." It's possible that Miss Jones' marginal utility of money at a weekly income of $200 is much higher than Mr. Smith's at a weekly income of $150. If this is true, to tax Miss Jones more heavily would involve a greater loss in total utility than to tax them both equally. Then, the progressive income tax could mean a greater loss of utility to the community than would an equal tax on all income earners.

Of course, there is no scientific answer to this question. Utility cannot be measured, so the argument for equalizing tax burdens cannot rest solely on the basis of diminishing marginal utility. And there is still another question. We cannot be certain that the marginal utility of money declines at all. Perhaps an extra dollar is just as precious to a rich person as to a poor one. If so, someone with a high income may miss the dollar paid in taxes just as much as someone with a small income.

Cite examples that confirm or refute diminishing marginal utility of money.

we are in equilibrium the marginal utility of money not spent ($MU_\$$) must be equal to the marginal utility gained for the last dollar spent on goods and services:

$$\frac{MU_a}{P_a} = \ldots = \frac{MU_z}{P_z} = MU_\$.$$

Following this principle ensures all consumers of maximum total utility through purchases of goods and services and through their money holdings.

As with other commodities, it is sometimes assumed that money provides diminishing marginal utility: The more we have of it, the less utility we gain from additional amounts. (This may not hold true for everyone; some people find money endlessly attractive and just can't get too much of it. But most of us spend more freely after payday than just a few days before payday!) It seems safe to say, as a rule, that persons with very small budgets probably attach a high MU to the last dollar held, and are reluctant to trade it away, while persons with large budgets probably attach a lower MU to the last dollar. Additional purchases will be made as long as the MU/P gained is greater than the marginal utility of the dollars given up.

Table 6 **Hypothetical Marginal Utilities for Pizza and Money**

	For Pizzas			For Money	
	MU (1)	P (2)	MU/P (3)	Consumer A $MU_\$$ (4)	Consumer B $MU_\$$ (5)
1st purchase	25	5	5	4	1
2nd purchase	20	5	4	4	1
3rd purchase	15	5	3	4	1
4th purchase	10	5	2	4	1
5th purchase	5	5	1	4	1

We can illustrate this with the example in Table 6. Columns 4 and 5 are the $MU_\$$ for consumer A and consumer B. Money provides greater marginal utility to consumer A, perhaps because consumer A's income is lower. The last dollar held over any particular time period is 4 times as satisfying to consumer A as to consumer B. This means that A's last purchase of an item must provide 4 times as much marginal utility per dollar spent as B's last purchase.

How many pizzas will consumer A purchase? Behaving like our previous consumers, A will equate marginal utilities per dollar for pizzas and for money: $MU_p/P_p = MU_\$ = 4$. The number of pizzas providing marginal utility per dollar of 4 is 2. The third pizza, with MU/P of only 3, would provide consumer A with less satisfaction than holding onto the money would provide, so A will buy only 2 pizzas. Suppose price falls to $2.50. Then MU/P for the first pizza will rise to 10, for the second pizza to 8, for the third to 6. The MU/P for the fourth pizza would rise to 4, consumer A's $MU_\$$; therefore, consumer A will buy a total of four pizzas at a price of $2.50. If price should rise to $6.25, consumer A will buy only one pizza. Can you show why?

By equating MU/P with $MU_\$$ at various prices, we are able to plot consumer A's demand curve for pizzas. Now, turning to consumer B, we can do the same. Remember that consumer B has a larger budget and a lower MU for money. Consumer B can continue to spend as long as each additional purchase provides MU/P greater than 1. At a price of $5, how many pizzas will consumer B purchase? Table 6 shows that the answer is five, because then $MU_p/P_p = MU_\$ = 1$. If the price of pizzas were to rise to $10, consumer B would purchase four pizzas. Can you show why? Figure 4 illustrates demand curves for pizzas for consumers with different money incomes and different $MU_\$$'s.

MARGINAL UTILITY AND CONSUMER'S SURPLUS

One interesting characteristic of the downward-sloping demand curve is that it gives the consumer a sort of bonus. If Miss Jones is prepared to buy eight opera tickets at $10 each, we know that the eighth ticket provides the same marginal utility per dollar as would any other purchase—say, a new scarf or dinner in a good restaurant. For Miss Jones the marginal utility of the eighth opera ticket is equal to the marginal utility of its $10 price. We know this because of the equal marginal utility principle. In equilibrium, consumer purchases are arranged so that

$$\frac{MU_a}{P_a} = \frac{MU_b}{P_b} = \ldots = \frac{MU_z}{P_z} = MU_\$.$$

Substituting,

$$\frac{\text{MU of 8th ticket}}{\$10} = MU_\$$$

or

$$\text{MU of 8th opera ticket} = \$10 \times MU_\$.$$

The eighth ticket gives Miss Jones precisely as much additional utility as the dollars she gives up do. But the principle of diminishing marginal utility reveals that each of the first seven opera tickets yields equal or greater utility than the eighth. The cost of the tickets is the same—$10—but marginal utility is greater. Therefore, the total utility of eight tickets must exceed their total cost. The difference between total utility and the utility of the amount spent is called **consumer's surplus.**

We can show this graphically. Figure 5 shows hypothetical demand curves for Miss Jones and Mr. Smith. Price and quantity are

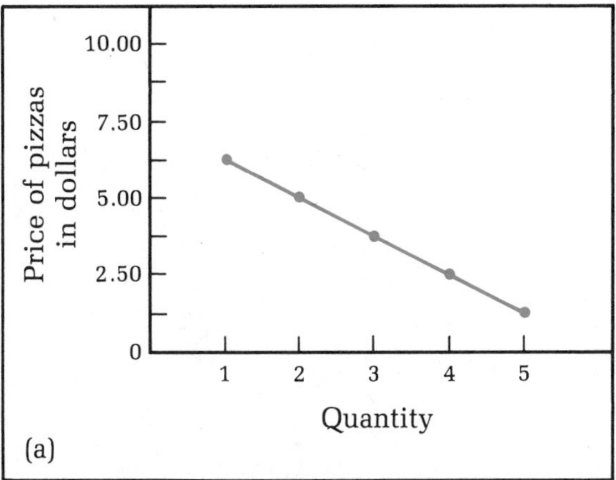

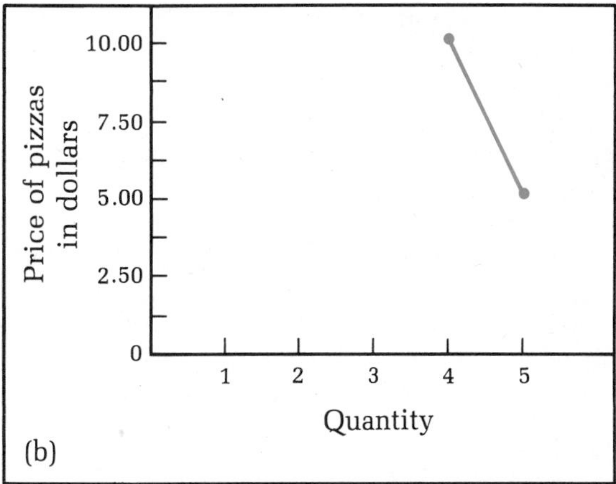

Figure 4 Consumer demand curves for pizzas: (a) consumer A; (b) consumer B. Consumer B has a larger budget than consumer A. The larger income allows consumer B to purchase a greater quantity of pizza at every price.

measured by drawing lines from the axes to the demand curve. A horizontal line has been drawn at $10 to show ticket price, a vertical line at 8 to show quantity. Miss Jones' total expenditure is calculated by multiplying price times quantity: P × Q. The values on the price and quantity axes form the rectangle *0ab8*. Because the area of a rectangle is the product of its two sides, Miss Jones' total expenditure can be represented by the area of the rectangle *0ab8:*

Total expenditure = P × Q
= 0a × 08
= area of rectangle 0ab8.

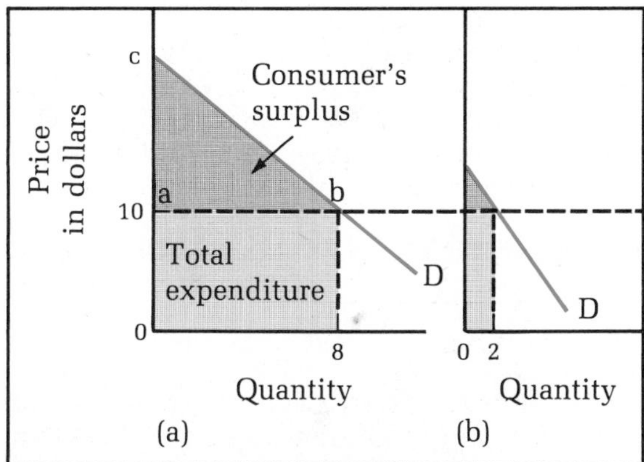

Figure 5 Demand curves for (a) Miss Jones and (b) Mr. Smith, showing consumer's surplus. The sum of the shaded areas under each demand curve constitutes total utility for that consumer. Subtracting the utility of the consumer's expenditure (bottom shaded rectangle) leaves consumer's surplus.

Miss Jones' expenditure appears as a rectangle formed beneath her demand curve. But her total utility from the purchase of tickets is shown by the entire area under her demand curve up to the quantity purchased. This is because total utility is the sum of all marginal utilities associated with additional purchases of an item. The sum of all the values under Miss Jones' demand curve is the entire area *0cb8*. Miss Jones would have been willing to pay more for the first seven tickets because they provide $MU/P > MU_{\$}$. The difference between her total expenditure and her total utility is the triangle *acb,* surplus utility over and above the utility of the dollars spent. For Mr. Smith, whose utility schedule is lower, the triangle is smaller, but even for him there is consumer's surplus.

USING MARGINAL UTILITY: SOME APPLICATIONS

Who thinks about marginal utility? Aside from economists, practically nobody. If you were to ask a friend to compare the marginal utility per dollar of a new sweater with that of a hockey ticket, you would get only a puzzled look. Even economists aren't really interested in measuring the additional satisfaction to be obtained from making another purchase.

The *concept* of diminishing marginal utility is of great importance nevertheless. Even though we aren't aware of it, we all consider marginal utility in making many of our daily

Economic Thinker William Stanley Jevons

Stanley Jevons (1835–82) was one of the great economic thinkers of the nineteenth century. He was known in his own day as an economic "scientist," pioneering in the use of mathematical methods in economics. Born in Liverpool, England, Jevons concentrated his early studies in the natural sciences: biology, chemistry, and metallurgy. However, he soon became interested in understanding the poverty he saw in London, where he attended school, and started writing on political economy.

Today Jevons is esteemed for his contributions to modern utility theory, in particular the marginal utility of income from work. He was the first to show that consumers would increase purchases of a good until the marginal utility gained from an additional quantity would be equal to the marginal utility of its price—the familiar $MU_a/P_a = MU_b/P_b \cdots = MU_\$$. The marginal utility theory of pricing contradicts Marx's *labor theory of value,* which claims that price is the value of the labor "embodied" in a good. Followers of Marx believed that a good is valuable only because labor is used to make it. Jevons turned this around and proved that a good is valuable only if it provides utility. Labor then becomes valuable when it is used to produce the good. Jevons showed that capital is also valuable for production; workers are not exploited by capitalists, as Marx had maintained.

Jevons accepted a job in Australia in 1853 and lived there for six years. His work in the Australian mint led to his studies of the determinants of the value of gold and of the effects of gold discoveries on the general price level. He was particularly interested in the social consequences of a change in the value of money. He wrote an early textbook on money in which he illustrated dramatically the disadvantages of barter. He played a major role in developing monetary theory.

Jevons made other important contributions to economic theory, particularly his work on fluctuations

in spending that lead to business cycles. His father had been a successful iron merchant until the depression of 1848 left him bankrupt. His grandfather was also bankrupt following a run on his bank in 1816. Both events stimulated Jevons' interest in business cycles. He applied the techniques of a natural scientist to investigating the causes of cycles and developed statistical series of prices and production in Great Britain back into the 1700s. Because of the regular appearance of economic depressions every ten or eleven years, he associated their occurrence with regular sunspot activity and the effects of weather on agricultural production. Later he changed this view to include many other causes.

Jevons' most famous work is his *Theory of Political Economy* (1871). His family had long been interested in social problems, but Jevons was himself opposed to public charity for the needy. He felt that social programs rendered the poorest classes dependent on the rich when they should be encouraged to provide for themselves.

choices. We have a limited budget which we try to spend in ways that will give us the greatest total satisfaction. We make our choices without consciously thinking about marginal utility.

Sometimes our choices involve time rather than money. When time is limited, we must decide how to use it so as to receive the largest total benefit. We still use the principle of MU/P for allocating our scarce time, but now P represents a quantity of time spent rather than money. For example, students must decide how to allocate their time among various campus activities: studying for a history exam, performing an experiment in chemistry lab, and practicing for a tennis tournament. The utility gained from each activity is the growing competence of the student. But as more units of time are consumed in any activity, marginal utility declines. Beyond a certain point, further study or practice within a particular time period adds little or nothing to the student's competence.

Can you express in symbols the equal marginal utility principle for allocating time?

SUMMARY

The theory of consumer choice explains how consumers help answer the question *What?* Consumers demand goods and services which provide certain desired characteristics. The satisfaction derived from these characteristics is called utility. Consumers try to maximize total utility within their limited budgets. As more units of a good are purchased in a single time period, each additional unit tends to provide diminishing marginal utility. The sum of marginal utilities is the total utility gained from consumption of all units owned.

A consumer's budget limits the number of units he or she can buy. However, within each consumer's budget, the greatest utility is achieved when units are purchased so that marginal utility per dollar is equal for all goods and for money: $MU_a/P_a = MU_b/P_b = \cdots = MU_z/P_z = MU_\$$. When all consumers observe the equal marginal utility principle it is possible to plot points on consumer demand curves.

Because marginal utility diminishes, some units of a good will provide greater utility than the utility of the money paid. The excess of utility is called consumer's surplus.

The equal marginal utility principle is used to allocate personal budgets and time.

Key Words and Phrases

characteristics properties of a good or service that affect consumer choice.

consumer's surplus total utility of a purchase minus the utility of the amount spent; surplus results because price is the same for all quantities of the good while utility is greater for all but the last purchase.

diminishing marginal utility when additional units of a good or service are acquired, each added unit contributes less utility than the one before.

equal marginal utility principle the consumer is in equilibrium when the marginal utilities per dollar spent on all purchases are equal.

marginal the increment, or additional amount, of something.

marginal utility the additional satisfaction (utility) that results when an additional unit of a good or service is consumed (purchased).

total utility the sum of satisfaction provided by the total quantity of a good or service purchased.

utility satisfaction obtained by a consumer from purchasing a good or service.

Questions for Review

1. Explain the relationship between total and marginal utility. Explain the effects of diminishing marginal utility on total utility. Demonstrate arithmetically and graphically.
2. What are the important characteristics a consumer would look for in a fishing boat, a pleasure boat, a TV dinner, a jogging suit?
3. How is it possible to get around the problem of measurement in evaluating the utility of an item? Describe how a typical consumer might decide on a particular combination of purchases within a fixed budget.
4. Using the consumer preferences of Table 5, graph the marginal utility and total utility for shirts.
5. True or false: Higher-priced items usually have a (relatively) low MU/P. Explain.
6. Under what circumstances might consumer's surplus be quite large?
7. The great architect Frank Lloyd Wright once said: "Give me the luxuries. I can do without the necessities." How would you describe his marginal utility choices? How would you describe your own?
8. Suppose you are packing a knapsack for a weekend camping trip. Describe how marginal utility analysis helps you decide what items to include. What is the cost of including each item? What corresponds in this problem to the consumer's budget in the text?
9. Define: diminishing marginal utility of money.
10. What utility calculations do you make when you go through a cafeteria line? What kinds of information are helpful in making your selections? How do your choices differ from those of your friends?
11. Suppose you could arrange your wants in the form of an inverted wedding cake. What wants would be included in the first (smallest) layer and in each successive layer? How would you describe total and marginal utility of the wants in each layer?
12. What marginal calculations should be included in our nation's decision to purchase (produce) larger amounts of energy?

Appendix

Another Explanation of Consumer Demand: Indifference Curves

Utility is a useful concept for explaining demand. Diminishing marginal utility helps explain the downward sloping demand curve: Because the utility of successive units of an item diminishes, consumers are willing to pay less per unit. Consumers compare the marginal utility per dollar of every item they buy and allocate their budgets so that $MU_a/P_b = MU_b/P_b = \ldots = MU_z/P_z$. In this way, consumers maximize the total utility possible within their limited budgets.

While utility is a useful concept, it does have a major disadvantage: Economists like to be able to measure variables, and utility is difficult to measure. A truly scientific approach to economics requires a uniform standard of measure which can be used to compare consumer behavior under alternative circumstances. All explanations of demand suffer from this fundamental weakness: They involve measurement which is imprecise and difficult to apply in empirical tests.

A CONSUMER'S INDIFFERENCE SCHEDULE

In this appendix we will consider a method of explaining demand that does not require actual measurement of the utility of alternative choices. To begin, we will assume that consumers may choose between two types of consumer goods. The two goods could be anything, but let's assume they are food and clothing. We use these goods as examples because they are not clearly substitutes or complements, conditions which would vary the results of our analysis. We ask a consumer to list the various combinations of purchases *per time period* which would provide the same level of satisfaction, or utility, ignoring for the moment such influences as price and income. Then we list all those combinations in a schedule. Each set of food and clothing combinations is chosen so that it provides the same total utility, U_0, as all other sets. We arbitrarily call these combinations A_0, B_0, C_0, D_0, and E_0 and show them in the following schedule:

	Combinations				
	A_0	B_0	C_0	D_0	E_0
Food	80	40	25	12	5
Clothing	5	14	25	40	55

We say the consumer is *indifferent* among any of these combinations. Why? Because, as we said earlier, the combinations in the *indifference schedule* provide the same level of utility; each combination satisfies the consumer as much as any other combination. Notice that it is not necessary that we measure the amount of utility provided, only that we accept the consumer's choice that combinations A_0 through E_0 provide equal utility.

Now let us ask the consumer for another set of combinations which provide greater total utility. All the combinations which provide U_1 utility are listed in the schedule below:

	Combinations				
	A_1	B_1	C_1	D_1	E_1
Food	90	55	27	15	8
Clothing	12	18	32	45	60

The consumer is indifferent among combinations A_1 through E_1. However, our consumer prefers any of these to combinations A_0 through E_0, because these combinations provide greater total utility.

GRAPHING A CONSUMER'S INDIFFERENCE SCHEDULE

All the combinations which provide equal utility can be plotted on a graph like Figure A.1. Units of clothing are plotted on the horizontal axis, and units of food are plotted on the vertical axis. The curve labeled U_0 shows all combinations of purchases which provide a particular level of equal utility. Likewise, the curve U_1 shows all combinations of equal utility which provide a particular level of total utility greater than U_0. We call these curves *indifference curves* because a consumer is indifferent among the quantities shown on any single curve. We could draw many more curves for any consumer and label them U_2 through U_n. Each successive curve would show greater total utility, but it would not be necessary that we measure the utility associated with any curve.

If we could plot indifference curves in three dimensions so that curves showing greater utility are shown at greater distances from the surface of the paper, the graph would look like a hill. In fact, each indifference curve would circle the hill at some particular altitude corresponding to a particular level of utility. Indifference curves are similar to contour lines on a geographical map, which are drawn to connect all points of equal altitude.

CHARACTERISTICS OF INDIFFERENCE CURVES

Let us notice some characteristics of indifference curves (see Figure A.1). First, *indifference curves cannot intersect*. This is so because all combinations on U_1 must provide more utility than those on U_0. Combination E_1, for instance, has more of both goods and therefore greater utility than combination E_0. Combination D_1 has fewer units of clothing than E_0 but substantially more food; D_1 provides more total utility. No point on U_1 can touch or lie below U_0 if it indeed provides greater utility than U_0.

If we could actually measure utility in utils, we might label the curves as follows: U_0 = 100 utils, U_1 = 200 utils, U_2 = 300 utils, and so forth. Each curve would show one hundred additional utils of utility, but *the curves would be drawn farther and farther apart*. This is because of the principle of diminishing marginal utility. As the consumer moves from combinations on U_1 to those on U_2, additional units of each good provide less additional utility than they did when the consumer moved from U_0 to U_1. Therefore, the consumer must purchase larger and larger quantities of both goods to achieve one hundred additional utils of utility.

A third characteristic of indifference curves is their shape. *Most indifference curves are convex to the origin*. This characteristic is also a result of diminishing marginal utility. To see why, consider a single indifference curve. Movement from one combination on the curve to another on the same curve requires that the consumer give up some goods for the sake of receiving others. If total utility is unchanged, the utility of goods given up must be equal to the utility of the ones gained.

Select a combination near the vertical axis representing a larger quantity of food units than clothing units. The large number of food units suggests that the last food unit is providing lower utility; meantime the small number of clothing units suggests greater utility for additional clothing units. If total utility is to be unchanged, the consumer must exchange a greater quantity of (low marginal utility) food for

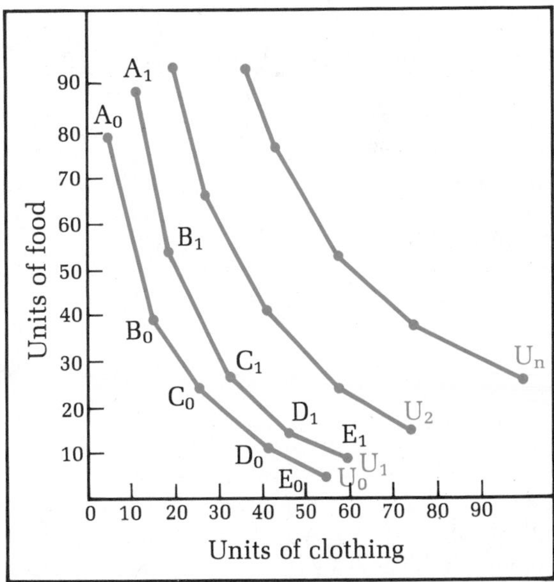

Figure A.1 All points on any single indifference curve provide equal utility. We can show different levels of utility by drawing different indifference curves: U_0, U_1, U_2, . . . , U_n. The farther a curve lies from the origin, the higher the level of utility it represents.

a smaller quantity of (high marginal utility) clothing.

As the consumer moves down the indifference curve, however, combinations include larger quantities of clothing relative to food. Along the lower portion of the curve, additional units of food provide more utility and additional units of clothing provide less utility. If total utility is to be unchanged, the consumer must exchange fewer quantities of (high marginal utility) food for larger quantities of (low marginal utility) clothing.

This principle can be explained algebraically. Along a single indifference curve the quantity of food given up for each unit of clothing gained is called the *marginal rate of substitution* of clothing for food:

$$MRS_{cf} = \frac{-\text{food units given up}}{\text{clothing units gained}}.$$

The marginal rate of substitution of clothing for food is negative over the entire length of the indifference curve. Moreover, as we have seen, the quantity of food given up per unit of clothing gained diminishes as we move down an indifference curve. Moving from A_0 to B_0 the marginal rate of substitution is MRS_{cf} = 40 units of food given up for 9 units of clothing gained = $-40/9 = -4.44$. The consumer gives up 4.44 units of food for each unit of clothing received, but total utility is unchanged. From B_0 to C_0 the $MRS_{cf} = -15/11 = -1.36$; from C_0 to D_0 the $MRS_{cf} = -13/15 = -.87$; from D_0 to E_0 the $MRS_{cf} = -7/15 = -.47$. Smaller quantities of food are exchanged for clothing as the utility of additional clothing decreases relative to the utility of food given up.

Test your understanding of the marginal rate of substitution. Begin with combination E_0 and calculate the marginal rate of substitution of food for clothing:

$$MRS_{fc} = \frac{-\text{ units of clothing given up}}{\text{units of food gained}}.$$

(Your answers should be -2.14, -1.15, $-.73$, and $-.23$.) The consumer is willing to give up fewer units of clothing for food as combinations include less (high marginal utility) clothing and more (low marginal utility) food.

The marginal rate of substitution defines the *slope* of an indifference curve. For most goods the slope is negative over its entire length. Beginning at A_0 the slope is very steep. When the combination includes substantially more food than clothing, a small gain in clothing offsets a large loss of food. As we move along the curve, however, each combination includes more clothing and less food. Along the lower right portion of the curve, combinations include substantially more clothing than food. When this is true, even small losses in food purchases must be offset by substantial gains in clothing; the slope of the curve becomes very flat. The slope of an indifference curve describes a consumer's relative preferences for the two goods.

Along a single indifference curve, total utility is unchanged. Therefore, the utility of the good given up must equal the utility of the good gained.*

We may summarize the characteristics of indifference curves as follows:

1. Higher levels of total utility are shown by indifference curves which lie farther to the right. No combination of goods on a higher curve can lie on or below a curve of lower total utility. Thus indifference curves cannot intersect.
2. If we could construct indifference curves to represent total utility in equal increments, the curves would lie farther apart as they moved farther right. This is due to the principle of diminishing marginal utility.
3. Most indifference curves are convex to the origin. This is because the marginal rate of substitution diminishes as combinations include substantially less of one good.

We might add another important characteristic of indifference curves. Since higher levels of utility are associated with higher indifference curves, consumers will normally prefer to select combinations which lie on the highest curve possible. To locate the actual combination chosen, it is necessary to know how much the consumer can spend. In the next section we will show how understanding indifference curves helps us draw an actual consumer demand curve.

*In our example, units of food given up × MU_f = units of clothing gained × MU_c, or $Q_f MU_f = Q_c MU_c$, which can also be expressed $Q_f/Q_c = MU_c/MU_f$. Since the $MRS_{cf} = -Q_f/Q_c$ is the slope of the indifference curve, the slope of the curve is also MU_c/MU_f, the ratio of marginal utility of the two goods in this consumer's preference map (when the good on the horizontal axis provides the numerator).

THE CONSUMER'S BUDGET

A consumer's indifference schedule defines his or her preferred combinations of goods. The consumer's budget and the prices of the two goods define the actual combination which he or she can purchase. Suppose the consumer's budget for the period is $150, the price of a unit of food is $2, and the price of a unit of clothing is $5. Some combinations the consumer could buy with this budget are shown below:

Possible purchases with a budget of \$150 and Price$_f$ = \$2 and Price$_c$ = \$5

Units of Food Possible	75	50	25	15	0
Units of Clothing Possible	0	10	20	24	30

Each combination listed would exhaust the consumer's entire budget: 50 units of food and 10 units of clothing would cost (50 × \$2) + (10 × \$5) = \$100 + \$50 = \$150. Many other combinations are also possible, some of which would not exhaust the entire budget. The maximum quantities possible within this budget are plotted in Figure A.2. The line *XY* is called the *budget line* because each combination on the line *exhausts* the budget; the shaded space includes all possible combinations that do not fully use up the budget. Combination *X* includes purchases of only food, and combination *Y*, only clothing.

The location of the budget line depends on the consumer's total budget, which determines the maximum quantities possible. The *slope* of the budget line depends on the relative prices of the two goods. This is easy to see with the help of a little algebra. We know that each point on the line *XY* exhausts the budget; thus at *X*,

$$\text{Budget} = \text{Quantity of Food} \times \text{Price of Food} = Q_f \times P_f$$

and at *Y*,

$$\text{Budget} = \text{Quantity of Clothing} \times \text{Price of Clothing} = Q_c \times P_c$$

or

$$\text{Budget} = Q_f \times P_f = Q_c \times P_c.$$

Rearranging terms:

$$\frac{Q_f}{Q_c} = \frac{P_c}{P_f}.$$

We know that the slope of the line $XY = Q_f/Q_c$.

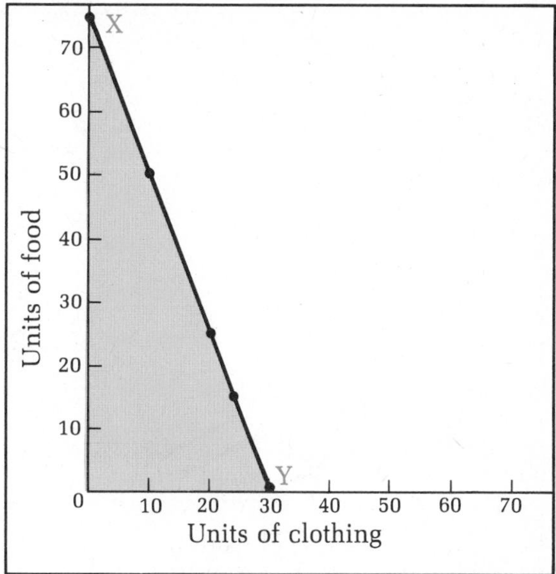

Figure A.2 Combinations of purchases on the budget line exhaust the consumer's budget. Any point in the shaded area is a possible combination the consumer could afford with a given budget, but it won't use up the entire budget. The above graph shows a budget of \$150 when the price of food P_f = \$2 per unit, and the price of clothing P_c = \$5 per unit. The slope of this budget line is $-P_c/P_f = -5/2$.

Therefore, the slope also equals P_c/P_f, or in our example $-P_c/P_f = -5/2$. The higher the price of clothing (the good on the horizontal axis), the steeper the slope of the budget line, such that fewer units of clothing can be purchased with any given budget.

Combining the budget line in Figure A.2 with the consumer's indifference map in Figure A.1 enables us to locate the actual combination of goods on the highest indifference curve possible within his or her budget. In Figure A.3 that combination occurs where budget line *XY* touches indifference curve U_0 at B_0, indicating purchases of 40 units of food and 14 of clothing. Combination U_0 exhausts the entire budget = (40 × \$2) + (14 × \$5) = \$150. Also, combination B_0 lies on the highest indifference curve possible within the consumer's budget. We can generalize this result and state:

A consumer maximizes satisfaction at the point where an indifference curve touches (is *tangent* to) his or her budget line.

At the point of tangency, the slope of the indifference curve is equal to the slope of the budget

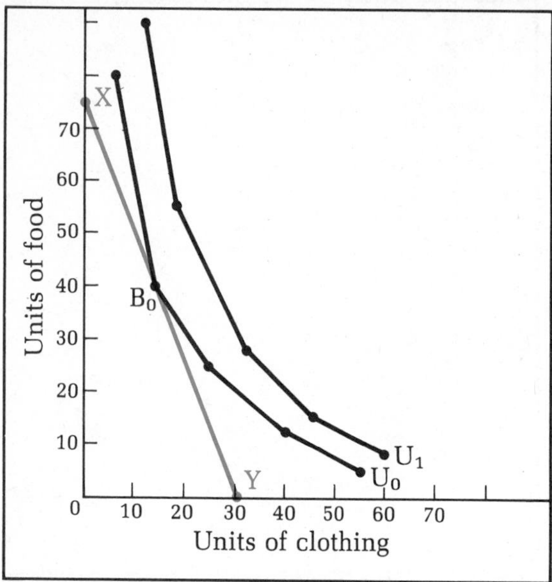

Figure A.3 The preferred combination occurs at the point where an indifference curve just touches (i.e., is tangent to) the budget line. Thus, point B_0 is the preferred combination.

line. Since the slope of the indifference curve reflects relative utility, MU_c/MU_f, and the slope of the budget line reflects prices, P_c/P_f, we can say $MU_c/MU_f = P_c/P_f$ or, rearranging terms, $MU_c/P_c = MU_f/P_f$. This equation satisfies the equal marginal utility principle and ensures that the consumer is maximizing total utility, given his or her preferences and budget and the prices of the two goods.

DRAWING THE CONSUMER'S DEMAND CURVE

Our consumer's demand curves for food and clothing can now be drawn. These demand curves would include point B_0 quantities: 40 units of food and 14 units of clothing. Figure A.4 shows the beginning of the demand curves: one point for each curve. Given the particular income and tastes of this consumer, he or she maximizes total utility by allocating his or her budget at these points.

A complete demand curve includes many more points, showing the quantities which would be purchased at various prices. Let us hold the price of food constant at $2 and see what happens when the price of clothing falls to $3. The new price ratio changes the slope of the budget line: $-P_c/P_f = -3/2$. With a budget of $150, maximum quantities of food (only) and clothing (only) would be 75 and 50 units, respectively. The new budget line is flatter because larger quantities of clothing can be bought at the lower price. Budget line *XZ* is drawn in Figure A.5; the new budget line intersects the horizontal axis farther to the right. The consumer will increase utility to U_1 (from U_0), moving along the new budget line to combination C_1 and purchasing 32 units of clothing. The lower price of clothing increases total utility by increasing quantity purchased, giving us a second point on this consumer's demand curve for clothing.

Many prices for clothing can be assumed and appropriate budget lines drawn for a budget of $150. In this way all relevant points may be plotted on the consumer's demand curve for clothing. Points on the consumer's demand curve for food can be determined in the same way: that is, holding the price of clothing constant and changing the slope of the budget line to reflect various prices for food.

You may have noticed that the lower price for clothing causes a change in food purchases also. A change in the price of one good will often affect purchases of the other good. Such changes in purchases are not a result of a change in the price of the second good; therefore, they

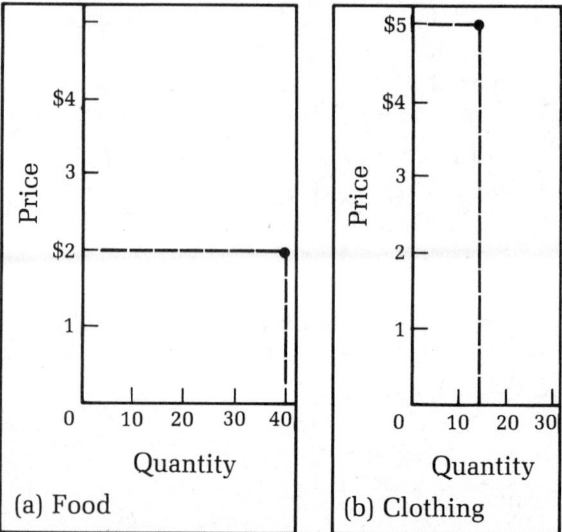

Figure A.4 Constructing demand curves. (a) The first point on our demand curve for food is plotted. We must add more points to draw the entire demand curve. (b) The first point on our demand curve for clothing is plotted.

do not belong on the same demand curve. Remember that a demand curve is drawn ceteris paribus, all other things remaining the same. A change in some factor other than the price of the good will cause a *shift* in demand. Some factors held constant for drawing a consumer's demand curve are the consumer's tastes, prices of other goods, and income. In the next section we will show how a change in income will also cause a shift in demand.

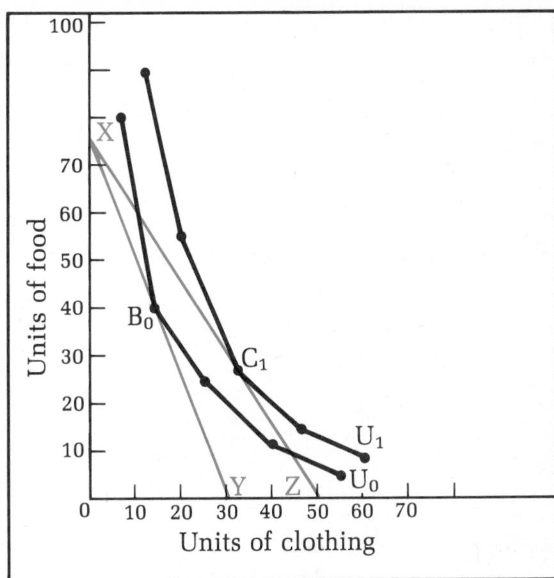

Figure A.5 A fall in the price of clothing means we can buy more clothing with our budget, and the budget line is flatter. Our new budget line is XZ and its slope is $-P_c/P_f = -3/2$. The consumer will now move to a higher indifference curve (U_1) and experience a higher level of utility ($U_1 > U_0$).

CHANGES IN A CONSUMER'S INCOME

A change in income will change the location of the consumer's budget line. Refer to Figure A.6. A larger income enables the consumer to move to a higher budget line $X'Y'$. The new budget line is drawn parallel to the old one if we assume that the price ratio remains 5/2. With a budget of \$200 the consumer in our example would select combination B_1, purchasing 55 units of food and 18 units of clothing for total utility of U_1. These points would lie on new, higher demand curves.

In this example, a higher income meant larger purchases of both goods. Indeed, most goods are preferred in larger quantities as incomes rise. We call such goods *superior* goods: autos, most items of clothing, steak, and wine are examples. As a consumer moves up his or her utility hill, larger quantities of superior goods are preferred.

For other goods the consumer may behave differently. An increase in income may mean fewer purchases of goods which are necessary at low incomes but become less preferred as income rises. We call such goods *inferior* goods: bus tickets, overalls, hamburger, and beer are examples for many of us. Higher levels of total utility are associated with fewer purchases of these goods as we satisfy our preference for superior goods.

When certain goods are classified as inferior goods, indifference curves must be drawn differently. The indifference curves in Figure A.7 converge more closely toward the vertical axis. If this graph could be drawn in three dimensions, the utility hill would rise closer to the vertical axis. Notice how increases in income affect purchases of both goods: As the budget line shifts to the right, purchases of the superior good increase, while purchases of the inferior good decline.

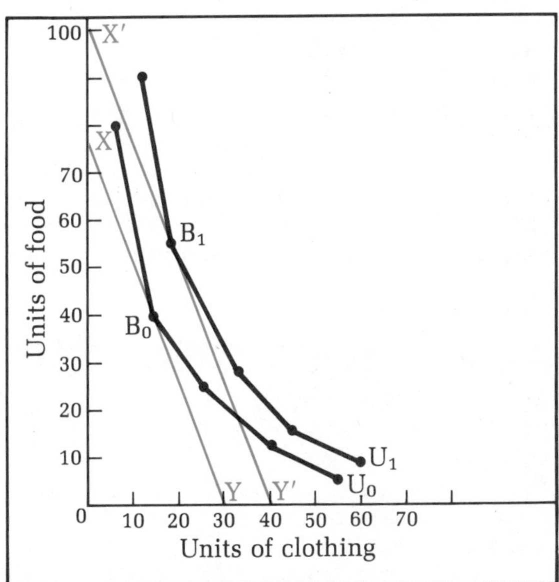

Figure A.6 An increase in the consumer's budget shifts the budget line to the right from XY to $X'Y'$. The larger budget enables the consumer to purchase more of both goods.

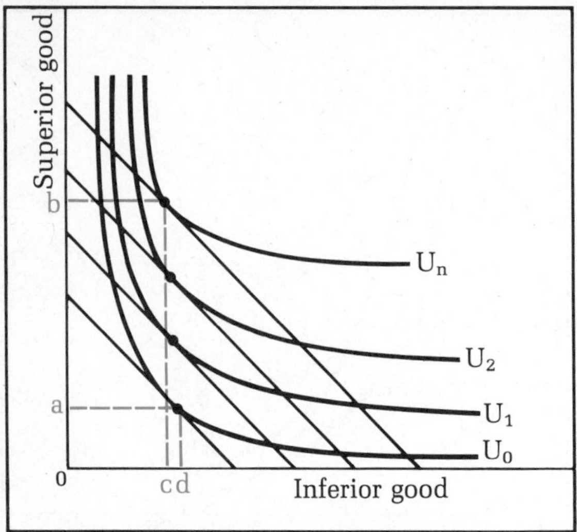

Figure A.7 An indifference map for two goods in which one is inferior and the other is superior. As the consumer's income increases and the budget line shifts outward, purchases of the inferior good decline.

OTHER TYPES OF INDIFFERENCE CURVES

Indifference curves for most goods have the convex shape shown in Figure A.1. Consumers prefer combinations with a balanced quantity of both items; they will require larger and larger gains in one good to offset the loss in another. When the goods are perfect substitutes or perfect complements, the curves will have different shapes.

Consider the case of substitute goods. Sweaters and jackets are reasonably good substitutes for most of us. For any period of time we may achieve a particular level of utility by purchasing a total of, say, two units: zero sweaters and two jackets, one sweater and one jacket, or two sweaters and zero jackets. Indifference curves showing these combinations and others for higher levels of utility are presented in Figure A.8. The marginal rate of substitution between the two goods is always $-1/1 = -1$ since they are perfect substitutes. Thus the indifference curves of perfect substitutes have a constant slope of -1 over their entire length.

Indifference curves for complementary goods also have a distinctive shape. Complementary goods must be used in some precise combination. Right and left shoes are examples. Figure A.9 shows indifference curves for right and left shoes.

THE CONSUMER'S BUDGET AND SUBSTITUTES OR COMPLEMENTS

For many combinations of goods, a fall in the price of one will lead to increased purchases of both. This is because the consumer's budget can be stretched farther for larger purchases of all goods. This is not true, however, when the goods are perfect substitutes or complements.

Figure A.10 illustrates the result when sweaters and jackets are perfect substitutes. A high price for jackets (steep budget line *XY*) causes the consumer to purchase combination *X*: two sweaters and zero jackets. A substantial fall in the price for jackets (flatter budget line *XY′*) will move the consumer to a higher indifference curve where three jackets and zero sweaters are purchased. For perfect substitutes a change in price leads to a total shift in demand to the less costly item.

Complementary goods must be used in some fairly constant proportion, like right and left shoes. Regardless of the price change for one good, the two goods will still be bought in that same proportion. Figure A.11 shows that a substantial fall in the price of left shoes would not affect the proportion of right and left shoes purchased.

SOME APPLICATIONS OF INDIFFERENCE CURVE ANALYSIS

1. In 1978 the Hertz Corporation reported that the cost of operating an automobile had almost doubled over the preceding five years. Relative to other items in the consumer's budget, the price of private transportation had increased twice as fast. This changing price ratio can be applied to an indifference map for predicting consumer behavior. First, however, it is necessary to know the shape of indifference curves; that is, to what extent are private automobiles clear substitutes or complements for other goods. Can consumers switch easily from high-cost automobile transportation to other low-cost items; or must autos be purchased in some roughly constant proportion with other goods?

Figure A.12 shows hypothetical indifference maps under both circumstances. Their shapes are drawn similar to the shapes of (a) perfect substitutes and (b) complements. Note the effect on purchases resulting from the rising cost of automobile transportation. Discuss the

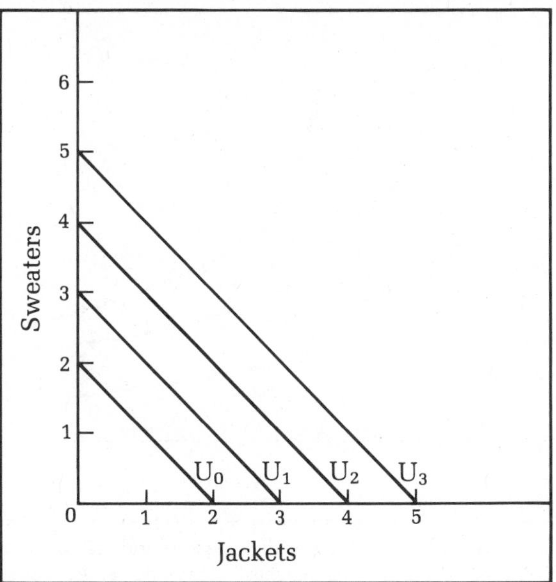

Figure A.8 The indifference map for substitute goods.

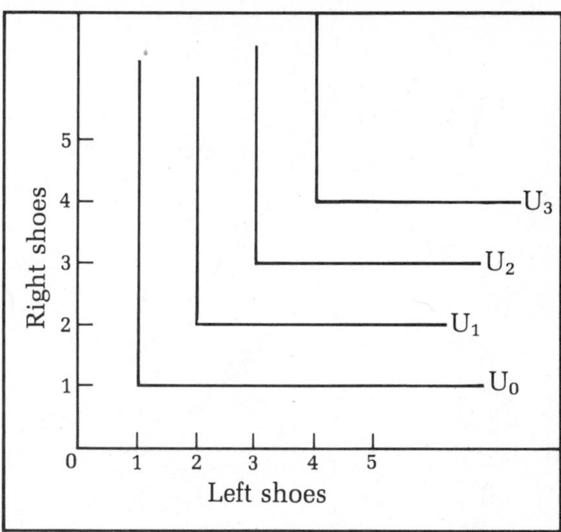

Figure A.9 The indifference map for complementary goods.

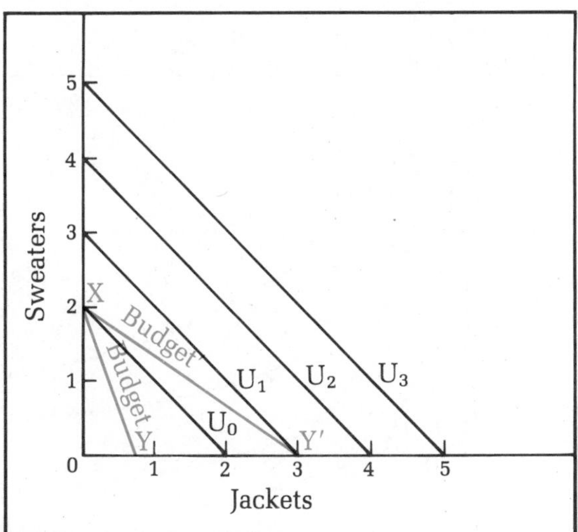

Figure A.10 An indifference map for perfect substitutes, along with two budget lines. For budget *XY*, the optimal combination is at point *X:* 2 sweaters and no jackets. If the price of jackets falls and the budget line rotates to *XY'*, the optimal utility choice becomes *Y'*: 3 jackets and no sweaters. What does this tell us? For *perfect* substitutes, a fall in the price of one good may lead to a *total* substitution of one for the other.

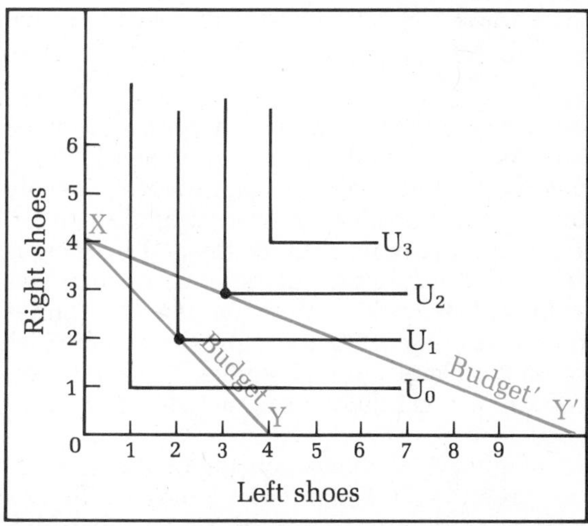

Figure A.11 An indifference map for perfect complements, along with two budget lines. Notice that each optimal utility combination has the same ratio of goods (equal number of left and right shoes), regardless of price.

implications in terms of changes in the level of economic activity over the period involved. How might the passage of more years affect consumer indifference maps?

2. Over the last thirty years a rising level of economic activity has meant higher incomes for most Americans. Our budget lines have been shifting to the right, enabling us to purchase larger quantities of most goods, depending on whether the good is considered superior or inferior. For superior goods the increase in purchases of one good relative to others depends on its degree of superiority relative to others.

An example of a highly superior good is housing. Generally, young American families

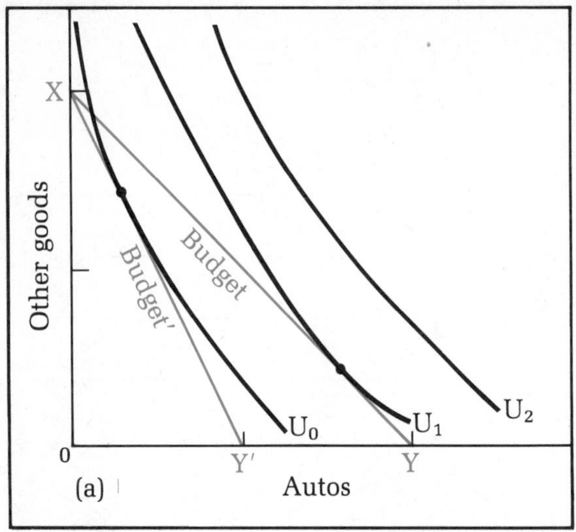

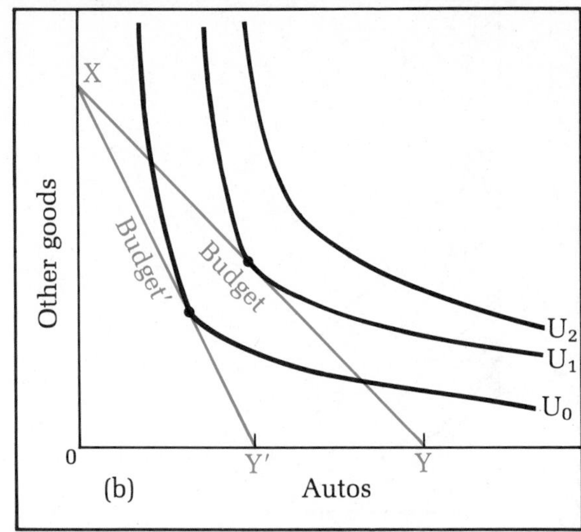

Figure A.12 Hypothetical indifference maps for autos versus other goods. (a) When other available goods and services are reasonably good substitutes for autos, if auto prices increase relative to other goods, their purchase greatly decreases while purchases of other goods increase. (b) When autos and other goods are complements, they must be used together in a fairly constant proportion. An increase in auto prices (a move from Y to Y') leads to a smaller drop in auto purchases than in (a). Purchases of other goods must fall also to maintain the desired proportion within the consumer's budget.

can afford only the minimum necessary housing. As their incomes increase, however, housing purchases are initially likely to increase more than proportionally as a percent of the budget. There are many reasons for this: (1) housing is seen as a secure asset whose value increases with inflation; (2) a growing family requires more living space; (3) more prosperous families come to desire more amenities like fireplaces, central air conditioning, garages, and lawn space.

Figure A.13 shows housing on the horizontal axis and all other superior goods on the vertical axis. With a budget of XY the consumer purchases equal quantities of housing and other goods. When the consumer's income rises to $X'Y'$, substantially greater quantities of housing are purchased. Although both types of purchases are superior, housing is clearly superior to other goods.

Will this result continue to be true for very high budgets? Probably not. Consider a very high-income family. It is unlikely that conditions (1), (2), and (3) above will continue to strongly encourage additional purchases of housing. After some very luxurious level of housing is reached, further improvements may become less superior than purchases of other goods. Figure A.13 illustrates the change in housing purchases when the consumer's budget rises to $X'''Y'''$. Housing is inferior over this range; ocean cruises, jewels, and yachts are clearly superior to housing.

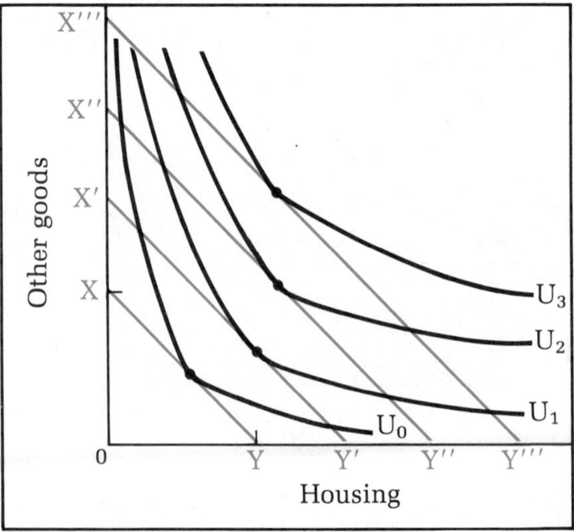

Figure A.13 Hypothetical indifference curves for housing versus other goods. Housing is strongly superior as the consumer moves from budget XY to budget $X'Y'$. Then housing becomes less superior (between budgets $X'Y'$ and $X''Y''$). Between budgets $X''Y''$ and $X'''Y'''$, housing is inferior.

CHAPTER 6

Measuring and Using Elasticity of Demand

Learning Objectives

Upon completion of this chapter, you should be able to:

1. Explain the income effect and substitution effect and how they can interact.
2. Define and calculate elasticity of demand.
3. Explain the effect of elasticity on a good's price, total revenue, and marginal revenue.
4. State four factors that determine elasticity and explain why.
5. Define and apply income elasticity of demand and cross elasticity of demand.

Understanding demand helps consumers analyze their own behavior and explain the effects of changing economic conditions on their own consumer choices. Understanding demand is also important to producers for predicting how changes will affect markets for their products. Workers and managers of business firms must look ahead if they are to meet new challenges effectively and take fullest advantage of new opportunities. For all these purposes, we must look more closely at demand. In this chapter we will describe how changing economic conditions affect demand for goods and services. Such information can help us, as consumers, to predict changes in our living patterns, and it can help us, as producers, to profit from change.

Understanding demand is especially important to governments for helping make economic policy. Decisions about government intervention in the marketplace depend on the character of demand and supply in particular markets. In general, our governments seek to direct government action so as to cause the least possible disruption of demand and supply. To accomplish this, it is necessary to analyze the response of consumers and producers to changes in the market environment.

This chapter continues our careful explanation of those factors that influence demand. In the next chapter, we will consider some parallel factors that influence supply. Throughout both these chapters, we will look at examples of how consumers, producers, and governments behave under various conditions of demand and supply.

THE DEMAND CURVE AGAIN

We have seen that demand for a good or service can be drawn in the form of a curve, showing how much consumers would buy at different prices during any given time period. Figure 1 is a typical demand curve. Quantity demanded is shown along the horizontal axis of the graph. Price per unit is shown on the vertical axis. Like most demand curves, this one slopes downward from left to right. Consumers would buy less at higher prices and more at lower prices.

For any certain period of time, the demand curve shows how consumers would respond to a change in price. It shows, at one end, the largest quantity that consumers would purchase if price is very low and, at the other end, the highest price they would pay to get any of the product at all. We assume that consumers always buy as much as they want at any particular price—that they are always on the demand curve rather than below it. Likewise, we assume that they never go above it, because, given their limited purchasing power, they prefer to use their income in other ways.

The central idea of the demand curve is that as the price of a good or service declines, more of it will be bought. Why? One reason we have already studied is diminishing marginal utility. Diminishing marginal utility means falling marginal utility per dollar (MU/P) spent on a particular good. If we are to buy more units of that good, price must also fall to bring its MU/P in line with the MU/P's of other goods we buy.

Diminishing marginal utility means that demand curves generally slope downward. They may not curve at all but may be a straight line like the one in Figure 1. Or they may level off at some price level. The shape of a demand curve depends on consumer response to changes in the price of the good. Responsiveness to price change depends on two effects: the *substitution effect* and the *income effect*.

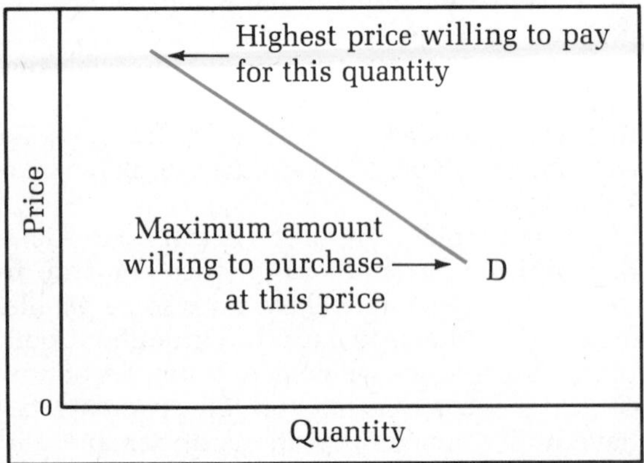

Figure 1 A typical demand curve.

The Substitution Effect

When a good is easily substituted for others in a typical market basket, consumers respond strongly to price changes. For useful substitutes, a fall in price may mean a substantial gain in marginal utility per dollar. Consumers can increase their total utility by buying more of this good and buying less of other goods with similar characteristics. If the price of beef falls, its MU/P will rise relative to substitutes for beef. We will buy more beef until its MU/P is equal to that of pork or fish. If the price of beef rises, we tend to eat less beef and more pork or lamb. When the **substitution effect** prevails, price and quantity purchased move in opposite directions: Consumers buy substantially more at lower prices but reduce purchases substantially at higher prices.

The Income Effect

Consumers also respond to price changes because of their effect on our incomes. If the price of a good falls, we have more income to spend on all the things we buy. It's like having an increase in pay. If the price of beef falls we will have more to spend for everything—and that includes steaks! The effect of a change in the price of a good on the consumer's purchasing power is called the **income effect.**

For many goods the income and substitution effects work together to increase or decrease quantity demanded. But for some the income effect works in the opposite direction from the substitution effect. Bread is an example. If the price of bread falls, consumers who buy a certain number of loaves a week will have income left over for spending on other things. The lower price for bread may make consumers so much better off that instead of substituting bread for, say, cake, they may buy *less* bread than before and eat out more often.

We have a name for goods that people buy more of when lower prices give them more spending power than before. These are called **superior goods.** Those that people will buy less of are called **inferior goods.** The distinction has nothing to do with the quality of the goods concerned. It is simply that as incomes rise, people tend to buy more of certain goods for which they have a higher preference.

Consider the consumption of protein. At low levels of income, people obtain protein from rice, beans, cheese, and cereals. As income increases, consumption of meat rises even more rapidly than income. Meat is a superior good, while other sources of protein are generally inferior. Likewise, some kinds of meat are preferred to others. In America steak is a typical superior good. Hamburger is a good that falls into both categories—it is superior at some levels of income and inferior at others. As people first begin to switch away from vegetable sources of protein, hamburger is a superior good, and its consumption rises rapidly. But as incomes increase further, hamburger becomes an inferior good, and consumers begin switching to steak.

The relationship between income and the quantity of a good or service consumed is shown by the curves in Figure 2. These curves differ from demand curves which show the relationship between price and quantity. They are called **Engel curves,** after the German mathematician/economist who first wrote about them. The curve in Figure 2a is that of a superior good. Notice that the quantity purchased increases faster and faster as income (Y) increases. The curve for an inferior good (Figure 2b) shows the opposite relationship: the quantity purchased decreases by larger amounts as income increases.

It's fun to classify various goods or services as inferior or superior. Bus transportation is inferior, since people use cars whenever they can afford them. Psychiatric counseling seems to be a superior good, and so are winter vacations in Mexico. Perhaps you can name others.

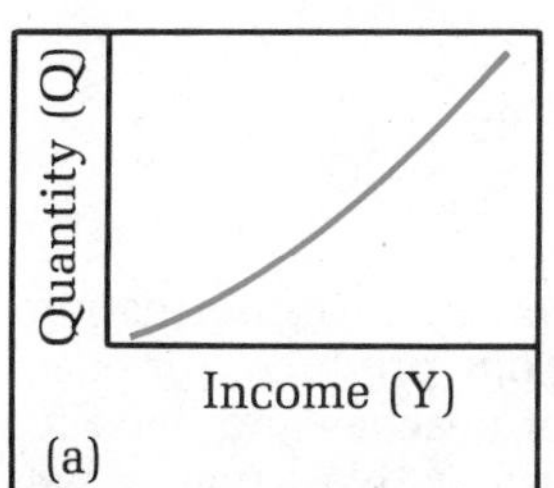

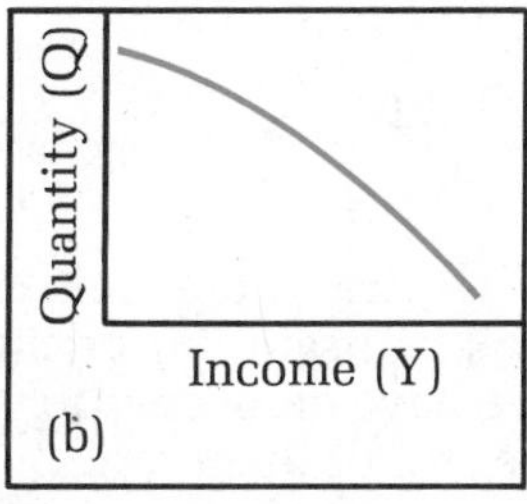

Figure 2 Engel curves for (a) superior good, and (b) inferior good.

Influence of Income and Substitution Effects

The relative strengths of the income and substitution effects determine the slope of the demand curve. In the case of a superior good, the income effect will reinforce the substitution effect. As price falls, consumers have more purchasing power and may decide to buy more of the superior good. And at the same time the lower price may encourage substitution of that product for other goods. Quantity demanded may increase substantially when price falls, and demand curves have the typical downward slope.

For an inferior good, however, the income and substitution effects are likely to work against each other. When a good is mildly inferior, the income effect may reduce the substitution effect only slightly. But for a strongly inferior good, the income effect is more powerful than the substitution effect. As price falls, consumers have more purchasing power and may decide to buy substantially less of the inferior good, buying more of other superior goods instead. In cases like this the demand curve will slope backward, to indicate that as price falls, fewer units will be demanded. On the other hand, a price increase will reduce consumers' income and lead them to buy more. Strongly inferior goods with an income effect stronger than the substitution effect are called **Giffen goods,** after Sir Robert Giffen, a Victorian economist. They are mostly an intellectual curiosity since there are very few goods which are strongly inferior.

ELASTICITY OF DEMAND

We have seen some of the factors that influence consumer response to price changes. Purchases of some goods change much more than purchases of others when their prices rise or fall. For instance, a price change for monogrammed T-shirts is likely to change sales substantially. On the other hand, a price change for calculus

Extended Example Calculating Elasticity

In the above example we computed price elasticity of demand for peaches: El = 2. But the formula we used has a flaw in it. Using simple percentages, you will get different answers depending on how you do your arithmetic. We figured a price change from 30 cents a pound to 15 cents a pound as being a 50 percent decrease. But suppose the price went the other way, from 15 cents to 30. That would be a 100 percent increase. Similarly, the change in quantity would be, instead of a doubling, a halving. Putting these figures into the equation we would get

$$\text{El} = \frac{\%\text{ change in quantity}}{\%\text{ change in price}} = \frac{50\%}{100\%} = 0.5.$$

Elasticity seems to have changed from 2 to .5. Which is right? We can't have it both ways.

We avoid this flaw in the simple percentage formula by using average values as the bases from which to figure our percentage changes. The percentage change in quantity can be stated

$$\%\text{ change in quantity} = \frac{\text{change in quantity}}{\text{average quantity}},$$

while, in like fashion,

$$\%\text{ change in price} = \frac{\text{change in price}}{\text{average price}}.$$

Now we can restate our equation:

$$\text{elasticity} = \frac{\text{change in quantity}}{\text{average quantity}} \div \frac{\text{change in price}}{\text{average price}}.$$

It will make things easier if we substitute the letters P for price and Q for quantity, and number them so we won't mix them up:

$$P_1 = \text{old price}$$
$$P_2 = \text{new price}$$
$$Q_1 = \text{old quantity}$$
$$Q_2 = \text{new quantity.}$$

Then, we can write the change in price as $P_1 - P_2$ and the change in quantity as $Q_1 - Q_2$.

Since the average of two numbers is their sum divided by two, we write

$$\text{average price} = (P_1 + P_2)/2$$
$$\text{average quantity} = (Q_1 + Q_2)/2.$$

Substituting these expressions into our previous elasticity equation, we now have

$$\text{Elasticity} = \frac{Q_1 - Q_2}{(Q_1 + Q_2)/2} \div \frac{P_1 - P_2}{(P_1 + P_2)/2}.$$

After we cancel the two's, we have

$$\text{Elasticity} = \frac{Q_1 - Q_2}{Q_1 + Q_2} \div \frac{P_1 - P_2}{P_1 + P_2}.$$

---

textbooks is not likely to have much effect on students' purchases. Economists say that the demand for T-shirts is more *elastic* than the demand for calculus textbooks. *Elasticity* measures the response of consumer demand to a change in price. More precisely, **demand elasticity** is the percentage change in quantity demanded for some good relative to the percentage change in price for that good. This relationship is described by a simple equation:

$$\text{Elasticity} = \frac{\%\text{ change in quantity demanded}}{\%\text{ change in price}}.$$

Elasticity is a number without units. It doesn't tell us the level of price or quantity but shows how quantity demanded changes when price changes. For example, if the price of peaches falls from 30 cents a pound to 15 cents, we can assume that consumers will increase their purchases. But we want to know more precisely what their response will be. Perhaps we know that, in the past, when prices fell by half, consumers doubled their purchases. We can put this information into our equation as follows:

$$\text{El} = \frac{\%\text{ change in quantity}}{\%\text{ change in price}} = \frac{100\%}{50\%} = 2.$$

If we are in the fruit business this information will be useful for pricing our product. Suppose we have an oversupply of peaches and need to get rid of them quickly before they spoil. If we know the elasticity of demand for peaches, we will have a better idea of how much we need to cut price.

Let's return to our example of the peaches and substitute figures in the equation. When the price of peaches rises from 15 cents a pound (P_1) to 30 cents (P_2), consumers reduce their purchases from 200 pounds (Q_1) to 100 pounds (Q_2):

$$\frac{200 - 100}{200 + 100} \div \frac{15 - 30}{15 + 30} = \frac{1}{3} \div \frac{-1}{3} = -1.$$

When the price of peaches falls from 30 cents a pound (P_1) to 15 (P_2), consumers increase their purchases from 100 pounds (Q_1) to 200 pounds (Q_2):

$$\frac{100 - 200}{100 + 200} \div \frac{30 - 15}{30 + 15} = \frac{-1}{3} \div \frac{1}{3} = -1.$$

Notice that, figured this way, elasticity is the same whether we're increasing price or decreasing it.

You may have noticed that our elasticity values are negative. Actually, price elasticity of demand is always negative,* since either the numerator or the denominator must be negative: either price falls or quantity falls. By tradition, however, economists ignore the minus sign, being interested mainly in the *magnitude* of the figure.

*Except for Giffen goods.

The Interpretation of Elasticity

Demand for a particular commodity is said to be **elastic** if the percentage change in quantity demanded is larger than the percentage change in price: consumers respond to price changes by changing their purchases significantly. If price is reduced by 1 percent, quantity sold will increase by a larger percentage, say 2 percent or 3 percent. Demand is said to be elastic for any value of elasticity greater than one (El > 1).

Demand is said to be **inelastic** if the percentage change in quantity demanded is smaller than the percentage change in price: consumers respond to price changes by changing their purchases very little, if at all. If price falls by 1 percent, quantity sold will increase by a smaller amount, perhaps as little as .2 percent. Elasticity is less than one. Demand is said to be inelastic for any value less than one (El < 1).

A special case worth noting is that of **unit elasticity.** This occurs when percentage change in price and percentage change in quantity demanded are the same. A 5 percent increase in price brings a 5 percent decrease in quantity sold (El = 1).

We can get a better understanding of elasticity if we apply our formula to a typical demand curve. Table 1 shows demand data in columns (1) and (2). At $12 one unit is sold, at $10 two units, etc. In column (3) are the elasticities, calculated from the formula for demand elasticity.

To calculate the elasticity of a price drop from $12 to $10, we begin with the values 12 (P_1), 10 (P_2), 1 (Q_1), and 2 (Q_2). We substitute these values in our equation and solve:

$$\begin{aligned} \text{Elasticity} &= \frac{1 - 2}{1 + 2} \div \frac{12 - 10}{12 + 10} \\ &= \frac{-1}{3} \div \frac{2}{22} \\ &= \frac{-1}{3} \times \frac{22}{2} = \frac{-22}{6} \\ &= -3.67\,. \end{aligned}$$

Repeating this for all the values in columns (1) and (2), we get the elasticity values in column (3).

You will notice that the demand schedule has different elasticities for different segments. In the $10–$12 price range, elasticity of demand is very high: 3.67. Elasticity falls as we go down the demand schedule—to 1.0 in the $6–$8 price range and to only .27 at the lowest price, where demand is very inelastic. Table 2 summarizes the values obtained from Table 1.

Table 1 **A Demand Schedule Showing Elasticities**

(1) Price	(2) Quantity	(3) Elasticity
$12	1	
		3.67
10	2	
		1.8
8	3	
		1.0
6	4	
		.56
4	5	
		.27
2	6	

Special Kinds of Demand Curves

If we were to draw the demand curve for Table 1, we would have a straight line sloping down to the right. This is the typical demand curve economists think about when they speak of demand curves. Such demand curves are called *linear* (straight) and are used in books like this quite often because they are easy to draw and they make explanations easier. Note that a sloping linear demand curve has a different price elasticity for every segment of the curve.

Vertical demand curves. If we tilt the linear demand curve until it becomes vertical, we have a curve with zero elasticity throughout its length. Such a demand curve implies that consumers insist on a certain quantity of a good whatever its price. They won't take more or less of it, regardless of how low or high the price. Few real commodities fit this case, though some may come close to it under certain conditions—perhaps tickets to the Superbowl or to a popular rock concert.

Examine the vertical demand curve shown in Figure 3a. Notice that quantity sold is always the same. This makes $Q_1 - Q_2$ equal to zero no matter what happens to price. The numerator of the fraction measuring elasticity will thus be zero, and the fraction itself will be zero (since zero divided by any number is still zero). Economists call this demand curve **perfectly inelastic,** or *absolutely inelastic:*

$$\text{El} = \frac{0}{\%\text{ change in price}} = 0\,.$$

Table 2 **Types of Elasticity**

Elasticity values	Interpretation	Condition
3.67	Elastic	El > 1
1.8	Elastic	El > 1
1.0	Unit Elastic	El = 1
.56	Inelastic	El < 1
.27	Inelastic	El < 1

Horizontal demand curves. At the other extreme is the horizontal demand curve shown in Figure 3b. This is important in economic theory because it is the demand curve facing a firm selling in a perfectly competitive market. It implies that firms are able to sell any quantity at the price indicated but are unable to charge a higher price because of competition. Along this demand curve, price does not change regardless of what happens to quantity. Therefore, $P_1 - P_2$ is zero everywhere. This means that in the formula for elasticity the denominator is always zero. Since such a fraction is infinitely large, we say that this demand curve has **infinite elasticity:**

$$\text{El} = \frac{\%\text{ change in quantity}}{0} = \infty\,.$$

Demand curves with constant elasticity. It is possible to draw a demand curve that has the same elasticity everywhere along it. One such curve is shown in Figure 3c. It is not a straight line but what mathematicians call a rectangular hyperbola. Economists say it has **unit elasticity:**

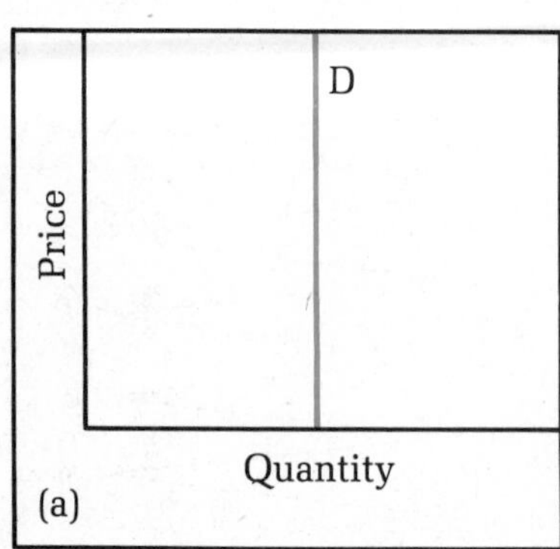

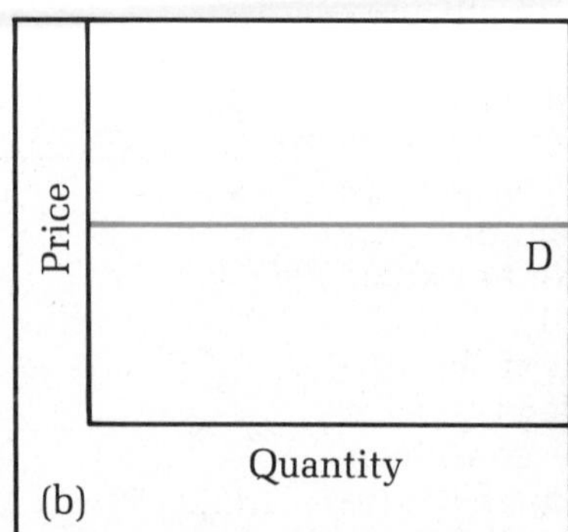

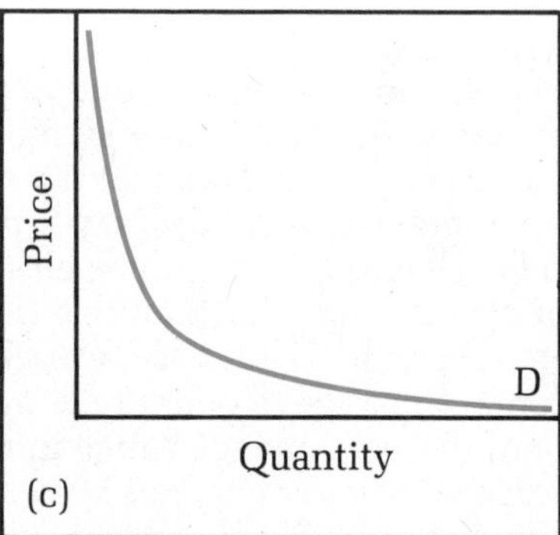

Figure 3 Three special demand curves: (a) perfectly inelastic; (b) infinitely elastic; (c) unit elastic at every point.

Extended Example Elasticity and Parking Fees

Sometimes we find that the price of a good or service varies depending on where we are or what time of day it is. The price of parking space in cities is an example. Parking fees seem to be cleverly arranged to hit our pocketbooks hardest when we most need to find a place to park. This is because prices are set to take advantage of different elasticities of demand.

During the main part of a business day, demand for parking is high and inelastic. Many drivers must visit urban offices even if the price is high. Owners of parking garages can charge high prices and still expect to fill all their spaces.

In the evening and on Sunday, offices are empty. Restaurants and shows attract fewer drivers relative to the available parking. Some spaces will remain unfilled, and parking rates are likely to reflect the lower and more elastic demand. Figure 4 shows demand curves for parking during the day and at night.

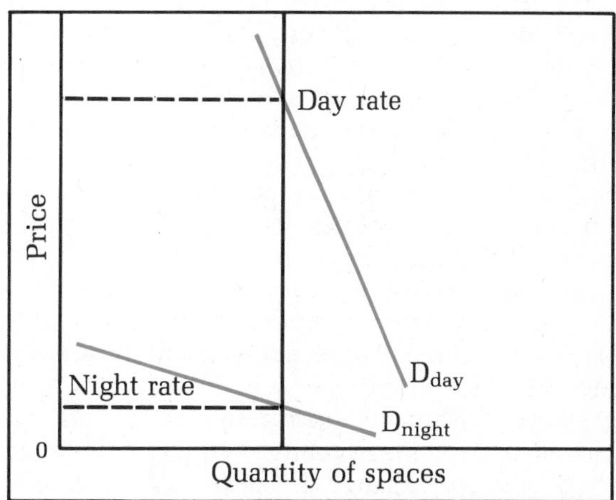

Figure 4 Demand for parking spaces during the day and at night. The demand curve for day parking is steeper and less elastic.

Sometimes drivers are allowed to park free. This only happens, however, where there is plenty of space and demand is highly elastic. Suburban shopping centers are glad to provide free parking in order to attract drivers who can readily change from one shopping center to another unless convenient parking is available. In the cities, some restaurants and shops will pay part of their customers' parking fees. In effect, they are persuading their customers to do business with them by subsidizing part of the expense of shopping.

Can you think of other charges that vary with the time of day or day of the week? Why do they vary? In what ways other than time can customers be classified and charged different rates?

Elasticity is equal to one everywhere along the curve. This means that percentage change in quantity demanded is the same as percentage change in price for any pair of points.

$$\text{El} = \frac{\text{\% change in quantity}}{\text{\% change in price}} = 1 .$$

ELASTICITY OF DEMAND AND A FIRM'S REVENUE

Business firms are concerned with elasticity of demand for their products. They must try to estimate the effect of a price change on sales. An increase in price will reduce quantity demanded, and therefore sold, but by how much? If demand is elastic, we can expect that a higher price will cause a substantial drop in sales. This is important because a large drop in sales may mean a decrease in the firm's total revenue, despite the higher price. On the other hand, if demand is inelastic, a higher price may not affect sales much. Total revenue may increase even though the volume of sales falls.*

Look again at the demand schedule of Table 1. You will recall that elasticity varies over the length of that schedule. At high prices demand is elastic. In the middle price range elasticity falls to unity. At very low prices demand is inelastic. These differences in elasticity as we move along the demand schedule are shown on the curve in Figure 5.

*Even an increase in revenue may not satisfy a typical firm's objectives, however. If costs rise faster than revenue, the firm's profit will fall. We will include costs in our model in a later chapter.

Total Revenue

The data underlying this demand curve are given once again in the first three columns of Table 3. Column (4) shows the effect of elasticity on a firm's total sales revenue. We calculate **total revenue** (TR) at every point on the demand curve by multiplying price times quantity sold: P × Q = TR. Total revenue is represented by the area of a rectangle formed by horizontal and vertical lines drawn from any point on the demand curve. The dashed lines in Figure 5 form such rectangles. Notice how the rectangles vary in size as we move along the demand curve.

Total revenue is greatest at the point where elasticity is equal to one. At that point the area of the rectangle under the demand curve is also greatest. Within the price range of $8 and $6, inclusive, percentage change in quantity is equal to percentage change in price. A 1 percent increase in price leads to a 1 percent drop in quantity sold; thus there is no change in total revenue. Likewise, a 1 percent decrease in price leads to a 1 percent increase in quantity sold; again there is no change in total revenue.

What happens to total revenue outside this middle range? Look first at the higher part of the demand curve, where elasticity is greater than one. In this range there will be a greater percentage change in quantity than in price. Within the range of $8 to $10, a 1 percent increase in price leads to a 1.8 percent decrease in quantity sold. The larger percentage drop in quantity means a reduction in total revenue. In the range from $10 to $12, elasticity is even greater. A 1 percent increase in price will bring a 3.67 percent decrease in quantity sold, and the reduction in total revenue will be still larger. On the other hand, if the firm reduces its $12 price by 1 percent, sales will increase by 3.67 percent, and total revenue will increase.

At the lower end of the demand curve, elasticity is less than unity. This means that percentage change in quantity will be less than percentage change in price. In the price range from $6 to $4, a 1 percent decrease in price leads only to a .56 percent increase in quantity. A drop in price will mean a drop in total revenue.

We have drawn Figure 6 immediately below Figure 5 to show how total revenue varies with changes in price. The two graphs have the same horizontal scales. Notice that total revenue increases as we reduce price, and keeps increasing until we reach the point on the demand

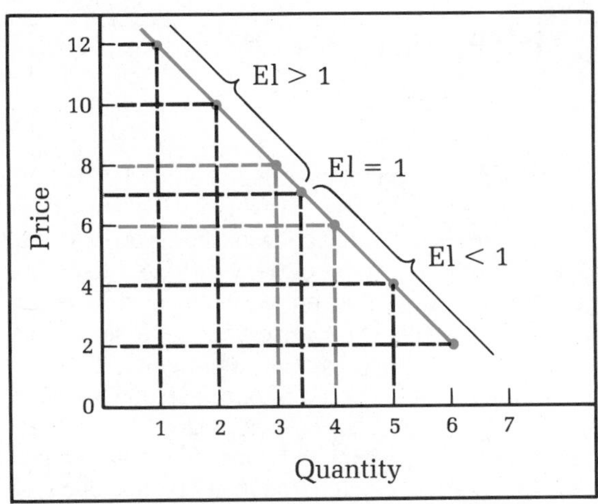

Figure 5 A hypothetical demand curve broken down to show the ranges of varying elasticities. At a high price, demand is elastic; at a low price, demand is inelastic.

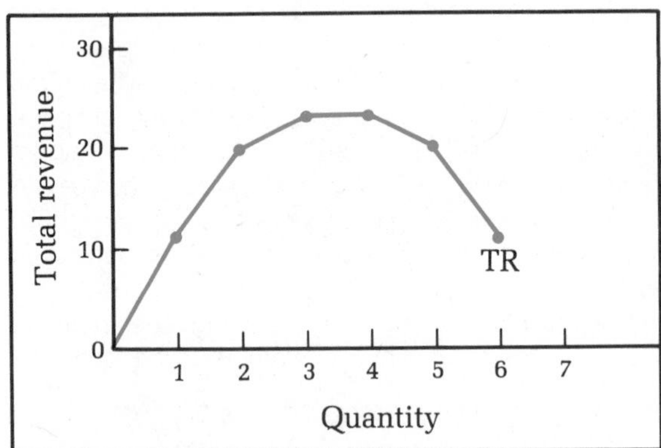

Figure 6 A total revenue (TR) curve. This curve is calculated from Figure 5, using the formula TR = P × Q. TR is greatest where elasticity equals one.

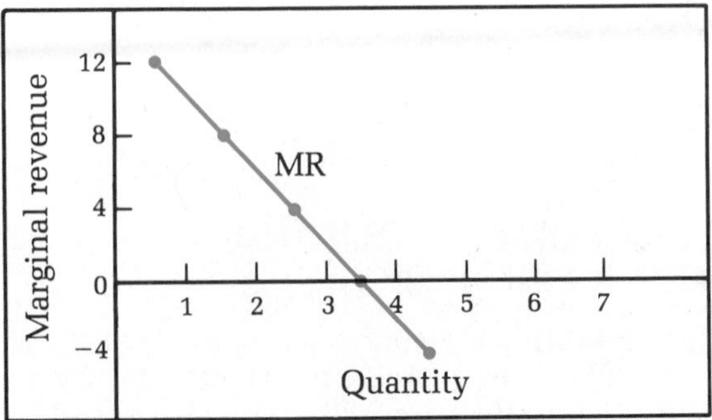

Figure 7 Marginal revenue (MR) curve for data presented in Figure 6. Where marginal revenue is zero (between 3 and 4 in quantity), total revenue is greatest.

curve where elasticity is equal to one. Beyond that point, total revenue decreases as we reduce price, even though the volume of sales is greater.

Retailers would not use the term *elasticity*, but they would explain its result in simple words: "If price is too high, it will discourage sales and keep total revenue low. If we cut price, volume will increase more than proportionately and total sales revenue will increase. At some point, however, further price cuts will lead to smaller proportionate increases in volume. Then total sales revenue will begin to fall."

If a firm wants to maximize its total revenue, it will sell its product at the price at which elasticity of demand is equal to one. At that level of price and output, no change in price can produce greater total revenue.*

Table 3 **Hypothetical Data for Market Demand**

(1) Price	(2) Quantity	(3) Elasticity	(4) Total revenue	(5) Marginal revenue
				$12
$12	1		$12	
		3.67		8
10	2		20	
		1.8		4
8	3		24	
		1.0		0
6	4		24	
		.56		−4
4	5		20	
		.27		−8
2	6		12	

Marginal Revenue

Business decisions typically involve small changes from current levels: small movements of price and small changes in quantity produced. The objective of change may be to determine the effect on total revenue. If a change causes an increase in total revenue, it will be continued and perhaps extended. If a change causes a decrease in total revenue, it will be reversed. The difference in total revenue that results from a unit change in quantity sold is **marginal revenue.** In Table 3 we show marginal revenue in column (5).

Marginal revenue is calculated by figuring the differences between total revenue in column (4) for each change in price. As price is reduced from $12 to $10, one more unit will be sold, and total revenue increases from $12 to $20. The difference between the total revenues, the marginal revenue, is $8. Further reductions in price increase total revenue, but the increments are smaller each time and eventually become negative. This is shown graphically in Figure 7. The curve of marginal revenue slopes downward until it plunges through the zero level and becomes negative. Beyond that point, reductions in price still increase quantity sold, but they reduce total revenue.

Compare Figure 7 with Figures 5 and 6. Notice that over the price range where demand is elastic, price reductions yield greater total revenue. For each additional unit sold, marginal revenue remains positive. Now look at the price range where demand is inelastic. Over this range, price reductions yield less total revenue. For each additional unit sold, marginal revenue is negative. Maximum total revenue occurs at the price where elasticity of demand is equal to one. This is also the price where marginal revenue is zero. If a firm wants to maximize total revenue, it will set price so that marginal revenue is equal to zero.

This can be stated another way. If the firm is operating in a price range where marginal revenue is positive, a price reduction will continue to yield greater total revenue. If the firm is operating in a price range where marginal revenue is negative, a price reduction will yield less total revenue.

Changing Elasticity to Increase Total Revenue

Many firms attempt to increase demand for their products in order to increase total revenue. Graphically, this means that demand curves shift to the right. If a firm's customers can be persuaded to purchase more units at every price, total revenue will increase.

Another way to increase total revenue is to make demand curves less elastic. Customers must be persuaded to reduce their purchases less than proportionately when price increases. Then, the firm can continue to raise price over

*But remember, the point of greatest total revenue may not be the point of greatest profit. We must also consider costs, as we will in a later chapter.

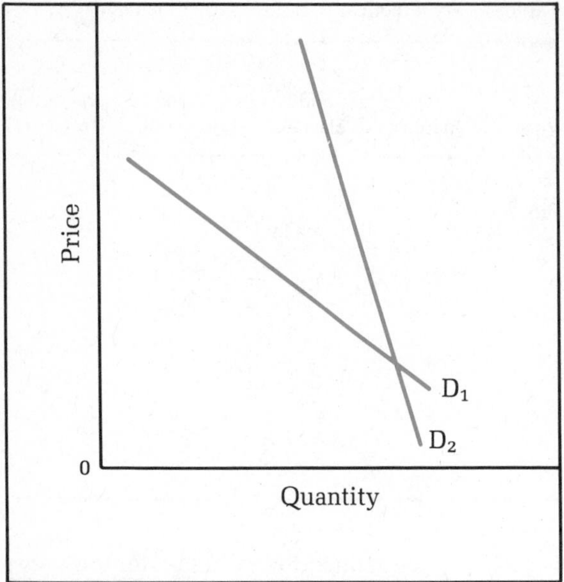

Figure 8 Changing elasticity to increase total revenue. Demand for a product increases and rotates from D_1 to D_2. Quantity demanded is less responsive to price changes.

the range of inelastic demand until it reaches the point of unitary elasticity, the point of greatest total revenue. Many companies have managed to tilt their curves so as to make demand less elastic at the current price level.

One way of doing this is to make sure the consumer thinks of the product as uniquely desirable. It is not just any loaf of bread, but it is Mother Porter's Cracked Wheat Bread with Molasses. Consumers are less sensitive to price changes for products that they identify through brand names. Advertising is a way of building loyalty to a particular brand.

The results of a successful marketing campaign are illustrated in Figure 8. This firm has tilted its demand curve from D_1 to D_2 and pushed it farther to the right. Consumers are less willing to accept substitutes, so the substitution effect is weak. Moreover, when higher prices reduce consumer incomes, purchases will not drop substantially. Demand has become more inelastic.

Once the demand curve is set, a firm must decide on a particular price and quantity. If the firm wants to maximize revenue, it will set price at a point on the demand curve where elasticity is equal to one. Figure 9 shows two curves of quite different slope, with the point of maximum revenue, or unit elasticity, for each. In each case, the revenue-maximizing firm will sell 0a units at a price 0b. Total revenue is the area of the rectangle under the curve. At any other price on these demand curves total revenue would be lower, and the area of a rectangle formed under the demand curve would be smaller. Try it.

Revenue Problems in Agriculture

A highly inelastic demand curve (i.e., a steeply sloping demand curve) is an advantage for a

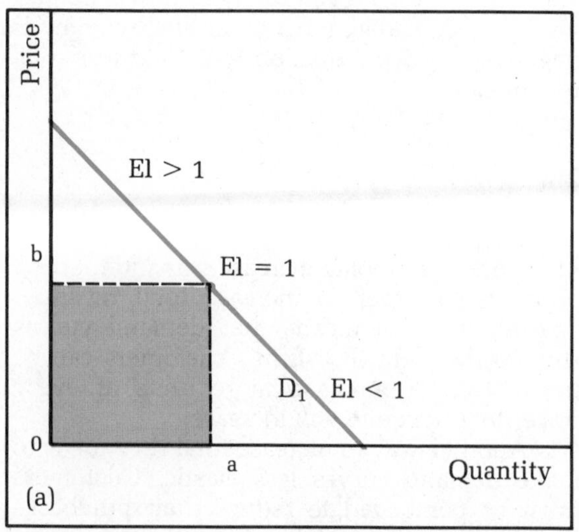

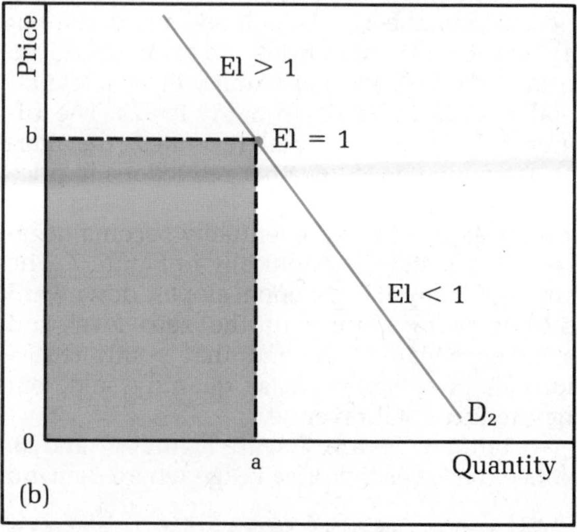

Figure 9 Two different demand curves. The shaded areas are the maximum total revenues for each curve. The point of unit elasticity (El = 1) determines the maximum total revenue.

business firm that wants to be able to increase its prices freely without reducing its sales volume very much. For farmers, however, inelastic demand curves often produce quite different results.

The demand for farm products tends to be inelastic: People will not buy much more food if prices are low, and they will not cut their consumption very much if prices are high. Meals aren't as easy to postpone as is the purchase of a house or a car or a microwave oven, and they can't be accumulated for use in the future. Because the demand for farm products is inelastic, a large drop in price is necessary if farmers are to sell only a small increase in output. And a large price increase is necessary to reduce consumption when food is scarce.

Farming is highly competitive, and individual farmers can't do much about the prices the market sets. An abundant harvest can be an advantage to consumers, who can buy larger quantities at sharply reduced prices. The consequences for farmers are less pleasant. The revenue they receive may fall below the outlays they have to make for machinery, fertilizer, and household supplies.

Governments have tried various ways of stabilizing prices in an effort to keep farmers' incomes from falling sharply in good crop years. In the United States, from the 1930s to the beginning of the 1970s, the federal government kept the prices of a number of farm commodities above a certain level by purchasing surplus farm output. The Department of Agriculture also tried to limit the production of some crops through restrictions on the acreage that could be planted. In 1973, Congress ended the policies of buying surplus output and restricting acreage for many farm products (but not all).

The European Common Market has a complex system of *price supports* on the crops grown by its member countries, as well as import controls to keep out farm products from other countries.

Some countries specialize in exporting agricultural commodities, or raw materials. As nations, these countries have the same problems that farmers have as individuals. When coffee-exporting countries have a bountiful harvest, they may face national disaster. The international price of coffee will plummet downward, while the prices of the goods these countries import may stay the same or even increase. A bad year, on the other hand, may bring prosperity to some farmers because the smaller quantity can be sold at premium prices. In 1976, frost in Brazil damaged much of the coffee crop. Prices soared in 1976 and 1977, enabling surviving producers to collect substantial revenues for their exports.

The problems of the raw-material–producing countries have been the subject of many international conferences and of many schemes for regulating the prices of commodities in international trade. With the exception of the Organization of Petroleum Exporting Countries (OPEC), there has not been much success in setting up arrangements to maintain high prices.

ELASTICITY OF DEMAND: SOME SPECIAL FEATURES

We have used the concept of elasticity to measure the responsiveness of consumers and of producers to price changes for various goods. Now we will see that elasticity is a way of comparing the demand for various kinds of purchases.

What Determines Elasticity?

Why is demand for some goods price elastic and for others price inelastic? Four important factors may be cited: (1) the availability of substitutes, (2) whether a good is a necessity or a luxury, (3) the proportion of consumers' incomes devoted to the purchase, and (4) the length of the time period involved in drawing the demand curve.

Availability of substitutes. The most important factor in determining the elasticity of demand for a good is the availability of substitutes. If the consumer can buy something else that will serve the same purpose just as well, a very small change in price may bring a large change in the quantity purchased. For instance, if the price of one brand of cola drink were to increase by a nickel a bottle, a lot of cola drinkers would switch to competing brands; demand would be quite elastic for that particular brand.

If prices for all cola drinks were to rise by a nickel a bottle, however, there might be very little decline in total sales, since many consumers feel there is no substitute for a cold bottle of pop

Extended Example Monkey Business

Some products are in demand not chiefly for their use by consumers, but because they contribute an important function in industry. Would you believe—monkeys?

Monkeys are an example of a good with particular characteristics needed for scientific research. Because their biological systems are so close to those of humans, monkeys react similarly to disease and to drugs. For example, the South American marmoset monkey is vital to experiments involving the liver disease hepatitis. Squirrel monkeys are useful for testing flu vaccine. Owl monkeys are vital to malaria tests.

These special properties of monkeys make the demand curve highly inelastic and enable suppliers to raise prices freely. In 1970 foreign suppliers in India, Brazil, and Peru cut their shipments drastically and raised price to $45, five times the previous price. With transportation and maintenance costs, the final cost rose to about $200 per animal.

Exporters of monkeys claimed they were forced to reduce shipments in order to conserve their monkey population. But U.S. buyers suspected the reduced supplies were actually the result of conscious decisions to exact higher prices for a product with inelastic demand.

Buyers have been willing to pay the price because (1) there are no suitable substitutes, (2) monkeys are essential to laboratory research, and (3) their cost still represents only a small part of a total research budget. The fourth determinant of demand elasticity is (4) time. It takes time to develop substitutes for imported monkeys; during short periods of time, demand is inelastic.

American biologists are already at work on the monkey problem. Scientists are encouraging development of domestic supplies. Breeding monkeys locally is costly because of the necessary controlled conditions and because of the high mortality rate of the infant animals. Current costs are estimated at about $1200 each. Experience—and cooperation from the monkeys—should soon bring down that figure, however. Then, there will be substitutes for foreign monkeys, and demand for imports will grow more elastic.

Cite other costly imports for which American producers and consumers have developed substitutes. Draw demand curves for short-run demand and long-run demand. How are the income and substitution effects significant in determining the demand for monkeys?

on a hot day. When there is no substitute for a good, buyers must purchase it without regard to price. Demand for the services of a kidney dialysis machine is quite inelastic for a patient whose kidneys have failed. Other goods and services with few substitutes include salt, insulin, and dental services. For these items, demand is relatively inelastic with respect to price changes.

Necessity or luxury. Some goods—like many foodstuffs—are necessary to life. Such goods have few substitutes, and we would expect the demand for them to be relatively inelastic. The substitution effect for luxuries is generally stronger. Demand for luxuries is relatively elastic because consumers can substitute among them as their prices change.

Luxuries can be classified as superior goods. Earlier we defined superior goods and showed how demand for these goods increases when lower prices increase consumer purchasing power. We called this the *income effect*. As prices fall, consumers have more spendable income and will use the extra income to buy larger quantities of goods they regard as superior. As incomes rise, consumption of luxuries will rise more rapidly than consumption of necessities. The income effect, added to the substitution effect, increases elasticity of demand for luxuries relative to demand for necessities.

Proportion of income spent. Price elasticity of demand for a good is directly related to the portion of the consumer's income spent on it. When the price of candy bars went from a nickel to a dime many years ago, that was a price increase of 100 percent. But demand proved inelastic; quantity purchased declined little, if at all. This was because the increase made practically no difference relative to the income people had to spend. In contrast, a 100 percent increase in the price of automobiles would reduce sales drastically.

Time. Another important determinant of elasticity is the length of the time period covered by the demand curve. If the time period is short, there will be less opportunity to find a substitute than if the need can be postponed a while. If we have a flat tire on the highway and need to replace it, we will buy a tire at the next gas station even though its price may be high. For a short time period there is no substitute, and demand is highly inelastic. For longer time periods, consumers can adjust purchases more freely in response to price changes.

In the case of new products in particular, consumers may have to learn to use them. Until this happens, demand is inelastic. Over time, demand for such items as microwave ovens and hand calculators responds more readily to price changes. It even takes time for consumers to adjust their life-styles to enjoy new luxury products. Over longer time periods, the income and substitution effects mean greater elasticity of demand for most goods.

Income Elasticity of Demand

We have been talking about the relationship between changes in price and changes in quantity purchased. Economists call this the *price* elasticity of demand to distinguish it from other kinds of elasticity. The concept of elasticity may also be applied to changes in purchases due to changes in income. **Income elasticity of demand** is computed like price elasticity:

$$\text{income elasticity} = \frac{\text{\% change in quantity demanded}}{\text{\% change in income}}.$$

As with price elasticity, we transform this formula into one based on averages:

$$\text{income elasticity} = \frac{Q_1 - Q_2}{(Q_1 + Q_2)/2} \div \frac{Y_1 - Y_2}{(Y_1 + Y_2)/2} = \frac{Q_1 - Q_2}{Q_1 + Q_2} \div \frac{Y_1 - Y_2}{Y_1 + Y_2},$$

where Y_1 is the old income and Y_2 is the new income.

For superior goods, rising consumer incomes lead to larger total purchases. We have classified steak and fur coats as superior goods. For goods like these, calculations of income elasticity involve the same sign for the numerator and the denominator. Thus income elasticity is positive for superior goods.

Inferior goods are those whose purchases decline as incomes rise. Potatoes, bologna, and bus transportation are often classified as inferior goods. An increase in income leads to a decrease in quantities purchased. For inferior goods income elasticity of demand is negative.

Income elasticity equal to one signifies equal percentage changes in income and purchases.

Long-range trends toward higher incomes in the United States have sharply increased purchases of superior goods like autos, quality restaurant meals, and home recreation equipment. For these goods income elasticity of demand is high and postive. Income elasticity is lower for most food items and basic clothing.

Short-range fluctuations in income also affect demand. Periods of recession or prosperity cause changes in sales, depending on income elasticities for various goods. Declines in income lead to sharp reductions in purchases of many durable consumer goods: appliances, furniture, and automobiles. These industries are hard hit during recession and may be slow to recover. In contrast, spending for nondurable consumer goods remains fairly steady.

Cross Elasticity of Demand

Another kind of elasticity involves demand for two related goods. Paint and paint brushes are examples. If the price of paint rises, we may expect that less paint will be sold and therefore fewer paint brushes will be demanded as well. The higher cost of paint discourages remodeling, and the demand curve for brushes shifts to the left.

We define **cross elasticity of demand** as the percentage change in quantity demanded for one good relative to the percentage change in price for another:

$$\text{cross elasticity} = \frac{\text{\% change in quantity (good A)}}{\text{\% change in price (good B)}}.$$

The calculations for cross elasticity of demand are similar to those for price elasticity and income elasticity. But in this case the two parts of our fraction refer to different goods:

$$\text{cross elasticity} = \left(\frac{(Q_1 - Q_2)}{(Q_1 + Q_2)}\right)_A \div \left(\frac{(P_1 - P_2)}{(P_1 + P_2)}\right)_B$$

In the case of paint and paint brushes, mentioned above, the cross elasticity of demand is negative. The increase in paint prices would

Extended Example Loss Leaders in Retail Stores

A marketing expert's version of Parkinson's Law might read:

Expenditures rise to absorb the capacity of the pocketbook.

At least that's what happens when many of us visit retail shops or supermarkets.

How often have you gone shopping for the "advertised special" and ended by filling your cart with a dozen other items you hadn't really planned to buy? This is precisely what the retailer expected you to do!

Retail shops and supermarkets often advertise a particular item with the hope of attracting customers. The item is called a "loss leader" because it may be sold at a loss. Nevertheless, the low price is expected to generate enough new sales for other, higher-priced items to more than offset the loss on the "bait."

Deciding on a loss leader involves consideration of demand elasticities. If demand is elastic, a very small change in price will elicit a great change in volume. Store traffic should rise and sales of other items increase in some proportion. If demand is relatively inelastic, store volume probably won't increase very much. Check your newspaper for the weekend specials. Very likely the advertised items will be characterized in the ways we have described goods in elastic demand:

(1) There are many substitutes. Customers can substitute the advertised product for other goods: economy-size bottles of soft drinks, chicken, etc.

(2) For most people the items are luxuries—fruit or ice cream—rather than essentials. Consumers who are undecided about indulging themselves will give in when price is reduced.

(3) They may even be items which involve a relatively large portion of a consumer's budget: meat. This way a price reduction will make a real difference in purchase plans.

Items for which demand is inelastic are not likely to be advertised as a loss leader. Consumers purchase the quantities they require of these items regardless of price. Few buyers are likely to respond to a special price when the need is not urgent. Some items in relatively inelastic demand might be auto repairs, diamond engagement rings, salt. Can you suggest others?

Demand elasticity plays an important part in a retailer's strategy in another way. Once the customer has taken the bait, prices for items in inelastic demand can be raised. It is assumed that customers must buy these items anyway, and a higher price will raise total store revenues. The store comes out ahead.

Think about this the next time you shop for notebooks at "one third off regular price" and buy, in addition, toothpaste or shaving cream at a substantial mark-up.

lead to a decrease in demand for paint brushes. But cross elasticity of demand is not always negative. Higher paint prices may lead to an increase in sales of wallpaper. We would then say that cross elasticity of demand for wallpaper and paint is positive. By the same token, a decline in wallpaper prices will probably lead to a decline in the demand for paint. Since the quotient of two negative numbers is positive, the cross elasticity will again be positive.

Complementary goods. We may characterize paint and brushes as *complementary goods:* they are used together. An increase in the price of paint reduces demand for its complement, paint brushes. Thus, when two goods are complementary, cross elasticity of demand has a negative sign.

Another example of complementary goods is biscuits and jam. What makes them complementary is that they are more desirable together than separately. You can, as any child knows, eat jam all by itself out of the jar. You can also eat biscuits by themselves. But putting the jam on the biscuits heightens the enjoyment of both. That is why a decline in the price of biscuits could easily lead to increased sales of jam, as well as of biscuits.

Substitute goods. Some goods replace others. Paint and wallpaper can be used in place of each other, and, therefore, we call them *substitute goods.* When two goods are substitutes, their cross elasticity of demand is positive. An increase in the price of one increases the demand for its substitute.

Manufacturers use the same principle to boost their revenues. This is possible when a single firm produces several items to be used together. Examples are cameras and film, razors and blades, and even electric stoves and electric power. Manufacturers of cameras, razors, or stoves have many competitors. This means there are close substitutes for the product and demand for a given brand is elastic. However, once a particular item has been selected, the consumer is locked into the purchase of the necessary complementary good. Demand for film, blades, or electric power becomes highly inelastic.

The clever manufacturer will take advantage of the difference in elasticities between the complementary goods. Price will be set quite low on the good for which there are rival producers. In fact, it may even be given away. The manufacturer can afford to take a substantial loss on the razor, knowing that the price of blades can be set quite high.

In the early 1970s the rising price of sugar raised the cost of producing many soft drinks. For the Coca Cola Company the cost of producing Cokes rose sharply relative to the cost of producing its sugar-free diet drink. Yet prices were raised for both. Can you explain this in terms of elasticity?

Years ago filling stations gave away free monogrammed glasses with each purchase. Why? Why did they discontinue this practice?

Substitutes have roughly similar characteristics. Whether they really replace each other depends on individual tastes. For some people bourbon would be an acceptable replacement for scotch, while for others it would do only as a last resort. Margarine and butter are very close substitutes for most of us. The various cola drinks are also very close substitutes. Slightly more distant substitutes for cola are other soft drinks, such as root beer or orange soda. More distant still are milk, coffee, orange juice, beer, wine, or—when we're desperate—water.

Cross elasticity is a useful measure of the *relatedness* of different goods and services. High cross elasticity indicates a close relationship: a change in the price of one has a significant effect on the demand for the other. In theory, any good may be related to any other good, if only distantly. To say that the cross elasticity of two goods is zero is to imply that there is no conceivable relationship between them. If the price of skis rises, we wouldn't expect the demand for country-fried chicken to be affected at all. But we can't be certain of this.

Remember the substitution and income effects. If the price of skis rises, skiers will be less well off and may have to restrict other purchases. The effect on demand for country-fried chicken will depend on whether it is a superior or an inferior good. If it's superior for buyers of skis, less will be purchased when their real income falls. If it's inferior, perhaps more will be purchased. The actual effect, of course, may be too slight for us to detect. It is best not to worry about this. For practical purposes we can think of some goods as being essentially unrelated in consumption and as having a cross elasticity of zero.

SUMMARY

Demand curves show the quantity of a good that would be purchased at every price during a certain time period. Demand curves slope downward for three reasons: (1) there is diminishing marginal utility for additional purchases of a good; (2) at lower prices consumers will substitute more of the lower-priced item for higher-priced ones; (3) lower prices increase incomes and allow consumers to purchase larger quantities of superior goods. Some goods are inferior; a lower price increases incomes and enables consumers to reduce their purchases of inferior goods.

Demand may be characterized as elastic or inelastic depending on the responsiveness of consumers to a price change. Demand elasticity is defined as the percentage change in quantity relative to a percentage change in price. Vertical demand curves are perfectly inelastic: $El = 0$. Horizontal demand curves are infinitely elastic: $El = \infty$. A rectangular hyperbola has constant or unit elasticity throughout: $El = 1$. Linear demand curves are elastic ($El > 1$) at high prices and inelastic ($El < 1$) at low prices.

Total revenue is represented by the area of a rectangle drawn beneath demand at the market price. Maximum total revenue is achieved when $El = 1$: A percentage change in price produces an equal percentage change in quantity purchased.

Marginal revenue is the change in revenue

Extended Example
Cross Elasticity and the Law

The question of relatedness among goods and services is of more than textbook interest. The U.S. Supreme Court has based decisions on the measurement of cross elasticity.

The Clayton Antitrust Act prohibits mergers of companies in the same industry if the effect would be to reduce competition. But what is an industry? Defining the industry was an important consideration in a Court decision in 1964. The second largest U.S. manufacturer of tin cans had purchased the third largest U.S. producer of glass containers. The firms claimed that each produced different goods; therefore, the merger did not reduce competition in the two separate industries. The Court decided differently, and the decision was based on cross elasticity of demand.

The Justices felt that users of cans and bottles could substitute between the two products fairly readily. With high positive cross elasticity of demand, the two goods were part of the same industry. To allow the merger would be to reduce competition in that industry. The expanded firm would control a substantial part of the market for containers and might increase price. For this reason the merger was not allowed.

Another famous decision involved the production of cellophane. A single firm produced almost all the nation's output of cellophane, which it sold at prices as much as seven times the prices of other wrapping materials. If the firm were judged to be a monopoly, then its pricing policy and even its existence would be illegal. The producer of cellophane claimed that all wrapping papers, such as waxed paper and brown wrapping paper, were essentially part of the same industry. That is, they were good substitutes for each other, and their cross elasticities were positive and large. Under this definition cellophane constituted only a small portion of industry output, and there was no monopoly in the industry. Would you agree that the cross elasticities among these products are high? The courts did. The case was decided in favor of the manufacturer of cellophane.

How does price elasticity of demand for cans differ from price elasticity of demand for containers? Illustrate graphically and explain.

which results from a change in price. When El > 1, marginal revenue is positive: A percentage decrease in price produces a greater percentage increase in quantity, and total revenue increases. When El < 1, marginal revenue is negative: A percentage decrease in price produces a smaller percentage increase in quantity, and total revenue falls. When El = 1, marginal revenue is equal to zero: A percentage change in price produces an equal percentage change in quantity, and total revenue is unchanged.

Advertising campaigns may shift demand curves to the right and make them less elastic. The result may be greater pricing freedom and larger total revenue.

Elasticity of demand depends on (1) the substitutability of the good or service, (2) whether the item is a necessity or a luxury, (3) the proportion of income spent for the item, and (4) the length of time for which the demand curve is drawn.

Income elasticity measures percentage change in quantity relative to percentage change in income. Superior goods have positive income elasticity of demand, and inferior goods have negative income elasticity of demand. Cross elasticity of demand measures the percentage change of quantity of one good relative to the percentage change in price of another. Complementary goods have a negative cross elasticity of demand, and substitute goods have a positive cross elasticity of demand.

Key Words and Phrases

cross elasticity of demand the percentage change in quantity demanded of one good relative to a percentage change in price of another.

demand elasticity the percentage change in quantity demanded of a good relative to a percentage change in its price.

elastic a condition of demand in which the percentage change in quantity demanded is larger than the percentage change in price: El > 1.

Engel curves graphs which show the quantity of a good purchased at various levels of income.

Giffen goods inferior goods whose income effect is stronger than the substitution effect; Giffen goods have backward-sloping demand curves.

income effect lower prices for a good increase consumers' purchasing power and enable them to purchase more of certain goods.

income elasticity of demand percentage change in quantity demanded relative to percentage change in income.

inelastic a condition of demand in which the percentage change in quantity demanded is smaller than the percentage change in price: El < 1.
inferior goods goods whose purchase declines when consumers' incomes increase.
infinitely elastic demand a condition of demand in which infinite changes in quantity demanded can take place with no change in price: El = ∞.
marginal revenue the difference in total revenue that results from a unit change in quantity sold.
perfectly inelastic demand a condition of demand in which a percentage change in price brings on no change in quantity demanded: El = 0.
substitution effect lower prices for a good encourage consumers to substitute the lower-priced good for other higher-priced ones.
superior goods goods whose purchase increases when consumers' incomes increase.
total revenue the product of price times quantity sold.
unit elasticity a condition of demand in which the percentage change in price and the percentage change in quantity demanded are the same: El = 1.

Questions for Review

1. Give examples and explain the effect of price change on quantity demanded when (a) the income and substitution effects work in the same direction and (b) the income and substitution effects work in opposite directions.
2. Draw a typical linear demand curve. Then, draw a second curve which lies exactly halfway between the demand curve and the vertical axis of your graph. This curve is your marginal revenue curve. Use the marginal revenue curve to explain changes in total revenue which would result from changes in price.
3. Use the following hypothetical data to compute price elasticity of demand for goods produced by firms A and B.

Firm A		Firm B	
Price	Quantity	Price	Quantity
100	5	100	11
80	10	80	13
60	15	60	15
40	20	40	17
20	25	20	19

What pricing policies would you recommend for maximizing total sales revenue?
4. Compare price elasticity of demand for each of the following pairs. In every case consider the four determinants of elasticity and discuss the significance of each for the particular good.
(a) a new auto—auto repair service.
(b) newspapers—*New York Times*.
(c) food—clothing.
5. Weather changes damage crops in many parts of the world and raise prices of basic foods. How is the income effect demonstrated by higher food prices for certain food purchases? What is the income effect of excise taxes? What type of industries are harmed most?
6. What types of goods would be expected to have negative cross elasticity of demand? Explain.
7. Define: income elasticity of demand, Giffen goods.
8. How have high oil prices affected demand for propane gas? How has the fast-food trend affected supermarket sales? What effect do high building costs have on the demand for mobile homes? Give other examples of interaction between markets.
9. Soaring coffee prices in the winter of 1977 discouraged consumption. What effect might this have on demand for muffins and doughnuts? Explain in terms of elasticity. What effect might this have on the demand for waitresses?
10. What is the mathematical shorthand for demand that is: (a) unit elastic; (b) inelastic; (c) elastic?
11. Ice-skating rinks must often operate twenty-four hours a day in order to cover their high costs. However, skating fees vary throughout the period and on different days of the week. Explain in terms of elasticity.
12. During the late 1970s the price of home heating oil doubled. Discuss the income and substitution effects of the price increase. Demonstrate graphically, under various assumptions about elasticity.
13. Explain why higher prices for U.S. autos caused a decline in revenues on U.S. auto exports, while an increase in Arab oil prices caused an increase in their revenues.
14. Why do baseball cards displaying Honus Wagner (Pittsburgh Pirates, 1911) sell for $3000? Illustrate this market graphically and explain in terms of elasticities.
15. Why are Americans more concerned about $1.50 a gallon gasoline than they are about $4 a gallon mouthwash?
16. How does a good's "storability" affect its elasticity of demand? How is storability related to substitutability?

Appendix

Elasticity and Indifference Curves

In the Appendix to the preceding chapter we used indifference curves as a device for explaining consumer demand. We showed how changes in prices or incomes would move consumers to new indifference curves. Consumers maximize total utility within their budgets by purchasing the combination of goods on the highest indifference curve touched by the budget line. Figure A.1 shows the changes in purchases that result from (a) a fall in the price of clothing and (b) an increase in income.

This chapter has focused on elasticity of demand. We defined price elasticity as the percentage change in quantity demanded relative to a percentage change in price. When a 1 percent drop in price produces a 1 percent increase in purchases, we say price elasticity of demand is equal to (minus) one, or unity.

PRICE ELASTICITY AND THE PRICE-CONSUMPTION LINE

It is interesting to illustrate *price elasticity of demand* with indifference curves. Look again at Figure A.1a. Successive declines in the price of clothing cause the consumer to increase clothing

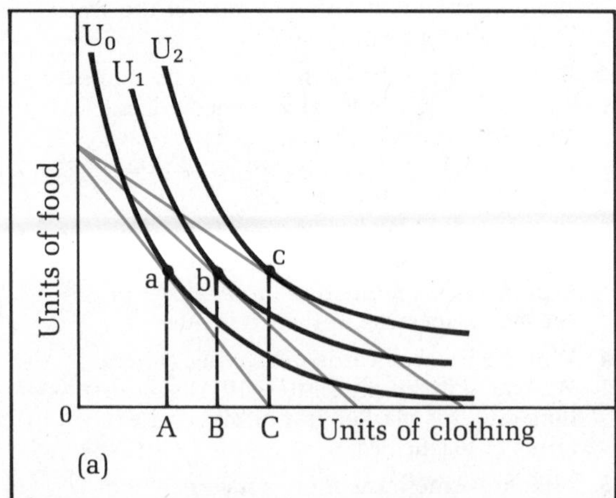

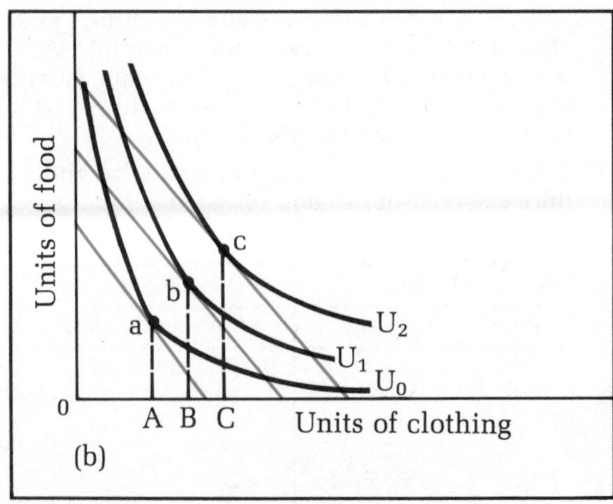

Figure A.1 As the price of clothing falls, purchases of clothing increase from *OA* to *OB* to *OC*. (b) As income increases, purchases of clothing increase from *OA* to *OB* to *OC*.

purchases from *OA* to *OB* and then to *OC*. The points *a*, *b*, and *c* define the preferred combinations of goods for various *price ratios*. In Figure A.2 we have connected these points with a dotted line. We might label the dotted line the *price-consumption line*. The behavior of the price-consumption line indicates the character of price elasticity for the good plotted along the horizontal axis.

In Figure A.2a the price-consumption line is horizontal. Purchases of clothing increase exactly in proportion to decreases in price. Thus we know price elasticity of demand is precisely equal to (minus) one. In Figure A.2b the price-consumption line slopes upward. Purchases of clothing, on the horizontal axis, increase less proportionally than decreases in price. Price elasticity of demand is less than one; how much less than one depends on the steepness of the slope of the price-consumption line. In Figure A.2c the price-consumption line slopes downward. Purchases of clothing increase in greater proportion than decreases in price. Price elasticity is greater than one; how much greater depends on the steepness of the slope.

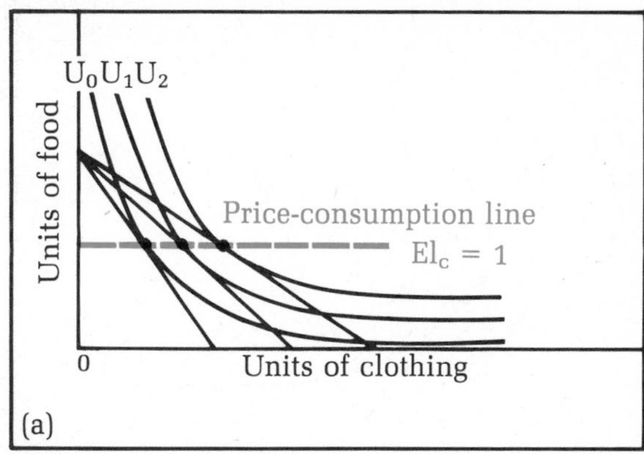

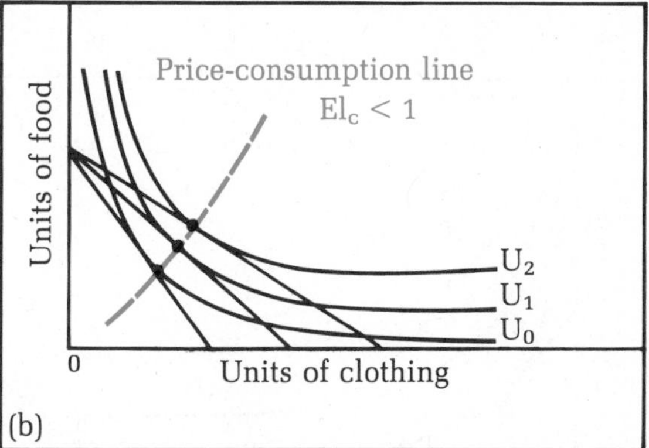

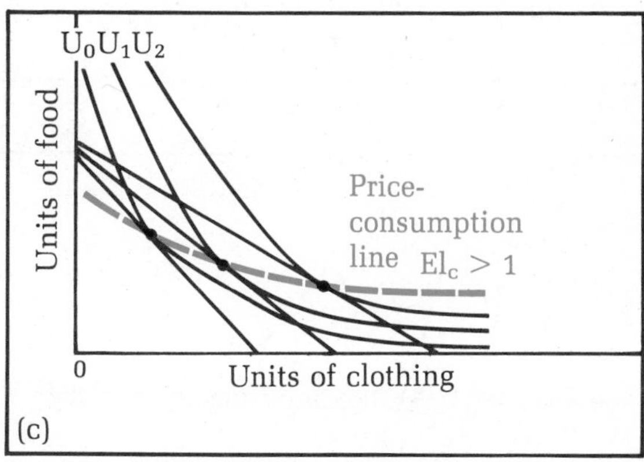

Figure A.2 Connecting the points of tangency with budget lines for various prices produces a price-consumption line. (a) A horizontal price-consumption line indicates price elasticity of clothing demand = 1. (b) An upward-sloping price-consumption line indicates price elasticity of clothing demand < 1. (c) A downward-sloping price-consumption line indicates price elasticity of clothing demand > 1.

Income Elasticity and the Income-Consumption Line

Similar interesting results are possible when indifference curves are used to illustrate *income elasticity of demand*. We defined income elasticity as percentage change in quantity demanded relative to percentage change in income. When a 1 percent increase in income produces a 1 percent increase in purchases, we say income elasticity of demand is equal to one, or unity. Income elasticity of demand is always positive for superior goods and negative for inferior goods. The size of income elasticity measures the strength of a good's superiority or inferiority relative to other goods.

Refer back to Figure A.1b. Successive increases in income cause the consumer to increase purchases of both food and clothing. The points *a*, *b*, and *c* define the preferred combinations of goods for various incomes. In Figure A.3 we have connected these points with a dotted line. We might label this line the *income-consumption line*. As you might have guessed,

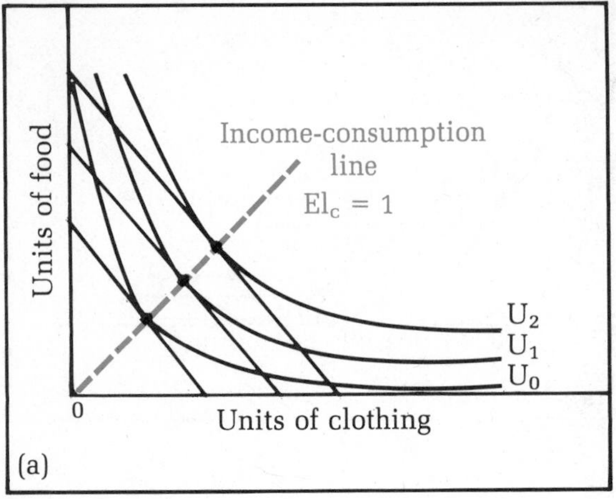

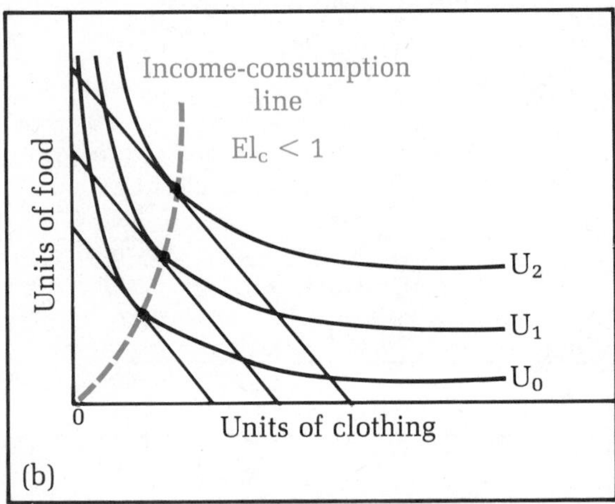

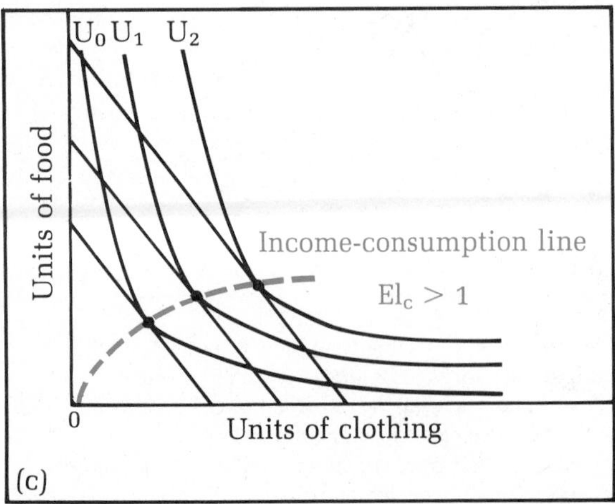

the behavior of the income-consumption line reveals something about the character of income elasticity over this range of incomes.

In Figure A.3a the income-consumption line rises from the origin with a constant slope; purchases of both goods rise equally in proportion to increases in income.* Thus income elasticity for both goods is precisely equal to one. In Figure A.3b the income-consumption line becomes steeper as it moves from the origin. Purchases of clothing, on the horizontal axis, increase in smaller proportion than income; income elasticity of demand for that good is less than one. If these purchases increase in lesser proportion than income, purchases of the good on the vertical axis must increase more than proportionally. Note that this is true on Figure A.3b. Income elasticity of demand for food must be greater than one. As before, the steepness of the income-consumption line reveals the magnitude of the deviation from elasticity = 1. Similar reasoning applies to Figure A.3c except the income-consumption line indicates income elasticity > 1 for the good on the horizontal axis and income elasticity < 1 for the good on the vertical axis.

Test your understanding of the income-consumption line. Construct a graph on which one of the goods is an inferior good. How does the income-consumption line behave on your graph?

*The income-consumption line need not have a slope of one for this to be true.

Figure A.3 Connecting the points of tangency with budget lines for various incomes produces an income-consumption line. (a) An income-consumption line which rises from the origin with a constant slope indicates income elasticity of clothing demand = 1. (b) An income-consumption line which rises with an increasing slope indicates income elasticity of clothing demand < 1. (c) An income-consumption line which rises with a decreasing slope indicates income elasticity of demand for clothing > 1.

CHAPTER 7

Supply Elasticity and Government Policy

Learning Objectives

Upon completion of this chapter, you should be able to:

1. Define and calculate elasticity of supply.
2. Indicate three basic factors that determine supply elasticity and explain why.
3. Explain how elasticity affects specific and ad valorem taxes and show how tax incidence depends on elasticity.
4. Explain the use of and effect of subsidies.
5. Define and graph price ceilings and price floors.
6. Explain agricultural problems in terms of elasticity.

The preceding chapter examined consumer response to price and income changes. We described *consumer* responsiveness in terms of elasticity of demand. This chapter will examine *producer* response to price change in terms of elasticity of supply. Then we will discuss the implications of elasticity for government policy.

Producers respond to market conditions differently, depending on the production characteristics of their industries. The result is various types of supply curves, with various levels of elasticity. We will study supply curves in detail in later chapters. However, at this point we will note some similarities between demand and supply elasticity.

SUPPLY CURVES: A REVIEW

We saw earlier how supply curves reflect the output decisions of producers. In general, producers would be willing to supply larger quantities at higher prices and smaller quantities at lower prices. If the price of tennis shoes is high, it would pay firms to operate their plant and machinery more intensively. They would hire more labor and purchase more materials with the object of meeting the demand and thus increasing their profits. If the price of tennis shoes should fall dramatically, then firms would operate their plant and equipment less intensively, hire fewer workers, and cut back their orders for materials. By reducing production, firms would seek to reduce their expected losses from low selling prices.

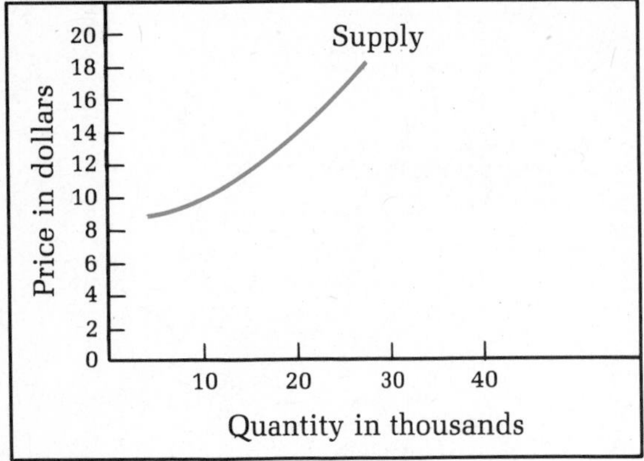

Figure 1 A typical supply curve slopes upward.

Figure 1 shows a typical supply curve drawn for some good or service over a given period of time. The upward slope shows that higher prices would mean higher production and lower prices would mean lower production. We say that there is a *positive* relationship between quantity and price: Larger values on the horizontal axis are associated with larger values on the vertical axis.

The points along the supply curve indicate the largest quantities that would be produced at every price level over a certain time period. There is another way of saying the same thing: The supply curve shows the lowest price for which a firm would be willing to produce a given quantity. Producers would not supply output below, or to the right of, the supply curve because the price would not be high enough to make it pay. They would, of course,

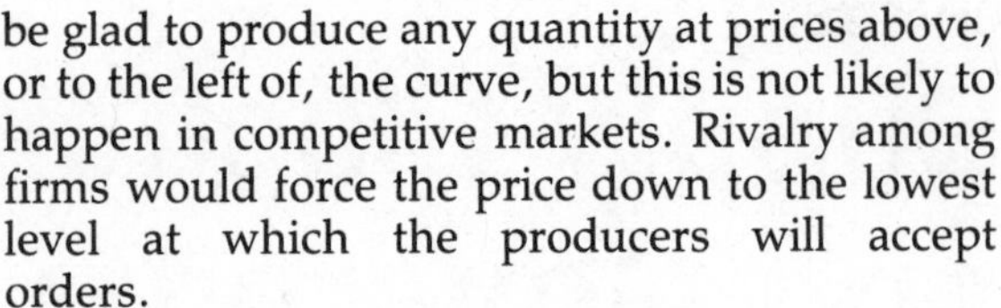

be glad to produce any quantity at prices above, or to the left of, the curve, but this is not likely to happen in competitive markets. Rivalry among firms would force the price down to the lowest level at which the producers will accept orders.

ELASTICITY OF SUPPLY

We saw that demand elasticity measures the response of quantity demanded to a change in price during a particular time period. Changes are stated in percentage terms, and we calculate elasticity by dividing percentage change in quantity demanded by percentage change in price. If the result is greater than (minus) one, we say that demand is elastic: Quantity demanded responds by a greater percentage than the price change. If elasticity is less than (minus) one, we say that demand is inelastic: Quantity demanded responds by a smaller percentage than the price change. **Supply elasticity** is calculated in the same way.

When we drew the supply curve, we pointed out the positive relationship between price and quantity supplied. An increase in price would lead to larger quantities, and a reduction in price would lead to smaller quantities. The positive relationship between price and quantity supplied means that supply elasticity will be a positive number. The numerator and denominator will have the same sign, and the quotient of two numbers with the same sign is always positive.

To illustrate elasticity of supply, let us look

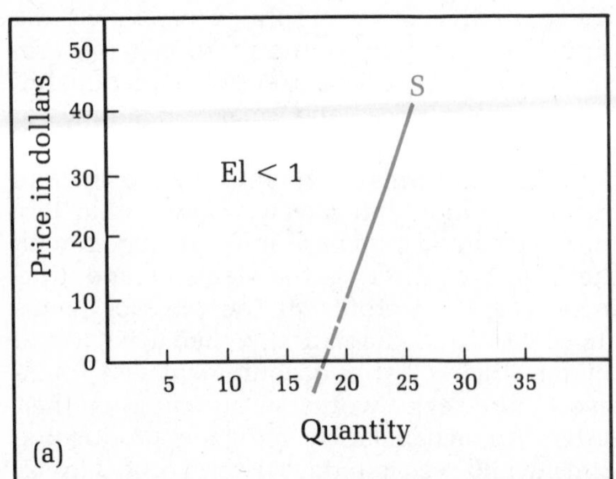

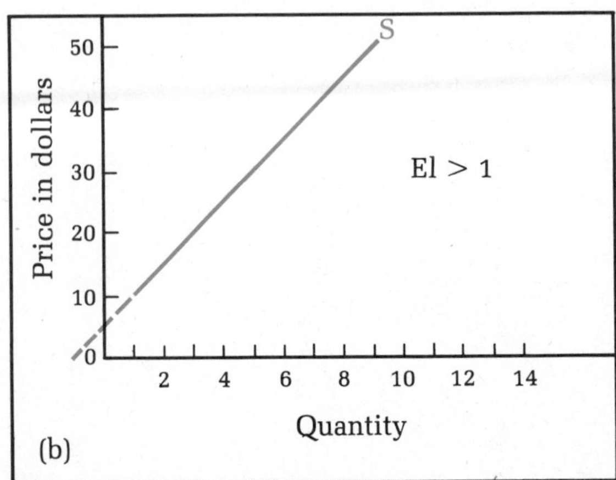

Figure 2 Supply of shoulder bags per month: (a) hand-tooled leather bags; (b) machine-made vinyl bags.

Extended Example Calculating Elasticity of Supply

If the price of hand-tooled leather handbags rises from \$40 to \$50, encouraging producers to make 28 bags instead of 26, what is elasticity of supply?

We use the same formula that we developed for demand elasticity. The percentage change in quantity is

$$\frac{Q_1 - Q_2}{(Q_1 + Q_2)/2}$$

and the percentage change in price is

$$\frac{P_1 - P_2}{(P_1 + P_2)/2}$$

Dividing the two percentages and cancelling the 2's leaves

$$\text{Elasticity of supply} = \frac{Q_1 - Q_2}{Q_1 + Q_2} \div \frac{P_1 - P_2}{P_1 + P_2}.$$

Using the values given above, P_1 is \$40 and P_2 is \$50. Likewise, Q_1 is 26 and Q_2 is 28. Substituting in the equation, we have

$$\frac{26 - 28}{26 + 28} \div \frac{40 - 50}{40 + 50} = \frac{-2}{54} \div \frac{-10}{90}$$
$$= \frac{-1}{27} \times \frac{-9}{1}$$
$$= \frac{1}{3} = .33.$$

This means that, along this segment of the supply curve, a 1 percent change in the price of leather bags will lead to a change in supply of only 0.33 percent. Thus we can say that the supply of leather bags is inelastic. Along other segments of this supply curve, supply is even more inelastic as we can see in Table 1.

Look at the price and output data for machine-made vinyl bags. If price rises from \$40 to \$50, quantity supplied will increase from 7000 to 9000. Substituting in the formula, we have

$$\frac{7000 - 9000}{7000 + 9000} \div \frac{40 - 50}{40 + 50} = \frac{-2}{16} \div \frac{-10}{90}$$
$$= \frac{-1}{8} \times \frac{-9}{1}$$
$$= \frac{9}{8} = 1.125\,.$$

The supply of machine-made bags is more responsive to price change; supply is elastic over the price range shown.

Table 1 **Supply Data for Shoulder Bags (one month)**

Price	Quantity of leather bags	Elasticity	Quantity of vinyl bags	Elasticity
\$50	28		9000	
		.33		1.125
40	26		7000	
		.28		1.167
30	24		5000	
		.22		1.25
20	22		3000	
		.14		1.5
10	20		1000	

at two hypothetical markets for shoulder bags. Table 1 shows price and quantity data for two kinds of shoulder bags: hand-tooled leather bags and machine-made vinyl bags. The quantities shown are the numbers of bags which would be produced for sale in a particular market during a given period of time.

Supply curves for leather and vinyl shoulder bags are drawn in Figure 2. As we know from Table 1, the supply of hand-tooled bags is price inelastic at all points on the curve, reflecting the difficulty of altering quantities when price changes. The supply of machine-made vinyl bags is price elastic, reflecting the ease with which factory output can be altered in response to price changes. An interesting characteristic of these curves is that if we extend them as shown in Figure 2, the inelastic supply curve cuts the horizontal axis to the right of the origin of the graph, while the elastic supply curve cuts the vertical axis above the origin.

What is the elasticity of supply for a curve that rises from the origin? If you answered El = 1, you are correct. In fact, El = 1 for every segment of such a supply curve, whatever its slope.

Perfect Inelasticity

Some goods and services are fixed in supply, and no increase in price will bring forth greater quantity. There will never be more Rembrandt paintings than exist now or another genuine 1926 Model T Ford. The supply curve for a good that is fixed in supply is shown in Figure 3a. It is drawn as a vertical line because quantity remains the same at all prices. Because the change in quantity is zero, the value of elasticity is also zero. (The numerator of the fraction measuring elasticity will be zero; hence the fraction itself must be zero.) Supply curves for which elasticity is equal to zero are said to be **perfectly inelastic:**

$$\text{El} = \frac{0}{\%\ \text{change in quantity}} = 0.$$

Infinite Elasticity

At the other extreme, supply of some goods and services can expand to almost any amount with no change in price. There is no human-made good with such a flexible supply, but pencils probably come as close as any other manufactured good. The supply curve for pencils may be said to be almost **infinitely elastic.** Referring to our formula, we see that this time the denominator will be zero since larger quantities can be supplied with no increase in price. A number divided by zero is infinitely large:

$$\text{El} = \frac{\%\ \text{change in quantity}}{0} = \infty.$$

Infinitely elastic supply curves are drawn as horizontal lines at whatever happens to be the established price for the good or service (Figure 3b).

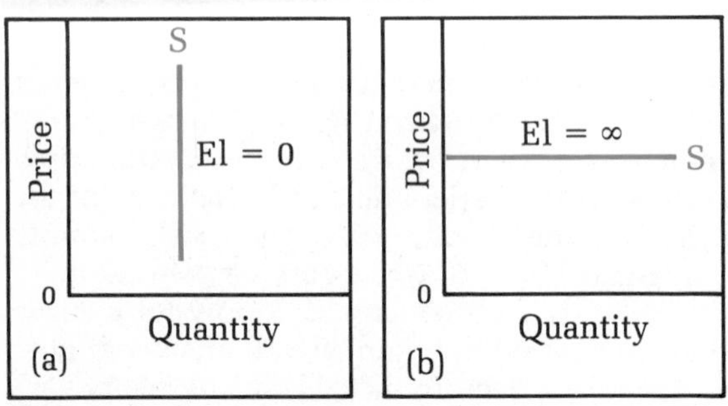

Figure 3 The two extremes in supply curves: (a) perfectly inelastic supply; (b) infinitely elastic supply.

Elastic and Inelastic Supply Curves

Classifying supply curves as elastic or inelastic enables us to say certain things about the nature of supply. We can say, in general, that inelastic supply curves reflect a relatively small response by producers to changes in price. For some reason producers are unable to take full advantage of price increases by expanding their output. On the other hand, when prices fall, producers are unable to make sharp cutbacks in their output. Perhaps the best example of this type of producer is a farmer who decides on production at the beginning of the growing season and can't change production plans until the following season. Whether farmers plant too many watermelons or too few, they have to live with their decision, at least until the next year.

Elastic supply curves reflect greater response to price changes. Producers are able to hire more workers and open more production lines when prices are rising and to cut back when prices are falling. Supply tends to be relatively elastic in many manufacturing industries. Elasticity of supply in service industries depends on the availability of necessary labor skills for performing the particular service.

WHAT DETERMINES ELASTICITY OF SUPPLY?

Suppose Pierre, the French baker, makes a batch of pastry. He puts the pastry in his window, and toward the end of the day there are a dozen unsold. He has a choice of eating them himself or marking down the price in hope of selling them before closing time. He won't make a profit selling them at half price, but he will get back some of his expenses. His supply curve for that batch of French pastry is perfectly inelastic; he can't supply any more apple tarts or chocolate eclairs that day even if someone were to offer him double the usual price, but he is willing to sell what he has, since it is too late to cut back production, at almost any price.

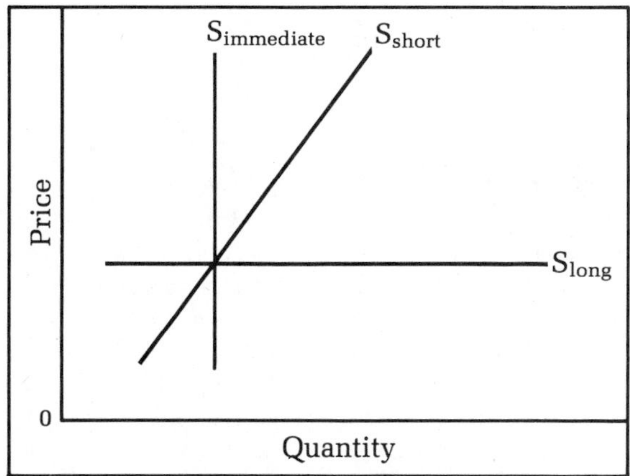

Figure 4 Elasticity of supply depends on the time period. Each of the three time periods may have a different supply curve and therefore a different elasticity.

This example illustrates one of the three important factors affecting the elasticity of supply: (1) time; (2) technology; and (3) price expectations. Let's look at each in turn.

Time

Our example of the French baker illustrates the first important determinant of supply elasticity: time. If we make the time period short enough, almost every supply curve becomes inelastic. There aren't enough materials or enough workers or enough machines to increase quantity supplied any further during a very short time period. It takes time to train new bakers (and leatherworkers, too). On the other hand, if we make the time period long enough, there is almost no limit to the possible increase in quantity supplied.

Economists distinguish three time periods when analyzing the behavior of supply. There is the **immediate time period,** in which the baker can make no more pastry because work is over for the day. (Likewise, leatherworkers can produce a limited quantity of bags.) There is the **short run,** in which the baker can increase output up to the limit of the existing plant—that is, by hiring more workers and putting in more hours a day baking tarts and eclairs. Finally, there is the **long run,** in which the baker can move to a larger plant and put in more ovens and more leather workers can be brought in.

Figure 4 shows three supply curves illustrating the immediate period, the short run, and the long run. Supply in the immediate period is perfectly inelastic: Producers can't increase quantity supplied no matter what price is offered. Therefore, the supply curve is vertical.

But over a period of a month or more, the supply curve will become more elastic, like the short-run curve in Figure 4. If prices are favorable, more goods can be produced with the existing plant. As the upward-sloping curve shows, supply is more responsive to a higher price in the short run.

If prices remain high, producers will increase their productive capacity. If, on the other hand, they face declining prices, some of them may leave their industry and try to make a better living in some other profession. This makes supply curves still more elastic in the long run, since quantity may expand or contract to almost any extent. Supply curves may approach infinite elasticity, as shown in Figure 4.

Technology

In an earlier example, we found that supply elasticity for hand-tooled leather bags was less than one (inelastic) while that for machine-made vinyl bags was greater than one (elastic). Over any particular period of time it will be much easier to expand the supply of machine-made bags than that of hand-tooled ones. To produce more hand-made bags it will be necessary to find additional skilled workers and set them to work. In contrast, the obedient machines stand ready at any time to labor a little harder or a little longer. Obviously, some technologies are more flexible than others for responding to price change.

In addition to including the technology of production, we should consider differences in the availability of resources used in particular industries. When resources are plentiful, the quantity of output is generally more responsive to price change than when necessary resources are scarce. If, in order to expand output, producers must use inferior materials, they may be required to develop new and more expensive production processes. Then an increase in supply would likely require a substantial increase in price.

Extended Example The Green Revolution

We have shown how supply curves become more elastic as producers adjust their output to accommodate consumer demand. Over time, supply curves may tilt from perfectly vertical to perfectly horizontal or, in terms of elasticity, from perfectly inelastic to infinitely elastic. The slope of the supply curve depends on the response of producers to price changes.

When producers are *responsive,* consumers are able to enjoy larger quantities of goods and services without having to pay higher prices. Is it possible, you may ask, for producers to be *so responsive* that consumers might enjoy larger quantities at even lower prices? In other words, is it ever possible for supply curves to slope *downward?* In one sector of the U.S. economy, conditions have been such as to bring about this pleasant result, largely because of the work of scientists like Norman Borlaug.

In 1970, Norman Borlaug received the Nobel Peace Prize. The unusual thing about this award was that Norman Borlaug is a botanist. Why should a *botanist* be awarded the *Peace* Prize?

More specifically, Borlaug is a plant geneticist. He specializes in plant mutations, plants which are superior to their ancestors in such things as protein content, fertility, and resistance to disease.

Borlaug's experiments helped change wheat from a tall, fragile plant which would collapse in bad weather to a more stable, shorter variety. The improved plant converts water and fertilizer into a larger kernel of grain, rather than into useless straw. Furthermore, the new plant is resistant to wheat rust and other plant parasites and can be grown over a wide range of climatic latitudes.

Borlaug's work began in Mexico, where crops had been regularly decimated by wheat rust. The research was long and painstaking. It required months of careful work followed by more months of patient waiting for new plants to mature. Plants of desirable characteristics had to be cross-pollinated with other plants to produce new seeds. Then Borlaug and his team of scientists would plant by hand thousands of new varieties of wheat—more than a million seeds in all. From dawn to dusk, the planting had to be done quickly; then the tiny sprouts had to be inoculated with a hypodermic solution of wheat rust. Plants that survived were retained for developing rust-resistant strains; they were further adapted to prepare them for the land and climatic features of particular countries.

Borlaug is part of a worldwide movement financed by U.S. foundations. The goal is to provide the collective wisdom and experience of American farmers to countries struggling with the problem of feeding their growing populations. World population is now about four billion. It is presently increasing about 2 percent annually; if it continues at this rate, population will reach about eight billion within thirty-five years. Demand curves for food are shifting to the right, and it is important that supplies of food grow at least as fast.

For the past two centuries the application of advanced technology to agriculture has accomplished sufficient growth to prevent mass starvation. Further improvements in productivity will be more difficult, however. This is because there is less tillable land remaining for cultivation and because costs of chemical fertilizers have been rising. Scientists are seeking new ways to expand agricultural output, but they worry that the world may be approaching absolute limits of production.

Currently, scientists are working on projects to:

(1) improve plant use of carbon dioxide for producing carbohydrates and for creating their own fertilizer, nitrogen, within the plant itself;

(2) produce improved plant strains in the laboratory

Expectations

Business firms are run by human beings, not machines, and changes in supply may depend on how people feel or think about the future. The fact that prices have increased may not be enough to start the wheels turning unless those in charge think the higher prices will continue. A sudden drop in prices may not discourage production very much either, unless business firms expect prices to remain low. The producer of hand-tooled shoulder bags or chocolate eclairs may not want to train additional artisans and set them to work unless the higher price is expected to continue. Thus business firms do not always adjust their production to market signals, rightly or wrongly. When they don't, supply may remain inelastic for some time.

rather than through the time-consuming process of crossbreeding;

(3) increase output per acre through use of high-yield planting techniques;

(4) increase beef and egg production through animal hormone treatments; and

(5) fatten cattle on a diet of garbage.

Unhappily, research and development spending in agriculture has declined (when dollar amounts are corrected for inflation). Failure to continue technical advance in farming will slow the growth of food supply and increase prices over the globe.

What are the implications of rising market prices for food? A larger portion of consumer budgets will have to be allocated toward fulfilling basic needs. Manufacturing industries will suffer a decrease in sales as consumers cut back spending for other consumer goods. Incomes to resource owners will change and resources will shift among industries according to changing consumer spending. Adjustments within food-producing nations like the United States will be gradual, but there will be some disruptions nevertheless. Those who are harmed by the changes will demand government action to protect their interests. Consumers may demand government-imposed embargoes on food exports and price controls on food. Food producers in this country and food importers abroad will resist these policies. Other nations may retaliate with embargoes on shipments of their basic raw materials to U.S. industry. The benefits of international trade will be replaced by the trauma of international conflict, possibly leading to outright war.

For these reasons we should recognize and encourage the work of "peace" scientists like Norman Borlaug.

Explain why farmers in many poor nations are sometimes reluctant to accept new agricultural techniques. Instead of sending our technology abroad, why don't we concentrate on producing more food and shipping food?

MARKET EQUILIBRIUM

Economists have compared supply and demand to the two blades of a pair of scissors. The action takes place at the point where the blades come together. When the quantity producers are willing to supply is just sufficient to satisfy the demand of those who are willing to buy, we say that the market has reached equilibrium. The *equilibrium price* is the price which brings buyers and sellers together in the right numbers to clear the market. It is the price at which the quantity suppliers want to sell is just equal to the quantity consumers want to buy.

Not everybody will be happy with the equilibrium price. Some producers may find that they must accept a lower price than they had hoped to get; their alternative is to hold off and wait for a better day. Some would-be consumers may find that price is higher than they had wanted to pay; their alternative is to refrain from buying.

Figure 5 shows three different equilibrium positions in the same market over various periods of time. The *immediate-period* supply curve, S_1, represents the limited quantity available at a particular moment (Q_1). Buyers must pay price P_1, which is determined by the intersection of the demand curve with S_1. Those who don't want to pay that price must go without. A high price in the immediate period may encourage producers to increase supply in the short run. Their response to the high price is shown by the *short-run* supply curve, S_2. At the new equilibrium point, determined by the intersection of the demand curve with S_2, a larger amount, Q_2, will be sold. Purchasers willing to pay price P_2 are able to buy. There are still potential customers, however, and producers may expand capacity to supply still more. The *long-run* supply curve, S_3, and the demand curve will intersect to

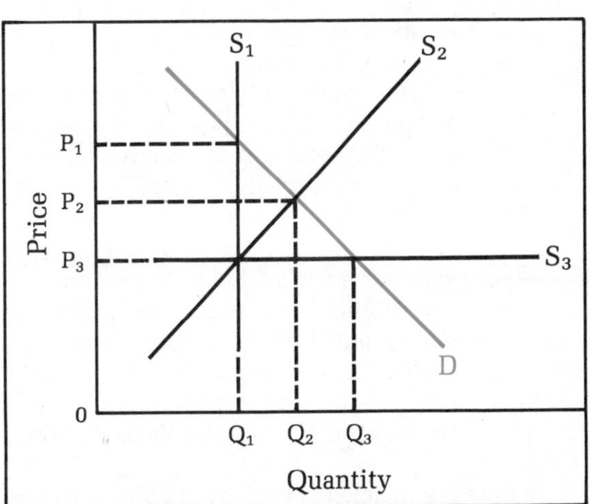

Figure 5 Equilibrium points for the immediate period, the short run, and the long run. Notice that equilibrium price may decline from P_1 in the immediate period to P_2 in the short run and P_3 in the long run.

form a new market equilibrium point. As producers adjust production over the longer time period, equilibrium price falls to P_3, and quantity increases to Q_3. More customers are satisfied and more goods are available at lower prices.

GOVERNMENT IN THE MARKET

Although our market system depends primarily on private decisions of consumers and producers, some government actions are necessary. Governments must levy taxes in such a way as to minimize interference with private decision-making. On the other hand, governments sometimes impose reverse taxes, or *subsidies,* with the clear intent of affecting private decisions. Elasticity is an important consideration for making these decisions.

Elasticity and Taxes

No field of economics is more controversial than the economics of taxation. What is the most efficient, most equitable way of paying for government? One mark of a successful tax is that it gets the maximum amount of revenue with the least disturbance to ordinary buying and selling.

An important source of tax revenue is sales and excise taxes added to the purchase price of a good or service. Refer back to Chapter 4 for definitions and discussions of these taxes. When demand is inelastic, consumers will buy roughly the same quantities regardless of price. A sales or excise tax will raise the selling price of such goods, but it will have little effect on the quantities produced and sold. Government will collect its revenue, and production will continue much as before.

Results are different if demand and supply are elastic. When a tax is added to the price of a good in elastic demand, consumers will reduce their purchases. Suppliers will produce less. Government won't collect as much revenue as it would have if demand and supply were inelastic, and the level of economic activity will decline.

A successful sales or excise tax will tax those goods characterized by inelastic supply and demand. We will examine this principle in greater detail below.

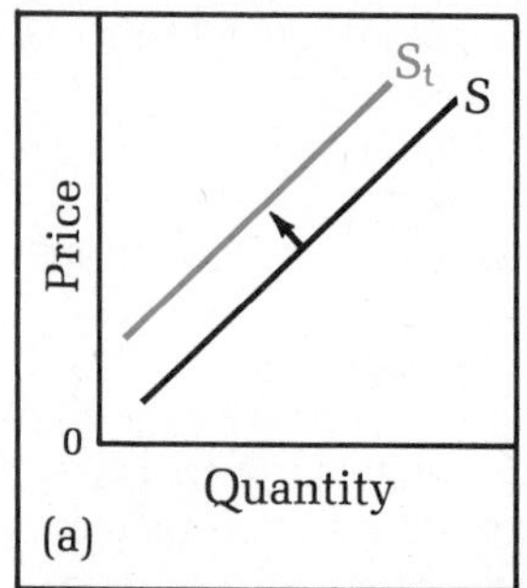

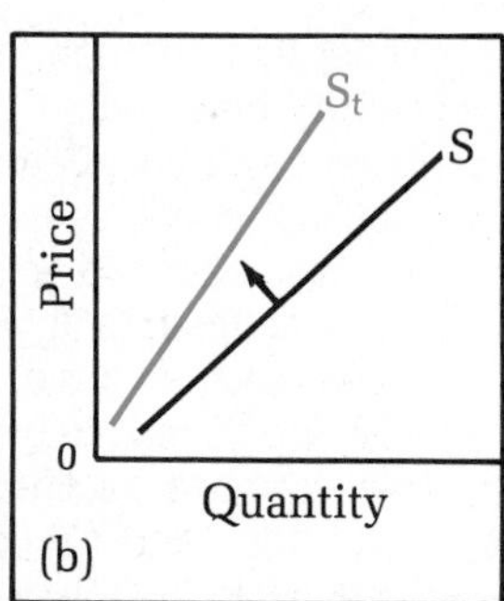

Figure 6 The effect on supply (S) of a good by imposing: (a) a specific tax; (b) an ad valorem tax. S_t (supply after tax) is parallel for a specific tax and diverges upward for an ad valorem tax.

Specific and Ad Valorem Taxes

A **specific tax** is a tax that raises the price of a good by a *fixed amount* per unit. Some taxes on cigarettes are specific taxes. A state may charge, say, $.10 per pack sold. A specific tax adds a constant amount to the supply price of each unit. The result is to shift the supply curve upward by the amount of the tax. Since a constant amount is added, the new supply curve is parallel to the old, as shown in Figure 6a.

An **ad valorem tax** varies with the value of the good: A fixed percentage is added to the value of what is sold. At low prices the percentage tax raises unit price by a small dollar amount. At high prices the tax raises unit price by a larger dollar amount. Sales taxes and property taxes are ad valorem taxes and so are most import duties. An advantage of ad valorem taxes is that government revenues automatically increase as prices go up. Of course, they also have the disadvantage that revenues fall if prices go down. Figure 6b shows the effect of an ad valorem tax. The supply curve tilts upward by larger amounts at higher price levels. As a result, supply curves become less elastic when ad valorem taxes are imposed.

State and local governments collect much of their revenue from taxes, both specific and ad valorem, on consumer purchases. The most commonly taxed goods are liquor, cigarettes, and gasoline. These are preferred sources of revenue because demand is inelastic, and the tax will have less effect on production.

Taxes where demand is inelastic. The effect on equilibrium price and quantity when demand is inelastic can be seen from Figure 7, using cigarettes as an example. The demand curve is steep, since the response of cigarette smokers to price change is relatively low.

Suppose the original market price is $3.00 per carton. At this price 1 million cartons are sold per time period. Now government imposes a specific tax of $.50 on each carton sold. Adding $.50 to the supply price per unit shifts market supply upward by $.50 at every quantity. What will the tax revenue be? After the tax, consumers move up their demand curves and purchase only .9 million cartons. Tax collections will be $.50 × .9 million = $.45 million, or $450,000. Consumers pay the value of the entire rectangle formed beneath the demand curve at Q = .9 and P = 3.50. Government revenue is the pink rectangle and cigarette producers receive the remainder.

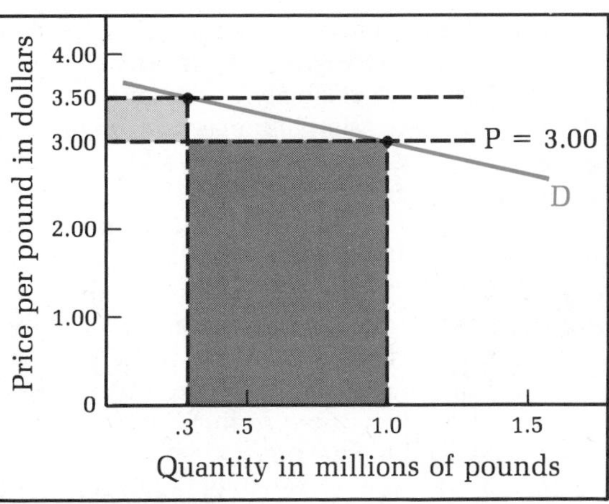

Figure 8 The effect of a tax on a good (cheese) for which demand is elastic. A $.50 tax on a pound of cheese causes price to increase to $3.50 per pound and quantity sold to fall from 1.0 to 0.3 million pounds. Tax revenue is shown by the pink shaded area, while total revenue lost by the cheese industry is shown by the gray area.

Taxes where demand is elastic. Demand for many consumer goods is more responsive to price changes. Figure 8 illustrates what happens when a tax is imposed on a good for which demand is relatively elastic, such as cheese. Cheese is a good for which there are many substitutes. Suppose, at a price of $3.00 per pound, cheese fanciers buy 1 million pounds per time period. When a tax of $.50 per pound is imposed, market supply shifts upward as before. But with elastic demand, quantity sold falls sharply to .3 million pounds. Government collects a tax revenue of $.50 × .3 million = $.15 million, or $150,000. Consumers pay the value of the entire rectangle at Q = .3 and P = 3.50. The higher price has turned off so many cheese consumers that tax collections are much lower than when the same tax is imposed on cigarettes. In addition, the cheese industry is now quite upset about the loss of its customers.

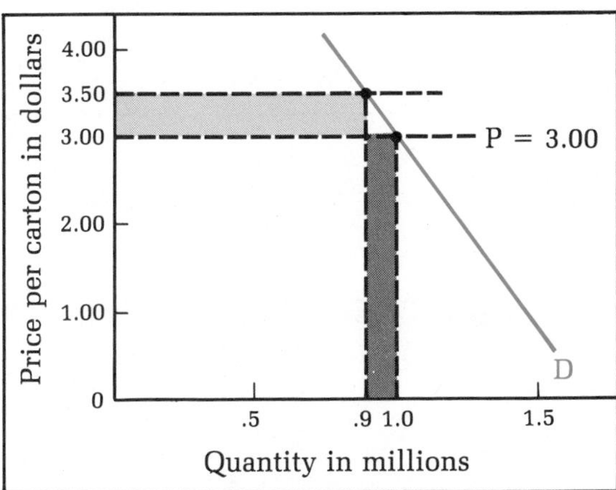

Figure 7 The effect of a tax on a commodity (cigarettes) for which demand is inelastic. A $.50 tax on cartons of cigarettes causes prices to increase to $3.50 per carton and quantity sold to fall from 1.0 to 0.9 million cartons. Tax revenue is shown by the pink area, while total revenue lost by the cigarette industry is shown by the gray shaded area.

Who Pays the Tax?

When we see the tax on our sales slips, it seems obvious that we consumers are paying it. From the standpoint of economics, however, the matter isn't that simple. The relative sacrifice made by consumers and producers is called the *incidence* of the tax. And tax incidence depends on elasticities of demand and supply.

The first thing that a tax does is to increase the price of the product. We can think of this as an upward shift in the supply curve, since the tax must be added to ordinary production costs to determine unit price. This is shown graphically in Figure 9, where S_t is the supply curve after a $.50 tax has been imposed. Given a relatively inelastic supply curve, the incidence of the tax will depend on elasticity of demand. In Figure 9a demand is relatively elastic: Consumers are able to substitute other products for the taxed item. Quantity purchased falls substantially (from Q to Q_t), and the equilibrium price only rises from $3 to $3.10. At this price, consumers are paying only $.10 more than they did before the tax—they are paying only $.10 of the tax. The remaining $.40 of the tax is the producers' contribution to the tax; producers now receive only $2.60 for the product, instead of the $3 they received before the tax.

When demand is relatively inelastic and supply elastic, as in Figure 9b, the opposite happens. Consumers continue to purchase roughly the same quantity, while selling price increases by almost the entire amount of the tax. The effect of relatively inelastic demand is to shift the greater part of the tax burden to the buyer. Forty cents of the $.50 tax is paid by the buyer and only $.10 by the seller, who keeps $2.90. You can visualize from the diagram the effect as demand becomes more or less elastic over the relevant range. When demand is more elastic than supply, the increase in price is less; consumers pay relatively less of the tax while producers pay more of it. When supply is more elastic than demand, price rises by almost the full amount of the tax; consumers pay more of the tax and suppliers less.

Suppose both demand and supply are highly elastic. Consumers and producers respond to the tax by reducing quantity significantly to avoid the tax. Price does not rise very much, production falls, and the tax is shared equally between buyers and sellers. With highly inelastic demand and supply, response to the tax is not as strong. Quantity falls only slightly, and price rises significantly. Again, buyers and sellers share the tax equally. Figure 10 illustrates these extreme market conditions. In general, the incidence of the tax depends on relative elasticity. Can you explain why?

Taxes and Disincentives

Taxes present difficult problems for governments. Tax revenues are needed to pay for public services, but the wrong taxes may discourage economic activity. There is a thin line between satisfying the needs of government and harming the economy.

Governments sometimes overlook the negative effects of taxes, with unhappy results. An example can be found in the recent history of New York City. In 1975 the city government levied a tax on its best known industry: the sale of stocks and bonds on Wall Street. A *transfer tax* of $.25 was imposed on each $1,000 sale of securities.

The transfer tax might have succeeded in

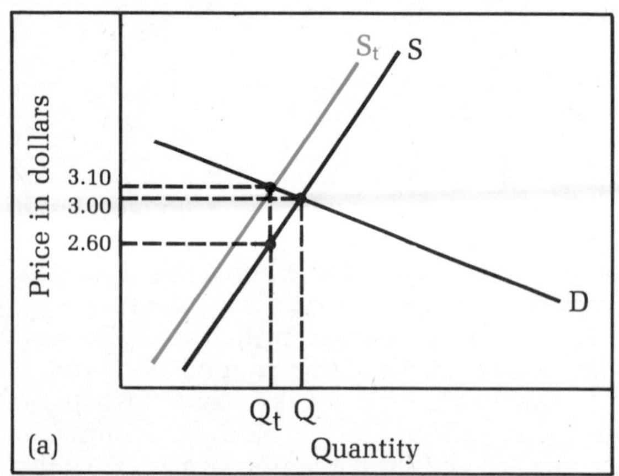

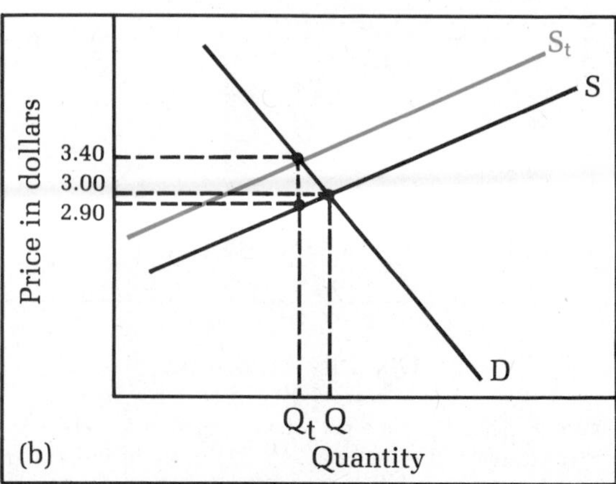

Figure 9 Tax incidence depends on elasticity of supply and demand. The effect of a $.50 tax is shown when: (a) demand is more elastic than supply; (b) supply is more elastic than demand. When demand is more elastic, producers pay more of the tax ($.40 of the $.50). When supply is more elastic, consumers pay more of the tax (also $.40 of the $.50).

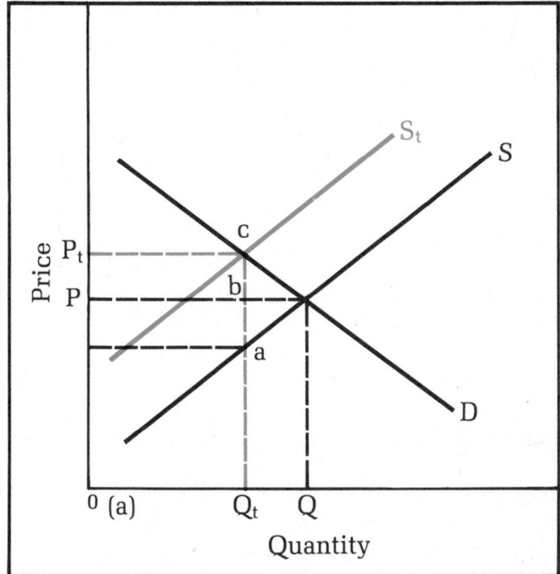

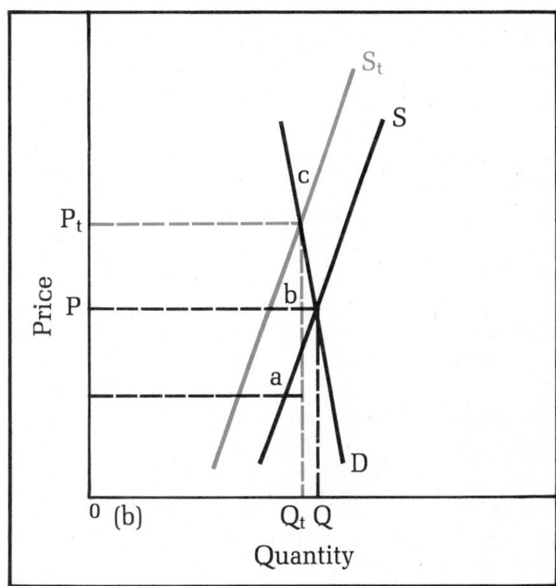

Figure 10 If supply and demand are equally elastic (a) or inelastic (b), a tax is shared equally between buyers and sellers. A tax of *ac* raises unit price from P to P_t. Buyers pay *bc* of the tax and sellers pay *ab*.

raising revenues if demand and supply had been inelastic. Unhappily for New York, securities buyers found they could trade just as easily in neighboring New Jersey, where there was no transfer tax. Securities dealers moved across the Hudson River and set up offices in New Jersey. What little was added to the city's revenues by the tax was more than offset by the flight of business from the city. The result was to aggravate the Big Apple's financial troubles.

The disincentive effect of taxes is particularly harmful in the case of ad valorem taxes such as sales taxes, excise taxes, and property taxes. Consumers will, if possible, make their purchases elsewhere. When Cook County, Illinois (which includes Chicago and many suburbs) imposed a tax on liquor sales, this was a bonanza for stores just across the county line; many people living in Chicago's suburbs transferred their liquor purchases to escape the tax.

Property taxes may produce especially harmful disincentives. Because property taxes increase with the value of the property, landlords may neglect to improve their buildings, thus encouraging the spread of slums.

Sometimes a tax is imposed with the *intention* of creating a disincentive. An example is the tax some states levy on styrofoam drinking cups. Styrofoam is not biodegradable; unlike paper it does not break down when exposed to weather. Styrofoam cups litter roadsides and recreation areas and must be removed at public expense. Imposing a tax on these cups raises their price to consumers. Because paper substitutes are readily available, many consumers will switch to these other containers. Those who continue to use the styrofoam cups pay the tax which helps pay the cost of cleaning up.

Subsidies

A **subsidy** is a payment by government to producers of some commodity to encourage them to produce more of it. In effect, it is a *reverse tax.* Whereas a tax increases the selling price of the good, a subsidy decreases price, allowing producers to sell more units. A subsidy may be a *specific* payment to the producer for each unit sold or an *ad valorem* payment based on the value of the good or service.

Payment of a **specific subsidy,** one of fixed amount, to a producer shifts the supply curve down by the amount of the subsidy at every quantity. An **ad valorem subsidy,** one of a percentage of value, shifts the supply curve down by larger amounts at larger volumes and thus makes supply more elastic.

Extended Example Taxes on Imports: The Case of Oil

In 1973, oil-producing nations stopped their shipments of oil to the United States and other industrialized countries and then resumed sales at much higher prices. In response, the U.S. government imposed a $1 tax on each barrel of imported oil. It was hoped that the higher price would discourage consumption and encourage production of domestic oil. This would make the United States less dependent on imported oil and less subject to the demands of foreign producers. What actually happened?

Consumer demand for oil was relatively inelastic in the short run. Americans were accustomed to having lots of gasoline available, to wearing synthetic clothing made from petrochemicals, and to using oil-based fertilizers in agriculture. There was no time to develop substitute goods or to find substitute raw materials.

The supply curve, on the other hand, was relatively elastic. The oil-producing countries had markets throughout the world; they were not limited to the U.S. market. For that matter, they could afford to leave their petroleum in the ground where its value would increase over time. Their small economies generally could not spend vast earnings all at once anyway.

We have already seen that when demand is less elastic than supply, the greater part of a tax will be shifted to the consumer. That was what happened in the case of the oil tax. The net effect was to channel heavy tax revenues to the federal government while substantial revenues continued to flow to oil producers. Consumers had less spendable income for other purchases. This had a contracting effect on other sectors of the economy, causing cutbacks in production and employment and contributing to the serious recession of 1973–75.

In 1979 oil producers raised prices again. Demand had become somewhat more elastic in the 1970s, as consumers learned to conserve and as some substitutes were developed. It had taken time for American consumers and suppliers to adjust. Auto manufacturers needed time to produce smaller, gas-efficient cars. (Actually, their response was slow enough to encourage an increase in Japanese gas-efficient imports.) Consumers needed time to wear out their gas-guzzlers. Although the tax revenues declined, the tax had its intended effect. Some policymakers proposed even higher taxes to discourage consumption further and to continue to provide revenues for energy research and development.

State and local governments often arrange subsidies to attract business firms so as to create jobs and to increase tax revenues. Subsidies sometimes take the form of property tax reductions, cheaper land, or low-interest loans.

Remember that taxes affect production more when demand and supply are elastic. Subsidies also affect production more when demand and supply are elastic. This is because quantities produced and sold will be more responsive to a change in price. If supply is elastic, quantity produced will increase substantially in response to a subsidy. If demand is elastic, consumers will buy larger quantities when price is reduced by a subsidy.

An industry may be subsidized because it is considered vital to the nation's security. For many years, United States agriculture was subsidized by means of price supports. Transportation is often subsidized, as the U.S. airlines used to be and as the airlines of other countries continue to be. Many foreign airlines are owned outright by their governments and operate consistently at a loss. This raises problems for competing U.S. airlines that must set prices to cover their costs without a subsidy.

Some countries subsidize their export industries. Without a subsidy these industries might not be able to compete in world markets against established industries in other countries. A subsidy enables firms in a developing country to meet world prices and earn foreign currency to pay for needed imports of food and machinery.

Like taxes, subsidies may have harmful effects on incentives. A subsidy makes life easier for the firms receiving it, but subsidized firms may grow dependent on government revenues and allow productivity to slip. Subsidies may also encourage too many firms to enter an industry, thus attracting resources that could be used more efficiently elsewhere.

WHEN GOVERNMENT SETS PRICES

The price system, as we have seen, is a useful means for guiding production. Changes in prices signal changes in consumer demand. Rising prices indicate that more is demanded, leading producers to expand output. Falling prices lead them to cut back. Market forces help direct productive resources to satisfy changing consumer tastes.

Sometimes governments interfere with the adjustment process and fix prices. In time of war, when resources are needed for war production, it is necessary to reduce production of consumer goods. To prevent prices from rising, government may set maximum prices *(price ceilings)* on scarce goods so that consumers will not bid up prices.

At other times, for other reasons, governments may set minimum prices *(price floors).* Both kinds of price controls have far-reaching economic consequences.

Price Ceilings and Shortages

Maximum prices set by government are called **price ceilings.** Because a price ceiling is almost always set below the equilibrium price, it places a lid on the price of a good. Price ceilings are necessary when the equilibrium price would be undesirably high.

During World War II, gasoline supplies were needed for the U.S. war effort. Fuel was needed for planes, ships, and tanks, with little remaining for civilian drivers. At the same time, rising incomes earned in war production had put greater purchasing power in the hands of consumers. Inflation was a real threat.

Figure 11 shows what might have happened if market forces had been allowed to work. The supply curve is vertical to show that the amount of gasoline available for civilian use was fixed. In the absence of price controls, equilibrium would have been at the intersection of the supply and demand curves, with price P_e. The ceiling imposed by government held price at only P_c. At this price demand for gasoline was *Ob*, a greater amount than the actual supply *Oa*. There was a *shortage* equal to *ab*. People didn't have to pay as much for gasoline as they would have if there were no price ceiling, but some weren't able to buy gas.

Price ceilings normally create shortages which must be corrected through **rationing:** allotting scarce items among buyers, generally on the basis of need. During the war, the U.S. government set up rationing boards to help distribute scarce items equitably among consumers. The boards issued coupons for use when buying rationed commodities. Every household received coupons according to the number of persons and their occupational needs. Doctors, for example, received more gasoline coupons than most other people. Large families received more coupons for sugar, meat, and shoes than smaller families. No purchase of a scarce item could be made without the proper coupon.

Another form of rationing is simply to let people stand in line. The British call this "queueing." Those first in line have first chance at whatever there is: first come, first served. In wartime many British people often stood in line throughout the night for the chance to buy sugar or meat, just as today people stand in line for World Series tickets.

In some countries you can still find people standing in queues to buy consumer goods that are in short supply. The command economies of the Soviet Union and most of the Eastern European countries have fixed ceiling prices for food and other commodities. Sometimes these consumer goods run short, with the result that lines form outside shops before daylight. Can you give a recent example of rationing by "queueing" in the United States?

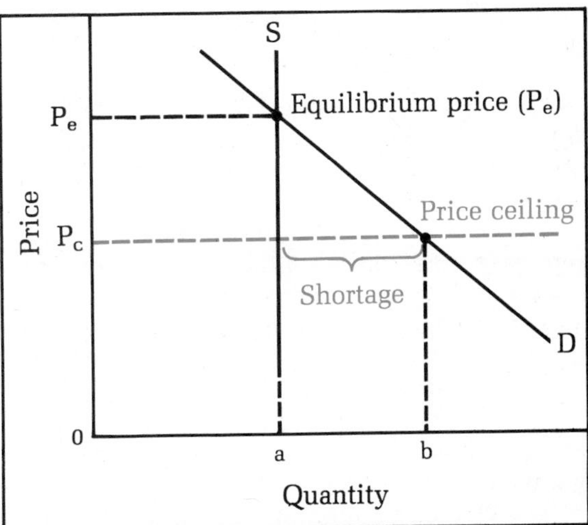

Figure 11 When a price ceiling is set below the equilibrium price, a shortage *ab* results. Often, the supply *Oa* will be rationed.

Viewpoint Rent Control

There are few public issues related to economics that are debated more hotly than price controls. Buyers vigorously defend ceilings on the prices they pay; sellers just as strongly demand price floors on the prices they receive. Many economists believe prices should be determined by market demand and supply alone.

Government must evaluate the total benefits and costs of nonmarket pricing and make the most efficient decision. Unfortunately, an efficient decision at one point in time may produce policy that lingers beyond the point when conditions require the policy. One single interference with the market may lead to reactions in the private sector that reduce the benefits and increase the costs of the nonmarket pricing. This leaves government with a more complex set of circumstances to evaluate. As time goes on, it becomes more difficult to measure precisely the gain or loss from any decision. Moreover, interest groups on both sides harden their positions, increasing the political problems with any government decision.

Rent controls are a prime example. During World War II, price ceilings were imposed on apartment rentals in New York City. Without controls, the high wartime demand for housing and the limited supply would have sent rates skyrocketing. The usual market response would have been for resources to move into the housing industry to take advantage of economic profits. But labor resources, raw materials, and power were critically needed for military production. Furthermore, higher rents would have pushed up living costs for workers, adding to their wage demands and aggravating inflation. Rent controls were supposed to be only a temporary measure to prevent these types of crises.

The temporary expedient has lasted forty years, and it has precipitated other crises not foreseen at the time. Rent control has protected middle-income residents from rent increases but only at a tremendous cost to landlords and mortgage lenders. Low rents have reduced funds for maintenance and capital improvements. Buildings have been allowed to deteriorate, and some have been abandoned. Low profits have discouraged new investment in the city. (What does this say about long-run supply curves for apartments?)

Although there has been some lessening of controls, to remove controls entirely is not a practical solution. If rents were allowed to rise to market levels, the higher living costs would drive more of New York's middle-income taxpayers to lower-cost housing outside the city limits. The loss of tax revenues would aggravate the city's already serious financial problems. (What does this say about long-run demand curves for apartments?)

Decontrol has gradually begun to affect rents. About a million and a half apartments are under control by New York State or City rent programs. Some rents have been allowed to increase by 7.5 percent a year, but most increases are permitted only when apart-

Another type of queue is the system of allotting scarce parking spaces at the curb in most U.S. towns and cities. The motorist drives around looking for a vacant space then parks and puts a few coins in a parking meter. Usually there is a one- or two-hour time limit, after which the driver is expected to move on and let someone else use the space. Some drivers try to circumvent this by simply putting more coins in the meter, but the time and trouble of returning every hour or two for this purpose discourages most of them. Parking space is rationed by inconvenience!

Scarcity and rationing sometimes encourage the growth of a *black market*. A **black market** is an illegal market in which goods are bought and sold outside normal channels of distribution at prices above the legal ceilings. Sellers in the black market manage to acquire items that are scarce and sell them at whatever the traffic will bear. During World War II, anyone willing to break the law could buy tires, gasoline, and quality cuts of beef on the black market. In the Soviet Union today the black market is so extensive as to constitute a complete counter-economy to the state-controlled economy. It is not confined to consumer goods but includes industrial raw materials, currency, personal services, and anything else that can be traded outside legitimate channels.

Price ceilings can be effective for short periods, holding down prices even when demand is

ments change hands. This means that apartments which have remained in the same hands for many years continue to rent at substantially below market rates. These apartments are generally in the more stable and more desirable neighborhoods, and their tenants are mostly middle-income families. Decontrol would bring abrupt rent increases in these areas. In addition, New York has a large population of elderly, many of whom live in inexpensive rent-controlled apartments. If rents rose suddenly, many elderly could not afford any housing. Rapid decontrol could lead to some difficult social problems.

All this brings to mind the statement once made by a prominent scientist: It is never possible to do *just* one thing. The scientist was referring to nature's ecological balance and the ripple effects any one action will have on every other life form in the system. But the statement is equally true about a market economy and government actions to control it. An action designed to accomplish one small result for a definite period of time will set in motion a whole series of reactions, some useful and some not so useful. Once the balance is destroyed, it becomes increasingly difficult to correct the situation. New York has been trying for forty years, and the end is not in sight.

Recently, Californians have been campaigning for rent controls, already in effect in some localities. What are the arguments for and against this policy?

great. This is particularly true in wartime when the public is willing to cooperate with government controls. But if price ceilings remain in effect over a long period, they may force prices to rise.

Since a price ceiling limits profits in the controlled market, firms are discouraged from investing in new productive facilities for expanding output. Instead, productive resources flow away from that industry to others where profits are greater. Output in the industry continues to decline as old equipment wears out in the remaining firms. Shortages worsen. Eventually, when price controls are removed, prices may rise more sharply than if there had been no controls.

Many economists believe that something like this actually happened in 1971–73. The federal government had clamped a lid on prices to hold back inflation. Shortages built up in some industries, and when controls were lifted there was a bulge in prices. That is why economists generally prefer to allow prices to be set in the market, except during periods of national emergency.

Price Floors and Surpluses

Sometimes governments try to prevent unusually low prices by setting minimum prices. A government-imposed minimum price is called a **price floor.** Price floors are used in sectors of the economy where incomes are considered too low, notably in agriculture.

Demand curves for agricultural products tend to be inelastic. This is because people consume a fairly stable quantity of food regardless of price. Supply curves are also inelastic in the very short run. Their position depends on growing conditions during each year. Since growing conditions change from year to year, supply curves may shift left and right as agricultural output changes. Inelastic demand and shifting supply make prices fluctuate widely from one year to another.

In the milk industry, price floors are used to stabilize prices and incomes for dairy farmers. Milk producers throughout the country are allowed to form associations or cooperatives to set prices. The object is to control supply and to keep prices from falling too low. Such agreements are illegal in most U.S. industries but milk-producing cooperatives are exempt from price-fixing laws. The result is illustrated in Figure 12. The demand curve is highly inelastic. Milk producers are willing to sell quantity *0b* at the cooperative's price floor, P_f. But at that price consumer demand for milk is less than the quantity supplied. There is a *surplus* of *ab,* the distance between demand and supply at the fixed price floor.

Free competition among milk producers would force price down to the equilibrium price, P_e. If price is to remain at P_f, some way must be found to sell the surplus at the fixed price. In the years when the federal government was supporting prices for a number of farm crops, the Department of Agriculture bought the surpluses and stored them. Now, milk cooperatives get rid

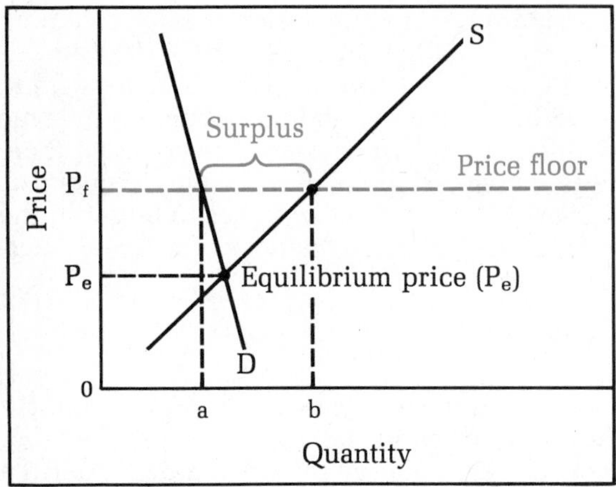

Figure 12 When a price floor is set above the equilibrium price, a surplus *ab* results.

of their large supply by selling "excess" at lower prices to manufacturers of milk products—cheese, condensed and powdered milk, butter, and ice cream. Manufacturers' demand for milk is more elastic than consumers; they will buy the remaining supply only if price is low enough. The cooperative maximizes its revenue by selling for a high price in the inelastic milk market and for a lower price in the elastic milk-products market.

In general, a price floor guarantees profits to firms in the industry concerned. But it has other, less desirable consequences. The artificially high price encourages existing firms to expand their production and encourages other resources to move into the industry. The result is growth in output with unusable surpluses. This is a misallocation of resources, since it doesn't reflect what consumers want.

Price Fixing and Elasticity

Success or failure of price ceilings and price floors may depend on elasticity. If both demand and supply are inelastic, roughly the same quantity will be sold regardless of the fixed price. With a price ceiling, the shortage will be small and black markets may not develop. With a price floor, surpluses will not grow as readily. The situation is different with relatively elastic demand. The wide gap between quantity demanded and quantity supplied at the fixed price makes black markets especially likely on the one hand, and surpluses, on the other.

We have seen that demand and supply tend to become more elastic with time. This suggests a possible course of efforts to fix prices. In the immediate period, when curves are inelastic, fixed prices may be effective. Over longer periods of time, however, the income and substitution effects will work to affect consumer demand at the fixed price. Low price ceilings will encourage demand, and high price floors will discourage it. On the supply side, expectations of continued fixed prices will tend to affect quantities offered for sale. In the long run, producers will alter their capacity for production. Worsening shortages and surpluses will increase pressures for removal of controls.

The responsiveness of buyers and sellers to fixed prices illustrates a fundamental characteristic of the U.S. economy. We rely primarily on free market decisions for establishing prices and quantities and for allocating resources. We expect government to intervene in free markets when it is absolutely necessary, but we won't tolerate prolonged intervention. Eventually, free market forces re-assert themselves (legally or illegally) until government intervention falls to a level that citizens willingly support.

AGRICULTURE AND SUPPLY ELASTICITY

We have already seen that supply is more responsive to price changes over a long period of time than it is at any particular moment. In agriculture, time plays a greater role in supply elasticity than it does in most other industries. The growing cycle for plants and animals makes supply highly inelastic over the time necessary for crops to reach maturity.

The supply of any farm commodity is the result of decisions made many months before the supply will be available to consumers and of changes in climate during the growing period. An unusually large harvest of eggs, strawberries, or calves' liver may cause prices to fall sharply. This is because demand is also inelastic and consumers will not stuff themselves with eggs simply because they are available, although they may purchase more after the price falls than they might have otherwise. These price changes may lead to new production decisions. Farmers will shift their resources to crops where they can get better prices. Over the long run, supply will become more elastic.

Extended Example Peanuts and Price Supports

Who would have thought that advances in scientific agriculture would virtually bury the United States in peanuts? In the last forty years new fertilizers, herbicides, and pesticides have increased peanut production in the Southeast from 700 pounds to 2500 pounds per acre. Under acreage allotment laws, farmers are allowed to plant 1.6 million acres, and that's a lot of goobers!

Twentieth-century technology has helped shift peanut supply curves to the right, often faster than demand has increased. The result has been falling market prices for peanuts and lower incomes for farmers. American consumers buy only about two thirds of our annual peanut output. Under farm price-support laws, the surplus is bought by the government at prices almost double the market equilibrium price. Surpluses acquired by government must either be sold on the world market at a loss or donated to domestic and foreign food-aid programs. The cost to American taxpayers is around $150 million each year.

The peanut problem has not escaped notice of the Department of Agriculture. Efforts are under way to increase consumer and industrial demand for peanuts. There is some natural growth in demand as population grows. Average consumption has normally been about 7½ pounds per person each year, but, unfortunately, weight-conscious Americans are becoming increasingly concerned about the high calorie content of peanuts and cutting back consumption. Also, the trend toward smaller families, with fewer peanut-butter-and-jelly sandwich eating children, is certain to reduce demand. Still, peanuts contain more protein, minerals, and vitamins per pound than beef; contain no cholesterol; and are a valuable, cheap food for poor people. In general, production of vegetable protein is more efficient than production of animal protein, since it requires one fewer step in the food chain. This makes peanuts an important source of nourishment in a world plagued by food shortages.

To attempt to stimulate the demand side of the market is more popular than to try to tamper with supply. It means cheap, healthful food for many low-income families. To correct supply problems would require massive cutbacks in production so that supply would come into equilibrium with demand at a market price acceptable to farmers. Before this could happen there would have to be an end to government price guarantees to farmers. If Congress repealed its price-support law, farmers would be forced to sell their surplus peanuts on world markets at market equilibrium prices. Many more farmers would go out of business entirely; others would cut back peanut production severely. Supply curves would shift to the left.

How would this affect American consumers? Shifts in supply would finally yield an uncontrolled market equilibrium price. At equilibrium, quantity supplied would be just sufficient to satisfy market demand. At the equilibrium price there would be no surpluses and no shortages. Furthermore, market price would be just high enough to cover all costs of production; otherwise farmers could not remain in the peanut business. Last and most importantly, the nation's scarce resources would be allocated toward producing the kinds of goods people want to buy.

How does this article illustrate the four important questions of the market system? How has government interfered with the market's answers to the four questions? Does the high fixed price serve a rationing function or an incentive function? Explain. What are the opportunity costs of peanut surpluses?

Throughout the twentieth century, U.S. agriculture has responded to price increases by massively increasing output. This response has been made possible by technological advances. Hybrid seed, new varieties of livestock, chemical fertilizers, pesticides, machinery, and scientific feeding processes have all helped farmers increase output enormously with very little increase in price. What has happened is summarized in Figure 13, where long-run supply has become infinitely elastic (as indicated by the horizontal supply curve).

This long-run elasticity of supply has been a great boon to the U.S. standard of living. It has enabled American families to live well while spending a much smaller proportion of their incomes on food than is the case in other countries. We enjoy a greater variety of food and more protein than most other people. We supply our food requirements and contribute heav-

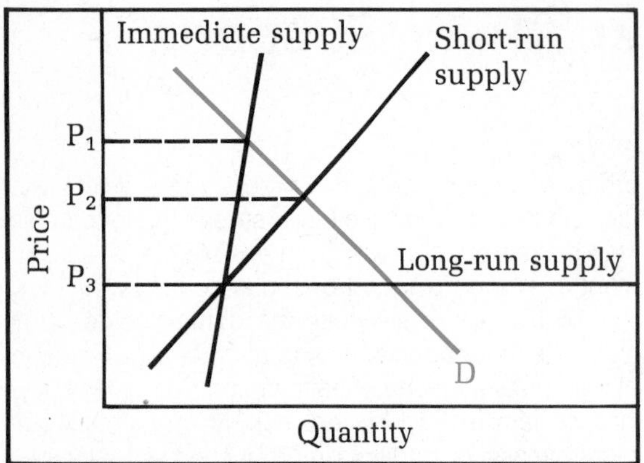

Figure 13 Elasticity of supply is shown for farm products for different time periods. Notice that in the long run, supply is infinitely elastic; larger quantities can be sold for the same low price P_3.

ily to supplying the rest of the world, while employing only about 5 percent of our labor force in farming. This allows us to devote most of our resources to the production of other goods and services.

While it is an advantage for consumers, the long-term elasticity of supply has been a serious disadvantage for many farmers. For them, relatively low farm prices have meant falling incomes. To make matters worse, the prices of manufactured goods essential to farming have risen. Farmers have often felt squeezed between the lower prices they receive and the higher prices they must pay. Many have been forced to leave farming altogether.

Moving people out of farming has been necessary for economic progress. Falling farm prices were a signal that supply was more than adequate to meet demand and that farm labor and capital could be put to better use elsewhere. But there have been strategic and economic reasons for government intervention to keep resources in agriculture.

Strategically, we recognize the importance in world affairs of a strong agricultural economy. Our farmers provide many poor nations with the means of survival. Our farm exports help earn foreign currencies to exchange for needed imports. Over the next century the ability to supply food may be a decisive factor in global strategy.

Economically, low food prices have helped keep down wage demands. Our low living costs relative to those in other countries have helped keep our costs of production lower. Thus our goods are more competitive in world markets, and our own standards of living are higher than they would be otherwise. Furthermore, to encourage farmers to leave agriculture might have dangerous consequences in years to come. Our abundant farm surpluses have provided a cushion against climatic disasters or other food crises. A severe drought or flood, an invasion of plant blight, a world war, or a collapse of world trade could bring starvation unless we encourage surplus production in good years.

For these and other reasons, the federal government has intervened over the years to prevent (or at least slow) the drift of people from farming. It has used tax revenues to supplement the incomes of farmers. It has provided extensive research services to improve farming methods. It has financed education and job training in rural communities. It has tried to encourage industry to move into rural areas where there is surplus farm labor. The "farm problem" has not been completely solved, as any working farmer will tell you. But much has been done to cushion the impact of economic forces upon the farmer.

SUMMARY

Supply curves show the quantities producers will supply at various prices over a certain period of time. Price elasticity of supply measures the percentage change in quantity supplied relative to the percentage change in price.

There are three factors that affect elasticity of supply. (1) The length of time determines the responsiveness of supply. In the immediate-time period supply is often highly inelastic; in the short run, supply is more elastic; and in the long run, supply may approach infinite elasticity. (2) Technology of production affects elasticity by limiting the substitutability or availability of resources needed for changing quantity of output. (3) Price expectations also affect the readiness to respond to price changes.

An efficient tax collects sufficient revenue without significantly altering production patterns. This result is achieved best by taxing the sale of goods and services with inelastic demand and supply. The less elastic is the demand for a good, the more revenue a tax will collect.

The incidence of a tax refers to the relative

Extended Example Trouble in Poland

In June 1976, the Polish government announced a drastic increase in food prices: Meat prices were to go up 69 percent, poultry 30 percent, butter 50 percent, and sugar 100 percent. The government soon found reason to change its mind.

The day after the announcement, violent demonstrations and strikes occurred in a number of Polish industrial centers. Workers destroyed railroad tracks outside of Warsaw, stopping the international express from Paris. In Radom, demonstrators set fire to the Communist party headquarters. Premier Piotr Jaroszewicz rushed to the television cameras and declared that the matter deserved further thought. The government had received a number of new proposals, he said, and several months would be needed "to reexamine the matter and work out a proper solution." Actually, the government postponed any decision.

The Communist government was understandably nervous. Twice before, in 1970 and 1956, top leaders had been given the ax when workers rioted over prices and living conditions. The trouble this time was not unique to Poland. It stemmed from inflation—the same illness that was afflicting the capitalist countries of the West.

Inflation was a problem not only in Poland, but in Hungary, Czechoslovakia, and other Eastern European countries. Ceiling prices in these centrally planned economies are fixed by the state, but ceilings on consumer prices did not prevent production costs from rising. Cost increases in Poland came from several sources. The prices of goods that Poland imported from Western countries had gone up in the previous two years, adding $7.4 billion to the import bill. At the same time, Poland's exports to Western markets had dropped by about $1 billion because of the worldwide recession of 1974–75.

What did this have to do with food prices? Poland, after all, is an agricultural country and doesn't have to import its food. The source of the problem was the way the centrally planned economy set its prices. Most of the food bought by workers in the cities was marketed through state purchasing agencies. Farmers in Poland sold their produce to the state, which then distributed it to city consumers at a fixed price. The state was taking a loss on this transaction. In short, it was subsidizing consumers by running large deficits, which had to be made up from other sources. The deficits had a tendency to grow because there was an upward drift in wages and industrial costs that were also being subsidized. Subsidies were paid from funds that might otherwise have been invested in factories and other productive facilities or in housing and schools.

The losses in foreign trade meant that the Polish government had to choose between cutting back its investment program or reducing its subsidies to consumers. Put simply, if economic growth was to continue, consumers would have to pay more for pork chops. Even a centrally planned economy cannot shelter its citizens indefinitely from economic forces.

In Poland the solution was postponed, but time would only make it more difficult. The Hungarian government went ahead and increased its meat prices, while in Czechoslovakia consumers were told they could expect a "restructuring" of wholesale prices at the end of the year.

What does this account suggest about the long-range results of government intervention in markets?

sacrifice borne by the buyer and the seller. If supply is less elastic than demand, the greater sacrifice is borne by the seller. If demand is less elastic than supply, the greater sacrifice is borne by the buyer. When both supply and demand are elastic, a tax can result in a disincentive to produce or to buy the item, and low tax revenues will result.

A subsidy is a reverse tax. A successful subsidy alters production patterns in certain intended ways. Subsidies work best when they are applied to production of goods and services with elastic demand and supply. Subsidies interfere with free competition by favoring particular industries or sectors.

Occasionally, government intervenes in markets to prevent price adjustments in the interests of particular groups. Government ceiling prices protect consumers from price inflation but generally lead to shortages and rationing. Government price floors protect farmers from falling incomes but often lead to surpluses.

Key Words and Phrases

ad valorem subsidy a subsidy based on the value of the good or service; a percentage subsidy.
ad valorem tax a tax which is based on the value of the good; a percentage tax.
black market illegal trading in scarce or rationed goods at prices higher than the fixed price ceiling.
immediate time period a short time period during which supply is relatively inelastic because it cannot be quickly increased.
infinitely elastic a condition where infinite changes in quantity supplied can take place with no change in price.
long run a long time period when supply may approach infinite elasticity because resources can be expanded to accommodate ever increasing output.
perfectly inelastic a condition where no change in supply is possible regardless of the change in price.
price ceiling a maximum price for a good set by government.
price floor a minimum price for a good fixed by government.
rationing allotting an item in scarce supply among buyers; often accomplished through assigning coupons by need or through queueing (first come, first served).
short run a time period during which output can be increased to some maximum limit of resource capability.
specific subsidy a subsidy of a fixed amount.
specific tax a tax of a fixed amount per unit purchased.
subsidy a payment from government to encourage a particular type of production.
supply elasticity the percentage change in quantity supplied of a good relative to a percentage change in price.

Questions for Review

1. Show how changes in the time period covered by a supply curve cause changes in the shape of the curve. Explain the process by which price changes serve as incentives to adjust output.
2. Use the hypothetical data below to calculate price elasticity of supply for firms A and B. Will the curves cut the horizontal or vertical axis?

Firm A		Firm B	
Price	Quantity	Price	Quantity
100	45	100	35
80	35	80	30
60	25	60	25
40	15	40	20
20	5	20	15

How would you characterize the two firms on the basis of the three important determinants of supply elasticity?
3. Describe the conditions which would give rise to market disequilibrium. Are there current examples of industries in which government has intervened to prevent equilibrium? What have been the results?
4. Demonstrate the effect of subsidies on supply curves. Explain why subsidies are most effective when supply is elastic.
5. Why are taxes more effective when demand is inelastic?
6. What are the economic benefits of smooth adjustments of supply over the long run? Cite specific industries in which supply has been slow to adjust and discuss the problems this creates for the economy.
7. Define: rationing, black market.
8. What are the purposes of a subsidy?
9. How can a tax "kill the goose that lays the golden eggs"?
10. Various government policies were proposed in 1977 to deal with the nation's growing energy problems. Evaluate each of the following, showing how the policy would affect supply curves in particular markets: (a) a tax on heavy, gas-guzzling automobiles; (b) a subsidy on home-insulating devices; (c) relaxation of environmental regulations in the coal industry.

Appendix

Problems in Agriculture

Agriculture in the United States is subject to an interesting paradox: We have the finest resources and technology in all the world for advanced agricultural production, yet many of our farmers suffer greater economic uncertainty than workers in many other industries. The reasons for the paradox are easy to see. We will discuss three important reasons in turn.

(1) *High productivity and low income elasticity cause farm incomes to fall.*

Productivity of farm workers has increased faster than productivity in the economy as a whole. At the beginning of this century, one American farmer produced enough food and fiber to supply eight people; today a farmer can supply more than thirty-five people. Americans are not consuming substantially more farm products, however. While our real disposable income has doubled, per capita consumption of food and fiber products has increased by only 17 percent. This is because our "income elasticity" of demand for farm products is low—less than 0.2 percent according to most studies: If income in the economy increases by 10 percent, food purchases will increase by only 2 percent.

Figure A.1 illustrates the effect of high productivity and low income elasticity over the long run. Increasing productivity on the farm has reduced costs, shifting marginal cost curves downward to the right. As a result, market supply of farm products has moved rightward fairly steadily, as shown by the movement of supply from S_1 to S_2. Demand has shifted to the right, too, but increased demand has come primarily from population growth. In Figure A.1 the long-run shift in demand from D_1 to D_2 is less than the shift in supply. As individuals we are not consuming substantially more food than at the turn of the century. The result of larger shifts in supply than in demand has been falling relative prices for farm commodities and lower incomes for many farmers.

(2) *Low price elasticity causes unstable prices and increases the uncertainties of farming.*

Apart from generally declining incomes, farmers have had to face another problem—that of price instability. Prices of farm commodities tend to fluctuate widely from year to year, adding to the uncertainty of farm enterprise. Price instability is a result of the relative price inelasticity of demand and supply in farm markets.

Figure A.2 illustrates the problem of price inelasticity. The demand curve in Figure A.2 has been drawn steeply to show that consumer response to price change is low: Some quantity of farm commodities is necessary for life regardless of high prices, but consumption will not increase substantially if prices are low. The sup-

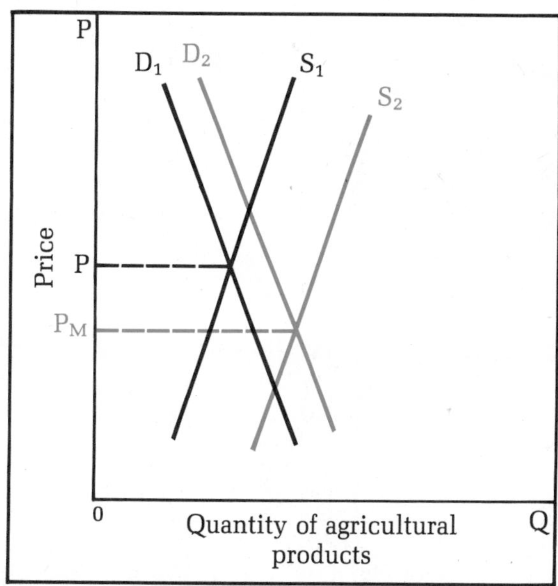

Figure A.1 Long-run shifts in supply and demand. Since early in this century, supply of agricultural products has increased faster than demand. Price falls from P to P_M, and farm incomes drop.

ply curve has been drawn steeply to show that producer response to price is also low in the short run: Regardless of price, many farm commodities must be taken to market before they spoil.

Supply is price inelastic in the short run, but supply is subject to extreme shifts from season to season. Favorable growing weather, crop disease, or early frost can cause abrupt changes in the available quantities of farm commodities. Note the effect of shifts in supply in Figure A.2. Suppose there are favorable growing conditions. This leads to an increase in farm commodities, which causes a substantial drop in price. Because of price inelasticity, however, consumption does not increase very much, and farm incomes drop from ($P_1 \times Q_1$) to ($P_2 \times Q_2$). Let's suppose the next year there are unfavorable growing conditions. This leads to a decrease in farm commodities, which causes a substantial price increase. Again because of price inelasticity of demand, consumption does not fall very much, and farm incomes increase from ($P_2 \times Q_2$) to ($P_3 \times Q_3$). Uncertainty about prices and incomes makes it difficult for farmers to plan future production.

Shifts in demand are another source of price instability. During the early 1970s, crop failures around the world caused a substantial increase in foreign demand for American grain. Moreover, the decline in the dollar made U.S. products a bargain in world markets, and increased purchasing power among the oil-producing nations allowed them to increase food purchases from the United States. All these factors contributed to a rightward shift in the demand curve for farm commodities, as shown on Figure A.3, and a tendency for market prices to rise. Even so, because supply is price inelastic in the short run, quantities brought to the market remained fairly constant. The result was substantial price increases, aggravating inflation in the United States.

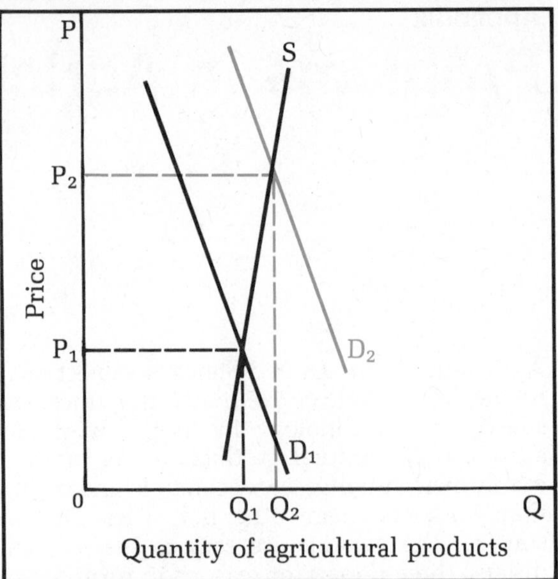

Figure A.3 Short-run shifts in demand. When supply is price-inelastic, season-to-season shifts in demand cause wide price fluctuations.

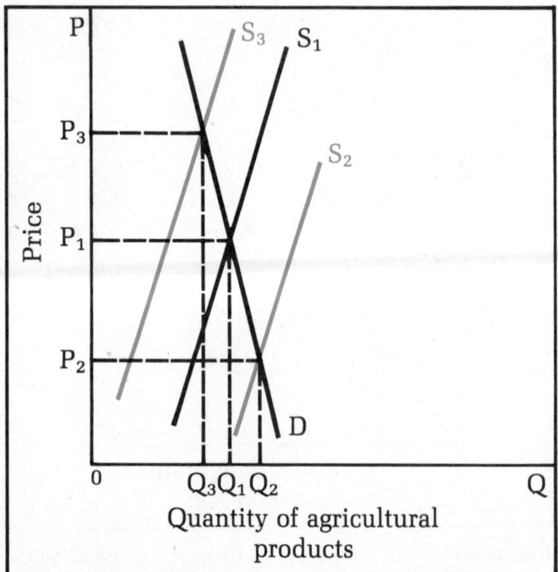

Figure A.2 Short-run shifts in supply. When demand is price-inelastic, season-to-season shifts in supply cause wide price fluctuations.

(3) *Changing technology has changed the character of farming.*

The kinds of resources used for farming have changed also. Machines have replaced labor, and chemical fertilizers and pesticides have made some farms more productive. Larger farms are providing larger fractions of total output. Most are family-operated businesses using the labor of the farmer working all year and an additional hired laborer for about half a year. Larger farms require greater amounts of financial capital, such that many farmers have gone heavily into debt.

Many of the remaining small, inefficient farms lack capital equipment to compete with larger ones. Low productivity increases the problem of rural poverty. Some small farmers can supplement their incomes with jobs off the farm, but many are too old or lack the skills to do so. Government-sponsored educational programs, regional development projects, and prosperity in the nonfarm economy encourage some movement off the farm. During the 1960s about 100,000 small farms went out of business every year or were absorbed into larger, more efficient units. A decline in the farm population helps increase the incomes of those who remain in farming by reducing excess capacity in the agricultural sector.

POLICY TOWARD AGRICULTURE

Why is our interest in farmers so strong? We do not get excited over the problems of people who run dry-cleaning shops! Tailors and TV dealers occasionally have financial problems; yet there is no mass outcry for policy in their behalf. Certain characteristics of the agricultural sector seem to call for particular attention. Maintaining a dependable source of food is certainly a worthwhile objective of policy, and maintaining a healthy farm sector is essential for this objective. There is also a certain sentimental feeling for farming as a pleasant way of life. Many of us (or our parents) came from farms and a few still have fantasies about going back to farming. For all these reasons, voters have generally supported policies to help farmers.

Occasionally the goals of U.S. farm policy have conflicted with other goals. Policy to protect tobacco farmers while simultaneously conducting antismoking campaigns is one example. Policy to raise farm prices and farmers' incomes while attempting to slow inflation is another. We will find in agricultural economics—as in other areas of economics—tradeoffs between goals. Thus, it is necessary to balance off the gains from agricultural programs against the costs in terms of other goals.

Since the 1930s government policy toward agriculture has been guided by two major objectives, determined mainly by circumstances of the times. In the early years, there was excess capacity in agriculture, with chronic farm surpluses to push prices down and depress farm incomes. During those years the objective of policy was to increase farm incomes. More recently, excess capacity has disappeared and the agricultural sector has experienced occasional scarcities with widely fluctuating prices. The objective has changed to the goal of stabilizing farm prices. In the future, policy may change again to deal with the changing technology of farming.

1933–73: Dealing with Excess Capacity

Agriculture was hit hard by the Great Depression. Increasing production and falling demand pushed farm prices down. Lower incomes left many farm families in poverty and forced others out of farming—often into worse poverty in urban ghettos. Economic distress in agriculture quickly spread to other markets, as farmers cut back their purchases of farm equipment, automobiles, household furnishings, and other manufactured goods. The drop in farm incomes contributed to a multiple decrease in incomes in other sectors, worsening the Great Depression.

In 1938 Congress passed the Agricultural Adjustment Act (AAA) which still serves today as the basis for most legislation on farm policy. The AAA allowed government to enter agricultural markets, established the means for computing the price which farmers should receive, and gave the Secretary of Agriculture power to control farm output and to purchase surplus farm commodities.*

An important feature of the AAA was its provision for *parity prices*. Parity pricing was government's response to farmers' complaints that farm prices were not increasing as fast as other prices in the economy. Low farm prices relative to prices of manufactured goods meant lower standards of living on the farm relative to living standards in other sectors of the economy. *Parity* is a ratio of farm to nonfarm prices computed in some base period—originally the years 1910–14. For any subsequent year a similar ratio of farm to nonfarm prices is computed and compared with the base year ratio. If farm prices have retained their same ratio to nonfarm prices, parity is said to be 100 percent. Fifty percent parity means that farm prices are half their former value relative to nonfarm prices. The parity ratio was only 58 percent in 1932 but rose to 93 percent in 1937. Under the Agricultural Adjustment Act, government would purchase farm com-

*The AAA of 1938 was almost identical to a law passed in 1933, but the early law was declared unconstitutional. Because of the dust bowl conditions, a law passed in 1936 (mainly intended to conserve the soil, but with output-control features) was allowed to stand. So was a law passed in 1937 which set up farm marketing agreements. By 1938 the Supreme Court had been expanded to nine judges and most of the new justices had a more favorable view of government involvement in agriculture.

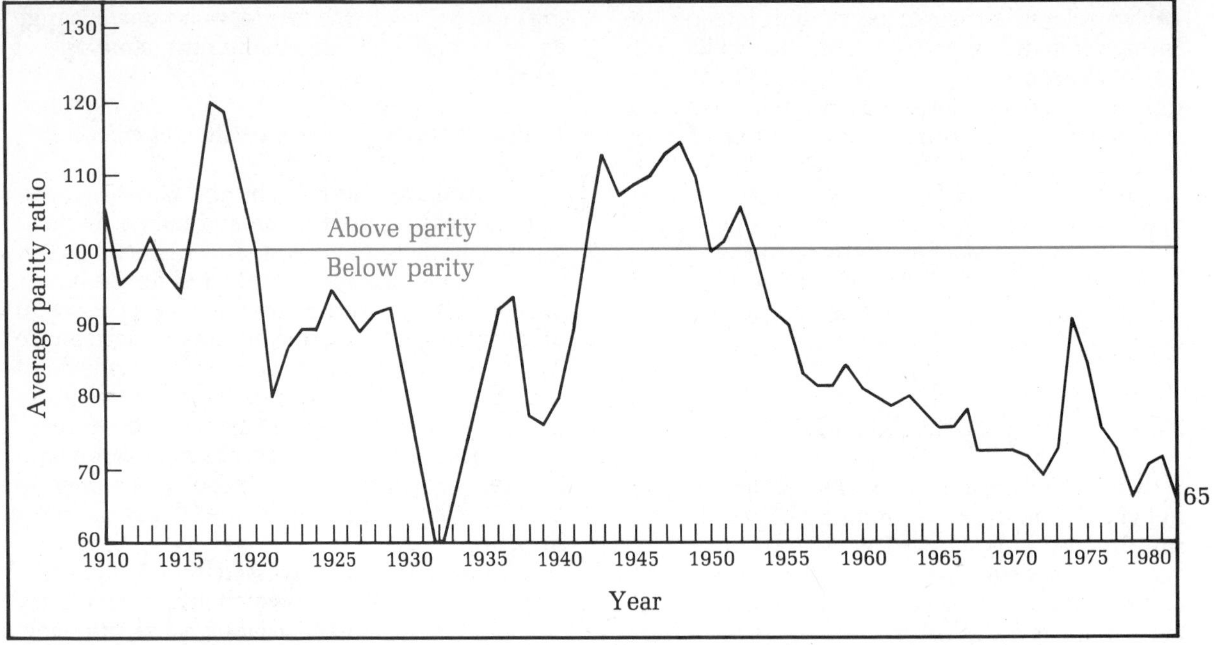

Figure A.4 Annual average for U.S. farm parity ratio (figures for 1979 and 1980 are estimates). The years 1910–14 equal 100. (Source: U.S. Department of Agriculture.)

modities in periods of excess supply so as to raise farm prices to some desired level of parity. Figure A.4 shows the behavior of the parity ratio since 1910.

The result of parity pricing was to place a floor under farm prices. In Figure A.5 price = P_m is the market price for farm commodities. If P_m is lower than the agreed-on level of parity, government may set a support price (P_s) consistent with parity goals. At price = P_s the quantity demanded in the market would be OQ_D and the quantity supplied would be OQ_S. The difference between quantity supplied and quantity demanded is the surplus, *ab*. If the support price is to be maintained, government must purchase and store the surplus or production will fall.

During the years of support prices, grain stocks built up so that in the late 1950s and early 1960s government-owned wheat stocks were equal to an entire year's consumption, and rice and feed grains were about one half of annual needs. Government owned almost $2 billion worth of cotton and enough dried milk to provide fifty pounds to every man, woman, and child in the United States. Because payments to farmers were based on quantity of output, they varied widely among small and large farmers. The result was greater income disparity, with some farmers receiving millions of dollars in government support payments.

Accumulating food stocks made other government programs necessary. Some government programs were aimed at increasing demand for agricultural products through research into new uses and through export promotion. U.S. farmers sold 400 million bushels of grain to Russia in 1972. Food for needy children, food stamps, and other domestic aid programs used $9 billion worth of food a year.

Another important government program was the *acreage allotment program,* limiting the amount of land farmers could plant. The objective was to reduce quantities of food and fiber crops brought to market. In fact, however, farmers removed from cultivation only their least productive land, cultivating the remaining land more intensively. Farm output continued to increase, filling up government bins and freezers. Many farmers complained that the existence of surplus products was keeping farm prices too low, because of the threat that all the surplus might be dumped on the market at any time. Meanwhile taxpayers were beginning to resist strongly any further programs to aid farmers.

Food and fiber stocks were depleted during the late 1960s, but there were no fears of shortage. It was felt that excess resources were still available for substantially increasing farm output, should a national or international emergency arise. In the 1970s, conditions began to change, and faith in the abundance of American agriculture began to fade.

1973–80: Dealing with Price Instability

The early 1970s may have been a watershed in U.S. agricultural history. Poor harvests worldwide eventually depleted U.S. food stocks, and the threat of famine emerged in many less developed countries. Growth in productivity slowed. Acreage removed from cultivation in the 1960s was returned to use, but much was found to be unproductive. The era of excess agricultural resources appeared to be over. Low farm incomes became less a problem than instability of agricultural prices. The object of recent farm policy has been to modify wide swings in supply and the accompanying price fluctuations.

New farm legislation passed in 1973 had two objectives: to reduce government involvement in agricultural markets and to stabilize farm prices. The Agriculture and Consumer Protection Act set target prices for wheat, feed grains, and cotton at roughly the level of production costs. Under the new law, if market prices are above target prices, crops will be sold

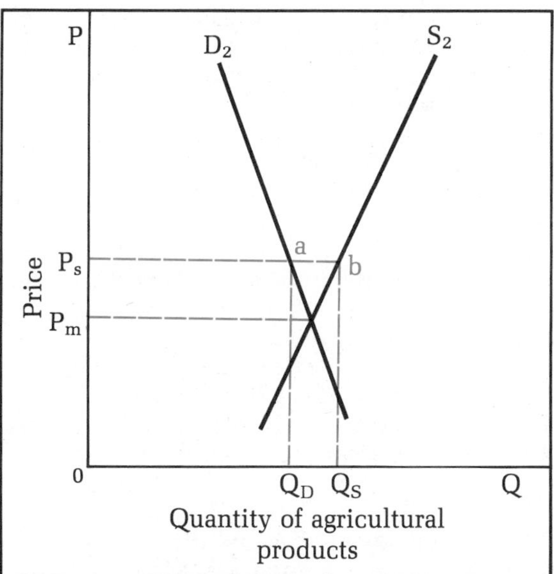

Figure A.5 When the support price is higher than equilibrium, there is a surplus which must be bought by government.

in free markets, and government will not intervene in agriculture. If market prices fall below target prices, crops will be sold at the low prices, and government will make "deficiency payments" directly to farmers. No farmer is to receive more than $20,000 annually. Only if prices fall to very low levels does government actually purchase farm commodities. This program was continued in the Farm Act of 1977.

The current program has some advantages. Production plans can be made on the basis of actual supply and demand in private markets. In general, consumers pay lower prices, since government is no longer supporting prices artificially. Smaller payments to farmers discourage excess production and may have caused some farmers to move out of agriculture into sectors where their resources are in greater demand.

There have been disadvantages, too. The absence of agricultural stockpiles has made consumers more vulnerable to abrupt changes in farm output. Poor harvests abroad in any year can put pressure on U.S. supplies and cause prices to rise sharply. Since food prices constitute a goodly portion of the average consumer's budget, rising food prices can aggravate U.S. inflation. All of this makes it especially necessary for farmers to have complete information on worldwide agricultural conditions or to engage in long-term sales contracts to stabilize supply.

The new Farm Act of 1977 included a program for accumulating privately owned grain reserves. Reserves would act as a buffer against either rising or falling prices. In surplus years, crops could be bought for adding to reserves. Later, in years of shortage, sales could be made from reserves. In both cases the effect would be to stabilize prices.

1977 was the worst year for farmers since the Great Depression. Three years of full production and bumper crops had pushed farm prices down 4 percent while other prices were rising by 14 percent. The parity ratio fell to 67 percent. Low farm prices and high fuel, fertilizer, and equipment costs, as well as high loan payments, pushed many farmers to the brink of bankruptcy. Farmers called a strike, and the American Agricultural Movement was organized to press for new farm policies. In 1978 farmers drove their tractors to the capitol mall in Washington, and in March 1980, Maine farmers dumped great piles of potatoes on the roads to keep Canadian potatoes from reaching U.S. markets.

AGRICULTURE IN THE 1980s

Many of our most cherished beliefs about agriculture may be challenged in this decade. Regard for farming as the good way of life and concern about small family farms may not be reasonable attitudes any longer. Farming has become big business. Less than 4 percent of the work force is engaged in farming; today about 160,000 farms, or only 6 percent of the total, produce more than half of all food grown in the United States. More than half of all grain-fed beef and lamb comes from fewer than 1000 farms. Most of our fruit, nuts, and vegetables are produced by a very small number of farms.

The remaining two thirds of the nation's farms produce less than $20,000 of gross sales annually. Half of the small farms are in the South, a remnant of the old policy of "40 acres and a mule" for freed slaves. For many of these small farms, the major portion of income is from nonfarm sources. If there is a problem of small farmers, it is less a farm problem than a regional development problem.

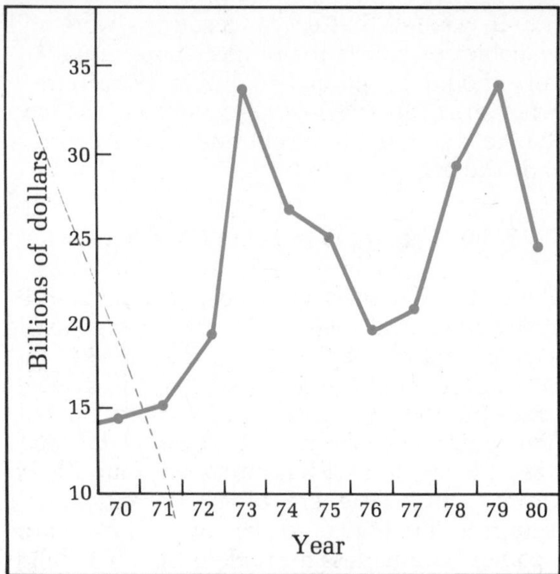

Figure A.6 Net farm income has fluctuated widely in the past decade. Income figures for 1979 and 1980 are estimates. (Source: U.S. Department of Agriculture.)

From 1940 to the latest available data, assets invested in farming have increased twelvefold. Still, growth in farm assets has been only 1/4 to 1/3 as fast as growth elsewhere in the economy. Farm debt has grown, too, but more slowly than farm assets. On the average, the debt-asset ratio of all farmers is about 15 percent, only half of what the debt-asset ratio is for other sectors. Most of the debt is owed by large farms with income and wealth enough to service the debt easily.

Even so, farmers are severely harmed by government policies to fight inflation. In early 1980, restrictions on short-term credit hurt many farmers who needed credit for purchasing seed, fertilizer, fuel, and pesticides for spring planting. Without credit, some farmers could not put in crops. Without crops, there was no income. And without income, some farmers were forced to sell their farms. Since farm costs were way up in 1980 and many agricultural prices were down, farmers who remained took another beating; 1980 was also not a good year for farmers (see Figure A.6).

Some things are clearly better in current agriculture. There is much less excess capacity, and the migration of labor from farms has slowed. Many farm families now have nonfarm income sources. Farm exports have increased significantly. Thirty percent of U.S. farmland provides products for the rest of the world, and twenty percent of farm sales are exports. Two thirds of the annual wheat and rice crops are exported, half of the soybeans, one third of the cotton, and one fourth of the tobacco. The United States produces almost half the feed grains traded in world markets. Rising incomes in other countries and increasing demand for higher quality foods should continue to increase export demand, raising farm incomes and improving our trade balance.

The future of agricultural policy will be different than in the past. Policies to aid middle-size farms will continue, but many small and inefficient farms will be allowed to fail. Improved consistency in farm policy should remove some of the uncertainties in agriculture. Environmental regulations which reduce productivity will be reevaluated and, where practical, liberalized. International trade will be encouraged. While this will mean more competition from imports, it will also mean more markets and higher demand for farm products.

What are the advantages and disadvantages of free trade in farm commodities? How might the economic interests of grain farmers differ from those of livestock producers? Small family farmers from large agribusiness corporations?

PART 3

Costs of Production and Product Markets

8 Perfect Competition: Costs and Production Decisions in the Short Run

9 Perfect Competition: Costs and Production Decisions in the Long Run

10 Monopoly

11 Imperfect Competition: Monopolistic Competition and Oligopoly

12 Market Power and Public Policy

CHAPTER 8

Perfect Competition: Costs and Production Decisions in the Short Run

Learning Objectives

Upon completion of this chapter, you should be able to:

1. Discuss the business hierarchy and state the advantages and disadvantages of the three different forms of business organization.
2. Explain the four basic conditions of perfect competition.
3. State the differences between (a) accounting costs and economic costs and (b) normal profit and economic profit.
4. Explain the principle of diminishing marginal product.
5. Discuss short-run costs, both fixed and variable.
6. Explain the relationships between MC and MR, including the rule of profit maximization.
7. State the conditions of equilibrium in the short run for perfect competition.

In the preceding chapters we examined consumer demand: the factors which influence demand and how changes in these factors affect market equilibrium. Then, we applied similar reasoning to supply curves. Supply curves reflect the willingness and ability of producers to respond to consumer demand. In this chapter and those that follow we will look more closely at the conditions which determine supply. We will be concerned first with how business organizes for production and arranges finances for business operation. Then we will discuss the behavior of costs at various levels of production. We will show how producers decide on a quantity of output and price under various types of market conditions.

Throughout the discussion, we will want to ask the questions: What does this mean for me? How does this situation affect my well-being? How does it strengthen or weaken our economic system? Sometimes, clear answers will be possible. But occasionally we will find even the experts in disagreement. Often the basis for disagreement is not the conclusions that result from economic analysis but the appropriate goals of our economic system itself. The experts may agree on whether one situation means higher costs but not on whether the higher costs may also yield other unmeasurable benefits.

BUSINESSES

The Business Hierarchy

Plants. The job of producing goods and services is carried out by business organizations in factories, or *plants*. A **plant** is a compact organization that produces a good or service over a range of output. A plant need not be a big building with tall chimneys. It is any single productive facility where goods or services are produced. It may be as small as a doctor's office, or it may consist of many buildings scattered over hundreds of acres of land. A university campus is a plant. So is a place that assembles automobiles or grinds flour or manufactures shoes.

Firms. Plants are operated and maintained by firms. A **firm** is a complete business enterprise including administration and long-range planning, production, and sales. When people speak of a *business,* they usually mean a *firm.* A firm may operate many plants or only one plant. One example of a firm is Standard Oil of New Jersey, which operates many plants for pumping, refining, and distributing petroleum and petroleum products. Another quite different kind of firm is Cinderella Rockefella, in a Chicago suburb, which operates a nightclub for celebrities—and for people who like to watch celebrities.

Industries. All the firms producing a particular good or service constitute an **industry.** The petroleum industry includes seven very large firms (often called the Seven Sisters) and many small firms. The telephone communications industry includes one giant (American Telephone and Telegraph Company) and several small independent telephone companies (like Winter Park Telephone Company in Winter Park, Florida). The clothing industry and the food-service industry include many small and some medium-sized firms.

Industries may be defined broadly as the energy-producing industry, the clothing industry, the construction industry, etc. Or they may be defined more narrowly as the coal, shoe, or homebuilding industry.

Sectors. A sector is a group of industries with some similar characteristics. The manufacturing sector includes all industries engaged in manufacture. Other sectors are the mining sector, the agricultural sector, the service sector, and the capital goods sector. Often it is convenient to speak of the *public sector* and the *private sector* to distinguish activities operated primarily by the government from those operating for private consumption. (In addition, economists in macroeconomics like to speak of the household sector, the business sector, and the government sector.)

Business Organization

Business firms differ in form depending on how they are owned and organized. They may be organized in one of three ways: as *single proprietorships,* as *partnerships,* or as *corporations.* These three forms of business organization are recognized by the laws of the United States.

The single proprietorship. The simplest form of organization is the single proprietorship, owned by one person. The proprietor makes the major decisions. The day-to-day operation may be supervised by a hired manager, or—as is more common—the proprietor may manage the firm personally. The single proprietor usually functions in several capacities, providing not only entrepreneurial services but most of the firm's capital and land resources and often much of its labor as well. For this reason the proprietor's income usually includes returns for all of these functions: profit for entrepreneurship; interest for the use of financial capital; rent for the land; and wages for the labor (though it will probably not be broken down this way in the firm's records).

Single proprietorships constitute the largest number of United States firms. They are usually found in agriculture, the services, and retail trade where small operations require little capital investment and can be run by a single person. They are the Mom and Pop groceries, the little restaurants, the dentists (some of them), and the shoe repair shops. The single proprietorship offers a person the chance to "be my own boss," which is very appealing to anyone who is tired of working as a cog in a big machine.

But competition is very keen and many of these businesses fail. Furthermore, single proprietorships are subject to *unlimited liability.* The individual proprietor is responsible for settling the debts of the enterprise, even if this means selling his or her personal possessions. A further drawback to the single proprietorship is that it is difficult to raise financial capital for expansion. The limited assets and riskiness deter banks from loaning much.

The partnership. Sometimes two or more persons may establish a **partnership** in which they share in the ownership and cooperate in the management. The partnership arrangement enables them to raise more financial capital than they could separately. It may also be a way of combining skills, as when lawyers or doctors with different specialties set up partnerships. This is a common form of business organization in building construction, law, medicine, and financial services. The partnership contract specifies the obligations of each partner and also what happens if one of them dies or if the company goes out of business.

One drawback of the partnership is that each partner is legally responsible for all the debts of the business. In case of failure, the partners' personal assets, such as homes, automobiles, securities, and savings accounts, may be seized to satisfy the obligations of the firm.

The corporation. To avoid the problem of legal liability, most large business firms use the *corporation* as their form of organization. A **corporation** may be owned by hundreds, even millions, of individuals and institutions who purchase "shares" of stocks. If the corporation is profitable, stockholders may receive dividends. (Individuals may incorporate as a firm and do business.)

Corporations issue two basic kinds of stock: *common* and *preferred*. Holders of **preferred stock** are guaranteed a regular, fixed dividend, if any dividends are paid at all. Holders of **common stock** are paid dividends only after all other obligations (including preferred stock dividends) have been met, and the amount of their dividend usually depends on how well the company is doing. (Firms try to pay regular dividends, so in good years they may hold back funds in order to pay comparable amounts in bad years.) If the corporation is doing very well, the common stock dividends may be greater than the preferred stock dividends.

Since the holders of common stock are legally the owners of the business, they may be entitled to attend stockholders' meetings and vote for a **board of directors.** The board of directors is responsible for hiring managers to conduct the day-to-day business of the corporation. In theory, common stockholders have the final say on how the business is being run and can vote the directors out of office if the enterprise has not been profitable. In practice, they seldom take advantage of this right. Most stockholders are too far removed from the operation of the business to have any opinion about it; if they are dissatisfied, the simplest way out is to sell their stock. Holders of large amounts sometimes get together and try to take control of the board. But if the stock is widely held, it is difficult for an outside group to get a majority of the votes. So a characteristic of large corporations is that ownership and control are usually divorced. Stockholders own the firm while managers control the firm. On occasion their goals may conflict.

Corporate law establishes the principle of **limited liability**—that is, owners are liable for the debts of the corporation only to the extent of their stockholdings. If the company fails, the stockholder loses only the amount paid for the stock, and the firm's debts have to be paid in other ways (for example, by selling the company's property). In Britain and Canada the word *Limited* or *Ltd.* is added after the name of the firm to show that it is a corporate organization. In the United States we use the word *Incorporated* or *Inc.*

Another peculiar characteristic of the corporation is that, in the eyes of the law, it is a person. It can sue and be sued, and what happens to it in the courts has no bearing on the lives of its owners and managers—unless they themselves have done something illegal.

Corporations have other advantages over partnerships and single proprietorships. They are continuing operations, unaffected by the deaths of shareholders or changes in stock ownership. And they can more easily raise funds for capital expansion and for investment in new research and development. A corporation can raise funds from (1) its own sales revenues or (2) by borrowing from banks or the public. Partnerships and single proprietorships can also raise funds in those two ways. But the corporation has a third way: (3) It can issue more shares of stock.

Corporations seldom sell their stock directly to the public. Usually a stock issue will be underwritten by an *investment bank,** which isn't a bank at all but a company that specializes in marketing new stock issues. The investment bank agrees to take the stock at a certain price and then tries to sell it to the public at a profit. Among the chief buyers of new stock issues are insurance companies, mutual funds, retirement funds, and universities which have large sums to invest for the dividends they hope they will earn.

There is an active market for stocks, espe-

*Stock may be underwritten by a syndicate of several brokerage firms.

Viewpoint Corporate Behavior

The separation of ownership and control provides the strength of the corporate form—and, some say, its potential for harm. Separation allows complete division of labor: Stockholders contribute their financial capital when they buy common and preferred stock; managers contribute their special expertise. Because of limited liability, other assets of stockholders are protected from loss in the event of corporate collapse.

Still, the corporate form was slow getting started in the United States. One reason was the restrictions many states placed on the size and practices of corporations. With the growth of the railroad, steel, and petroleum industries in the late 1800s, firms sought to expand beyond state lines. New Jersey and Delaware led in chartering enterprises that were headquartered there but conducted operations in many states. Both states tried to outdo the other in the leniency of laws regulating corporate behavior. Eventually, New Jersey was earning so much from license fees charged to new corporations that it was able to eliminate all property taxes and pay off its entire state debt besides. Between 1913 and 1934 almost one third of state revenues in Delaware came from corporate fees. By 1974 nearly 76,000 corporations were chartered in tiny Delaware; this figure included more than half the nation's largest firms.

Other states have not passed up the opportunity to enrich state revenues through liberal corporation laws. The result has been a wide variety of practices with little consistent supervision of the growth of corporate powers. Corporate behavior came into the spotlight in the mid-1970s with the disclosure of widespread corporate bribery of foreign officials and "customers." The theory of shareholder control through corporate democracy has not worked out in practice. Boards of directors are generally composed of corporate executives and others sympathetic to the aims of management. Management's increasing independence from stockholders has produced, in the words of a former corporate board chairman, "a totalitarian system in industry, particularly in large industry."

Ralph Nader and the Corporate Accountability Research Group have proposed a remedy to limit corporate power. According to Nader, the solution lies in federal chartering of the nation's largest corporations. Each corporation would still be required to comply with state chartering rules, but it would be subject to additional federal requirements:

(1) Managers would have to practice corporate democracy by shifting more control to directors and stockholders. Corporate employees and citizens of neighboring communities would also be permitted to vote on certain corporate practices.

(2) Firms would be required to disclose practices that are potentially damaging to the environment.

(3) Consumers, workers, and shareholders would be able to use the courts to protect their rights against unresponsive corporate management.

(4) Finally, and perhaps most importantly, the nation's largest corporations would be prohibited from acquiring other firms to increase their market power.

Competition would be strengthened so that consumers might enjoy lower prices, greater product variety and more innovations. Federal antimonopoly laws would be strengthened by closer supervision of corporate practices. Some restraints on corporate growth might actually reverse current trends toward industrial concentration which, if continued, might lead to complete nationalization of some industries in the future.

Can you think of any arguments against federal licensing of corporations?

cially in years when business is good, because stocks are easy to sell when the holder needs cash. If you put your money into real estate or collections of art, you may not be able to get it out quickly. Stocks may also increase in value over a period of years, especially if the firm has been very profitable.

When you are able to sell the stock for more than you paid for it, you have made a **capital gain.** Holders of stock can sell through a broker who has a seat on one of the stock exchanges: the New York Stock Exchange, the American Stock Exchange, or a regional stock exchange in another large city.

PERFECT COMPETITION

Our market system is based upon the freedom of buyers and sellers to pursue their own interests. This fundamental principle was first stated by Adam Smith. Smith argued that a system of free markets would permit buyers and sellers to pursue their own interests and benefit not only themselves but all of society. In pursuing individual interests, he wrote, each person "is led by an invisible hand to promote an end which was no part of his intention." The kind of market structure Adam Smith described was essentially what modern economists call **perfect competition.**

Four Basic Conditions

Since nothing in this world is perfect, we should not expect to find many actual markets that conform precisely to the theory of perfect competition. But if markets were perfectly competitive, the following four conditions would have to be true.

(1) *There must be many small buyers and sellers in the market.* All buyers and sellers must function *economically:* They must rationally seek their own self-interest by weighing the costs and benefits of each alternative action. Buyers seek their own self-interest by demanding the maximum quantity of useful goods and services for every dollar spent. Sellers seek their own self-interest by producing goods and services at the lowest cost in terms of scarce resources. When many small buyers and sellers behave in this way, no single individual or group has power to influence the market: The actions of one are balanced by the actions of others; what happens in the market is not the decision of any one person.

Few markets have so many buyers and sellers as to be perfectly competitive. Markets for most products are generally too small for many buyers and sellers to operate. Farming probably comes closest to satisfying this condition, with some types of farming still carried on by many small operators selling to many small buyers. As long as there are many small buyers, no single buyer can force price down by refusing to buy. And with many small sellers, no single seller can force price up by refusing to sell at the market price.

(2) *Products for sale in the market must be homogeneous—that is, identical or undifferentiated.* The market for automobiles would not meet this condition, since nobody is likely to confuse a Ford with a Cadillac. The market for coffee wouldn't meet it either, since coffee producers try very hard to persuade consumers that Brand X is different from Brand Y. Products of every seller in an industry must be equally acceptable to buyers if the industry is to qualify as a perfectly competitive one. If a product is unique in any way, it may be able to attract buyers even when its price is higher than competing products. Its seller becomes the *single* supplier, thus breaking the first condition that there be many sellers. But if all firms are selling an identical product, no one firm has an advantage over the others.

In most markets, products are not identical. They differ in color, taste, design, or function. Some products may look alike and may even be chemically identical, but in some way they *appear* to the buyer as different. Advertising often creates the illusion of differences among products. Most shops and stores are unique in particular ways. One may provide services that competitors do not: delivery service, easy credit, or more friendly salespeople. Differences among products are inconsistent with perfect competition.

(3) *Buyers and sellers must have equally complete knowledge of market conditions.* Buyers must understand what products are available, how they are to be used, and what their prices are throughout the market. Complete information allows shoppers to buy the most wanted goods in markets where they are the most plentiful and are selling at the lowest prices. Sellers must also have complete information about prices and production costs throughout the market. This allows sellers to supply goods to markets where they are scarce and are selling at the highest prices and it allows them to use low-cost production techniques and low-cost resources. The market for corporate securities probably comes closest to the ideal of free access to information for all buyers and sellers.

Modern communications help speed the flow of information throughout an industry. But technology changes quickly, and those who have the newest methods may try to keep them secret from competitors. Sometimes the battle for control of information goes to great lengths. Companies install security precautions, such as identification badges, guards, and combination locks. Their competitors hire spies. One of the best-known kinds of espionage is carried on by large retail chains that employ comparison shoppers to go around and find out what their competitors are selling at what prices. Occasionally, a disloyal employee with access to vital information will sell it to other companies.

Patent laws are a way of protecting information. They protect an inventor from competition in the use of a new process or product for a period of time. Whenever information is concealed, condition (3) is not satisfied.

(4) *Buyers and sellers must be able to react quickly to news of market conditions.* Buyers must move to areas of abundance, where prices are low, while sellers must move to areas of scarcity, where prices are high. Production must be carried on in places where resources are plentiful and costs are low. Any obstacle to mobility raises costs of production above their lowest possible level. Since conditions are always changing, it is important that buyers and sellers be able to move as freely as possible in order to make the most of new possibilities.

In the short run, mobility is always limited. Restaurants cannot move quickly to new locations. Manufacturing firms cannot move quickly into production of new goods. Farmers cannot quickly become dentists. School buildings cannot become oil tankers. Workers' skills are fixed; they require retraining before a change of occupation.

The theory of perfect competition requires smooth, costless, and almost instant adjustment to changes in economic conditions. Resources must flow smoothly from one location, product, or occupation to another. The ultimate mobility would be the instant creation of firms to meet new demands and the instant disappearance of firms that are no longer needed. In reality, it takes time to create a new firm and to begin operations. It even takes time—years perhaps—to dissolve a firm, as we saw in the mid-1970s in the case of the W. T. Grant variety-store chain. There are always many legal claims to settle and much physical property to dispose of.

Putting the Conditions Together

We have seen that a perfectly competitive market must meet four conditions: (1) it must have many small buyers and sellers, (2) the product must be homogeneous, (3) buyers and sellers must have equally complete knowledge about market conditions, and (4) they must be completely mobile in the marketplace. Let's put these conditions together and see what they mean in terms of economic efficiency.

We have described a mechanism that will respond quickly to changes in demand. If the demand for leather bags increases, manufacturers will notice an increase in total revenue received. This will cause them to increase output in order to increase their incomes further. The news of this opportunity will spread quickly, and other manufacturers will start producing leather bags. Every firm will be under pressure to adopt new methods of production in order to produce still more bags at even lower cost. Competition will drive price down to the minimum for which bags can be produced. Manufacturers whose costs are higher will be forced out of the industry. Surviving firms must operate at their most efficient level of output, achieving the lowest unit costs of production.

Without even thinking about it, consumers will have voted to have the economy produce more leather bags and a little bit less of something else—shoes or vests or whatever else manufacturers could have produced. So far as this industry is concerned, consumers are getting maximum output at the lowest possible cost. Competition *forces* firms to operate efficiently and to produce the goods consumers want and are able and willing to pay for.

Demand Curves in Perfect Competition

The assumptions of perfect competition are unrealistic, especially in industries outside agriculture, but they give us a starting point from which to explore how things actually work. As we will see, perfect competition is a useful *model*.

Let's think for a moment about the demand curve in a perfectly competitive industry. Remember, from Chapter 3, our model of the market for ski weekends? We added all consumer demand curves to arrive at total demand in the market as a whole. Market demand for the industry was shown as a downward-sloping curve. This was because at lower prices there would be more customers for ski accommodations. Likewise, market supply for the entire industry was shown as an upward-sloping curve—because at higher prices more ski accommodations would be offered for sale.

Table 1 **Demand for and Supply of Ski Weekend Accommodations**

Price	Quantity demanded	Quantity supplied
$100	20,000	50,000
90	25,000	40,000
70	30,000	30,000
60	35,000	20,000
50	40,000	10,000

The model of the market for ski accommodations is shown again as Figure 1. Table 1 lists the data on which the curves are based. Equilibrium price is $70. That is the price at which demand for ski weekends is equal to supply. A total quantity of 30,000 ski weekends would be sold at that price.

Figure 1(a) shows the market demand curve. But this is not the demand curve facing an individual firm. When there are many firms in a perfectly competitive industry, the equilibrium price is the result of decisions of all buyers and sellers. This means that each individual firm is faced with a single price at which it can sell its output. Even though the demand curve for the industry is downward sloping, the demand curve for the individual firm is a horizontal line drawn at the level of the market equilibrium price. This is because in a perfectly competitive industry no individual firm is strong enough to affect market price.

A horizontal demand curve is drawn on Figure 1(b) at the equilibrium price of $70. This is the demand curve facing Wonderland resort. Figure 1(b) also shows Wonderland's individual supply curve drawn from data in Chapter 3. At the equilibrium price of $70 Wonderland must decide on a level of output. It has no choice as to price: If there is perfect competition, no single firm can set price higher than equilibrium. This is because there are (1) many other small sellers who are (2) selling identical products and have (3) perfect information and (4) ease of mobility into this market. Under these conditions Wonderland will decide to provide 475 units of accommodations, as shown in Figure 1(b). Refer to Figure 1(c) to determine the quantity supplied by Alpine resort.

We say that the individual firms in this situation are "price takers." Price is set by the interaction of decisions of many buyers and sellers, each too small to affect price. This is true only when there is perfect competition or a situation very close to it. In other market structures, we will see that price and output decisions are made differently.

MEASURING COSTS OF PRODUCTION

We have seen how an equilibrium price is determined in the market as a whole and how an individual firm decides on quantity to be supplied at that price. Now we will look at this decision in more detail. We will be concerned with the costs of producing output and the profit associated with the firm's production decision.

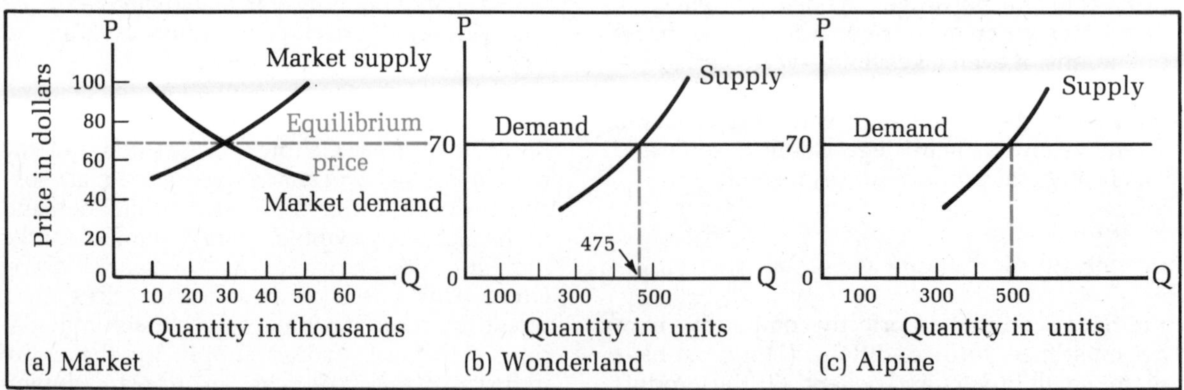

Figure 1 (a) Competitive market for ski accommodations; supply and demand determine the equilibrium of $70. (b) At $70, Wonderland resort supplies 475 accommodations. (c) At $70, Alpine resort supplies 500 accommodations.

Business firms are always thinking about costs and prices. If a firm is of sufficient size, there will be employees whose job it is to analyze the data on costs paid out and revenues taken in. On the basis of this information, management will evaluate the firm's performance.

There are two approaches to the task of measurement. One is that of the *accountant* and the other is that of the *economist*. The accountant is mainly concerned with seeing that the firm meets its financial obligations—that it pays its bills on time and maintains a good credit standing. The economist is more concerned with the way the firm uses its resources—that is, with its performance in terms of economic efficiency. Because accountants and economists measure costs in different ways, they often reach different conclusions about the health of the firm and the value of its operation.

Accounting Costs: The Bottom Line

A firm must meet its **accounting costs,** its financial obligations, if it is to remain in business. Accounting costs are the **explicit costs** of carrying on operations. Every month revenues must be accumulated and paid out to the resources used in production. Each resource must be paid the going rate for its employment.

Net income after taxes, or **profit,** is what is left after all explicit costs have been paid. This is the amount available for distribution to the owners of the business—to the sole proprietor if there is one, or the partners, or the owners of stock in the corporation. Eventually, the owners expect to receive at least some gain to compensate them for putting their savings into the company or for devoting their energies to the business. Otherwise it would pay them to use their resources in some other firm. The firm will usually not pay all its profits to the owners. It will retain a portion of earnings for future needs: as a reserve against a temporary decline in income or for future expansion.

A successful firm will show a large net income as its "bottom line," one that grows from year to year. If the amount gets smaller or is negative, the firm is in trouble. A negative figure for net income means that the firm's costs are greater than its income from sales. If the firm continues to lose money, certain changes will be necessary.

Economic Costs: Efficient Resource Allocation

When economists speak of costs, they are likely to be thinking of something more than the costs we have been discussing. Economists are concerned with full *opportunity costs.* **Opportunity costs** are the trade-offs we experience when resources are used in one type of employment instead of another. The costs are the sacrifice of other goods and services which could have been produced.

To economists, total costs include the total value of forgone production. This means that production decisions must be based on the opportunity cost of all resources, whether purchased from other resource owners or supplied by the business firm itself. The costs of resources owned by the firm are called **implicit costs;** although they may not actually be paid out, they still reflect the income a resource could be earning in another employment.

If a firm rents a piece of land for parking its trucks, its *explicit cost* is the rent paid. But even if the firm owns the land itself and no rent is actually paid, its *implicit cost* is still the full opportunity cost of the land—the amount the owner could get by renting the land as an amusement park or a vineyard. Similarly, if the firm borrows financial capital, it must pay lenders at least as much interest as they could earn on other investments of equal risk. But if the firm uses its own funds, it must also, in effect, *pay itself* for the use of its own financial capital. Interest on its own funds is an implicit cost of doing business.

These are the full opportunity costs of productive resources. Gross income from sales must be great enough to cover the opportunity costs of *all* resources used in production: the explicit costs paid to other resource owners and the implicit costs of using the firm's own resources in some way. If sales revenue fails to cover full costs, then it would be wiser to use the resources in another firm where income is greater.

The Costs of College, Strawberries, and Other Things

Have you considered the total costs of your college diploma? Probably you are aware of the explicit costs: tuition fees, the cost of books, and dormitory rents (to the extent that these payments exceed what you would pay outside college). But there are implicit costs, too. While you are busy attending classes you may be sacrificing opportunities to earn an income. If so, the full cost of your education includes the forgone income from that job you didn't take. (This may explain why golf pros, opera singers, and Hollywood stunt extras don't find it practical to pursue advanced college degrees.)

What are the total costs of strawberries grown in your neighbor's yard? They include the explicit cost of seed, fertilizer, and garden tools. But suppose your neighbor is a respected lawyer whose time is valued at $100 an hour. Each hour spent tending strawberries adds an implicit cost equal to the most productive use of your neighbor's own labor. Thus the full opportunity cost of those strawberries from the garden may be substantially higher than the supermarket price.

Many less developed countries face important decisions involving full opportunity costs. Often their resources are severely limited, and it is important to use them in the most productive way. The resources may seem cheap because their explicit costs are low. But to use those resources unproductively will mean large implicit costs. If land is used for parade grounds instead of for farms, the full opportunity cost will include the forgone agricultural production. If strong youths are made to walk around carrying guns, their labor power is lost to the manufacturing industry. If funds are used to build magnificent office buildings or sports stadiums, the country will be poorer by the number of power plants that might have been built instead. Each of these examples of patriotic display involves a heavy implicit cost which must be borne by the nation's people.

Defining Profit

Normal profit. An important implicit cost is the cost of using the firm's own entrepreneurial resources. Just as land, labor, and capital must be paid, respectively, rent, wages, and interest, the entrepreneur must be paid a return. For the entrepreneur, the necessary return is called **normal profit.** To economists, normal profit is the opportunity cost of entrepreneurship. Normal profit enables those who provide entrepreneurial ability to continue to use their resources in a particular way. It is considered a cost.

Along with other explicit and implicit costs, normal profit must be subtracted from revenues in order to evaluate the performance of the firm. Total revenue must be enough to cover all costs, including rent, wages, interest, and normal profit, if the firm is to remain in business. (Many economists would also consider dividends paid to stockholders a part of normal profit.)

Economic profit. If normal profit is treated as part of costs, what do we call the firm's earnings above total costs? We have another term for this: **economic profit.** Economic profit is a return to the entrepreneurial resource over and above the necessary normal profit. Later we will see that in perfect competition firms will not make economic profit in the long run. This is because competition from other firms will reduce market price to the point at which each firm covers its full opportunity costs (including normal profit but no economic profit).

In the short run, economic profit may result from abnormally high demand or from restrictions in supply. For instance, if a firm introduces a new product and captures the entire market, it may be able to set price well above total costs of production. It will earn large economic profits until other firms succeed in marketing a similar product at a lower price. Eventually, competition will drive price down; economic profit will decline and perhaps disappear. Something like this happened in the pocket calculator industry in the mid-1970s. The price of the first simple calculators was high, but prices fell as competing firms struggled for a share of the market. Then, more complex calculators were introduced at higher prices and another round of competition began.

Economic profit serves two important functions in the market system. (1) Economic profit is a reward for firms that develop new products and technical processes which reduce production costs. (2) Economic profit is an incentive for firms to move into expanding industries, aiding the growth and technical development of U.S. industry.

What if economic profit is negative? This happens when revenue from sales is not enough to pay all production costs, including normal profit. (1) Negative economic profit is the penalty for producers who make mistakes. It is their punishment for being wrong about the profitability of new products and methods. (2) Negative economic profit provides the incentive for firms to move out of unprofitable industries. Thus, it ensures that valuable resources will not be used for producing goods and services consumers do not want.

RESOURCES IN THE SHORT RUN

We have already distinguished two important time spans for making economic decisions: the short run and the long run (the immediate period leaves no time for making decisions). They differ because of the character of resources available to the firm. During the short run, a firm will have a certain stock of **fixed productive resources:** a plant with machinery, an office building, and salaried administrative personnel. These resources are fixed in the short run because plant and equipment cannot be expanded or cut back very quickly, and because a salaried staff is often hired on a contract basis.

Along with its fixed resources, the firm will employ **variable resources:** hourly paid production workers, electric power, raw materials, and component parts. These are called variable resources because their quantities can be adjusted fairly quickly, depending on the level of production required.

The length of the short run differs among firms. For some service firms, the short run may be only a few weeks; operations require only a small quantity of capital that can be readily increased. A city taxicab company, for example, can expand its operations rather quickly by buying more cabs and hiring additional office personnel. For a subway system the short run is much longer. It may take ten years to make the decisions, acquire the land, sign the contracts, and construct new subway lines. In the meantime, the subway's existing equipment can be operated more or less intensively by running trains more or less frequently, by hiring or laying off hourly workers, and by using varying amounts of electric power.

In some manufacturing industries the short run depends on the time it takes to hire and train skilled labor. Chemical engineers, aeronautical designers, and financial analysts must train for years before their skills are available to business. In small firms the most important limitation in the short run may be the time and ability of the individual entrepreneur. A person who runs a small business may not want to assume heavier burdens or may lack the training to adapt to new developments easily.

We generally think of the short run as the time period over which fixed resources cannot be *increased*. But the short run also involves decisions to *reduce* fixed resources—or even to go out of business altogether. Reducing productive capacity takes time, too, although the duration may be different from the time required to expand. After the decision has been made to contract operations, a firm may continue to operate its fixed resources until it is able to dispose of them on satisfactory terms. In the meantime it can increase or decrease output by changing the quantity of variable resources it uses.

PRODUCTION DECISIONS IN THE SHORT RUN

We have defined the various forms of business organization, and we have described four conditions for perfect competition. In perfectly competitive markets, business firms respond to consumer demand by supplying goods and services. Economic profit depends on revenues and costs—both explicit and implicit. In this section we will show how firms make their production decisions in the short run and how their decisions affect profit. We will use a hypothetical firm to illustrate this process.

Principle of Diminishing Marginal Product

The Golden Sands Dune Buggy Company had a plant with capacity for operating five assembly lines. For several months business had been slow, and production was less than capacity. But consumer spending began to increase, and orders for dune buggies came in faster than they could be filled. The production manager hired more workers and increased the pace of operations. Business continued to improve; soon orders were piling up again, so additional workers had to be hired. Then the firm's sales manager received an important order from a large amusement park. "We've got to fill it fast," the company president said. "I don't want to lose this customer."

The production manager pointed out that

Extended Example Decision-Making at the Margin

"Natura non facit saltum." After having read this chapter you must surely agree this is true. It is an old Latin saying and it means, "Nature doesn't take leaps."

People do not take leaps either. People make small decisions a little at a time. They make decisions at the margin. They decide on a little more or a little less, and they balance off the benefits gained against the costs given up. This is what we mean by *marginal analysis*.

Marginal analysis is important to consumers as they allocate their budgets. Marginal analysis requires measurement one step at a time. Comparisons are made *incrementally:* the incremental change observed when one small step is taken. Consumers use marginal analysis to make buying plans; they compare the incremental change in utility with the price of one more unit. Because of diminishing marginal utility, the incremental change in utility is smaller with each additional unit purchased.

Marginal analysis is especially important to business firms as they make decisions to allocate their budgets for producing output. Many U.S. retailers were faced with an interesting marginal question during the recession of 1973–75. High unemployment and inflation had led to sharp cuts in consumer spending. Retailers began to accumulate unsold stocks of merchandise and their revenues fell. How could they encourage consumers to begin buying again?

Marketing departments hit on a revolutionary new idea: Sunday shopping for some, all-night shopping for others. It was hoped that the added convenience would stimulate sales and increase consumer loyalty to particular retail stores. Of course, once a single retailer in an area opened at odd hours, others were forced to follow or risk losing many of their own customers.

Retailers used marginal analysis to determine how many additional hours to offer. Each additional hour was expected to yield greater sales, but operating costs would rise, too. How many extra hours should the store provide?

To evaluate the profitability of longer hours, it was necessary to compare the incremental *gains* with the incremental *cost* of each additional hour of operation. The first extra hour may indeed have brought in more customers: those whose work schedules prevented shopping during regular hours, familes who enjoyed shopping together in the evenings, and last-minute gift buyers. But retailers considered another possibility. Many, if not most, of the extra shoppers probably would have managed to do their shopping during regular hours if they had had no other choice. Part of the

the firm's equipment was already pushed to normal full capacity. Expanding production further would involve some overtime work and the possibility of costly breakdowns. To hire still more workers to operate a fixed number of machines would reduce plant efficiency: Each additional worker would add less to monthly output than those already working. The result would be higher unit costs of production for additional units.

The company president thought it over and decided to go ahead. "The cost of filling this order will be higher than for our other orders, but the price will just cover the additional cost."

The principle we have been describing is the **principle of diminishing marginal product.** (This principle is also known as the **law of diminishing returns.**) **Marginal product** is the contribution to output of the last unit of a variable resource hired—in this case, the number of dune buggies produced by the last worker hired.

In any production process, the quantity of marginal product behaves in a particular way as variable resources are added to some quantity of fixed resources. The behavior of marginal product is a result of limitations imposed by the fixed quantity of certain resources. Golden Sands' experience is typical of most manufacturing enterprises. Let us recall in detail the changes in output that result from adding various quantities of labor to Golden Sands' fixed plant and equipment.

We begin by adding zero units of a variable resource to our stock of fixed resources. Without

late night shopping probably replaced shopping which would have been done anyway, and the marginal benefits to the store were probably slight. The same cannot be said of store costs. Much higher wage costs and utility bills and the added cost of security at night probably added significantly to operating expenses. The net result may actually have decreased the profitability of some firms.

Marginal analysis requires a cutoff at the point where incremental gains fall below increased costs. Unfortunately, other considerations entered retailers' decisions. Each retailer hesitated to change the policy for fear of losing customers. It is ironic that efforts like this were continued in spite of widely accepted agreement that they were futile. Customers continued to shop at odd hours and to pay the high costs in the form of higher prices on merchandise.

Actually, the late-night shoppers do not pay the full costs of their shopping. Who pays? How would you describe the equity of this result; that is, how would you describe the relative distribution of benefits and costs among all classes of shoppers? Why didn't the stores get together and agree to abandon the policy when profitability fell?

some quantity of the variable resource, there can be no output; therefore, total product is zero. This would be the case when none of Golden Sands' assembly lines is working.

When a small quantity of the variable resource is hired, total product begins to increase. Moreover, each additional unit of variable resource hired may add more to total product than the one before. We say that the marginal product of the variable resource increases. Marginal product increases because, over some range of employment, more workers can operate the fixed equipment more efficiently. They can divide tasks and smooth the flow of materials from one process to another.

Some quantity of the variable resource is optimum in terms of the design of Golden Sands' fixed equipment. In fact, there may be a range of employment for which the marginal product of the variable resource is maximum and constant: Each additional unit hired will add the same to total product as the one before. Over this range, the combination of variable and fixed resources is most appropriate, and production is most efficient.

At some level of employment, the quantity of variable resource will become excessive relative to the design features of the fixed equipment. Adding more units will yield smaller additions to total product, and we say that marginal product diminishes. Diminishing marginal product is the result of a combination of variable and fixed resources that is beyond the optimum combination of the plant. For Golden Sands, extra shifts and overtime produced smaller gains in output and reduced plant efficiency.

Finally, for some quantity of the variable resource, total product reaches its maximum. Adding more variable resources beyond this level might reduce efficiency to such an extent that total product would decline. We say that marginal product becomes negative beyond the absolute limit of plant capacity.

Total, Marginal, and Average Product

The principle of diminishing marginal product is illustrated in Table 2. **Total product** (TP) is the level of output associated with any quantity of variable resources. Total product, column (2), increases with every increase in the quantity of the variable resource, labor, column (1), over the range of operation for which the plant and equipment are designed. Beyond this quantity of labor, total product reaches a peak and levels off. Then, adding more labor will cause total product to decline.

Marginal product (MP) is the change in total output which results from the addition of a unit of variable resource. At first, each additional unit of labor adds more to total product than the one before, column (3). But beyond a certain level of operation, marginal product begins to decline. In Table 2 this point is reached when the fifth unit of labor is added: total product increases from ten to thirteen, a smaller amount than when the fourth unit was added. If as many as eight units are employed, the eighth will add nothing to total product; a ninth will cause total product to decrease.

Table 2 **Production (per month) from the Use of Variable Resources with a Fixed Quantity of Plant and Equipment**

(1) Quantity of labor (Q)	(2) Total Product (TP), dune buggies per month	(3) Marginal Product (MP), change in total product, $\frac{\Delta TP}{\Delta Q}$	(4) Average Product (AP), product per worker, $\frac{TP}{Q}$
0	0		0
		1	
1	1		1.0
		2	
2	3		1.5
		3	
3	6		2.0
		4	
4	10		2.5
		3	
5	13		2.6
		2	
6	15		2.5
		1	
7	16		2.3
		0	
8	16		2.0
		−1	
9	15		1.67
		−2	
10	13		1.3

The algebraic formula for marginal product is

$$MP = \frac{\text{change in total product}}{\text{change in variable resource}}$$

$$= \frac{TP_2 - TP_1}{Q_2 - Q_1} = \frac{\Delta TP}{\Delta Q}$$

where the symbol Δ stands for "change in," TP stands for total product, and Q stands for variable resource (quantity of labor). Using the data in column (2), the marginal product of the fourth worker is

$$\frac{10 - 6}{4 - 3} = \frac{4}{1} = 4 \text{ units of output.}$$

Marginal product is written between the lines because it represents the differences between two amounts in column (2). Thus the marginal product of the fourth worker is written between the fourth and fifth lines of column 2.

It is useful to know how much each unit of labor produces on the average—that is, total product divided by the number of units employed. **Average product** (AP) is defined as output per unit of variable resource employed. The algebraic formula is

$$AP = \frac{\text{total product}}{\text{units of variable resource}} = \frac{TP}{Q}.$$

Using the data in Table 2, average product per worker when four workers are employed is

$$\frac{10}{4} = 2.5 \text{ units of output.}$$

Average product is shown in column (4). Up to some level of employment, increasing the number of variable resources causes average product to increase. Average product reaches a peak and then starts to decline as more labor is added.

The data in Table 2 are graphed in Figure 2 with output on the vertical axis and units of the variable resource on the horizontal axis. The three curves for total product, marginal product, and average product have characteristic shapes in the short run. Their shapes result from the principle of diminishing marginal product.

Figure 2 is divided into three stages, showing the typical behavior of total product, marginal product, and average product. Note the general shapes of the three curves. Then, look closely at stage 1. Over most of stage 1, total product is rising at an increasing rate, and marginal product is increasing as the use of labor resources approaches the optimum combination of fixed and variable resources. Even when marginal product begins to fall, additional units of labor continue to add enough output to increase average and total product.

At the end of stage 1, marginal product falls below average product and begins to pull the average down. Throughout stage 2, each additional unit of labor adds less to total product. Total product is still rising, but it rises by smaller amounts with each unit of labor added.

The absolute limit of plant capacity is reached at the end of stage 2 when total product reaches a peak. Beyond this limit, marginal product is negative and additional units of labor would cause total product to fall. Production may still be carried on, but the combination of variable and fixed resources is clearly inefficient.

There is a special relationship between marginal product curves and average product curves: The marginal product curve always lies above the average product curve over the range for which average product is rising and below the average product curve over the range for which average product is falling. This is because marginal product tends to pull up the average when it is above the average, and tends to pull down the average when it is below the average.

An illustration may be helpful. Suppose you are recording test scores. Scores are listed in any order and cumulative totals recorded. As each score is added, it is the marginal score.

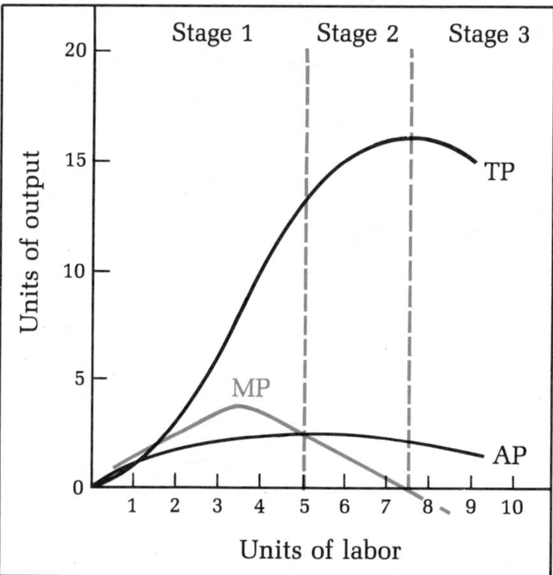

Figure 2 Short-run production function for a hypothetical firm. The top curve shows total product (TP), while the lower two curves are average product (AP) and marginal product (MP). Stage 1 is characterized by rising AP; stage 2 begins where AP and MP intersect; stage 3 begins where TP starts to decline and MP moves below zero.

Average score is computed by adding all scores and dividing by the number of students: average score = total scores ÷ number of students. A high score* adds a high marginal score and pulls the average up. A low score** adds a smaller marginal score and pulls the average down. If you list all students' marginal scores and calculate the average score at every point you will find this is always true.

There is another characteristic of marginal product and average product curves: A marginal product curve will always intersect its average product curve at the highest point on the AP curve. Why is this? It is because when marginal product falls below average product it begins to pull average product down. This can also be seen in Table 2. Notice that marginal product is above average product over the range of one to five units of labor and that average product is rising. When a sixth worker is added, marginal product falls below average product and begins to pull the average down. Marginal product crosses average product at its highest value: AP = 2.6. The point at which MP intersects AP defines the end of stage 1 and the beginning of stage 2. The point at which MP becomes negative and total product begins to decline defines the beginning of stage 3.

Firms are not likely to operate in stage 3. But they will generally not continue to operate in stage 1 either. Since average product is increasing in stage 1, the firm would be wise to continue to add variable resources as long as average product is increasing. This means that firms will prefer to operate in stage 2, where average product is falling, marginal product is below average product, and total product is moving toward its peak.

COSTS IN THE SHORT RUN

Now we are going to change our language. Instead of talking about units of output, we are going to talk about costs. This isn't a change of subject. When we say that marginal product and average product decline beyond a certain point, it is the same as saying that production costs increase. From now on we will look at the cost of producing goods rather than at the goods themselves.

*higher than average

**lower than average

Table 3 **Hypothetical Cost Data for Producing Dune Buggies (per month)**

(1) Quantity of output, Q	(2) Total Fixed Cost, FC	(3) Total Variable Cost, VC	(4) Total Cost, TC	(5) Average Fixed Cost, AFC	(6) Average Variable Cost, AVC	(7) Average Total Cost, ATC	(8) Marginal Cost, MC
0	$5,000	0	$ 5,000	—	—	—	
1	5,000	$ 2,000	7,000	$5,000	$2,000	$7,000	$ 2,000
2	5,000	3,000	8,000	2,500	1,500	4,000	1,000
3	5,000	4,000	9,000	1,667	1,333	3,000	1,000
4	5,000	5,000	10,000	1,250	1,250	2,500	1,000
5	5,000	7,000	12,000	1,000	1,400	2,400	2,000
6	5,000	10,000	15,000	833	1,667	2,500	3,000
7	5,000	14,000	19,000	714	2,000	2,714	4,000
8	5,000	19,000	24,000	625	2,375	3,000	5,000
9	5,000	31,000	36,000	555	3,444	4,000	12,000
10	5,000	45,000	50,000	500	4,500	5,000	14,000

If you look at the data in Table 2 you will see that average product, column (4), rises in stage 1 as more workers are hired. As this happens, average labor cost must be falling: When workers produce more units apiece, each unit costs less in labor time. When average product starts to fall in stage 2, it must be true that average labor cost must be rising: When workers produce fewer units apiece, each unit costs more in labor time.

Diminishing marginal product means increasing marginal cost. In fact, if we reverse the marginal product curve, we will get a curve that looks very much like marginal cost.

Total Costs

In Table 3 we present some figures to show the relationships among different cost concepts. Certain costs remain the same throughout the short run, regardless of the quantity of output. Such costs are called fixed costs (FC) and include such fixed expenditures as rent, interest and repayment of debt, and depreciation of equipment. In general, fixed costs refer to the costs of a firm's fixed plant and equipment. Moreover, larger firms usually include the salaries of top management as part of fixed costs. In column (2) fixed cost is $5000 for any quantity of output produced in the short run.

Other short-run costs, however, do vary with the quantity of output. Variable costs (VC) include total expenditures for labor, raw materials, fuel, and any other variable resources that are used along with the firm's fixed resources. The behavior of marginal product determines the behavior of variable costs. Total variable costs increase as output increases, column (3), but for small quantities of output, total variable costs increase by a constant amount. This corresponds to the range of output over which marginal product is also constant. At some level of output, total variable costs begin to rise by larger amounts. This corresponds to the range in which marginal product is falling. Can you find the quantity of output at which this starts to happen in Table 3?*

The sum of fixed cost and variable cost is **total cost** (TC), shown in column (4). We can write the relationship in shorthand form:

$$\text{TC} = \text{FC} + \text{VC}.$$

Like variable cost, total cost rises slowly at first and then more rapidly. In fact, since fixed cost remains the same, any change in total cost must reflect a change in variable cost.

Average or Unit Costs

If we divide fixed cost (FC) by the quantity produced (Q), we get **average fixed cost** (AFC):

$$\text{AFC} = \frac{\text{FC}}{\text{Q}}.$$

*Total variable cost rises more steeply when monthly output increases to five dune buggies.

Unlike all other costs, average fixed cost declines over the whole range of output, as shown in column (5). This is because fixed cost is a constant amount; as total output increases, each unit of output bears a smaller portion of the cost of fixed plant and equipment. Business firms refer to this as "spreading the overhead" over a greater number of units.

The **average variable cost** (AVC) is calculated similarly, by dividing total variable cost by the quantity produced:

$$AVC = \frac{VC}{Q}.$$

For small quantities of output, average variable cost declines as more units are produced. This corresponds to stage 1 when average product is rising. But when average product starts to fall, average variable cost starts to rise. AVC is shown in column (6).

The **average total cost** (ATC) is the sum of average fixed cost and average variable cost:

$$ATC = AFC + AVC.$$

Since ATC measures average cost of production per unit of output, it can also be calculated by dividing total cost at every level of output by quantity of output:

$$ATC = \frac{TC}{Q}.$$

Thus column (7) is the sum of columns (5) and (6), or it is column (4) divided by column (1).

ATC combines unit fixed costs, which decline as output increases, and unit variable costs, which first decline and then rise when average product starts to decrease. Note that ATC declines over the range of output where AFC and AVC are falling. Beyond some level of output, however, increases in AVC are greater than decreases in AVC, and ATC rises. Thus, when graphed, ATC becomes a U-shaped curve (see Figure 3).

Marginal Costs

The last column of Table 3 gives marginal cost for every quantity of output. **Marginal cost** (MC) is defined as the additional cost of producing an additional unit of output. It is the change in total cost resulting from a unit change in output:

$$MC = \frac{\text{change in TC}}{\text{change in Q}} = \frac{TC_2 - TC_1}{Q_2 - Q_1} = \frac{\Delta TC}{\Delta Q}.$$

In Table 3, the figures for MC in column (8) are the increases in TC in column (4) for each unit change in Q. They are also equal to the increases in total variable cost in column (3). This is because, as we have already seen, the only cost that increases as production increases is variable cost. In the short run, fixed cost

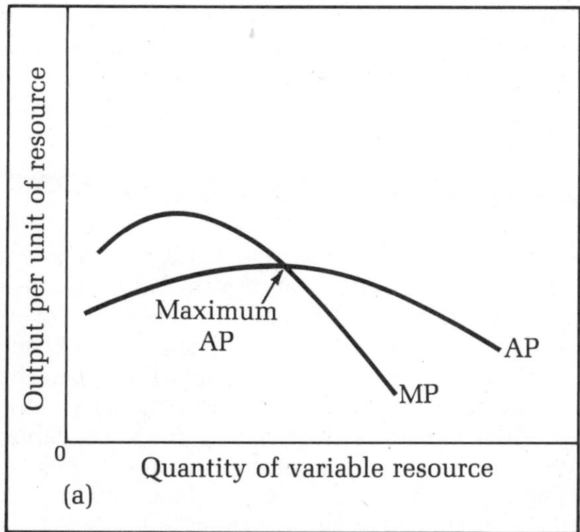

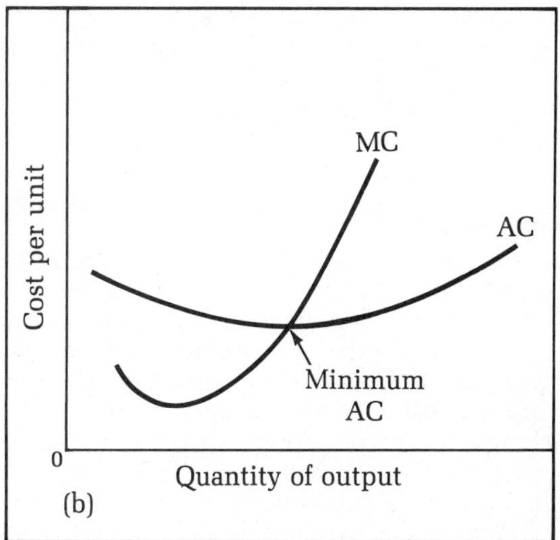

Figure 3 The relationship between average and marginal curves. When average is rising, marginal is above average. When average is falling, marginal is below average. The intersection of the two curves shows the maximum or minimum average.

Extended Example Production Costs in the Food Industry

You may have noticed as you grow older that birthdays have become more expensive. The suede jacket or typewriter that you want this year will cost substantially more than the chemistry set or wagon you wanted as a child. Not only will your gifts be more costly but your birthday cake has risen in price too!

Prices of baked goods have risen along with the rising cost of ingredients and of the processing which goes into the finished product. Even when some costs have fallen, others have generally increased in greater proportion, and total price has continued to rise.

A layer cake selling for $1 yields the farmer only about $.10. Furthermore, the "spread" between the supermarket price and what the farmer receives has been widening. The main ingredient provided by the farmer is wheat. Wheat prices fluctuate according to world supply and demand. A plentiful supply in one year may push price below average total costs of producing wheat, leaving the farmer with negative profit, or loss, in the short run. As a result, production may be cut back the next year and price will rise. It takes 2.3 bushels of wheat to make 100 pounds of flour. In 1979 wheat was selling for about $2.50 a bushel, or about $.07 per pound of flour. This was about double the price on your birthday in 1970.

Wheat must be cleaned, ground, and sifted for an additional cost of $.01 per pound. Sugar, shortening, and eggs add more costs, and all these ingredients must be transported to bakeries. The flour must be shipped in special wax-coated rail cars so that it won't stick. Transport costs comprise about $.30 of the price of your birthday cake.

Baking the cake requires human labor at almost every stage. Rising wage rates and worker fringe benefits have more than doubled in the last decade. Packaging costs have risen also, partly because of shortages and higher prices for paper and petroleum-based plastics. Between 1973 and 1975 alone, packaging material costs rose about 35 percent. Of course, energy costs are another major part of baking the cake, and energy costs have soared.

Finally, transport costs to retail outlets claim a large part of the cake price. Delivery is highly fuel-intensive and labor-intensive, and both fuel and labor are scarce and costly resources. As a result of their high costs, bakers themselves receive less than $.01 for each dollar's worth of cake they sell. Retailers add a mark-up of about $.20 to cover their fixed overhead costs: rent, labor, utilities, taxes, and so forth.

All in all, family food budgets will continue to increase between 3 percent and 5 percent yearly, largely as a result of higher processing and marketing costs. The only hope for lower production costs seems to lie in labor-saving technologies along the entire chain of processing activities. Greater standardization of containers would also help reduce average costs and permit more efficient arrangement of warehousing and trucking space.

Use a series of graphs to show the effect of rising average and marginal cost on short-run supply curves for bakery products, What is the effect on equilibrium price and output? Is the result efficient? Is it equitable? Discuss.

doesn't change and total cost is the sum of FC and VC.

Marginal cost bears the same relationship to average cost as marginal product bears to average product. That is, over the range for which marginal cost is below average cost it pulls the average cost curve down; over the range for which marginal cost is above average cost it pulls the average cost curve up. It follows that marginal cost curves must always intersect AVC or ATC curves at their lowest points.

Figure 3 illustrates the similarity between product curves and cost curves. Note the position of the marginal curves relative to the average curves. The curves are mirror images of each other, but there is one important difference. The horizontal axis (and the denominator) for the product curves is the variable resource, labor; thus "quantity" here means *quantity of resource.* The horizontal axis (and the denominator) for the cost curves is output; thus "quantity" here means *quantity of output.*

Cost Data Summary

We will hear more about marginal cost in the pages that follow. MC is one of the most important concepts in economic theory. It underlies many economic decisions because the decision maker wants to know the cost of a change in a program or an activity. What will it cost to fill a new order for dune buggies? The company may have to hire additional workers to use equipment in less efficient combinations than currently used. The contribution to output of additional workers will be less than that of those already working, and—another way of saying it—the unit cost of the additional output may be greater than the unit cost of the present output. Marginal cost will rise. Since the price at which the firm sells dune buggies will have to remain the same under perfect competition, management must decide whether the cost increase is acceptable.

To summarize, the behavior of marginal product determines the behavior of marginal cost. When MP is increasing, MC declines along with average variable cost and average total cost. Over some range of output, marginal product and marginal cost may be constant, as the firm uses the most efficient combination of variable and fixed resources. When marginal product begins to fall, marginal cost increases: each unit of output begins to cost more. In the short run, marginal cost always increases after a certain point because production approaches the limits of available resources or the capacity of the plant itself. By resorting to various makeshifts, total production can be increased further. But these makeshifts involve additional expenses or inefficiencies that raise unit costs. If the greater demand for dune buggies continues over a long time, the company may decide to build an addition to its plant; then it will be able to move to a larger scale of output. Long-run production decisions are the subject of the next chapter.

PROFIT MAXIMIZATION IN THE SHORT RUN

Suppose you are the president of the Golden Sands Dune Buggy Company. You ask the company economist to give you some figures on the firm's monthly production costs and economic profit at various levels of output. The economist brings you the data in Table 4 and points out that cost figures include both explicit payments made by the firm and implicit costs of using the firm's own resources. Among implicit costs is the cost of the firm's entrepreneurial resources: the normal profit which must be paid if these resources are to remain in use.

Costs, Revenue, and Profit

Cost figures in Table 4 show that marginal cost decreases as output increases to the level of two dune buggies per month, remains constant over a range of output, and then increases by larger and larger amounts until a production level of ten dune buggies is reached. Dune buggies sell at a price of $4000. Therefore, **total revenue** (TR) increases by $4000 for each dune buggy. Eco-

Table 4 **Monthly Data for Dune Buggies**

(1) Output	(2) Total Cost	(3) Marginal Cost	(4) Total Revenue	(5) Marginal Revenue	(6) Economic Profit
0	$ 5,000		0		−$5,000
1	7,000	$ 2,000	$ 4,000	$4,000	− 3,000
2	8,000	1,000	8,000	4,000	0
3	9,000	1,000	12,000	4,000	3,000
4	10,000	1,000	16,000	4,000	6,000
5	12,000	2,000	20,000	4,000	8,000
6	15,000	3,000	24,000	4,000	9,000
7	19,000	4,000	28,000	4,000	9,000
8	24,000	5,000	32,000	4,000	8,000
9	36,000	12,000	36,000	4,000	0
10	50,000	14,000	40,000	4,000	-10,000

nomic profit for any level of output is the difference between total revenue and total cost, when cost includes all implicit costs, including normal profit:

economic profit = TR − TC.

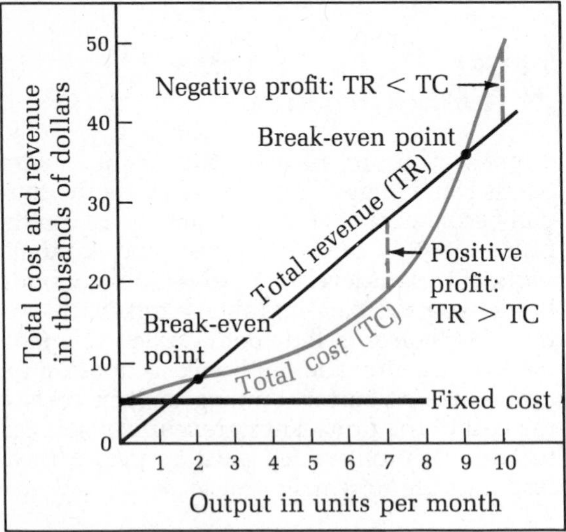

Figure 4 Comparison of total cost and total revenue shows total economic profit. When TR is greater than TC, economic profit is shown by the distance between the two curves. When TC is greater than TR, there is negative economic profit or loss.

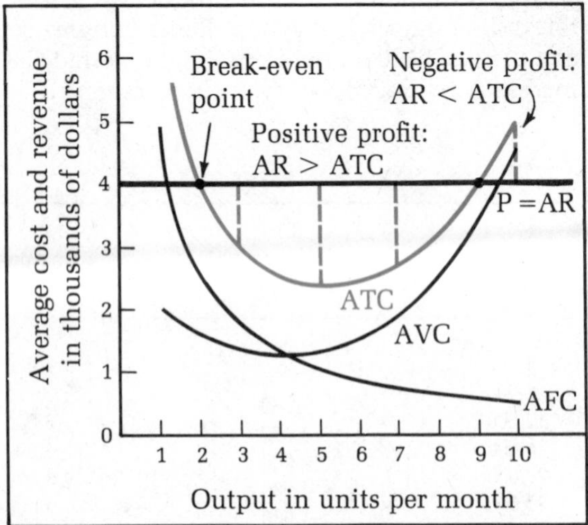

Figure 5 Comparison of average total cost (ATC) and price (average revenue) shows economic profit: positive when AR > ATC; negative when AR < ATC. Average fixed cost declines through the short run.

Compare total cost with total revenue in Table 4. Economic profit is shown in column (6).

Table 4 shows that production of fewer than three dune buggies per month produces no economic profit. If the firm produces two a month, it would just break even: total cost would equal total revenue, and economic profit would be zero. This is called the **break-even point**—the quantity of output at which total revenue just covers full costs.

Increasing the level of production would increase revenue faster than costs increase; economic profit would be earned, rising to a peak of $9000. Beyond this level of output, however, increasing production would cause total cost to rise so that, at nine units of output, the firm would just break even, and for larger outputs it would incur losses.

Figure 4 is a graph of total cost and total revenue for the dune buggy company. Fixed cost is the horizontal line at $5000, and variable cost is added to fixed cost to produce the total cost line. Total cost rises slowly at first as the plant is used more efficiently. Beyond five units total cost rises faster. Because total revenue increases at a constant rate ($4000 for each dune buggy), it is shown in Figure 4 as a straight line beginning at the origin. At every level of output economic profit is measured by the vertical distance between total revenue and total costs: economic profit = TR − TC.

The firm's break-even point is the quantity of output at which the total revenue line crosses the total cost line. Revenue is just enough to pay all explicit and implicit costs, including normal profit. Notice that there are two break-even points.

A production level of fewer than two dune buggies per month will result in *negative economic profit* (or loss) as total cost lies above total revenue. The same is true for a production level of more than nine units per month. Negative economic profit means that some resources are not earning their opportunity cost. If resources are not paid their opportunity cost, they must eventually leave their current employment. We will have more to say about this later.

Average Cost and Average Revenue

Another way of measuring profit is to compare average total cost with the price (P) at which the product sells. This is the purpose of Figure 5, which shows three average cost curves and market price. Remember that average total cost (ATC) is the sum of two components: average fixed cost and average variable cost (ATC = AFC + AVC). Moreover, ATC includes implicit costs, in particular normal profit. In Figure 5, average fixed cost is shown as a curve which declines over the entire range of output. Average variable cost declines at first and then rises. It is shown in Figure 5 as a U-shaped curve. Average total cost is the sum of AFC and AVC and is shown as a U-shaped curve lying above them. Price is shown as a horizontal line drawn at $4000. Price is also called **average revenue** (AR). This is because

Total revenue = price x quantity sold

Rearranging terms,

$$\text{price} = \frac{\text{total revenue}}{\text{quantity sold}} = \text{average revenue.}$$

Economic profit per unit is shown in Figure 5 as the difference between average revenue (or price) and average total cost:

unit economic profit = AR − ATC.

Where average revenue lies above average total cost, unit economic profit is positive. Where average revenue lies below average total cost, unit economic profit is negative. Where the two are equal, at production of two and nine dune buggies, unit economic profit is zero, and the firm is just breaking even. However, all costs are covered, including normal profit.

Making Production Decisions at the Margin

If we are given all the information in Tables 3 and 4, it is easy to locate the range of output over which the firm can earn economic profit. But all this data may not be available to the managers of a firm. It is not always possible to determine the variable costs associated with each level of output. Often the firm must base its decisions on just the cost data that are within its immediate range of operation. Management can estimate how much more it will cost to produce one more dune buggy per month, or one less. In short, it can estimate marginal cost.

The firm also knows how much it can add to total revenue by producing one more dune buggy per month. The change in total revenue associated with a unit change in output is called **marginal revenue.** We can express marginal revenue (MR) in terms similar to those for marginal cost:

$$MR = \frac{\text{change in TR}}{\text{change in Q}} = \frac{TR_2 - TR_1}{Q_2 - Q_1} = \frac{\Delta TR}{\Delta Q}$$

In competitive markets marginal revenue is the same as price. This is because a perfectly competitive firm is a price taker; price is set in the competitive market. Sale of an additional unit causes total revenue to increase by the market price. Thus under perfect competition P = MR, which also equals average revenue since each additional unit sells for the same price.

The firm makes its production decision by comparing MR with MC. When marginal revenue is greater than marginal cost, the firm will decide to expand production. By doing so it will add more to revenue than to costs, and economic profit will increase.

MR > MC: Expand output.

When marginal revenue is less than marginal cost, the firm will want to contract output. That is because a reduction in output will reduce costs more than it will reduce revenue. Contracting production will allow economic profit to increase.

MR < MC : Contract output.

It follows that when marginal revenue is just equal to marginal cost, the firm will maintain its output at that level—where the last unit produced adds the same to total cost as it adds to total revenue. At this quantity of output the firm is earning maximum economic profit. In Table 4 the firm's maximum output consistent with maximum economic profit is seven dune buggies a month. The marginal cost of the seventh unit is $4000. The seventh unit also adds $4000 to total revenue.

MR = MC: Maximum profit level of output.

The rule of setting production at the quantity where MR = MC is a fundamental principle of microeconomics. When MR = MC, the firm is

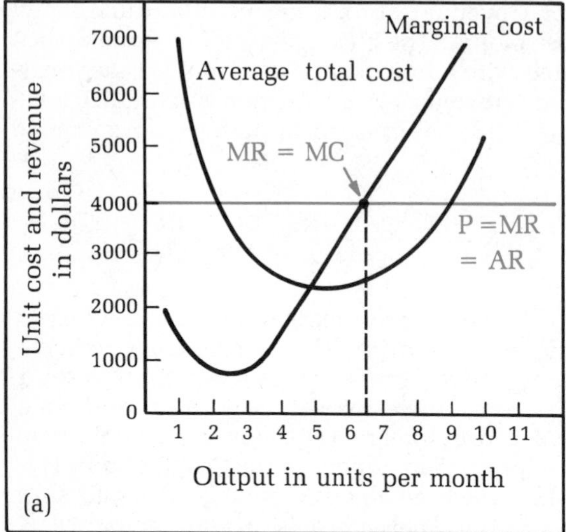

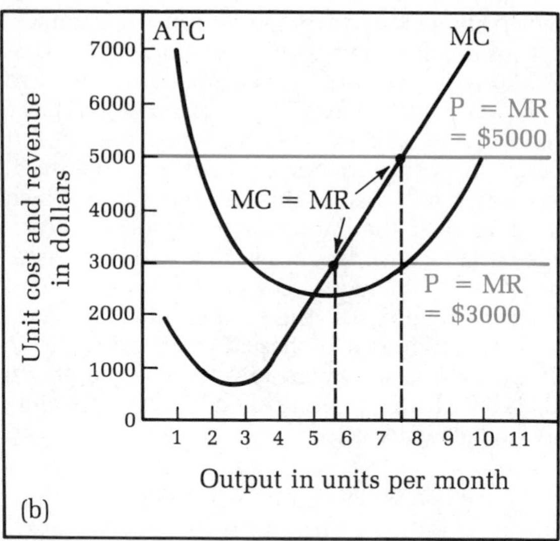

Figure 6 (a) Marginal revenue and marginal cost determine the quantity of output a firm will produce to maximize profits. A firm seeks to produce where MR = MC. Here that point means an output of 7 dune buggies per month when price is $4000. (b) When price changes, the firm will adjust output. If price rises to $5000, our firm moves up its marginal cost (supply) curve to a new equilibrium—output is now 8 dune buggies. When price falls to $3000, equilibrium output is 6 dune buggies. (*Note:* Output can't be in fractions and is given in whole numbers.)

earning maximum economic profit. This holds true for all forms of competition—imperfect as well as perfect. (We will see later how the rule applies when markets are not perfectly competitive.)

Figure 6 illustrates these production decisions at the margin. Output per month is measured on the horizontal axis and unit cost on the vertical axis. The marginal cost curve declines at first and then begins to rise. Market price is shown as a horizontal line drawn at a price of $4000 (Figure 6a). This is also marginal revenue and average revenue, because, under perfect competition, price is not affected by the level of the firm's output. Each unit sold adds the same amount to revenue.

Compare marginal revenue with marginal cost. Increasing production from four dune buggies to five adds $4000 to revenue and $2000 to costs. Because MR is greater than MC, the firm will want to expand output beyond five units per month. As the seventh unit is added, MR is equal to MC, and this is the firm's profit-maximizing quantity of output. To produce more than seven units would add more to costs than to revenue. At a monthly output of seven units, therefore, the firm will have no incentive to contract or expand its output.

Now suppose market price rises to $5000. This can be shown in Figure 6b by drawing the marginal revenue (price) line at $5000. The firm will now decide to expand production of dune buggies from seven per month to eight. How would the firm adjust its output if price falls to $3000?

Have you noticed that the quantity of out-

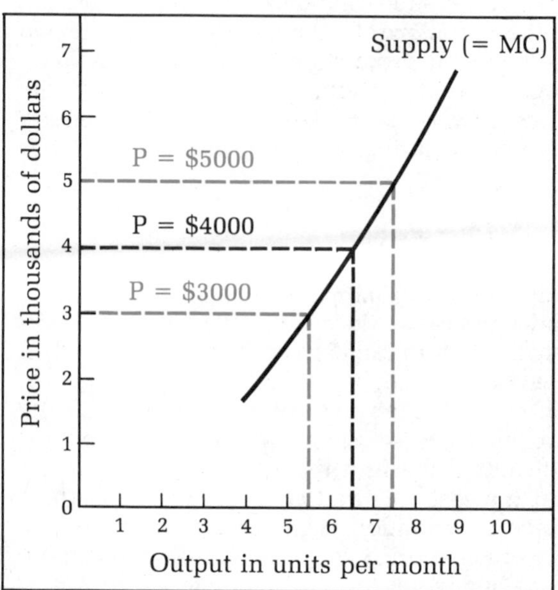

Figure 7 A part of the rising portion of the firm's MC curve is its supply curve.

put the firm will supply can be read from its marginal cost curve? In fact, a portion of a firm's MC curve constitutes its supply curve. In Figure 7 we have reproduced part of the rising portion of the firm's marginal cost curve and labeled it supply. This portion of the MC curve tells you the maximum quantities of output that the firm will supply at different prices. At every price, quantity supplied can be read on the horizontal axis.

Throughout this explanation we have considered the effect of a change in output on total profit: the difference between total revenue and total cost at various levels of output. Maximum total profit is not the same as maximum profit per unit. Maximum profit per unit occurs where ATC is lowest relative to AR. In our example, the greatest unit profit (or profit *margin*) is associated with output of five dune buggies per month. This is also the level of output at which ATC is lowest (refer again to Figure 5).

Producing five dune buggies per month would not yield maximum total profit, however. By expanding production as long as MR > MC, the firm can increase total profit, even though ATC may be increasing. Still, if additions to revenue are greater than additions to costs, production should be increased.

ECONOMIC PROFIT AND SHORT-RUN DECISIONS

Measuring Economic Profit

We have been describing how a firm decides what quantity to produce per month. It decides on the quantity that will maximize total economic profit. This is the quantity of output at which MR = MC. But this doesn't tell us how much economic profit the firm will actually make. To determine total profit, the firm first calculates economic profit earned per unit of output. Average economic profit (AEP) is found by computing the difference between average revenue and average total cost: AEP = AR − ATC. By multiplying average or unit economic profit by the number of units produced, the firm obtains the figure for total economic profit: EP = AEP x Q.

The quantity of output which maximizes economic profit is seven dune buggies per month. Referring to column (7) of Table 3, we find that the average cost of seven units is $2714. Since the buggies are selling at a market price of $4000 each, unit economic profit is AEP = AR − ATC = $4000 − $2714, or $1286. Multiplying unit economic profit by the number of units sold gives us total economic profit: EP = AEP x Q = $1286 x 7 = $9002, or, rounded off, $9000. At this level of output, the firm is paying all costs of production, including normal profit, and earning maximum economic profit above that (see Table 4).

Losses in the Short Run

But suppose business is bad. Consumer demand curves shift to the left and price falls. Now instead of earning economic profit the firm incurs losses. Average revenue minus average total cost becomes a negative number. What should the firm do?

A glance at Figure 8a shows the situation if market price falls as low as $2000. Management compares marginal revenue (price) with marginal cost (supply) and moves down the marginal cost curve. Marginal revenue is equal to marginal cost at an output of five dune buggies per month. This level of output maximizes economic profit (or, rather, minimizes loss). Average total cost at this level of production (see Figure 8b) is $2400. This means that the firm is suffering a loss of $400 on each dune buggy: AEP = $2000 − $2400 = −$400. Total loss is −$400 × 5 = −$2000.

Can the firm continue to operate in the face of such losses? In the short run the answer depends on the relation between price and average variable cost. The firm's fixed costs are constant in the short run and must be paid regardless of the quantity of output. If the firm stops production altogether, it will still owe the entire amount of its fixed cost for the remainder of the short run. If it keeps on producing some quantity, it may earn enough to pay variable cost and perhaps make some contribution toward payment of fixed cost.

This is precisely the case for our dune buggy firm, as we can see from Figure 8. If the firm produces five units, the price of $2000 covers average variable cost of $1400 (see Table 3) and leaves $600 per unit to apply to payment of fixed cost. Even if the firm stopped production entirely, it would still have to pay fixed costs of $5000 per month. By producing five dune buggies and selling them for $2000 each, it obtains $600 × 5 =

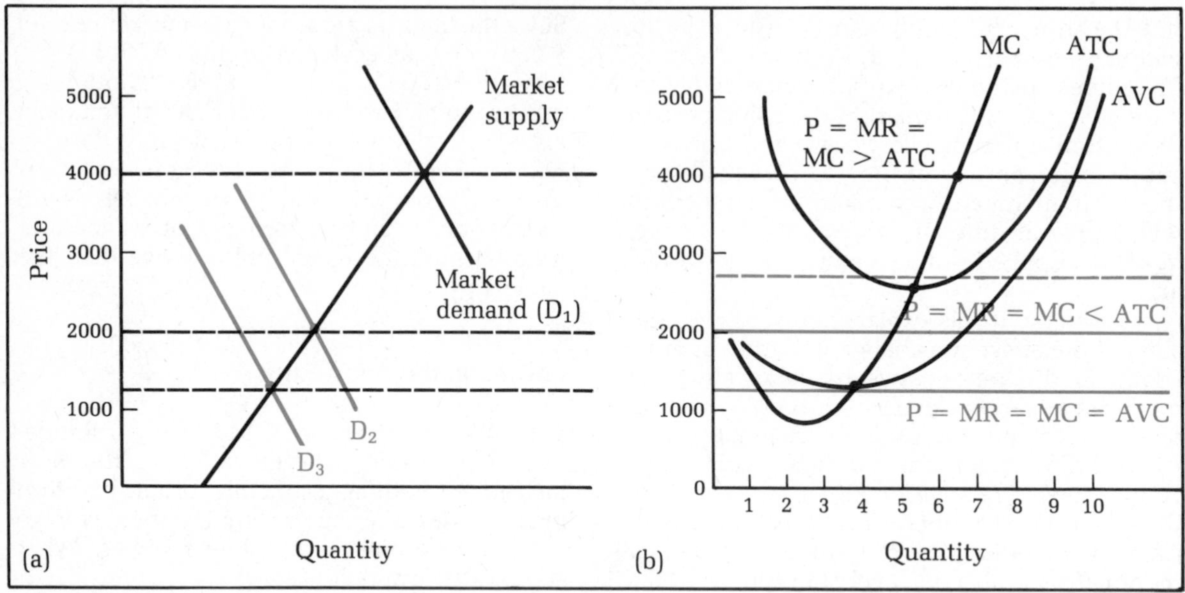

Figure 8 (a) As market demand declines to D_2 or D_3, price falls. (b) The price that covers full costs is \$2400, where MC = ATC. The shut-down point occurs at a price of \$1250, where MC = AVC.

\$3000 to apply toward fixed costs of \$5000. Thus the loss is held down to only \$2000 per month. The firm can pay the cost of labor, electric power, raw materials, and component parts—that is, all variable cost. The remainder will go toward paying fixed charges for plant and equipment, office space, and administrative staff. The \$2000 loss may be covered temporarily by borrowing or by selling other assets owned by the firm. This is better, in the short run, than stopping production entirely.

Shut-Down Point in the Short Run

The firm cannot produce forever at just any price. If demand keeps falling, market price may fall so low that the firm can't cover average variable cost. It will have to shut down. By shutting down, the firm will incur a smaller loss than to go on producing and selling for a price lower than the cost of variable resources. Losses will be limited only to fixed costs contracted for the short run. Thus, when price falls below AVC, the firm reaches its **shut-down point.**

You can locate the shut-down point on Figure 6b by following the firm's marginal cost curve down to the point at which MC is equal to average variable cost. To produce and sell for a price lower than average variable cost would add more losses to what the firm is already losing on its fixed cost. The lowest average variable cost of producing dune buggies is \$1250 (see Table 3), when four units are produced each month. As long as price is at least \$1250 the firm minimizes losses by continuing to operate in the short run.

The shut-down point sets the minimum conditions for operating in the short run. Producing above this minimum helps the firm fulfill its obligations over the period for which some resources are fixed. If the firm continues to incur losses over the short run, it cannot remain in business indefinitely. At the end of the short run, a firm incurring losses must finally go out of business. The decision to enter or to leave an industry is a long-run decision. We will deal with long-run decisions in the next chapter.

Equilibrium in the Short Run

You will recall that market equilibrium is the level of price and output at which all buyers and sellers are satisfied with the price and quantity of their transactions. Producers have no incentive to expand or contract the operation of their fixed plant and equipment. At equilibrium, all firms are producing a level of output that yields maximum economic profit (or minimum loss). In short-run equilibrium the following conditions are true:

(1) MR = MC. Firms are producing a quantity of output at which marginal revenue is equal

Economic Thinker Alfred Marshall

Alfred Marshall (1842–1924) was probably the greatest microeconomist of the last one hundred years. His reputation rests mainly on his *Principles of Economics* (1890), which was used as a textbook in many English (and some American) universities for nearly fifty years. Even now, much of modern microeconomic theory can be described as "Marshallian."

Marshall was educated at Cambridge, England, and was a lecturer in political economy at Oxford. He was primarily a mathematical economist, able to think through economic relationships mathematically. Then, he would express economic principles in clear and precise detail. His skills were appropriate for the new wave of economic thought (the neoclassical theory) that occurred at the end of the nineteenth century.

Marshall was especially interested in the subjective process by which consumers determine the utility of a good or service. Using calculus, he was able to explain the *paradox of value:* Diamonds are worth more than water even though water is essential to life. Marshall showed that value is determined by the *marginal* utility of a good and that the intensity of wants decreases with each unit acquired. Diamonds have great marginal utility because few units are owned. Water has less marginal utility because it is relatively more plentiful. The price of each depends on its marginal utility.

Although he introduced the concepts of demand elasticity and consumer surplus to economic theory, Marshall's most important contribution to economic theory was in applying marginal analysis to income distribution. Whereas earlier economists had described diminishing marginal productivity of land, Marshall showed that the marginal product of *all* resources tends to diminish as variable resources are combined with fixed amounts of other resources. Business firms try to combine factors of production so as to achieve greatest profit. In competition, resource prices are bid up or down until price is precisely equal to the value of marginal product. This view gave support to the idealistic view of income distribution according to each resource's productivity in the free market system.

Marshall also showed how demand curves are the result of many psychological factors and how production responds to consumer demand. Demand determines price and output in the short run, and firms may collect economic profit or suffer loss. But in the long run, firms enter or leave the industry, affecting quantity supplied until price just covers full costs of production.

He went on to develop the neoclassical view of the relationship between quantity of money and level of economic activity. The Cambridge theory of "cash-balances" eventually became an important part of much of today's business cycle theory.

to marginal cost. The last unit of output adds the same amount to revenue as it adds to costs. At this level of output the firm is maximizing economic profit (or minimizing loss). A portion of a firm's MC curve constitutes its supply curve.

(2) MR = P = MC. Under perfect competition, marginal revenue is equal to price. Equilibrium price is just enough to cover the marginal cost of additional resources used to produce the last unit of output.

(3) P ≥ AVC. The firm is covering its variable cost for the short run. In the short run, firms may earn economic profit or they may experience losses. Nevertheless, in the short run firms will continue to operate as long as price is at least as great as average variable cost.

These features of short-run equilibrium are favorable for consumers and business firms. This is because consumers are able to satisfy their needs at acceptable prices, and business firms are able to conduct their operations and pay their suppliers.

Table 5 **Income and Expense Statement for Golden Sands, Inc.**
January 1, 1981 to December 31, 1981

(1) Gross Revenue from Operations		$ 336,000
(2) Operating Expenses:		
Administrative Salaries	$ 50,000	
Wages to Production Workers	90,000	
Contributions to Social Insurance	10,000	
Costs of Materials	35,000	
Property Rentals	2,500	
Interest on Bank Loans	7,500	
Total Out-of-Pocket Expenses	195,000	
Depreciation on Capital Equipment 1/10 ($500,000)	50,000	
Total Expenses		−245,000
(3) Net Income from Operations		91,000
Income Taxes payable (46%)		− 41,860
(4) Net Profit After Taxes		49,140
(5) Dividends Paid to Stockholders		30,000
(6) Retained Earnings: to Surplus		19,140

But the short-run equilibrium may not be ideal for our economic system as a whole. Total revenue may exceed total cost, or it may be less than total cost. When total revenue differs from total cost, firms will either be earning economic profit or suffering loss. From the standpoint of the industry as a whole, the number of firms in the industry is either too small or too large. If there are too few firms to satisfy demand, price will be high and firms will collect economic profits. If there are too many firms for the existing market, price will be low and firms will suffer economic losses. In either case, resources are not used efficiently.

BUSINESS ACCOUNTING*

Whatever the price and quantity of output, a business firm must have a system for measuring the flows of receipts and expenditures for any business period. Accounting statements for measuring *flows* are called *income and expense statements*. Accounting statements for measuring the *stock* of assets owned by the firm are called *balance sheets*. Tables 5 and 6 are hypothetical accounting statements for our hypothetical dune buggy firm.

*This section is optional at the discretion of the instructor. No loss of continuity will be incurred by omitting it.

The Income and Expense Statement

A firm's **income and expense statement** is a record of flows: flows received from the sale of output and flows paid for the use of productive resources. The amount remaining after all expenses and taxes is available for distribution to stockholders.

Look at Table 5, which shows Golden Sands' income and expenses for the year. The first item of interest is (1) Gross Revenue from Operations. This represents total receipts from sales of goods or services. As such, it tells us not only how much money the firm has received but the value of Golden Sands' output.

Most of Golden Sands' production costs, (2) Operating Expenses, are out-of-pocket payments made to the suppliers of resources: land, labor, and capital. One important cost is not paid to a supplier in the current period. **Depreciation** of capital equipment represents the estimated cost of the plant and equipment which wears out during each production period. It is a cost of current production even though an out-of-pocket payment is not made. A firm must allow for the fact that machinery, buildings, vehicles, and other capital equipment are used up over a period of years. To do this, the firm assumes that a certain amount of depreciation will take place each year and sets aside a sum of money to replace the equipment when it is worn out. Firms generally estimate the usable life of each piece of equipment and then arrive at some reasonable figure to be set aside each year for capital depreciation (in Golden Sands' case, one tenth of the equipment's original cost). An allowance for depreciation is set aside in a special account, creating a fund for eventual replacement of the equipment. The depreciation account is a type of business saving, corresponding to the saving that a household does when it sets aside money to replace its old car.

When total costs, including depreciation, have been deducted from income, the result is (3) Net Income from Operations, or operating profit. In the United States, corporations have to pay income taxes just as people do, and the tax bite may be almost 50 percent of profits.

After deducting the amount of taxes paid, Golden Sands is left with (4) Net Profit After Taxes. Part of net profit goes to stockholders in the form of (5) Dividends Paid to Stockholders. How this flow is distributed among stockholders depends on the kind of stock they own. Preferred stockholders are paid first, at a guaranteed rate, and common stockholders are paid from what is left of net profits. (This may mean that they receive more than preferred stockholders, if it has been a profitable year, but it often means that they receive less). Since most common stockholders buy stock with the expectation of participating in the profits of the firm, management tries to pay dividends regularly. People sometimes pay more for the stock of firms that pay good dividends; and high stock prices make it easier to raise funds with new stock issues when the firm wants to expand.

Not all the firm's net profit will be paid out in dividends. A portion will be held in the corporation as a source of funds for future growth. Stockholders like to see the firm grow because growth is likely to raise the value of their shares. Business saving for growth is called (6) Retained Earnings, or undistributed profits.

The Balance Sheet

In contrast to the income and expense statement, which is a record of *flows*, a balance sheet is a record of the *stock* of assets owned by a firm on a certain day. Assets are the property of a firm, including land, buildings, equipment, cash, and bank deposits. It is called a *balance sheet* because the total value of **assets** and the total claims against assets must be equal. The left side of a balance sheet shows the value of the assets a firm *owns*. The right side may be considered the amounts the firm *owes*—that is, the firm's total liabilities or claims (including those of stockholders) against its assets. Look at Table 6. Among (1) Assets, the value of Golden Sands' buildings and equipment is the largest item. The firm also owns small amounts of financial assets: cash and a checking account for immediate needs and a savings account which can be drawn on for extraordinary needs. The sum of Golden Sands' assets is $1,416,000.

Claims against the firm's assets are of two types. Promises to pay the firm's creditors, (2) Liabilities (or Debt Claims), are the firm's IOUs issued to banks and to suppliers who have delivered component parts, electric power, and other

Table 6 **Balance Sheet for Golden Sands, Inc.**
December 31, 1981

(1) Assets		(2) Liabilities (or Debt Claims)	
Buildings and Equipment	$1,250,000	Bank Loan	$ 150,000
Land	150,000	Accounts Payable to Suppliers	10,000
Cash on Hand	1,000	*Liabilities*	*160,000*
Checking Account	5,000		
Savings Account	10,000	(3) Net Worth	
		Capital (or Equity Claims)	1,000,000
		Surplus and Reserves	256,000
		Total Net Worth	*1,256,000*
Total Assets	**$1,416,000**	**Total Liabilities**	**$1,416,000**

materials for operations. If the firm were to go out of business, it would have to sell its assets and pay all debt claims first before any other claims were satisfied. This action is called **liquidation.** The firm would liquidate its assets and pay off all the claims of its creditors. It is important that the value of assets be greater than the value of debt claims. Otherwise, the firm is said to be **insolvent.** Fortunately, Golden Sands' debt claims are only $160,000.

The third group of items on a balance sheet represents (3) Net Worth. Net worth is the net value of assets after all debt claims have been paid, the amount which would be available for the stockholders if the firm were to liquidate all its assets and pay its creditors. The firm's net worth of $1,256,000 would be divided among its shareholders.

The largest claims against the assets of Golden Sands are the equity or ownership claims of its stockholders, included as part of (3) Net Worth. When Golden Sands began operations it issued a million shares of common stock at $1 each. The one million dollars in financial capital, together with a bank loan, enabled the firm to purchase land and construct a plant. Over the years, operations have been profitable. The firm gradually reduced its bank loan and consistently paid dividends to its shareholders. Each year it set aside an allowance for depreciation and retained some of its earnings after taxes and dividends. As a result, the total value of the firm's assets grew to be larger than the sum of its debt and equity claims. The difference between total assets and total liabilities plus stockholders' equity appears on the balance sheet as the firm's surplus. Adding surplus to the right side of the balance sheet ensures that the total values on each side will indeed balance.

SUMMARY

Business firms are organized for supplying the goods and services consumers demand. Firms operate plants, and all firms producing a particular output constitute an industry. Similar industries constitute a sector of economic activity. Firms may be single proprietorships, partnerships, or corporations. Corporations have limited liability and can acquire investment funds through the sale of corporate stock.

For an industry to be perfectly competitive it must include many small buyers and sellers, produce a homogeneous product, have free flow of market and technical information, and enjoy maximum mobility of resources. Perfectly competitive firms cannot affect price but face a horizontal demand curve drawn at the market equilibrium price. Costs determine quantity of output at the equilibrium price. Full costs include both explicit out-of-pocket costs and implicit or opportunity costs. Normal profit is a necessary implicit cost.

In the short run, some resources can be varied for producing different quantities of output with existing fixed resources. When variable resources are expanded beyond some optimum combination of variable and fixed resources, the result is diminishing marginal product. The behavior of total, marginal, and average product determines the behavior of total, marginal, and average costs. Firms will choose to produce a quantity of output in the range of increasing marginal costs where marginal revenue is equal to marginal costs. This is the profit-maximizing output. Unit economic profit is the difference between price and average cost, and total economic profit is unit profit times quantity of output.

Firms may enjoy economic profit in the short run. Or price may be so low as to yield negative economic profit, or loss. However, firms will continue to operate as long as price covers average variable cost. In this way, the firm can allocate some revenues toward fixed cost and minimize losses. If price falls below average variable cost, the firm reaches its shutdown point.

Short-run competitive equilibrium provides some favorable results. Marginal revenue is equal to marginal cost and to price. Price covers average variable costs. But economic profit or loss may lead to long-run changes in industry productive capacity.

Business firms measure revenues and costs for any production period and report them in an income and expense statement. The current financial condition of a firm is reflected in its balance sheet: a statement of assets and claims against assets at a particular point in time. A healthy firm will have ample assets to use for long-run expansion.

Key Words and Phrases

accounting costs costs actually paid or allocated as a result of business activity over a particular time period.
assets the value of things a firm owns.
average fixed costs total fixed costs in a particular period of time divided by the number of units of output produced: AFC = TFC/Q.
average product output per unit of variable resource employed.
average total costs total costs in a particular period of time divided by the number of units of output produced: ATC = TC/Q = AFC + AVC.
average variable costs total variable costs in a particular period of time divided by the number of units of output produced: AVC = TVC/Q.
balance sheet a record of the value of assets owned and of debt owed by a firm at a particular point in time.
board of directors a group of decision makers decided upon by vote of the stockholders of a corporation.
break-even point the quantity of output at which revenue from sales just equals total costs of production.
capital gain an increase in the value of an asset from the time of buying to the time of selling.
common stock a stock certificate which entitles the holder to vote in stockholder meetings and to receive dividends at the discretion of management.
corporation a business firm owned by stockholders.
depreciation the decline in value of an asset (such as a capital good or a durable good) as it wears out.
economic profit total revenue above the necessary amount needed to reward productive resources; negative economic profit indicates loss.
explicit costs costs actually paid or allocated in the course of business activity; these costs are the same as accounting costs.
firm a complete business organization, including all activities of administration, planning, production, and sales.
fixed costs the unchanging costs of a business firm's plant and equipment in the short run.
fixed productive resources resources such as plant, equipment, and management staff, all of which are fixed in the short run.
implicit costs the opportunity costs of a firm's own resources; these are costs the firm owes to itself.
income and expense statement a record of the flow of funds to and from a business firm over a particular period of time
industry all the firms producing a particular good or service.
insolvent a condition in which the value of a firm's assets is less than the value of its liabilities.
investment bank a financial institution which specializes in marketing new issues of corporate stock.
liabilities amounts a firm owes; debt claims against a firm's assets.
limited liability a condition in which owners of stock are not held liable for the debts of the corporation beyond the extent of their stockholdings.
liquidation the process of selling a firm's assets in order to satisfy its liabilities.
marginal cost the additional cost of producing an additional unit of output: MC = $\Delta TC/\Delta Q$.
marginal product the change in total output that results from adding a unit of variable resource.
marginal revenue change in total revenue associated with a unit change in output.
net worth the net value of a firm's assets in excess value of its liabilities.
normal profit a necessary return in payment for entrepreneurial resources.
opportunity cost the forgone production from using resources in a particular way.
partnership a business firm owned by more than one individual.
perfect competition the free market structure described by Adam Smith in which buyers and sellers pursue their own interests and benefit themselves and all of society.
plant a single productive facility.
preferred stock a stock certificate which entitles the holder to receive regular, specified dividends, if any dividends are paid at all.
principle of diminishing marginal product above some level of output, a firm's total output will increase by smaller amounts as variable resources are added; the additional output from each additional unit of variable resource tends to decrease.
net income, or accounting profit the remaining revenue after paying all explicit costs.
sector a group of industries with similar characteristics.
shut-down point the level of output at which revenue from sales is just sufficient to cover a firm's variable costs of production.
single proprietorship a business firm owned by a single individual.
total product level of a firm's output.
variable costs the total costs of variable resources employed in the short run.
variable resources resources which are quickly adjustable in the short run; some variable resources are fuel and energy, labor, and raw materials.

Questions for Review

1. Outline the principal forms of business organization and describe advantages and disadvantages of each. Give familiar examples of each type.
2. Distinguish between accounting costs and economic costs. What resource costs are included in each?
3. State clearly the principle of diminishing marginal product. Does this principle apply over all ranges of output? Explain.
4. Use the hypothetical data below to construct a graph of revenue, cost, and profit at all levels of output.

Quantity	*Price*	*Fixed Cost*	*Variable Cost*
1	5	3	4
2	5	3	7
3	5	3	9
4	5	3	13
5	5	3	19
6	5	3	27
7	5	3	37

5. Use the data from question 4 to calculate average total cost and marginal cost. Plot on a second graph directly below your graph for question 4. Verify that MC = ATC at its lowest point. Verify that profit is maximum at the level of output at which MC = MR.
6. Use the data from questions 4 and 5 to demonstrate two ways of calculating profit at the maximum profit point.
7. What is the lowest price the firm in question 4 will accept in the short run? Suppose price does fall to this level. What is the total amount of the firm's loss? State clearly the conditions which would cause the firm to shut down in the short run.
8. Draw up a hypothetical income and expense statement for a firm producing economics textbooks. Include all explicit costs and depreciation incurred during the period.
9. We have defined a firm's supply curve as a portion of the rising part of its marginal cost curve. Why is only a *portion* of the curve involved in supply decisions? What part of the MC curve is *not* part of its supply curve?
10. Consider the following industries. Can you identify the resources that are likely to be fixed in the short run? How long do you think the short run would be?

steel production	coal production
soybeans	dental services
ladies' clothing	auto manufacture
college textbooks	catering services

11. Distinguish between common and preferred stock. What are the advantages of each to the issuing firm? to the holder? How do stockholders differ from partners and how are they similar?
12. List the four basic conditions of perfect competition and explain why each is necessary. What circumstances in today's economy enhance or endanger the conditions of perfect competition?
13. Select a familiar business firm and list its costs under the headings Explicit Costs and Implicit Costs. What are the firm's opportunity costs?
14. Explain the economic function of economic profit—both positive and negative. What circumstances within an industry may result in persistent positive or negative economic profit?
15. State clearly the relationship between average cost and marginal cost. Explain why this relationship is always true.
16. Explain why a firm's income and expense statement is said to measure "flows" while its balance sheet measures "stocks." What is the significance of the following terms: liquidation, insolvent?
17. Corporate profits and dividends for the years 1972–79 are shown below. Compute the ratio of dividends paid to total profit for each year and comment on the results. What can be said about the absolute level of dividends and of undistributed corporate profits?

	1972	1973	1974	1975	1976	1977	1978	1979
After-tax profits (billions of dollars)	50.5	50.4	31.2	46.1	63.0	77.3	83.2	85.8
Dividends paid	24.6	27.8	31.0	31.9	37.5	42.1	47.2	52.7

18. In 1979 sales of all manufacturing corporations were about $437.5 billion. Profits before income taxes were $38.3 billion and taxes amounted to $13.5 billion. The value of outstanding stock in 1979 was $609.2 billion. Compute the after-tax return on stockholders' investment for the year. What was the ratio of after-tax profits to total sales?

APPENDIX

Isoquants and Isocosts

This chapter has discussed production costs in terms of diminishing marginal product. When variable resources are added to a fixed resource, total product tends at first to increase. The reason has to do with the proportion of variable to fixed resources. As the proportion approaches the optimum, total product increases by larger amounts with each additional unit of variable resources. We say that marginal product increases.

Beyond some optimum proportion of variable and fixed resources, additional units of the variable resources produce smaller changes in total product. We say that marginal product declines. At some proportion of variable to fixed resources, marginal product may become negative.

We have shown how changes in marginal product are reflected in costs. When marginal product is increasing, total costs increase at a decreasing rate (marginal cost declines). When marginal product is falling, total cost increases at an increasing rate (marginal cost increases). The firm produces the quantity of output at which MC = MR.

This analysis suffers from the assumption that one resource is fixed and another variable. When both resources are variable, the firm's choice of resources becomes more complex. In this appendix we will describe a method of analysis similar to indifference curve analysis. The process of selecting quantities of resources is similar to the process of selecting quantities of consumer goods. Business firms respond to price and budget circumstances in much the same way as consumers do.

ISOQUANTS

Most manufacturing processes can be carried out through a variety of combinations of productive resources. Various combinations of labor and capital, for example, can be used to produce leather bags. Some possible combinations for producing one hundred bags per week are shown in the schedule below.

	Combinations for producing 100 units per week				
	A_1	B_1	C_1	D_1	E_1
Labor hours (in thousands)	4.0	3.0	1.5	1.0	.8
Equipment hours (in thousands)	.5	.7	1.5	3.0	4.0

Note that no combination includes zero units of either resource since some quantity of labor and equipment is necessary for production. All the combinations shown can be used for producing 100 units of output. Combinations for producing 200 units are shown below.

	Combinations for producing 200 units per week				
	A_2	B_2	C_2	D_2	E_2
Labor hours (in thousands)	6.0	4.5	3.0	1.0	.8
Equipment hours (in thousands)	.8	1.0	2.0	5.0	8.0

Schedules can be drawn up for producing 300, 500, 675, or any number of units per week. Then all combinations for producing an equal quantity of output can be plotted on a graph.

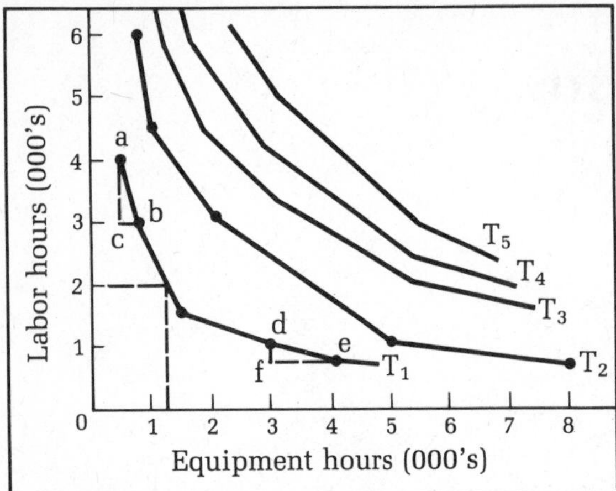

Figure A.1 Curves T_1 through T_5 are isoquants. Of the five curves, T_1 represents the lowest output and T_5 the highest output.

Combinations for producing 100 and 200 units per week are graphed in Figure A.1. Connecting the points showing combinations for producing 100 units yields the curve T_1.

All combinations on T_1 produce an *equal quantity of output*. T_1 is called an *isoquant*. An isoquant is a curve of all efficient combinations of inputs producing an equal quantity of output. T_2 is the isoquant of all combinations producing 200 units per week.

The isoquants in Figure A.1 suggest that 100 units of output could be produced using combinations of labor and capital equipment not shown in our schedule: Any point on the curve is a possible combination. In fact, there is a large number of possible combinations on any single isoquant.

A series of isoquants could be drawn for all possible levels of output. The result would be an isoquant map similar to a contour map (and to a map of indifference curves). Isoquants for larger quantities of output would lie farther to the right. We may suppose that business firms would prefer to operate on the highest isoquant possible, producing the largest quantity of output possible within the firm's resource budget.

Isoquants have certain characteristics:

(1) We have noted that zero resource units do not appear in any resource combination. We may assume that within a reasonable range of production, some quantity of both equipment and labor is needed. This means that our isoquants will not touch either axis.

(2) Isoquants may not touch or cross each other. This is because each represents a unique quantity of output. Unless more units of labor and equipment produce *fewer* units of output, isoquants cannot cross.

(3) Isoquants representing larger quantities of output lie farther to the right. A larger quantity of either resource yields greater total output. Larger quantities of both resources yield greater total output.

(4) Isoquants are *convex* to the origin. Convexity is the result of diminishing marginal product. To see why, select a point, *a*, on T_1 near the vertical axis, including a large quantity of labor and a small quantity of capital. The principle of diminishing marginal product suggests that the large amount of labor will yield small marginal product and the small amount of capital will yield large marginal product. Moving from point *a* on T_1 to another point, *b*, farther down the isoquant leaves total output unchanged. Therefore, the marginal product of the labor given up must be equal to the marginal product of the capital added. For this to be true, the quantity of labor given up, *ac*, must be greater than the quantity of capital added, *cb*. This means that near the vertical axis, isoquants are relatively steep.

As points are selected farther down T_1 (say, at *d*), combinations include less labor and more capital. The marginal product of labor must be larger relative to that of capital. Therefore, to remain on the same isoquant, less labor must be given up as larger amounts of capital are added. This means that isoquants become quite flat near the horizontal axis.

The quantity of labor given up per unit of capital added is the *marginal rate of technical substitution* (MRTS) of labor (L) for capital (K):

$$MRTS_{LK} = \frac{-\text{ labor units (given up)}}{\text{capital units (added)}}.$$

The $MRTS_{LK}$ is negative over an entire isoquant. Moreover, as we have seen, the $MRTS_{LK}$ diminishes as points are selected farther down the curve. The $MRTS_{LK}$ defines the slope of the isoquant.

The slope of an isoquant may be described another way. Between two points, total product is unchanged. Therefore, labor units given up × marginal product of labor = capital units added

× marginal product of capital. Rearranging terms,

$$\frac{\begin{array}{c}-\text{labor units}\\ \text{(given up)}\end{array}}{\begin{array}{c}\text{capital units}\\ \text{(added)}\end{array}} = \frac{\begin{array}{c}\text{marginal product}\\ \text{of capital}\end{array}}{\begin{array}{c}\text{marginal product}\\ \text{of labor}\end{array}}.$$

This equation can be expressed symbolically as

$$\frac{-Q_L}{Q_K} = \frac{MP_K}{MP_L}$$

where Q_L and Q_K stand, respectively, for quantity of labor and quantity of capital. Since the expression to the left of the equality is the slope of the isoquant, the expression on the right must also measure the slope. Thus the slope of an isoquant measures the productivity of the resource on the horizontal axis relative to the productivity of the resource on the vertical axis. To summarize:

$$\text{slope} = MRTS_{LK} = \frac{-Q_L}{Q_K} = \frac{MP_K}{MP_L}.$$

ISOCOSTS

An isoquant map illustrates the possible combinations of resources for use in production. The actual combination used depends on the prices of resources and the firm's budget for operations. The relative prices and total budget can be shown on the firm's budget or *isocost* line. An isocost line marks all resource combinations that are possible within a firm's budget constraint.

Suppose the price of labor in our example is \$8 per hour and the price of capital is \$4 per hour. The firm's budget is \$18,000 per hour. Some possible combinations of labor and capital are shown below.

Possible combinations with a budget of \$18,000: P_L = 8 and P_K = 4

Labor hours (in thousands)	2.25	2.0	1.5	1.0	.5	0.0
Capital hours (in thousands)	0.0	.5	1.5	2.5	3.5	4.5

An isocost line for \$18,000 is drawn on Figure A.2. All points on the isocost line are possible resource combinations, as well as all points within the shaded budget space. However, points not on the isocost line do not exhaust the entire budget. The slope of the isocost line is

$$\frac{-\text{labor hours (given up)}}{\text{capital hours (added)}}$$

for a given budget. The slope also reflects the prices of the two resources. Since every point on the line exhausts the entire budget, movement from one point to another on any isocost line leaves total expenditure unchanged. Therefore, labor hours given up × price of labor = capital hours added × price of capital. Rearranging terms,

$$\frac{-\text{labor hours (given up)}}{\text{capital hours (added)}} = \frac{\text{price of capital}}{\text{price of labor}}.$$

Once again, this can be expressed symbolically as

$$\frac{-Q_L}{Q_K} = \frac{P_K}{P_L}$$

where P_K and P_L are, respectively, the prices of capital and labor. Thus the slope of the isocost is also the ratio of the price of the resource measured on the horizontal axis relative to the price of the resource measured on the vertical axis. Since relative prices remain constant for drawing a single isocost line, the line has a constant slope.

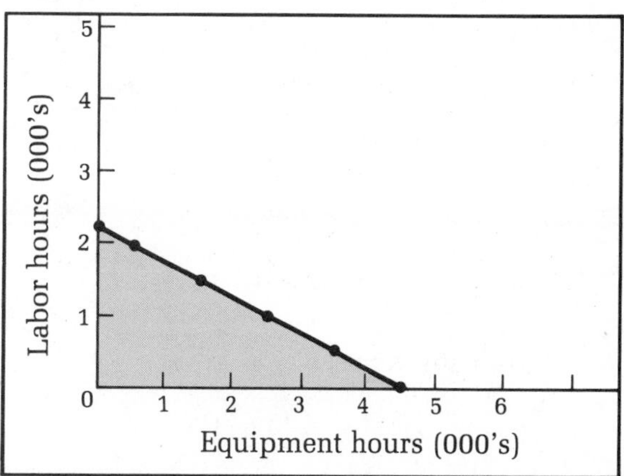

Figure A.2 Combinations on the isocost line exhaust the entire budget. Combinations in the shaded area use less than the full budget.

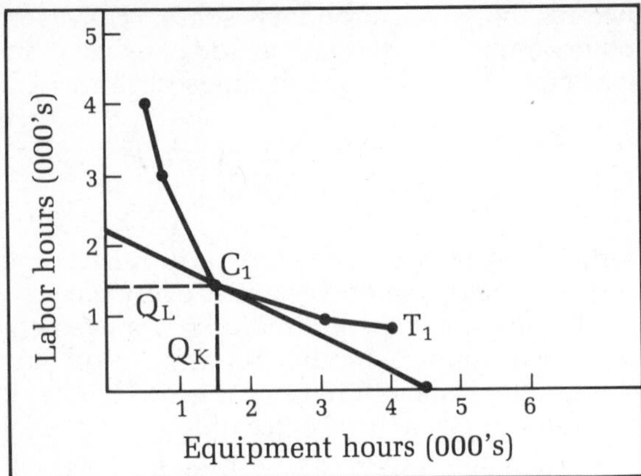

Figure A.3 Maximum output with the given budget occurs using resource combination C_1, where isoquant T_1 is tangent to the isocost line.

Equilibrium

We may assume that a firm will allocate its budget so as to produce the largest quantity of output. Stated differently, the firm will select the combination of labor and capital equipment which lies on the highest isoquant touched by its isocost line. On Figure A.3 the maximum output combination is C_1, including 1.5 thousand labor hours and 1.5 thousand equipment hours.

At the point of tangency, the slope of the isoquant T_1 is equal to the slope of the isocost line. In terms of our analysis, the marginal rate of technical substitution is equal to the price ratio:

$$MRTS_{LK} = \frac{\text{marginal product of capital}}{\text{marginal product of labor}}$$

$$= \frac{\text{price of capital}}{\text{price of labor}}$$

$$= \frac{MP_K}{MP_L} = \frac{P_K}{P_L}$$

or, rearranging terms,

$$\frac{MP_K}{P_K} = \frac{MP_L}{P_L}.$$

This equality is known as the *equal marginal productivity principle*. It states that the firm is using resources so that output per dollar spent on all resources is equal. If this were not so, the firm should increase the use of the resource for which MP/P is greater than MP/P of another. The use of the more productive resource should be expanded until diminishing marginal product makes MP/P equal for all resources.

Changing Prices and Budget

Changes in prices or in the firm's budget are represented by changes in the isocost line. *Changes in relative prices change the slope of the isocost curve, and changes in the total budget shift the isocost curve.* Suppose, first, the price of capital falls from \$4 to \$2 per hour while the price of labor remains at \$8 per hour. Total budget is still \$18,000 per hour. Some possible combinations of labor and capital are shown below.

	Possible combinations with a budget of \$18,000: $P_L = 8$ and $P_K = 2$					
Labor hours (in thousands)	2.25	2.0	1.5	1.0	.5	0.0
Equipment hours (in thousands)	0.0	1.0	3.0	5.0	7.0	9.0

The isocost line has been shifted in Figure A.4 to show possible combinations with the new prices. Note the flatter slope of the isocost line. Recall that its slope equals P_K/P_L; the lower price of capital reduces the value of the ratio and lowers the slope of the isocost line.

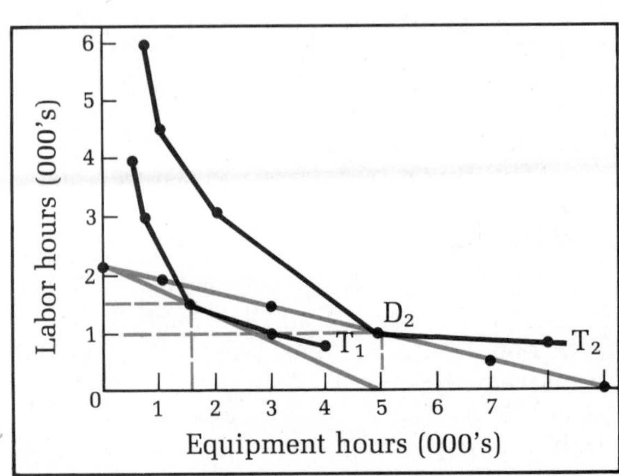

Figure A.4 Lower prices for capital equipment lead to a new, flatter isocost line and encourage substitution of capital for labor. Total output increases as the firm shifts to a new isoquant, T_2.

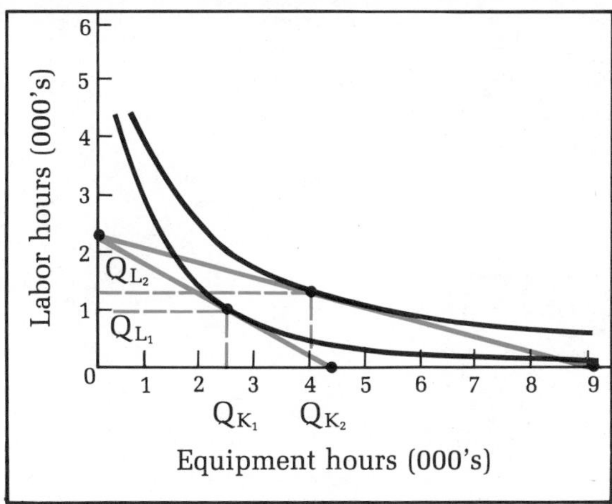

Figure A.5 Lower prices for capital equipment can also yield scale effects, increasing the use of labor as well as capital.

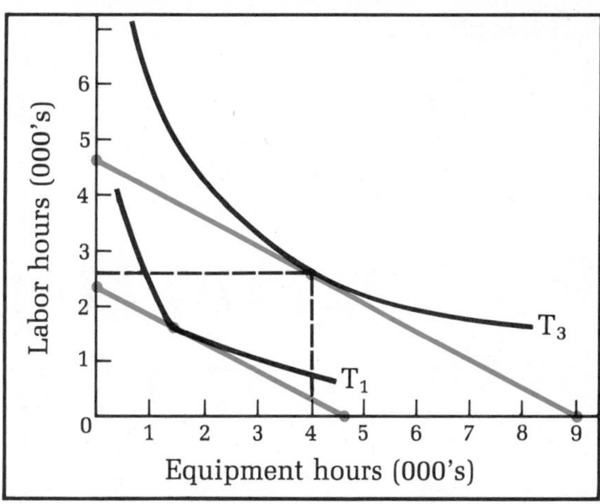

Figure A.6 A larger budget shifts the entire isocost line. Output increases as the firm shifts to a new isoquant, T_3.

Again we will assume that the firm attempts to produce the largest possible quantity within its budget. The combination for greatest production is D_2, where 200 units of output are produced per hour using 1000 labor hours and 5000 equipment hours. At the point of tangency of the isocost line with isoquant T_2, their slopes are equal. Therefore, $MP_K/MP_L = P_K/P_L$ and $MP_K/P_K = MP_L/P_L$. This combination satisfies the equal marginal productivity principle and ensures maximum efficiency in the use of resources.

Note that the lower price for capital enables the firm to substitute capital for labor in production. The most efficient combination of capital and labor is that at which $MP_K/P_K = MP_L/P_L$. The firm moves down the isoquant to reach that proportion of resources. (The firm moves down its demand curve for capital while its demand for labor shifts backward.)

The curves in Figure A.5 suggest a different outcome. In Figure A.5, relative prices of capital and labor have changed as before so that the firm's isocost line becomes flatter. But in this case, the lower price of capital enables the firm to use larger quantities of both resources. The larger quantities are a result of: *substitution* of the lower priced resource for the more costly one and an effective increase in *scale* which results from lower capital costs. The substitution and scale effects are similar to the substitution and income effects we have associated with consumer choice.

An increase in the total budget shifts the entire isocost line to the right at a slope corresponding to the existing price ratio. The isocost line for a budget of $36,000 per hour is shown in Figure A.6. The most efficient combination of resources enables the firm to produce 300 units per hour. Tangency of the new isocost line with isoquant T_3 ensures that $MP_K/P_K = MP_L/P_L$, for maximum efficiency.

Recent increases in energy prices are raising the cost of operating capital relative to labor costs. How would you expect changing resource costs to affect employment? Be careful. Consider various possibilities and be prepared to illustrate your conclusions graphically.

CHAPTER 9

Perfect Competition: Costs and Production Decisions in the Long Run

Learning Objectives

Upon completion of this chapter, you should be able to:

1. State several advantages of long-run competitive equilibrium.
2. Relate plant size to both economies and diseconomies of large scale.
3. Explain what an envelope curve is.
4. Explain the conditions for profit maximization in the long run.
5. Discuss the concepts of external economies and diseconomies.

The Golden Sands Dune Buggy Company enjoyed several prosperous years. The market for dune buggies was excellent. At the going price of $4000 the company earned economic profit on every vehicle it sold. But after several profitable years the president reported to the board of directors that competition was beginning to move into the market. The firm would have to expect declining sales in the future and lower prices for each unit sold.

The president was right. Economic profits on dune buggies had led new firms to enter the industry and other existing firms to expand plant capacity. Competition drove price down until, by the following year, dune buggies were selling for only $3000. Figure 1a shows the marginal cost and average cost curves for Golden Sands. You will remember from the last chapter that the firm established its output at the level at which marginal cost was equal to marginal revenue (or to price since there is perfect competition): MC = MR = P. At a price of $4000 the firm was producing seven buggies per month. For each unit sold, the firm earned economic profit equal to the difference between price and average total cost: AEP = AR − ATC. In Figure 1a economic profit on each dune buggy is the distance *ab*, and total economic profit is represented by the rectangle *abcd:* EP = AEP × Q.

But this was only the short run. Over the short run some resources were fixed. In the short run output may sell for a price greater than average total cost, providing economic profit. Or price may be less than average total cost (while still covering average variable cost), and economic profit may be negative. In either case firms will continue to produce in the short run.

But over the long run it is possible to change the quantity of resources considered fixed in the short run. Firms may enter or leave the industry in response to positive or negative economic profit; or existing firms may expand or contract productive capacity.

As production increased in the dune buggy industry, the market supply curve shifted to the right, to S_1 in Figure 1b. A larger quantity of output was now supplied at every price level. This forced market price down to $3000, as shown in Figure 1b. Individual firms' demand curves moved down to the horizontal line drawn at P = $3000. Golden Sands cut back its production, moving down its MC curve until MC = MR at P = MR = $3000. With output of six units per month, the firm is still able to earn economic profit. If industry supply were to increase still further, the supply curve would shift again, to S_2. Price would continue to fall and Golden Sands would cut production again. At a market price of $2400 Golden Sands would still be in business but producing only five units monthly, where MC = MR = $2400. With production of five units, average profit is AR − ATC = $2400 − $2400 = 0. Economic profit is zero. Golden Sands would still earn what we have called "normal profit"—enough to pay full opportunity costs to entrepreneurship—but the company's great days would be over.

LONG-RUN COMPETITIVE EQUILIBRIUM

The decision to expand or contract industry capacity is a long-run decision. In the short run, a firm may earn economic profit or suffer loss, but it will continue to operate as long as price covers variable cost. Over a longer period, economic profit approaches zero. All this is true if conditions for perfect competition exist in the industry.

Figures 2 and 3 summarize the process by which an industry moves toward long-run equilibrium. In Figure 2a, as supply curves of new firms are added to existing industry supply, the market supply curve shifts to the right, from S_1 to S_2. As market supply increases, price falls. Consumers can buy larger quantities at lower prices. To an individual firm, the falling market price appears, in Figure 2b, as a downward shift in the horizontal line drawn at market price. The firm moves down its marginal cost curve and produces a smaller quantity. Until market price

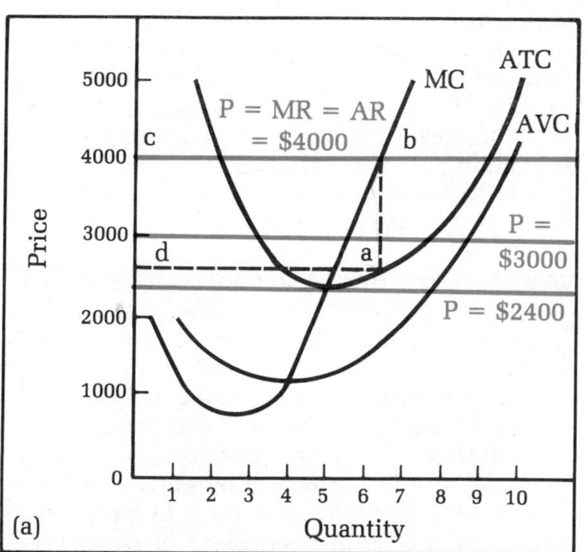

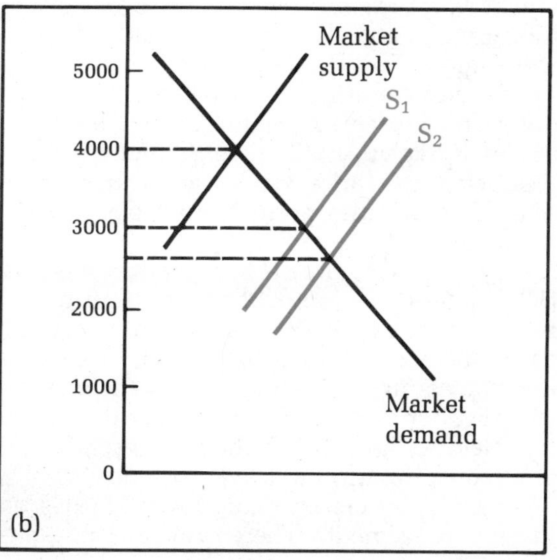

Figure 1 (a) Marginal cost and average cost curves for producing Golden Sands dune buggies. The distance *ab* is the average economic profit when 7 dune buggies are sold at a price of $4000. (b) As new firms enter the market, market supply expands to S_1 and then to S_2. Equilibrium price falls, and the firm's economic profit declines to zero.

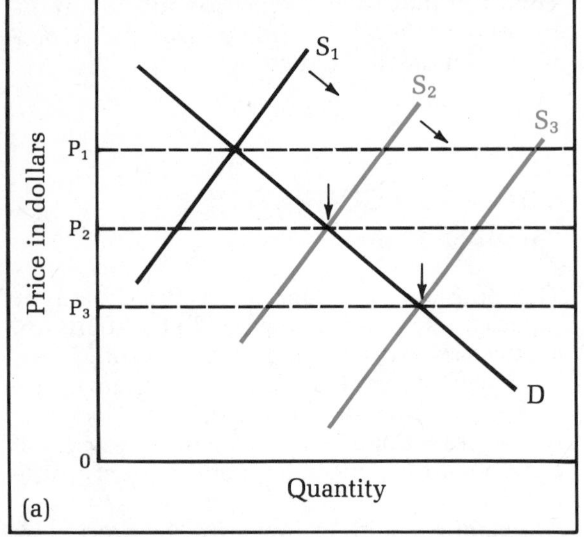

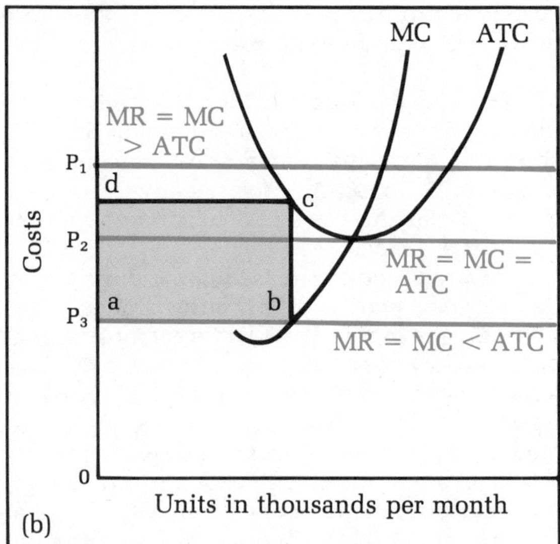

Figure 2 (a) As new firms are added to an industry, the market supply curve moves to the right. (b) As supply expands, unit price falls. At a price of P_3, the firm's average economic profit is *–bc* and total economic loss is the shaded area *abcd*.

falls to P_2 there is still economic profit. But below this price the firm would suffer loss. At a price of P_3 the loss on each unit is the difference between price and ATC. Total loss is the rectangle *abcd*.

We have seen that firms may accept losses in the short run. But when their short-run obligations expire, new long-run planning decisions will have to be made. Firms experiencing losses must contract firm capacity or drop out of the industry entirely. As they do so, market supply will begin to fall. Figure 3a shows the industry supply curve shifting back to the left as firms leave an industry. In Figure 3b, market price moves up again, until all remaining firms are producing at a price that covers average total cost. This includes normal profit but no economic profit.

At a market price of P_2, the industry is said to be in **long-run competitive equilibrium.** All firms are earning revenue sufficient to pay full costs, including normal profit. But, since they are not earning economic profit, there is no incentive for any new firms to enter the industry. Neither, however, is there an incentive for any remaining firms to leave the industry.

For producers and consumers, this is an ideal arrangement. There are five reasons why.

(1) Consumers are satisfied; they are getting the product at minimum long-run price. There is enough output to fill demand at a price buyers are willing to pay.

(2) Producers are satisfied; price is sufficient to cover the cost of the last unit produced: P = MC. Furthermore, the entry and exit of firms have stabilized price at a level that covers average total cost, including normal profit: P = ATC. (But there is no economic profit or loss for any firm.)

(3) The number of firms in the industry is just enough to satisfy market demand at lowest average total cost. No firm is operating at less than or greater than its minimum cost rate of operation.

(4) Competition has compelled firms to build plants that are neither too large nor too small. All plants are designed to produce at minimum cost; they would not be more efficient if they were larger or smaller. (We will study the question of plant size in the section that follows.)

(5) The economy as a whole benefits from industries that are in long-run competitive equilibrium. Such industries produce at the lowest possible cost in terms of the scarce resources they use. They pay a return to productive resources that is just sufficient to cover their opportunity costs—that is, they do not attract resources that could be better employed elsewhere.

PLANT SIZE AND THE LONG RUN

What about the size of plants in long-run competitive equilibrium? For maximum efficiency should plants be small or large? The answer is: It depends. As larger plants are built, production costs per unit of output often tend to fall. But beyond some level of plant size, costs per unit may increase, as we will see.

Long-run average costs are all variable. There are no fixed costs in the long run. In the long run, variable costs include all costs of plant, equipment, and administrative personnel, costs which are considered fixed in the short run. The shape of the long-run average cost curve depends on the behavior of these and other costs for plants of various size.

Economists refer to the size of plant as *scale.* In some industries the scale of plant may have no effect on unit costs. Then we say that production involves *constant returns to scale,* or *constant average costs* at every plant size. In the more usual case, however, larger plants experience increasing returns to scale, or lower average costs, up to some level of plant size. Beyond that size, larger plants may have decreasing returns to scale, or higher average costs.

When average costs are lower in large plants, we say that production involves **economies of large scale.** When average costs rise with larger plant capacity, we say that production encounters **diseconomies of large scale.**

Economies of Large Scale

Why do larger plants sometimes have lower production costs? There are four basic advantages of large size, technological and administrative.

(1) A large plant may be able to use more advanced and specialized equipment. Some equipment requires a large production run if it is to be efficient.

(2) With a larger plant, a firm may be able to buy its materials in larger quantities, at a price discount.

(3) A large plant may make more profitable use of by-products. It may even develop subsidiary plants, using by-products to produce other goods. A large petroleum refinery, for instance, may produce chemicals derived from oil. A fish-packing plant may process the heads and tails and sell them as fertilizer. Some large plants may use excess heat from production for "co-generating" their own electric power.

(4) Large plants provide many opportunities to increase efficiency through better organization and administration. Production can be organized into specialized divisions so that less time is lost shifting workers from one operation to another. The work force may become more specialized and develop higher skills. Staff members can be trained for particular functions such as production planning, market research, cost accounting, and finance. The flow of materials can be regulated more carefully so that less time is lost waiting for parts to arrive.

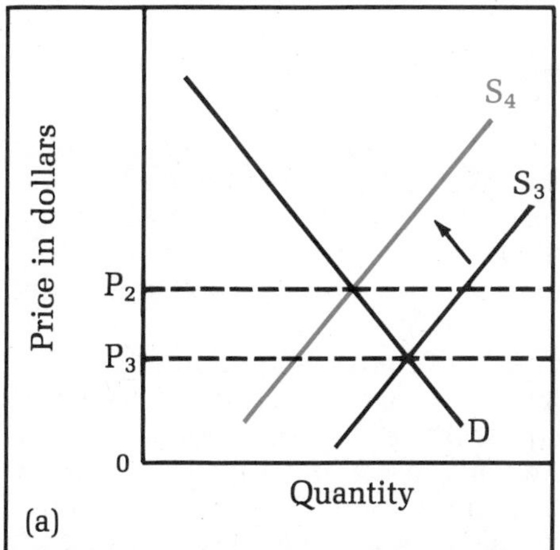

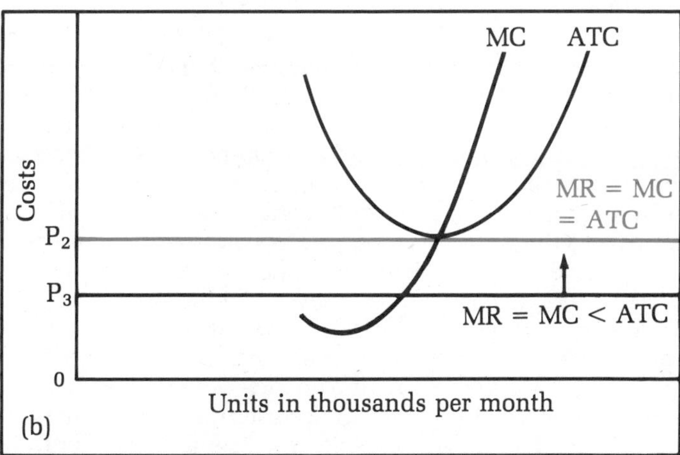

Figure 3 (a) Economic loss forces firms to leave the industry, and the market supply curve moves to the left. (b) As supply falls, unit price increases. Negative economic profit rises to zero.

Extended Example The Bicycle Boom

Until the 1970s, bicycle production in the United States was somewhat less than exciting. Between 6 million and 7.5 million units were produced each year, mostly by eight small, family-held firms. But the relative tranquility changed in 1971, and the industry hasn't been the same since.

Suddenly, adult Americans began to buy bikes. Sales to adults now account for more than half of all bikes sold and pushed industry sales to 15.2 million in 1973. The physical fitness fad was partly responsible. Also, the energy crisis and the emphasis on protecting the environment led many young adults to take up cycling to work and for play.

The surge in demand surprised bike manufacturers. Their frantic efforts to fill orders for 10-speed adult bikes led to sharply rising costs and falling quality. Limited by their fixed productive capacity, firms moved up their marginal cost curves and prices rose.

Foreign producers jumped at the chance to penetrate the booming U.S. market and to fill the gap left by inadequate domestic capacity. Imports rose 20 percent in one year, capturing 37 percent of the market by 1972. Foreign manufacturers continue to supply almost 30 percent of component parts, including all multispeed gear systems, 80 percent of tires, and 75 percent of bike chains.

Bike sales took a beating in the recession of 1973–75. The adult market was saturated. Sales growth depends on replacements, and good 10-speeds can last up to ten years. Fortunately, the average child outgrows two or three bikes before reaching the 10-speed model. Domestic firms are particularly adept at gauging the tastes of the young and capitalizing on new fads. The "Motocross" bike became especially popular; it sports racing plates, an extra cross bar, and sometimes a fake fuel tank.

Industry prospects look favorable for the future. The Federal Highway Administration has appropriated $6 million for demonstration bikeways to supplement the 25,000 miles of bike routes now in use. With the greater area for bike riding, demand is expected to stabilize at about 16 million units per year.

Cyclists are adding accessories to their equipment and fueling a prosperous new industry. Some of the extras include locks and lights, pole banners that glow in the dark, snap-on baby seats, flower baskets, and strap-on duffel bags. Accessories add up to $100 million in sales a year. Annual growth in sales is expected to continue at about 8 percent to 10 percent, with industry revenues of $1 billion yearly, and manufacturers will turn out thirty thousand bikes a day.

Illustrate graphically changes in market conditions for bicycles. What is the effect of imports on the industry supply curve? What happens to economic profit as the industry approaches long-run competitive equilibrium?

In some types of production there is almost no limit to the economies of scale. Long-run average costs continue to fall as plants increase in size. Figure 4a shows the *long-run average cost (LRAC) curve* for a transportation firm. By expanding its plant and equipment to a very large size, the transportation firm is better able to use modern technology to reduce costs. A firm's average cost curves may continue to decline as capital and development costs are spread over more and more passengers or tons of freight. Airlines or railroads can increase their capital stock greatly without encountering diseconomies of scale. Automobile and steel factories are other examples of increasing returns to scale. In fact, the history of modern mass production is largely a story of increasing returns to scale in industries where vast amounts of capital investment have increased productivity and reduced unit costs. Your Chevy could be made in a small factory employing a few hundred workers, but not for a price that you would want to pay.

Some types of production seem to be characterized by the curve in Figure 4b. Average costs decline at first and then remain about the same over a wide range of plant sizes. In many manufacturing industries, plants of quite different sizes manage to be competitive with each other. Some minimum size may be necessary in order to enjoy the available economies of scale. But beyond that point, whatever economies there may be from growing larger are offset by diseconomies—such as higher costs of management. As a result, large producers cannot undersell small ones. The printing industry furnishes a good example: a few giant firms exist side by side with a large number of medium-sized and small firms. If you want to print a large metropolitan telephone directory you will go to one of the giants. But if you're the editor of a small magazine with a limited press run you may find that a small printer will give more individual attention to your order. In many industries, a purchasing firm may find it practical to establish a customer relationship with a supplying firm of roughly similar scale. This ensures that the resources of the supplying firm are adequate for the needs of the purchasing firm.

Diseconomies of Large Scale

In some industries the long-run average cost curve rises after a certain size of plant has been reached. The costs of maintaining the larger size begin to outweigh the economies of large scale. This may happen because of administrative problems: there may be too many employees for easy supervision, or there may be so many supervisors that it is difficult to coordinate them all. Or diseconomies may result from resource problems: the use of poorer quality resources may push up a firm's production costs. For example, a coal mine may be able to expand only by working seams of coal that are less productive or more difficult to mine than those currently in use. Or a farm, if it is to grow much larger, may have to cultivate land that is less fertile or is farther away. Figure 4c shows a long-run cost curve for an industry that experiences decreasing returns to scale.

Plant Size and Optimum Scale

If you were the president of an ice-cream company and were thinking of building a new plant, how would you decide on its size? Which plant size would have the **optimum scale**—that is, the scale that offers lowest average total costs? Let us suppose that the long-run average cost curve for ice-cream plants resembles the curve in Figure 4c. A small plant can supply its local area, but a larger one could supply the whole town at lower unit cost. Beyond a certain plant size, problems of supervision develop, as well as higher costs of transportation and product handling. Thus average costs will be higher for very large ice-cream plants.

In Figure 5 we have drawn short-run average total cost curves for plants of different sizes. An ice-cream plant of size *A* is designed to produce 5000 gallons of ice cream per month. In the short run it could produce up to 10,000 gallons, but this would exceed its design capabilities, and average total costs would increase. A plant of size *B* is designed to produce 25,000 gal-

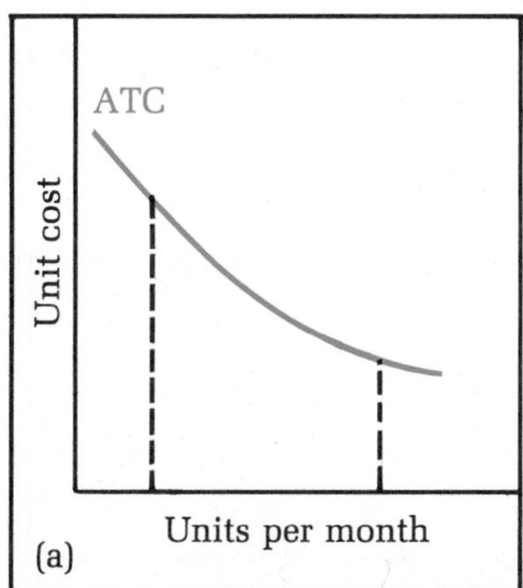

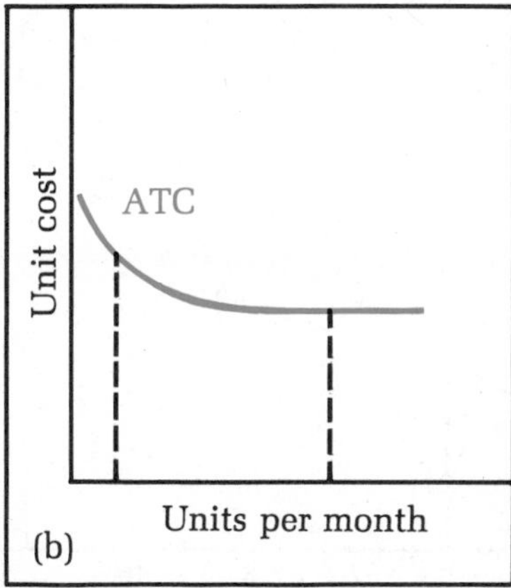

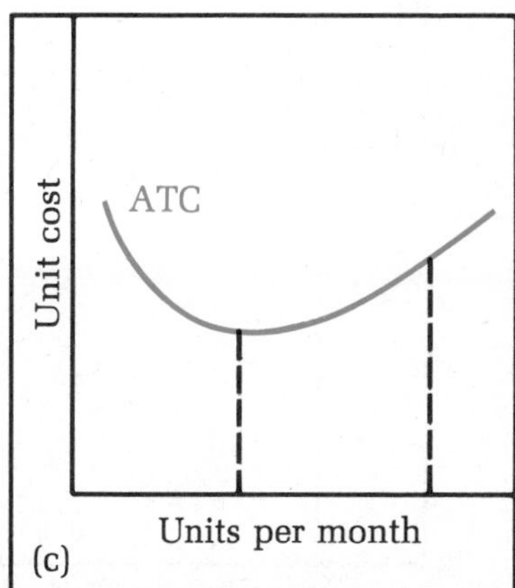

Figure 4 Long-run average cost curves show scale economies: (a) an industry with economies of scale; unit costs decline as plant size increases; (b) an industry with initial economies of scale and eventual constant average costs; (c) an industry with initial economies of scale and eventual diseconomies of scale.

lons per month. At its optimum level of operation, average total costs are lower than those of plant *A* because of the economies of large scale. Plant C could be built to produce 50,000 gallons per month, but it would have to seek markets outside the metropolitan area, and that would increase average total costs. It would experience diseconomies of scale.

You decide to build a plant of size *B*, because you expect to operate within a range of output around 25,000 gallons per month. Although you may sometimes produce as much as 35,000 gallons per month, your unit costs will still be lower than if you were operating plant *C*. In slow times you may reduce production to 15,000 gallons, but unit costs will be lower than if you were operating plant *A*.

The Long-Run Planning Curve

Before you decided on the optimum scale, you had engineers prepare cost estimates for plants of various sizes. The picture they presented may have resembled the diagram in Figure 6. Plant A_5 is designed to produce 5000 gallons of ice cream a month, plant A_{10} will produce 10,000 gallons, and so forth. An **envelope curve** has been drawn to enclose the individual plant curves. This envelope curve is the *long-run average cost (LRAC) curve,* sometimes called the *industry planning curve.*

The long-run average cost curve is *not* a separate, independent curve. It is drawn from short-run average total cost curves for plants of every conceivable size. Every point on the long-run curve represents the lowest average cost for which that quantity of output could be produced. Thus, an infinite number of short-run curves would be drawn and a single point taken from each to construct the long-run curve.

This is why the envelope curve *touches (is tangent to)* the short-run average cost curves for plants of various sizes. But notice that, except for the B_{25} curve, the LRAC curve is *not* tangent to them at their lowest points. This is significant because it shows that a plant designed to produce exactly 25,000 gallons per month will achieve lowest average cost for firms in the industry. It represents the *optimum* scale of plant. Smaller plants fail to enjoy all the potential economies of larger scale. Larger plants encounter diseconomies. Except for plant B_{25} the envelope curve touches average cost curves

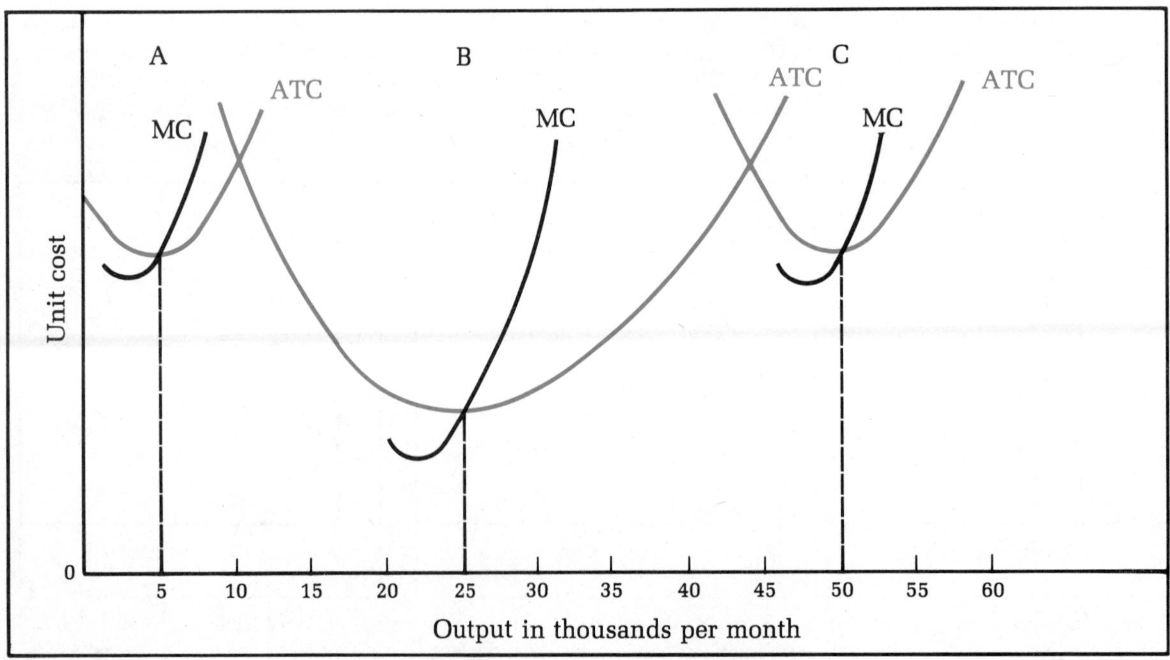

Figure 5 Short-run average total cost curves for ice-cream plants of different sizes. Plant *A* is desirable for small output; its minimum costs per unit occur when producing 5000 gallons. Plant *B* operates most efficiently at an output of 25,000 gallons. Plant C operates most efficiently at 50,000 gallons; notice, however, that plant C has higher unit costs than plant *B* at its most efficient volume of output.

Extended Example The End of the Short Run

Nostalgia buffs know about them.

There aren't many left, and soon they'll probably be extinct. But they used to be the favorite meeting place for teenagers after school, businessmen at lunch, and couples out for an evening stroll.

Of course, I'm referring to the drugstore soda fountain.

There was a distinctive odor about them—a combination of fizz-water and bubbly fudge sauce. And they served real, honest-to-goodness milkshakes—poured thickly from metal shakers with beads of condensation running down the sides. For lunch, a crisp club sandwich or a slaw dog, so rich with filling that you had to eat it with a fork. And through it all a feeling of personal attention to your individual tastes.

They're almost all gone now. The short run has come to an end and they're dropping away. They've been victims of the inexorable force of supply and demand. Demand first. Population growth has certainly increased the potential market. But the growth of the automobile, suburban sprawl, and the faster pace of modern life have sent customers to the fast-food franchised eateries. The tastes of today's young adults have become accustomed to standardized food, often ordered through a microphone and shoved at you through a slot!

As soda fountain customers drifted away, demand curves shifted back, revenues fell, and normal profit changed to economic loss. Many establishments remained in business as long as revenues were sufficient to cover variable costs. Fixed costs were low for their aging capital equipment; losses at the soda fountain could often be subsidized by profits at the prescription counter.

What was happening to supply over these decades? Remember that a supply curve is the rising portion of marginal cost, above average variable cost. How have modern conditions affected the position and shape of marginal cost?

The answer requires a word about scale of plant. Optimum scale for drugstore lunch counters is rather small. Small scale limits the use of specialized labor, equipment, and management. The problem of scale is a real disadvantage in competition with new forms of food service where optimum scale is very large. Mass techniques of organization, purchasing, and production in large volume have enhanced efficiency far beyond what is possible at the lunch counter. The predictable result has been a wide difference between the average and marginal cost curves for the two types of service. In terms of supply price, the old couldn't compete with the new.

To make matters worse, the industry was experiencing long-run diseconomies of growth. Growth of industry in general was increasing the cost of resources. Old drugstores are generally located on high-cost, highly taxed urban land. Opportunity costs are high, excluding all but the most profitable enterprises. Utility rates and materials costs have risen similarly. Furthermore, general wage inflation in urban areas has been especially hard on such a labor-intensive activity. Diseconomies of economic growth have shifted long-run average cost (LRAC) curves upward for the drugstore lunch counter.

For any business enterprise, the end of the short run brings on the sometimes painful question of long-run planning. One by one these establishments have faced up to the economic facts of life. We are witnessing the sad demise of an American institution.

Often the decision to purchase food involves more than simple nutrition. What bundles of characteristics are included in purchases at the soda fountain and at the fast-food eatery?

at levels of output less than or greater than short-run minimum cost. This means that, say, 10,000 units per month may be produced more cheaply by plant A_{13}—built to produce 13,000 units but operated at less than full capacity—than by plant A_{10}. Likewise, 35,000 units can be produced most cheaply by Plant C_{33}, operated at greater than minimum cost. In fact, for all quantities of output less than that associated with optimum scale, plants should be built larger than necessary to capture additional economies. For quantities greater than optimum scale, plants should be built smaller than needed to minimize diseconomies. In both cases, plants would operate at higher than minimum total cost.

PROFIT MAXIMIZATION IN THE LONG RUN

In a perfectly competitive industry, firms will tend to build plants of optimum scale in the long run. That is, their short-run average cost curve will be tangent to industry long-run average cost at its lowest point. In Figure 6, all firms would build plants of size B_{25}. When the industry is in long-run competitive equilibrium, price will have fallen to the point where no firm earns economic profit—that is, price will also be tangent to the long-run average cost curve at its lowest point. We can abbreviate this statement to read:

$$P = AR \begin{array}{l} = \text{minimum ATC} \\ = \text{minimum LRAC.} \end{array}$$

But each firm will also be in short-run equilibrium. As we saw earlier, this means that marginal cost (MC) is equal to marginal revenue (MR). Since average cost is at a minimum, marginal cost must be equal to average cost. The complete statement of the conditions of long-run equilibrium for a firm in perfect competition thus becomes

$$MC = MR = P \begin{array}{l} = \text{AR} \\ = \text{minimum ATC} \\ = \text{minimum LRAC.} \end{array}$$

How Realistic Is This View of the Long Run?

The picture of firms in a state of perfect competition is not a photograph of firms in the real world. The theory of perfect competition is a model. It is a description of a theoretical world in which no firm has control over price and nothing prevents firms from entering or leaving an industry. Economists study this ideal world because it shows how resources would be allocated efficiently under perfect competition.

In most industries long-run adjustments are constantly occurring. Firms enter or leave an industry on the basis of profitability. Where demand is growing, new firms will try to establish positions. Some will succeed. Others will fail and be forced to withdraw, or they may be absorbed by established firms.

Seldom, if ever, will an industry reach the point that we have called long-run equilibrium. This is because conditions in the economy are

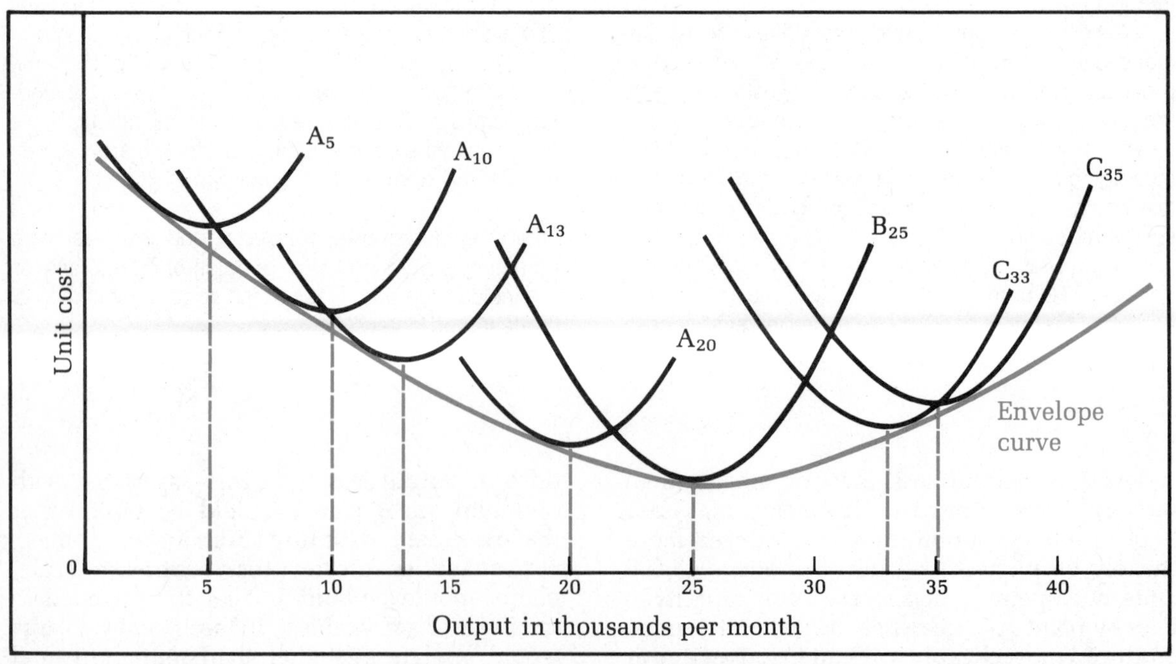

Figure 6 An envelope curve is drawn by taking a single point from the short-run average total cost curve for every possible plant size. The envelope curve is tangent to all the short-run curves and is called the long-run average cost curve.

Extended Example Market Changes in the Long Run

Sometimes changes in consumer demand can change a dying industry into a booming one. The ice for your beer keg was very likely the product of a $175 million a year industry—an industry which faced possible extinction only thirty years ago.

In the early 1800s ice was made in the United States by cutting natural ice from ponds and storing it in icehouses for use throughout the year. The first ice plants were built in 1869 and used the principle of ammonia absorption to freeze water. Output was about fifty million tons a year, and the iceman was an important part of American life.

All this changed in the 1920s with the appearance of home refrigerators. Ice-making firms began to go out of business. It looked as if market demand would never again be high enough to justify long-run plans to produce this very basic product.

Who could have predicted the tremendous changes in the United States social environment since World War II? Americans have been earning more and spending more. They've been partying and picnicking and stocking their freezers with processed foods. With no room for storing ice for peak needs they've turned to self-service dispensers, and the ice-making industry is off and running.

Small firms have combined into larger ones with greater financial capital for new, fast-freezing equipment. The Turbo method freezes layers of water in sheets like plywood; the sheets are then broken into chips. The Voght method freezes ice around a metal tube which is then slipped out; the resulting ice cylinder is sliced into many circular pieces for a larger cooling surface. Both methods require only about twenty-five minutes. A total of about five million tons of ice is produced annually, with about two thirds considered "social ice" and the remainder used to supplement mechanical refrigeration in railroad cars, trucks, and storage depots.

Increasing consumer demand provided the incentive for technological change in this industry. External economies of growth shifted long-run planning curves down. Supply has become more elastic over the long run.

Construct a series of graphs illustrating shifts in demand and supply for ice over time. Show how supply curves reflect long-run average costs and how optimum scale has increased. What has happened to industry planning curves? What has happened to price? How does this article illustrate the responsiveness of industry to consumer preferences in the short run and in the long run? Why is it correct to say that industries seldom actually reach long-run competitive equilibrium?

dynamic, i.e., ever changing. Market demand changes, and prices change with it. New developments in technology and resources cause industry cost curves to move up or down. It would be quite remarkable if any industry were to reach long-run competitive equilibrium and remain there. Rather, an industry will move toward what would be a long-run equilibrium position *if no further changes were to occur;* it will not reach that position because some change will occur and send it off in another direction.

In some industries, adjustments to changing conditions may be slow because of rigidities within the industry. Long-run plans require large commitments of costly resources for a long time period. The short run thus becomes very long, and firms may show economic profit (or loss) for long periods. This seems to be true of the steel industry in the United States. Because of heavy financial commitments made years ago, many mills operate equipment that is technologically obsolete. Technologically backward firms may suffer loss over many years before they finally leave the industry or update their capital equipment.

In some industries market demand may be too low relative to optimum scale, so plant size must be less than optimum. In others, market demand may be high, but barriers to entry keep out new firms. In both cases, production is less than perfectly efficient. Although existing firms earn no economic profit, costs and prices are still higher than minimum.

Competitive Equilibrium: A Standard of Efficiency

Economists are interested in the theory of long-run competitive equilibrium because it offers a standard of economic efficiency. In long-run competitive equilibrium, industries would be producing the goods most desired by consumers at the lowest possible prices. Firms would be building plants of optimum scale and operating them at minimum cost per unit of output. Moreover, they would be producing just the collection of goods and services that the market wants—not too many of some things and too few of others. There would be no economic profit—only normal profit.

This state of affairs would be ideal in many ways. Consumers could buy goods and services at the lowest possible prices. Any improvement or new discovery would be reflected quickly in lower prices and greater output. And no government board or planning authority would be needed to tell firms how to go about it. Of course, no economy in the world has ever attained this kind of efficiency and none ever will. But economists often use long-run competitive equilibrium as a standard by which to judge the actual performance of an industry. We can say, for instance, that an industry in which most of the output is produced by two or three large firms is rather far removed from the ideal of perfectly competitive equilibrium. In the following chapters, as we study monopoly and imperfect competition, we will see in what ways such an industry is likely to fall short of the perfectly competitive ideal, and why.

What Determines the Number of Firms?

This is an important question for two reasons. First, the number of firms affects the level of competition in U.S. industry and thus the power of firms to restrict output and to keep price above average total cost.

Second, the number determines the efficiency of firms. When there are many firms in competition, they will tend to construct plants of optimum scale and operate them at lowest average total cost. Without competition there is no necessary drive to maximize output per unit of scarce resources.

In Table 1 we have listed some U.S. industries, together with certain of their characteristics. Column (1) is the number of firms in each industry in 1972. Column (2) is the percentage of the market supplied by the fifty largest firms in each industry. Wherever the figures in column (2) are low, it means that the largest fifty firms supply only a small proportion of the industry's output. Wherever the figures in column (2) are high, a few large firms dominate the industry.

Table 1 **Degree of Competition in Industry (1972)**

Industry	(1) Number of firms	(2) % of market supplied by 50 largest firms
Motor vehicle parts	2610	85
Radio/TV equipment	10,043	75
Meatpacking	2580	65
Food preparation	2113	65
Paints and allied products	1576	65
Bread and cake	3062	60
Newspapers	8815	60
Milk	1923	55
Soft drinks	2193	45
Plastic products	10,043	35
Women's dresses	6989	28
Special dies, tools	7154	20
Machinery, except electrical	19,160	12

From the standpoint of our perfectly competitive model, the best industries are those for which the figures in column (2) are low. Where there are many firms, competition will be greater. Firms will tend to construct plants of optimum scale and operate them at minimum average total cost. Where there are relatively few firms, they may use market power to restrict output and keep price above average total cost.

What determines the number of firms in the industry? One factor, of course, is the quantity of output demanded by consumers. If market demand is only ten units per month, one firm can usually satisfy it by operating a single plant. The plant will probably be smaller than the optimum and will operate at greater than minimum average cost. If market demand is five hundred units per month, two firms operating two plants of optimum scale may suffice. If demand is five thousand units per month, the market may require twenty plants of optimum scale operating at minimum cost. This would be closest to the perfectly competitive model and best for consumers and society. In many U.S. industries large numbers of firms do exist, as Table 1 shows.

Another factor that determines the number of firms in an industry is the shape of the long-run average cost curve. In Figures 4b and 4c we saw that in many industries average total costs

Extended Example Sugar Elasticity and the Long Run

If you have a "sweet tooth" you may remember with horror the sudden increase in sugar prices in 1974. The price of raw sugar in the United States jumped from $.11 to $.60 per pound in only ten months. Bakers, bottlers, and candymakers all over the country passed on their higher costs to their customers.

After a few years, price declined. By 1977 sugar was selling for less than $.08 a pound. But the wide price gyrations of the past continue to make sugar producers and consumers nervous.

Sugar markets have been coping with problems of elasticity. Demand and supply curves have been going through a painful process of adjustment to new conditions in the world economy. Demand for sugar has been relatively price inelastic. This is because there are few substitutes, sugar purchases comprise only a small portion of the budget, and more and more people are beginning to regard sugar as a necessity rather than as a luxury. Demand curves have been shifting to the right, along with rising incomes and growing population. Consumption has been increasing at a fairly steady rate of about 2 percent a year. In 1978 Americans used an average of 129 pounds of sweeteners in processed foods and beverages for a total of 13.2 million tons. Rising affluence and population growth have increased appetites for luxury foods in developing nations as well. This is particularly true in the newly rich Arab nations, where sugar is clearly a superior good. The worldwide inflation of the 1970s also fed the demand for sugar. Many commodity speculators purchased salable products, including sugar, as a hedge against falling currency values.

All these factors contributed to high and rising demand for raw sugar. The sudden surge in demand bumped up against the typical problem in agriculture: inelastic supply in the short run. The world's supply of raw sugar depends on production and investment months or years in advance. In 1973 the Soviet Union experienced a severe crop failure in its valuable sugar beet producing region. Supplies on the world market dropped sharply, and sugar producers throughout the world were able to raise prices repeatedly to ration their limited supplies.

High prices should serve an incentive function, and supply curves should become more elastic as producers adjust their production plans. Unhappily, land suitable for sugar cane is in short supply. To increase output, it is necessary to increase yields from existing acreage. Better irrigation systems and improved planting and harvesting techniques help, but such improvements are costly. New processing mills for the increased yield cost $30 million to $50 million each. Sugar producers were slow to make these investment expenditures until they were sure the higher demand would be permanent. In the meantime, short-run supply curves remained inelastic and prices soared.

The long run provides time for changes in demand as well as supply. Users of a scarce commodity will seek substitutes. Fortunately, there is a plentiful alternative to sugar beets and cane in—would you believe?—corn. The Japanese have developed a new technique for liquifying corn starch to produce a sugary syrup nearly twice as sweet as sugar. Under normal circumstances, its high cost would keep it from competing with sugar; but its cost was 10 percent to 15 percent below the high sugar prices of 1974. Corn syrup became an especially attractive substitute for sugar in making jam and cola drinks. Americans reduced their average consumption of sugar in recent years and made up the difference by consuming more of the new sweetener.

Demand curves for sugar were shifting to the left at just about the time that expanded sugar production was finally hitting the market, and prices dropped sharply. But the story doesn't end here. Once producers have expanded their productive capacity, they are back in their short run. When new capital improvements are in place, short-run supply again becomes fairly inelastic, and suppliers are subject to wide price fluctuations.

These adjustments in sugar markets are typical in agriculture, where demand and supply curves tend to be inelastic. Prices vary widely as farmers adjust production. But in agriculture the adjustments always come too late—a sad result of the growing cycle. The expected profitability of increased output occurs only for the very first farmers to bring increased supplies to market. For the rest, there may be losses and severe cutbacks, setting the stage for another boom and bust cycle in the future.

What other agricultural markets are subject to extreme fluctuations as a result of short-run supply inelasticity? What implications does this problem have for long-range food supplies? How has government helped farmers deal with this problem?

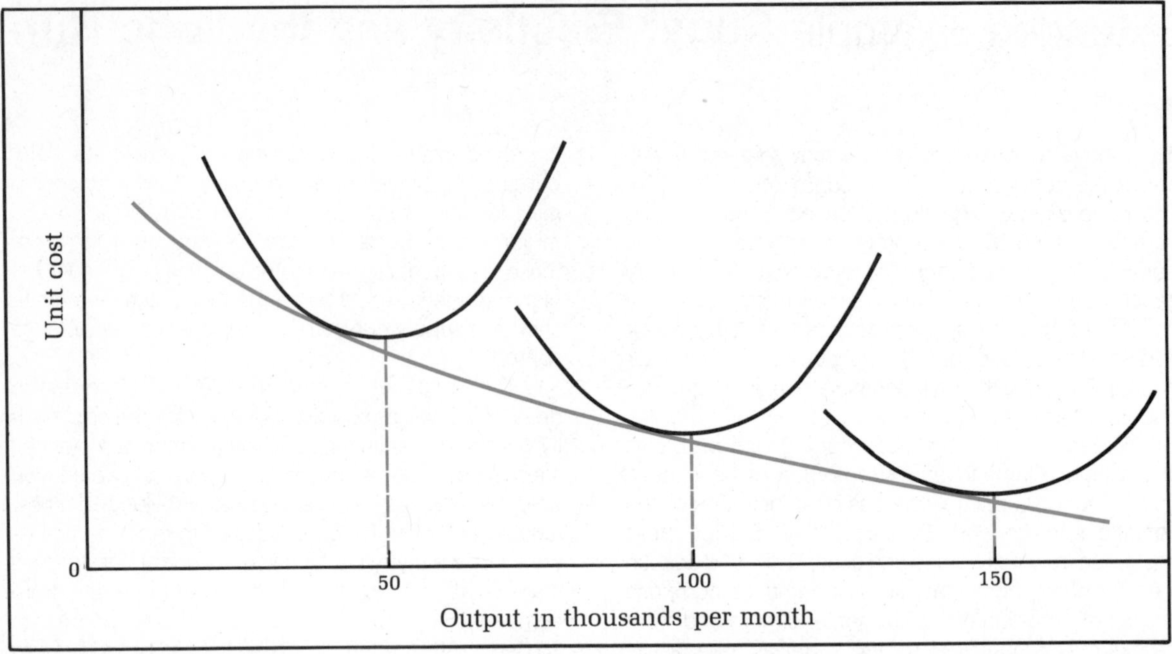

Figure 7 This long-run average cost curve slopes downward. This curve illustrates economies of scale for plants designed to produce larger quantities.

tend to be about the same for different sizes of plants or to increase for plants larger than a certain scale. But suppose an industry has a long-run average cost curve that slopes downward over its entire length, like the one in Figure 4a. In Figure 7 the long-run curve is drawn on the assumption of continuing economies of scale for plants of larger and larger size. Plants producing 100,000 units per month have lower average total costs than plants producing 50,000. Plants producing 150,000 units have even lower average total costs. Thus even if market demand is for 150,000 units, only one plant will be needed for efficient production.

Something like this happens in industries requiring much capital equipment with high fixed costs. As output increases, the costs of fixed equipment are spread over a larger and larger volume. Industries that are characterized by economies of very large scale include steel, autos, aircraft, tires, and organic fibers. In these industries fewer than fifty firms supply almost the entire U.S. market.

Economies of large scale have important consequences for consumers and for society. If larger and larger volume can be produced for lower unit cost, then the ideal plant is one large enough to produce for the entire market—that is, a single monopoly firm. Industries that experience continuing economies of very large scale are often called **natural monopolies.** Technical conditions within such an industry lead to dominance by one firm. Examples of natural monopolies are electric power and telephone service. It is easy to see why they are generally run as monopolies if you try to imagine several telephone companies competing for customers on the same block, each stringing its own lines. Natural monopolies are discussed in the next chapter, along with ways of regulating them.

INDUSTRY GROWTH AND CHANGING COSTS

We have been discussing the pattern of costs *within* a firm for various scales of plant. We found that in long-run competitive equilibrium each firm will build plants that can be operated at minimum average total cost. But sometimes as an industry grows, changes in costs occur as a result of actions of other firms. The existence of many firms in an industry may affect the supply and the price of needed productive resources. For example, as an industry grows, the available

Extended Example
Franchises and Ray Kroc's Burger Stand

Most of us feel that we deserve a break—if not today, at least once in a while. Millions take their breaks at McDonald's and contribute to one of the nation's grandest success stories since World War II.

The "McDonald's Experience" is based on an image of fun and healthy, family-oriented food service. Fast feeding was a natural in the United States. Eating in defense plants and military camps during the war had accustomed Americans to standardized foods. New techniques of mass production and blitz media advertising had been developed in manufacturing industries and were waiting to be applied to food service. Moreover, the device of franchising revolutionized marketing arrangements throughout consumer industries generally.

Ray Kroc didn't foresee all this when he began his selling career. He began with only a large share of persistence and determination and a fierce drive to succeed. Selling paper cups and milkshake machines took him into restaurants around the country, where he gradually became acquainted with some of the problems of the fragmented food industry. He saw the potential profitability of streamlining food service: eliminating waste and increasing efficiency through mass production; relieving dependence on temperamental cooks through prepackaged, premeasured foods; and providing food of consistent quality at lowest prices.

In 1954 Ray Kroc found just the spot for beginning his venture. It was a hamburger stand in San Bernardino, California, and it caught his attention because the owners wanted to buy equipment for preparing forty-eight milkshakes at one time! The stand was the property of Maurice and Richard McDonald and already bore the distinctive golden arches trademark. It was located at the end of U.S. Route 66 and captured the bulk of east-west traffic in the area. The name was appealing, having the charm of a child's nursery rhyme. Kroc persuaded the brothers to sell all trademarks, copyrights, formulas, arches, and the name for $2.7 million. Then he launched into the sale of licenses entitling *franchisees* to share in the benefits of assembly-line methods in food service.

The word *franchise* comes from a French word meaning *to free.* Franchising was intended to free enterprising workers from dead-end jobs and allow them to own and operate their own businesses. The first major franchiser in the United States was General Motors, which began to license its automobile dealers in 1898. The sale of dealer franchises helped overcome some of GM's distribution problems. It was a source of financial capital for the manufacturer and a source of highly motivated salespeople who were working for their own interest. The drive to "be your own boss" accelerated in the 1950s, fueled by production of cheap, mass-produced goods. By 1967, total sales of franchised businesses mounted to $90 billion and accounted for one fourth of all retail sales.

Of course, franchising also created some problems. It was driving independent "Mom and Pop" enterprises out of business. Frequently it also milked franchisees. Many enthusiastic newcomers invested their life's savings and the labor of their families to get their franchise outlet going, often to lose their entire investment if the business failed. A Congressional investigation into some shady franchising operations slowed the pace of growth in some industries during the 1970s.

Franchising was appropriate for hamburger sales because the product could be standardized, produced efficiently on a large scale, and sold through mass-selling techniques. McDonald's franchisees were required to follow definite product standards and selling practices. They were instructed in all aspects of the industry at Hamburger University outside Chicago. Although anti-trust legislation prohibits the franchiser from selling supplies to the franchisee, unwritten agreements were made for purchasing premeasured, prepackaged supplies from approved suppliers. Franchisees pay $15,000 initially, to be rebated without interest in twenty years. Many franchisees also rent their building and equipment from McDonald's for annual rent of a percentage of gross revenues. They also pay a yearly franchising fee. In the 1970s McDonald's began gradually buying back its franchises and by 1973 was operating a third of the stands itself.

In 1974 total sales were $2 billion with the average stand grossing $600,000. McDonald's is big business. The chain buys 1 percent of all beef wholesaled in the United States and provides more meals than the U.S.

Army. Its stock trades on the New York Stock Exchange and in 1973 was considered a "glamour" stock along with AT&T, Polaroid, Xerox, and Sears.

At McDonald's the economies of large scale reduced costs through use of mass-production technology. Production was streamlined from patty to patron, and price remained for years at only $.15. Equipment is designed for maximum efficiency, and operators are trained for maximum productivity. The norm is to serve a burger, fries, and shake within fifty seconds. New products are tested exhaustively before they are introduced. Every aspect of the business is carefully studied and standardized for psychological appeal.

The drive to keep price low means low unit profits; so volume is important for maximum total profits. High volume depends on advertising, and McDonald's has been innovative here, too. The economies of large scale yield efficiencies in advertising budgets. Franchisees pay a percentage of gross revenues into a central fund that supports McDonald's displays in parades and state fairs. The fund also provides free hamburgers to various customers (such as victims of natural disasters—always well publicized). Advertisements stress McDonald's family-oriented image and point up associations with popular charities, politicians, movie stars, and sports figures.

All has not been unmitigated success, however. In recent years McDonald's has redirected its growth away from the suburbs and back to the central cities. The result has been exposure to some of the nation's urban problems. Complaints have arisen from groups who resist changes in neighborhood quality. Blacks have been critical of the small number of black franchisees. Nutritionists and environmentalists have campaigned against poor food quality and gaudy design. Unions resent the use of teenage labor at wages lower than the legal minimum wage.

Nevertheless, Ray Kroc is a multimillionaire as a result of his innovation. He owns 20 percent of the company's stock, worth almost half a billion dollars in 1977. In fact, McDonald's has made many millionaires. Kroc's secretary in the early years accepted stock instead of wages. Her share is now worth $70 million!

supply of skilled machinists may increase so that an individual firm's costs of hiring and training workers will fall. Or specialized firms may spring up that concentrate on supplying low cost materials or parts the industry needs; examples are piston rings for use in auto manufacture and memory chips for producing pocket calculators.

Changes in costs associated with industry growth are called *external economies and diseconomies*. When such costs fall, we say that there are **external economies.** When they rise, we say there are **external diseconomies.**

External Economies in the Very Long Run

External economies of growth may be of several kinds. We have already mentioned economies that come from establishing new supplying firms. Firms that make memory chips and piston rings may be able to supply these inputs at lower cost than if the buying firms made their own. Such specialized firms achieve economies of scale that are passed on to their customers in the expanding industry. Moreover, supplying firms may respond to industry growth by developing more advanced technology and improving their equipment for still lower costs.

When growth brings on external economies, long-run average cost curves shift downward. Downward-shifting long-run average costs will permit construction of new plants at lower costs for every scale. The entire array of cost curves will shift downward to reflect new cost patterns.

When production costs decline with growth, the industry is called a *decreasing cost industry*. With industry growth, larger quantities of output can be supplied at lower and lower prices. Over time, the industry long-run supply curve *slopes* downward. (In terms of elasticity, price elasticity of supply has a negative sign over the very long run.)

Figure 8 illustrates a decreasing cost industry. Industry growth yields external economies so that long-run costs fall to $LRAC_2$. Plants built at optimum scale can satisfy demand at lower prices. In the very long run, the industry supply curve slopes down.

Decreasing costs in the very long run are characteristic of young industries employing new technologies. In the earliest stages, produc-

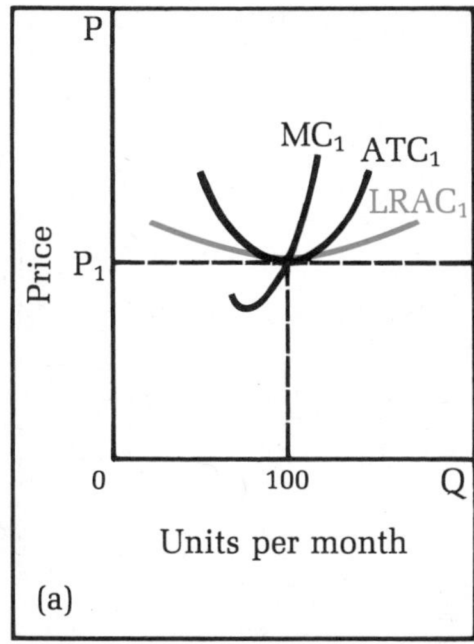

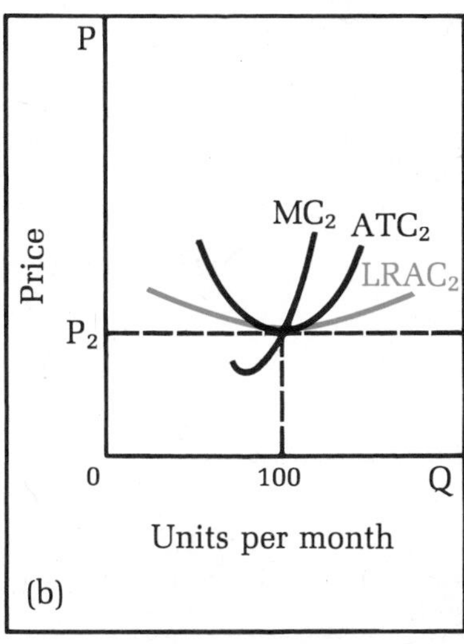

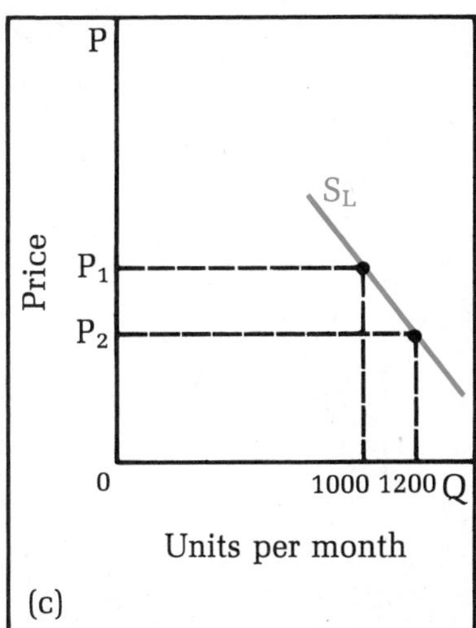

Figure 8 (a) Each of 10 firms faces the cost curves shown and maximizes profit by producing 100 units per time period. (b) When the number of firms in the industry increases to 12, cost curves shift. External economies result and LRAC declines to $LRAC_2$. Total production increases from 1000 to 1200 units per period. (c) The long-run market supply curve (S_L) shows that price = LRAC after industry growth. S_L slopes downward because the industry is a decreasing cost industry.

tion involves high-cost skilled labor and primitive technology; unit cost is high. As consumer demand increases, however, firms are encouraged to develop more complex technology, often operated by lower-cost labor. Production can be divided into specialized operations, and product flow can be regulated for greater efficiency. Supplying firms compete to provide materials and parts at lower prices. Finally, product price is forced down—all to the benefit of the consuming public.

The automobile industry was once a young industry. Autos were made mostly by hand at extremely high cost. Henry Ford pioneered mass production of autos. He saw that a wider consumer market would encourage the development of external economies. So he raised the wages of his work force to an unheard of $5 a day! And he encouraged others to do the same. As spending increased generally throughout the economy, demand for autos increased. Industry growth enabled the auto industry to turn out a better quality product at prices which fell relative to prices of other consumer goods.

Probably the best recent example of a decreasing cost industry is the industry producing pocket calculators. From an initially high price and small quantity, industry output grew through the stages described above, until calculators are now available at much reduced prices.

External Diseconomies in the Very Long Run

In some industries, growing consumer demand may have the opposite effect on costs. Many firms in the industry may cause resource prices to rise. For instance, if the number of firms engaged in lobster fishing increases off the Maine coast, a point may be reached at which overfishing reduces the supply of lobsters so severely that they become more difficult and more costly to find. This is why governments regulate fisheries so as to ensure plentiful supplies at reasonable costs.

External diseconomies may result from the limited supply of mineral resources, the overuse of transportation facilities, or from rising wage rates for certain types of skilled labor. When resource prices rise, production costs and the prices of finished goods must also rise.

There are other external diseconomies that may increase production costs in the long run. The community may require that firms install antipollution equipment to avoid depleting the area's scarce air and water resources. Or it may levy taxes or fines to remedy past offenses. All these changes will push long-run average cost curves upward with industry growth. Firms will operate with higher average cost curves.

When production costs increase with growth in the number and size of firms, the

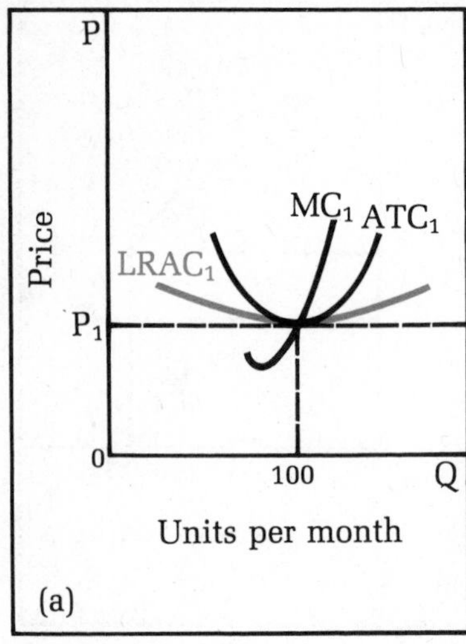

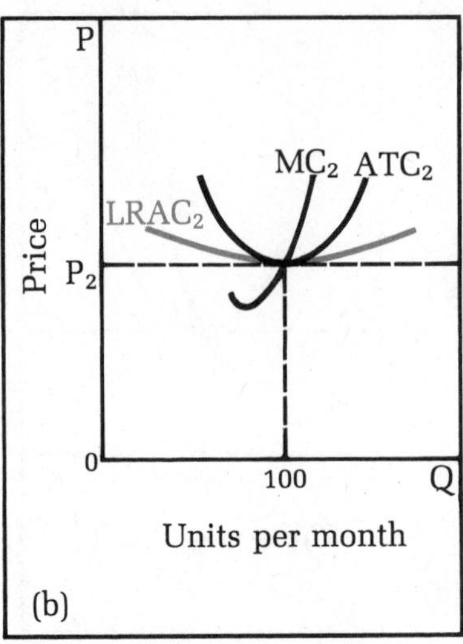

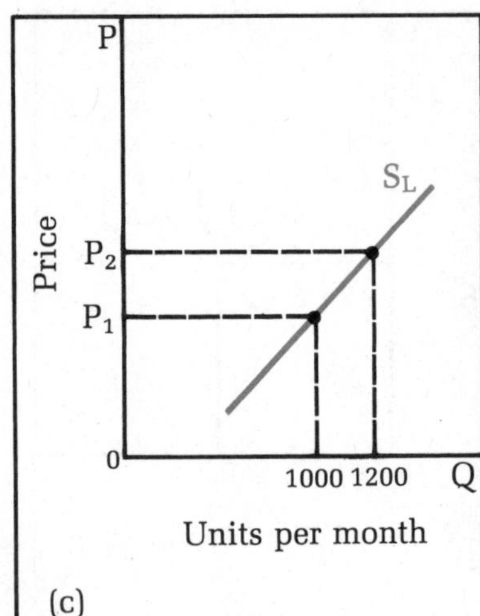

Figure 9 (a) Each of 10 firms faces the cost curves shown and maximizes profit by producing 100 units per period. (b) When the number of firms in the industry increases to 12, cost curves shift. External diseconomies result and the LRAC rises to $LRAC_2$. Total production changes from 1000 to 1200 units per period. (c) The long-run market supply curve (S_L) shows that price = LRAC after industry growth. S_L slopes upward because the industry is an increasing cost industry.

industry is called an *increasing cost industry.* Its very long-run supply curve slopes more steeply upward as larger quantities are supplied at higher costs. (In terms of elasticity, supply curves become less elastic over the very long run.)

Figure 9 illustrates an increasing cost industry. Growth yields external diseconomies and long-run costs increase to $LRAC_2$. With higher production costs, very long-run supply curves slope upward.

Increasing costs in the very long run are characteristic of old industries employing obsolete technologies and using basic materials in increasingly limited supply. In industries like these, all opportunities for productivity gains have been fully exploited. Entry of new firms has reduced economic profits so that research and development funds are scarce. Increased demand for resources enables suppliers to raise prices for materials, which may be of poorer quality. Higher production costs must be passed on to the consumer in higher prices.

The most obvious recent examples of increasing cost industries are those which supply energy: the electric power generating industry and the petroleum industry. The use of high-cost, low-quality coal and petroleum has raised unit costs, since output per unit of input is less. High capital costs aggravate the problem. Furthermore, environmental restrictions have complicated the cost picture, adding to the costs of capital equipment for new or expanding firms.

In some industries, diseconomies of growth are precisely offset by economies. For *constant cost industries,* very long-run supply curves are horizontal at minimum long-run average cost.

Social Economies and Diseconomies

We have discussed external economies and diseconomies as if all cost changes from growth were actually paid and received by firms in the industry. This is not always the case. Long-run growth in one industry may produce benefits or costs outside the industry which apply to the community as a whole. These economies and diseconomies are said to be external to the industry and are often referred to as **externalities.** Externalities may either be *social benefits* or *social costs.*

Growth in one industry may produce technological benefits for other industries. New job skills and resource development may mean lower production costs for other industries. The entire community will benefit from social externalities. A fully employed labor force, buying from local merchants and paying higher taxes, contributes to the general prosperity of the community. Moreover, a prosperous and well-managed industrial expansion can attract other activities which give balance to the community's economic structure. When industry growth yields external economies, the community receives benefits for which it does not have to pay. Many communities seek the social benefits of growth through tax incentives to industry and through government programs sympathetic to the needs of business.

Sometimes growth in one industry produces higher costs for other industries. This is often the case when two or more industries compete for a particular resource. Growing demand for scarce materials or labor can lead to higher production costs and higher prices for consumers. When external diseconomies extend to the community as a whole, they are called social costs. Social costs occur when industry growth puts too much pressure on the resource capabilities of the community. The result is higher production costs for other industries, higher living costs for workers, and higher wage demands in a continuing upward spiral. This time the community pays a price greater than the benefits it enjoys from industrial expansion. The cost of growth may be a lower quality of life for local citizens. When growth reaches this stage, communities may act to restrain further expansion through higher business taxes and limits on new business licenses.

Internalizing Externalities

One way of making industry aware of its externalities is to require each firm to pay for its own social costs. This changes these costs from social to private costs so that firms see them as part of their costs of operation. In other words, the externalities are "internalized."

In recent years many communities have established regulations to limit the social costs of industrial growth. Firms have been required to install "scrubbers" in their smokestacks to remove injurious chemicals and to run their waste water through purification systems. Mining firms have been required to restore the topsoil where they have used strip-mining and to landscape the surface before they leave. Some communities require that new plants be designed to fit into an established pattern of development.

Naturally, these restrictions raise costs for the firms involved. Consumers in turn must expect to pay higher prices for the products. The long-run average cost curves will shift upward to reflect the full costs of these industries. If consumers are unwilling to pay the increased prices, then sales will fall (or fail to increase). Internalizing externalities ensures that the price system can work efficiently to allocate all resources the way consumers want.

SUMMARY

In the short run, market price may exceed average total cost and firms may receive economic profit. Or price may be less than average total cost and firms may operate at a loss. But in the long run, new firms can enter or old firms leave an industry; firms can expand or contract output, shifting supply until price is finally equal to average cost and only normal profit remains.

In long-run equilibrium, the product is sold at minimum price, firms are earning normal profit, and the number of firms is sufficient to fill market demand. Furthermore, plants are constructed to optimum scale: the scale of plant is large enough to enjoy all economies of large size but not so large as to experience diseconomies. At optimum scale, production can be carried on at minimum average total cost and maximum economic efficiency. Technical factors determine the optimum scale of plant and thus the optimum number of firms in an industry. The number of firms is important for maintaining a competitive industry structure.

A firm's long-run average cost (LRAC) curve is an envelope curve. It consists of points taken from short-run average total cost curves for different size plants. In long-run equilibrium, the point of greatest profit occurs when MC = MR = P = AR = minimum ATC = minimum LRAC. In the real world, long-run equilibrium is seldom actually achieved, because conditions in the economy keep changing. In addition, there are, within some industries, rigidities and barriers to entry that prevent long-run equilibrium.

When an industry grows, changes in cost patterns for the individual firms may result. External economies of growth yield lower costs through improvements in the production and use of necessary resources. External diseconomies yield higher costs through excessive pressure on limited resources. Growth may yield social externalities which are not actually received or paid for by the growing industry.

Key Words and Phrases

economies (or diseconomies) of large scale the decrease (or increase) in average total cost which results when plants are constructed of larger size.

envelope curve a graph which traces the lowest average total cost for producing any volume of output in plants of various sizes; long-run planning curve.

external economies (or diseconomies) the decrease (or increase) in average total cost which results from industry growth.

externalities advantages or disadvantages which come to a community because of industry growth; social benefits and costs of industry growth.

long-run competitive equilibrium a condition in which entry and exit of firms in an industry have eliminated all economic profit and have forced firms to produce at minimum average total cost.

natural monopolies industries in which economies of large scale continue for plants of very large size.

optimum scale the size of plant which achieves minimum average total cost.

Questions for Review

1. List characteristics of an industry which would tend to yield economies of scale in the long run. What characteristics would lead to diseconomies?
2. Suppose optimum scale of plant is 100 units of output per week, but the market will only absorb 75 units. You must choose to build either of the following plants: Plant A, designed to produce 60 units but operated beyond maximum efficiency; Plant B, designed to produce 75 units and operated at maximum efficiency; Plant C, designed to produce 90 units but operated at less than maximum efficiency. Which plant would you choose and why?
3. Refer again to question 2. Suppose the market would absorb 500 units. How would you describe long-run competitive equilibrium in the industry?
4. Explain the following:

   MC = MR = P = AR
   = minimum ATC
   = minimum LRAC.
5. Cite examples from current news of external economies and diseconomies resulting from industry growth.
6. "The best cure for higher prices is high prices." Explain.
7. Explain precisely what is meant by "internalizing" external diseconomies of industry growth. Can *economies* also be "internalized"? Once they are internalized, can such benefits and costs be termed externalities?
8. How realistic is the theory of long-run competitive equilibrium? Cite recent examples of industries whose movement toward long-run equilibrium was interrupted, causing a new series of market adjustments. One suggestion: digital watches.
9. Define: social benefits and social costs.
10. Suppose the long-run average cost curve for a certain type of production slopes downward over its entire length. What does this imply about the size of plant and the level of operation of plants for maximum efficiency? Explain.

Appendix

The Cobweb Theorem of Agricultural Prices

Among all the sectors of the U.S. economy, the agricultural sector experiences the greatest price instability. The reason has to do with elasticities of demand and supply, both in the short run and the long run. In this appendix, we will look into these characteristics of farming in detail.

In the short run, demand for agricultural products is relatively price inelastic. A certain amount of food and fiber products is necessary for life and must be consumed regardless of price. Beyond this necessary quantity, some additional units may be consumed at lower prices, but consumer response to price change is small. As a necessity, with few substitutes in the short run, agricultural products experience relatively inelastic demand. Through time as population grows, demand curves shift to the right, but short-run demand curves continue to be relatively steep.

Elasticity of supply of agricultural products differs in the short and the long run. In the short run, quantities supplied are determined by production decisions made months or years in advance. The short-run supply of apples, beef, butter, and wine, for instance, depends on planting and breeding decisions rather far in the past. As a result, short-run supply curves tend to be relatively steep.

Over the long run, changes in the availability of resources for use in agriculture and changes in the technology of farming may bring on higher or lower costs. Or improvements in production methods may be precisely offset by cost increases. Thus, long-run supply may be perfectly elastic, negatively elastic, or positively elastic, depending on particular characteristics of the product itself.

Variable supply elasticities have significant effects on price and quantity adjustments in the agricultural sector. The reason has to do with attempts by farmers to satisfy demand when price is high or to withhold supplies when demand is low. The time required for adjusting supplies to demand means that price may remain at one extreme level for a substantial time and then move abruptly to the other extreme.

Beef production provides a common example. Large demand and high prices will encourage producers to increase output. But once the production decision is made, approximately three years are required to bring to market the additional quantities. During the time required for adjustment, price will remain high, adding to farmers' incentives to expand output. Finally, a substantial increase in quantity will be brought to market, pushing price down, often to a level which will not cover total average costs.

Low beef prices will set in motion the opposite series of responses. Large supply and low prices will discourage production. Farmers will sell off their breeding stock in an attempt to cut losses. Price is depressed further, and production plans are reduced again. Ultimately, the reduced quantity brought to market will push market price up, and the entire process will be repeated.

Price fluctuations can be demonstrated graphically. On Figure A.1 demand is shown as relatively inelastic. Supply is shown as taking

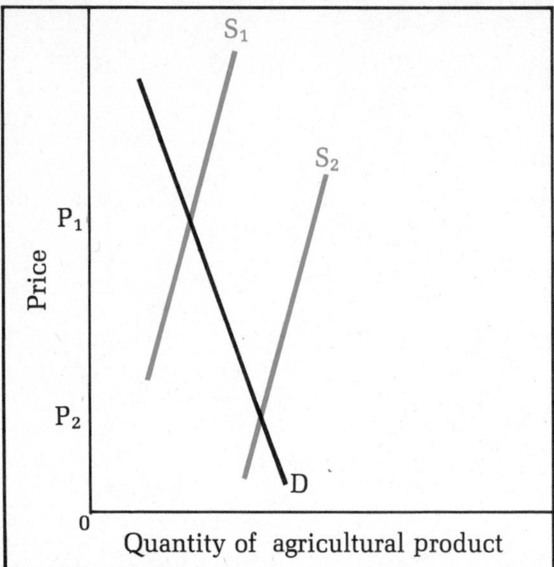

Figure A.1 Demand curves for farm products are inelastic in the short run and move slowly to the right as population grows. Supply curves may shift abruptly because of biological factors and changes in weather. The result is wide fluctuation in farm prices.

either of two positions: relatively inelastic in the short run and shifting from left to right over time. Begin with supply curve S_1 and price P_1 and assume that the high price yields positive profits. Expectation of economic profit encourages an increase in quantities supplied at every price level, and supply shifts to S_2. The magnitude of the shift depends on long-run elasticity of supply. In any case, the greater quantities brought to market force price down to P_2. If the new price is below average total costs, farmers will experience economic losses. Some will go out of business, and supply will eventually shift backward; again the magnitude of the shift depends on long-run elasticity of supply.

Figure A.1 illustrates the basis for price fluctuations in agricultural markets, with continual movements from high to low prices and back again. Price instability would create continuing problems of adjustment with substantial disruption in the agricultural sector. The level of disruption depends on shifts of supply and, in turn, on long-run supply elasticity. The greater the elasticity of long-run supply, the greater the response of producers and the wider the price fluctuations. The reverse is also true, since slower response to price would tend to push price closer to a stable equilibrium.

Figure A.2 illustrates the character of price fluctuations *in the long run.* In Figure A.2 demand and supply curves represent long-run demand and supply. Demand is shown as relatively price inelastic; long-run supply is more elastic. Let us assume that short-run supply has shifted such that supply exceeds demand at a price of P_1. Excess supply, *ab,* forces price down to a level at which demand is equal to supply at P_2. (Follow the dashed line at Q_2 down to the demand curve at *c.*) The entire quantity $0Q_2$ is sold, but the low price reduces production incentives and short-run supply shifts back to Q_3. At a price of P_2, quantity demanded exceeds quantity supplied, by the amount *dc,* and the existence of a shortage pushes price up. Price rises to the level at which consumer demand is equal to quantity P_3Q_3. (Follow the dashed line at Q_3 up to the demand curve at *e* where price = P_3.) Notice that in both cases supply has been relatively inelastic in the short run and rises or falls abruptly after the necessary time for adjustment.

At a price of P_3, supply incentives will cause output to increase until supply exceeds demand. Efforts to sell unsold surpluses, *ef,* will push price down to P_4 and lead to new produc-

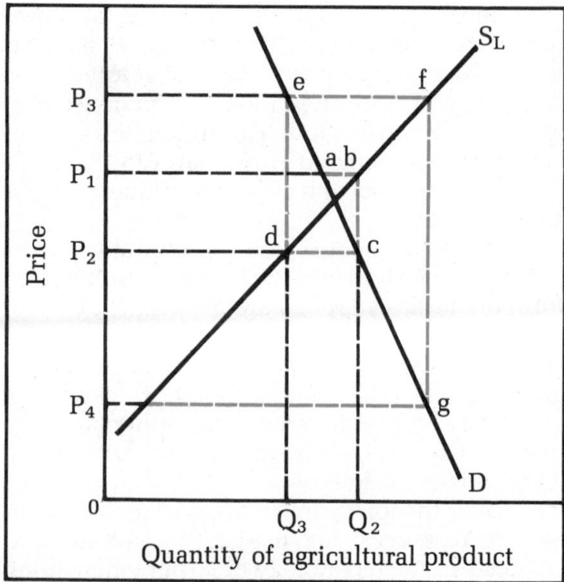

Figure A.2 Response of producers to shortages and surpluses pushing prices beyond equilibrium. The greater the elasticity of long-run supply, the wider the price fluctuations.

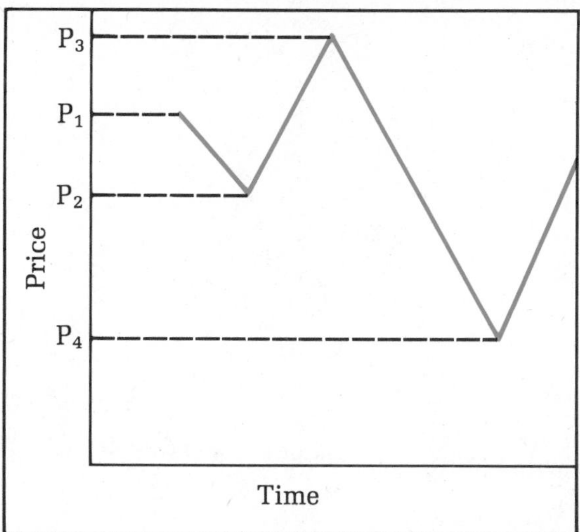

Figure A.3 If suppliers respond significantly to the existence of a surplus or shortage, price will fluctuate widely.

tion cuts. We might expect this process to continue, with price moving beyond equilibrium each time a supply adjustment is completed. Failure to reach equilibrium is a result of lagged response to surpluses and shortages, such that price cannot move smoothly to a market-clearing level. By the time price has moved to a level consistent with current demand, producers have reversed production plans and prices begin to change again.

In Figure A.2 the pattern of price adjustments circles equilibrium like a cobweb—giving this phenomenon the nickname the ***"cobweb theorem."*** In the example, price fluctuations become wider with each adjustment, as shown in Figure A.2. Wider fluctuations are a result of the shape of demand and supply. The relatively greater elasticity of long-run supply means larger changes in quantity and therefore wider price movements. If we had assumed relatively greater elasticity of demand, supply adjustments would be inadequate for demand, and price fluctuations would become smaller. The cobweb would circle closer around equilibrium until an equilibrium price was actually achieved. In this case, farmers are unable to overreact to high or low prices, and the result is smaller shortages and surpluses.

Agricultural price fluctuations over time are shown on Figure A.3. If suppliers respond significantly to the existence of a surplus or shortage, price will fluctuate more and more widely, as shown in our example. On the other hand, if long-run supply is relatively inelastic, shifts in short-run supply will be smaller, and price fluctuations will become narrower with each shift.

CHAPTER 10

Monopoly

Learning Objectives

Upon completion of this chapter, you should be able to:

1. Explain ways of evaluating our economy and industry structure.
2. State four characteristics of monopoly and explain how natural and artificial monopolies are formed.
3. Discuss characteristics of the monopolist's demand curve and cost curves.
4. Explain both verbally and graphically the pricing and output decisions of a monopolist.
5. Discuss the shortcomings of monopoly.
6. Explain why and how government regulates monopolies.

The last two chapters looked closely at competitive markets. We examined in detail the way firms make price and output decisions in the short run and in the long run. We saw that free competition encourages decisions which move an industry to long-run equilibrium: maximum output, minimum costs and prices, and the appropriate number of firms operating at optimum levels of output. Adam Smith's "invisible hand" helps bring about these results. The "invisible hand" helps promote two major goals of our economic system: efficiency and equity.

EFFICIENCY AND EQUITY

We may define economic **efficiency** very broadly as getting the most output from our resources. Any change that increases total output without increasing the amount of resources used may be said to increase economic efficiency. A change that diminishes output per unit of resource decreases economic efficiency.

The concept of efficiency is important today more than ever because our nation is growing more concerned about the problems of poverty and resource depletion. While resources are becoming scarcer, we are finding more and more things that we want to do with them. If we are to continue raising the living standards of all our people, it will be necessary to improve the efficiency of our economy.

A second important goal of our economic system is **equity**—the extent to which the economy rewards people fairly for their efforts. *We must distinguish between equity and equality. Equity* implies fair (but usually unequal) shares, while *equality* implies identical shares. No industrial society—market system or communist—distributes output equally among all its citizens. Some degree of inequality is believed to be fair. Most people consider it fair for the president of a company to be paid more than the janitor. The principle of equity does not require that rewards be equal.

Most people also feel that it is fair to help those at the bottom of the income pyramid, particularly those who are unable to support themselves. We expect our government to transfer income from those who have plenty to those who are poor. It does this through income taxes, unemployment benefits, public welfare assistance, and in other ways. So while we don't think income must be distributed equally to all, we do feel that justice requires us to adjust the distribution of income that the market system provides—to smooth out the peaks and valleys. In this way we help make our unequal distribution of income more equitable.

If perfect equality were the only concern, we could change the distribution of income even more than we have already. But beyond some pattern of distribution, greater equality would interfere with economic efficiency. If rewards were precisely equal, it would no longer be in anyone's interest to work hard and save for the future. The result would be a slower rate of economic growth. Equal rewards would damage our system of economic incentives. Production would not be as high as it might, and total income would be lower.

Whereas some inequality is necessary to encourage greater productivity, extreme inequality may also discourage productivity. Poor rewards at the bottom of the range do not offer much incentive for achievement, since people have little hope of improving their standard of living. And excess rewards at the top of the scale may also stifle initiative and reduce effort.

Thus we are safe in assuming that both perfect equality and extreme inequality would reduce the efficiency of our economic system. We choose some level of inequality, and a corresponding level of efficiency, that we believe to be equitable. It is not for economists to make a final decision about the proper level of equality. Economists can estimate what the effects of more equal distribution are likely to be. But it is up to us as voters to decide how much equality we want—based on considerations of efficiency and equity.

Efficiency and equity depend strongly on the **structure of industry** in our economy. The structure of an industry involves the size distribution and market power of firms. Structures range from a single firm producing the entire industry output to many firms, each producing only a small portion of the total. In the United States most industries fall somewhere between the two extremes.

Industry structure is important because it may influence the **conduct of firms** in the industry. A firm's conduct often depends on whether it is the only firm in the industry or whether there are many rival firms. Its conduct with respect to efficiency and equity is important to all consumers.

If industry structure leads to particular types of conduct, then conduct is important in influencing the **performance of firms** in an industry. *Performance* refers to the ability of firms to fulfill the long-range goals of efficiency and equity with no external diseconomies. Industry structure should contribute to efficient and stable growth in production. In this way it will enhance the security of the community and establish the basis for equity in the distribution of output.

DEFINING MONOPOLY

Most of us think we know how monopoly works—after years of landing on Boardwalk and Park Place. In the game of Monopoly the idea is to accumulate property and then charge high rents to our customers. Under the rules of the game they have no choice but to pay our price. Monopoly like this is hard to find in the real world. People don't have to stay at the Ritz or the Waldorf-Astoria unless they want to; there are other hotels that will be glad to accommodate them at a lower price. We don't have to buy Cadillacs—Mustangs may do as well. In our discussion of the economics of monopoly, therefore, we will be dealing with an extreme case. Pure monopoly, like perfect competition, seldom exists in the real world.

We are interested in monopoly, however, because by studying how monopolists behave we learn a good deal about how other firms behave. Later we will use the term *monopolistic competition* to describe an industry in which there are elements both of monopoly and of competition. As we shall see, most business firms fall between the two extremes of pure monopoly and perfect competition.

What is a pure monopoly? We define a **monopoly** as a firm that is the only producer of a product for which there are no acceptable substitutes. Consumers must purchase that company's product or go without. Examples of pure monopoly are public utilities, such as electric, gas, water, and telephone companies, and many railroads and bus companies. Outside the public utility field it is hard to find a pure monopoly in this country. One near-monopoly is the service provided by Red Adair's oil-well firefighters. For major oil fires, oil executives seem to feel only Red Adair can do the job safely—and he can thus command six-figure salaries for a major fire. At one time the Aluminum Company of America had a monopoly in the production of aluminum, but there are now three large firms in that industry. Federal laws make it illegal for any firm to try to set up a monopoly. Even agreements among several firms to restrict competition are against the law.

Monopolies are of two kinds: natural and artificial. **Natural monopolies** result from certain technical conditions in the market, while **artificial monopolies** result from deliberate efforts to keep out competition.

Characteristics of Monopoly

Single seller. In a monopolized industry, one seller supplies the industry's entire output. The single seller may achieve its monopoly position through the absence of any one of the other three conditions that characterize perfect competition. That is, it may provide a unique good or service, it may have information that is not available to other firms, or it may be taking advantage of a lack of mobility.

Unique good or service. The product of the monopoly firm is different from products offered for sale by all other firms. As the only supplier of the good, the monopoly firm has the power to set price at any point on the product demand curve. (Notice we didn't say "set any price." As we shall see, even a monopolist has a demand curve, bcause consumers won't—and can't—pay any extremely high price.)

Information barrier. The monopoly firm may have information that is not readily available to other firms wanting to enter the industry. This could be knowledge of particular geographic markets where sales are greatest or knowledge of strategic resources, formulas, or designs. Without information, rival firms are unable to enter the market, and the monopoly firm can set price and output for the entire industry.

Another barrier to entry may be the high costs of advertising the new product. If a new firm is to capture part of the market, it must provide buyers with information and incentives to buy. Heavy advertising expenses may discourage new competition.

Lack of mobility. Finally, difficulties of movement may prevent new firms from entering the industry to take advantage of profitable conditions. If substantial investment is required to start up production, this may be a serious barrier to new competition. Moreover, the existing monopoly may enjoy economies of large scale with low unit costs. A new, smaller firm would have higher production costs and could not compete.

An example of lack of mobility can be seen in the U.S. automobile industry. While the industry is not a monopoly, the four U.S. firms are so thoroughly entrenched that they need fear no *domestic* rival. The costs required to challenge General Motors would be too great, and so would the risks. Only foreign manufacturers with established plants, ample financial assets, and secure markets have been able to expand into the American market.

Methods of Monopoly

Back in the late nineteenth century, some U.S. firms used ruthless methods to acquire market positions close to monopoly. Sometimes they did so by driving rival firms out of business. Or a dominant firm might force small firms into mergers. One way to do this was to engage in *predatory price cutting*. In areas where there was competition, the dominant firm would reduce its price far below costs, making up the loss by setting higher prices in areas where it faced no

Economic Thinker Thorstein Veblen

Thorstein Veblen (1857–1929) was probably America's greatest political economist. Sharp and incisive, he said much about contemporary economics that angered and upset his academic colleagues. To many, his views represented a total rebellion against the "given economic wisdom" of his day. Veblen was never bothered by the hostile reception of his ideas, but delighted in disturbing the intellectual peace of his time.

Born of Norwegian immigrant parents, Veblen spent his boyhood in rural Wisconsin. He studied at Carleton College, Johns Hopkins, Cornell, and Yale University, where he received his Ph.D. in economics. He taught at Chicago, Stanford, and Missouri universities, and, in his later years, at the New School for Social Research in New York. Never a popular instructor—his students complained that he mumbled rather than lectured—his teaching career was undistinguished. His unconventional social behavior and maverick ideas also contributed to his lack of professional success. He died, alone and impoverished, in 1929.

Veblen's best-known work, *The Theory of the Leisure Class,* was first published in 1899. In it he coined the still widely used term "conspicuous consumption." The phrase refers to how the "leisure class" tends to spend its wealth on unproductive goods and services designed solely to impress others. Vulgar ostentation becomes the road to social acceptance. Whenever possible, the middle class, and eventually even the poor, imitate the wealthy by also spending money wastefully in the illusory hope of becoming true members of the leisure class. Such behavior, Veblen contended, disputes the notion of diminishing marginal utility, a basic cornerstone of microeconomics. Diminishing marginal utility holds that the more an individual has of some good, the less satisfaction is provided by additional amounts. Thus diminishing marginal utility supports the law of demand. However, Veblen said, more goods might be sold at higher than at lower prices when "conspicuousness" replaced value as the criterion for purchase; this kind of behavior could undermine many economic theories.

Veblen believed that the evolutionary process in the United States had brought about an economic system motivated solely by profit. Its ultimate object was to produce gain, not goods. When the captains of industry found they had produced too many goods and services to maintain their profit margin, they used their power of monopoly or near-monopoly to restrict production. If necessary, they would use the power of their wealth to maintain profits through unproductive military expenditures and even war.

According to Veblen, profit seeking produces a predatory economy in which the power of profits takes

competition. In this way a "robber baron" might force rival firms to sell out.

Another strategy was the *squeeze operation.* Suppose a giant firm bought raw materials from many small suppliers and sold its finished output to many small buyers. As the largest buyer of materials, the firm could offer to pay low prices to its suppliers; lacking other markets for their materials, the suppliers would be forced to accept. As the largest seller of the finished good, the firm could charge high prices to its buyers; lacking other suppliers, the buyers would be forced to pay. The dominant firm could thus collect large profits. It could then complete the

precedence over the production of goods and services—no matter what the cost to society. The ethics of the marketplace is the ethics of the jungle. In such an economy, the laissez-faire theories of the classical economists were, to Veblen, an invitation to social disaster. The power of the community at large must be brought to the marketplace to counter the power of the trusts and monopolies. Technology, Veblen believed, could bring about necessary political, social, and economic reform. But the people must have social control over technological change to prevent its being used to enhance the power of profit seekers.

Veblen wrote many books attacking the economic and social institutions of his day. Institutions themselves, he said, were little more than widespread habits of thought. They were not fixed in place for all time as many economists of his day seemed to believe. They were, instead, subject to evolutionary change in a constant power battle between those who wished to reform them and those who sought to keep them unchanged. Among such institutions, he said, were the universities.

Universities had evolved into fiefdoms of administrators more concerned with intrigues and conspicuous extracurricular activities than with scholarship. The "captains of industry" wielded the real power through endowments and governing boards. Scholars had to defer to this power in order to maintain their positions. What was taught in the universities was what the business leaders wanted to have taught—conformity to accepted social behavior and to the "given wisdom" of economic thinkers who considered contemporary capitalism a near-perfect system.

Veblen argued this position in a book called *Higher Learning in America* (1918). It is interesting to note that he chose as subtitle for the book "A Study in Total Depravity." Although he later dropped this subtitle, the book's uncompromising tone is a measure of Veblen's uncompromising and hard-hitting criticism of the institutions of his day.

squeeze operation by using the profits to buy out small suppliers and purchasers.

Through tactics like these a firm (or a group of firms) might secure control of production in an industry. Once a monopoly position was certain, the firm could raise price above its full production costs and cut back quantities offered for sale. With control over market supply, the monopoly could collect economic profit without fear of competition. Of course, having a monopoly on a product doesn't guarantee profits. There must be sufficient demand for the monopoly product.

Few pure monopolies actually exist in the United States. Some firms may enjoy small, temporary monopolies. A restaurant or shop, for instance, may dominate a local market area. But as population grows, there is room for competition, and rival firms will move in. Even a single railroad may not monopolize transportation services between two cities. When traffic builds up, buses, airlines, and trucking firms will enter the market and provide competition. A single electric power company may monopolize the supply of electricity in an area, but it will not monopolize the supply of all energy; the local gas company will provide some competition. For many decades the American Telephone and Telegraph Company (AT&T) provided almost all the nation's telephone communications. But now other firms supply some communication services that were formerly in the exclusive hands of AT&T.

How an industry is defined also affects the degree of monopoly. When an industry is narrowly defined, one firm may be dominant; for example, single firms provide Atlanta–New Orleans passenger railroad transportation; telephone service in Winter Park, Florida; and custom-made hiking boots. However, when industries are defined more broadly, as transportation, communication, or recreation equipment, it is difficult for a single firm to control supply.

Market growth provides opportunities for competitors to invade the area of a monopoly and reduce its power. As substitutes become available, the monopoly firm loses its power to set prices. Substitute forms of transportation, energy, and communication develop as an economy grows. New supplies of strategic resources or synthetic materials reduce a monopoly's hold on factors of production. Research and development programs create new products and new production techniques to undermine the monopoly's power.

Natural monopolies. Some markets lend themselves to monopoly because of their limited size. The dining car on a passenger train serves a limited market. It wouldn't be practical to have two competing dining cars on the same train. The same may be true of a tourist hotel on a small island or a television repairman in a rural community. When a market is small, a single supplier may be the *natural* result. In these situations a **natural monopoly** is formed.

Most communities in the United States have only one electric company, one gas company, and one telephone company. It would be very wasteful to have two or three electric companies competing in the same neighborhood, each with its separate power lines. Also, because of economies of scale, public utilitites tend to have decreasing average costs for larger quantities of output. One big generating station or gas plant can easily provide service to a sizable community at low unit costs.

Even the entire United States may not be large enough to ensure competition in some industries. If the optimum scale of production is very large relative to the size of the market, then the market may support only one giant producer.

Artificial monopolies. There are other monopolies that are created as a matter of public policy. These legal monopolies are *artificial* in the sense that government declares them monopolies by its will. An **artificial monopoly** results from legal barriers or government policy. Many artificial monopolies are either government monopolies or government-regulated monopolies. For example, most governments have made delivery of letters a government monopoly. Most local governments in the United States operate their own water and sewer systems and often garbage collection as well. Because these services are essential to the community, it is felt that they should be provided at the lowest cost—with no monopoly profit. If we thought it would be more efficient, we might want our government to own the telephone, electric power, gas, and transportation systems, as is true in many European countries. In the United States these systems are generally operated by privately owned firms that are allowed a legal monopoly. Government regulates their prices and output, however. When a railroad or a phone company wants to raise rates, it must get approval from the appropriate public commission.

Another kind of legal artificial monopoly results from our patent system. A **patent** is a temporary monopoly granted by the federal government, which gives an inventor the sole right to manufacture and sell a new invention. In order to patent an invention, you must show that it is a new and significant development in its field. A patent is property and can be sold or inherited during its lifetime (seventeen years in the United States). The purpose of patents is to stimulate invention and to encourage their use in production.

The most valuable patent ever issued in the United States was the one for Alexander Graham Bell's telephone. More recently, companies such as Xerox (in photocopying), Hewlett-Packard (in electronics), Digital Equipment (in minicomputers), Polaroid (in instant photography), and IBM (in computers and typewriters) have used patents to protect themselves from competition while they established strong market positions in their industries. But a patent only provides a monopoly of a specific invention; it doesn't prevent competitors from producing substitutes for it.

Extended Example
Monopoly in Dolls

One U.S. toy company hired Muhammad Ali to knock out its competitors. Back in the 1960s, Mego International, Inc., was just another merchant importing cheap dolls from factories in Hong Kong. It marketed low-priced counterparts of the G.I. Joe and Barbie dolls, only to find that its competitors were copying its copies and selling them at even lower prices. Looking around for something that couldn't be copied, the new young president, Martin B. Abrams, decided to acquire licenses to make dolls resembling famous TV personalities. One of the new creations was a Muhammad Ali doll that fought with an opponent in a miniature boxing ring. There were also Sonny and Cher dolls, Wizard of Oz dolls, and Superman dolls.

The company paid $100,000 or more, along with 5 percent royalties, for the exclusive rights to each well-advertised name. This strategy helped it climb into the top ten companies in the toy business within four years. Not only did its sales shoot up, but its prices went up along with them. One of the company's top executives pointed out what the rights to famous names had done for its products: "They can't be copied by others, so our prices—and our profits—are higher than otherwise."

How would you describe demand elasticity in this case?

DECISION MAKING BY THE MONOPOLIST

We have all had fantasies of being the sole producer of something the world wants—a self-emptying mousetrap or the secret of changing sand into gold. We imagine ourselves becoming immensely rich, the money pouring in faster than we can spend it. Let's pursue this dream for a moment and ask ourselves how we could earn the greatest economic profit from our monopoly. "That's simple," you say. "Just charge all the traffic will bear." How much the traffic will bear depends on the monopolist's demand curve.

The Monopolist's Demand Curve

How much will the traffic bear? If we set our price very, very high probably nobody will buy. People can live without our self-emptying mousetrap if need be. If we set price at, say, $100, we may sell one or two of our mousetraps to people who have everything. The money won't exactly be pouring in. We reduce it again and sell more. If we keep on reducing our price, we will sell more and more mousetraps until we reach a point where the additional revenue we get from selling another one won't cover the additional cost of making it. In economists' language, we have reached the point where marginal cost equals marginal revenue.

Notice that we have followed the same rule that sellers follow in a perfectly competitive market. We have expanded output to the point where MC = MR. The difference is that under perfect competition, price is not affected by the actions of a single seller. A competitive firm's demand curve is a horizontal line drawn at the level of the equilibrium price. By contrast, *the monopoly firm is the industry*, and like the industry it faces a downward sloping demand curve for its output. It must base its output decision on market prices which are different at every level of output. The monopoly firm can choose between selling a few units at a high price or many units at a low price.

For pure monopoly to exist there must be no acceptable substitute for the good or service. Without substitutes consumers cannot readily shift to another supplier if price rises. If the electric company raises its rates, we can't change to another source of light and power. If the bus company's fares go up, not many of us will choose to walk or ride a bicycle. Of course, we may use somewhat less of these services, and if prices get very high some alternatives will be found. Natural gas may substitute for electricity for some uses, and private autos can be used instead of buses or trains.

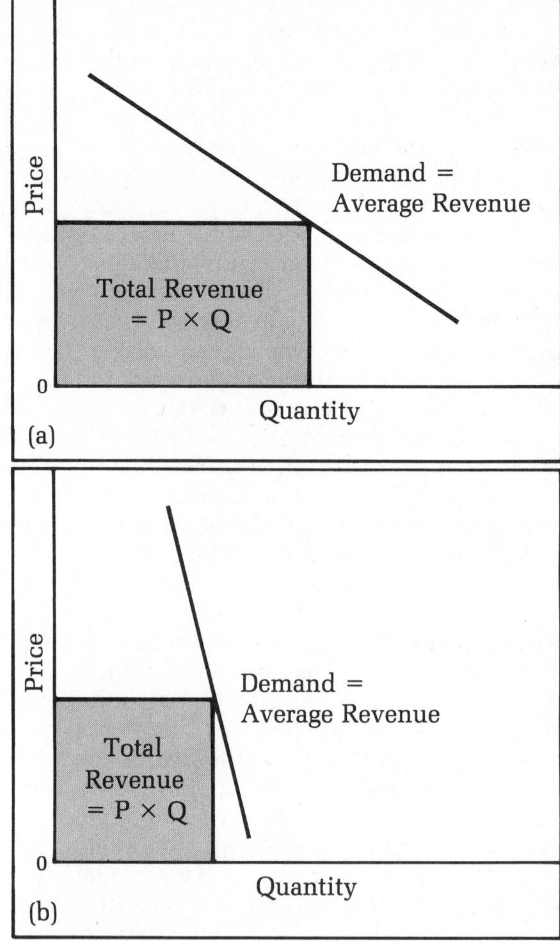

Figure 1 Demand curves for a monopolist: (a) demand for a good with many substitutes; (b) demand for a good with few substitutes.

Poor substitutability also affects demand when prices are low. Electric power and mass transportation are not themselves good substitutes for other services. Therefore, consumers will not increase their purchases significantly when prices are reduced.

Table 1 **Hypothetical Sales and Cost Information for Autographed T-Shirts**

(1) Quantity, Q	(2) Price	(3) Total Revenue, TR	(4) Marginal Revenue, MR	(5) Total Cost, TC	(6) Average Cost, AC	(7) Marginal Cost, MC	(8) Profit
0	$10	$0		2	—		−2
			$9			7	
1	9	9		9	9		0
			7			5	
2	8	16		14	7		2
			5			1	
3	7	21		15	5		6
			3			3	
4	6	24		18	4.5		6
			1			4.5	
5	5	25		22.5	4.5		2.5
			−1			7.5	
6	4	24		30	5		−6
			−3			19	
7	3	21		49	7		−28

Figure 1 shows two possible demand curves for a monopolist. For simplicity, the demand curves are shown as straight lines. The good with few substitutes has a steeply sloping demand curve, and the good with many substitutes has a demand curve with flatter slope. In either case, the quantity the monopolist can sell is greater at lower prices. At any point on the demand curve, average revenue is equal to price. Total revenue is the number of units sold times price, or average revenue. Total revenue is represented by a rectangle drawn beneath the demand curve with base equal to quantity sold and height equal to price, or average revenue.

The monopolist is interested not so much in the level of total revenue as in the level of profit. To determine the profit-maximizing price and quantity, we must look at costs. To illustrate we will use the hypothetical sales and cost data in Table 1.

The firm in Table 1 is the sole producer of autographed T-shirts. As a monopoly, the firm faces the *industry demand curve.* Like the demand curves in Figure 1, this one slopes downward to show that larger quantities can be sold only if price is reduced. In Table 1, columns (1) and (2) give data on demand. Column (3) is the product of price (2) times quantity (1). Thus Total Revenue = P × Q. The change in total revenue from each change in sales is shown in column (4). Changes in total revenue constitute the firm's marginal revenue from sales and are written between successive values of total revenue.

Remember that under perfect competition marginal revenue is the same as average revenue or price. This is because the demand curve for the individual firm is horizontal. The perfectly competitive firm can continue to increase sales without affecting price. On the other hand, a monopoly firm can sell a larger quantity only if price is reduced. Average revenue falls with every increase in the quantity sold. Because price must fall with a larger volume of sales, *marginal revenue for the monopoly is always less than average revenue or price.* To sell the third unit requires a lower price on all units sold—on units one and two as well as on unit three. Marginal revenue for the third unit is not its price. Marginal revenue is the price of that unit *minus* the price reductions on units one and two. In Table 1 the marginal revenue of the third T-shirt is $5, which is its price, $7, minus the price reductions of $1 each on units one and two.

We have drawn the average and marginal revenue curves for T-shirts in Figure 2. Notice that the MR curve is always below AR and falls faster as quantity sold increases. Marginal revenue eventually becomes negative. This is because for the monopoly to sell six units requires a price reduction that yields less total revenue than would be received for five units.

The Monopolist's Cost Curves

Cost data for the T-shirt firm are shown in columns (5), (6), and (7) of Table 1. In Figure 3 we have drawn the marginal and average cost curves just as we drew them for a competitive

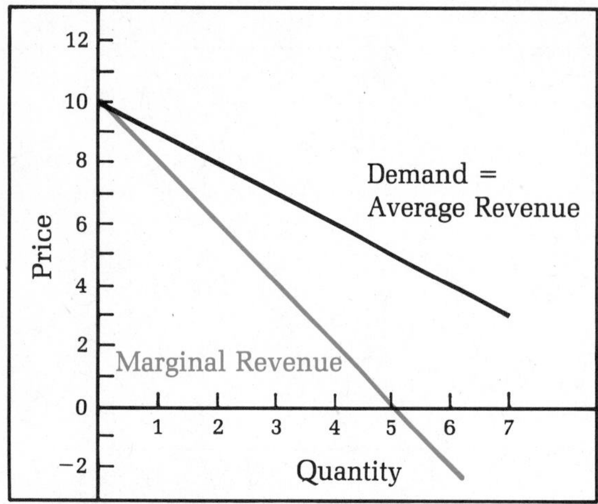

Figure 2 The average revenue and marginal revenue for our monopoly selling T-shirts. The MR curve is always below the AR curve.

firm. The AC curve is saucer shaped. Marginal cost is high for a small volume of output but falls sharply. Beyond some level of output, MC begins to rise and passes through the AC curve at the lowest point of the saucer.

The monopoly is now faced with the same decision as any competitive firm. Assuming that management wants to maximize profit, it will continue to supply additional units of the good or service as long as each additional unit sold adds more to revenue than it adds to cost. When marginal cost rises and is just equal to marginal revenue, the profit-maximizing level has been reached and the monopolist will not sell more. In Figure 3 the profit-maximizing level of output is four T-shirts. If the monopoly firm were to sell a fifth T-shirt, marginal revenue would be less than marginal cost and profit would be less. If the firm were to sell only three T-shirts, marginal revenue would be above marginal cost. Economic profit would be greater if sales were increased to four units.

Maximum profit occurs at sales of four units. But what price will the monopoly firm set? We find price by drawing a line up from the horizontal axis to the demand curve and reading price on the vertical axis. The four shirts can be sold at a price of $6. If the monopoly tries to sell more shirts, revenue will increase by less than costs. If it sells fewer shirts, revenue will fall by more than costs. In either case, profit will be less than maximum.

Economic Profit for the Monopolist

Economic profit for our T-shirt monopolist is shown in Figure 3 as the shaded rectangle. The length of the rectangle is quantity sold, and height is the difference between AC and AR at the point where maximum profit occurs (here, an output of four). Given the cost structure shown in Figure 3, no other combination of price and output would yield greater economic profit. At any other output, the area of the shaded rectangle would be smaller. Profit per unit might be greater at some other level of output, but the monopolist is seeking to maximize *total* economic profit, not *unit* profit. At some other level of output the difference between average revenue (AR) and average cost (AC) might be greater. But the total-profit rectangle is greatest at the profit-maximizing output.

The point of maximum economic profit is easy to see if you examine the cost data in Table 1. Compare marginal revenue (4) with marginal cost (7). The firm continues to expand output as long as marginal revenue is greater than marginal cost. To expand output to five units would add more to costs than to revenue. The profit-maximizing output must be four units per time

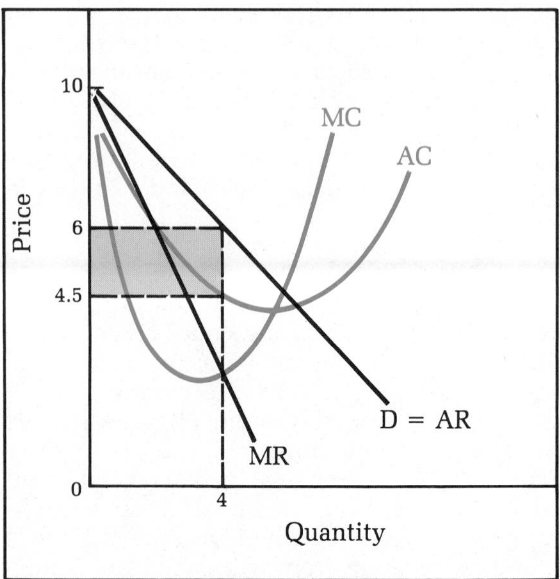

Figure 3 The intersection of marginal cost and marginal revenue curves determines the profit-maximizing point for our T-shirt monopoly.

Extended Example Shopping Malls and Monopoly

When the history books are written about the last half of the twentieth century, one of the most significant economic developments will be said to have been the shopping center. Ownership of automobiles has enabled us to live in suburbs, away from the urban centers of commerce. Business has responded by following the market to suburbia, building ever more lavish and more complete shopping malls for middle-income Americans.

Less noticed than the growth of shopping malls has been the boost they have given to local monopolies. Malls are generally built around a few big "anchor" stores. The large space occupied by these stores gives them the power to demand certain conditions in their lease agreement. One important specification has been that certain competitors not be allowed to rent space. Discount stores, for instance, and aggressive promoters of other kinds are often excluded; small specialty shops may be restricted to handling only a single line of merchandise—like clothing or books or jewelry or food.

Exclusionary contracts like these have the effect of establishing a monopoly. They reduce the available supply of certain goods and services to only the amount provided by a single merchant. Customers are attracted to the mall by the convenience of one-stop, nearby shopping with ample parking. Their demand curves become highly inelastic when there are no substitute suppliers of particular items. A monopolist can move up consumer demand curves to the point at which marginal revenue is equal to marginal cost and profits are maximized. The result is higher prices and smaller quantities sold.

In the beginning, exclusionary contracts were considered necessary by landlords and tenants alike. Landlords needed assurance of stable renters if they were to obtain long-term financing for the project. Tenants wanted a guaranteed market if they were to undertake the large investment and the risks involved in a new and unfamiliar marketing arrangement. To limit competition enabled a project to get on its feet financially and to become established as a viable institution in the community.

But by the 1970s, the Federal Trade Commission was charging that exclusionary contracts violate laws prohibiting restraint of trade. State attorneys-general and attorneys for small business firms also brought suit against mall developers. In most cases the complaints were settled through "consent decrees" which carry no penalties for past offenses. The consenting firm simply agrees to cease certain forbidden practices in the future or it will suffer heavy fines.

A major case was settled in 1976 with Sears, Roebuck and Co. Sears operates 900 stores throughout the United States and is the major tenant in more than 265 shopping centers. Sears' contracts have excluded competitors and discounters and have limited competition from other tenants. A consent decree settled in 1976 provided for fines up to $10,000 for any similar practices in the future.

What are other long-range effects of the movement to shopping malls? What are some benefits and costs? What has been the course of shopping-center development in your town?

period. Four units is the greatest level of output for maximum economic profit.*

Economic profit is shown in column (8). Economic profit is equal to total revenue less total cost: TR − TC = $24 − $18 = $6. Or, economic profit is unit profit times quantity of output:

$$(AR - AC) \times Q = (\$6 - \$4.50) \times 4 = \$1.50 \times 4 = 6.$$

From the standpoint of the monopolist, this level of output is ideal. Since economic profit is at a maximum, the monopolist has no incentive

*A more precise cost analysis would locate the profit-maximizing output between 3 and 4 units. This is because MC refers to the *process* of adding another unit. In an actual production decision, the units of output might be stated in thousands and the maximum profit position would be 3.5 thousand units.

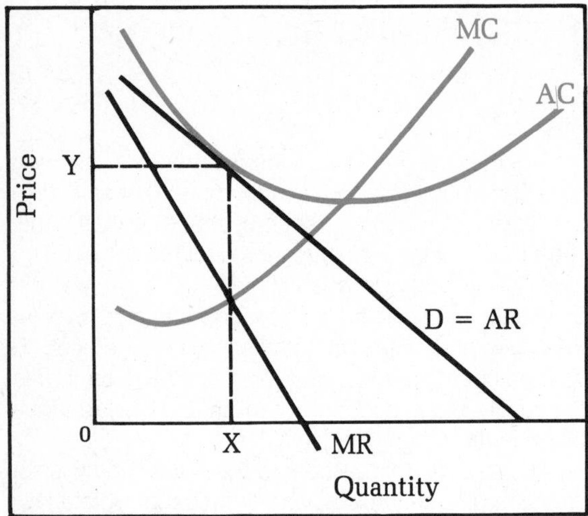

Figure 4 Cost curves for a monopolist. For this monopoly firm, AC = AR = P. The profit-maximizing quantity is $0x$, where MC = MR. Price is determined by the intersection of the dotted line at X and the demand curve. Total revenue equals the area of the rectangle formed by the dotted lines.

to change. From the standpoint of the economy as a whole, however, the situation is not ideal. The reason is that T-shirts are not being produced at the lowest possible cost. From society's standpoint the point of maximum efficiency would be 5 units of output, where MC = AC. This is because unit costs are lowest at that output. For the monopolist, economic profits are gained at the expense of efficiency in the use of productive resources.

The profit-maximizing rule holds true even when the monopolist doesn't earn economic profit. Consider the market conditions illustrated in Figure 4. This monopolist maximizes profit at an output of $0x$, which is where marginal cost is equal to marginal revenue. This happens also to be the point at which average cost equals average revenue or price. Price just covers full costs, including normal profit, and there is no economic profit. Still, under existing demand and cost conditions, this is the profit-maximizing quantity. Note that this result resembles perfect competition in that only normal profit is earned. Unlike perfect competition, however, the minimum point on the AC curve has not been reached.

Elasticity Again

The ability of a firm to influence the market in which it sells its product or buys its resources is called **market power.**

The market power of the monopolist depends in part on the shape of demand for the product. When demand is relatively inelastic, the monopolist is in a very strong position. Customers are willing to purchase roughly the same quantity of the product regardless of its price.

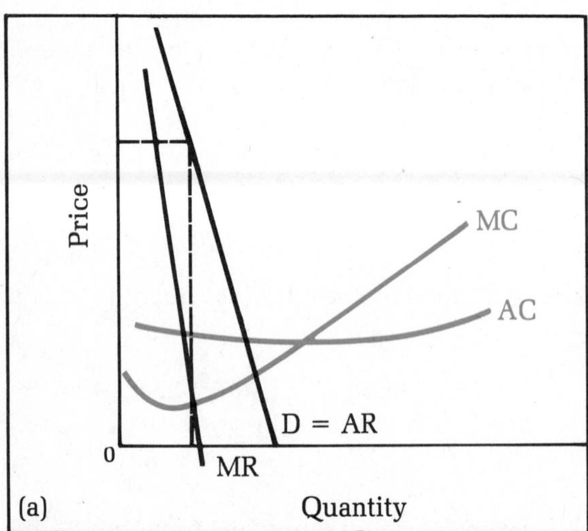

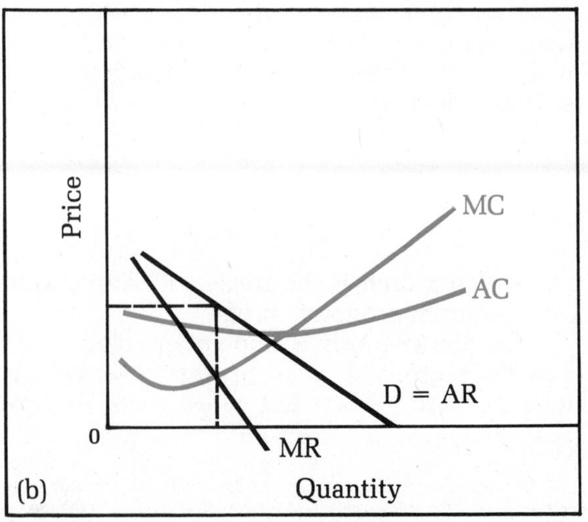

Figure 5 The demand for a monopolist here is (a) inelastic; and (b) elastic. Compare the distances between MR and AR for (a) and (b). For inelastic demand, marginal revenue is much lower than price (AR). If cost curves are identical in the two markets, this means lower output in (a) and higher prices. The result is higher profits for the monopolist facing inelastic demand.

Viewpoint
Do Monopolies Really Maximize Economic Profits?

In this chapter we've analyzed the behavior of monopolies with the assumption that a rational monopoly will try to make as much economic profit as possible. This implies that top executives sitting in their offices are able to tell exactly where the point of maximum profit is. When they are asked, most executives say they don't know where that point is. They may not even know what their demand and cost curves look like. To maximize profits all the time, executives would have to know exactly how many units they can sell at any given price. Many firms have marketing departments that study the buying habits of consumers. But consumer preferences change from time to time, and market data may be obsolete by the time it gets to the decision makers.

Economist Herbert Simon (who was a 1978 Nobel Prize winner) declares that the complexities of economic decision-making lead business firms toward "satisficing" rather than maximizing. Because of the high cost of acquiring all the information needed for perfectly correct decisions, business managers look only for solutions that will keep them out of serious trouble.

Information about a firm's cost conditions may be just as elusive as data on consumer demand. When a firm produces a variety of products, it is difficult to tell how much of the firm's overhead costs belong to each one. It may also be difficult to predict how a change in the number of units produced will affect costs. It is the job of cost accountants to figure out these things, but they often disagree over how best to go about it.

Let's suppose, however, that the firm making autographed T-shirts knows exactly what its demand and cost curves are. It still may not try to maximize economic profits; instead it will *satisfice* profits (i.e., try to earn satisfactory profits). There are good reasons why. If the company does too well, it may encourage potential competitors to enter the field. History shows that monopolies don't last indefinitely. Sooner or later other firms make their way into the business, and the more profitable the business is, the harder they will try. Another reason why a monopolist may not pursue maximum profits is the fear of attracting public criticism, which may lead to government investigations.

In the next chapter, we will take a look at that very large segment of business activity that doesn't fit into the framework of either pure monopoly or perfect competition. We will see that monopolistic behavior is found to some extent in almost every industry. Most companies charge higher prices than they would if they were perfectly competitive. But in setting their prices they take into account the reactions of other companies in the same industry, as well as federal laws and the general state of the market.

When a good or service is essential and has few substitutes, demand tends to be less elastic than for other goods. The demand for housing, electric power, and gasoline tends to be relatively less elastic than demand for nonessential goods.

When demand is relatively inelastic over the relevant price range, the demand curve will be steep, and a monopolist will have greater power to raise price. The result may be high unit profit and high total profit even when the volume of sales is low. Figure 5 shows how the slope of the demand curve in different markets affects price, quantity, and economic profit.

The monopolist will have less power to set price when demand is more elastic. If there are many substitutes, or if the product is easily given up, consumers will cut their purchases sharply when price increases. Economic profit will be less. Look again at Figure 5. Note that costs are identical in the two markets while price is different. The monopoly firm may earn substantial economic profit when product demand is inelastic.

Price Discrimination

Sometimes a monopoly can increase economic profit by charging different prices to different classes of customers. This practice is called **price discrimination.** Price discrimination is possible only if markets can be separated in some way, so that buyers in the low-priced market aren't able to resell their purchases in the higher-priced market. By charging different prices in different

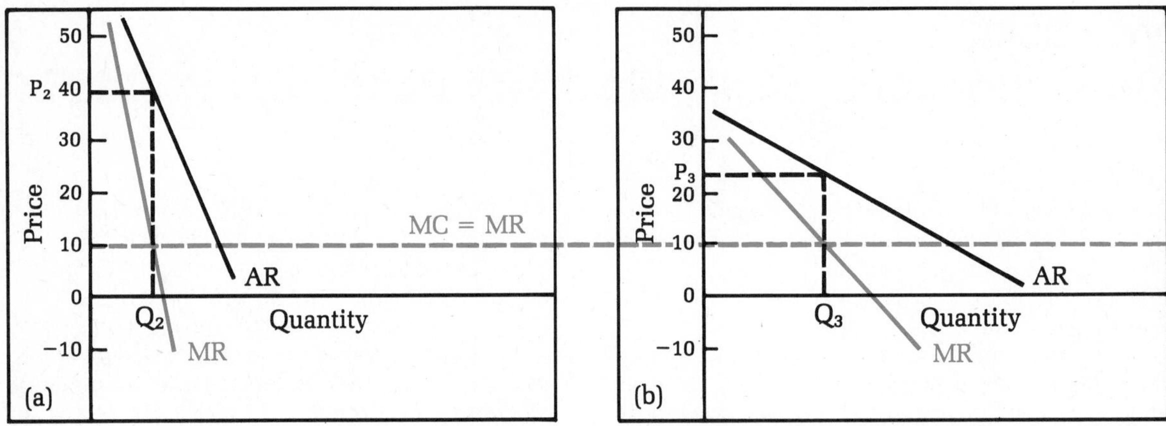

Figure 6 Price discrimination in air fares for: (a) adults, and (b) children. Where demand is inelastic, price can be set higher.

markets a firm can take advantage of differing elasticities of demand. In markets where demand is relatively inelastic, a firm can charge higher prices and reap larger profits. An airline company, let us say, may charge different rates for adults and for children. Adult demand is relatively inelastic, since many travelers on business or vacation must fly, regardless of price. The demand for children's flights is relatively more elastic: children may or may not be brought along, depending on price. Figures 6a and 6b show how this difference affects pricing decisions.

How does the firm determine the fare for two different groups of customers? It will figure its marginal revenues in both markets and then determine the point where combined marginal revenue is equal to marginal cost. This is shown in Figure 7. The AR and MR curves in Figure 7 are obtained by adding together those in Figures 6a and 6b: we simply add the quantities demanded at each price in 6a and 6b. There is no need to add marginal costs for the two markets, since there is only one marginal cost for the service regardless of the market in which it is sold. Figure 7 shows that marginal cost is equal to combined marginal revenue at output Q_1. From the vertical scale we see that MC equals MR at 10.

But where will we set our prices? How will total sales be divided between the two markets? Return to Figures 6a and 6b. Price and quantity will be determined by a vertical line passing through the MR curves at the point where MR is equal to 10. The airline will sell OQ_2 tickets to adults at a price of OP_2, because that is where marginal revenue in that market is equal to marginal cost. It will sell OQ_3 tickets to children at a price of OP_3 because that is where marginal revenue in that market is equal to marginal cost. Notice that price is higher in the market in which demand is relatively inelastic.

Some other examples of price discrimination include: lower-priced ladies' tickets at ball games; lower prices for movie matinees; no cover charge for ladies in singles' bars; special rates for nighttime phone calls; lower off-season prices at hotels and beach resorts. Quite often price discrimination is practiced without customers even knowing it. Large appliance manufacturers commonly sell part of their output to mail-order houses such as Sears, Roebuck and

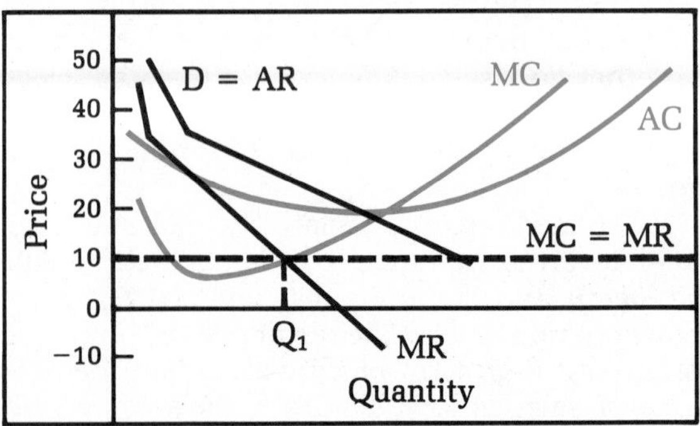

Figure 7 Combined demand for airline travel. The MR and AR curves are the sums of quantities for both markets. The intersection of MC and MR determines equilibrium quantity. Prices depend on demand in the separate markets.

Montgomery Ward, but the item is sold under different brand names and at lower prices. Manufacturers of auto tires, batteries, and other products do the same. From the manufacturer's point of view this is efficient because it makes use of excess production capacity that would otherwise remain idle. Some people might say that it is equitable, since higher prices charged to those who can afford to pay more make it possible to charge lower prices to others.

When price discrimination is practiced by firms engaged in international trade, it is sometimes called **dumping.** The word has a negative connotation and means that the producer is unloading goods on foreign markets in order to keep prices higher in the home country. Sometimes dumping is even used as a means to destroy foreign competitors so that a monopoly in one nation will become an international monopoly. Dumping is possible because demand curves in distant markets are often more elastic. Foreign customers are able to choose among several producers, substituting readily if price is high. From the point of view of foreign producers, American dumping looks like unfair competition. And U.S. companies don't like dumping when foreign companies do it here. Congress has passed legislation penalizing foreign manufacturers who sell at lower prices in the U.S. market than in their home markets. Not long ago Poland was fined for dumping golf carts in the U.S. market.

We've seen that the monopolist has to divide the market in order to discriminate successfully. For simplicity's sake we've used only two markets in the foregoing examples. But in reality, price discrimination may be practiced in several markets at the same time. Each additional market segment increases the firm's potential for economic profit. An airline may have market segments for businessmen, children, tourists (excursions fares), standby passengers, and charter groups. At the very extreme, a firm may be able to treat each individual customer differently, thus dividing the market into innumerable segments. This is unusual, but doctors and lawyers have been known to do it. The country doctor who charges patients according to what they are able to pay, perhaps accepting several bushels of apples instead of cash, is actually a highly discriminating monopolist.

Price discrimination works for airlines, ball games, and doctors for an important reason. It is not possible for buyers to purchase the service and resell it themselves. To buy at low prices in one market and resell at high prices in another is called arbitrage. Arbitrage raises the low price in the first market and reduces it in the second, almost immediately pushing them to the same level. When arbitrage can take place, price discrimination is not possible.

SHORTCOMINGS OF MONOPOLY

How does monopoly affect us? Economics is not an exact science. An economist cannot measure the precise effects of economic actions in the same way that a chemist measures a chemical change. Even so, an economist must not fall into the trap at the other extreme, basing conclusions on purely subjective standards of judgment. We must look for objective criteria by which to judge the effects of monopoly.

Two broad and important criteria have been emphasized: efficiency and equity.

The need for efficiency is a result of the economic problem. Because our resources are scarce, we must use them wisely. We must produce the maximum output per unit of input. If resources are used for maximum production, we have achieved efficiency.

Remember that equity refers to the distribution of output among participants in the economic system. Distribution takes place according to the values and goals of the society. Values and goals may be primarily material or primarily ethical or a combination of the two. Emphasis on material values will reward individuals on the basis of their material contributions to output. Emphasis on ethical values will reward on the basis of the community's particular ethical standards.

Of the two criteria, efficiency is more easily measured. This is because many benefits and costs can be measured for comparing the results of various economic actions. Judgment based on the equity principle is more difficult. It requires that there be agreement on values and goals. To advocate particular ethical positions is beyond the scope of a positive science.

With these qualifications in mind, let us summarize the harmful effects of monopoly on our economic lives. Later we will consider arguments in favor of bigness in industry.

Economic Thinker Paul Sweezy

Paul Sweezy (born 1910) is one of the nation's most distinguished Marxist economists. His economic philosophy was strongly affected by the Great Depression of the 1930s. He saw monopoly capitalism as the principal cause of economic crises. As a Harvard professor from 1934 to 1942, he wrote articles and books which applied Marxist theory to American economic institutions. He helped found the *Monthly Review,* the leading Marxist journal in the nation, and is still one of its editors.

Sweezy's most famous book, *Monopoly Capitalism* (1966), was co-authored by Paul Baran. In it Sweezy and Baran claim that the United States is *not* an effective capitalist economy where all productive resources receive their just rewards. Instead, the authors argue, monopoly conditions prevail in much of the American economy. Giant corporations have captured increasingly large shares of business through monopoly strategies. These corporations also help influence American foreign policy toward militarism and imperialism.

An earlier work by Sweezy, *The Theory of Capitalist Development* (1942), is a restatement and updating of Marxist theory. Sweezy believes that events in today's world economy are proof of the dynamic processes Marx described. Marxist economists see social reality as a process of change. Economies go through a definite and predictable life cycle. According to the Marxists, it is a mistake to take capitalism—or any other "ism"—as something immutable. An economic system is not fixed like the orbits of the planets but moves from one stage to another.

Sweezy believes that the prosperity of today's developed nations is based on exploitation of other, more primitive economic systems. Preexisting societies were destroyed and reorganized to serve the purposes of capitalist invaders. Then the wealth was transferred to the industrial powers to serve as a basis for capital accumulation and growth. Just as individual capitalists exploited workers and accumulated greater capital, capitalist nations have achieved economic growth through imperialist ventures into weaker lands. But in both cases, exploitation creates tensions that will eventually bring on collapse of the dominant powers. The change may be gradual or it may be violent and abrupt, but it is inevitable.

Sweezy doubts that attempts at economic reform can actually reverse this historical process. This is because the economic system is part of the entire social structure and cannot be repaired independently of the rest. Government is part of the social structure and is the means by which capitalist rule is ensured. Total change will begin gradually, with a series of socialist revolutions in separate countries. Finally, a worldwide socialist system will develop, capable of eliminating world capitalism in one final struggle.

Inefficiency of Monopoly

Misallocation of resources. Monopoly violates the principle of efficiency by misallocating resources. This is easy to see if we compare costs and revenues at the monopolist's equilibrium level of output. The profit-maximizing monopolist produces the quantity of output for which MC = MR. But because price is greater than MR, price is also greater than MC. When price is higher than marginal cost, this should be a signal to increase output. Consumers value the product enough to pay the cost of additional output. The principle of efficiency would require that more resources be allocated to this industry. A monopoly will not do this. The monopoly restricts output so as to maintain a high price and to maximize economic profit.

Average revenue greater than average cost. Monopoly violates the principle of efficiency by charging a higher price than minimum average costs. In monopoly there is no competition to force the firm to expand output to a level of production consistent with minimum average costs. When unit costs are not pushed to the minimum, society's scarce resources are used inefficiently.

Restriction of new technology. A monopoly may attempt to protect its market power by restricting new technological development. When a monopoly controls productive capital, strategic resources, and technical knowledge, it may limit their use for innovation. The result is prolonged inefficiency, with the waste of scarce resources for years to come.

Inequities of Monopoly

Price higher than marginal cost. Monopoly violates the principle of equity by maintaining price higher than marginal cost. A high price for a monopolist's product reduces the real income of consumers. If buyers are to continue to consume the monopolist's product, they must reduce their purchases of other goods and services. Demand curves in other markets must shift to the left. The result is distortion in production and in incomes throughout the economy. Differences in income come to be based not on different contributions to production but on the existence of monopoly power. In addition, wealth accumulated by monopoly-owners further distorts income distribution.

Concentration of power. Monopoly may undermine the principle of equity by financing political power in the hands of a few. Concentration of power is a threat to equity, however it is acquired.

GOVERNMENT AND MONOPOLIES

Government Regulation of Monopolies

Most monopolies in the United States are "natural monopolies"—electric companies, telephone companies, railroads. The city you live in probably has just one electric company, one gas company, and one phone company. We call these firms *public utilities* and regulate their price and output policies. (Regulation attempts to reduce or prevent the inefficiencies and inequities we have just discussed.) The advantages of large scale production make monopoly the most efficient structure for providing these services: Capital costs are high, and unit costs to the consumer are lower if a single firm is able to spread its capital costs over a large volume of output. Once a firm is operating successfully, others cannot easily enter the market because of the necessary heavy investment in vehicles and rights of way, in telephone lines and switching equipment, in power plants and cables.

Local utilities in this country are regulated by public service commissions. At the federal level the Interstate Commerce Commission (ICC) regulates interstate transportation by rail, bus, and truck; the Civil Aeronautics Board (CAB) regulates the airlines; the Federal Communications Commission (FCC) regulates telephone, television, and radio service; and the Federal Power Commission (FPC) regulates the price and output of electric power. The purpose of regulation is to prevent natural monopolies from exploiting their market position at the expense of consumers.

Regulated Prices

Under regulation, utility prices are based on costs of production. Generally the firm is allowed to charge rates that cover its full costs

Extended Example
Price Discrimination by a Regulated Monopoly

Some regulatory commissions permit a public utility to discriminate among customers in setting its rates. One reason for doing this is to permit the company to provide a larger quantity of service and to earn more total revenue than it could if it charged a single rate. Like the doctor who charges his patients according to how much each can afford to pay, the utility company tailors its rates to its customers. Figure 8 shows how this is done in the electric power industry.

Some users of electric power are willing to pay a high rate for small amounts of power. Their demand appears at the highest point of the curve. Some are willing to pay a moderate rate, and others would use more power if rates were low. Their demand appears in the lower range of the curve. By setting different rates, the power company is able to satisfy all these demands at the highest rate each class of user is willing to pay: high rates at the highest point of the demand curve and lower rates farther down. The firm's total revenues are shown as the entire shaded area under the demand curve.

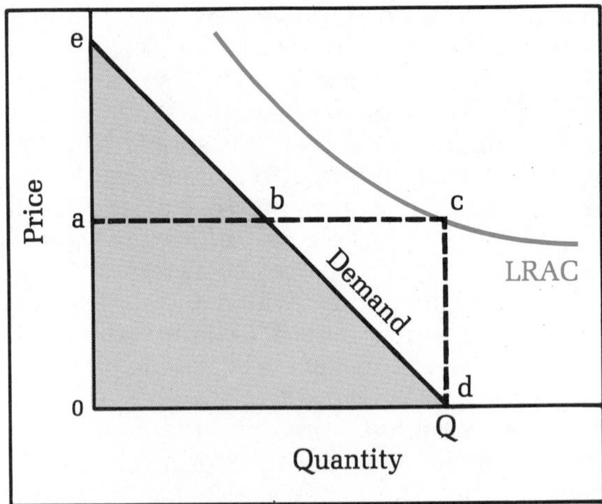

Figure 8 Price discrimination with a rate schedule. Total revenue equals the shaded area under the demand curve. Total costs equal the area of the rectangle *Oacd*.

Now look at the long-run average cost (LRAC) curve. You'll notice that it lies above the demand curve. No single user is willing to pay rates that will cover the full costs of providing individual units of service. But with a discriminatory rate schedule, the company will be able to cover its costs at quantity *OQ*. This is not magic. It is because those who pay the higher rates will provide enough revenue to make up for those who pay the lower rates. Total costs are shown by the rectangle *Oacd*, with base equal to quantity, *OQ*, and height equal to average total cost, *Oa*. Total revenues are shown by the entire area under the demand curve up to quantity *OQ*. The revenue area appears to be of about the same area as the cost rectangle. This means that total revenues are about equal to total costs. We can say that as long as the triangle *abe* is at least as large as the triangle *bcd*, the regulated utility will be able to cover its costs.

plus a reasonable rate of return on its capital investment. The rate of return must be high enough to compensate savers for the use of their funds—that is, the utility must be able to pay enough interest and dividends to encourage investors to buy its securities.

Often the firm's rate of return depends on the volume of output. An airline may be permitted to charge fares that will enable it to earn 9 percent on its capital investment if its planes are averaging 60 percent of capacity. If planes are more than 60 percent full, earnings will be greater than 9 percent. One difficulty with calculating the permitted return is getting everybody to agree on the value of the invested capital. What is the value of a five-year-old Boeing 707 or a two-year-old baggage cart? In times of inflation it may be necessary to figure what it would cost to replace equipment at current prices. When prices are going up, the utility will ask the regulatory commission to increase the value of the base for determining rate of return so as to allow for the eventual replacement of its capital equipment.

Subsidies

There is more than one way of setting prices for public utilities. Lawmakers may decide that a service is of such value to the community that it should be provided at less than its full cost.

Figure 9 shows the market demand for first-class mail delivery in the imaginary country of Atlantis. You'll notice that demand is relatively elastic over the range shown. At lower postage rates, people would send more letters, business firms would send advertising circulars, and politicians would mail campaign literature. Notice also that as the volume of mail increases, the average total cost of providing mail service declines. This is because of economies of large scale; the fixed cost of vehicles, sorting machines, and office space can be spread over many pieces of mail. Marginal costs drop with greater volume, up to a certain level, and average cost declines throughout the range shown.

If the postal service of Atlantis wants to maximize its profits, it will set its price at OP_1 and handle the volume OQ_1. At this point, MC = MR. Profits are shown by the shaded rectangle formed between the demand curve at (P_1) and (Q_1) and ATC.

A regulatory commission might say, "This is a public service, and the people of Atlantis don't want the post office to collect economic profit. They want postal rates to cover full costs and no more." The commission will look for the point at which ATC = AR, where full costs are covered, but there is no economic profit. The price at which ATC intersects AR is P_2. At that price, the volume of mail would increase to Q_2. Economic profit is zero, but since price covers full costs, the firm still earns normal profit. To force production to this level achieves some of the efficiency of a free and competitive market without substantial government control.

Nevertheless, the *value* of the postal service to each user is still greater than the cost of providing additional units of service. We know this because the demand curve for postal services lies above the marginal cost of producing postal service. Atlantis may decide to reduce price still further and provide greater service. At a price of OP_3 the volume of mail will be OQ_3, and the price will cover the additional cost of the last unit of mail delivered (MC = AR). But the price OP_3 won't cover full costs, including the cost of the postal service's fixed equipment. You can see this by comparing total revenue (the rectan-

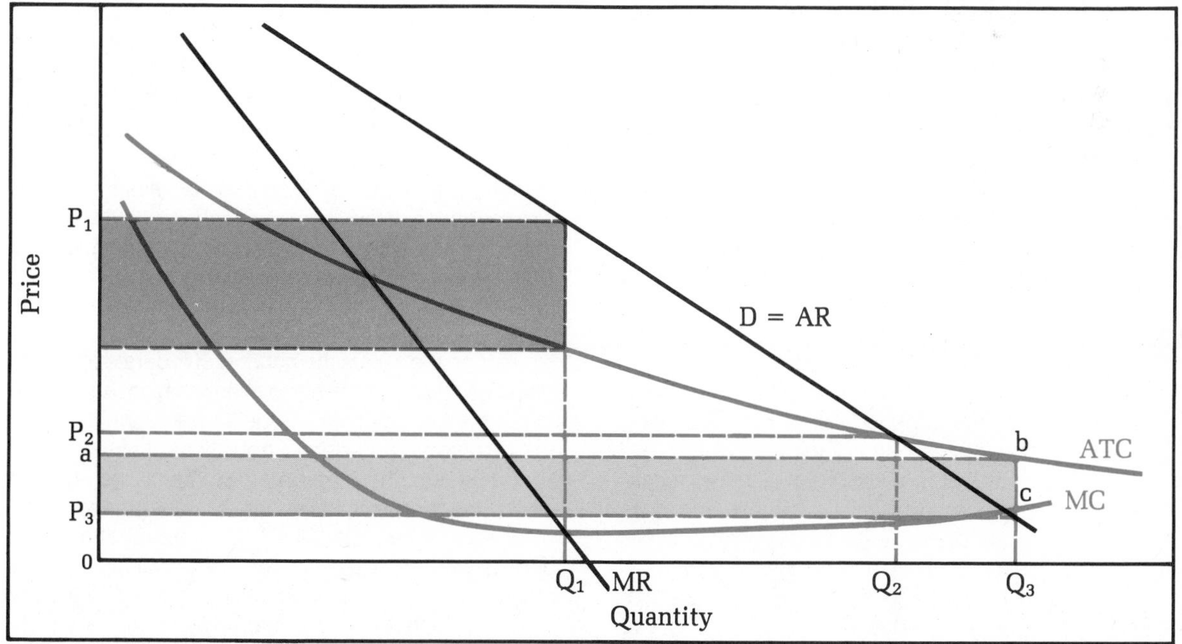

Figure 9 A regulated monopoly, such as the post office. At a price of P_1, profit is equal to the gray rectangle, but monopoly pricing is not permitted by the regulatory agency. At a price of P_2, the regulated monopoly is covering only its full costs; a subsidy is necessary equal to the area of the rectangle P_3abc.

Viewpoint Regulation or Strangulation?

It is said that your freedom to do as you please ends precisely at my nose! Government helps protect your freedom—and my nose—particularly when the overwhelming strength of one adversary would give it unfair advantage over a weaker opponent.

John Kenneth Galbraith popularized the phrase "countervailing power" to illustrate the need for a strong government to balance the power of strong industrial corporations. It was for this purpose that regulation of private business firms began in the late 1800s. Since that time, regulatory activity has increased, and lately efforts to evaluate the results of regulation have increased as well. Today's policymakers are aware of the costs of regulation and are proposing reform or even elimination of the regulations that have governed many industries.

The first regulatory agency was the Interstate Commerce Commission (ICC), established in 1887 to regulate U.S. railroads. In 1935 its authority was extended to regulate trucking. Its purpose was to ensure fair conditions of freight service for all customers whether large or small. In 1914 the Federal Trade Commission (FTC) was set up to preserve competition among industrial firms and to protect consumers from deceptive advertising. In the 1930s the Securities and Exchange Commission (SEC) was established to prohibit fraud and unfair practices in the exchange of securities. These and many other federal agencies have worked to protect the interests of individual consumers and small business firms against an unfair use of power by large enterprises.

Regulatory agencies established in recent years have focused on environmental issues, including health and safety and energy policy. Probably the agency most hated by American business is the Occupational Safety and Health Agency (OSHA). The purpose of OSHA is to set standards for employee health and safety and to fine employers if these guides are not followed. For strict compliance with OSHA standards, employers must spend billions of dollars every year, consuming a large part of their total investment budget. Few deny that regulation of health and safety standards are needed. But many business and government administrators argue that the present arrangement is costly and unworkable and should be overhauled. In response to administration pressure, OSHA began a program in 1978 to remove needless job-safety rules.

The Environmental Protection Agency (EPA) is also criticized for setting impossible or undesirable standards for industry. It has set maximum noise levels for newly produced locomotives, power saws, motorcycles, snowmobiles, and other noise polluters. And it is currently involved in setting noise standards for autos and commercial aircraft. Its air and water standards are expected to cost $500 billion over the next decade, or more than $230 a year for each American. Hundreds of foundries in the United States have been closed down for failure to meet environmental safety and health standards.

The Federal Energy Administration was established in 1975 and became the Department of Energy in 1978. The DOE has set standards for manufacturers of major appliances calling for a 20 percent overall reduction in energy use. The change required new appliance designs and materials and major retooling of factory equipment.

The immediate effect of recent environmental and energy regulations has been to increase the uncertainties of private business managers. Without clear information on current and future regulations it is difficult for firms to plan ahead. As a result, new investment may have been cut back so as to minimize exposure to agency pressure.

Improvements in industrial safety are costly, adding a hidden tax to every item produced. If consumers are to accept the higher-priced products they must be convinced they will receive superior benefits. True benefit-cost analysis is necessary to justify the higher prices, higher costs to business, and lower productivity. Some benefits of regulation are difficult to measure against costs, however. How do you measure the one third reduction in the American highway death rate following auto safety regulation, for example? Or progress in cleaning the nation's air and water of harmful chemicals or improvement in the safety of consumer products?

During the 1970s the number of federal regulatory agencies rose from twenty to twenty-seven, and by the end of the decade their budgets approached $10 billion. The Code of Federal Regulations grew to almost 30,000 pages. Should such growth be allowed to continue? One proposal, called the "Sunset Amendment," would require that agencies "self-destruct" after a certain specified period of time unless Congress makes a definite effort to continue them. Another would require the President to offer yearly plans to eliminate unneeded regulation; the President's recommendations would go into effect unless Congress acted to overrule them.

In 1978 Congress began deregulation of the nation's airlines. Since 1938 the Civil Aeronautics Board (CAB) had regulated routes and fares for all airlines that flew interstate (between states). Fares were often double the fares on unregulated lines flying intrastate (within a single state). The reason was the need to guarantee service to small isolated communities, possible only if airlines were allowed to make up those losses on other routes. The frequent result of regulation was that too many flights were scheduled and capacity was underutilized, wasting fuel and pushing up fares.

In the first year after deregulation, airline traffic on the nation's major airlines increased 10 percent. Average fares dropped 1.7 percent, saving consumers $2.8 billion. Profits soared to record levels. In the following year, the picture changed. High fuel prices and a worsening economic climate for the nation cut into profits. Fares rose, but by less than airline costs were rising. Competition increased on heavily traveled routes, and many unprofitable routes were abandoned.

Deregulation of the trucking industry has faced opposition from the Teamsters Union and from trucking companies. For forty-five years the ICC regulated routes and classes of commodities, effectively reducing competition in the industry. Rates were set by *rate bureaus:* organizations of trucking companies immune from the antitrust laws. As a result, rates were higher than they might have been and inefficiency was encouraged. Regulation added billions of dollars a year to trucking costs and an estimated one half percent to consumer prices. President Carter urged gradual decontrol of the trucking industry and in the summer of 1980 Congress moved to lift certain regulations.

It may be surprising that some of the chief opposition to deregulation comes from the regulated industries themselves and from organized labor. They argue that deregulation would bring ruinous competition, price wars, and bankruptcies. The result would be a decline in service and no service at all for some markets. The public, too, is not convinced of the need for deregulation: Studies show that a majority of Americans want more regulation. Other objections come from the regulatory agencies themselves, which provide jobs for more than 64,000 people.

Consult current news items for information about the progress of deregulating American industries. What groups support and oppose deregulation? What types of firms will benefit? How will consumers be affected? What are the results in terms of efficiency and equity? Are there also externalities?

gle formed beneath the curve at P_3 and Q_3) with total costs (the rectangle formed beneath the ATC curve at Q_3). The excess of costs over revenue must be paid by the government in the form of a *subsidy* to the postal service. Receipt of a government subsidy places the firm more closely under the control and protection of government. It may mean reduced incentives to innovate or to hold down costs, but it provides service to more people.

Government Monopolies

We encounter many forms of government monopoly every day. As you leave your home in the morning, you give a letter to the national post-office monopoly. You may be driven to work or to school by a municipal transportation monopoly. Very likely, the price you pay does not cover the full costs of providing these services. You probably don't give this much thought until someone asks why the postal service and the bus and subway should be run by a public authority and subsidized by all the taxpayers.

The philosophy of these matters is not consistent, but a reasonable explanation would probably include *externalities.* When a service provides social benefits over and above the benefits paid for in the market, there may be justification for providing it at public expense.

Railroads have long been government monopolies in most countries. In the United States most freight railroads are still privately owned, though heavily regulated by the federal government. But if you've recently taken a long ride on a passenger train, you've been a customer of Amtrak. Amtrak is a public corporation set up in 1970 to provide railroad passenger service when privately owned railroads found they could no longer do so. If Amtrak had not been formed, nearly all intercity passenger rail service would have disappeared. Amtrak's passenger coaches ride over privately owned rails and are repaired, at public expense, in the private shops of the railroad companies. Passenger service is still unprofitable, since most people prefer other modes of transportation. Congress underwrites Amtrak's deficits, which amount to about two fifths of the total cost of carrying passengers.

Municipal and interurban transportation in the United States was once privately owned and subject to regulation as a public utility. In the last few decades, however, most of the systems

Viewpoint The U.S. Postal Service

Benjamin Franklin started it all. Then in 1847 the postal service became a federal responsibility, with establishment of the Post Office Department. The objective of the coordinated postal service was to stimulate national communication and commerce and to aid national defense. It was felt that federal government subsidies should be used when necessary to further the process of integrating and strengthening a nation of such diverse needs and concerns.

Postal service revenues increased regularly as the nation grew, but so did the deficits financed by federal subsidy. The growing volume of mail required substantial investments in new equipment and technology, raising unit costs. Even with substantial automation, labor costs continued to amount to 85 percent of costs. In the 1970s rising wage demands and rising gasoline costs added to the problem of higher costs.

In order to protect the postal service from competition and to encourage investment in modern equipment, the U.S. government gave the Post Office a legal monopoly on first-class mail delivery. With its protected market in letter handling, the postal service was able to practice price discrimination. Markets could be separated easily: first-class letters, second-class bulk mail, and parcels. Then prices could be set on the basis of elasticity of demand: higher relative prices where demand was less elastic.

The U.S. Post Office monopoly on first-class mail makes demand highly inelastic. Because there is no suitable substitute, users will pay a high price to acquire the service. On the other hand, business bulk mail and parcels may be sent by alternate means. In order to compete, the price for handling packages must be lower than rates charged by other carriers. The result is a *cross subsidy* within the postal service. High first-class letter charges help pay the costs of carrying other mail at rates below cost.

In recent decades there has been growing criticism of high postal rates and poor service. In 1971 the service was removed from federal government responsibility. The Post Office Department was abolished and the U.S. Postal Service was established as a quasi-private corporation. It was to receive a temporary government subsidy to ease the transition, but it was assumed that the Postal Service would be self-supporting by the year 1984.

Unfortunately, other factors have intervened to worsen the financial plight of the sick service. Over time, demand has become more elastic. Rising bulk rates led many business firms to use other means of communication. Private parcel carriers and electronic communications are modern substitutes for the mail service, especially for the most profitable types of mail: Telephone communications are a substitute for business letters, and electronic fund transfers allow users to deposit checks and pay bills without use of the mail.

have been sold to government and reorganized as public enterprises. Private companies found it difficult to obtain the high fare increases that became necessary to cover rising costs and stay in business. Metropolitan Chicago has a Regional Transit Authority that doesn't own any of the interurban systems it governs but subsidizes them from local tax revenues. This enables the Authority to plan rail and bus services without regard to whether any particular route is profitable.

Socialists have traditionally favored turning large sectors of industry over to public ownership. In Britain, after World War II, the Labor government nationalized basic industries such as coal, railways, and trucking. In 1976, however, British socialists changed their minds about the benefits of nationalizing competitive industry. Government monopoly has been found to work best in industries that were already monopolies under private ownership. Most West European socialists would probably agree with a leading member of Parliament, R. A. S. Crosland, that industries should be nationalized only when this will improve them—that is, "where the existing industry is clearly performing poorly, when competition either cannot or is not permitted to enforce an improvement, where physical or fiscal controls are incapable of curing the situation, and where public ownership will not bring attendant disadvantages of its own."

Some consumers avoid higher postal rates by paying bills in person. Publishing companies distribute magazines and advertising material door-to-door through independent companies or through subsidiaries. Business firms insert their advertisements in newspapers for cheaper distribution. Greater elasticity of demand in these markets has meant lower volume and higher unit costs.

While the volume of mail has declined, the number of homes and business addresses the Post Office must serve has continued to rise. This increases unit costs further. As a result, the postal service continues to run a deficit in most years.

Nobody seems to know the solution to the problems that plague the postal service. Raising letter rates again is apparently not the answer (though in 1981 postal authorities were ready to raise the 15¢ letter rate to 18¢). Some policymakers have suggested eliminating Saturday delivery in order to reduce costs. In terms of the efficiency principle the postal service is a failure; the value of benefits purchased is less than the cost of providing the service.

Perhaps the postal service should be evaluated in terms of a third criterion. Recall that production of certain goods and services imparts benefits to the society over and above the explicit benefits purchased in the market. We have referred to these unmeasured benefits as *externalities:* the external benefits that accrue to a society as a result of particular economic activity.

External benefits are difficult, if not impossible, to measure correctly. Still, when production adds to a community's living standards, an effort should be made to evaluate the full effects. Some of the external benefits of cheap postal service might include:

integration of a diverse society into a coherent unit;

dissemination of advertising information to increase the market for mass-produced goods;

exposure to cultural and political information for isolated areas;

employment for many low-skilled workers.

You may be able to add more external benefits—and perhaps some external costs as well. The important question would be whether *total benefits* of cheap postal service exceed *total costs.* If this is indeed the case, then a strong argument could be made for continuing to subsidize the service from public funds. Like the public school system, the postal service would be operated as a service whose total benefits to the society as a whole justify making it a public responsibility.

What would be the likely effects of allowing free competition in carrying first-class mail (letters)? In what sense would this be more efficient? In what sense would it be more equitable?

SUMMARY

Competitive markets come close to satisfying the goals of efficiency and equity in the long run. The structure of an industry affects the conduct of firms and, in turn, their performance in terms of these goals. Structure determines the performance of monopoly firms, too.

A monopoly is the single supplier of a good or service without acceptable substitutes. Information barriers may interfere with the mobility of firms into the monopolized industry. Predatory pricing or squeeze operations may eliminate competitors. Natural monopolies result from technical conditions of production; because of economies of large scale, a single producer is more efficient than many small competitive firms. Some artificial monopolies are granted by government when the service is believed to be essential to the community; patents create artifical monopolies and help encourage invention.

The demand curve for a monopolist slopes downward because it is the industry demand curve. The result is that a monopolist's marginal revenue is not the same as price. When MR = MC, the level of output is lower and price is higher than under competition. The monopoly firm may continue to collect economic profit in the long run because of the absence of competition.

A monopoly firm has greater power to raise

price when demand is relatively inelastic. Price discrimination is possible when elasticity differs among separate markets.

Monopoly violates the principle of efficiency by producing less output at higher resource costs than under competition and by limiting incentives for innovation and communication of new technology. Monopoly violates the principle of equity by distorting the distribution of real income. Natural monopolies are often regulated by government agencies. Regulated monopolies may expand the volume of service so that price covers marginal cost but not average total cost. When this happens, a subsidy must be paid. The postal system is an example of a regulated monopoly which is believed to provide external benefits in return for the subsidy it receives.

Key Words and Phrases

artificial monopolies monopolies which result from deliberate efforts to keep out competition.

conduct of firms behavior of firms with respect to competition.

dumping the practice in international trade of setting lower prices in distant markets than in the home country.

efficiency using resources so as to achieve maximum output per unit of scarce input.

equity distributing benefits and costs from production in a way that society regards as fair.

monopoly an industry in which a single seller controls the entire output of a product for which there are no acceptable substitutes.

natural monopolies monopolies which result from technical factors within an industry.

patent a legal monopoly over the use of an invention for a fixed period of time.

performance of firms behavior of firms with respect to efficiency and equity.

price discrimination use of different prices in different markets.

structure of industry arrangement of firms in an industry according to size and market power.

Questions for Review

1. Explain why the concepts of structure, conduct, and performance are critical to a study of industrial organization in the United States.
2. During what stage of American economic development did monopoly occur? How was it achieved?
3. List as many advantages and disadvantages of monopoly as you can think of. Be careful to state the conditions under which the advantages would exist.
4. Use the following hypothetical data to determine a monopoly firm's price and output. First you must calculate total revenue, marginal revenue, and marginal cost for every level of output. What is the monopolist's profit at the profit-maximizing output?

Quantity demanded	*Price*	*Total cost*
1	10	6
2	9	11
3	8	15
4	7	20
5	6	26
6	5	33

5. Refer again to the data in question 4. Assume the industry is competitive and new firms can enter the industry and also produce under the cost conditions given. What would a perfectly competitive firm's long-run price and output be?
6. The data in question 4 can also be used to illustrate price discrimination. If the firm is able to discriminate completely among buyers, charging a different price to each one, what would be its total revenue? What would be its economic profit? On a graph of demand, what geometric space represents total revenue under conditions of perfect price discrimination?
7. Define: patent, marginal cost pricing in regulated industries.

CHAPTER 11

Imperfect Competition: Monopolistic Competition and Oligopoly

Learning Objectives

Upon completion of this chapter, you should be able to:

1. Distinguish monopolistic competition and oligopoly from the other product market structures, emphasizing both differences and similarities.
2. Graph demand and cost curves for both monopolistic competition and oligopoly.
3. State conditions of long-run equilibrium in monopolistic competition and explain the shortcomings.
4. Graph and explain the kinked demand curve.
5. Discuss the forms of competition in oligopoly and explain the shortcomings of oligopoly.
6. Discuss the pros and cons of advertising.

We have studied two quite different forms of economic behavior: perfect competition and monopoly. In perfect competition there are many sellers, all producing identical products. In monopoly there is only one seller, providing a unique good or service. The monopoly firm has control over the price at which its product sells, but producers in a perfectly competitive market have no such control.

There are few pure monopolies in our economy and few markets in which perfect competition can be found. Most markets are somewhere in between. Economists refer to all forms of industrial organization other than monopoly and perfect competition as **imperfect competition.*** This is an odd name to use for everyday economic activities. It's like saying, "You understand what we mean by perfect competition, don't you? Well, this isn't it."

One reason we do this is that the theory of perfect competition was developed first, and for a long time was the only theory to explain economic behavior. Economists knew that perfectly competitive markets were few and far between. In analyzing the real world they didn't expect firms to behave exactly as they would in the world of economic theory. Only fairly recently did economists begin to develop a theory based on less-than-perfect competition. This proved to

*Some economists lump monopoly in the pot of imperfect competition.

be a step forward in our understanding. The theory of imperfect competition helps explain things that happen in real life. It explains such things as the tendency of prices in some industries to rise together in spurts, or the existence of four gas stations at one intersection, or the huge sums of money spent for advertising beer and pet foods.

Two kinds of imperfect competition may be distinguished: *monopolistic competition* and *oligopoly*. **Monopolistic competition** resembles perfect competition in that *many firms* compete with each other; it resembles monopoly in that each firm has *some power* to influence the price at which it sells, because it offers a differentiated product. A firm in monopolistic competition affects price by trying to convince buyers that its product is the only one that will meet their needs. To the extent the firm succeeds in this, it establishes a monopoly and can set a monopoly price. Henri's Delicatessen is the only Henri's Delicatessen around, just as Maude's Dress Shop is different from any other dress shop. If you're loyal to Henri or Maude, you'll patronize them rather than their competitors, even if their competitors' prices are somewhat lower.

Oligopoly is a situation in which the market is dominated by a *few firms*. This is typical of industries producing automobiles, steel, and soap, and of other large-scale industries. Oligopoly differs from monopolistic competition in that new companies find it difficult to enter these fields. Almost anybody can start a little shoe store or some other small business, but few people would think seriously of setting up a new auto company to compete with General Motors.

Both monopolistic competition and oligopoly are characterized by a particular type of competition. Price competition is *not* significant. Instead, firms in monopolistic competition and oligopoly engage in other forms of competition. This chapter will provide some examples.

MONOPOLISTIC COMPETITION

Probably most U.S. firms could be characterized as monopolistically competitive. Monopolistic competition develops in industries having a simple technology and requiring relatively small capital investment. This allows many small firms to enter. Thus we notice another characteristic of monopolistic competition: there are few barriers to entry. (Monopolistic competition resembles perfect competition in this regard.) Vigorous competition may result.

Because many firms are competing, each will try to distinguish its product from the products of others. A firm in monopolistic competition may give uniqueness to its product in either of two ways: through design or service features that improve the usefulness of the product, or through appeals to buyer psychology that give the *appearance* of greater usefulness. The process of creating uniqueness is called **product differentiation.**

Product differentiation allows a firm to establish a degree of monopoly control over price. In monopolistic competition, some buyers will remain loyal to a particular brand even if price is slightly higher. For this reason the firm in monopolistic competition is not forced to produce and sell at the very lowest cost. And by the same token it faces less pressure to develop newer and cheaper production techniques.

Where do we find monopolistic competition? Almost everywhere. Grocery stores, restaurants, dry cleaners, stationery stores, book publishers, and most small shops are monopolistic competitors. In manufacturing, we find monopolistic competition in industries where there are large numbers of small firms: women's clothing, shoes, wood furniture, men's and boys' suits and coats, among others. Firms engaged in monopolistic competition tend to be limited to local, rather than national, markets.

Under monopolistic competition it pays to advertise, but often on a limited scale. Since most of the firms are small, they can't afford lavish expenditures. Their ads appear in local newspapers, not in important magazines. They use direct mail. Sometimes they buy spots on local radio and TV broadcasts.

There are seldom too few firms in this type of market. On the contrary, monopolistic competition tends to draw more firms than necessary to satisfy market demand. This is because it is so easy to enter the field and because the business appears so profitable. Every year thousands of shops and small businesses are established, and every year thousands fail. In a new industry with a growing consumer market, profits will be adequate for the first firms that enter the industry. But profits will soon attract competition, each new firm supplying a product somewhat different from the others. New firms must

Economic Thinker Joan Robinson

When Joan Robinson (1903–) began studying economics in England during the early 1900s, there was substantial agreement among economists about the structure of the market system. It was assumed that markets were fundamentally competitive. Somewhere in the textbooks reference was usually made to monopoly, but this was "a hard, indigestible lump" which never quite fit in with the competitive analysis. The logical consistency of the competitive model was so attractive that economists tried not to notice that it didn't fit the real world.

The problem could not be ignored forever, though, and eventually the modern theory of monopoly was developed. Monopoly is different from competition because of a "gap in the chain of substitutes" for some good. When the output of a firm is bound on all sides by such gaps, the firm is a monopoly. If entry of new firms is restricted into this industry, profits may continue to be greater than normal for some time.

Joan Robinson was significant for her work in the theory of how monopoly firms behave. But she went much further than this. She saw that goods in real markets are often *partial substitutes* for other goods. They may not be *perfect substitutes* but they are reasonably substitutable so that absolute monopoly is rare. The real world is characterized by monopolistic competition among firms selling similar but differentiated products. It is her path-breaking work in the theory of monopolistic competition for which Robinson is best known—especially in her book *The Economics of Imperfect Competition* (1933).

She also analyzed the effects of imperfect competition on income distribution. A firm in monopolistic competition restricts output in order to maintain price. The result is a lower level of plant operation than optimum and lower employment of factors of production. The final result of imperfect competition is a greater

return to entrepreneurs relative to the incomes of other factors of production. The gap between industry's ability to produce goods and workers' ability to purchase them will bring on periodic depressions. This conclusion led Robinson to accept Marx's predictions of change in economic systems.

As a Reader of Economics at Cambridge, Robinson has continued her work in the theory of imperfect competition, employment, capital accumulation, and economic philosophy, including Marxist economics.

often set lower prices to attract a share of the market. Competitive price cutting will reduce the profits of all. Finally, many firms will share a market that isn't quite large enough for them all, each charging a price that just covers full costs of production and none collecting substantial profits.

It may appear that these results are the same as results under competition, but this is not the case. In perfect competition there are only enough firms to supply the entire market at lowest costs of production. Each firm produces enough output to achieve minimum costs and maximum efficiency. In monopolistic competition there are too many firms. Each has a smaller share of the market than would be true under perfect competition. The existence of product differentiation enables firms to set price a little higher than would be true under perfect competition, but each monopolistically competitive firm will produce too little output to enjoy minimum costs. Their prices must cover their higher production costs and also the cost of advertising. Product differentiation interferes with competition, so that firms in these industries operate at less than maximum efficiency.

Demand Curves in Monopolistic Competition

Demand curves for firms in monopolistic competition slope downward. The steepness of the slope depends on the characteristics of the product. If a product is highly differentiated—that is, if it appears to consumers to be completely different from competing products—demand will be relatively inelastic and the downward slope will be steep. Demand for the product will resemble the demand curve of a monopolist, since there are no close substitutes. A less differentiated product will have some acceptable substitutes, so its demand curve will be flatter—more nearly like a demand curve in perfect competition.

Figure 1 shows a hypothetical demand curve for an imaginary cola drink, Pepto-Fizz. For many consumers Pepto-Fizz is a beverage that has no substitute. Others will substitute Coke or Pepsi if price is less. The marginal revenue curve lies below the demand curve to show

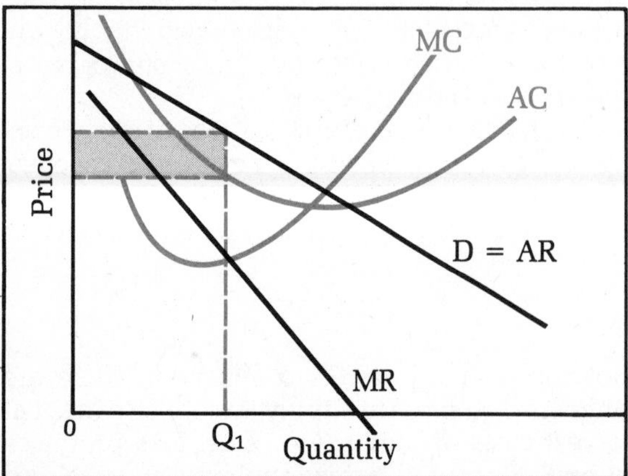

Figure 1 Market for the cola drink Pepto-Fizz. A firm in monopolistic competition faces a downward-sloping demand curve. Marginal revenue lies below average revenue. Total profit is shown by the shaded area.

Extended Example
How to Be Successful in Monopolistic Competition

Find a product that can be sold through food and drugstore outlets, that is purchased primarily by women, that sells for less than $3, that can be easily and distinctively packaged, and for which there is at least a $500 million market not already dominated by one or two producers. Then take aim and fire.

That is how Hanes Corporation broke into the consciousness of American women with L'eggs, the cleverly packaged pantyhose that captured 13 percent of the market in its first five years. By 1976 the company was already looking for new worlds to conquer in socks and underwear. According to Hanes' president, Robert Elberson, "The only way we can continue to grow in women's hosiery is to continue to take away from somebody else. And that gets progressively tougher and more expensive."

In its invasion of the women's hosiery field, Hanes spent heavily on advertising. It had previously been an apparel manufacturing company, but in 1969 management decided to become a consumer goods marketing company. It hired experts from companies like Procter & Gamble, General Mills, and R. J. Reynolds—firms which also stress the importance of marketing. The marketing approach begins with the customer rather than with the product. Hanes started by finding out what consumers disliked about existing goods or about the way they were merchandised. Once it spotted an opening, it developed an approach, and a product, to fill it. That was followed by test marketing, to see how the public reacted, and, finally, by planning sales and distribution methods. Between 1969 and 1975, Hanes raised its advertising budget from 5 percent of sales to 13 percent.

In the crowded market for consumer goods the motto seems to be: If you can't be new, be different.

How does advertising affect a firm's demand curve? Show the effect of an advertising campaign on a firm's profits. What is the result if other firms counter with a similar advertising campaign? Illustrate graphically.

that the firm has a degree of monopoly power. Each reduction in price produces a smaller increase in revenue.

Costs in Monopolistic Competition

Costs in monopolistic competition have the same characteristics as costs in other market structures. Short-run average cost curves are saucer-shaped, and marginal cost curves rise after some optimum level of production has been reached. The output that maximizes profit is at the point where MC = MR. Selling price is determined from the point on the demand curve directly above MC = MR. Profit per unit is the difference between price, or average revenue, and average cost: AR − AC. In Figure 1, total profit is the area of the rectangle whose base is quantity sold (OQ_1) and whose height is AR − AC.

Long-Run Equilibrium in Monopolistic Competition

The fact that firms are in monopolistic *competition* with each other affects what happens to them over time. In the short run, a firm may receive economic profit, as shown by the rectangle in Figure 1. But since the industry is imperfectly competitive, this profit cannot last. Unlike the situation in monopoly, conditions in monopolistic competition permit relatively free entry of other firms. Initial capital requirements are low, encouraging people to go into business on a small scale. Technical information is widely available. Even though products are similar, there is often room enough in the market for one or two more firms producing slightly different versions of the same good or service.

As new firms enter, the industry moves toward long-run equilibrium. But long-run equilibrium under monopolistic competition lacks the ideal characteristics of perfect competition. As new firms enter, they take away part of the market from existing firms. Each firm's demand curve shifts to the left, eliminating some economic profit. In Figure 2 the entry of new firms has reduced each firm's sales by half. There is still some economic profit, however, and new firms continue to enter. When each firm's sales have fallen to the position shown in Figure 3,

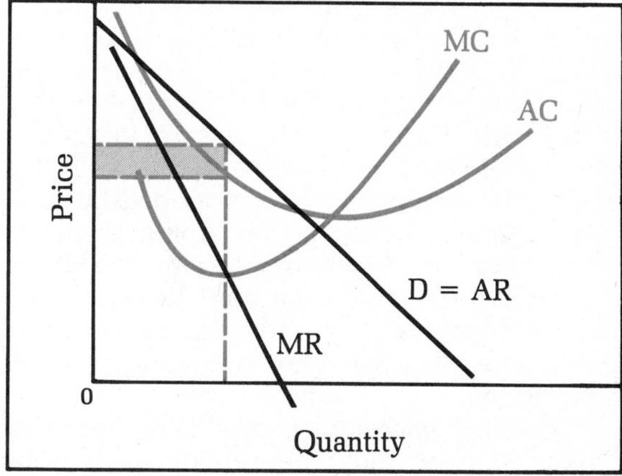

Figure 2 Economic profit attracts new firms into the industry. The individual firm's demand curve shifts to the left. Economic profit is reduced.

there is no longer any incentive for new firms to enter. The industry has reached long-run equilibrium.

What are the characteristics of long-run equilibrium under monopolistic competition?

(1) At equilibrium, there is only normal profit. The disappearance of economic profit removes the incentive for new firms to enter the industry. There are no losses either, because firms with losses have withdrawn. So, average revenue must equal average cost: AR − AC = 0. Price is just enough to cover full costs.

(2) Because the demand curve slopes downward, the average cost curve must also slope downward at the point where AR = AC. That is the only way the two curves can just touch with-

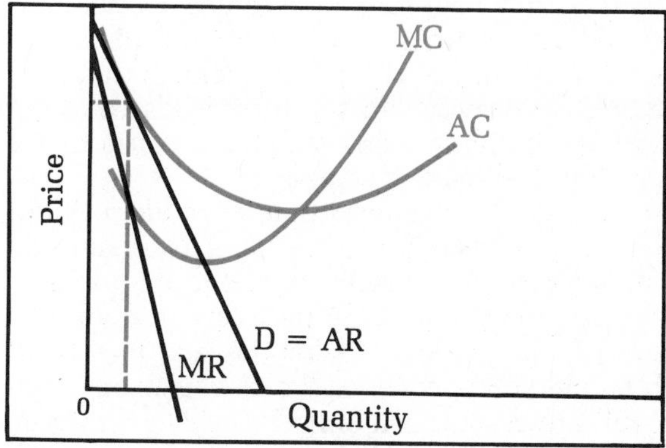

Figure 3 Long-run equilibrium under monopolistic competition. Economic profit is eliminated and firms operate at less than their lowest cost level of output.

out crossing each other. This is significant. It means that firms are not producing at their minimum-cost level of output. If they produced more, AC would be lower. Remember that under perfect competition, firms are in equilibrium at the lowest point on the AC curve. To the extent that unit costs under monopolistic competition are higher than they would be under competition, the economy is using too many resources to produce each unit. Resources are being used inefficiently, and consumers are paying a higher price than they would under perfect competition.

(3) Since each firm is producing less than the optimum quantity, there are too many firms in the industry. The same quantity of output could be supplied by fewer firms. This means that more capital resources are being allocated to this industry than would be necessary for maximum efficiency. Many communities have small stores that sell substantially the same goods or two barbers on opposite sides of the street where one barber wouldn't be kept busy full time. Still, their loyal customers help keep them in business.

(4) Because their very existence depends on distinguishing themselves from their competitors, firms in monopolistic competition must allocate resources for product differentiation. A retailer can attract customers in various ways: through better service, more accessible shelves, a greater variety of brands, special sales, and heavier advertising. In some manufacturing industries the options are fewer. A manufacturer of electric drills for home carpenters may sell a product that is practically identical to that of competitors. In order to carve out a place in the market, this firm may have to use special merchandising techniques to get its drills displayed so that customers will notice them. It may also advertise heavily. All these methods can help shift an individual firm's demand curve to the right and to make it steeper.

The most common route to product differentiation is through *advertising*. Advertising can often persuade consumers of the uniqueness, the superiority, and the necessity of owning a product, regardless of what the facts may be. If total market demand for the good is fixed, however, advertising can only shift customers from one product to another. A rightward shift in one firm's demand curve will mean a leftward shift in another's. A barrage of advertising from one producer must be countered by similar barrages from others. The result may go far beyond what could reasonably be considered product information. Much of the effort will be devoted to confusing consumers or to diverting or entertaining them.

Advertising is expensive. It increases average cost curves and increases the price of the product. The final result of heavy advertising may be that total industry sales remain the same but unit costs rise for every firm. Again, the result is inefficient use of the nation's resources.

SHORTCOMINGS OF MONOPOLISTIC COMPETITION

How does monopolistic competition affect us?

Monopolistic competition should be evaluated in terms of the principles of efficiency and equity. Because monopolistic competition is similar to monopoly in product uniqueness, it has some of the same disadvantages as monopoly (refer to the previous chapter). There are other disadvantages which grow out of particular features of monopolistically competitive markets.

Efficiency

Monopolistic competition violates the principle of efficiency because it allows too many producers in the industry. When initial capital requirements are low and technical information readily available, many firms can enter the market. The result is too many firms, each producing less than the optimum quantity of output. At low levels of operation, unit costs are higher than necessary. Plant and equipment are underutilized and prices are higher than necessary. Productive resources are used wastefully, and the industry is inefficient.

In monopolistic competition some resources are used for nonprice competition: product differentiation, including advertising. Using resources in this way may be a net benefit to society if the result is greater information, greater variety of products, and a wider range of qualities to choose from. However, if the result is false advertising claims, superficial product gimmickry, or rapid obsolescence of products, then there is a net loss.

Extended Example Monopolistic Competition in Ladies' Apparel

The ladies' apparel industry is described as a *fragmented industry:* It is broken into many small firms, each supplying a small fraction of the market. Initial capital costs are low, encouraging entry of new firms and increasing competition among them. Not only must firms compete among themselves for customers, they also must compete for sales against the customer's existing wardrobe. As a result, the apparel industry reflects all the characteristics of monopolistic competition. There are many firms, each producing a smaller volume at higher prices than would be true under perfect competition. Firms differentiate their product through design changes and heavy advertising, pushing average costs up and profit margins down.

In order to increase demand and make demand curves less elastic, the industry must constantly create new fashions. New fashions render the customer's existing wardrobe out-of-date and shift demand curves to the right. New fashions create urgency in the mind of the fashion-conscious consumer and make demand curves steeper. In the markets for high-fashion clothing, firms are often able to sell more units at higher prices.

In recent years fashion-conscious American women have been urged to emulate the Argentine ranchero, the guerrilla fighter, the Russian streetsweeper, and Annie Hall. Many consumers have gone along with current fads, willingly paying the higher prices and discarding last year's clothes. But occasionally they have rebelled. In the early 1970s, American women refused to accept the maxi-skirt, and clothing manufacturers lost millions of dollars.

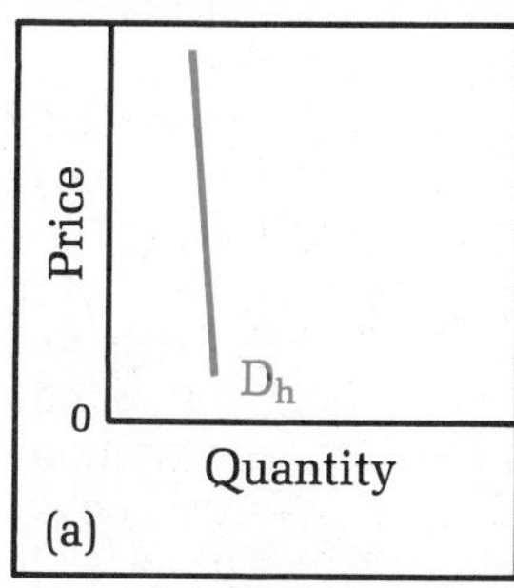

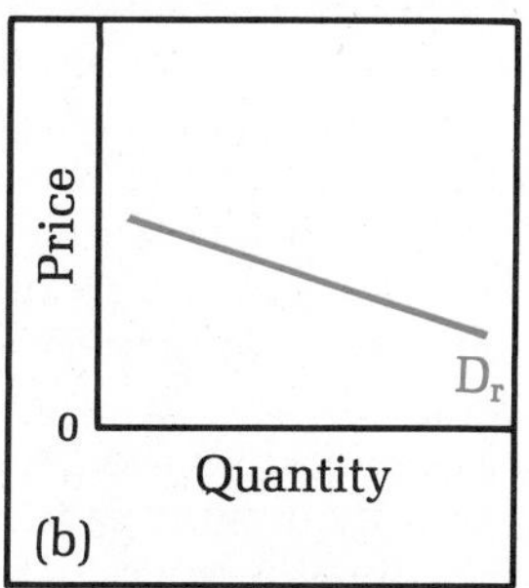

Figure 4 A clothing retailer sells in two markets: (a) high-fashion clothing; (b) ready-to-wear clothing.

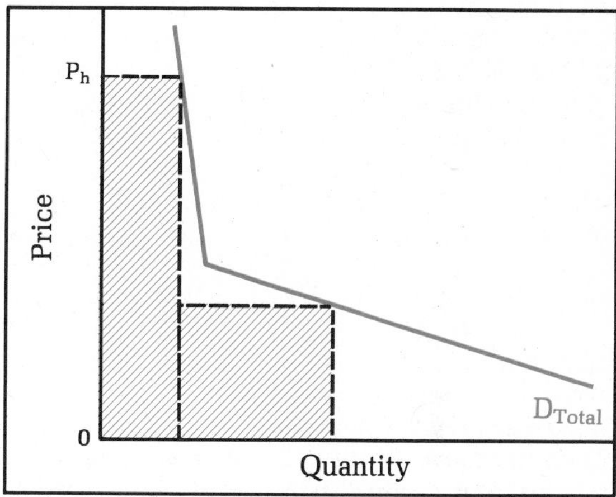

Figure 5 The separate market demand curves shown in Figure 4 are combined to give total market demand. Total revenue is the sum of the shaded areas.

If the maxi-skirt was the Edsel of the clothing industry, the pantsuit was its Mustang. Once American women grew accustomed to its comfort and wearability, they could not be persuaded to discard it completely in favor of new dresses. To the extent that consumers regard their pantsuits as acceptable substitutes for skirts, demand curves for dresses will remain more elastic.

The apparel industry provides another example of how firms use knowledge about demand to increase revenues. High-fashion apparel firms sell their "original" creations to wealthy women for as much as $5000 a garment. At that price, volume is so low that total profits are minimal. Therefore, the same firms market a separate line of ready-to-wear at much lower prices (see Figure 4). Total market demand is the sum of the two curves, and there are two prices instead of one. Total revenue is the sum of two rectangles formed beneath the two demand curves (see Figure 5).

Describe how firms in other industries increase total profit by selling similar products to different classes of buyers. Some examples are airlines, football teams, vacation resorts. What is the significance of demand elasticity in these cases? How can profits from one product be used to "subsidize" production of the other?

Equity

Monopolistic competition may enhance equity in a society, but in a way which damages the principle of efficiency. The lure of monopoly profits and the small capital investment encourage entry of new firms. Entrepreneurs seeking business opportunities find a wide range of possible activities. Regrettably the same factors which encourage entry make continued prosperity less certain, and many of these small enterprises soon succumb to market forces. Ultimately, the waste of human and capital resources may be substantial.

OLIGOPOLY

Oligopoly differs from monopolistic competition in that there are fewer firms. The word *oligopoly* means "few sellers." There may be as few as two, or there may be twenty or thirty with just two or three dominant firms. These are the glamorous companies of American industry, the firms with executive suites and company airplanes. Their production is carried out on a large scale; their sales efforts are nationwide. Some oligopoly firms produce industrial commodities for which product differentiation is not practical: steel, aluminum, copper, and petroleum are examples. Others produce differentiated consumer goods: automobiles, TV programming, cigarettes, cereals, classical records, movies, and tires.

Oligopoly firms tend to grow through **merger,** as small firms join or are absorbed by bigger firms to combine their productive assets. They have high overhead costs for plant, equipment, advertising, and executive salaries, but their large volume permits them to spread fixed costs over a large number of units, keeping unit production costs down. Even so, their market power often enables oligopoly firms to keep prices higher than full costs of production.

Oligopolists find other ways of competing than through price. Aggressive selling and advertising are important nonprice methods of competition in oligopoly. The Bic company competes by comparing its ballpoint pens to bananas. The four American automobile firms compete by emphasizing superficial differences in design.

Product differentiation is less important for oligopoly firms that sell homogeneous materials such as steel, cement, or aluminum. Among these firms, nonprice competition takes the form of service or credit arrangements on behalf of customers. Firms use "institutional" advertising to inform buyers about the industry as a whole and the nice people who work in it. In some industries, firms run informational advertising in which highly technical messages are aimed at specialists who use the product.

In general, the closer an industry is to the consumer, the more advertising and product differentiation it will do. Automobiles have already been mentioned. Aspirin is another example. Although all aspirin is identical in substance, we would scarcely be aware of this from the TV ads. Similarly, automobile rental firms rent the same kinds of cars but plug their services relentlessly on TV.

Regrettably, competitive advertising may take the place of research and development for oligopoly firms. Research and development is costly and involves substantial risks, but it probably produces more benefits to our economy than competitive advertising.

Oligopoly prices are higher than prices would be under perfect competition, and they tend to be rigid. To the extent that firms coordinate their policies, the harmful results of monopoly will follow. Price is higher and output lower than in perfect competition, and production costs may not be pushed to the minimum. Without competition, firms may not be forced to operate efficiently.

Price and Output in Oligopoly

The unique thing about oligopoly is that one firm's price and output decisions depend on the decisions of others. There are so few firms that no single firm can ignore the actions of others. If Avery Company should reduce its price and take away part of the market from Bates Company and Clark Company, then Bates and Clark would be forced to reduce their prices, too. Soon the three companies would be back with the same share of the market as before, except that each would sell its product for less and none of the firms would gain. Of course, Avery knows that the others would match its lower price, so it doesn't reduce it. It won't raise price either. A higher price would mean the loss of its share of the market to the others.

Extended Example Oligopoly in Chips?

When is a potato chip not a potato chip? When it's stackable.

In the past, most potato chips were produced by about a hundred firms scattered around the United States. Total sales ran about $1.5 billion a year, primarily from small plants close to consumer markets. Chips break easily and packages are bulky, so they cannot be shipped very far. This kept production on a small scale.

In 1969, however, Procter & Gamble, the large food and housewares firm, began to test market its "new-fangled potato chips." P & G dehydrated its potatoes, ground them and pressed them flat, and then fried them. The finished "chips" were uniform in size and shape and could be stacked in sealed cans similar to tennis ball cans.

The new process had several advantages. It permitted substantial cost savings through large-scale processing and packaging. The new compact containers could be shipped longer distances, and the product had a shelf life of about a year. Whereas most markets for conventional potato chips were served by about five local plants, the new product could be provided economically by as few as three or four nationwide giants.

Fighting back, traditional chip makers petitioned the Food and Drug Administration to prohibit the use of the term "potato chip" on any product not made in the conventional way. After much consideration, the agency finally ruled that the new product could be labeled "potato chips made from dried potatoes." The ruling was a setback for the conventional chip producers, some of whom set out to develop a similar product.

This case illustrates that innovative activity can occur in oligopolistic industry. Large firms can afford to make heavy outlays for product development, capital equipment, and sales promotion. When they succeed, the result is a restructuring of the industry.

What are the efficiency and equity arguments for small-scale chip manufacturers versus large nationwide suppliers?

This sort of testing of the market and backing down is fairly common in oligopolistic industries until firms learn how their rivals will probably respond. Then price tends to stabilize, and firms decide it's better not to rock the boat. Oligopoly firms are interdependent. Each firm must base its decisions on the actions and reactions of others. If you have played bridge or poker or chess, you know what it means to base your decisions on the expected reactions of others: you can't decide beforehand on the proper strategy to adopt, but must be prepared to follow a different strategy depending on what the others do.

It is not surprising that interdependence among large oligopoly firms might lead eventually to agreements to fix price. To agree in advance on price or output is called **collusion.** Oligopolies certainly prefer collusion over ruinous price wars and industry-wide losses. Collusion might take place through industry trade associations. Member firms submit price lists to the association's trade journal; when members know what other firms are charging, they are likely to charge the same. In other industries, rate schedules are readily available for making comparisons.

Collusion is illegal under U.S. antitrust laws, to be discussed in the next chapter. However, it is often difficult to determine whether firms in oligopoly are actually agreeing to fix price or only making intelligent business decisions.

Duopoly

Suppose there are two firms in an industry, both with long experience and loyal customers. They divide the market, behaving like monopolists in their own parts of the market. They don't do this by agreement or collusion but by long practice. Together, they maximize their joint profits.

This form of oligopoly is called **duopoly**—the prefix *duo* meaning two. If the firms have identical cost curves, they will equate MC with MR, and each will produce half of total industry output. Unit profit for each firm is the difference between price and average cost at the profit-maximizing level of output. The existence of

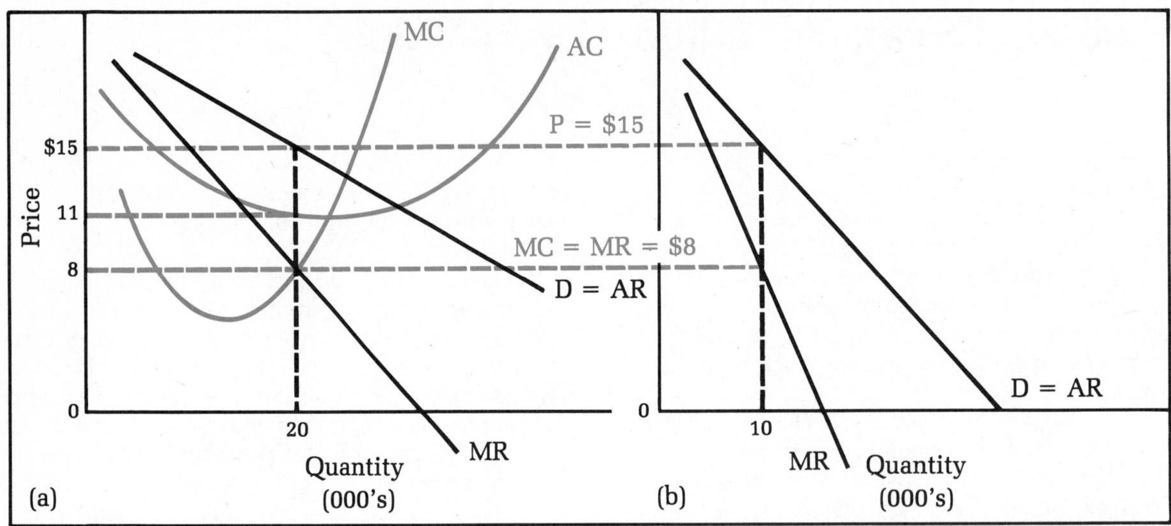

Figure 6 In a duopoly, market demand is shared by two firms. (a) Total industry output is 20,000 units, where the firms' combined MC = MR. (b) Each firm produces 10,000 units, one-half total industry output. Price P is read from the demand curve. Profits are maximized for the industry.

economic profit does not attract other firms to the industry because of the high capital investment needed to gain entry. The situation is diagrammed in Figure 6.

Total demand is shown as D = AR in Figure 6a. At a price of $15, twenty thousand units will be sold. If two firms divide the market, each firm's demand curve will be D = AR in Figure 6b. At a price of $15, each firm will sell ten thousand units. With MC = MR = $8 and AC = $11 the two firms will receive economic profit of $4 for each unit sold. Economic profit is $4 × 10,000 = $40,000 for each firm.

Duopoly has the same disadvantages as monopoly. Price to consumers is higher than the perfectly competitive price and quantity is lower. Unit costs of production are higher than the minimum, since MC = MR at a point where the average cost curve is still falling. This means that plants are producing less than optimum quantity. Resource allocation is distorted: inputs are not used as efficiently as they would be under perfect competition.

We have assumed that the duopoly firms have identical cost curves and that they have developed a practice of dividing the market between them. If their cost curves are different, however, or if they haven't worked out a way of living together in peace and harmony, there is nothing to prevent one firm from deciding to reduce its price and go after a bigger share of the market. If the other firm responds by doing the same thing, then more goods would be produced at a lower cost. This would be fine for consumers, but the two firms would no longer be maximizing profits.

Price Rigidity and Kinked Demand Curves

When there are more than two firms in an industry, the problem of determining a firm's equilibrium price and output becomes more difficult. There is no method by which we can assign particular shares of the market to particular firms. Still, each firm is affected by the decisions of other firms: Each must consider what other firms will do before deciding on its own price and output. The situation is shown by the peculiar looking demand curve in Figure 7. We call this a **"kinked" demand curve** because it is bent in the middle.

The kink in the demand curve occurs at the customary market price. At prices higher than $8 in Figure 7, demand is highly elastic. This is because if a single firm raises its price, other firms will not follow, and the high-priced firm will lose customers to them. If the firm raises its price as high as $10, it will lose all its customers. The behavior of buyers at prices above $8 is shown by movement off the dashed curve onto the more elastic kinked curve.

At prices below $8, on the other hand, demand is highly inelastic, because other firms in the industry will resist being undersold and will tend to match a price reduction by any single firm. Even a price reduction to $6 will gain only a few customers. The behavior of buyers at prices below $8 is shown by movement off the dashed curve onto the less elastic kinked curve.

The existence of a customary market price discourages price competition in an oligopolized industry. The kink in the oligopoly demand curve means that price will not change often, even when costs are falling or rising. Such prices are said to be *rigid*. Figure 8 illustrates **price rigidity** in oligopoly. Notice how costs can vary widely without affecting a firm's equilibrium point. Say the firm's costs were originally reflected in curves MC and AC, but then rise (because of increasing energy costs) to MC′ and AC′. The firm will *not* raise its price or lower output, because of the kinked demand curve. Conversely, if the firm's original costs were shown by MC′ and AC′, but then fall (because of a technological innovation) to MC and AC, the firm will not lower price or increase output—again because of the kinked demand curve.

Thus, the profit-maximizing output and price remain the same at both levels of MC and

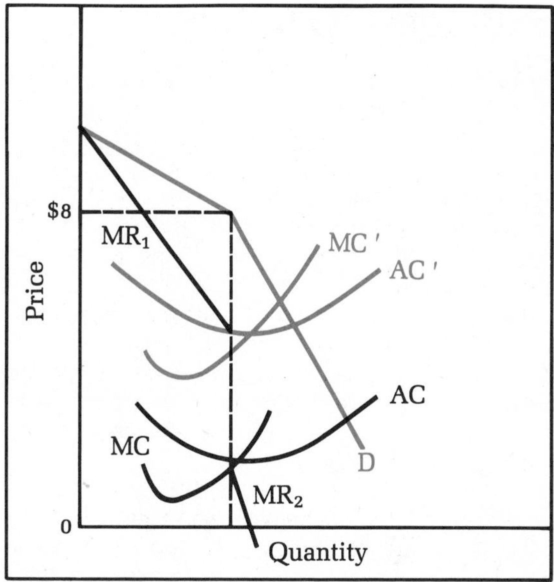

Figure 8 Large changes in AC and MC do not affect the profit-maximizing output. Prices tend to remain rigid.

AC. When cost curves shift up or down, only the amount of economic profit is affected. Price remains rigid.

In Figure 8 economic profit per unit may be as much as $6 or as little as $2, depending on whether costs are AC or AC′. Still, the oligopoly firm will not change the level of output. It will not change price, either, until another firm does so. This is one reason why automobile prices (in oligopoly) fluctuate much less than the price of pork (in competition).

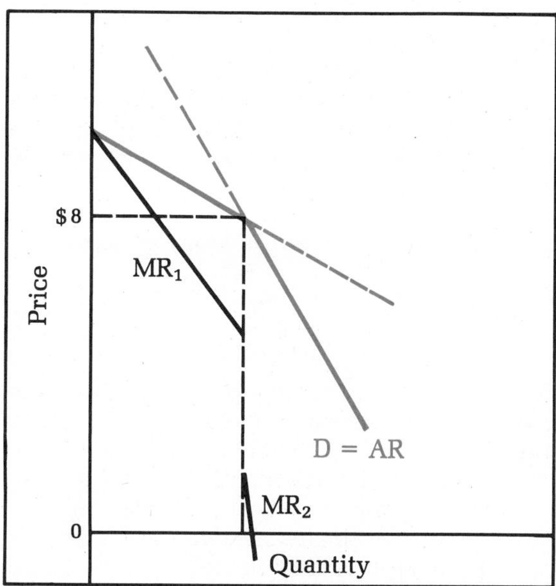

Figure 7 An oligopoly firm faces a demand curve with a kink at the customary price.

Price Leadership

Oligopoly prices may remain rigid over long periods. Still, if costs continue to rise throughout the market, oligopoly prices must finally rise, too. Pressure will build up within the industry for a price change, but each individual firm will be reluctant to be the first to raise price. Each will fear the loss of its customers if other firms do not follow the price increase. Often the firms in the industry look to one firm to make the first move. This firm is called the **price leader.** The other firms don't get together and agree to follow the leader; the practice just evolves over the course of time. In the steel industry, for example, United States Steel is considered the price leader, and in tobacco the leader is R. J. Reynolds.

Extended Example
Concentration in the Aluminum Industry

Efficient markets depend on price flexibility. Changes in demand are communicated to producers as their inventories pile up or are depleted. In perfect competition, firms react by changing their prices: They reduce prices to avoid accumulating unwanted inventory, or they raise prices to ration their limited supply among their most urgent buyers. When markets are free and competitive, prices serve as incentives to increase or decrease output in line with the changing needs of the economy.

When competition is imperfect the automatic adjustment of output to demand works less efficiently. Large firms in concentrated industries can avoid price cuts without worrying about losing sales to rival firms. All the firms need a steady flow of high sales revenues if they are to maintain and expand their large capital investment. The aluminum industry provides a recent example.

Beginning with World War II, aluminum has been a miracle metal. Made from bauxite extracted from clay, this lightweight metal conducts heat and electricity well, reflects light and heat, and resists corrosion. It is an important material in the production of cans, appliances, autos, and building construction. Over recent decades aluminum production in the United States has become concentrated in three large firms. Together Alcoa, Reynolds, and Kaiser account for about 70 percent of the nation's capacity for producing aluminum.

The recession of 1973–75 hit hard at firms producing durable goods and housing—two of the principal users of aluminum. Demand curves for aluminum shifted to the left. A competitive industry would have reacted by reducing price, with the expectation that lower prices would increase sales. But the president of one of the three major firms revealed, "I don't think I'd sell one extra pound of metal if we cut the price." Apparently, aluminum producers believed that the industry demand curve was inelastic; a price cut would reduce revenues for all the firms rather than expand sales.

The firms reacted to the decrease in demand by a series of price increases amounting to more than 50 percent in 1974 (from $.25 to $.39 per pound). By selling a smaller quantity at a higher price, they expected to maintain sales revenue. By early 1975, sales had plummeted by almost half and firms cut operations to only three fourths of productive capacity.

Observers grew concerned about rising unemployment in the aluminum industry. Moreover, they saw that high aluminum prices were causing higher production costs in many other industries. Their higher

The price leader may be the largest firm in the industry, the most aggressive firm, the one having the lowest costs, or the firm with the longest experience in estimating costs. The leader can set its price as if it were a monopoly, at a level that maximizes its own profits. Other firms will then follow, though they may have to accept somewhat less than maximum profits for themselves.

Price leadership is most common among firms that sell undifferentiated products, such as industrial commodities. Without some sort of coordination among them, individual price setting could disrupt the established pattern of market shares and lead to a price war—a cat-and-dog struggle over which firm is to get what share of the market. Formal agreements are not really necessary as long as each firm understands how to behave so that every firm benefits.

Attempts at price leadership don't always work. Occasionally an oligopoly firm will have to take back a price increase when its competitors refuse to go along.

Mark-Up Pricing

A common practice in oligopoly is **mark-up pricing:** Firms set price at a fixed percentage above average cost. Most business firms don't know enough about their costs and revenues to draw the neat diagrams we have presented here. In practice, they estimate sales for the upcoming period and then estimate cost per unit. To unit cost they add a percentage mark-up to arrive at price.

For instance, suppose a firm makes metal

costs meant even more price increases, lower sales, and lower employment. Concentration in the aluminum industry seemed to be aggravating both inflation and unemployment throughout the economy.

With recovery from recession in early 1976, demand for aluminum began to pick up. This time it was *higher* demand which became the motivation for higher prices. Ingot prices rose to $.48 a pound, a further increase of about 20 percent.

In the long run it is likely that high prices will affect the shape of demand curves for aluminum. The development of substitutes will increase user resistance to higher prices, and demand curves will become more elastic. Plastics are already filling many uses, and other industrial users are turning to steel. Competition from other materials may prove to be the important force for holding down materials prices in the future. But in the 1970s, concentration in this and other basic industries probably worsened the nation's economic problems.

Illustrate graphically the response of aluminum producers to a leftward shift of demand in the short run. What roles are played by mark-up pricing and price leadership in this article?

rods for use in manufacturing. At the current level of operation, unit costs include:

labor	$3.50
materials and power	1.50
fixed costs	.50
Total unit cost	$5.50

If firms agree on a standard mark-up of 10 percent, rods will be sold for $5.50(1.10) = $6.05. Any change in production costs throughout the industry will lead to similar price revisions in all firms.

The amount of the standard mark-up varies from one product to another. Economists have found that the greater the elasticity of demand the smaller will be the mark-up. For instance, suppose this firm also makes metal sheets to be used along with the rods in certain manufacturing processes. The rods have special qualities and are essential in the making of certain products. The sheets, on the other hand, are not essential; other firms produce substitutes that will do just as well. The firm will be able to charge a higher mark-up on the rods, for which demand is less elastic. Elastic demand for sheets may justify only a 5 percent mark-up to maximize revenue.

When a company produces a large variety of products, its market analysts must try to determine the relative elasticities of the different items. If the firm were to use the same mark-up for all its products, it would fail to maximize revenues. Some prices would be too low and others too high.

The use of standard mark-ups helps explain why prices under oligopoly remain stable over a long period. If average cost curves are fairly flat over a wide range of output, firms will not necessarily increase their prices when there are increases in demand. The result may be very different if there is a substantial drop in demand. In fact, a drop in demand may lead to a price increase. This is because unit costs are often higher at a low volume of output. As volume falls, the fixed costs of capital equipment must be spread over a smaller number of units. To add a standard mark-up will mean higher prices—an especially serious problem at a time when consumer spending is already low. In 1980, one of the worst years in recent history of the automobile industry, manufacturers raised prices, even though auto sales were declining.

Cartels

If oligopolists were free to do as they chose, most of them would probably enter into *formal pricing agreements*. Then they would know exactly what to expect from each other. Such an arrangement is called a *cartel*. A **cartel** is a *formal* agreement among producers aimed at regulating prices and output and dividing markets. At one time steel production in the United States was operated as a cartel, and prices were regulated according to the **basing-point** system. All steel was priced according to its production cost at its base (Pittsburgh) plus the cost of transportation to its destination. Early in this century, Judge Gary of the United States Steel Company held dinners at which representatives of the leading companies met to decide on price. All such arrangements are now illegal in the United

Extended Example The Rent-a-Car War

Life is never very quiet among the big car-rental companies, but in the fall of 1975 price discounts began flying like shrapnel. National Car Rental System announced in October that it was charging a flat rate for its subcompacts, without the usual separate charge for mileage. The rate was about $5 less than Hertz and Avis were charging.

Why did National cut its price? According to industry analysts, National had been losing some of its market share to fourth-ranked Budget Rent-a-Car Corporation. In the preceding three years, Budget claimed to have increased its share of the important airport market from 5 percent to 11 percent, largely at National's expense.

National's price cut was soon met by its competitors. One industry representative said, "You've got to meet competition first and worry about profits later." The war raged in the subcompact sector, comprising about 10 percent of the market, with the losses being made up on the more profitable standard-size cars. The leading companies not only cut prices but raised their advertising budgets. The president of Hertz even declared that it was "an advertising war more than a price war."

Some bystanders shared in the casualties. Small independent car-rental agencies lost business to the heavily advertised price-cutters. The little agencies, with a third or more of their fleets in small cars, lacked the resources to compete. One harassed president, quoted by *Business Week,* predicted that in the course of the struggle "they are going to destroy a lot of small competitors."

Illustrate the effect on Avis' demand curve of an advertising campaign claiming "We try harder because we're number 2." What is the likely effect of competitive advertising on profits?

States, except when they are believed to aid small competitors. This is the case in many communities where the price of milk is fixed by dairy associations, legal under current law.

Cartels are legal in many other countries. One famous cartel is the Organization of Petroleum Exporting Countries (OPEC), led by the Arab oil-producing countries of the Middle East. In 1974–75, OPEC was able to quadruple the price of oil sold in world markets.

Cartels are usually set up to prevent what producers regard as ruinous competition. Members agree to reduce output and keep price high. Each firm is guaranteed a share of the market and promises to abide by common arrangements on price and output. As long as the members of a cartel stick together, they are able to function as a monopoly. Eventually, conflicts are likely to occur among the members of a cartel, and sooner or later some of them find it in their interest to leave the group. As a result, cartels are often short-lived.

The Payoff Matrix

In oligopoly, each firm must consider the reactions of other firms to a change in its price. If one firm cuts price, competitors may cut price, with the result that all will end up with the same share of the market as before but with lower profits. The *payoff matrix* in Figure 9 illustrates this interdependence.

Suppose there are two firms in an industry. At a uniform price of $10, firm A's profits are $40,000 and firm B's are $60,000. If A reduces its price to $8 while B keeps its price at $10, A will gain some of B's customers and make profits of $60,000 while B's profits will fall to $50,000. If A then reduces its price to $5 while B stubbornly maintains its price of $10, A will gain still more of B's customers. But the lower price will reduce A's profits to $50,000. The best possible situation for A would be the price of $8, provided B were to remain at $10.

Of course, B won't let A take its customers away. B can always fight back by reducing its own price. If B follows A to a price of $8, A's profits will be only $30,000 as against B's profits of $40,000. This isn't satisfactory for A, which can raise its profits to $40,000 by going to a price of $5. At this price, B can't improve its profits by any price change. Knowing that price competition helps no one—except the consumer—most oligopoly firms prefer to compete in other ways.

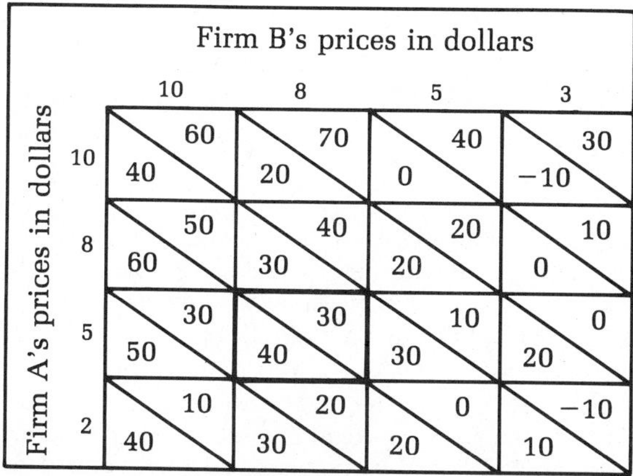

Firm A's prices in dollars	Firm B's prices in dollars: 10	8	5	3
10	60 / 40	70 / 20	40 / 0	30 / −10
8	50 / 60	40 / 30	20 / 20	10 / 0
5	30 / 50	30 / 40	10 / 30	0 / 20
2	10 / 40	20 / 30	0 / 20	−10 / 10

Figure 9 A payoff matrix. Firm A's profit is shown below the diagonal in each square. Firm B's profit is shown above the diagonal. The payoff matrix demonstrates why oligopolistic firms are often reluctant to cut prices—even when price cuts might seem to increase profits.

Other Approaches to Pricing

The foregoing approach to pricing assumes that the firms want to live with each other. In some markets one firm may decide to underprice the other until it has forced the rival out of business. For example, if A sets its price at $2, no pricing policy will enable B to earn more than $20,000. Low profits may eventually force B to leave the industry. In the meantime, A may make up its losses from economic profits elsewhere.

Still another solution would be for the two firms to merge. Prices could then be set to maximize total profits. The merger would bring maximum returns if the A part of the new company sets its price at $8 and the B part sets its price at $10.

NONPRICE COMPETITION

Advertising

There are other ways of competing than through price. In both oligopoly and monopolistic competition, many firms turn to advertising as a way of persuading customers that their products have something special about them. The simplest form of advertising is to put a label on the product to distinguish it from its competitors. Consumers who like Orchard Farm canned peaches will look for the label whenever they buy canned peaches; it saves them the trouble of choosing among perhaps half a dozen brands of different prices and qualities. The next step is to bring Orchard Farm products to the attention of the general public through newspapers, radio, or television.

The media used by advertisers vary with the kind of product. Producers of industrial equipment don't advertise in *Newsweek* or *Time*, and supermarkets don't advertise in *Fortune* or *Business Week*. Beer companies advertise on TV sports programs, soap companies on women's daytime programs, and deodorant manufacturers on the family hour. Hobby items are most often advertised in specialty magazines, and industrial commodities in trade journals.

The introduction of an entirely new product is sometimes accompanied by tremendous advertising outlays. Menthol-tipped cigarettes were popularized with heavy advertising. Substantial outlays may also be used to introduce an old product to a new market—to sell cigars to women, for example.

Advertising expenditures amount to between 2 percent and 3 percent of all income earned in the United States. The percentage falls slightly during periods of rising sales and rises when sales are falling. In some industries, notably cigarettes, soap, food, and drink, the sums spent on advertising are a substantial proportion of total costs.

Is advertising good or bad? It would be difficult to conceive of a modern capitalist economy without any advertising at all. Every business firm needs to tell the public about its products, and the defenders of advertising stress this information-giving function. However, most advertising seeks to persuade rather than inform, like the ads for painkillers that tell you Brand X works faster than Brand Y. Some ads tell you nothing at all; they use psychological tricks to make you feel good about their beer or their toothpaste so that you will unconsciously prefer those brands when you see them in the store.

Defenders of advertising say that advertising helps support our communications system. Newspapers, magazines, radio, and TV get most or all of their revenue from advertising. In this way, advertising pays for much of our information and entertainment. This is true, reply the critics, but they point out that

Extended Example
Advertising as a Factor of Production

The biggest advertisers in the nation's economy are the food producers. Food manufacturing firms and retailers pay advertisers almost $3 billion a year. Advertisers tell **you** what to buy and add the cost to **your** food bill!

The average food budget for a typical family is about $3000 a year. Of that $3000 about $28 goes to advertisers, especially for television ads, which account for almost one fourth of all television advertising. Magazines, radio, newspapers, and billboards consume the remaining advertising dollars.

Most food advertising aims at creating images rather than at informing the consumer. Highly processed foods are advertised heavily. Television ads create an image of healthy funseekers, quenching their thirst with soft drinks as their raft plunges down the rapids. Or they create an image of the active professional woman with no time for food preparation before rushing off to the evening's entertainment. Or they might show us popular teenagers with an insatiable appetite for snacks while studying for exams. Viewers have no trouble at all imagining themselves a part of scenes like these.

Nonfood items sold in grocery stores account for another $3 billion annually in advertising costs. Health and beauty aids, alcoholic beverages, pet foods, and tobacco are the most heavily advertised nonfood items, all substantially increasing your living costs.

Consumers in a free market system, such as we Americans, are the most heavily "promoted." Why is this so? Advertising is a factor of production like any other resource. It is subject to derived demand like labor, materials, or any other resource used in production. If manufacturers plan their advertising expenditures carefully, they will purchase advertising up to the point where the gains from the last advertising campaign are just equal to its cost. The quantity purchased will reflect our responsiveness to the message advertisers are sending. If we are willing to buy an image along with a soft drink, we will continue to hear the message—and pay a higher price.

Actually, we may have little choice in the matter. The food industry is typical of monopolistic competition, with many small sellers and slim profit margins. Under monopolistic competition all firms must advertise to differentiate their products and keep their place in the market. We have a wide choice in the variety of food items available—but only if we're willing to buy the image, too.

What is the effect of heavy advertising on marginal cost curves? On average costs? How do shifts in costs affect long-run equilibrium? What are the results in terms of efficiency?

communications might be paid for in other ways. The new cable TV systems that are now spreading through the country charge their users a direct fee. If the entire communications system were supported directly by its users, the resources that now go into producing those expensive beer commercials could be devoted to producing quality programs. In short, say the critics, advertising represents waste.

Waste? Not so fast, reply the defenders. Advertising is beneficial to the economy in several additional ways. Advertising may increase demand and enable companies to expand their production. Since under imperfect competition average cost curves decline with increases in output, firms could sell more products at lower prices—even after adding the cost of advertising. Figure 10 illustrates this result.

Also, advertising helps market new products. If a company couldn't acquaint the public with a new product, it couldn't sell enough to cover the costs of developing it. Defenders of advertising also argue that it actually stimulates the development of new products, since in order to advertise effectively a company needs to have something new and better to offer.

Critics don't buy these arguments either. They say that for every company that reduces its costs and prices through advertising, there are others that raise their costs and charge the consumer more. Certainly it would be hard to prove that automobiles would cost *more* if they weren't

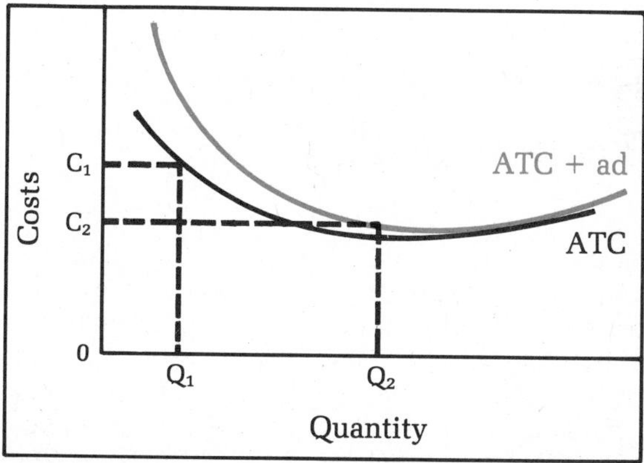

Figure 10 An advertising campaign increases fixed costs and shifts ATC up to ATC + *ad*. But advertising increases sales volume from Q_1 to Q_2 and unit costs fall. When firms set MC = MR, the result may be lower prices and higher volume as consumers move down their demand curves.

advertised! And in some industries one company's advertising is cancelled out by another's. Cigarette advertising probably doesn't sell more cigarettes; it only helps keep the major producers from losing sales to other cigarette producers.

Advertising may help capture a share of the market for a new product or a new firm, but this isn't necessarily beneficial to consumers. Perhaps the old product was just as good as the new one. John Kenneth Galbraith says that advertising stimulates people to want goods that they wouldn't want otherwise. Thus advertising has helped build up a transportation system based on the private automobile, a more costly form of transportation than commuter railroads and buslines.

The issues are complex and highly debatable. However the benefits and costs of advertising may balance out, it's safe to say that advertising will be around for a long time. It's built into our capitalistic economy.

Misleading or unethical advertising is prohibited under the Wheeler-Lea Amendment to the Federal Trade Commission Act, passed in 1938. The Commission often issues orders to advertisers to cease and desist from advertising practices it considers illegal. Not long ago, for example, the FTC ordered producers of headache remedies to admit that their product is no faster or more effective than simple aspirin. The manufacturers of Listerine and Wonderbread were ordered to broadcast commercials correcting false claims made in previous advertising. And some years ago Geritol was fined $50,000 for advertising that its product cured "tired blood."

Even socialist and communist economies find a place for advertising. In 1966 the Soviet government set up an ad agency called Soyuztorgreklama (National Trade Advertising) to help create demand for new types of consumer goods. One of its clients is a factory in Minsk that produces TV sets. The factory has placed ads in trade magazines describing its latest models: "The novelty of the year—Horizon 107," or "Horizon 104—the only first-class TV set in the country." Some Soviet factories spend relatively large sums of money on multimedia campaigns in newspapers, magazines, movie-theater commercials, and television. Foreign companies, including U.S. firms, are also beginning to advertise in Soviet magazines. Most of the advertising in communist countries so far is still of the informational type, designed to sell goods that might not otherwise find buyers or to inform the consumer that the shortage of some good is over.

Trademarks

A **trademark** is a word, emblem, or symbol used to identify a product or a service. Because it immediately identifies a product with a particular company, a trademark is a type of advertising and a form of nonprice competition. Some trademarks are very old. The Nabisco trademark is based on an old religious symbol: the orb and cross. Shell Oil's trademark goes back to the early nineteenth century, when the founder of Shell got his start selling shell-covered boxes to tourists. The Prudential Insurance Company's symbol, adopted in 1896, is the Rock of Gibraltar.

Oligopoly firms often spend vast sums of money to develop a corporate symbol appropriate to the firm's image. In recent years oligopolies like A&P, Exxon, and United Airlines have employed specialized research organizations to determine the most attractive company trademark or "logo." In one case, however, results of the corporate design campaign were somewhat embarrassing.

In the mid-1970s, the National Broadcasting Company spent fourteen months and an estimated $750,000 to replace its old NBC emblem with a simple N composed of red and blue wedges. The design was believed to impart "the bold look of strength and modernity." It was flashed on television screens 1150 times in the first month in an effort to implant the new image firmly in the consciousness of the viewing public. Too late, NBC learned that substantially the same design had earlier been adopted by the Nebraska Educational Television Network. To add insult to injury, the competing design had been developed in only one day at a cost of less than $100! Eventually, NBC made an out-of-court settlement to the Nebraska station in return for exclusive use of the expensive trademark.

Like a patent, a trademark is property and may be sold or licensed. Manufacturers often license companies in other countries to use their trademarks, thus giving others the advantage of their own international reputation and enhancing it at the same time. A company may lose its right to a trademark if the mark becomes part of everyday language. Aspirin, cellophane, and thermos were once trademarks, but they are now only words referring to types of products. The courts have said that a trademark ceases to be private property when the public no longer associates it with a specific company.

Extended Example
How Sacred Is a Trademark?

One of the world's most valuable trademarks is the one owned by Britain's Rolls Royce, Ltd. The manufacturer of fine automobiles distinguishes its product through the use of a unique radiator grill and "Flying Lady" hood ornament. The most famous Rolls Royce to bear this trademark is the Silver Cloud. In 1980 new Silver Clouds were selling for more than $100,000.

An enterprising Florida manufacturer noticed the similarity between the Silver Cloud and old models of the Chevrolet Monte Carlo. The company began manufacturing and selling, for $3000, a customizing kit for use on the Chevrolet. The kit included a similar grill and hood ornament and was designated the Custom Cloud.

Rolls Royce was not amused. The firm brought suit in federal district court for trademark infringement. The court ruled against the Florida firm, barring further use of the distinctive emblem and name.

Oligopoly firms take their trademarks seriously!

What characteristics of perfect competition are nullified by trademarks?

Differentiated and Undifferentiated Oligopoly

Oligopolies take different forms. They vary because they serve different kinds of markets. Some oligopoly firms produce industrial commodities for other manufacturing firms. Some produce goods or services for sale at retail to final consumers. For these different markets, different selling techniques are appropriate, and different forms of competition develop.

Firms producing for industrial markets often produce an undifferentiated product: aluminum, copper, steel, chemicals, construction equipment, and electrical apparatus. These commodities are fairly uniform among producers. A firm producing such products is known as an *undifferentiated oligopoly.* Because these oligopolies are reluctant to engage in price competition, they compete by offering better service or more advanced research and development. They work closely with customers to fill the needs of each more completely than rival firms.

Firms producing for final consumers have greater opportunities for nonprice competition. The product of one firm can be more easily distinguished from others. Oligopolies producing such products are known as *differentiated oligopolies.* The national TV networks, camera film manufacturers, and large-scale computer firms are all examples of differentiated oligopolies. Product loyalty can be established through advertising and product differentiation. Product uniqueness helps move a firm's demand curve to the right and protects its market share.

Positioning

Firms in oligopoly or monopolistic competition often compete for a position in the market. **Positioning** is a way of aiming a product at a particular segment of a larger market. In this way a product is differentiated from rival products aimed at consumers in general. Thus aspirin can be advertised as especially effective for arthritis pain, for women, or for adults under particular stress. Cough medicines can be billed as nighttime remedies or as especially effective for coughs accompanied by a runny nose. The phrase, "We're number two. We try harder" was very effective for a car-rental firm that wanted the public to think of it whenever it thought of the number one firm. Some beer is sold for the sports lover, some for the hard worker, and some for the sophisticate (though few beer drinkers can tell one brand from another if they're blindfolded). In the same way, manufacturers of perfumes and hair colorings aim their products at the simple country lass, the career woman on the go, or the modern mom.

Apparently, it is more profitable for some firms to have an ensured position in one segment of a market than to compete over a wide range with all the other firms in the industry. If you can convince modern moms that your hair preparation is necessary for them and that it is the only one worth buying, your firm's demand curve will shift rightward and become less elastic. This will enable your firm to make greater economic profit than it might otherwise.

PROS AND CONS OF OLIGOPOLY

How does oligopoly affect us? Oligopoly should also be evaluated in terms of the principles of efficiency and equity.

Efficiency

Oligopoly may improve efficiency in the economy. Oligopoly industries are often characterized by high initial capital requirements, effectively barring entry of excess firms to the industry. A few large firms may serve the entire market at lower unit costs by operating fixed capital at a larger volume of output. Price may still be greater than minimum average costs, yielding economic profit. Oligopoly firms may compete for greater market share by investing their profits in research and development; over time, oligopoly profits may finance technical progress, although sometimes there may be wasteful duplication of research efforts.

In the short run, oligopoly may have a worse effect on efficiency. Efficiency in the use of productive resources depends on steady growth in employment and output. When demand fluctuates, price changes would help prevent sharp changes in production. In particular, a decline in demand should lead to a price reduction to stimulate sales and to maintain plant operation at optimum levels. This is not likely to happen in an oligopoly industry. We have seen how a kinked demand curve encourages price stability. When demand falls, oligopoly firms are likely to reduce production and employment rather than price. The result is to aggravate the problem of reduced demand, increasing unemployment and intensifying a recession.

When prices rise independently of a rise in demand, the economy is said to be experiencing *cost-push inflation*. Cost-push inflation often originates in strongly unionized industries and in industries producing basic industrial commodities. The market power of oligopolies allows them to pass on their higher labor costs to their industrial customers. Therefore, there is less incentive to resist union demands and high materials prices. Because all firms in the industry are equally affected by most cost increases, they may be expected to follow closely the pricing policy of the industry price leader. Again, the effect is to aggravate cost-push inflation and worsen the tendency toward instability of output and employment.

Equity

Oligopoly is harmful to equity in many of the same ways as monopoly. In addition, the economic power of oligopoly firms may lead to the development of offsetting power elsewhere in the industry. Economist John Kenneth Galbraith coined the phrase **countervailing power** to describe the power of industrial unions and of government regulatory agencies. These giants may serve to hold down the power of each other. On the other hand, their power may overwhelm individual consumers, who have no similar means of combining to achieve common goals.

SUMMARY

Most imperfect competition is described as monopolistic competition or oligopoly. In monopolistic competition many firms compete to sell differentiated products. Demand curves slope downward, but the easy entry of new firms pushes individual demand curves to the left. The result may be no economic profit in the long run. Firms will be producing less than their optimum level of output and at higher than minimum costs. There will be too many firms for efficient operation and heavy expenditures for product differentiation.

Monopolistic competition violates the principle of efficiency by misallocation of resources. It may enhance the principle of equity by allowing small businesses to operate, but many will not be profitable and must fail.

In oligopoly a few large firms control industry output. Capital costs are high and technology is complex, discouraging entry of competing firms. The small number of firms means that pricing and output decisions in one firm depend strongly on decisions in the others. The result may be a degree of formal or informal collusion.

Duopoly is a condition where the market is divided between two large firms. When there are several firms, a firm's demand curve is kinked at the customary price. Firms resist price changes; price rigidity means that cost changes will affect only profits in the short run. Price changes ultimately depend on action by the industry price leader. Oligopolies sometimes practice mark-up pricing.

A cartel is a formal agreement to fix price and output among firms, but cartels are illegal in the United States. Oligopolies may compete through nonprice competition: advertising, trademarks, customer service, research and development, and positioning.

Oligopoly may improve efficiency by operating few plants at optimum volume. But oligopoly contributes to instability in resource use by maintaining prices in a time of falling demand and by aggravating cost-push inflation. Oligopoly violates the principle of equity by encouraging the growth of "countervailing power."

Key Words and Phrases

basing point production costs at a geographic location, used as the basis for setting price plus transportation charges to the point of delivery.

cartel a formal agreement among producers to regulate prices and output.

collusion an agreement among two or more firms to cooperate in setting price and output.

cost-push inflation price increases that result from higher resource prices, often higher wage rates, without an increase in demand.

countervailing power the development of organized power to offset power elsewhere in industry.

duopoly a condition in which two large firms share the market for a particular good.

imperfect competition industrial organization other than monopoly or perfect competition.

kinked demand curve a demand curve for oligopolies with a bend (kink) at the customary price; above the kink, demand is elastic, and below the kink, demand is inelastic.

mark-up pricing practice of adding a fixed percentage to the average cost of producing a good or service.

merger a combination of the productive assets of two or more firms into a single larger firm.

monopolistic competition a condition in which many small sellers compete to sell differentiated products.

oligopoly a condition in which a few large sellers control most of the output of an industry.

positioning aiming a product at a particular segment of a larger market.

price leader a firm which normally is the first to signal a price change in a particular industry.

price rigidity a tendency for customary prices to remain constant in spite of a change in demand or costs.

product differentiation efforts to distinguish a product from another similar one.

trademarks distinguishing symbols used to promote identification of a particular firm and its product.

Questions for Review

1. Explain the process by which ease of entry in monopolistic competition eliminates economic profit. Why is the final result zero economic profit, but still higher prices than the competitive price?
2. Discuss the advantages and disadvantages of monopolistic competition in terms of efficiency and equity.
3. How is duopoly different from other forms of oligopoly? How does the difference affect demand curves?
4. Discuss the advantages and disadvantages of price rigidity. Why is price leadership important in oligopoly?

5. Use the following hypothetical data to calculate elasticity for every price change along the demand curve. What is the marginal revenue associated with every price change? What price will the firm set?

Price	Quantity Demanded
20	0
15	50
10	100
5	125

6. How is a payoff matrix useful? Under what condition can a firm avoid the uncertainties associated with a payoff matrix?
7. Define: collusion, differentiated oligopoly.
8. We have shown how price rigidity increases oligopoly profits when new technology reduces costs of production. Are there some benefits for consumers when the opposite takes place: that is, when inflation *increases* costs of production? How do oligopoly firms deal with this situation?
9. What are the characteristics of convenience food stores that make them monopolistically competitive rather than perfectly competitive? What about New York's fabulous Fifth Avenue department stores?
10. Describe the conditions which lead to formation of a cartel. To its collapse.

CHAPTER 12

Market Power and Public Policy

Learning Objectives

Upon completion of this chapter, you should be able to:

1. Discuss the various forms of merger and how they are established.
2. List several pieces of antitrust legislation, discuss the philosophies of antitrust, and evaluate the effectiveness of antitrust action.
3. Define and discuss concentration ratios and evaluate trends in concentration.
4. Give arguments in favor of and against large firms.

Is big business good or bad? Americans tend to distrust big business, and we were the first nation to pass laws restricting the growth of business firms. Our courts have forced some big firms to break up and prevented others from merging. By limiting the power of big business, we have sought to prevent the growth of monopoly and oligopoly in our economy.

OUR CONTRADICTORY ATTITUDES

Still, we have some of the world's largest corporations. Every year *Fortune* magazine publishes a list of the 500 largest corporations in the United States. These corporations control about two thirds of the assets of American industry. One percent of the country's business firms employ 60 percent of the workers employed in business. General Motors alone employs hundreds of thousands of workers; its total output is roughly equal to the total annual production of Belgium.

Some of our most important industries are dominated by just a few companies. No more than four large companies in each industry account for at least 75 percent of total production in aluminum, light bulbs, flat glass, breakfast cereals, chewing gum, cigarettes, sewing machines, automobile tires, and motor vehicles. One company alone produces about a third of the pig iron made in the United States and more than a quarter of the steel ingots.

Yet in a land of bigness we honor the small firm. Most Americans have at some time in their lives had an ambition to go into business for themselves, and many of us have done so. Our government has a Small Business Administration to help small, struggling firms survive. At the same time, we admire the executives who manage large corporations and fly from city to city in company planes.

These contradictions are rooted deep in the history of our country. For our first hundred years, the United States was a land of small farmers and traders. Even the plantations of the old South, worked by black slaves, were small by today's standards. The political views of Americans reflected the conditions of their economic life.

After the Civil War great changes began to take place in the U.S. economy. Railroads were laid from the Atlantic to the Pacific, bringing the grain of the Midwest to the growing cities of the East. New business firms began to view the whole country as a potential market. The wider market encouraged mass production, using machines that could turn out a much greater flow of goods. At the same time a revolution was taking place in agriculture: The reaper, the combine harvester, and steam-powered threshing and husking machines greatly increased output per farm worker. Americans began to leave the farms for cities, where they became industrial workers and consumers for giant manufacturing firms.

THE FIRST GREAT MERGER MOVEMENT

The late-nineteenth century was a period of phenomenal growth, particularly in the industries producing raw materials and transportation. Between 1878 and 1898, the volume of industrial production, the number of industrial workers, and the number of factories more than doubled. Railroad mileage increased from 93,262 miles in 1880 to 190,000 miles in 1900. A group of creative entrepreneurs developed who soon became famous for their aggressive pursuit of wealth and power. Among them were the oilman John D. Rockefeller, the steel magnate Andrew Carnegie, and railroad builders Cornelius Vanderbilt, Leland Stanford, Collis P. Huntington, Henry Villard, and James J. Hill.

The vehicle these men used to build their empires was the corporation. The corporate form enabled entrepreneurs to raise large amounts of capital through the sale of stock. It also made it easy for large enterprises to acquire small, specialized firms and to build powerful market organizations.

Organizations called **trusts** enabled one individual or group to control a number of separate corporations. The stockholders of several corporations turned their stock over to the individual or small group, who would control the stock as *trustees*. The trustees had the power to elect directors of the corporations and were thus able to manage the combination of firms as if it were a single unit. A trust was not a corporation and produced no good or service; it was created solely for the purpose of owning a majority of the stock in each subsidiary company and influencing operations for the sake of profits.

An early trust was the Standard Oil Company of Ohio, created by John D. Rockefeller to own many small operating companies producing petroleum products.

Many large corporations were formed through **merger:** a combination of two or more independent firms into one. In general, all but one firm loses its identity, and operations are carried on together. The American Tobacco Company and the American Sugar Refining Company were formed by mergers in 1890 and 1891. Mergers were of two kinds: **horizontal** when the merging firms were direct competitors, and **vertical** when one firm was a supplier or customer of the other.

Horizontal Mergers

Horizontal mergers are combinations of firms in the same industry, producing the same good or service.

Horizontal mergers were most common in railroading and in the telephone industry where it was important to have smooth coordination among different parts of the country. Furthermore, firms in these industries required large amounts of investment in capital equipment before they could begin to function. This made it necessary for small firms to combine their resources to provide dependable service over a larger geographical area. Horizontal mergers also helped reduce duplication of facilities. Two separate railroads serving the same route would be economically inefficient unless demand was high enough to keep both operating at full capacity.

Horizontal mergers help firms reduce costs through economies of large scale. Figure 1 shows the effect of market size on average total cost. Suppose there are two firms in an industry, each facing average total costs shown by ATC. Market demand is 10,000 units. If the two firms divide the market equally, each would produce 5000 units with average total costs of $2. But if only one firm produces all 10,000 units, average total cost drops to $1. This market is too small for several competing firms to operate at lowest average cost. A single firm producing larger volume can spread the fixed cost of capital equipment over many more units. Mergers would be profitable in this industry for market demand up to 30,000 units, at which point diseconomies of large scale begin.

The railroad builders were the first to take advantage of these economies of scale. Cornelius Vanderbilt established the first through-route from New York to Chicago. He acquired ownership or control of many railroad lines connecting the rich agricultural and manufacturing areas of the Northeast. Along routes where he faced competition, he would reduce freight charges below costs and drive his weaker rivals out of business. He would make up his losses by charging higher freight rates on other routes. He bought the stock of failing roads at low prices: the New York and Harlem Railroad, in 1862, and later its competitors, the Hudson River Railroad and the New York Central Railroad running from Albany to Buffalo. He tried unsuccessfully to take over the Erie Railroad, but his acquisition of the Lake Shore and Michigan Southern, in 1873, extended his route to Chicago.

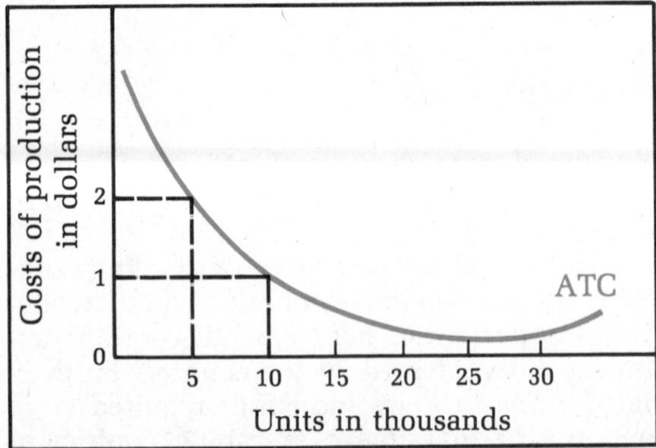

Figure 1 The effect of market size on cost. Suppose 10,000 units are to be produced and sold in one market. If firms A and B each produce 5000 units, unit cost is $2; however, firm A alone could produce all 10,000 units at a unit cost of only $1. Beyond production of 30,000 units, mergers are no longer efficient, although they do increase market power.

Price discrimination. Vanderbilt was able to maximize revenues through a complex structure of discriminatory freight rates. Different rates were possible because of differences in the elasticity of demand along different routes and among different commodities. The elasticity of demand for rail service depended on (1) the availability of substitutes and (2) the value of the freight.

If customers could choose between competing rail lines or between rail and barge, they would be more sensitive to changes in rates charged by any one company. For instance, ore shippers in the Mesabi Range of Minnesota could choose to send their iron ore by lake and canal transport to foundries in Pennsylvania. This kept railroad freight rates fairly low along this route. On the other hand, cotton producers in the deep South had fewer alternatives for shipping their cotton to textile mills in the North. They could be charged higher freight rates. Moreover, the high rates charged on northbound cotton made it possible for the railroads to reduce southbound rates on manufactured goods. This gave northern manufacturers a cost advantage over competitors in the South and held back the industrialization of the South.

The second factor in price discrimination, freight value, was equally important. Manufactured goods are more compact than bulky commodities like ore, grain, and other primary products; hence they tend to be higher in value per carload. Also, large manufacturers could often create their own transportation services if they chose. For these reasons the rates for manufactured goods produced in the Northeast tended to be lower than for bulky raw materials from the West and South. Since the shipment of low-value, bulky commodities to eastern factories often left freight cars empty for the "back haul," it cost the railroads very little to carry manufactured goods southward and westward.

In both these ways discriminatory freight rates had significant effects on the prosperity and growth of industry in different regions of the country. The result was growing political pressure among farmers of the South and Midwest against horizontal railroad mergers.

Vertical Mergers

Vertical mergers are combinations of firms producing materials or services used by each other.

Vertical mergers occurred in industries that needed a dependable supply of inputs at every stage of processing. Steelmakers needed a steady supply of iron ore and coal for making pig iron and basic steel. The steel itself then had to be rolled or drawn into rods, sheets, beams, and other structural forms. Many small firms joined together to form vertically integrated companies for producing steel products.

Andrew Carnegie was an industrial organizer in iron and steel who created and combined many different firms. He finally sold his interests to J. P. Morgan, the financier who formed the United States Steel Company. Carnegie began by investing in a firm that built railroad bridges. This led him into steelmaking and the manufacture of locomotives. Carnegie and his associates soon acquired a leading position in the manufacture of steel. In 1870, with the building of the Lucy Furnace, they began turning out their own pig iron, from which steel is manufactured. By 1877 the Carnegie mills were making about one seventh of the Bessemer steel produced in the United States. In 1882 the company acquired a major interest in the H. C. Frick Coke Company, which controlled deposits of good coking coal needed for blast furnaces. The final step in the process of vertical integration was taken in 1896 when Carnegie obtained a lease on iron ore fields in the Mesabi area of Minnesota. Ore was transported by company-owned boats and railroads to the coke ovens in Pittsburgh. The only stage of production not included in Carnegie's empire was the large-scale rolling of steel products, such as tubes and wire.

John D. Rockefeller used vertical mergers to establish the Standard Oil Corporation. Rockefeller began as the operator of pipelines carrying crude oil from the oil fields to refineries. Since his pipeline enterprise was the only outlet for crude oil, well owners were forced to sell at low prices. Since delivered crude oil was available only from the pipeline, refiners were forced to buy at high prices. High profits on pipeline operations enabled Rockefeller to buy up oil wells, on the one hand, and refineries, on the other.* By the early 1880s he had brought approximately 80 percent of the nation's refining capacity and 90 percent of the pipelines within the scope of his organization. Moreover, he had acquired a large interest in railway tank cars for transporting the products. By a series of vertical mergers, Rockefeller achieved nearly complete monopoly in the petroleum industry.

Holding Companies

As we saw earlier, John D. Rockefeller established Standard Oil of Ohio as a trust (1882). His example was widely followed, and by 1890 there were trusts in sugar, lead, whiskey, cottonseed oil, and salt. In 1892 the Supreme Court of Ohio declared trusts to be illegal. Rockefeller reorganized the company as a *holding company* under the more relaxed laws of New Jersey, naming it the Standard Oil Company of New Jersey. A **holding company** was a corporation with power to hold stock in other corporations, achieving certain advantages in administration, production, and sales. Eventually the remaining states passed laws permitting holding companies, and the trust form of business organization faded into history.

ANTIMERGER LEGISLATION

The great merger movement of the late 1800s aroused much public opposition, particularly from those who felt they had been treated unfairly by giant corporations. Farmers of the Midwest were especially angry about the discriminatory freight rates they had to pay for shipping grain. Their protests led to a Populist movement demanding government control over the industrial giants. The farm vote was important to many members of Congress. Under Populist pressure, two important laws were enacted: the Interstate Commerce Act of 1887, establishing the Interstate Commerce Commission (ICC) with the power to control rates and practices of interstate railroads; and the Sherman Antitrust Act of 1890.

*This is an example of a "squeeze operation."

Extended Example Giant of the Steel Industry

The nation's economy is built on iron and steel. We live in it, ride on it, and cook on it. Iron and steel form the building blocks of modern industry. Iron was produced in America as far back as colonial times. Forges turned out many of the plows, hammers, and machines needed by our developing nation. Production was small scale, using local ores and charcoal and serving local markets. Production costs were high because of heavy initial capital investment and the heavy use of labor. Labor was essential for pounding the pig iron to produce wrought iron. The Bessemer process and the open-hearth process, developed in the late 1800s, removed the impurities from iron through less costly methods and yielded finer grades of metal.

Andrew Carnegie grew up with the iron and steel industry. His family migrated from Scotland in 1848 and settled near Pittsburgh. Pittsburgh was becoming an important center of iron production and of rail traffic because of its location near the major coal fields. Carnegie quickly saw the potential profitability of combining the two industries. With his brother and some friends, he established firms for producing iron rails, railroad bridges, locomotives, and sleeping cars.

Carnegie was less interested in the purely technical aspects of production than in developing long-run strategy. He hired experts to operate the enterprises so that he could concentrate on financial planning. His acquaintance with banker Junius S. Morgan introduced him to the world of finance.

The earliest Carnegie enterprises were parterships; but in 1874 Pennsylvania passed a law authorizing "limited partnership associations" similar to corporations, and the firms were reorganized. Then followed expansion into production of raw materials: coking coal to fuel the new furnaces and limestone and ore mines on Lake Superior. The process of vertical integration was completed with the acquisition of ore shippers on the Great Lakes and firms producing all the major end products. Finally, the separate operating companies were brought together under New Jersey corporation law into the Carnegie Company.

In the meantime, competitors were also establishing fully integrated steel firms. One strong competitor was J. P. Morgan, son of Junius Morgan. Under competition, rate of production was highly unstable because of instability in manufacturers' demand for

Andrew Carnegie

capital equipment made from steel. When sales dropped, overhead costs per unit of steel output soared. Firms tried to increase volume by drastically cutting price. But demand was inelastic in the short run, and weak firms were forced into bankruptcy. Informal agreements were made to allocate market shares, but these were not always successful.

Competition was worrisome to the steel giants, so in 1901 the three major steel producers joined to form the United States Steel Corporation, with outstanding capital stock worth more than a billion dollars and with control of three fifths of the nation's steel business. The goal of the new combined firm was "a completely rounded system of coordinated plants adapted to the entire process of mining and transportation, and of [transformation of] raw materials into . . . highly finished products . . . at the lowest cost." Plants were modernized and made more efficient, new technology was installed, and a complete system of cost accounting was introduced. Perhaps the most significant innovation was the introduction of a bonus system for rewarding employees on the basis of merit.

The great steel combination was more profitable than competition had been. By operating its facilities at full capacity, the firm was able to supply 70 percent of the nation's steel output and to achieve substantial cost reductions. But it faced a delicate problem: Dominance of the steel industry left the firm open to attack from the Antitrust Division of the Department of Justice. Judge Elbert H. Gary, U.S. Steel Board Chairman in the early 1900s, believed that the firm would not be dissolved if "the intentions of the managers are good, [and] . . . there is no disposition to exercise a monopoly or to restrain legitimate trade." Competitive *conduct,* not its monopoly *structure,* would justify U.S. Steel's existence.

U.S. Steel did not attempt to monopolize output completely but instead encouraged competition. By its pricing policies it aimed at securing stable and profitable revenues for all firms in the industry. When demand fell, it kept prices high to avoid bankruptcies among small firms. When demand rose, it avoided price increases so as to discourage new entry and excess capacity. Chairman Gary hosted a series of dinners for industry executives and helped make U.S. Steel the price leader in the industry. Identical prices were established through the basing-point system, which set all delivered prices in the nation a price plus freight charges from Pittsburgh.

The administration of President Theodore Roosevelt went after antitrust violators with vigor. U.S. Steel had always believed that responsible business giants should cooperate with government, turning over their records freely and explaining their policies. In this way, they believed they could counter the efforts of some groups to break up large firms. In 1911, when steel's anticompetitive practices were challenged by the Justice Department, the judgment went in favor of the company. The Supreme Court ruled that the Sherman Act could be used only against unreasonable restraints of trade. Standard Oil and American Tobacco Company were found to be illegal under the law, but U.S. Steel had not abused its power to restrain competition.

During World War II, U.S. Steel continued as the nation's largest single producer of steel products. After the war, the firm diversified into chemicals, cement, natural gas, electric cable, and mining equipment. (By 1975 more than half the firm's profits came from its nonsteel divisions.) Yet the firm has been slow to modernize since the war, and imported steel has gained a foothold in American markets. Foreign producers supplied as much as one fifth of the American market in 1978. U.S. Steel complains that Japan and Common Market countries use illegal trade practices to undercut American-made steel. Steelmakers abroad receive government subsidies for their exports so as to keep price low and maintain employment in the domestic steel industry. But American steelmakers must pay a tax when they sell in foreign markets.

The result has been lower sales and falling profits at precisely the time when steelmakers critically need funds for new capital investment. During the 1970s, profits have been less than \$.03 per dollar of sales. The years 1979 and 1980 saw several plants closed and thousands of steelworkers thrown out of work. The American steel industry has asked government help to prohibit imports from nations which use unfair practices, to guarantee loans for modernizing steel capacity and diversifying output, to retrain workers for new jobs, and to relax some environmental rules. Such actions would improve profitability for the industry but with a possible cost in reduction of competition. Government has been reluctant to comply.

What does this article demonstrate about the course of monopoly over time?

The Sherman Antitrust Act

Section 1 of the Sherman Act declared illegal "every contract, combination in the form of trust or otherwise, or conspiracy, in restraint of trade or commerce among the several States, or with foreign nations." Section 2 forbade any person to monopolize or to attempt or conspire to monopolize trade. Although trusts are specifically mentioned in the law, it has been applied more generally to the now more common holding companies or mergers.

The intention of the law was to condemn all actions designed to achieve a monopoly structure in industry. But because the language was broad, it was also vague. The law failed to spell out exactly what actions were forbidden. It left to the courts the responsibility for interpreting the law, case by case, and applying it where market power was found to be excessive.

The courts have not been consistent. In one early decision, the Supreme Court held that the first section of the act could not be read literally as outlawing "every contract . . . in restraint of trade" since every business contract restrains the parties to some degree. That section, the Court declared, should be understood to prohibit only unreasonable restraint. This declaration came to be known as the "rule of reason." It left the way open for many new combinations and further growth of market power.

Prosecution under the Sherman Act was uneven, and mergers continued. In 1899 the number of new mergers reached 1208, and giants like International Harvester and National Biscuit Company were formed.

During the administration of Theodore Roosevelt (1901–1908), antitrust activity increased. Roosevelt moved against combinations in a number of industries and was supported by the Supreme Court. In 1911 the Court ordered Standard Oil of New Jersey and the American Tobacco Company to break up into smaller competing enterprises and to cease certain "unfair competitive practices."

The Clayton Antitrust Act

In 1914, during the administration of Woodrow Wilson, Congress passed new legislation defining certain business practices which were to be forbidden. The Clayton Act prohibited the following practices "where the effect may be to substantially lessen competition or tend to create a monopoly":

Discriminatory price cutting where rivals may be forced out of business, leaving one firm in control of the market;

Tying contracts, under which buyers are required to purchase the entire line of a supplier's products, thus closing out competition from other suppliers;

Interlocking directorates, when directors serve on the boards of several firms in the same industry, with power to direct pricing and output policies as if for a single firm; and

Stock ownership in competing companies where this would enable the companies to be operated as a monopoly.

The Federal Trade Commission

At the same time, Congress established the Federal Trade Commission (FTC) as a watchdog to seek out unfair methods of competition in interstate commerce. The FTC was given two powers: (1) to investigate trade practices and report its findings, and (2) to issue a complaint against any firm that it found to be practicing unfair competition. After considering testimony by those concerned, the Commission might either dismiss the complaint or issue an order to cease and desist the unfair practice. Over the years the FTC developed a system of trade practice conferences through which members of an industry are guided as to what constitutes unfair competition.

In 1938 the *Wheeler-Lea Act* gave the Federal Trade Commission power to forbid false or misleading advertising. Congress specifically made it illegal to publish false claims for food, drugs, cosmetics, and therapeutic devices.

THE SECOND GREAT MERGER MOVEMENT

Experience showed, however, that antitrust laws could not prevent the growth of market concentration. The Clayton Act specified certain actions as illegal, but this encouraged firms to find other ways to increase their size and power. Furthermore, the courts still clung to the "rule of

Extended Example Menace at the Breakfast Table

"If the FTC can convince the courts of the validity of its shared monopoly theory, it can declare over half of all the industries in America—producing over two thirds of our manufactured products—guilty and break all of them, and along with [them] the free market system," said William E. LaMothe, president of Kellogg Company.

It is natural that business firms should feel threatened by a government regulatory commission. In fact, they are supposed to be adversaries. Business firms have as their objective to serve the public by providing goods that can be sold at a profit. A regulatory commission has as its objective to serve the public by protecting consumers against unfair business practices. To determine the precise point at which business methods become unfair practices is not a simple task. Occasionally, it may seem that business firms are penalized for performing too well—for meeting too completely the needs of the market and for being too successful at earning a profit.

The issue then becomes: *At what point does success become a threat to competition?*

The question has become important in recent years because of the increasing size of the U.S. market and increasing opportunities for business diversification. With more efficient transportation and communication facilities, firms have been able to consolidate many operations under a single management. Centralization of financial decision-making, purchasing, and advertising has reduced unit costs and increased profits. When profits are reinvested to diversify and expand, then success yields more success.

A 1976 case still before the Federal Trade Commission illustrates the complexity of the problem. According to FTC and Justice Department lawyers, the breakfast cereal industry in the United States is a "shared monopoly." A shared monopoly exists when a few large companies use their market power to collect monopoly profits and to exclude competition. Through their diversified products, Kellogg, General Mills, General Foods, and Quaker Oats provide more than 90 percent of our breakfast cereals. The suit now before the Commission asks that the first three, the largest, firms be required to sell one or more of the brands they now produce. If the Commission agrees, this will establish a significant precedent in antitrust law. The precedent could then be used in other industries in which a few large firms produce a number of diversified products. Some possible targets might be autos, steel, and electrical goods.

Seven out of ten Americans consume cereals, at least occasionally. Industry sales grew from $165 million in 1950 to almost $3 billion in 1979. The largest firm is the price leader, Kellogg, which supplies 56 percent of the U.S. market, including seven top-selling brands. Profits were $162 million in 1979 on sales of $1.8 billion. General Mills is next with 21 percent of the market, and General Foods accounts for 16 percent. Quaker

reason" in deciding whether or not combinations were in restraint of trade. In 1920 a case was brought against United States Steel, which then had 60 percent of the nation's iron and steel capacity. The Supreme Court ruled that the company had not committed specific illegal acts. It found no reason to break up the corporation as long as the firm did not abuse its market power. Bigness in itself was not illegal.

The Clayton Act may even have encouraged mergers. The act made it illegal to acquire control of a competing corporation through ownership of its stock, but it did not prohibit buying the firm outright. The 1920s saw a new growth of industrial concentration. In 1929 the number of mergers reached a new peak of 1245—largely in the new communications and automobile industries. Markets were becoming larger, increasing the need for large-scale industrial operations. Typical of the times was the growth of radio broadcasting and the stimulus this gave to nationwide advertising by the industrial giants.

The Great Depression Antitrust Action

The 1930s brought new concerns about the plight of small business firms, pushed to the wall by the depression and by the growing power of the giants. Franklin Roosevelt's New Deal tried to protect weak firms by encouraging industrial cooperation rather than competition. The *National Recovery Act* set up industry boards

Oats supplies 9 percent and is not included in this suit.

The FTC claims that increased competition in the industry would save customers $128 million each year. The Commission charges that the firms maximize monopoly profits through tacit agreements not to cut price. "Gentlemen's agreements" have also eliminated the use of package premiums and coordinated advertising budgets of cooperating firms. Firms have set up barriers to entry by brand proliferation, by control of supermarket shelf space, and by extensive advertising. New firms in the industry would have to spend millions of dollars to introduce a cereal to compete with the more than one hundred well-known brands. Recently, when small firms tried to introduce new granola cereals, the big four introduced their own brands and captured most of the market.

The President's Council on Wage and Price Stability is also interested in the outcome of the FTC suit. The Council believes that shared monopoly and administered prices are partly responsible for the recent surge of price inflation. In fact, during the recession of 1973–75, grain prices declined, but the prices of cereals continued to rise.

What are the important characteristics of the cereal industry? What market structure does it resemble most closely? How can you explain rising cereal prices when grain prices were falling?

to stabilize business practices and keep prices at a level that would enable small operators to stay in business.

The *Robinson-Patman Act of 1936* amended the Clayton Act specifically to forbid price cutting by large retail stores when used as a weapon to destroy competitors. Chain stores had used their market power to cut prices and force small retailers out of business.* The law forbade wholesalers from giving discounts to large retailers, unless it could be shown that discounts were justified by lower costs. The stated aim of the Act was to preserve competition, but it may have protected inefficiency since many small firms could not have survived in perfect competition against more efficient large-scale retailers.

The *Miller-Tydings Act of 1937* went still further in the direction of regulating prices. It put the stamp of federal approval on state **fair trade laws.** These laws permitted manufacturers of brand-name items to set the prices at which retailers could sell their goods. Under the fair trade laws, retailers who cut price were subject to prosecution. In the 1930s most states passed laws requiring *all* dealers to sell at a manufacturer's recommended price if *some* dealers did. Fair trade laws applied mainly to drugs and pharmaceuticals, books, photographic supplies, liquor, some household appliances, radios, watches, jewelry, and bicycles. Their effect was to keep prices high so that small retailers could compete against the more efficient giants.

Post–World War II Antitrust Activity

In the 1950s and 1960s the fair trade laws became unpopular. The growth of discount stores increased the public's sensitivity to higher prices, as did the inflationary trend of the 1970s. Moreover, the whole principle of fair trade laws ran counter to antitrust laws promoting price competition. A Department of Justice study of the question estimated that "fair trade" was costing consumers $2.1 billion a year. In 1976 Congress repealed the Miller-Tydings Act.

The strength of the second great merger movement led to another important piece of legislation in 1950: the *Celler-Kefauver Amendment* to the Clayton Act. The new law closed the loophole which had allowed firms to expand by buying competing firms. It forbade any acquisition or merger which would "substantially . . . lessen competition, or tend to create a monopoly."

The Celler-Kefauver Amendment seemed to focus antitrust law back toward the *structure* of an industry. Supporters of the law felt that to permit monopolistic *structure* would eventually bring on monopolistic *conduct*. Therefore, they sought to prevent the growth of monopoly in its earliest stages. Horizontal mergers are now forbidden, except where the merger of two very small firms will help them compete more successfully against a large firm. Vertical mergers are examined closely and forbidden where the effect is to give one firm a substantial advantage and to close out competition from other firms.

*This is an example of predatory pricing.

THE THIRD GREAT MERGER MOVEMENT

Despite all this legislation, another period of mergers and acquisitions came, beginning in the 1960s. In the years 1948 through 1959, corporate mergers had averaged 428 per year, fewer by far than in the 1920s. But in the 1960s the average rose to more than 1250. These new combinations took a different form, however; corporations expanded by acquiring firms in totally unrelated fields.

Conglomerate Mergers

The name **conglomerate** was given to a combination of firms in unrelated industries. For example, Radio Corporation of America (RCA) bought the Hertz car rental agency, Columbia Broadcasting System bought Creative Playthings, and Greyhound acquired the Armour meat-packing company. Of the 4003 mergers in 1969, 90 percent were classified as conglomerates.

There were several reasons why corporations expanded in this way. One was that the antitrust laws prohibited all horizontal and many vertical mergers, but they did not explicitly prohibit acquisitions in other fields. Another reason was that a corporation seeking to grow often found more profitable opportunities in other industries than its own. A third reason was the development of computers and the scientific management techniques they made possible. It became cheaper and easier to carry on planning, control, organizing, and other centralized functions of management, so large conglomerates could operate efficiently.

Not all conglomerates were successful. A few mergers turned out to have been based on hopeful enthusiasm rather than real business prospects. Some of the firms used accounting techniques that made their earnings look larger than they really were. Afterward, of course, some acquisitions were found to be less profitable than expected.

The Goliaths

The most spectacular of the new conglomerates was the International Telephone and Telegraph Corporation (ITT). Between 1955 and 1978, ITT's annual sales rose from $450 million to $15.3 billion. During this period ITT absorbed Sheraton hotels, Avis car rentals, Bobbs-Merrill publishers, Levitt and Sons builders, Continental bakeries, Smithfield hams, and other firms in the cellulose, vending-machine, and fire-protection fields.

Another famous conglomerate was Ling-Temco-Vought (LTV), founded by a World War II Navy electrician and school dropout, James J. Ling. Ling began with a small electrical contracting business in 1946. By 1967 he had acquired eighty companies in eighteen industries, including meat packing, sporting goods, airlines, and steel. LTV's total sales were $2.8 billion in 1968, making it twenty-fifth in the nation's top 500 industrial corporations. In 1969 the Department of Justice brought suit under the Sherman Act to force the company to divest itself of some of its acquisitions, and the firm's creditors got control of the board of directors. Ling left the company, but most of the structure he had created remained. By 1979 LTV had slipped to thirty-first among the country's top 500 industrial corporations.

Litton Industries began with $3 million in sales in 1953 and grew to $4.1 billion in sales in 1979. Litton is noted for its pioneering research and development, particularly in advanced military technology. It includes firms producing foods, missile guidance systems, business furniture and equipment, nuclear submarines, electronics, textbooks, and even economic development advice to foreign governments.

Textron began in 1923 as a textile firm, but it no longer produces any textiles. The company operates 27 divisions with 113 plants producing electronic equipment, aircraft, drugs, machine tools, marine engines, and helicopters.

Managing a conglomerate is a difficult job. The diversity of its operations requires special talents on the part of top management, talents which are costly and place heavy burdens on a firm's finances. But diversity is also an advantage, in that poor performance in one subsidiary may be offset by very good performance in another.

Attacking the Conglomerates

By the late 1960s the public was becoming alarmed about the power of conglomerates. Pressures mounted in Congress for changes in

Extended Example Merger Strategy in Japan

Big business in Japan is big by any standards. In 1967 Japan's one hundred largest companies had 36 percent of total manufacturing assets. Concentration was highest in iron and steel, shipbuilding, automobiles, electrical machinery, and home appliances.

After World War II, the U.S. Army of occupation brought American antitrust philosophy to Japan and broke up the big family-owned holding companies like Mitsui, Mitsubishi, Sumitomo, and Yasuda. Soon, however, these conglomerates began to recombine, and new industrial giants appeared as well. Much of the impetus for their formation came from departments of the Japanese government, particularly the powerful Ministry of International Trade and Industry.

The recession of 1973–75 hit hard in Japan and accelerated the trend toward combining firms in financial trouble. Firms with excess capacity sought mergers that would permit them to lay off workers and shut down high-cost plants. Others sought agreements or cartellike arrangements to control prices and output.

Some Japanese economists are opposed to the trend toward bigness, and the Fair Trade Commission has been investigating mergers to make sure they are legal. Most observers believe that industrial concentration will continue to grow, because otherwise many weak firms will simply go out of business.

Several different types of industrial reorganization have been taking place. One is in strategic industries, such as computers. The government has played a leading role in the reorganization of computer manufacture because the industry is felt to be important to national economic growth and because it requires large capital outlays. A second group of industries, including petrochemicals and steel, has needed coordination among firms to prevent the development of cutthroat competition. A third category of old, labor-intensive industries, such as textiles, plywood, and fishing, has been losing ground to competitors at home and abroad. Their reorganization has involved shifting capital out of low-profit areas into new lines of production; there have been gentlemen's agreements, mergers, and even bankruptcies. A fourth category, overlapping with the third, consists of firms needing some kind of rescue operation to survive. Often the reorganization, requiring mergers and other strong measures, is led by banks. This category includes small steel companies and the sugar industry.

Thus the government and the banks in Japan are playing an active part in changing the structure of industry. The law may have been inspired by American antitrust philosophy, but the world of business is being run along Japanese lines.

How is international competition affected by differences in U.S.-Japanese attitudes toward industrial concentration?

tax laws which had favored conglomerate mergers. The Department of Justice filed cases against several of the largest conglomerates, testing whether the courts would find them in violation of antitrust laws.

The case against ITT drew the greatest public attention. The Department of Justice petitioned the Supreme Court to require ITT to divest itself of several recent acquisitions. Then, reports appeared in the newspapers that ITT was applying political pressure to force the Department to settle the case in the conglomerate's favor. As a result of the publicity, ITT finally agreed to divest itself of all the recent acquisitions except the largest one—the Hartford Fire Insurance Company.

In recent years, antitrust actions have focused on *preventing* concentration in industry rather than attempting to break it up after it has developed. On balance, however, it would seem that the total effort at enforcing the antitrust laws so far has been quite small.

The Changing Philosophy of Antitrust

We have seen how the courts have interpreted antitrust laws differently in different periods. They have focused either on the *structure* of an industry or on the *conduct* of firms in the industry. The early emphasis on structure led to the breakup of such firms as the Standard Oil Company of New Jersey and the American Tobacco Company. Then followed a long period when the **rule of reason** was the guiding principle: A giant firm might avoid prosecution by refraining

Viewpoint Antitrust in the Oil Industry

Over the last several years, Congress has been cooperating with the Justice Department and the Federal Trade Commission to draw up powerful new antitrust legislation. Since 1974 the FTC has had the power to: (1) block mergers before they take place so that investigation into their probable effects can be completed, and (2) give state attorneys-general power to file class-action suits for triple damages in cases of price fixing or other monopolistic practices. Under the new law, the maximum fine for disobeying an FTC order rose to $1 million for a firm and $100,000 for an individual.

The new emphasis on antitrust action is probably an outgrowth of the inflation of the 1970s. Steadily rising prices in the face of declining demand have aroused suspicions of collusive pricing among large firms in concentrated industries. Food and fuel are among the main targets. Alleged price fixing in sugar, bread, coffee, beer, and breakfast cereal is currently under investigation. Severe penalties and damages have been assessed firms in the forest products industry. Manufacturers of drugs and hospital supplies have also been subject to complaints, along with professional associations and local real-estate boards.

But in the mid-1970s the greatest attention of the trustbusters was focused on allegations of monopolistic practices in the petroleum industry. In 1974 the FTC charged Exxon, Texaco, Gulf, Mobil, Standard Oil of California, Shell, and Atlantic Richfield with following a "common course of action" in production, transportation, and supply of crude oil to the "detriment of independent refiners."

The FTC complaint actually involves two subsidiary issues: Is competition among the majors—the "Seven Sisters"—really effective? And should the federal government continue to protect smaller, independent refiners from competition with the majors?

Of the top ten U.S. corporations, five are oil companies. Exxon is the world's largest company, with revenues (in 1979) greater than those of the hundred countries in which it conducts operations. Critics claim that the major oil producers use profits from the first stages of petroleum processing to subsidize inefficient refining and marketing operations. Their mark-up on a gallon of gasoline was three times as much as the mark-up of independent companies.

Under a bill introduced in Congress in 1976, the twenty-two largest companies would have to divest themselves of properties worth $28 billion. Each firm would be allowed to operate in only one of three stages of petroleum processing: production, transportation, or refining and marketing. Another bill would require oil companies to dispose of their interests in competing energy sources. Oil companies account for about 18 percent of the nation's coal production and 32 percent of uranium production. Critics suspect that oil company investment in alternative energy sources is designed to slow the development of competing fuels which could undermine their oil monopoly.

Defenders of the petroleum industry claim that competition is vigorous, with 10,000 companies producing oil and gas, 131 operating refineries, and 15,000 wholesaling and 200,000 retailing gasoline. The top eight firms control only 57 percent of the market, compared with 65 percent in steel, 98 percent in copper, 98 percent in motor vehicles, and 87 percent

from specific acts of monopoly conduct, regardless of whether or not it had a monopoly structure.

In 1945 the courts changed direction again. The Aluminum Company of America (Alcoa) was charged under the Sherman Act with monopolizing the manufacture of aluminum ingots and the sale of aluminum products. The firm had achieved market power through a basic patent and then had expanded by reinvesting its profits. Its large and efficient operation discouraged the entry of other companies, and, since the late 1930s, Alcoa had supplied more than 90 percent of the market for aluminum. Alcoa was not accused of unfair business conduct; the courts ruled against the firm on the grounds that the law prohibited the existence of so much market power. Structure, rather than conduct, was again to be the test of legality.

Recent rulings have continued to follow this principle. Some mergers have been prohibited in order to prevent monopoly "in its incipiency"—before monopoly structure can develop. Even small firms have been prohibited from merging. In 1962 Brown Shoe Manufacturing Company produced only 4 percent of the

in aircraft. Nevertheless, the major firms are interlocked into joint ventures which enhance their individual market power. They have combined their resources in major projects like the Alaska pipeline and offshore oil-producing leases. Small firms could not accumulate the funds or absorb the risks involved in such enterprises. Oil company profits have averaged 13.1 percent of net worth, compared with 13 percent for U.S. industry as a whole.

Defenders also claim that a large, vertically integrated firm can coordinate more efficiently the flow of oil to consumers. In this view, restructuring the industry would so disrupt production as to reduce supplies and force prices up. It would cause duplication of facilities and research efforts and reduce capital available for development of alternate energy sources. If these claims are true, breakup would prevent the United States from achieving energy independence in the next decade and would be detrimental to the nation's security and defense.

The tremendous power of the major oil firms has been one of the reasons for the preferential treatment given small producers. The 123 independent petroleum companies are able to acquire oil cheaply under the present system. From 1959 to 1973 they were allowed favorable licenses to import crude oil under the import quota system. Then in 1974 the Federal Energy Administration adopted a cost-sharing "entitlements" program to guarantee low-priced domestic oil equally to all firms. The independents are permitted to buy about half of their crude oil from the major producers at controlled prices. The entitlements program helped independents increase their market share from less than 20 percent in 1968 to almost 30 percent in 1975. Gradual decontrol of oil prices will mean that independents will have to pay more for their oil and compete on less favorable terms.

Independents were also helped by favorable tax arrangements in former years. The oil-depletion allowance encouraged major producers to construct surplus oil-producing capacity. When demand for oil fell, the majors would sell oil cheaply to independents. But when the energy crunch came in 1973, this supply was not available to the independents.

It seems safe to say that, over the next decade, pressure to break up the "Seven Sisters" will continue. An energy-conscious nation will be watching their every move. As oil firms move into exploration and development of alternate energy sources, public pressure will increase. This is as it should be. Even if the oil firms are not broken up, their business is so central to our national interest as to deserve constant public scrutiny and accounting.

Do you think the "Seven Sisters" should be broken up? Will this increase efficiency? Would such an act lead to lower prices? Explain.

President Carter has stated that divestiture by the oil companies might be avoided by closer regulation of company profits. What are the advantages and disadvantages of this approach?

Explain how oil firms are both vertically and horizontally integrated. What are the implications of this?

nation's output of shoes; Kinney was the eighth largest retailer. But the Supreme Court ruled that a merger would give the combined firm power to exclude competitors and would be a start toward greater concentration in a fragmented industry.

If structure is to be the test, then what about industries in which most of the market is already in the hands of a few large firms? While structure may not be precisely that of monopoly, *performance* may resemble it. In industries characterized by oligopoly, firms may perform like monopolists without ever committing an illegal act. Because the firms are aware of their interdependence, they base their price and output decisions on the expected reactions of other firms. **Parallel performance** among separate firms produces results similar to monopoly even without a formal agreement.

The courts have hesitated to tackle this problem. The only significant case was the one against the three big tobacco firms in 1946. American Tobacco, Liggett & Myers, and R. J. Reynolds were accused of monopoly performance because of their nearly identical prices. The Supreme Court ruled that "conscious parallelism of action" is illegal and that "no formal agreement is necessary to constitute an unlawful conspiracy." Since then, the courts have retreated from the rigor of this decision, leaving the problem of parallel performance still unsolved.

In 1977 the Carter Administration began a new drive to increase competition in highly concentrated industries. "Shared monopolies" were to be the focus of attack, with stiff penalties for such actions as price fixing through public statements (press conferences and speeches rather than through private agreements). Professional codes that restrict entry and forbid advertising were to be examined also.

Viewpoint Advertising in the Professions

"Upper and lower dentures; half price, this week only."

"Year-end sale—divorce proceedings handled cheap."

"Lost our lease—appendectomies performed at cost."

These advertisements are only imaginary—and frankly ridiculous. But it was partly to prevent such appeals that professional associations have generally prohibited advertising among their members. The public, it was said, does not have the necessary knowledge to evaluate the quality of professional services. Professional people must follow a rigid code of professional ethics in order to protect consumers from incompetent practitioners. Professionally determined standards of excellence in every field prevent the entry of those who might lower the quality—and the price—of medical, dental, or legal services.

These views came under attack in the recent climate of concern about the rising prices of professional services. In many communities young doctors, dentists, pharmacists, and lawyers challenged the rules prohibiting advertising. They opened "clinics" in which a large volume of professional services could be handled at low unit cost. Professional clinics provide basic services to a wide range of urban low- and middle-income consumers. A high volume of business depends on advertising to get the word out.

Enterprises like these have run afoul of state licensing boards, composed entirely of members of the profession. State boards have used their power to restrict entry to the professions and to prevent the sale

REGULATION TO CURB MARKET POWER

The aim of the antitrust laws is to maintain competition and prevent monopoly. Nevertheless, in some industries we accept monopoly and try to regulate it through public commissions. These industries include the public utilities—electricity, telephones, local transit, water, and gas. These are the natural monopolies we discussed earlier. There is another group of industries that aren't monopolies but that are regulated because this is believed to be in the public interest. They include railroads, oil pipelines, motor carriers, airlines, and radio-TV communications.

The problems of regulation are too complex to cover adequately in an introductory textbook. But a brief look at the railroads will give you a very small bird's-eye view of what is involved.

The Interstate Commerce Commission

Even before passage of the Sherman Antitrust Act, state and federal governments had been regulating the railroads. The public had grown angry over collusive agreements among railroads and their practice of discriminatory pricing. In 1887 Congress created the Interstate Commerce Commission (ICC) and directed it to prevent such practices. Other legislation in 1906 and 1910 strengthened the ICC. By the 1920s the ICC had taken over many of the functions of railroad management. The original aim of the ICC was to protect the customers of the railroads from monopoly practices and to see that the roads earned no monopoly profit. The ICC determined railroad rates and decided who could enter the industry, what services could be offered or abandoned, and whether mergers could take place.

In the 1930s railroads began to face increasing competition from pipelines, highways, waterways, and air transport. By 1939 the railroads were carrying less than 63 percent of the intercity freight and only 66 percent of the passenger

of services through high-volume, low-cost methods. They want to reserve for professionals the right to perform even simple routine services that could be performed by lower cost paraprofessionals.

Monopoly in the professions may be largely responsible for their sharply rising prices. Price inflation is most notable in the health services. During much of the 1970s health care costs rose at twice the rate of average consumer prices. The President's Council on Wage and Price Stability blamed the price rise on the physician's power to determine the scope and method of care provided. Lacking incentives to improve efficiency and install cost-reducing innovations, professionals constitute, in the words of G. B. Shaw, a "conspiracy against the laity."

The legal profession has prohibited advertising among lawyers since 1908. However, in 1977 the Supreme Court ruled that bans on professional advertising are illegal under the First Amendment. Some lawyers argue that advertising will raise the price of legal services, give large firms an advantage over small ones, and perhaps even persuade customers to buy services they don't need. Furthermore, advertising may destroy traditional lawyer-client relationships. Others say that advertising might provide the incentives for improved efficiency. Meaningful advertising would provide a responsible method of communicating price. (In states where pharmaceutical advertising is permitted, average prices of drugs and eyeglasses have fallen significantly.) Misleading advertising is already prohibited by existing laws.

What are the likely effects of advertising on elasticity of demand for professional services? Under what circumstances can advertising strengthen competition or weaken it?

traffic. Matters grew worse after World War II, and by the 1970s the railroads had only 30 percent of intercity freight traffic and about 2 percent of passenger traffic. Return on invested capital was among the lowest in all American industry, providing insufficient funds for maintaining and modernizing capital equipment.

The railroads found that progress had passed them by. Who was at fault? There was blame enough for everyone: the railroads for becoming rigid and bureaucratic; the unions for insisting on outmoded work rules and for keeping labor costs high; the ICC for preventing the railroads from adjusting rates and service so as to compete with other forms of transportation; and Congress and the public for failing to see that a useful national asset was being squeezed out of existence.

Slowly Congress took steps to rescue what was left. In 1964 it appropriated money to help state and local governments develop mass transit systems in urban areas. In 1970 it established Amtrak to take over the passenger business of the railroads. And in 1976 it set up Conrail to absorb the freight lines of the failing northeastern railroads. None of these public enterprises was expected to show a profit; all would require billions of dollars in government subsidies for many years.

By 1980 the U.S. Department of Transportation was demanding an end to regulation. Congress began work on a new law which would allow greater flexibility in rate-making, including the possibility of discounted rates for large shippers. Under the proposed law railroads would be permitted to charge higher rates on unprofitable lines. Grants and low-interest loans might be provided for modernizing rail facilities. If the anticipated changes take place, independent railroads would be operated like any other large firm, subject only to the provisions of antitrust laws.

Inherent Weaknesses of Regulation

Regulation of the railroads has been costly and has tended to perpetuate inefficiency. How well does regulation work in other industries? There are many critics. Some say that commissions set up to do the regulating often end by becoming captives of the interests they are supposed to control. Others say that regulation takes away the incentives of private enterprise.

Regulation is a poor substitute for competition. It cannot require quality or force efficiency or innovation. Competition does. Regulation cannot force firms to sell at prices below production costs, even when costs are too high. Competition does. It forces the high-cost company to discover means whereby its costs can be reduced. Regulation does not always set prices at the lowest level consistent with a fair return. Competition does. Regulation does not offer rewards and penalties to encourage performance. Competition does.

Extended Example The Little Engine That Could?

On the first working day of 1973 President Nixon signed into law an act which revolutionized rail transportation in the United States. The Regional Rail Reorganization Act was designed to restructure the railroad industry in the nation's industrial heartland. By this Act, six bankrupt railroads operating in the East and Midwest were absorbed into a single quasi-government corporation known as the Consolidated Rail Corporation, or Conrail.

Most of the new system (94 percent) represents lines formerly operated by the Penn Central Railroad. Penn Central operated 20,000 miles of routes and carried 228,000 tons of coal, 65,000 tons of ore, 55,000 tons of food, 44,000 tons of pulp and paper, and 24,000 tons of grain *each day*. Other railroads in the new system are the Reading, Lehigh Valley, Central of New Jersey, Ann Arbor, and Lehigh and Hudson River lines. Although the new Conrail system is intended eventually to earn a profit, its first years of operation were highly unprofitable.

Not all the nation's railroads are losing money. The most profitable roads are in the West and South where there is less competition from barges, trucks, and other railroads. Railroads which carry coal and grain to the West Coast and farm and industrial commodities among the Middle Atlantic states, as well as long-haul carriers of heavy industrial goods, have remained profitable.

But Northeastern railroads had been suffering from the movement of factories to the South and from the growth of services and light industry which use less rail transport. Coal could be transported by barges on the nation's rivers, where costs are lower than on the rail lines. The interstate highway system and St. Lawrence Seaway drained off other profitable freight.

Railroads also suffered from stringent union work rules which kept productivity low and maintained inefficient duplication of rail facilities. As an example, in the early 1970s, there were still 3000 ways to route freight from Washington, D.C., to St. Louis.

Rail traffic is highly sensitive to economic recession because of the types of freight carried. Autos, auto parts, and coal account for about a third of railroad freight business. Major strikes in these industries and declines in consumer spending had a disastrous effect on revenues.

Another problem facing the railroads was deteriorating tracks, terminals, and other facilities. During years of declining revenues, railroads cut back on maintenance of equipment and improvement of facilities. Other forms of transportation often receive government subsidies from tax revenues for operating their service. Commercial airlines use government-financed systems of airways; water freight uses rivers maintained by government; trucking companies use tax-supported highways; and users of private autos benefit from controlled gasoline prices.

In 1972 the six failing railroad lines were operating 26,000 miles of track for gross revenues of $2.3 billion. To allow these firms to collapse would have choked industrial activity in the seventeen affected states and would have thrown 2.7 million railway employees out of work. Reorganization into the Conrail system in 1976 consolidated routes and permitted roads to abandon some unprofitable lines for greater efficiency.

Conrail was financed by federal grants of approximately half a billion dollars and by sale of $1.5 billion worth of government-guaranteed securities. Existing

The Carter Administration has pledged to reduce regulation where such action would increase competition. The process has already begun in the trucking industry and is substantially complete in the airlines.

THE DEBATE OVER BIGNESS

We saw at the beginning of this chapter that 500 large corporations control about two thirds of the assets of American industries. This implies that much of the economy no longer fits the competitive model as described in economic theory. Is this a serious problem? Is industrial concentration something to be feared? Is it increasing, as some people say, or is it staying about the same or even decreasing? What ought we to do?

Measuring Concentration

Numerous efforts have been made to measure the degree of concentration in various industries and in the economy as a whole. Measurement is

lines were bought outright or absorbed through exchanges of stock in Conrail. At some time in the future the government might take over entirely all track and roadbed and allow Conrail to run the trains without bearing the financial burden of maintaining the track. More than 6000 miles of unprofitable track will be abandoned or else subsidized by federal, state, or local governments. Workers displaced by reorganization will be eligible for financial support while out of work.

Passenger traffic is practically nonexistent in the Conrail system. In 1969 most of the nation's passenger rail traffic was placed under the quasi-government corporation Amtrak. Amtrak continues to require subsidies to offset intercity operating losses amounting to hundreds of millions of dollars a year. The new rail act will provide $800 million in additional expenditures to make tracks smoother and safer and to provide new cars, locomotives, and stations.

The railroad reorganization plan was designed to preserve competition by preventing the collapse of major roads. However, profitable roads continuing under private ownership resent having to compete with a road that can cover any losses with a federal subsidy. Other competing forms of transportation may also demand subsidies, leading to further government intervention into the private economy. Eventually, the entire industry may be nationalized.

In most of the world, railroads are already nationalized. Still, there is a high degree of innovation—the bullet trains in Japan are a prime example. In Britain, France, and West Germany there are plans for trains capable of speeds up to 150 miles an hour. Traffic is high along the nationalized systems, but deficits are common.

difficult because the structure of industry is so complex. Some firms produce a variety of goods for sale in many different markets. In one market a firm may face substantial competition, while in another it may have a degree of monopoly power. If it serves a large geographic area, it may face heavier competition in one region than in another.

Concentration may be defined as the extent to which the largest firms dominate an industry. This is usually expressed as a *concentration ratio.*

A **concentration ratio** measures the percent of industry output of the four (or eight) largest firms in an industry compared to all the firms taken together. Thus if the four largest firms account for 90 percent of an industry's sales, we can say that the industry is highly concentrated. If the four largest firms account for only 2 percent of sales, the industry is not concentrated at all. Concentration ratios may measure sales as a percent of total sales, productive assets as a percent of total industry assets, or value added in production as a percent of total value added. (*Value added* is the difference between the dollar value of a firm's output and the amount paid to other firms for inputs such as materials, parts, and energy.)

A concentration ratio for the cigarette industry in a recent year is calculated as shown in Table 1. The four largest firms were R. J. Reynolds (32.5 percent of total sales), Philip Morris (23.8 percent), Brown & Williamson (17.0 percent), and American Brands (14.2 percent). Together the four firms accounted for 87.5 percent of industry sales.

Latest census figures compiled by the Department of Commerce show that the four largest (and only) aluminum producers have 100 percent of the market. The four largest auto firms supply 92 percent of the domestically produced market. The production of electric light bulbs has a concentration ratio of 91 percent, and sewing machines, 81 percent. On the other hand, the women's dress industry has a concentration ratio of only 7 percent. The great majority of U.S. industries have concentration ratios less than 50 percent.

There are certain difficulties with the concentration ratio. First, what is an industry and who belongs to it? Does a company making floor tiles belong to the tile industry or to the floor-covering industry or to the home-products industry? If the firm is thought of as belonging to the tile industry, it may have a large share of the market. But if it is thought of as part of the floor-covering industry, it may be far less important.

A second problem is that we calculate a concentration ratio only for the largest four or eight firms. It doesn't give us a picture of the whole industry. For example, a study in the 1960s showed sales concentration ratios of 70 for the tire-and-tube industry and 31 for the meatpacking industry. The ratios suggest that tires and tubes is the more concentrated industry.

Table 1 **Concentration in the Cigarette Industry**

Company	Sales (billions of cigarettes)	Market share (percent of total sales)
R. J. Reynolds	193.6	32.5%
Philip Morris	141.7	23.8
Brown and Williamson	101.3	17.0
American Brands	84.5	14.2
Total industry sales	596.0	—
Concentration ratio		87.5%

But the figures conceal the fact that in tires and tubes there are only 105 firms, while in meat packing there are 2833. So in the meat packing industry the four largest firms are very large compared to the other 2829 and therefore command much greater market power.

Finally, a concentration ratio doesn't show the actual level of competition in small, local markets. It usually is calculated for the country as a whole. In any particular locality or region, one or two local firms may have overwhelming market power because other firms are too far away to compete with them. This would be the case in such industries as sand and gravel, hardware supplies, plant nurseries, supermarkets, and mobile homes.

One way to escape the limitations of the industry concentration ratio is to include all industries in a single ratio. The *aggregate concentration ratio* measures the level of concentration in the economy as a whole. It can be used to compare the importance of big firms over time and to measure the trend toward greater or less concentration. In a sense, it is a way of evaluating the effectiveness of antitrust legislation. The aggregate concentration ratio is usually calculated for the nation's 50, 100, and 200 largest firms.

Trends in Concentration

The important question is whether industry is becoming more or less concentrated. A study published in 1979 reported significant changes in aggregate concentration ratios over the past several decades.* The data showed that the share of productive assets owned by the 50 largest U.S. firms grew from 31 percent of total manufacturing assets in 1947 to 39 percent in 1977. The data for the 50 largest, 100 largest, and 200 largest firms are summarized in Table 2. Concentration ratios expressed as shares of total manufacturing sales also increased over the period (see Table 3).

Much of the early growth in concentration among the 200 largest firms can be attributed to newly formed conglomerates. In recent years, growth is associated primarily with growth of petroleum and chemical firms.

If industry is indeed becoming more concentrated, what ought to be done about it? Even in the most concentrated industries, there are still several firms, and the customer can choose among them. You aren't compelled to buy a car made by Ford or General Motors or Chrysler; you can buy a foreign car, as many people do, or one made by American Motors. In fact, in many industries there are growing numbers of large firms, all competing vigorously against each other. There is also competition between industries, as between steel and aluminum or between glass and plastics.

*Betty Bock, Jack Farkas, and Deborah S. Weinberger, *Aggregate Concentration*, The Conference Board, #57, May 1979.

Bigness Defended

Large size is not universally condemned. Many nations protect and encourage combinations of enterprises into giant firms. Some groups in the United States point to the advantages of large

Table 2 **Ratio of Assets to Total Assets of All Manufacturing Corporations**

	1947	1977
50 largest	31%	39%
100 largest	39	50
200 largest	46	62

Table 3 **Ratio of Sales to Total Sales of All Manufacturing Corporations**

	1947	1977
50 largest	22%	36%
100 largest	29	46
200 largest	36	57

Viewpoint How Big Does a Company Have to Be?

One of the arguments for giant firms is that production of some goods requires large-scale production. Economic efficiency, it is said, requires a large output relative to the size of the market. Small firms cannot achieve the same economies of scale, and their costs will be higher than those of the giant firms.

How big does a firm have to be to achieve economies of scale? In 1956 an important study was made of this question. Although that was more than twenty-five years ago, the fundamental conclusions are still significant. The research showed that there were only two industries in which ten or more firms could not supply the market at lowest cost. Only in typewriters and cigarettes did a firm have to produce at least 10 percent of industry output to achieve maximum efficiency.

In each of the industries in Table 4, maximum efficiency was attainable with less than 10 percent of the market in sales volume.

A small percentage in column (1) means that a firm can be small relative to the size of the market. Many firms can operate efficiently, and competition is possible. Where only 1/4 percent of the market is needed for efficient operation, the industry can include as many as 100%/1/4% = 400 firms. Where 20 percent of the market is needed for efficiency, only 100%/20% = 5 firms should operate. Vigorous competition may not be possible.

Table 4

Industry	Percent of market needed for efficiency	Number of firms needed for lowest costs
Steel	2–20	5 to 50
Soap	8–15	7 to 13
Cement	2–10	10 to 50
Rayon	4–6	17 to 25
Tires and tubes	1 3/8–2 1/4	approx. 50
Petroleum	1 3/4	approx. 60
Distilled liquor	1 1/4–1 3/4	approx. 60
Canned fruits and vegetables	1/4–1/2	200 to 400

*From Joe S. Bain, *Barriers to New Competition: Their Character and Consequences in Manufacturing Industries* (New York: Cambridge University Press, 1965), pp. 80, 861.

size and recommend relaxing the antitrust laws.

One argument in favor of bigness stresses the international competitiveness of U.S. firms. Small U.S. firms may be unable to compete against giant firms in foreign markets; they should be allowed to develop the cost advantages of large scale.

Secondly, strong firms should be allowed to merge with weak firms, spreading their better management techniques, more dynamic production planning, and more efficient operations to other firms. Permitting mergers may actually encourage innovative and efficient management techniques.

Thirdly, larger firms can better afford an aggressive research and development effort. In large firms the risks and costs of research and development can be spread over a greater volume of output. Many large firms keep constant watch on their rivals' successes and work vigorously to develop ways to keep costs down and to maintain market share. Their awareness of potential competition from new products keeps big firms on their toes. Government policy to penalize growth would thwart this stimulus to innovation.

Finally, the visibility of large firms helps monitor their activity. Industry performance and methods of competition are more easily regulated among large firms, and steps can be taken to correct anticompetitive practices. Defenders of bigness say that the important question is not "Is the firm big?" but "Is bigness in the public interest?" When bigness reflects greater efficiency, they would answer "Yes."

Living with Bigness

Some economists believe that we should learn to live with big business. A well-known economist of this school is John Kenneth Galbraith, whose books have had considerable influence among the general public. Galbraith sees bigness as an inevitable result of modern technology. Modern technology has made Adam Smith's competitive model obsolete, he says. Today's large organizations can produce and sell goods more efficiently than small ones. Instead of being controlled by the competitive market, large firms have used advertising and marketing techniques to take control of the market themselves. Furthermore, they are largely immune from antitrust laws, since government lawyers are

Economic Thinker John Kenneth Galbraith

You may have seen John Kenneth Galbraith (1908–) on his Public Television series "The Age of Uncertainty," a lively, thirteen-part history of economics. Galbraith is one of the best-known economists of today. He was a professor of economics at Harvard, has served as ambassador to India (during Kennedy's administration), and has even dabbled as a novelist. Some of his best-known books are *The Affluent Society: The New Industrial State; Money;* and *Economics, Peace, and Laughter.*

John Kenneth Galbraith was born on a farm in Ontario, Canada. After studying at the universities of Toronto and California, he began his career as an agricultural economist. This was during the Great Depression of the 1930s, and agriculture was suffering heavy losses. Farm prices were dropping sharply while the prices farmers paid for manufactured goods were rising. Galbraith concluded that the market economy of the United States is actually divided into two parts: the competitive sector of small farmers and shopkeepers and the monopoly sector of industrial giants. The giants are the major cause of inflation and of fluctuations in output and employment, he said, and the competitive sector has to bear the costs of depression. To break up the giants is not the answer. According to Galbraith this would only produce oligopoly, which is not much better. Furthermore, the system actually works rather well most of the time. Technical innovation by large firms has yielded unprecedented gains in real incomes, while the growth of unions has helped spread these gains more equitably among working people. In fact, it was the power of the giants that brought on the development of union "countervailing power."

Galbraith believes that the power of large firms can best be checked by encouraging development of other forms of countervailing power. The nation should aim not to eliminate power but to increase the power of those groups which lack it: agriculture, consumers, and small business. Galbraith urges that we face up to the new realities of modern life—the technical and organizational benefits which bigness produces. Large-scale firms should not be broken up. When necessary, they should be regulated so that their policies cannot injure other groups in the economy.

Galbraith has also attacked American capitalism for what he believes is one of its greatest flaws: too little is allocated to the public sector. This idea, which was present in his earlier works, emerged to form the core of his most recent and controversial book, *Economics and the Public Purpose* (1973). He sees the public sector—housing, education, public transportation, urban services, health services—as underfunded and sees too much emphasis placed on private-sector activities. The private sector dominates, partly because of the power of the big corporation. Galbraith would do away with current antitrust laws in favor of nationalization of industries in the public sector and wage and price controls in much of the private sector.

more likely to go after small- and medium-sized firms that cannot afford a strong defense. Galbraith says our current antitrust policy is like locking the barn door after the horse has been stolen.

Galbraith does not advocate breaking up large firms, however. He believes that dissolving large firms would sacrifice the benefits of modern technology which created bigness in the first place. Instead, he points to ways of balancing and controlling the power of big business for the benefit of society. He recommends government ownership, or *nationalization*, of highly concentrated industries so that they can be run according to the national interest. He would also build up the *countervailing power* of labor unions, consumer groups, and government regulatory bodies as a way of balancing the power of big business. Bigness doesn't worry Galbraith as long as other bigness grows up to offset it.

Another view of big business was offered by the important economist and social thinker Joseph A. Schumpeter (1883–1950). Schumpeter studied how a capitalist society grows and develops through the work of entrepreneurs. He described economic development as a process of **creative destruction.**

"The fundamental impulse that sets and keeps the capitalist engine in motion," Schumpeter wrote, "comes from the new consumers' goods, the new methods of production or transportation, the new markets, the new forms of industrial organization that capitalist enterprise creates." Every new creation *destroys* old ways and opens the door to progress. According to Schumpeter, it is innovation that strengthens competition and limits monopoly power. Even the largest monopoly is vulnerable to this kind of competition; the constant threat of newness is sufficient to discipline large firms and keep them on their toes.

Bigness Opposed

Monopoly and innovation. One argument in favor of bigness stresses the ability of large firms to conduct research and develop new products. But there is some question whether large firms have actually promoted technological progress. In fact, of sixty-one important inventions made since 1900, only eleven came from research teams in large industrial laboratories. More than half were the product of independent inventors working alone: air conditioning, automatic transmission, power steering, cellophane, the helicopter, the jet engine, streptomycin, insulin, and continuous steel casting. Several other inventions came from small- or medium-sized firms: DDT, the crease-resistant process for fibers, continuous hot-strip rolling of steel sheets, and shell molding. Many inventions came from university research.

Why have many large firms generally been slow to innovate? Why has their market power not been used for imaginative entrepreneurship? The answer lies partly in the large bureaucratic structures needed to run these firms. Bureaucracies are not often the source of creative thinking. Furthermore, as Schumpeter noted, creation destroys—and a giant firm has a vested interest in continuing past products and processes. A small firm, on the other hand, may leap at the chance to adopt new techniques and products as a way to undersell its competitors and increase its share of the market.

Bigness and the market system. Another school of economics wants to fight industrial concentration. One of the best known of this group is George J. Stigler of the University of Chicago. He acknowledges that large firms may be more efficient in terms of lower production costs, but he maintains that their cost advantage comes from market power. Large firms are able to buy their materials for less than competitive market prices. Their actual production costs are probably no different from those of small- and medium-sized firms. In fact, the giants are often composed of numerous divisions that operate independently, almost as separate firms. Each division may be economically viable and efficient on its own.

Stigler fears the growth of economic power in the hands of big business. Economic power is a potential source of political power—power to undermine individual liberties and stifle participatory democracy. But Stigler also fears government regulation of business. His prescription is simple: bust the trust. He would apply the Sherman Act vigorously to break up existing concentration, as well as to prevent new concentration from developing. If the laws are enforced vigorously, says Stigler, a competitive structure would result. A competitive *structure* is better than regulating business *conduct*. With industries of small- and medium-sized firms, the final result would be competitive *performance* in industrial markets.

Economic Thinker George Stigler

In the economics profession, disagreement is healthy. Economists have traditionally brought their ideas into the open to encourage debate. Vigorous debate is in some ways a substitute for the laboratory experiments which are not possible in a social science. When many active minds examine a question, they can expose the flaws in logic behind a particular conclusion.

There is probably no greater opponent of Galbraith's acceptance of big business than George J. Stigler. Stigler is one of the staunchest supporters of the free market, whose invisible hand works to the benefit of all. The invisible hand works best in perfect competition. So, according to Stigler, the greatest enemy of our capitalistic system is not the economic systems of other countries but the monopoly and oligopoly elements of our own economy.

Born in the state of Washington in 1911, George Stigler has taught economics at the London School of Economics and Columbia and Brown universities. He has been Professor of Economics at the University of Chicago since 1958. Stigler has observed the growing power of large manufacturing firms and finds it dangerous. Whereas small-scale competition is responsive to consumer demand, he says, large firms are able to control output and prices, reaping monopoly profits. Whatever cost advantages there are in large size are generally a result of the use of monopoly power to force down the prices of material inputs. Under imperfect competition resources are misallocated and the community suffers a loss in efficiency. Stigler believes that equity is harmed, too, because of the dominance of powerful institutions in our political system.

Professor Stigler is opposed to the recent emphasis on monopoly conduct in enforcing antitrust laws. He believes that large firms can always discover new tactics to accomplish their monopoly purposes without ever being judged in violation of the laws. The only effective remedy to their power is to attack monopoly structure, to break up large-scale manufacturing firms and enforce competition throughout U.S. industry.

The military-industrial complex. Shortly before he left office, President Dwight D. Eisenhower spoke of "the conjunction of an immense military establishment and a large arms industry" which had developed after World War II and the Korean War. He urged the nation to "guard against the acquisition of unwarranted influence, whether sought or unsought, by the military-industrial complex. The potential for the disastrous use of misplaced power exists and will persist . . . we should take nothing for granted." President Eisenhower's message was all the more remarkable in coming from a five-star general and former chief of staff of the armed forces.

Eisenhower was thinking of the network of common interests among Pentagon officials, defense contractors, and certain members of Congress whose reelection often depends on defense contracts for their districts. The implication is that their common interests may at times take precedence over the interests of the nation, particularly when it comes to deciding how big the military budget should be.

In reality, the size of military expenditures seems to depend on a number of factors, the most important of which is the current international situation. Expenditures rose greatly during the Vietnam War, dropped in the early 1970s, and then began to rise again in response to increased Soviet military spending. In 1973, about 30 percent of federal government outlays went for national defense, but the percentage fell to 23 percent in 1980.

Some critics say that corporations doing most of their business with the Department of Defense, such as General Dynamics, Lockheed, and others, are almost extensions of the government rather than private firms. As Galbraith has pointed out, these firms often use plants belonging to the government, get their working capital from the government in the form of "progress payments," receive management guidance from the Defense Department, are required to follow government accounting rules, and are heavily staffed with former military personnel.* Their plants are regarded as a national defense resource. It has been charged that military contracts are awarded to the leading firms on the basis of available capacity rather than competitive bidding. One author analyzed the awarding of aerospace contracts in the years 1960–72. He found that when a major production line was available, it would receive a new military contract for a product resembling that of its previous contract. In this way all of the eight major aerospace production lines were kept busy from 1960 to 1972.**

What you think about the military-industrial complex is likely to depend on how you feel about national defense. If you feel that our international obligations require all the strength we possess and perhaps more, you will be less inclined to criticize the way security is achieved. You may want government to own or control all defense production, regulating costs and profits. If you feel, as some of the critics do, that the defense system is like any other big enterprise in wanting to grow as large as it can regardless of whether growth is needed, you will worry about how to control it. You may want to enforce vigorous competition in defense as in any other industry.

The question has been a key issue in several presidential campaigns. In 1960 John F. Kennedy and the Democrats charged that the United States was falling behind the Soviet Union in the production of nuclear missiles. In 1975 the administration of Gerald Ford was attacked both by some Democrats and some Republicans for "weakening" the country's military posture. In 1979 the Senate appeared willing to refuse the SALT treaty on strategic arms control unless defense spending increased beyond what even some military authorities believed to be necessary.

SUMMARY

Advances in technology and the great size of the American market were factors in the trend toward industrial concentration. In the late-nineteenth century, firms combined through merger or acquisition and through trusts. Mergers were horizontal or vertical. Monopoly power permitted price discrimination, particularly in railroads and petroleum pipelines. The first antitrust laws were aimed at regulating railroad monopoly—the Interstate Commerce Act—and at preventing monopoly structure throughout industry—the Sherman Antitrust Act. The Clayton Antitrust Act of 1914 prohibited specific types of monopolistic conduct: discriminatory price cutting, tying contracts, interlocking directorates in the same industry, and stock ownership in competing companies. The Federal Trade Commission was established to investigate and to prosecute violations.

The *rule of reason* refers to Supreme Court interpretation of antitrust legislation where only monopoly *conduct* was ruled illegal. The result of such lenient interpretation was a new wave of mergers in the 1920s. Automobiles and communications were the major new industries. Antitrust laws of the 1930s aimed at protecting small business firms by prohibiting price discounting by large retailers—the Robinson-Patman Act and the Miller-Tydings Act. In 1950 the Celler-Kefauver Act amended the Clayton Act to prohibit acquisition of firms where the effect would be to reduce competition.

Business firms of the 1960s turned to con-

*John Kenneth Galbraith, *The New Industrial State* (Boston: Houghton Mifflin Company, 1967), p. 314.

**James R. Kurth, "The Political Economy of Weapons Procurement: The Follow-On Imperative," *American Economic Review*, LXII No. 2, May 1972, 304–11.

glomerate merger: International Telephone and Telegraph, Ling-Temco-Vought, Litton, and Textron. But again the Supreme Court changed direction and began to focus on monopoly structure. The aim has been to prevent the formation of new monopolies by carefully investigating all new applications for merger. The most difficult problem facing the courts is parallel performance among firms where no formal price and output agreement has taken place. Some large and concentrated industries are regulated by public commissions; the Interstate Commerce Commission regulates rail and water transport.

There are disagreements as to the relative merits of bigness versus small-scale competition in the United States. Some economists believe bigness provides greater opportunities for research and development and enhances our competitive position in international trade. They believe large-scale enterprises should be regulated in the public interest. Others claim large enterprises have been slow to innovate and should be broken up.

Key Words and Phrases

aggregate concentration ratio the percentage of our economy's output produced by the 50, 100, or 200 largest firms.

concentration ratio the percent of industry output produced by the four (or eight) largest firms.

conglomerate mergers combinations of firms producing unrelated goods and services.

creative destruction the process of innovation which makes old processes and products obsolete.

fair trade laws laws permitting manufacturers to set retail prices as a means of protecting small retailers from price competition.

holding company a corporation which is established for the purpose of holding voting stock in other operating firms.

horizontal mergers combinations of two or more independent firms into one when the merging firms were direct competitors.

interlocking directorates the practice of a single individual serving on the boards of several firms in the same industry and influencing their market behavior.

parallel performance similar pricing practices resulting from similar market conditions rather than from actual collusion.

rule of reason a court practice of judging only monopoly behavior, without regard for monopoly structure, in industry.

trusts holdings of voting stock in several corporations for the purpose of controlling price and output, allocating markets, and reducing competition.

tying contracts contracts requiring the purchaser of a particular type of output to purchase an entire line of goods from the same supplier.

vertical mergers combinations of two or more independent firms when the merging firms were suppliers or customers of each other.

Questions for Review

1. Outline three historical periods of significant merger activity. What were the characteristics of mergers in each?
2. Show how the major antimonopoly legislation grew out of industry conditions in each of the periods discussed in question 1.
3. Discuss the problems of legislating controls over conglomerate mergers. What are the advantages and disadvantages of conglomerates?
4. List important legislation by which government attempted to prevent monopoly price reductions. What is the long-term basis for forbidding price reductions, even if they reflect lower production costs? State your answer in terms of structure, conduct, and performance.
5. Discuss the major arguments favoring and opposing industrial concentration.
6. Define: price discrimination, interlocking directorates.
7. What are the limitations of the concentration ratio as an indicator of market power?
8. Discuss the effects on the national economy as a whole of concentration of market power. How are efficiency and equity affected by industry structure?
9. Consider the fundamental economic circumstances that often underlie industrial concentration. Can you project any trends in these circumstances for the future? What do your predictions imply about market power and the future role of government in the economy?
10. On the basis of the following concentration ratios, how would you describe trends in the beer industry?

Year	Percent of Total Shipments		
	4 largest	8 largest	50 largest
1958	28	44	88
1963	34	52	94
1967	40	59	98
1972	52	70	99

PART 4

Resource Markets

13 The Marginal Productivity Theory of Resource Allocation

14 Employing Labor Resources: Unions, Work, and Wages

15 Employing Land, Capital, and Entrepreneurial Resources

16 Poverty, Discrimination, and Public Assistance

CHAPTER 13

The Marginal Productivity Theory of Resource Allocation

Learning Objectives

Upon completion of this chapter, you should be able to:

1. Explain the theory of marginal productivity.
2. Graph the demand for resources.
3. Discuss the three basic determinants of demand for resources and the four basic factors affecting elasticity of demand for resources.
4. Explain and apply the equal marginal productivity principle.
5. Discuss how government subsidies and taxes affect resource use.
6. Explain how resources and income are allocated in a perfectly competitive market.

We have been looking at the ways in which firms price and sell their finished goods to consumers. Now we must turn to the beginning of the production process. We will examine how firms combine their resources to produce the final product.

An economic system, you will remember, must answer four questions: What is to be produced? How is it to be produced? For whom is it to be produced? When may goods be enjoyed? In the preceding chapters we saw how the first question is answered as consumers express their demand for goods and services in the marketplace. The second question is answered in the chapter before us now: How is production to be carried out?

In this chapter we will describe the markets where resources are hired for use in production. We will show how demand and supply interact to determine resource prices and the incomes of resource owners. In the two chapters that follow we will examine separately the markets for the four classes of productive resources: land, labor, capital, and entrepreneurship.

RESOURCE ALLOCATION: THE BACKGROUND

Economic relationships play such an important part in our productive lives that it is not surprising to find a strong influence on our political lives as well. Certainly our political views influence and are influenced by our economic arrangements. This was never truer than in the early years of the Industrial Revolution, a time during which nations experienced the upheavals and distortions of fundamental change. Changing class structures made life insecure, and new learning shattered old beliefs. Philosophers tried to interpret the causes and predict the results of economic change.

Two of these philosophers had especially great impact on the societies they described. One was Adam Smith, whom we have already met. Adam Smith's theory of production was based on the economic relationships which developed during the Industrial Revolution. Smith saw that goods and services were created through the use of productive resources. He divided these productive resources into the familiar classifications: land, labor, capital, and entrepreneurship. And he showed that production depends on the combined efforts of all four types of resources. This was particularly important because it showed that profit received by the entrepreneur was actually *earned* income—income earned through directing the use of other productive resources. In Adam Smith's view, the value of the finished product embodied the value of all resources used in production.

Smith was optimistic about the results of economic growth. He predicted that improvements in technology and greater division of labor would help increase the productivity of all resources. Then a growing consumer market would lead to increased profits, increased demand for labor, and higher wages. The result would be population growth with further increases in demand and supply. Thus, the prosperity of each group of resource owners was linked through interdependence with all other groups.

Adam Smith was optimistic about other results of the market system, too. He believed that free markets would allocate scarce resources efficiently toward the kinds of products people want. Business firms would strive to produce the greatest output of goods and services at the lowest cost. Moreover, rewards for production would be distributed to resource owners in fair proportion to their contribution to output.

The other giant of early economic philosophy was Karl Marx. He began writing his famous economic treatise *Capital* nearly seventy years after Smith wrote *The Wealth of Nations*. By the time Karl Marx was writing, the Industrial Revolution seemed to have caused more misery than good. Marx observed the suffering of working people and built a theory of class exploitation and a prediction of violent revolution to come. To Marx it appeared that labor was not receiving its fair share of output from production.

Marx began with an idea developed earlier by David Ricardo. Ricardo believed that the output of industry is entirely the result of labor; therefore, the value of goods and services is only the value of the labor required to produce them. This **labor theory of value** was an outgrowth of the simpler times when production was indeed largely the result of human effort. But the new capitalist system had brought changes in economic relationships. Workers were no longer individually responsible for planning production and for marketing their output. In the industrial era they became dependent on capitalists who owned the *means of production*—the factories and machines of the new technology. The capitalist owners of industrial plant and equipment used their productive property to serve their own interests and the interests of the capitalist class. Thus, according to Marx, the "propertyless proletariat" became subservient to the wishes of the owners of capital.

Without bargaining power relative to their employers, many industrial workers were forced to accept wages barely above subsistence. Improvements in technology increased their productivity, but the growing surplus of goods and services was taken over by the capitalist owners. Marx called this excess of value produced by labor the **capitalists' surplus.** According to Marx, there would be a larger and larger imbalance between the incomes of these groups. Workers would have less to spend, but capitalists would have more savings to invest in productive equipment. In fact, the availability of funds for investment would worsen the position of workers, as machines would gradually replace labor in production. A reserve army of unemployed workers would develop from which capitalist employers would draw workers at lower and lower wage rates.

Marx believed that all this was inevitable. It seemed to him that capitalism carried within itself the "seeds of its own destruction." Eventually, the great bulk of the working proletariat would rise up against these injustices and overthrow the capitalist class. Following violent revolution the means of production would be taken over by workers and operated in the interests of the working class alone. Then capitalism would disappear, and all people would work together for common purposes. Marx's influence on the politics of his era and of years since has been enormous.

The life of the average worker improved greatly after the time Marx was writing in the 1840s and 1850s. By the 1870s, followers of Adam Smith went on the counterattack. They became known as **neoclassical economists,** and they were especially significant for developing a new theory of income distribution. They showed that income depends not on class conflict but on relative productivity. The economist Alfred Marshall analyzed the important relationships within resource markets more precisely than Smith had done. He and John Bates Clark went even further. They stressed the ultimate justice of a system that rewards participants according to their contribution to work.

In fact, the ideas explored by the neoclassical economists are the basis for our theory of resource markets. Now we can answer the question: How is production to be carried out?

THE THEORY OF MARGINAL PRODUCTIVITY

Suppose you are the production manager of a bicycle factory. You run an assembly line, and you employ workers who put together the bicycles. There are separate departments for making wheels and forging frames and another where paint is sprayed and trim applied. As the production manager, you are responsible for getting everything together at a minimum cost. If sales of bicycles go up, you have to hire more workers, buy more materials, and perhaps even put in another assembly line. When you go out to buy more resources, you do so because you need them for making bicycles. Your demand for resources depends on the technology of bicycle manufacture and on the demand for bicycles. We say that your demand for resources is a **derived demand** because it is derived from the demand for finished goods.

Much of the demand for industrial resources is derived demand. Most primary products such as cement, steel, aluminum, and copper are purchased not for themselves but for use in making other products. Some of these other products may not be consumer goods either, but producer goods, which in turn are used to make goods for final consumption. This is important to remember because changes in the demand for consumer goods sometimes cause much greater changes in the demand for producer goods and for primary products.

Usually an enterprise owns a certain amount of fixed plant and equipment. The bicycle company has its buildings and assembly lines and machines. It also has a staff of managers who run the business. These fixed resources do not change in the short run.

When demand for its products increases, the firm enters resource markets to purchase variable resources for use in combination with its fixed resources. Labor and materials are variable resources because they are employed in varying quantities together with the firm's fixed resources.

Resource Demand in Perfect Competition

Let us begin by examining derived demand for resources in a perfectly competitive market. Competition means that firms will be price takers. They will buy inputs and sell output at a constant price determined in the market.

Suppose your bicycle firm enters the market for labor. In this case labor is a variable resource to be used with the firm's fixed quantity of plant and equipment. We will assume that there is a range over which the firm can vary its output by varying the quantity of labor hired. (The firm also varies the amount of some other resources, such as materials and energy, but for simplicity we will consider only labor.) Because plant and equipment are fixed, there is an upper limit to the output the firm can produce in the short run. This brings us to our old friend, the *principle of diminishing marginal product:* when successive units of a variable resource are added to a fixed resource, the result at some point will be smaller and smaller additions to total product. Thus if we add more units of labor to a firm's fixed plant and equipment, the additions to total product will eventually decline.

Table 1 shows a hypothetical schedule of the *marginal product of labor.* **Marginal product** is the change in total product resulting from the addition of one more unit of a variable input. The schedule is drawn up for a time period during which some of the firm's resources are fixed. For simplicity we have begun our computations at the point at which marginal product begins to decline. Actually, marginal product might increase as labor is added, up to some point, then remain constant for a bit, and then start to decline. In Table 1, the figures for marginal product (MP), shown in column (3), are written between the lines to show that they represent the differences in total product (TP), listed in column (2).

Marginal Revenue Product

As the production manager of the bicycle company, you are interested in producing as many bicycles as you can sell at a price that covers the costs of production. You will hire another unit of labor if it contributes more to the value of total output than it adds to total costs. In Table 1, columns (3) through (6) help us see how much each additional unit of labor (Q_L) adds to the value of output. Because the product is sold in a perfectly competitive market, price is the same no matter how many units the firm sells. The value of the marginal product in column (6) is called labor's **marginal revenue product** (MRP). It is calculated by figuring the *change in total revenue* that results from adding one more worker:

$$MRP = \frac{\text{change in TR}}{\text{change in } Q_L} = \frac{\Delta TR}{\Delta Q_L}$$

Marginal revenue product declines because marginal product declines. If the firm hires three additional workers, the third will contribute $40 to the value of the firm's output. A fourth would contribute $30, and a fifth only $25. MRP for a seventh worker would be only $5.

The actual quantity of labor hired depends in part on how much it contributes to production. But it depends also on the cost of labor. The firm will keep hiring workers as long as the last one hired adds more MRP than the firm must pay in wages. Column (7) shows that the market price of labor is $15 for the given time period. The firm should hire six workers, since the cost of the sixth is just equal to that worker's MRP of $15. Workers one through five add more MRP than their cost, and workers seven through nine add less. The sixth worker adds just enough revenue to justify hiring him or her.

A firm will hire a variable resource up the point at which the marginal revenue product of the last unit hired is just equal to its price. Glancing at Table 1 again, we can see that hiring seven workers would gain MRP of only $5, which would be less than the wage cost. The optimum number of workers to be added is six.

Demand Curve for Resources

Graphs of the data in Table 1 will help us visualize the relationships between total quantities and marginal quantities. Figure 1 shows what happens to total product and marginal product when more workers are hired. From zero to seven workers total product rises, but by smaller quantities for each additional worker. Total product levels off at eight workers and declines when more than that number are hired. The marginal product for each worker, shown by the lower line in Figure 1, declines throughout. If more than eight workers are hired, marginal product becomes negative.

Table 1 **Hypothetical Production Data for the Use of Labor Resources in Perfect Competition**

(1) Quantity of labor Q_L	(2) Total product TP	(3) Marginal product MP	(4) Product price P_P	(5) Total revenue TR	(6) Marginal revenue product MRP	(7) Price of labor P_L
		10			$50	
1	10		$5	$50		$15
		9			45	
2	19		5	95		15
		8			40	
3	27		5	135		15
		6			30	
4	33		5	165		15
		5			25	
5	38		5	190		15
		3			15	
6	41		5	205		15
		1			5	
7	42		5	210		15
		0			0	
8	42		5	210		15
		−2			−10	
9	40		5	200		15

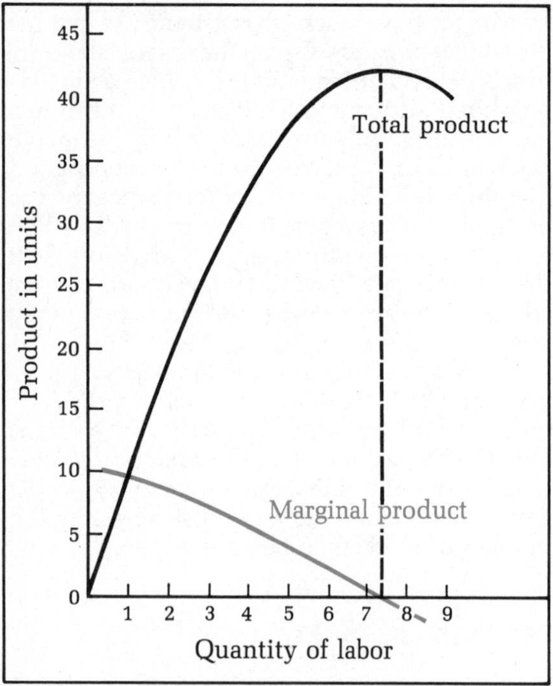

Figure 1 Production from the use of variable quantities of labor with a fixed quantity of other resources.

Figure 2 is a similar graph for total revenue and marginal revenue product. As additional workers are hired, total revenue rises, reaches a peak, and then starts to decline. MRP declines continually. The curves in Figure 2 have exactly the same shape as those in Figure 1, since they are based on the same quantities of output multiplied by the constant price for which the product sells ($5).

Figure 3 shows the MRP curve alone. We have drawn MRP separately to show that the MRP curve for a resource is the same as the firm's demand curve for this resource. The horizontal line at $15 represents the price of labor. At that price the firm will hire six workers. To hire fewer than six would sacrifice greater revenue than the cost of additional labor. To hire more than six would add more to costs than the firm would receive in additional revenue.

If the wage rate rises to $25, the firm moves back up its MRP curve and hires only five workers. The value of the fifth worker's MRP is just enough to offset the higher wage rate. If the wage rate falls to $5, the firm moves down its MRP curve and hires seven workers. At every wage rate, the firm hires workers until MRP is equal to the wage rate.

We have been discussing the firm's demand for labor. But of course there are other variable resources; materials, fuel, and power are examples. Exactly the same analysis applies to each of them. Each resource contributes its output and thus helps increase the firm's total revenue. Each resource has its MRP curve, which is the same as the firm's demand curve for that resource.

MARKET DEMAND FOR RESOURCES

No resource is used by just one firm. The market demand for any resource is the sum of the demands of all the firms using it. The bicycle company hires workers for its assembly line. So do other bicycle companies. Supermarkets, department stores, and the post office also hire workers in resource markets. The demand for workers of a particular kind will be the sum of the demands of all the firms employing them.

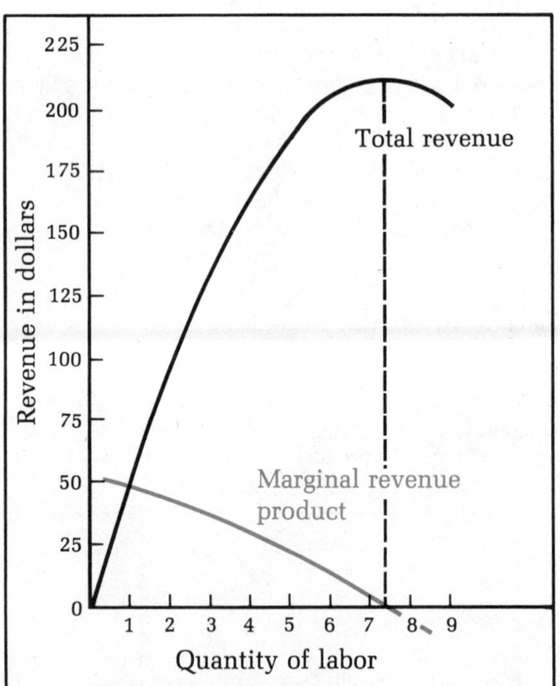

Figure 2 Revenue from the sale of output when variable quantities of labor are hired. Price of product = $5.

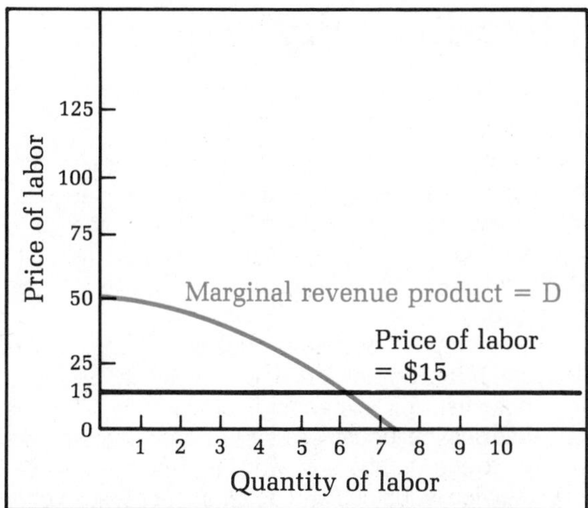

Figure 3 Demand for labor. A firm compares labor's marginal revenue product with its price and hires the quantity of labor at which MRP = P. At a labor price of $15, the firm will hire six workers.

Determinants of Demand

We have shown that demand for any resource reflects its contribution to output. In economic terminology a resource's contribution to revenue is its marginal revenue product:

$$\frac{\text{the change in total revenue}}{\text{the change in quantity of resource}}.$$

In perfect competition, the change in total revenue is determined by the marginal product of the resource and the price of output. This means that resource demand depends on resource productivity and consumer demand for output.

In a dynamic economy like ours, demand for a resource is never constant. It changes over time, depending on changes in productivity and in consumer markets. The more productive a resource becomes, the greater will be the demand for it. The greater consumer demand becomes, the greater will be the demand for resources used in production. In addition, the demand for any resource is affected by changes in the availability and prices of other resources. Let's look at these three determinants in more detail.

Resource productivity. The more productive a resource is, the greater will be the demand for it and the higher will be its price. Its productivity often depends on its quality and on the quantity of other resources used with it.

Workers in advanced industrial countries are more productive than workers elsewhere. They benefit from an educational system that stresses science and vocational training. Some nations, like Sweden, Germany, Japan, and the United States, reward individual achievement by providing achievers the opportunity to enjoy higher standards of living. Attitudes toward work are important too. People in the industrial countries believe that work is a good thing; they agree to sacrifice leisure in the present so as to enjoy higher income in the future.

Workers in the industrialized countries are fortunate also in the rich supplies of resources other than labor for use in production. The advantages of fertile land, minerals, water power, and specialized capital equipment help them be more productive. Even in nations like Japan, which much import most of its raw materials, the people have used initiative and entrepreneurial ability to develop highly productive economies. Human creativity is important for raising a country's productivity; it leads to better products and processes so that greater output can be obtained from a limited quantity of material resources.

In many nonindustrial cultures, productivity is much lower because the conditions mentioned above are lacking. Many people manage only to survive from one day to the next or from one year to another. They lack capital equipment and other resources. Few are able to get the kind of training that is available in industrialized countries. The economic conditions of masses of people are not much different from those of their ancestors hundreds of years ago.

Consumer demand. Because demand for resources is a derived demand, it depends on conditions in markets for consumer goods. When consumer incomes are rising, demand for many goods and services is likely to rise too. As firms are able to sell more goods, they are encouraged to hire more resources and to increase production. Thus the demand curve for a resource is likely to shift to the right over the course of time. The result is greater employment and sometimes higher pay as well.

Time doesn't always bring higher demand for a particular resource. Sometimes the demand curve for a resource may shift to the left.

Extended Example Trends in Productivity

The *quantity* of a nation's resources is limited by nature and by the ability to increase capital stock. Growth in output depends largely on improvements in *quality*. Improved quality enables a single unit of a resource to produce greater output. We say there has been a gain in *productivity*. In the United States productivity increased by an average of 3.2 percent yearly from 1950 to 1968. Since then, output per worker hour has grown only 1.4 percent on the average each year.

Productivity gains shift marginal revenue product curves to the right and increase equilibrium prices of resources. Higher resource prices mean higher incomes for American households. Moreover, when productivity increases, the gains in spendable earnings are *real* gains. Higher productivity means more goods and services without inflationary pressures. *Real* incomes increase along with *money* incomes.

During the 1970s, the United States experienced a reversal in the trend toward higher productivity. If the lower trend continues, we will have to adjust our lifestyles to a stationary or declining economy in the future. What are the reasons for the change?

Advances in learning are the fundamental source of productivity growth. Regrettably, the massive advances in technological knowledge of the post-war period may have been only a brief spurt in the long sweep of history. Furthermore, the major gains from extending basic education to all levels of the work force may already be behind us. Similarly, the gains from shifting large numbers of agricultural workers into manufacturing industries are not expected to be repeated.

The composition of U.S. industry is changing, too. The emphasis on service employment has reduced the potential for expanding productivity. This is because service industries use less capital equipment relative to the numbers of workers employed. Moreover, service industries and government services offer fewer opportunities for research and development of cost-saving technologies.

One basis for increasing productivity involves improvements in the way resources are combined for work. What are the potential advantages and limitations of combining resources in new ways?

Show how increases in productivity affect the nation's production-possibilities curve. How is the greater output distributed among households?

Service industries (such as health care, education, and travel agencies) have experienced lower gains in productivity than manufacturing. Can you suggest ways in which service jobs can be made more productive?

This may happen because the resource becomes less productive than other resources. Or it may be the result of a decline in consumer demand for the finished product. This can be a serious problem in a resort town, for instance, where the fading popularity of a certain tourist attraction leaves local workers without a livelihood. An oil spill on a beach may bring unemployment to workers in hotels and restaurants. Or the claim that eggs contain harmful amounts of cholesterol may reduce the derived demand for resources in the dairy and poultry industry. Perhaps you can name other resources that have been displaced by declines in consumer demand.

Prices of other resources. When we studied demand for goods, we found that demand for one good might be strongly influenced by a change in the price of some other good. For instance, an increase in the price of beef may cause consumers to eat more pork. Or an increase in the cost of vacations may cause a fall in the demand for beachwear. A similar relationship holds among resources: the demand for one resource is often related to the price of another.

The best-known relationship is that between the price of labor and the demand for labor-saving machinery. The mechanization and automation of U.S. industry over the past century were in part a result of the high cost of labor. In railroading, labor had been used to fire the coal boilers that produced the steam to run the locomotives. When wages rose among railroad workers, railroads switched from steam power to electric or diesel-electric. The result was a decrease in demand for locomotive firemen. For years the railway unions sought desperately to hold back this decline in demand for labor. In the same way, the development of television and, more recently, the popularity of discos reduced demand for live entertainers. These resources are substitutes; an increase in the price of one will increase demand for its substitute.

Not all resources are substitutes. Quite often they are complementary; that is, they must be used together. If the price of electricity rises, demand for electrical equipment will probably fall. On the other hand, if some new technical process reduces the price of steel, this might increase the demand for auto assembly-line workers. Can you see why?

Elasticity of Demand for Resources

The demand curve for a resource may slope downward very gradually or very steeply. The shape of the curve reflects the elasticity of demand for the resource. When demand is very elastic, a change in the price of the resource will have a more than proportionate effect on the quantity purchased. An increase in teenagers' wage rates, for example, would probably reduce their employment greatly. In contrast, consider the demand for skilled machinists who assemble bicycle transmissions. If the wages of such workers were to double, bicycle factories would still continue to employ them. In economists' language, demand for teenage workers is elastic and demand for machinists is inelastic.

Elasticity of demand for a resource differs just as it does among consumer goods. For resources there are four basic factors affecting elasticity of demand: (1) the rate of decline in the marginal revenue product; (2) substitutability among resources; (3) elasticity of demand for final product; and (4) percentage of total costs used for hiring the resource.

MRP rate of decline. If marginal productivity of a resource falls rapidly, demand will be inelastic. This can be seen from Figure 3, showing the demand curve for labor based on its marginal revenue product. The less rapidly the marginal revenue product falls, the more the demand curve will approach the horizontal and the more elastic will be the demand for the resource. Employers will hire substantially more workers if wage rates fall.

Substitutability. A second basis for a resource's elasticity of demand is the ease with which other resources can be substituted for it. A farmer may work a field with two laborers and two machines, five laborers and one machine, or ten laborers without a machine. Demand for workers or machines will depend on their prices. If the price of farm labor rises, farmers will switch to machines; if the price of machines rises, they will switch back to workers. Thus the demand for both labor and machinery is relatively elastic in this case. On the other hand, if resources must be used in fairly rigid proportions, a change in their prices will bring no significant change in employment. Some machine tools must be operated with a constant quantity of labor. Trucks and airplanes require crews of specific sizes. In these employments, technical factors limit substitutability and keep labor demand curves inelastic.

Final-product demand elasticity. A third basis for the elasticity of resource demand is elasticity of demand for the final product. If an increase in the price of the product causes a sharp drop in sales, this will be reflected in the demand for resources to make that product. The demand for many consumer durables is relatively price elastic; this is because purchases of durable goods may often be postponed until the price is right. As a result, rising prices may cause severe cutbacks in production and throw many factory workers out of work.

Percentage costs. A fourth determinant of elasticity of demand for a resource is the proportion of total costs accounted for by that resource. If labor is only a small part of total costs, a wage increase will have less effect on production costs than if labor accounts for a large part of total costs. Suppose two firms each have to pay a wage increase of 5 percent. In one firm labor costs amount to only 10 percent of total costs, but in the other labor costs amount to 80 percent. The costs of one firm will increase by $.05 \times .10$, or by only ½ percent, while those of the other will increase by $.05 \times .80$, or 4 percent. Resource demand will be more elastic for the firm whose costs are affected more strongly by changes in resource prices.

Demand Under Imperfect Competition

We began by examining demand for resources in perfect competition. In perfectly competitive

Table 2 **Hypothetical Production Data for the Use of Labor Resources in a Firm Under Imperfect Competition**

(1) Quantity of labor Q_L	(2) Total product TP	(3) Marginal product MP	(4) Product price P_P	(5) Total revenue TR	(6) Marginal revenue product MRP	(7) Price of labor P_L
1	10	10	$10	$100	$100	$15
2	19	9	9	171	71	15
3	27	8	8	216	45	15
4	33	6	7	231	15	15
5	38	5	6	228	−3	15
6	41	3	5	205	−23	15
7	42	1	4	168	−37	15
8	42	0	3	126	−42	15
9	40	−2	2	80	−46	15

markets, sellers have no influence over price. Price is uniform throughout the market and for any quantity sold by an individual firm.

Actual markets, as we know, are likely to be less than perfectly competitive. In the chapter on monopoly we saw that when one firm controls the output of an industry, its demand curve is the demand curve for the entire industry. The firm can sell a small output at a high price or a larger output at a lower price. If the monopoly firm wants to increase its sales, it must reduce its price. This is true for all firms in imperfect competition.

The declining product-demand curve under monopoly and imperfect competition has important consequences for the firm's resource

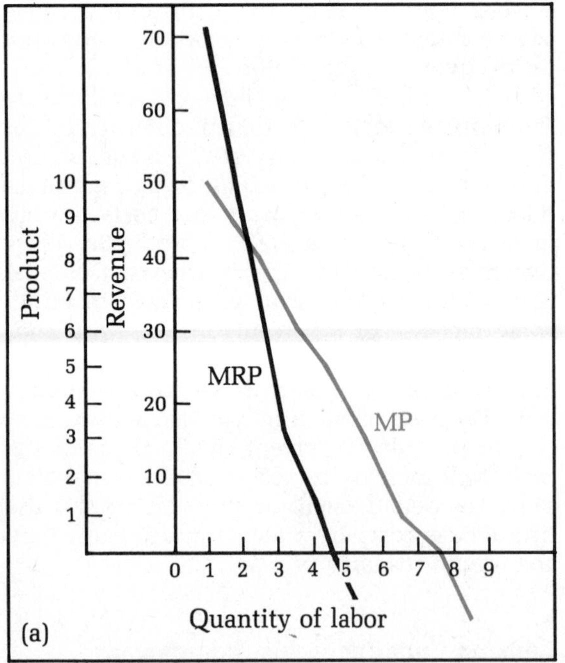

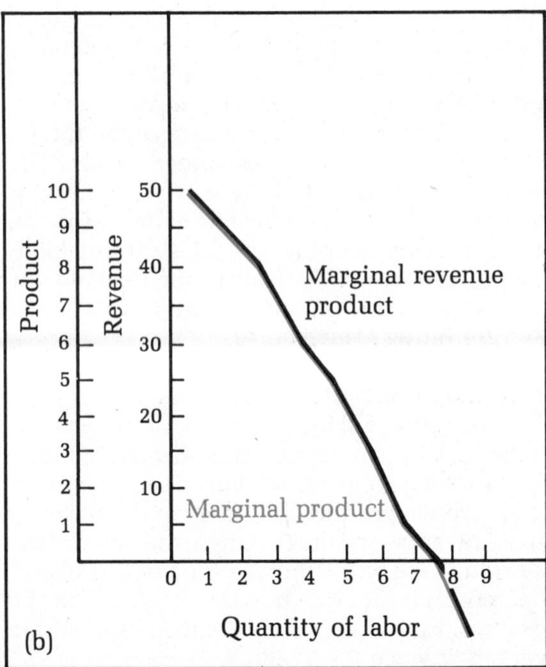

Figure 4 Comparing marginal product (MP) and marginal revenue product (MRP) for: (a) a monopoly firm; (b) a competitive firm. In (a), MRP declines more rapidly than MP because price must be reduced to sell more output. In (b), MP and MRP coincide.

demand curve. When we calculate the marginal revenue product, we can't use the same price for additional units of output as we did for the firm in perfect competition. We must use a declining range of prices for calculating MRP.

Table 2 shows data for a firm in imperfect competition. It is almost the same as Table 1, except that product price in column (4) decreases with greater output. Ten units of output can be sold for a price of $10 each. But if the firm is to sell nineteen units, it must reduce price to $9. Total revenue at different prices is shown in column (5). Changes in total revenue give us the marginal revenue product, shown in column (6).

If we compare the MRP schedule for the firm under imperfect competition with that for the perfectly competitive firm in Table 1, we find that the imperfectly competitive MRP curve falls more steeply. This is because of the downward sloping product-demand curve under imperfect competition. Figure 4 shows the difference graphically. The competitive firm's MRP curve is shown in Figure 4b. MRP is parallel to MP because product price is constant. Figure 4a presents the same MP curve for a firm under imperfect competition. But this firm's MRP curve declines more rapidly, because larger outputs can be sold only if price is reduced. Thus under imperfect competition the demand for resources is relatively inelastic.

HIRING RESOURCES FOR MAXIMUM PROFIT

A firm can continue to hire variable resources up to the point at which the MRP of the last unit hired is just equal to its cost. In this way the firm maximizes economic profit from the use of a single variable resource.

The hope of making a profit drives the firm to hire resources. A firm that wants to maximize profit will hire variable resources on the basis of marginal revenue product (MRP). The procedure it will follow is illustrated in Table 3, which is drawn from the data in Table 1. This time we have added column (8), showing total labor cost (VC), and column (9), giving the cost of the firm's fixed resources (FC). (Remember, VC stands for variable cost, and in our example labor is the variable resource and the variable cost). Column (10) is total resource cost (TC), equal to the sum of columns (8) and (9): TC = FC

Economic Thinkers
Frank and Lillian Gilbreth

Good things come in pairs—and sometimes even in dozens!

It was a pair of industrial engineers around the turn of the century who pioneered in the development of techniques for increasing the productivity of labor. Frank and Lillian Gilbreth used scientific methods to analyze and improve work processes. They were the first "efficiency experts." The Gilbreths were marriage partners as well as professional partners. They produced twelve children, and their unusual family life was the subject of their son's book, *Cheaper by the Dozen*.

The Gilbreths called their industrial experiments Time and Motion studies. They saw that most industrial jobs could be performed in numerous ways. But, according to Frank, there was always "one best way." Scientific methods could be used to discover that one best way, the way most conserving of time and motion. Scientifically designed work methods could help workers produce more than they could through individual ingenuity alone.

The studies began simply. Small lights were attached to the hands of a worker performing a single task. The operation was photographed by a still camera with an open shutter. The resulting picture would show a series of dots reflecting the speed and direction of hand movements. Then, the analysts could study the picture for clues for improving the procedure and for training new operators to perform the job better.

After years of studying work, the Gilbreths developed a list of seventeen basic hand movements that are common to all human activity. They named the seventeen classifications "therbligs"—Gilbreth spelled backwards (roughly). Therbligs provided a framework for classifying and improving work procedures. Some of the classifications are pinch grasp, wrap grasp, and hold.

Each work activity was broken down into tiny units, or therbligs, and the series of actions recorded on a chart. Often the chart was divided into two columns and the actions of both hands recorded as they worked together. The chart helped define and explain job requirements clearly and consistently.

The Gilbreths' objective was not to have workers work harder or faster, but to reduce wasted motion so that workers would produce more units of output per

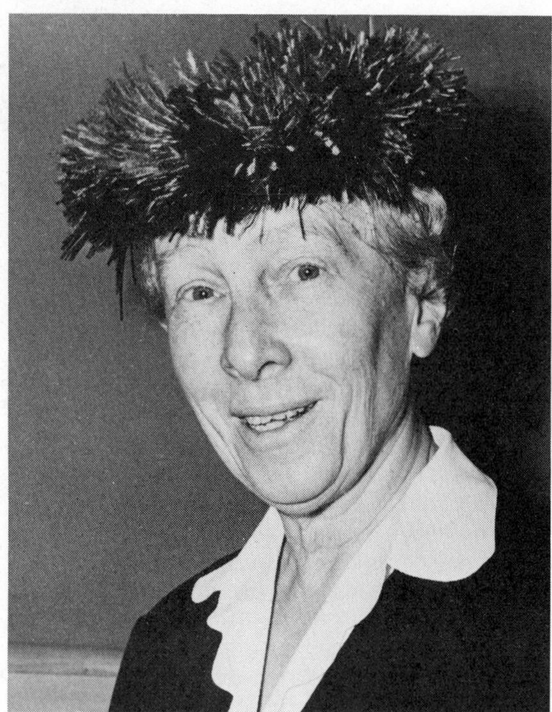

time period. Their experiments were especially useful in routine procedures where a large volume of units must be processed. The original studies were done in bricklaying, but the techniques soon spread to iron and steel, shoe manufacture, book binding and printing, and office work. Workers were shown how to place materials conveniently to minimize wasted motion. The order and arrangement of motions were simplified so that often the quantity of output increased by as much as four times.

Many workers reacted favorably to the new procedures. They developed a healthy pride in their productive ability and often contributed suggestions from their own experience for further gains in productivity.

Industrial engineers continue to work toward improving the applications of technology to industrial jobs. Every gain in productivity reduces costs of production and moves production-possibilities curves to the right. The result is lower prices for the consumer and larger output from the nation's scarce resources.

+ VC. Finally, the firm's economic profit is shown in column (11) as the difference between total revenue and total resource cost: economic profit = TR − TC.

The highest level of employment consistent with maximum economic profit occurs with six units of the variable resource. Total revenue at this point is $205. Total resource costs are $180. Economic profit is $205 − $180 = $25. The cost of hiring the sixth unit of labor is $15 (since labor costs are $15 per unit), and the MRP of the sixth unit is $15 (obtained by subtracting total revenue of $190 from total revenue of $205). If a seventh unit of labor were added, its MRP would be only $5, and the firm's economic profit would fall to $15. The optimum level of employment is that at which six units of labor have been hired.

The profit-maximizing quantity of labor is shown graphically in Figure 5a. As more units of labor are hired at $15 each, total variable cost rises along the straight line from the origin. The total resource cost curve (TC) is parallel to the variable cost curve (VC) but higher because of fixed costs of $90 at every level of employment. Total revenue (TR) rises by varying amounts, depending on total product price. The TR curve reaches a peak when seven units of labor have been hired, levels off, and then declines as total product and product price fall. The firm's economic profit is the difference between the TR curve and the TC curve at every level of employment. The difference is shown separately in Figure 5b. Economic profit is negative at low levels of employment, becomes positive over a middle range, peaks over the range of five to six units of

Table 3 **Profit for the Competitive Firm**

(1) Q_L	(5) TR	(8) Labor cost VC	(9) Fixed cost FC	(10) Total cost TC	(11) Profit TR − TC
1	50	$15	$90	$105	−55
2	95	30	90	120	−25
3	135	45	90	135	0
4	165	60	90	150	15
5	190	75	90	165	25*
6	205	90	90	180	25*
7	210	105	90	95	15
8	210	120	90	210	0
9	200	135	90	225	25

*The two maximum profit points arise from the use of whole units of labor. Most resources can be used in fractions; even a single worker can be hired for part of a day. The unique profit-maximizing point for this firm would occur with 5½ workers, and profit would be slightly greater than $25.

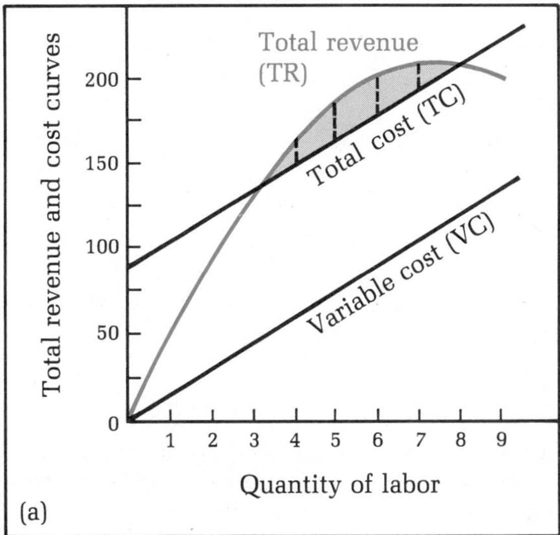

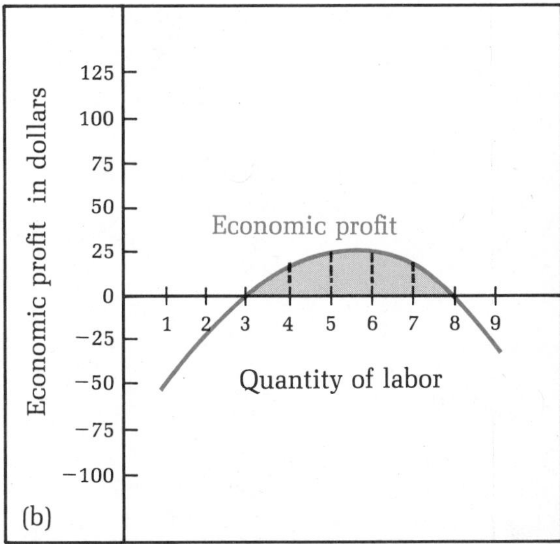

Figure 5 (a) Comparing the total revenue and total cost curves shows economic profit or loss. Economic profit at every level of employment is the vertical distance between the two curves. Positive economic profit is shown in the shaded area; the longer the broken line in the shaded area, the greater the amount of profit. (b) Only economic profit is shown. Normal profit is included in total cost.

labor, and then declines. If the firm wants to maximize its profit, it will choose to employ between five and six units of labor.

Hiring More Than One Variable Resource

The real-world decision is a little more complicated, of course, because production generally involves the use of several variable resources. The firm must select the proper combination of resources for lowest-cost production. The optimum resource combination will be the one at which the firm produces the desired quantity of output at the lowest resource cost.

A farmer, for example, may use a number of resources in various combinations. The farmer may combine labor, machinery, land, and fertilizer in different proportions to achieve the same quantity of output. The pròportion used of each resource depends on its contribution to total revenue together with its price. The farmer begins by hiring the resource that produces the greatest output per dollar of cost. A hay reaper and binder may do the work of hundreds of hours of labor but may cost thousands of dollars. The farmer has to figure the addition each resource makes to total revenue relative to its price.

The numerical comparisons are shown in Table 4. P_L is the price of one unit of labor while P_K is the price of one unit of capital. Suppose the marginal revenue product of labor (MRP_L) is equal to \$50—that is, one unit of labor adds \$50 to total revenue in a given time period. If it costs the farmer \$15 to hire one unit of labor (P_L = \$15), then the contribution of labor per dollar is 50/15 or \$3.33, as shown in column (4). In the same way, if one unit of capital equipment adds \$100 to total production (MRP_K = 100) and costs \$40 per time period, its contribution per dollar is 100/40 or \$2.50, as shown in column (7).

In this example labor is a more productive resource than capital: its marginal revenue product per dollar is \$3.33 compared to only \$2.50 for capital. This farmer would want to hire more labor. As a general principle, we can say that *as long as one resource produces more revenue per dollar than other resources, more of it should be hired.* If labor adds more to total revenue per dollar spent than machines do, the farmer should hire more labor and fewer machines. If a dollar spent on machines adds more to total revenue than a dollar spent on labor, the farmer should use more machines. The farmer will continue to adjust employment of variable resources until the marginal revenue product per dollar of every resource is the same. Only at that point can there be no further gain from changing the combination of resources used. The last dollar spent on every resource should add an equal amount to the value of total product.

Table 4 **Hypothetical Data for Labor and Capital Productivity**

(1) Quantity of resource	(2) MRP_L	(3) P_L	(4) $\frac{MRP_L}{P_L}$	(5) MRP_K	(6) P_K	(7) $\frac{MRP_K}{P_K}$
1	50	15	3.33	100	40	2.5
2	40	15	2.67	80	40	2.0
3	30	15	2.00	60	40	1.5
4	25	15	1.67	40	40	1.0
5	20	15	1.33	30	40	0.75
6	15	15	1.00	20	40	0.5

Suppose the farmer were employing four units of labor and one unit of machinery. Looking again at Table 4, we see that the marginal revenue product per dollar for four units of labor is $MRP_L/P_L = 1.67$, while the marginal revenue product per dollar of one unit of machinery is $MRP_K/P_K = 2.50$. Clearly this is not the optimum combination of resources. If the farmer spends one dollar less on labor and one dollar more on machinery, the loss in output from the marginal dollar's worth of labor is $1.67 but the gain in output from the additional dollar's worth of capital is $2.50. It will pay to keep shifting dollars from labor to capital until $MRP_L/P_L = MRP_K/P_K$.

This result can be generalized to include all productive resources. Resources should be employed in proportions such that

$$MRP_A/P_A = MRP_B/P_B = \ldots = MRP_Z/P_Z,$$

where A is the first resource, B the second resource, and so on through resource Z (if required). This rule may be called the **equal marginal productivity principle.** In our example with the farmer, there are only two resources: Resource A is labor (L),and resource B is capital (K).

In Table 4, if the farmer reduces employment of labor from four units to three and increases employment of machinery from one unit to two, the result is the optimum combination of resources for that level of output. At three units of labor and two of machinery, the last dollar spent on each resource adds the same amount to total product. Satisfying the equal marginal productivity principle ensures that there is no way the farmer can gain by shifting expenditure from one resource to the other. At the optimum combination of resources, the farmer's output is produced at minimum cost.

But we should not stop here. Remember that a firm maximizes profit by employing resources up to the point at which the MRP of each resource is equal to its price. The farmer in our example has not yet reached that point. Every dollar spent on both resources is returning two dollars of MRP. The farmer can afford to keep on expanding employment up to the point where six units of labor have been hired and four units of machinery. At that point, a dollar spent on labor will add a dollar's worth of output, and a dollar spent on machinery will also add a dollar's worth of output. Thus, $MRP_L = P_L$ and $MRP_K = P_K$ and

$$\frac{MRP_L}{P_L} = \ldots = \frac{MRP_K}{P_K} = 1.$$

When this second condition is satisfied, (1) the farmer is using the least-cost combination of resources and (2) is realizing a maximum economic profit from the use of all resources.

RESOURCE SUPPLY

We have seen how the independent decisions of business firms determine market demand for a resource. A firm employs every resource up to the point where its MRP is equal to its price.

What Determines the Equilibrium Price of Resources?

As in other markets, resource prices are determined by the interaction of supply and demand. The market for a resource reaches equilibrium where quantity demanded is equal to quantity supplied. The individual business firm then becomes a price taker. For a firm in perfect competition resource supply becomes horizontal at the market price. The competitive firm can hire any quantity at that price, but the firm alone is too small to affect market price. Later we will show how resource supply is different when resource markets are not perfectly competitive.

A low market price for a resource is often the result of a bountiful supply and a high price the result of a more limited supply. In our economy there is often an overabundance of particular resources. The most obvious examples are unskilled labor, which is usually in excess supply, and even skilled labor of types that are no longer needed. Certain kinds of capital are sometimes overabundant too: office space or apartments in undesirable locations or obsolete factory equipment that is still usable. An overabundance of resources relative to demand keeps their market supply curves far to the right, as shown in Figure 6a, holding price down.

An interesting example of shifting resource supply is in the market for teachers. Several generations ago, elementary and high-school teaching was considered a woman's job. In many communities, in fact, it was the only acceptable employment for women. The steady flow of women who were widowed, divorced, or helping support their families kept supplies abundant and salaries low. All this changed in the period after World War II. Women began to find other employment opportunities that were as challenging as the teaching profession. Supply curves for teachers shifted to the left in some cities and more slowly to the right in others. At the same time, the demand for teachers was increasing with the postwar baby boom and with adults attending school for more years. Many teachers formed unions and pushed for higher pay scales. Eventually, better pay made teaching an attractive career for both men and women, and supply began to increase. The field seemed to be heading toward a high-employment, high-salary equilibrium.

Unfortunately for would-be teachers, derived demand began to shrink at the very time that more people were entering the profession. By the 1960s the birthrate had begun to fall, and by the 1970s there were empty classrooms in many elementary schools. Today many teachers have lost their jobs. Some cannot find teaching jobs and are retraining for new professions.

While teachers are overabundant, some other skills are in short supply. Labor-market forecasts for the 1980s suggest that there will be shortages of accountants, engineers, social workers, and health-care personnel. People having these skills may find that resource prices are high in those fields. Other scarce resources include capital equipment needed for energy development and for meeting environmental standards in production. Figure 6b illustrates price determination when resource supplies are low relative to demand.

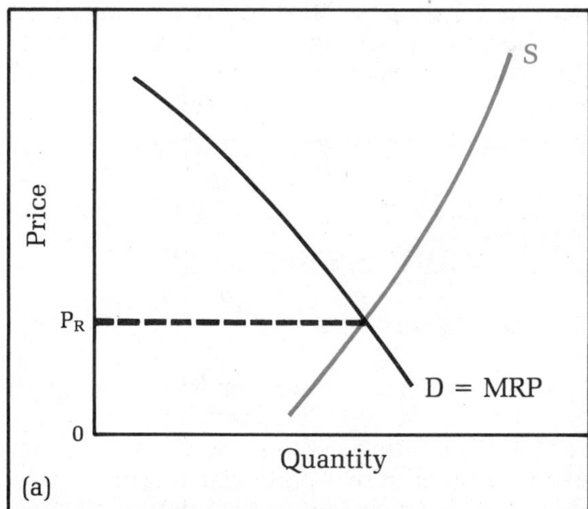

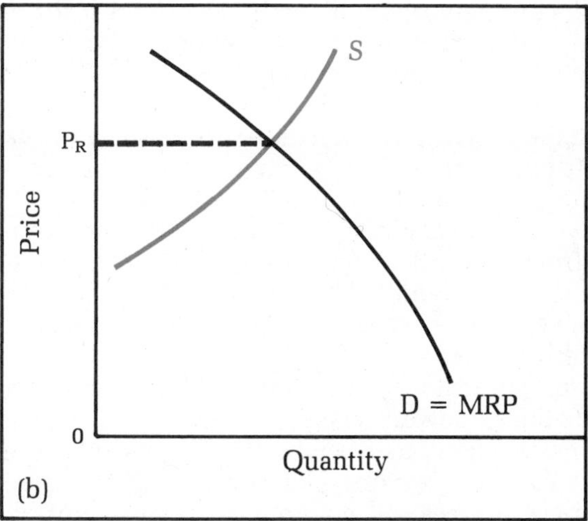

Figure 6 (a) When a resource is abundant, its supply curve is far to the right and equilibrium price is low. (b) When a resource is scarce, its supply curve lies to the left and equilibrium price is high.

Government Subsidies for Resource Development

As our population grows and as we demand more and better goods and services, we must ensure that our supply of productive resources grows also. The federal and state governments have tried to encourage development of new resources in order to prevent bottlenecks and hold down costs of production. Government aid to producers often takes the form of *subsidies.* These subsidies can be grouped together as contributions to factors of production, especially land, labor, and capital.

Subsidies to land resources. Agricultural scientists provide information to farmers, helping them use land more efficiently. Governments provide low-cost loans for irrigation and land reclamation. Emergency aid is available in the event of weather disasters, such as droughts or heavy frosts.

Subsidies to labor resources. Government also underwrites training programs for labor in several ways. It subsidizes vocational training. It gives tax credits to private employers who provide on-the-job training. Laws that prohibit discrimination in hiring on the basis of race or sex also help enlarge the labor supply.

Subsidies to capital resources. A number of government tax and spending programs are aimed at increasing the supply of capital. Corporations are allowed credits on their income taxes when they invest in new plant and equipment. Government agencies make low-interest loans in certain sectors of the economy: the Small Business Administration, the Federal National Mortgage Association, the Government National Mortgage Association, the Farmers Home Administration, Banks for Cooperatives, Federal Land Banks, and others.

Some federal funds go directly into construction of plant and equipment. When Congress appropriates money for research and development, it is spending money to create new capital. Other capital investments by government include construction of docks and port facilities, power generation plants, and transmission equipment. Education loans (like the well-named National Defense Education Loans) are examples of government investment in human capital.

In 1980 Congress was considering President Carter's proposal to appropriate billions of dollars for joint public and private development of new energy resources. The President hoped that activities such as these would help shift resource supply curves to the right, thus reducing resource costs and holding down the prices of final products.

Taxes to Discourage Resource Use

Governments may sometimes take steps to reduce resource use. One way is to tax resources, thus making their employment more costly.

The effort to stop water pollution is an example. Many local governments now impose a tax on firms that discharge industrial wastes into rivers and streams. Or they require the offending firms to install corrective equipment. The effect is to shift water supply curves backward to the left, adding the cost of water purification to a firm's total production costs.

The energy crisis of the 1970s provides another example of a government policy directed at reducing the use of a resource. The growing dependence on imported oil was seen as a threat to the long-range security of the United States. In order to discourage the use of foreign oil and to encourage domestic producers to expand their output, President Ford imposed a tax on each barrel of imported oil. The effect was to raise production costs in industries using petroleum products. Unfortunately, because the demand for oil is relatively inelastic and the tax was small, the tax had no appreciable effect on oil consumption in the short run. In 1980, President Carter proposed further taxes on imported oil. The object of this proposed tax was, in part, to increase the costs of gasoline by at least $.10 per gallon and thereby cut gasoline consumption.

EARNINGS OF RESOURCE SUPPLIERS

Determining Incomes

We have seen that the demand for productive resources is derived demand. A firm hires resources according to their contribution to total revenue. It will hire a particular resource up to the point at which the contribution of the last unit is equal to its price. The price of the resource, in turn, is determined by demand and supply in the resource market. The chain of events is summarized in Figure 7.

All suppliers of resources—land, labor, capital, and entrepreneurship—receive incomes that depend on equilibrium price in their respective markets. The incomes of all resources add up to the total national income. The share of total national income received by each resource supplier depends on (1) the productivity of the resource, (2) the price of the final product, and (3) the price of the resource as determined in the resource market. This is how a competitive economy answers the third fundamental economic question: *For whom is output to be produced?*

Consider Figure 7. At the market equilibrium price of P_M the firm hires the quantity of resource for which MRP = P_M. The firm's total resource cost is shown on Figure 7b as the rectangle with sides $0P_M$ and $0Q_F$. That is the price of the resource multiplied by the number of units hired. Figure 7a shows total market demand for the resource in question, and the rectangle ($0P_M \times 0Q_T$) shows total income received by this particular resource.

We know that if the incomes of all resources are added together, they must equal total national income. Each resource will be paid according to its contribution to total production. This is easy to see if we suppose that only two kinds of resources are employed. Figure 8 allows us to compare income shares for two kinds of resources: labor and capital. Demand for each resource reflects its marginal revenue product. Total income is the sum of the two rectangles: income to labor = $0P_L \times 0Q_L$ and income to capital = $0P_K \times 0Q_K$. But we know that the value of total output must be equal to the entire shaded area under each curve. How do we explain the difference between the rectangle and the whole shaded area under each curve?

Look at Figure 8a. Total product is equal to the entire shaded area. Of this total, the income paid to labor is represented by the rectangle. What is left over goes to the owners of capital. Now look at Figure 8b. Total product is again equal to the entire shaded area. Of this total, the income paid to owners of capital is represented by the rectangle. What is left over goes to labor. Thus each resource is paid according to its MRP, and the total payments add up to the value of the total product.

This is significant because it contradicts Marx's labor theory of value: Income shares are paid to all resources according to their contribution to output. It shows that a perfectly competitive market system distributes income according to productivity. Resource owners are encouraged to cooperate to produce the nation's economic "pie." Then they are rewarded by slices equal in value to their marginal product. The implication of this idea is clear: if you don't like the size of your slice (i.e., your income), you should seek a different type of job.

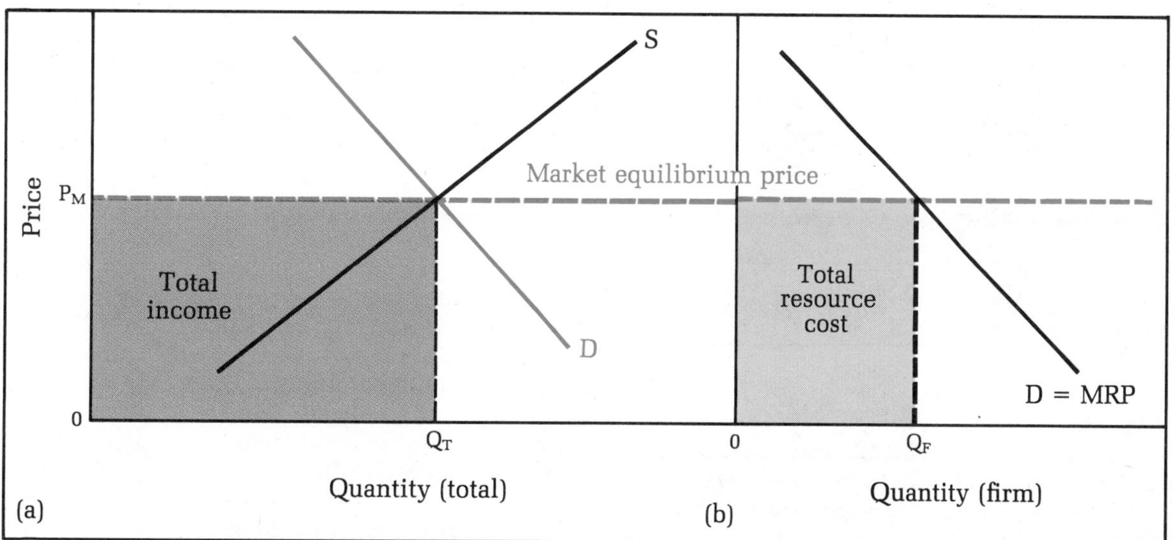

Figure 7 (a) The market for a resource. (b) A firm's demand for the resource. A profit-maximizing firm compares the market equilibrium price of the resource in (a) with the resource's MRP. Then it selects the quantity of resource, in (b), for which P_M = MRP.

Marginal Revenue Productivity and Incomes

The relative shares of resources do not remain fixed. They vary from time to time or from place to place, depending on resource productivity and on the value of final product. Highly productive workers who have the advantages of specialized training or better equipment are likely to get a larger share of total output. This doesn't mean that they work harder or are better citizens; it means only that they have a higher MRP.

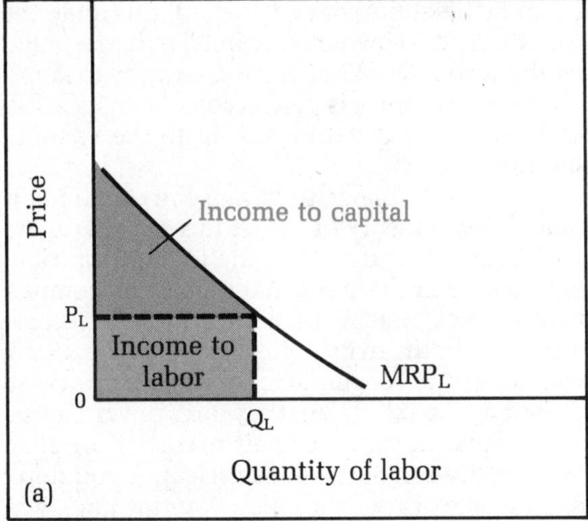

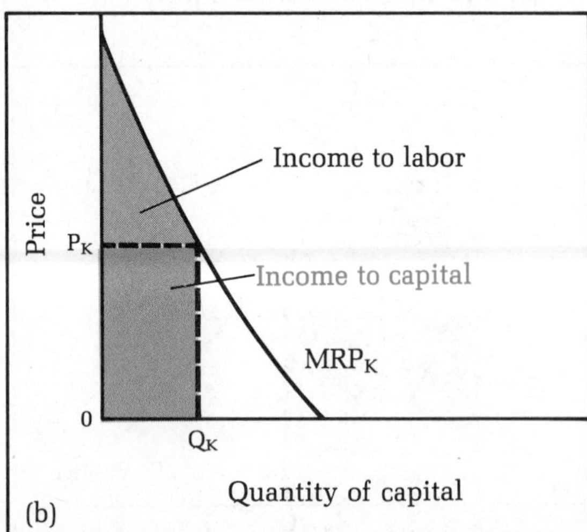

Figure 8 A firm's MRP curve for: (a) labor, and (b) capital. Total product is the entire shaded area in each graph. Since each resource is paid the value of its marginal product, total product is distributed according to each resource's contribution to output.

But workers may also have a higher MRP if the price of their finished product is high relative to other products. Some popular musicians have a higher MRP than others mainly because consumers are apparently willing to spend more for their recordings than for others'. Other high-priced items that earn high incomes for their producers are health care, electronic equipment, and legal services.

Many workers are aware of this, and their unions or professional associations devote much effort to keeping the prices of their products high by excluding low-priced competition. Labor unions have been among the strongest supporters of trade barriers against foreign manufacturers. Likewise, many resource owners in North Carolina, who depend for their incomes on high consumer demand for tobacco, are less than enthusiastic about advertising the harmful effects of smoking on people's health.

Changes in Resource Prices over Time

How high a price can the owner of a resource charge? Of course, it depends partly on the MRP of the resource. But other factors also affect resource price. In the long run, prices of resources depend on the ease with which other resources can be substituted for them. Another way of saying this is that the behavior of resource prices over time depends on long-run elasticity of demand and supply.

When a resource is essential to an operation, it must be purchased regardless of price. The result is relatively inelastic demand: A change in the price of the resource will have little effect on the quantity purchased. But if a resource has many substitutes, quantity demanded will vary widely with a change in price; demand will be relatively elastic.

When resource demand is inelastic in the short run, price may fluctuate widely. A temporary shortage means that buying firms must bid vigorously, pushing the price up. On the other hand, an abundant supply will not lead to greater employment in the short run, and price will fall. Certain metals are essential in producing alloys for the manufacture of stainless steel. When supplies are interrupted for any reason, their prices may rise sharply. Certain specialized labor skills are essential in some manufacturing processes and can command high prices. In both cases, a sudden increase in supply may cause price to fall but will bring no substantial increase in employment.

Demand may be inelastic in the short run, but in the long run firms can develop substitutes, and demand becomes more elastic. For instance, in the nineteenth century, labor was scarce in the United States and wage rates high. Instead of continuing to bid up the price of labor, employers began to substitute machines. The result was substantial technological development of our nation's industries. A more recent example involves the nation's new subway systems. Many of these trains are run without human operators in order to avoid paying the rising wage scales of municipal employees.

The longer the time period, the easier it becomes to substitute resources. Business firms confronted with a rising wage trend can develop alternative means of production. As a result, demand for resources is likely to be more elastic over longer periods of time. This has been true of the demand for labor in the coal-mining industry. Following World War II, the high wages won by John L. Lewis and the United Mine Workers gave the owners an incentive to mechanize their mines wherever they could and to close those they couldn't. Employment in coal mining fell sharply in the postwar decades.

More recently, new health and safety standards for mining coal have pushed its costs up. Users of coal converted their power plants to use cheaper substitutes: oil or natural gas. Now many of these same firms are facing a new adjustment as oil and natural gas become more costly.

Inelastic supply may also cause wide variations in resource prices. If a given price increase causes quantity supplied to increase more than proportionately, we say that supply is elastic. If the change in quantity supplied is smaller in proportion than the change in price, we say that supply is inelastic.

Inelastic supply curves may be the result of restrictions in the resource market. For example, the supply of workers may be limited by discriminatory hiring practices, by inadequate educational opportunities, or by restrictive job requirements. When supply is inelastic, wage rates may rise sharply without producing a significant increase in the quantity of labor supplied. Meanwhile, workers who are excluded from certain jobs compete strongly in other markets and keep wages there low.

The civil rights acts of recent years have helped reduce discriminatory hiring practices and have made labor supply more elastic. Regrettably, many restrictions on educational opportunities remain. Furthermore, some employers still set unrealistic job qualifications, such as requiring a college diploma for jobs of relatively low skill. The result is to keep supply more inelastic and wage rates higher than they would be otherwise.

The Politics of Elasticity

The relative elasticity of demand and supply curves has important results in terms of the relative power of demanders and suppliers of resources. If a resource is essential to production, buyers of resources are often helpless to resist high resource prices. Relatively inelastic demand makes its employment necessary without regard for price. If supply is also inelastic, resource owners can command high prices when demand shifts to the right. On the other hand, a drop in demand will reduce resource price sharply as the inelastic supply competes for the few available jobs.

During periods of growth in production, resource buyers have stronger positions when supply is relatively elastic. They can increase resource employment without offering substantial wage increases. Conversely, a strong union of resource suppliers is more powerful when demand is relatively inelastic. When buyers have rigid resource requirements, sellers can command higher resource prices for roughly the same quantity.

Elasticities in resource markets have significant macroeconomic effects as well. Relatively elastic demand and supply curves imply greater ease in allocation of resources among alternative employments. Quantities respond readily to small changes in price. As a result, incomes to resource owners remain fairly stable.

SUMMARY

Employment of resources helps determine income shares among owners of factors of production. The neoclassical economists developed the theory of marginal productivity to explain the hiring decision. Demand for a resource is a derived demand and depends on the marginal product and the marginal revenue product of the resource. A variable resource's MP and MRP decline because of the limitations of fixed resources; the resource's MRP is its demand curve. A firm will demand more units of a resource as long as its MRP is greater than its price.

The determinants of demand for a resource include: its productivity and the quantity and quality of other resources used with it; consumer demand for the finished product; and prices of substitute or complementary resources. Demand elasticity is affected by the rate of decline of MRP, the substitutability of the resource, elasticity of demand for the finished product, and the percentage of total costs represented by the resource. When the final product is sold in imperfect competition, resource demand is less elastic; this is because larger quantities of the finished good can only be sold at lower prices, reducing a resource's MRP more rapidly than in competition.

A profit-maximizing firm will hire resources up to the point at which MRP is equal to price. Price is determined by the intersection of resource demand with supply. The firm will choose among alternate resources so that the last dollar spent on every resource adds an equal amount to the value of total product. For example, a firm will choose labor and capital so that $MRP_L/P_L = \ldots = MRP_K/P_K$. The profit-maximizing combination of resources is the one at which $MRP_L/P_L = \ldots = MRP_K/P_K = 1$. Government helps increase supplies of some resources by offering subsidies. Government attempts to reduce the use of some resources by taxing them.

The share of national income going to a particular resource is its price times the quantity hired. Income shares of all resources equal the entire national income. Basing resource incomes on marginal productivity ensures that all resources are compensated according to their contribution to production. Shifts in demand and supply may cause changes in resource earnings over time.

Key Words and Phrases

capitalists' surplus according to Marx, the excess of value produced by labor but retained by the capitalist.

derived demand demand for a resource that results from consumer demand for the finished product.

equal marginal productivity principle the rule that resources should be hired in combinations such that MRP per dollar spent is equal for all resources.

labor theory of value Marx's theory that all value is fundamentally the result of the productivity of labor.

marginal product the change in total product that results from employment of an additional unit of a variable resource.

marginal revenue product the change in total revenue that results from employment of an additional unit of a variable resource.

neoclassical economists economists who expanded the work of the classicists (Smith, Ricardo, etc.) and gave it mathematical precision; economists who developed the theory of marginal productivity.

Questions for Review

1. Discuss the important political debate that has centered around payment for productive resources. Who were the major contributors to the debate?
2. List the determinants of demand for a productive resource. Give examples, showing how changes in these determinants affect demand elasticity.
3. When the telephone company began charging for information calls, the union representing information operators complained. Explain in terms of demand elasticities and shifts in demand.
4. The following equation is an important guide to the profit-maximizing use of resources: $MRP_L/P_L = \ldots = MRP_K/P_K = 1$. Explain why.
5. Explain why the marginal revenue product (MRP) curve slopes more steeply when output is sold under conditions of imperfect competition.
6. Define: derived demand. Give some examples.
7. In 1977 Americans suddenly discovered that their homes were poorly insulated. Rising costs for heating and air-conditioning led many homeowners to increase insulating material in their attics. Was limited insulation ever an economically efficient decision? Explain in terms of MRP/P.
8. For years one of the few acceptable employments for women was teaching. What did this mean in terms of elasticity of supply? What effect would you predict on pricing in this market?

CHAPTER 14

Employing Labor Resources: Unions, Work, and Wages

Learning Objectives

Upon completion of this chapter, you should be able to:

1. Understand the various tools of power that unions wield, explain basic labor legislation, and indicate present trends in union membership.
2. Explain the factors affecting labor supply and labor demand.
3. Show how wages are determined in a competitive market and in a monopsonistic market.
4. Show graphically the effect of unions on wages and labor supply.

Our work shapes our lives. It affects more than our income and social status; it affects how we think and behave and grow. More than that, occupational status even affects our role in history: the part we play in our nation's progress and development.

Philosophers of the past have set forth their theories about how the character of work influences historical change. Adam Smith's views were optimistic. He believed that increasing specialization in work and interdependence among producing groups would enhance a sense of community and provide a better life for all. Karl Marx was pessimistic. Marx described history as a series of conflicts between those who own the means of production and those who work. Periodically, according to Marx, workers would rise up and overturn owners until finally all work would be shared "in common." Work and rewards from work would be based on the rule "from each according to ability, to each according to need."

Thorstein Veblen had a different theory about work and historical change. He agreed that conflict over occupational status would bring revolution, but workers would not be responsible. The highly trained engineers would be the ones who would take control from capitalists. They would establish a new society based on engineering efficiency rather than on purely market considerations. More recently, John Kenneth Galbraith developed a similar theory: Specialized management and scientific and engineering personnel will come to dominate economic life. Galbraith called the new class the *technostructure* and foresaw that their emphasis on economic growth might endanger the quality of life.

Other analysts include labor in their definition of the dominant class in industrial society. They believe that economic power is shared within a syndicate of strong unions and management. The *syndicalists* see decisions increasingly made outside the market through agreements between these great power blocks.

The relationship between work and historical change is an important one and worthy of the attention of scholars. But it is risky to accept too completely ideas that reflect conditions only at the time of writing. The tendency among social scientists is to extend and apply current conditions to their theories of the future. No one can correctly predict all the new possibilities for a society as changeable as ours.

This chapter will focus on labor. We will begin with a look at the institutions that affect working relationships. Then we will examine some current problems and policies for work in the coming decade. The next chapter will examine the other three factors of production: land, capital, and entrepreneurship.

We will find marginal productivity theory useful for analyzing allocation of labor. We will see that demand for all resources depends on productivity. Along with demand, resource supply determines equilibrium price. That price determines the incomes of resource owners and the distribution of goods and services. We will find differences between the results of economic analysis and actual arrangements in the real world, however. Just as was true in product markets, we will find that institutional factors interfere with perfect competition in resource markets. One of those institutions is labor unions.

LABOR UNIONS

A Brief History

Labor unions began early in the Industrial Revolution. In the early years of our nation **craft unions** were formed by shoemakers, carpenters, printers, and other artisans having a particular skill or trade. Craft unions were exclusive organizations, having only skilled artisans as members and maintaining rigid standards of apprenticeship and control. Because worker organizations interfered with perfect freedom in working arrangements, they were regarded as illegal conspiracies, and many operated in secret. Unions were not legalized until 1842.

By the late 1800s U.S. industry was expanding and nationwide *federations* of unions were formed. The *Knights of Labor* flourished briefly. It was a secret organization that aimed to organize all workers—skilled and unskilled—for the sake of their common objectives. The *American Federation of Labor* (AFL) was more enduring. The AFL was formed by Samuel Gompers in 1886. Gompers was a cigar maker, and his union, along with harness makers, organ workers, and other craft unions, constituted the first nationwide federation of craft unions.

Around the turn of the century, the growth and occasional abuses of big business stimulated a new burst of union activity. New mass-production industries like steel and automobiles called for a new type of union. **Industrial unions** were inclusive organizations, having as members all workers in a particular industry or sometimes even a group of industries. For example, all auto workers, from sweepers to assembly-line workers to tool-and-die makers, were eligible to become members of the United Auto Workers. Industrial unions of railroad workers, construction workers, and miners came to dominate the AFL.

A wave of union organization began in the 1930s, encouraged by the Norris-LaGuardia Act and the National Labor Relations Act (Wagner Act). These laws forbade employers to interfere with the right of workers to form unions and required employers to bargain in good faith with unions once they were established.

In 1931 the Davis-Bacon Act was passed as a basis for improving wages of construction workers. Under this law, contractors working under a federal government contract must pay workers the "prevailing wage" in the community. Determining the prevailing wage is difficult; so in practice the union wage rate is the usual standard. The result is to raise nonunion wage costs and eliminate the cost advantage of nonunion construction firms.

By the 1940s many people had come to feel that unions were getting too strong. There was widespread resentment against strikes and rising prices, as well as outrage over certain union practices that were regarded as unfair. This antiunion sentiment culminated in the Taft-Hartley Act of 1948, intended to regulate collective bargaining between labor and management. The Taft-Hartley Act contains provisions designed to prevent abuses of union power.

(1) It outlaws closed shop agreements among workers and employers engaged in interstate commerce. **Closed shop** is an agreement that allows a firm to hire only workers who already belong to the union.

(2) The law permits **union shop** arrangements (requiring workers to join the union after they are hired) unless these are prohibited by state law. A number of states (twenty-one in 1979) have passed **right-to-work laws,** which make compulsory union membership illegal. In those states, mostly in the South and West, **open shop** prevails; employers may hire union or nonunion workers as they please, and no worker is required to join a union. As a possible consequence, wage rates in these states tend to be lower than in the heavily unionized industrial states of the Midwest or Northeast.

(3) The Taft-Hartley Act granted the President power to issue a court injunction against a strike when the strike is believed to be contrary to the nation's health and safety. An **injunction** is a court order to refrain from or cease a certain action. A labor injunction forbids the union to strike for an eighty-day "cooling off" period. To disobey an injunction would risk contempt of court charges, with heavy fines and possible imprisonment.

The injunction has been used only thirty-six times since the law was passed. A President who issues the antistrike order takes a risk that the order will not be obeyed. This happened in 1978 when coal miners disobeyed President Carter's injunction, and a federal judge let the order lapse. The President has the power to call in the National Guard to operate an industry paralyzed by strikers. But when the jobs are skilled or dangerous—which is true of coal mining—this may not be possible. John L. Lewis, organizer of mine workers in the 1940s, used to say "you can't mine coal with a bayonet."

(4) In recent years labor has attempted to reverse Taft-Hartley's prohibition of secondary boycotts. To **boycott** is to withhold cooperation from a business in order to pressure it to accept union demands. In a **secondary boycott** workers withhold cooperation from a business firm in order to pressure it to accept the demands of another union. It is a way of enforcing demands through worker solidarity. Secondary boycotts could seriously interfere with production in firms not directly involved in the primary dispute.

A bill to permit secondary boycotts was vetoed by President Ford in 1976; it failed to pass Congress again in 1977. The bill would have permitted "common situs" picketing on construction jobs. A union of electricians, for example, could surround a construction site with striking pickets. Then cooperating members of other unions (plumbers, floorers, and roofers) could refuse to cross the picket line and bring the entire operation to a halt. "Common situs" would give substantial new power to unions and is hotly denounced by business management. Secondary boycotts would be particularly damaging in the construction industry, which accounts directly for about one tenth of annual national output and provides employment for additional millions of workers in steel, lumber, cement, transportation, and other related industries.

Defenders of "common situs" argue that the principle of united action requires that workers be permitted to use all reasonable means of pressure. Otherwise employers could substitute nonstriking workers for strikers and win any dispute with the union.

Antiunion sentiment intensified during the 1950s. Widespread corruption and fraud in union finances led to a Congressional investigation and, in 1959, passage of the *Landrum-Griffin Act*. This law requires democratic election of union officers and regular reporting of union finances. A notable use of the law was against Teamster President James Hoffa, who was convicted in 1969 of misappropriation of union funds. More recently, Teamster President Frank Fitzsimmons has been the subject of investigations because of possible Mafia connections.

Union Activity

In general, unions try to resolve their differences with management peacefully, without strikes. The most common form of bargaining is called **collective bargaining,** where union representatives and their lawyers meet with management representatives and their lawyers. Through collective bargaining, unions help draw up regular contracts which specify terms of employment: hours and wage rates, vacations and sick leave, seniority rights and retirement benefits, grievance procedures, and the time period or dura-

Extended Example Labor/Management Cooperation to Increase Productivity

One way to increase the demand for labor is to increase worker productivity. Managers of business firms frequently find the key to increasing productivity in employer-employee relationships. Changing from a rigid authoritarian work relationship to a cooperative one has had positive results for many.

One particular plan originated with Joseph Scanlon in the late 1930s. Scanlon was an employee of the United Steel Workers union. Many of his union members faced the loss of jobs with the imminent bankruptcy of their employer, a small steel company. Scanlon developed a plan for worker participation in management with the goal of reducing labor costs and increasing job satisfaction. The hope was that employer-employee cooperation might raise productivity and prevent bankruptcy.

The "Scanlon Plan" has been adopted by many small companies. Workers are encouraged to contribute their ideas for improving production techniques and for reducing costs. Suggestions range from proposals for new work tools to proposals to drop suppliers of poor quality materials. Gains from cost savings are distributed among employees. In addition to these material rewards, workers appear to enjoy the opportunity to participate in work decisions.

Some firms encourage increased productivity by such devices as "well pay," "safety pay," and profit-sharing plans. Employees are paid a bonus for being neither absent nor late for a full month. Bonuses are paid also for perfect safety records that bring savings in company insurance premiums. After-tax profits above a certain percentage of sales are distributed to workers according to a formula measuring their contributions to production.

U.S. firms have generally not moved as far as West Germany in allowing workers to participate in company policymaking. In 1951 West Germany adopted a system of "co-determination" to forestall a move toward nationalization in major industries. Under current German law, representatives of labor constitute half the members of a firm's board of directors. In the beginning, critics predicted that labor would use the system to disrupt production and gain unfair advantage over shareholders. But, in fact, differences have generally been worked out through compromise. Moreover, the sectors where co-determination prevails have experienced generally greater productivity than other industrial sectors.

Illustrate graphically the effect of increasing productivity on the market for labor.

Do you think co-determination would work as well in the United States as in West Germany? Why or why not?

In what ways do the interests of workers and shareholders coincide? How do they conflict?

Explain the following paradox: Increased productivity means that fewer workers can produce the same quantity of output; yet increased productivity generally means *more* workers will be hired.

tion of the contract. If representatives of both groups are unable to agree on the terms of the contract, they may hire an impartial *mediator* to attempt a compromise solution.

Contracts may run for as long as three years. During the life of a contract, disagreements, or **grievances,** may arise over interpretation of contract clauses. Minor disputes can be settled by an established *grievance committee* of workers and employers. A union representative or **shop steward** will usually discuss the complaint first with the immediate superior. If the worker and the union representative are not satisfied with the supervisor's response, the union representative can submit the grievance to the plant superintendent. Sometimes a grievance will be appealed all the way up to top management. If satisfaction is still not achieved, the grievance may be submitted to an **arbitrator,** an impartial outsider jointly chosen by the employer and the union. If the arbitrator's decision is binding, this procedure is called **binding arbitration.**

A **strike** is the halting of work indefinitely by the union's members and is a union's ultimate tool for advancing the interests of labor. When a reasonable period of collective bargaining fails to produce an agreement, the union may call for a strike. Sometimes the decision to strike is made by the local union, but more often today it is decided, or at least approved, by the national union of workers involved. When a contract is finally agreed on, the union guarantees not to call a strike for the life of the agreement. Sometimes a local union may call a **wildcat strike,** one that disobeys the no-strike provision. This action is generally opposed by the national union.

A historical peak in strike activity occurred in 1934 when there were almost two thousand work stoppages nationwide. That same year, San Francisco experienced our nation's only successful *general strike,* in which members of many unions walked off their jobs in support of striking longshore workers. Some radical groups believed that the era of revolution, predicted by Karl Marx, had at last arrived.

Employers can use a form of strike, too. When employers close down an operation in defense of their position, it is called a **lock-out.** Employers in some industries may join together in a *Mutual Assistance Pact* (MAP) to provide funds for firms paralyzed by strikes. Since railroads and airlines suffer severely when a union calls a strike, they have been most active in MAPs. Unions are understandably opposed to MAPs.

Trends in Union Membership

From a low of 2.7 million in 1933, union membership has grown to a new peak, 22.8 million workers in 1979. Still, this number represents a declining share of the nonfarm labor force: 26.6 percent in 1979, down from 35 percent in 1945. The United States now ranks fifteenth among nations in the percent of nonfarm workers who are organized.

The 1970s were hard on the labor-union movement. Three recessions reduced job opportunities for union members. High wage demands aggravated inflation and priced many workers out of the market. The public grew hostile to union wage demands, particularly the demands of public employees. Longtime leaders of major unions retired because of age or because of competition for top union offices.

Even more serious for unions are the long-run problems of automation, the growing relative power of industrial conglomerates, and the shrinking share of manufacturing jobs in the work force. Additionally, the auto and steel industries have suffered in competition with foreign manufacturers. As imports have risen dramatically in the last decade, jobs have declined here. Thus there are fewer union members in these industries.

One reason for the decline in union strength has been a failure to keep up with the times. While significant changes were taking place in the composition of labor, unions continued to follow the same old organizing strategies. For years they concentrated on blue-collar *manufacturing* workers and ignored the growing numbers of *service* workers. That emphasis is finally changing. Today the Service Employees' International Union and the Retail Clerks International Association are organizing service workers in retail trade, health, finance, insurance, publishing, and real estate. Government employees are also beginning to form unions. More than a million federal government employees are covered by union contracts and the American Federation of State, County, and Municipal Employees (AFSCME) has around a million members. AFSCME members include janitors, clerical workers, technicians, and hospital personnel. Teachers, farmworkers, ballplayers, nurses, and doctors are joining unions, and workers in the Southern states, who have long resisted union organizing efforts, are finally beginning to join unions. Only white-collar office employees have generally resisted unionization. Perhaps they feel they receive the same benefits as unionized employees without having to pay union dues. Table 1 lists the nation's largest unions along with their membership.

Some unions are attempting to increase their power by merging. The two large federa-

Table 1 **Major Unions in 1979**

Union	Membership
Teamsters	2,000,000
National Education Association	1,700,000
Auto Workers	1,524,717
Steelworkers	1,300,000
AFSCME	1,000,000
Brotherhood of Electrical Workers	924,000
Machinists	917,000
Carpenters	820,000
Retail Clerks	637,980

tions of unions merged in 1955: The American Federation of Labor and the Congress of Industrial Organizations joined to form the AFL-CIO. Until 1979, its president was George Meany, a former plumber from the Bronx. George Meany was considered the granddaddy of unionism by many of the fourteen million members of AFL-CIO affiliated unions. The only major challenge to his long reign was the withdrawal of the United Auto Workers union by its president Walter Reuther in the late 1960s. (In 1957 the AFL-CIO expelled the mammoth International Brotherhood of Teamsters for corrupt practices.)

What accounted for Meany's long dominance of the labor movement? In general, he was respected by representatives of labor, management, and government alike. He was often called a labor diplomat, one who could perceive and defend the interests of his constituents without endangering the national interest. His rules of operation were: "Never beg, never threaten, never think you're right all the time." These rules and his philosophy of unionism helped him achieve a degree of industrial peace while defending the interests of union members. Most important, his influence helped persuade wage earners not to ask for wage increases in excess of gains in productivity.

Public Employee Unions

Today if you deal with a public employee (i.e., someone employed by local, state, or federal government), the odds are better than fifty-fifty you're dealing with a union member. Public employee unions are becoming more aggressive in their wage and benefit demands at a time when the public sector is starved for funds. Postal employees, air-traffic controllers, teachers, hospital employees, firefighters, police, and sanitation workers have been responsible for more and more work stoppages in recent years. Most of the strikes were illegal under local or federal law, and some strikers were jailed.

Currently, the fastest growing union of all is the American Federation of State, County, and Municipal Employees (AFSCME). It is the largest union in the AFL-CIO and the largest union of public employees. Its president is Jerry Wurf, a union organizer for twenty-five years. Wurf has impressed friends and foes alike with his aggressive support of policies favorable to labor.

Citizen support for unions of public employees waned during the recession of 1973–75 with the increasing financial problems of state and local governments. Public workers were accused of excessive wage demands, unwarranted strikes, and too little work. Wurf complained that many of the problems of state and local finances were the result of mismanagement by government officials. Many local government officials are inexperienced in the area of labor relations, he said, and are strongly influenced by local political considerations. When politicians promise lower taxes and better public services, they naturally create unreasonable attitudes in the minds of voters. Wurf believes that unions can help plan government services and tax policies more systematically. Unions have the research staffs and the expertise in industrial relations to make public decision-making more scientific. Wurf favors collective bargaining and binding arbitration, rather than strikes, in unions like police and firefighters where strikes might result in death or serious injury. He believes that moderation in these areas would promote fair practices in other areas of public employment.

As the 1980s began, one of the largest areas of labor unrest and battle was with public employee unions, especially those of local government. The so-called tax revolt movement of the late 1970s and early 1980s combined with inflation to put nearly all American cities in fiscal trouble. The cities' greatest outlay of budget expense is for the services provided by labor—often union labor. The first few months of 1980 witnessed strikes by firefighters in Kansas City and Chicago.

Labor Issues for the 1980s

Wages and hours have always been a primary concern of labor organizations. But efforts to raise the general level of **wages,** the payment made to households in exchange for their labor resources, will be self-defeating if wage gains exceed worker productivity. Over the 1970s, hourly wages rose 90 percent while productivity increased only 13 percent. Excess wage increases can be paid in either of two ways: by the consumer in the form of higher prices or by the employer in the form of lower profits. Inflationary price increases threaten the nation's economic health by distorting relative values and disrupting normal production relationships. On

Extended Example COLAs and Inflation

Rising wage rates do not necessarily mean rising costs of production. An employer's costs depend on worker productivity. To see why, consider a lollipop factory where workers produce an average of ten thousand lollipops a week and earn $100. Now, suppose a union is formed and workers demand a 10 percent wage increase. Will paying workers $110 a week raise production costs and require a lollipop price increase?

If worker productivity increases at the same rate as wages, there is no increase in production costs. When workers produce eleven thousand lollipops a week, the labor cost of each lollipop is unchanged. Greater total output means that workers can receive higher pay without pushing up average costs. On the other hand, producing fewer than eleven thousand lollipops raises the labor cost of each one. Wage increases in excess of productivity gains can be paid in either of two ways: (1) wages absorb a greater share of total revenues, diminishing the share going to profit and perhaps reducing the flow of new investment expenditures; or (2) prices must rise.

Since 1967 annual productivity gains have averaged about 1.6 percent, but wage increases have ranged from 6 percent to 11 percent. The major cause (and result) of excessive wage increases has been inflation. Union negotiators in particular are sensitive to the behavior of *real* wages and insist on "catch-up" raises and cost-of-living-adjustment clauses (known as COLAs) to keep money wages rising with inflation. The big gainers have been workers in primary metals, mining, transportation, utilities, transportation equipment, and manufacturing. All are strongly unionized. Less organized services and retail and wholesale trade fell far behind.

Generally, COLA clauses in union contracts perpetuate inflation. A one-time boost in inflation is followed by an automatic wage increase which gives inflation another boost and stimulates more inflation. It becomes a repeating cycle. Many union officials realize this and would like to stop the cycle, but they worry about being voted out of office by disgruntled union members.

Suppose lollipop production increases by 10 percent and wages rise by 10 percent. How does the change affect the compensation of other resources used in production: land, capital, and entrepreneurship? Are these resources also entitled to a higher return? Explain.

the other hand, falling profits reduce the ability to invest in new plant and equipment.

There is another side to the issue of wage inflation. Unions argue that progressive income-tax rates have actually reduced worker take-home pay so that real wages are no higher today than in 1968. Many unions have demanded escalator clauses, keyed to changes in the *consumer price index* (CPI), in order to protect their purchasing power. These escalator clauses are known as **cost-of-living adjustments** (COLAs). Escalator clauses have the advantage of extending contracts over longer periods without risk of loss of purchasing power. But they have the disadvantage of accepting the inevitability of inflation and the loss of purchasing power that non-covered workers suffer as a result. About nine million American workers are covered by COLAs.

Wage rates in the United States exceeded those of most other industrial nations for many years. This was not a serious problem because output per worker in the United States was also higher. With high worker productivity, labor costs per unit of output were low. We could produce goods of high quality at prices that were competitive in world markets.

Accelerating wage inflation in the United States during the 1950s, 1960s, and 1970s and rising productivity in other nations changed all this. The United States suffered a gradual weakening in world trade, and unions complained that corporations were establishing plants abroad to take advantage of cheap foreign labor. The picture may be changing again. In fact, by the late 1970s increasing wages in other industrialized nations had overtaken U.S. wage rates.

Another important reason for the change in relative wage rates has been increasing fringe benefits for workers in other countries. **Fringe benefits** include paid holidays and vacations, pensions and health insurance, and unemploy-

Extended Example Fringe Benefits

Probably the fastest growing element of worker income is *fringe benefits.* On the average, the value of fringe benefits adds about one third to a worker's money wage. Fringe benefits include health and other insurance programs; pensions, including the employer's contribution to social security; paid vacations and holidays; unemployment benefits, including employer contributions to unemployment insurance; severance pay; supplemental unemployment benefits; bonuses; profit-sharing plans; and other benefits. Many fringe benefits are now taken for granted, although they were unheard of only a few decades ago. For example, without pension plans, many workers of years past retired to live off their meager savings or moved in with employed sons and daughters. As American workers have become more affluent, they have demanded new kinds of nonwage compensation. Moreover, since many fringe benefits are not taxed, workers enjoy higher total benefits as a result. Also, employers can purchase services like insurance more cheaply in large amounts than an individual worker can.

Some important fringe benefits are shown below, along with their percentage of total payroll expense in large firms:*

Total employee benefits	35.4%
Pension plans, insurance programs, and goods provided by company	11.6%
Paid vacations, holidays, sick leave	10.1%
Employer share of social security contributions, unemployment compensation, and workmen's compensation	8.0%
Paid rest periods and travel time, etc.	3.6%
Profit-sharing, bonus, education expenses	2.1%

*Richard B. Freeman, *Labor Economics, 2nd Ed.*, Prentice-Hall, Englewood Cliffs, N.J., 1979, p. 84.

ment benefits. Fringe benefits, or *indirect labor costs,* add about 30 percent to basic wages in the United States but more than 50 percent to wages in many European nations. The higher cost of these benefits in European nations has driven many foreign firms to seek cheap labor in the United States!

After wage negotiations, the next biggest issue of collective bargaining concerns the length of the workweek. The current forty-hour week in manufacturing was an accomplishment of the 1940s. Now the thirty-two-hour week without a reduction in pay is an important goal of unions, particularly the United Auto Workers (UAW). Improvements in productivity, the increase in numbers of part-time employees, and the growth of service industries have already reduced the average workweek in nonfarm employment to about thirty-six hours. High unemployment during the recession of 1973–75 spurred a new drive to reduce regularly scheduled hours in manufacturing. The hope was that shorter hours would help put more people back to work. Of course, it might have the opposite result in increasing "moonlighting" or second jobs among persons already employed.

The labor contract between Ford Motor Company and the UAW in the fall of 1976 promised workers forty paid days off a year, in effect reducing the average workweek substantially. Whether the agreement adds to costs of production, and thus to auto prices, will depend on trends in worker productivity. Some auto workers prefer shorter hours to more pay. They see their wage gains eaten up by inflation and prefer to enjoy the gain of greater leisure instead.

Probably the most serious problem facing labor is the dynamics of job opportunities. Every year jobs are wiped out because of automation, increased efficiency, or declining demand for the products or services of an industry. At the same time, the labor force grows and new industries and jobs are created. Structurally, our labor force has changed dramatically with the entry of millions of women. Labor force trends suggest that the United States must create an average of 72,100 new jobs every week for the next ten years. This is twice as many jobs as the number generated weekly during the past decade.

Each new job requires investment in capital equipment averaging $40,000. To generate investment on this scale requires a high level of saving so that resources can be used for producing human and material capital. Tax and spending programs of the federal government can help stimulate job-creating investment. Business can be given tax incentives to invest in plant and equipment expansion and modernization, particularly in industries where demand is pushing against the ceiling of productive capacity. Employment subsidies can be awarded to private firms that provide on-the-job training. Government can subsidize public service jobs to provide employment for workers who lack industrial skills. Government can sponsor skill-development programs to prepare workers for productive employment.

Whatever the means employed, it is important that the nation provide useful work for our growing labor force. In the words of Charles L. Schultze, President Carter's Chairman of the Council of Economic Advisers: "The single most important contribution toward solving the major social problems of this generation—deteriorating inner cities, inequality among the races and between the sexes, high and still-rising crime rates, poverty, insecurity, and hardship for a minority of our citizens—would be a high level of employment and a tight labor market."

THE MARKET FOR LABOR: LABOR SUPPLY

The supply of labor depends fundamentally on two variables: the size of the adult population and the percentage of the population that wants to work. In 1980 the U.S. labor force was more than 100 million people, out of a total population of about 220 million. Economists use the term "labor" to include all persons who work for pay. The repair person who comes to your home is a member of the labor force. So are your dentist and your stockbroker. Your boss is a member of the labor force and her boss is, too, all the way up to the company president.

The adult population for the 1980s is simple to predict, since most were born in the 1950s and 1960s. Participation depends on social factors as well as conditions of work and income. Women are now a major component of our labor force. So, in most families, there are now at least two potential wage earners: husband and wife. But will both work?

Work Vs. Leisure

Deciding to work requires individual choice, much like the choice we make as consumers. As consumers we select among a variety of goods according to the relationship between gains in utility and product price:

$$\frac{MU_a}{P_a} = \frac{MU_b}{P_b} = \ldots = \frac{MU_z}{P_z},$$

where MU is marginal utility and P is price. We increase purchases in a certain proportion until we have exhausted our entire budget. In this way, we achieve maximum utility with our limited funds.

Deciding between work and leisure involves a similar process. Since our time is limited, we can achieve maximum utility by spending for work and leisure according to the marginal benefits of working or not working. We weigh our own preferences for leisure against the things we could consume with added income:

$$\frac{MU_L}{MU_G},$$

where MU_L is the marginal utility of leisure and MU_G is the marginal utility of consuming goods. Then we compare this ratio with the price of leisure: P_L. The price of leisure is the wage we would earn if we were working instead of resting. (More precisely it is the quantity of consumer goods we could purchase with our earnings from work.) If $MU_L/MU_G > P_L$, we would gain more utility from increasing leisure; if $MU_L/MU_G < P_L$, we should increase work. When $MU_L/MU_G = P_L$, we are allocating our limited time so as to achieve maximum total satisfaction.

People differ as to their preferences toward work and leisure and as to the price of leisure (the wage). These differences explain the willingness of some to spend afternoons picnicking in the park while others lunch on yogurt at their desks. Individual preferences change slowly, but changes in the wage rate take place frequently. When the wage rate increases, $MU_L/$

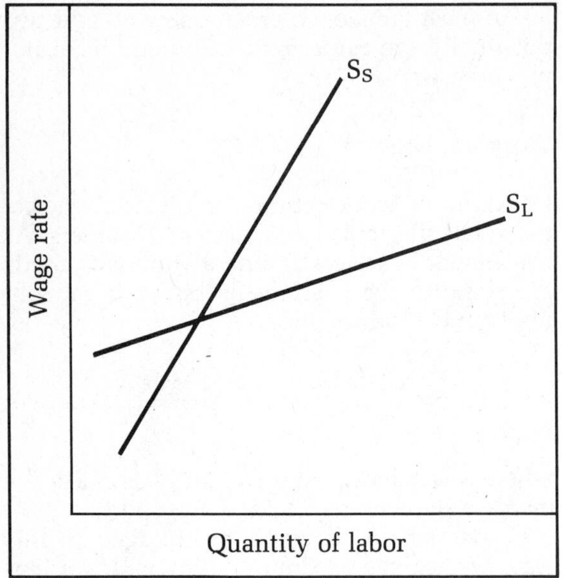

Figure 1 Short-run and long-run supply curves for labor. Both curves slope upward, but long-run supply (S_L) is more elastic than short-run supply (S_S).

$MU_G < P_L$, and hours of work increase. When the wage rate falls, $MU_L/MU_G > P_L$, and hours of work fall. The result is an upward-sloping labor supply curve.

In the short run, there are limits to the increase in supply: the available population and the number of hours in the day. In the long run, higher wage rates may encourage population growth, so that supply curves become more elastic. Figure 1 shows short- and long-run supply curves of labor.

Whereas total supply is relatively inelastic in the short run, supply in particular employments is more elastic. In this case, workers must compare the attractiveness of various employments with their relative wage rates. If job markets are competitive and if there are no restrictions on mobility, some workers will move freely among markets in response to wage changes. Supply elasticity will be greater in occupations that require relatively common skills and that have similar nonmonetary characteristics. Figure 2 shows hypothetical supply curves for labor in two different fields of employment.

Backward-Bending Supply Curves

Labor supply differs from the supply of other resources in that the owner *is* the resource. When workers work, they are in effect selling a part of their own lives. This fact can cause labor supply curves to take on an unusual shape.

For most goods and resources, supply curves slope upward to reflect the higher quantities offered at higher prices. This characteristic may be true of labor supply only up to a certain wage rate. Beyond some level of income, workers may choose to work fewer hours. If at high incomes workers place a higher value on leisure, the result may be $MU_L/MU_G > P_L$, whatever the value of P_L. In fact, higher wage rates may allow

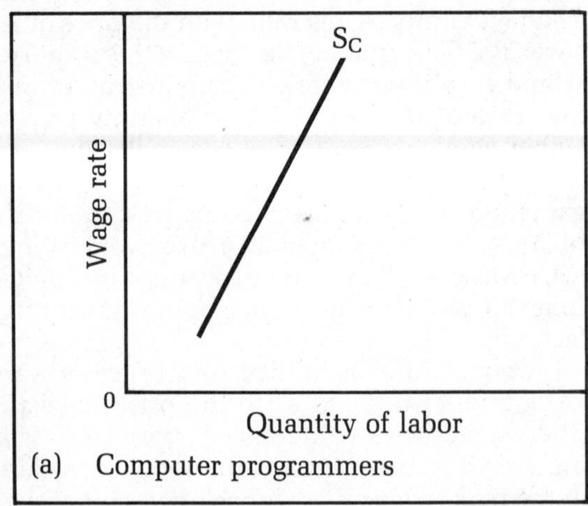

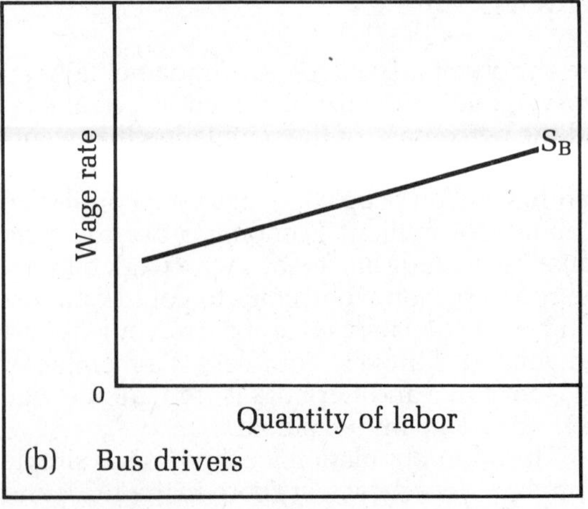

Figure 2 Short-run supply curves for: (a) computer programmers, and (b) bus drivers. Because the job market for bus drivers is highly competitive and demands relatively few skills (compared to computer programming), S_B is more elastic than S_C.

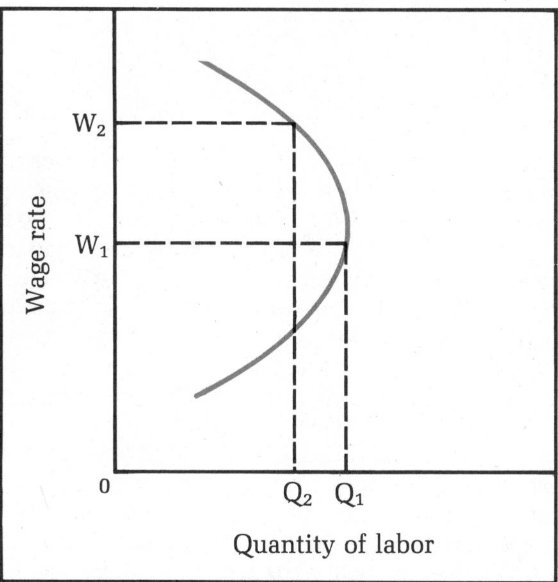

Figure 3 A backward-bending supply curve for labor. If the wage rate rises from W_1 to W_2, workers can decrease the number of labor hours they supply from Q_1 to Q_2 and still earn sufficient income to satisfy their needs.

workers to work only a few hours a day and still earn sufficient income to satisfy their needs for goods and services.

When workers behave this way, the supply curve of labor may bend backward, as in Figure 3. At higher rates of pay, fewer hours are worked. This is often true in primitive economies, in the tropics, and in rural areas of developed countries. Something similar may happen at a very high level of affluence, when workers prefer leisure to working extra hours of overtime. Nevertheless, for most purposes of economic policy in the United States, we are safe in assuming that the supply curve of labor slopes upward to the right.

LABOR DEMAND AND EQUILIBRIUM IN THE LABOR MARKET

Together with supply, demand for labor determines employment and wage rate. The wage rate times the number of workers employed constitutes labor's share of national income: 76 percent in 1979 in the United States.

Members of the labor force may be paid in various ways: wages, salaries, commissions, or bonuses. Whatever their pay is called, it is classified as *wages* because it is payment for labor resources. Wages do not include the returns that go to capital or land or entrepreneurship; we don't count interest or rent or profits as pay for labor. In general, people who own their own businesses may receive a *salary* for their labor, as well as *profits* from owning and managing the business. Top executives in a corporation may receive regular bonuses in addition to their salary. In companies that have profit-sharing plans, employees receive profit in addition to their wages and salaries. In the pages that follow we will use the term "wages" to refer to payment for labor resources alone. Rent, interest, and profits will be discussed in the next chapter.

We should also distinguish between money wages and real wages. **Money wages** are actual earnings in dollars and cents for any given time period—say a week, a day, or an hour. **Real wages,** on the other hand, are earnings expressed in terms of what they will buy. It is possible for your money wage to go up while your real wage is going down; this happened to many workers during the 1970s because of inflation. If the boss gives workers a 10 percent raise but prices go up by 15 percent, real wages have clearly fallen. In our discussion we will assume that prices remain the same, unless we specify otherwise; when we speak of wages, we will mean real wages.

The Productivity of Labor

Demand for labor depends on productivity. An individual firm's demand curve is labor's marginal revenue product (MRP_L). The market demand curve is the sum of all individual demand curves. Equilibrium in the market determines the quantity of labor employed and the wage rate.

By now you are aware that workers in the developed industrial countries earn higher wages than workers in most parts of Asia or Africa. This is because total output in developed countries is so much higher than in other countries, and there is more to be divided among those who work. Workers in the developed countries are more productive because their health is better, they have better education and training, and they have acquired attitudes toward work that cause them to work more effectively. But beyond that, workers in the

Extended Example Minimum Wage Laws

Since 1938 the federal government has set minimum wage rates for workers outside agriculture. In 1980 the legal minimum wage for workers covered by the Fair Labor Standards Act was $3.10 an hour. The purpose of the law is to "put a floor" under the wages of the lowest-paid workers. Over most of the last forty years, the wage floor has been set at about half the average wage.

What is the effect of the minimum wage law? If we assume a competitive labor market, the effect is to raise the wage of the lowest-paid workers. But because employers make their hiring decision according to MRP = wage, the result is also a drop in employment.

Those who favor minimum wage laws disagree with this analysis, however. They argue that the labor market is not competitive for many workers. Many labor markets are characterized by monopsony, so employers can actually hold wages below the competitive level. To the extent that this is true, a minimum wage law can bring these workers up to the market level without any reduction in employment.

A number of statistical studies have been made of industries in which the law has forced employers to raise the wages of the lowest-paid workers. These studies indicate that the minimum wage does lead to reductions in employment. The workers most affected by the minimum wage law are those in small-scale industries such as retailing, domestic service, cigars, fertilizers, sawmills, seamless hosiery, men's and boys' shirts, footwear, and canning. The minimum wage hits hardest in low-wage areas of the country, mainly in the South, while it has relatively little effect in other areas. The loss of employment is most severe among the unskilled, the nonwhite, and teenagers. Some economists have proposed excluding teenagers from the minimum wage law, or providing a lower minimum for them than for others, in the hope that this might reduce the high rates of unemployment among young people.

Explain why minimum wage laws are especially hard on teenage workers. How does elasticity of resource demand affect the results of the minimum wage?

developed countries have much more to work *with*, in the form of capital equipment and advanced technology. The average worker in the United States or Germany, for example, uses machinery and equipment worth thousands of dollars.

You will see a number of these causes of higher productivity the next time you call someone to fix your refrigerator or washing machine. The repair person will drive up in a truck, carrying tools and spare parts; he or she will have at least twelve years of schooling, plus additional training in the field; and he or she will watch the time carefully so as not to waste it. Perhaps you will also sense other things that aren't as obvious, such as the existence of managers who organize the repair service and hire the workers as well as a concern on the part of management for earning the goodwill of customers. If you talk to the repair person, you may learn that he or she used to do something else and moved into this work because of particular skills and because of the opportunity to earn a higher income.

The earnings of labor, by and large, depend upon productivity. If we were to look at a chart showing the trend in real earnings of American workers over the last century together with the trend in output per worker, we would find that the real-earnings curve and the output curve practically coincide. In some periods output would have grown faster than real earnings, and in others it would have grown more slowly. But over the long run, their growth patterns would have been very close.

We mentioned *output per worker.* If output per worker has risen, this means that total output has risen faster than the number of workers. Each of today's 100 million workers is more productive on the average than one of the 50 million workers of fifty years ago. Does this disprove the principle of diminishing marginal product? Recall that our analysis of resource markets showed that adding larger and larger quantities of labor to a fixed quantity of land or capital will result in smaller and smaller additions to total product. When other resources are fixed in amount, the *diminishing marginal product of labor* will limit its employment and its earnings.

The marginal product of labor need not

decline, however, if the quantities of other resources increase. In the long run, a growing population means more consumers, more producers, and larger consumer markets. Growing markets provide the incentives for business to invest in new capital equipment and new scientific technologies. Better education and training add more human capital to our stock of resources. In the long run, more and better capital resources may offset the tendency toward diminishing marginal productivity of labor. As a result, output per worker can increase along with the growing labor force, and all can enjoy higher real wages. (All this is consistent with Adam Smith's optimism about the progress of a market economy.)

Wage Determination in Labor Markets

Even though the general level of real wages has risen over the years, what about wages for particular occupations and skills? Typists enjoy higher real earnings now than they did thirty years ago. So do engineers, psychologists, and sanitation workers. Workers in other occupations have gained less. What determines the rate of pay that any particular kind of labor can earn?

There is no single answer to the question of how wages are determined in labor markets. There are a number of answers, depending on conditions in particular markets. We will first look at two basic types of labor markets: the competitive model and monopsony. Then we will study the effect of unions on wages.

The competitive model. It is helpful to begin with a perfectly competitive labor market. For the labor market to be competitive, we must assume: (1) a large number of buyers and sellers, (2) homogeneity of labor resources, (3) perfect information about market conditions, and (4) perfect mobility among markets. The market for restaurant cooks is fairly competitive. No buyer of restaurant cooks (that is, no employer) is able to influence the wage rate. No single seller of labor (that is, no cook) is able to influence the wage rate either. When markets are competitive, the wage rate is determined in the market by the intersection of market demand and market supply.

Hypothetical market demand and supply curves for restaurant cooks are shown in Figure 4a. Market demand is the sum of all individual demand curves for labor. The market demand curve slopes downward because of diminishing MRP_L in the short run. Market supply represents the number of cooks that would be available in the market at different wage rates. The supply curve slopes upward, since more workers would be drawn to restaurant jobs at higher wage rates. The market equilibrium wage for this type of labor is shown as OW.

For any individual restaurant manager, the demand for labor is a single marginal revenue

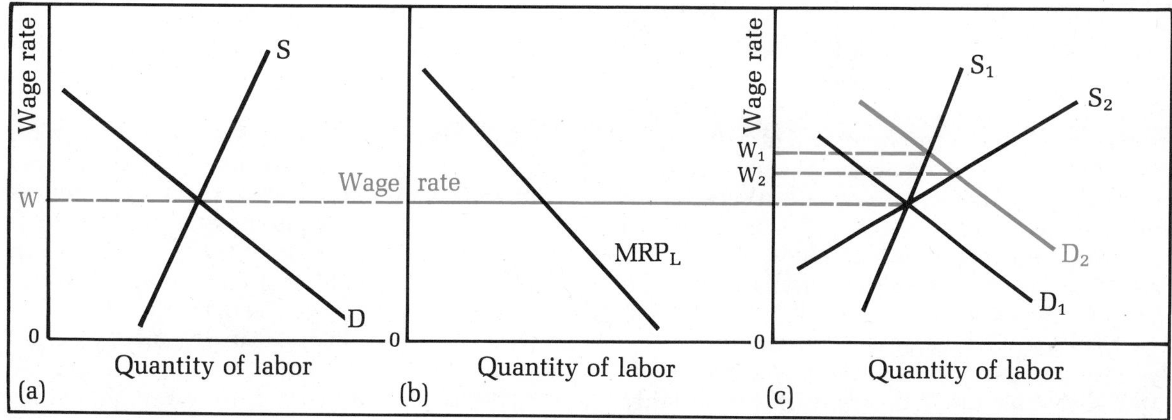

Figure 4 (a) Market demand and supply for restaurant cooks determine the industry wage rate W. (b) The number of cooks hired by the firm is determined by the intersection of the wage rate with the firm's marginal revenue product curve for labor. (c) If industry demand for cooks rises from D_1 to D_2, the wage rate will rise initially from W to W_1. Over time, however, the supply of cooks—drawn by higher wages—will rotate from S_1 to S_2. Now there is a new—and lower—equilibrium wage, W_2.

Viewpoint Worker Mobility Across Borders

High labor productivity in the United States depends on the quality and quantity of other resources available for use by workers. Fertile land, a good climate, and advanced human and material capital help increase the output of American workers and push labor demand curves to the right. Other nations are not so fortunate. Poorer resources and a low level of capital formation in many parts of the world keep employment and incomes low. The result has been massive shifts of population in search of economic opportunity.

Estimates are that twenty million workers with "untold numbers of dependents" are now living outside their native countries. Migrant workers from Mexico into the United States are the most immediate and visible example of this movement. Western Europe receives migrants from Southern Europe and the Eastern Mediterranean region. Kathleen Newland of the Worldwatch Institute in Washington, D.C., believes this new mobility may have these results:

(1) The receiving country benefits from the use of workers with a wide variety of skills. A flexible supply of labor keeps wages stable during expansion and helps reduce the problem of unemployment in recession: Unemployed workers can just be sent home. But social tensions frequently result from the presence of foreign nationals.

(2) The sending nations benefit from the earnings which are often sent back home and from lower levels of domestic unemployment. But since their strongest and most productive workers are the first to migrate, these countries lose the contributions the workers could make to their economic growth. Moreover, when growth slows in the receiving country, whatever benefits had existed will cease. The result could be economic crisis.

The problems associated with labor migration are likely to intensify over the 1980s and 1990s. Less developed nations will be unable to provide jobs for their rapidly growing populations, and developed nations will not be able to absorb all the excess. The tendency will be to erect barriers to international mobility, a course which will reduce efficiency in the allocation of labor resources. A healthier approach would be to deal with the causes of movement: poverty and lack of economic opportunity. The goal should be to encourage the free movement of investment capital toward nations experiencing a capital shortage. International grants and loan guarantees might be needed to establish the foundation for normal growth and economic opportunity worldwide.

Illustrate graphically the effects of labor mobility on labor markets in developed and less developed nations. Discuss the implications of the results.

How does this article illustrate the working of perfect competition in resource markets? the lack of perfect competition?

product curve for labor, MRP_L in Figure 4b. Since supply is perfectly elastic at the equilibrium wage, supply is shown as a horizontal line drawn at OW. Each employer will hire the quantity of labor for which marginal revenue product is equal to the market wage rate. Workers are paid the value of labor's marginal product.

Suppose there is an increase in demand for restaurant meals. Consumer prices rise and the marginal revenue product of labor increases. The result will be increased demand for cooks. The demand curve in Figure 4c shifts from D_1 to D_2. In the short run, the supply of labor is fairly inelastic. The quantity of workers hired will rise only slightly, but the wage rate will rise sharply, to W_1. The higher wage for cooks will begin to draw more workers into that occupation, but it will require time for many of them to learn the trade. As they do so, the supply of labor curve will rotate to S_2, and the wage rate becomes W_2.

As everyone knows, wage rates differ for different kinds of work. Even under perfect competition we would expect some differences to exist. Jobs that are particularly unpleasant or dangerous, such as coal mining or working with explosives or building skyscrapers, must pay more in order to induce people to do them. Otherwise, workers will prefer to find more pleasant jobs.

We would also expect to find higher wage rates in jobs requiring more training; workers have to be compensated for the time and money invested in acquiring the necessary skills. Workers such as bricklayers or carpenters, who can't work during bad weather, must receive higher hourly rates to make up for the days when they are idle. Difficult or more responsible work may be paid more than easy work.

These differences in wage rates can be explained by differences in supply. Supply curves for dangerous and difficult jobs lie higher and farther to the left of supply curves for pleasant and safe jobs. Of course, no theory will explain all the many differences in wage rates; some differences seem to be accidental. If you go around a large city checking the wages of secretaries, for instance, you may find that they vary considerably. Some secretaries earn more than others because they happened to be in the right place at the right time. Others earn more because they have been on the job longer. A few may earn more simply because someone likes them.

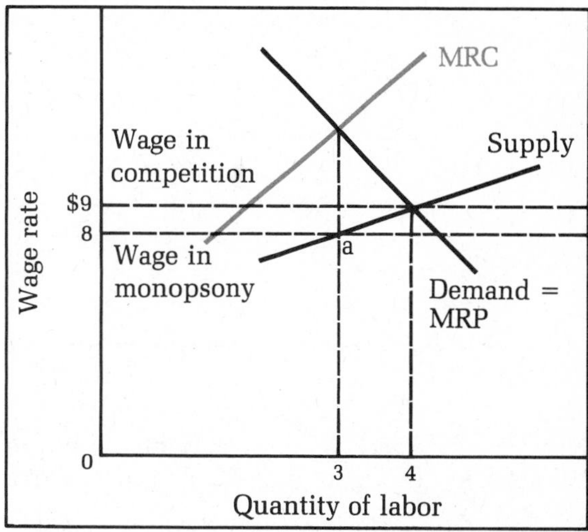

Figure 5 As the only employer of labor, the monopsonist hires labor according to its marginal resource cost (MRC) curve. Under this monopsony, quantity hired is three and the wage rate is $8. The competitive market equilibrium would lead to more workers hired (here four) and a higher wage paid ($9).

Monopsony. So far we have been assuming perfect competition in the labor market. There are many employers, and workers can choose among many jobs at the market wage rate. But quite often a worker has little or no choice among jobs. There may be only one employer for a certain kind of labor. A firm that is the single buyer of a resource is called a **monopsony.** A monopsony is similar to a monopoly, except that it is on the buying side of the market. It doesn't have to bid against other firms for the resource in question.

A common example of a monopsony is the one-factory town. Residents depend for employment on a single enterprise. As sellers of labor, they face a monopoly buyer. Career diplomats and military personnel experience the same problem, since their only employer is government. When one buyer faces the entire resource supply curve, the equilibrium level of employment and the wage rate are determined differently than in competition. Figure 5 illustrates the difference between competitive and monopsonistic labor markets.

In Figure 5, labor demand and supply have the same shapes as in competition. Recall that in competition the equilibrium wage is determined at the point where market demand and supply curves intersect. Then, the supply curve facing an individual firm is a horizontal line drawn at the equilibrium wage. The individual firm under perfect competition is a price taker; it can acquire any quantity of labor without affecting the market price.

The result is different when the buyer is a monopsony. Since the monopsony firm is a single buyer, it faces the entire upward-sloping market supply curve of labor. If the monopsony firm wants to hire more labor, it must offer a higher wage—both to the new units of labor *and* to all previously employed units of labor.

The additional cost of hiring workers means that we must add another curve to Figure 5. The *marginal resource cost* (MRC) is the additional cost of hiring one more unit of labor. In competition any quantity of labor can be hired for the same wage; therefore, marginal resource cost is equal to the wage rate. In monopsony, additional quantities of labor mean a higher wage must be paid to *all* workers; therefore, marginal resource cost is greater than the wage.

A numerical example will help make this clear. Table 2 shows hypothetical cost data for a monopsony firm. Suppose the firm decides to increase employment of labor from three units to four. The wage rate rises from $8 to $9. What is the added cost to the firm? It is the higher price of $9 for the fourth unit plus the additional $1 which must be paid to each of the other three units. The addition to total cost with each added unit of labor is shown in column (4), labeled "Marginal resource cost." MRC of the fourth unit is $12 and that of the fifth unit is $14.

In monopsony, the marginal resource cost associated with increasing employment is always greater than the supply price. This is dif-

Table 2 **Hypothetical Cost Data of a Monopsonist Acquiring Labor**

Quantity of Resource (1)	Price (2)	Total Cost of Resource (3)	Marginal Resource Cost (4)
0	$ 5	$ 0	
1	6	6	$ 6
2	7	14	8
3	8	24	10
4	9	36	12
5	10	50	14

ferent from perfect competition, when firms are price takers. In Figure 5, MRC is drawn above the supply curve.

A monopsony firm will read its equilibrium level of employment where its resource demand curve intersects MRC: At equilibrium the last worker hired adds the same to revenues and to costs. In Figure 5 this is the point at which the quantity of labor hired is three and the wage rate is $8. The equilibrium level of employment is less than under perfect competition, and the equilibrium wage is lower. (Read the market price of three units of labor at *a*.) To hire more than three units would add more to costs than to the value of output; thus fewer workers will be employed than under perfect competition and for less pay.

Note the similarity between the monopsonistic employer of labor and the monopolistic seller of goods. Just as the monopolistic seller is led to produce less than a firm in competition and to set a higher price, so the monopsonistic employer will tend to hire fewer workers and to pay lower wages. Note also the difference between the wage rate and labor's marginal revenue product. Under monopsony, a larger portion of total output is retained by the monopsony employer than under competition.

Unions and the labor market. Monopsony illustrates imperfect competition on the demand side of the labor market. Unions illustrate imperfect competition on the supply side. One purpose of unions is to achieve wage rates and working conditions different from those provided by the intersection of supply and demand in a competitive market. When there is no union, each worker makes his or her own agreement with the employer in competition with other workers. But a union bargains on behalf of all its members, giving them monopoly power over the sale of their labor. If employers refuse to meet union demands, the union can call a strike and withhold all labor from the job.

There are three ways a union can raise wage rates. One is to raise the demand for labor. If the union can cause demand to increase, as in Figure 4c, the equilibrium wage for workers in the union will be higher. The number of workers hired will also increase. In some industries unions have tried to do this. These are primarily industries in which the demand for labor has been declining because of technological changes or because of competition from imports. Garment workers' unions have tried to help their employers produce and sell more clothing; they have cooperated in increasing worker productivity and in helping advertise the products. Unions of steelworkers have pressed for higher tariffs to keep out competing products from abroad and thus to increase demand for American workers. Railway unions were able for a long time to force their employers to hire workers who were no longer needed; stokers on diesel engines were a significant example.

Generally, these efforts have only limited success. In the long run, the demand for labor depends on its MRP, which depends on production and prices of finished goods. Increased production may be achieved by increasing other resources with which labor works, primarily capital equipment, and by improving organization of work. As more-productive industries expand relative to less-productive industries, the economy as a whole enjoys greater total production and higher real wages.

A second way that a union can raise wage rates is by restricting the supply of labor. This has been the approach used by *craft unions*—

Extended Example Efficiency in the Military*

For almost a decade the United States has had a volunteer army. Like any other employer, the Department of Defense enters the market to purchase quantities of various types of labor at the going wage rate. Workers are hired on the basis of the equal marginal productivity principle. Furthermore, since capital is employed on the same basis, the combination of labor and capital is most efficient: $MRP_L/P_L = MRP_K/P_K$.

It has not always been this way. During most of the nation's wars and for many years of peacetime, army personnel were acquired by draft. Whether by lottery or by systematic selection, labor was employed through nonmarket means. There are several important consequences of an army draft:

(1) Since workers are acquired involuntarily, there is no need to pay a market wage. A low wage increases MRP_L/P_L relative to MRP_K/P_K, encouraging greater use of labor and less use of capital. The result is an inefficient allocation of the nation's resources.

(2) Army pay is uniform for persons of similar rank. Without pay differentials for workers of superior skills, all workers will be assigned to similar jobs. Workers whose productivity in civilian jobs is high will be likely to perform jobs of low productivity. The result is a loss of output for the economy as a whole.

(3) The cost of reduced output is shared inequitably. The loss to productive workers is the difference between the value of their alternative production and the value of their contribution to defense. Thus, the cost is a kind of tax on the nation's most productive resources.

(4) In general, army draftees spend only two years in the military. Much of this time is involved in training programs that involve considerable expense. After costly investment in training, the high turnover of army personnel increases significantly the total costs of defense.

Early in our nation's history, draftees were allowed to buy their way out of the army. Presumably, persons whose skills were in great demand in civilian labor markets could pay less productive workers to take their places. While this practice might improve the efficiency of resource allocation, it did not appear equitable and has since been abandoned.

This article has described only the benefits of a volunteer army. What are some costs?

*For further reading on this topic, see Douglass C. North and Roger LeRoy Miller, *The Economics of Public Issues,* Harper & Row, New York, 1971.

organizations of workers having a particular kind of skill, such as bricklayers, carpenters, electricians, and plumbers. Craft unions restrict their membership by requiring long periods of apprenticeship, by setting high initiation fees, by admitting few new members, or all of these. Figure 6 illustrates a typical market for artisans. In the absence of restrictions, the competitive supply curve for labor would be S. The craft union, by restricting the supply of labor, succeeds in achieving the curve S_u and in pushing the wage level up from W to W_u. It does this, of course, at the cost of fewer jobs and lower total production.

Unions have also tried more socially desirable ways of reducing the supply of labor. They have favored laws to limit child labor, to raise the school-leaving age, and to make it possible for workers to retire earlier. They even agreed to a *mandatory* retirement age, which is now seventy for most forms of labor. Unions have also favored shorter workweeks and longer vacations. All of these have helped reduce the supply of labor below what it might otherwise be and have helped keep wage rates higher.

A third way that a union can raise wage rates is by getting employers to agree not to pay less than a certain wage. This can be done through legislation or through a labor-management contract spelling out what the union wage will be for particular kinds of labor.

The effect on wage levels is shown in Figure 7. Under competitive conditions the wage would be W, determined by supply and demand. But the union contract sets the wage at W_u. Firms will hire the quantity of labor at which MRP equals the cost of an additional unit of labor. This is given by Q_u. The higher the union wage level, the lower the quantity of labor hired.

Several things should be said about this.

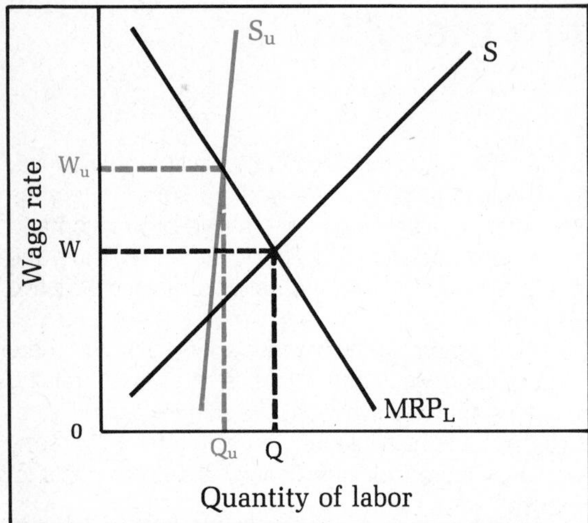

Figure 6 A craft union restricts supply to keep wage rates high. S represents free market supply, which leads to wage W and quantity of workers hired Q. The supply of labor from a craft union is S_u. The union wage rate W_u is higher than W, and the quantity of union workers hired Q_u is smaller than Q.

Figure 7 exaggerates the extent to which most unions are able to raise wages. Probably most labor-management contracts set union wage rates at about what the market would pay anyway. Union negotiators generally ask for more than they expect to get, and management responds by offering less than it is willing to settle for. The wage they finally agree upon will depend on the strength of the union and the aggressiveness of its leaders, as well as on the resistance of management. Often it is not very different from wages under competition.

Even when unions succeed in raising the *money* wage rate, their victory will not amount to much unless productivity increases, too. Without gains in productivity, prices of many finished goods will also rise. If a number of unions in basic industries sign agreements for excessive wage increases, the resulting price increases will spread throughout the economy to the goods that workers buy. Their *money* wages will increase, but higher prices will mean that their *real* wages increase less or not at all.

Again, the result may be different when a union deals with a monopsonistic employer. The union may be able to raise wages without raising prices by forcing the employer to pay the wage that would be achieved under competition. Left to itself, the monopsonist would pay less than labor's marginal revenue product, as we saw in Figure 5. Thus the union is able to achieve better terms for its members than they could get if they were left to bargain as individuals. This may often be the case in small towns or in industries where a few giant firms employ many semiskilled workers.

Sometimes unions help raise the wages of some workers at the expense of others. For instance, if a union is able to achieve higher than average wages for its members by restricting employment, many workers will have to find other kinds of work and perhaps accept lower wages. In some industries, such as steel, powerful unions have been able to achieve wage increases that their employers then passed on in the form of higher prices to consumers. Workers in lower-wage industries do not benefit from the higher wages won by unionized workers. But, like all consumers, they have to pay higher prices for the products of those industries. Something like this happened in the late 1970s, a period of high inflation. Many strong unions were able to protect their workers against inflation. The net result was greater inequality in incomes among various types of jobs.

Most union workers are better paid than

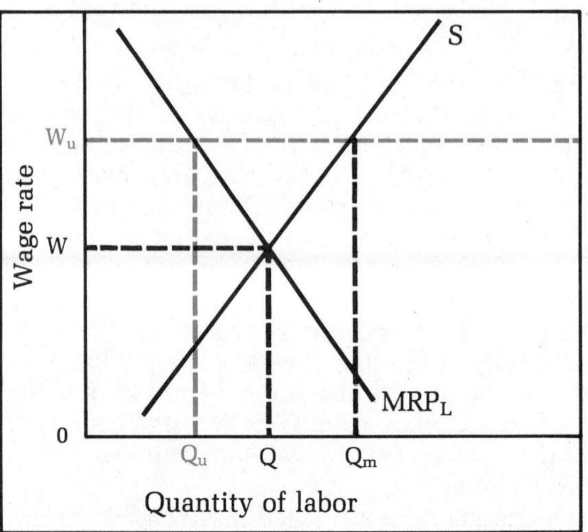

Figure 7 Unions bargain for a minimum wage (W_u) higher than the competitive wage (W). The industry demand curve is the MRP_L curve. At W_u, the number of laborers seeking work (Q_m) is larger than the number hired (Q_u). In fact the number of workers hired (Q_u) is smaller than it would be under competition (Q).

nonunion workers. The highest wage gains have been achieved by coal miners, airline pilots, teachers, merchant marines, and construction workers. Among the lowest paid are nonunionized farm laborers, domestic servants, store clerks, and laundry workers.

Unions have other purposes, of course, than to raise wages. Unions have done much to eliminate unpleasant and dangerous working conditions, establish rules for promotions and layoffs, and prevent hard-driving employers from speeding up the work excessively.

SUMMARY

Unionism grew slowly in the United States until the 1930s with the development of mass production and with passage of the Norris-LaGuardia and National Labor Relations acts. The Taft-Hartley Act of 1948 curbed some unfair practices of unions and gave the President power to issue an injunction against strikes. Collective bargaining is a means of achieving labor-management agreements without strikes. Unions also arrange a grievance procedure for arbitrating disagreements between labor and management. In general, union power failed to grow significantly in the 1970s; AFSCME is the nation's fastest growing union. Labor unions currently face problems of declining real wages and declining job opportunities.

The supply of labor depends on the size of the adult population and its participation in the labor force. Participation depends on preferences as to work and leisure and may decline at higher incomes.

Demand for labor depends on labor's MRP when it is used along with certain fixed resources. In competitive labor markets, employment and wages are determined by the intersection of demand and supply. Where there is a single monopsony buyer of labor, employment is determined by demand and marginal resource cost. Because MRC is greater than supply price under monopsony, employment and wages are lower than in competition.

Unions are a means of monopolizing the supply of labor and controlling its price. Unions attempt to raise wages by increasing demand for labor, restricting the supply of labor, or establishing a minimum wage rate.

Key Words and Phrases

arbitrator an impartial outsider who settles disputes between unions and management.

binding arbitration a settlement by an impartial outsider that is binding to both union and management.

boycott a refusal to patronize or cooperate with a business for the purpose of applying pressure.

closed shop an agreement forbidding hiring of workers who do not belong to the union; closed shops are now illegal.

COLAs cost-of-living adjustments that raise wages in line with increases in consumer prices.

collective bargaining a process by which labor and management agree on wages and work practices.

craft unions organized groups of workers having a particular skill or trade.

fringe benefits extra benefits provided to labor over and above the established wage.

grievance a disagreement between a worker and the management of a business firm regarding interpretation of a union contract clause.

industrial unions unions of all workers within a particular industry.

injunction a court order to restrain or to cease a particular activity; a labor injunction forbids strikes within 80 days of the order.

lockout a tactic of management to halt work as a means of pressuring a union to accept management's demands.

money wages wages in terms of actual dollar amounts.

monopsony a condition in which a single buyer faces the entire supply of a resource.

open shop a condition in which union membership is not considered in hiring or employment.

real wages wages measured in terms of real purchasing power.

right-to-work laws state laws forbidding union membership as a requirement for new employees; these laws make the union shop illegal.

secondary boycott a withdrawal of support from a particular business firm because of that firm's dispute with another union.

shop steward the union's representative within the work force of a particular business firm.

strike a union's most powerful tactic; the union halts work at target firms by having its members stop working indefinitely.

union shop an agreement requiring all employees to join the union after they are hired; union shops are illegal in some states.

wages payments made to households in exchange for labor for use in production.

wildcat strikes strikes called by a local union without approval of the national office of the union.

Questions for Review

1. Explain the derivation of the marginal resource cost (MRC) curve. What is the MRC curve when a firm buys resources in a competitive market?
2. Use the following hypothetical data to determine equilibrium employment and wage. Then, suppose unions impose a minimum wage of $15 per day. What is the result in terms of employment?

Quantity demanded	*Wage/day*	*Quantity supplied*
4 labor days	$20	14 labor days
5	15	10
6	10	6
7	5	2

3. Refer again to the data in question 2. Suppose union members participate in technological progress that doubles their productivity. Show the results arithmetically and graphically.
4. List the major pieces of labor legislation in the United States and the important provisions of each.
5. Discuss the significant problems that are facing unions today.
6. Suppose that your living requirements can be fully satisfied with a wage of $150 a week and that you desire no more material goods and services than this. Draw your supply curve of labor for a wage of $5, $10, and $15 an hour.
7. Real wages are determined by dividing money wages by a price index. Compute the level of real wages for the years shown in the table below and comment on the results.

Year	*Price index (1972=100)*	*Average money wage*	*Real wage*
1968	82.57	107.73	
1973	105.80	145.39	
1978	152.09	203.34	

8. Compute the marginal resource cost associated with the following levels of employment.

Wage rate	*Quantity supplied*	*Marginal resource cost*
$ .50	1	
1.00	2	
1.50	3	
2.00	4	
2.50	5	
3.00	6	

Explain why a legal minimum wage might not reduce employment in this case.

CHAPTER 15

Employing Land, Capital, and Entrepreneurial Resources

Learning Objectives

Upon completion of this chapter, you should be able to:

1. Explain the theory of rent.
2. Discuss the advantages and disadvantages of Henry George's tax on land.
3. Explain verbally and graphically the concept of economic rent.
4. Explain how firms make investment decisions.
5. Discuss the determinants of interest rates.
6. Discuss the functions of profit.
7. Explain why profit is important to a market economy.

Workers in the United States live better than workers in most other parts of the world today. Output per capita is greater and real incomes are higher, in part because of the institutional factors which affect working relationships in this country. Political and cultural institutions of U.S. life provide incentives and opportunities to enjoy high standards of living. Worker prosperity has contradicted Karl Marx's predictions about increasing misery and class conflict in market economies.

Aside from these institutional advantages, however, the United States has enjoyed other sources of high productivity. Our workers have a wealth of other resources with which to work.

We have enjoyed fertile and abundant *land,* including a variety of forest and mineral resources. The productivity of our land has enabled us to produce surplus food and fiber crops; production of a surplus enables us to release workers from basic production to produce another important resource, capital.

We have produced *capital* equipment, buildings, and social overhead for increasing total output. Capital per worker ranges from about $4,500 in apparel manufacturing to $104,700 in petroleum and coal. Our capital stock per worker increases about 2.2 percent a year, allowing workers to increase total production about 3 percent a year.

Institutional factors have made the United States rich in *entrepreneurial talent,* too. Our system encourages the exercise of free, individual enterprise and rewards economic achievement.

Striving entrepreneurs have helped make the best use of our other resources.

This chapter will focus on land, capital, and entrepreneurial resources. We will consider the *institutions* which affect their use and the *analysis* which determines their prices. In general, we will use marginal productivity theory to explain demand for resources, and we will show how resource owners choose to supply various quantities. Then, we will observe how equilibrium price determines the income share for each.

LAND: THE THEORY OF RENT

The market for land differs from that of other resources because the supply of land is fixed. The total amount of land in the United States, for example, cannot be increased or decreased in response to a change in price. The supply curve of land is vertical. This means that the value of land is determined by demand alone, as shown in Figure 1. The demand curve for land, like demand for other resources, slopes downward, reflecting the principle of diminishing marginal revenue product. As larger quantities of land are used in combination with certain fixed resources, output increases by smaller and smaller amounts.

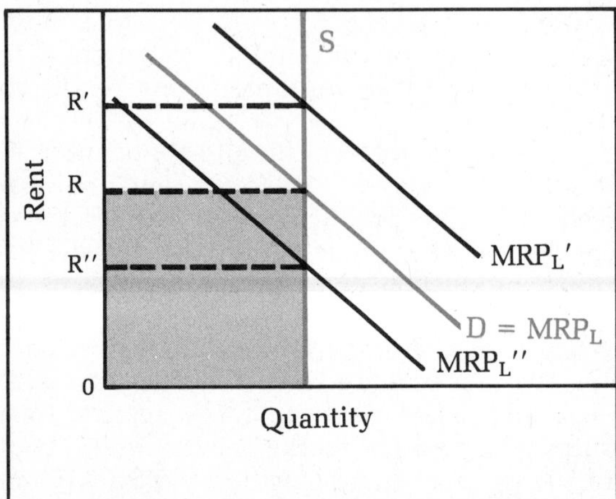

Figure 1 The market for land. The total supply of land is fixed, making the supply curve vertical (i.e., perfectly inelastic). When supply is perfectly inelastic, price is determined by demand alone. The demand curve for land equals the marginal revenue product (MRP) curve for land. For MRP_L', the rent equals R', while for MRP_L'', the rent equals R''. The total rent paid is represented by a rectangle formed beneath the intersection of MRP and the supply curve.

Differences in the productivity of land resources or a change in the market price of output will cause a shift in demand and a change in the price buyers are willing to pay. In Figure 1, land yielding an MRP of MRP_L' will earn a price OR'. Land yielding MRP_L'' will earn only OR''.

The classical economists referred to the income from the use of land as **rent.** David Ricardo (1771–1823) observed that agricultural land would be cultivated up to the point at which the value of output from the poorest acre used just covered the nonrent costs of cultivation. The value remaining for rent would be zero. More fertile land would produce a surplus above the nonrent costs of cultivation. The surplus would be collected by the landlord as rent. As demand for food rose, less fertile acreage would be brought into use. The value of its production would just cover nonrent costs, and its rent would be zero. But the surplus collected on good land would increase.

From the standpoint of an individual user of land, its price is a cost just like the cost of any other resource. The renter must pay this price for its use. From the standpoint of society, the price of land is a surplus that accrues to owners because the supply of land is fixed and immutable. Land would not diminish in supply if no rent were paid, as would be the case for labor and capital if wages and interest were not paid. In this respect, land has a unique quality compared to the other resources.

Alternative Uses for Land

Resource prices normally perform two important functions: an incentive function and a rationing function. The first of these is not relevant in the market for land, since no amount of incentive can increase the quantity of land available. However, the second function is especially important. With a limited supply of land it is important to ration the existing quantity wisely among all possible uses. The fixed quantity of land must be allocated toward those types of production which produce the greatest value.

Although the total supply of land is fixed, the supply available for particular employments is variable. Land may be shifted from use as parking lots to tennis courts to condominiums. The quantity available for any particular employment varies with the rent paid.

Dividing land among many different uses

Viewpoint Speculating in Urban Land

"I would not call owning land a good way to become wealthy; I would not call owning land the best way to become wealthy; owning land is the *only* way to become wealthy."

He may have overstated his case a little, but Chicago businessman Marshall Field accumulated a vast fortune by speculating in urban and suburban land.

The value of land is a result of supply and demand. Supply is fixed: The Lord ain't making any more. And demand increases as population grows and as scientific advances increase land's productivity. The selling price of an acre of land reflects its earning capacity or rent. A seller must receive a price equal to the sum of expected future rentals, discounted by the rate of interest the seller's funds could earn in other employments. The formula for the price of land is:

$$P = \sum_{t=1}^{n} \frac{R_t - C_t}{(1 + i)^t}$$

where P = price, R_t = expected rent earned in period t, C_t = maintenance costs paid in period t, i = interest rate available on other investments, n = the number of periods over which rent will be received, and Σ is a summation sign. Suppose a piece of property yields a rental return over costs of $100,000 for the next five years, when it will be sold for $500,000. The going rate of interest is 10 percent. The current value of the land is:

$$P = \frac{\$100{,}000}{1.10} + \frac{100{,}000}{1.10^2} + \frac{100{,}000}{1.10^3} + \frac{100{,}000}{1.10^4} + \frac{100{,}000 + 500{,}000}{1.10^5}$$

$$= 90{,}909 + 82{,}645 + 75{,}131 + 68{,}301 + 372{,}553 = \$689{,}539.$$

Land differs from other resources in that its value may increase through no effort of its owner. Urban and suburban lands increase in value as a region's economy develops. Many improvements made at the expense of all taxpayers actually increase the wealth of property owners. Streets, airports, schools, water systems, police and fire systems, civic centers, and sports arenas make land sites accessible and more valuable. These improvements constitute the city's social overhead capital or *infrastructure*. The infrastructure is the city's stock of basic services. *The New York Regional Plan Commission* found that the city's

allows renters to express their demand for land according to the value of its output in many different employments. And it allows owners of land to vary the quantity they supply in each of many different markets. The result will be a wide variety of rents paid. Land suitable for growing a strain of grapes for fine wine will command a higher rent than swamp land. Land adjacent to a large amusement park may command even greater rent as a parking lot. This suggests two reasons for high MRP and high rent: (1) the value of the output of land and (2) its location. A favorable location allows land to deliver its good or service with a greater net gain to its user. The payment of rent serves to allocate land to its best uses in terms of productivity and location.

The possibility of alternative uses of land complicates our definition of rent. When there are alternative uses, the payment necessary to keep land in its current employment is the amount it could earn in its next most productive use. By this definition the payment to landowners includes an opportunity cost. The user of land must pay the land's opportunity cost in order to attract land for a particular use. Any excess income over its opportunity cost is the landowner's surplus, or rent. In Figure 2 the landowner's surplus is FP, the excess earnings of land used as an amusement park over its productivity as a tree farm.

A Tax on Land

Since land rent is a surplus that the owner gets simply from being the owner, some people have favored taxing the surplus away. The American economist Henry George (1839–97) proposed that government tax away all the rent from land and use it to finance social programs. He pointed out that economic progress would lead to a growing demand for land. Landowners would reap ever greater returns as land rents rose. The

infrastructure costs taxpayers more than $30,000 for every residential homesite in the metropolitan area. A land speculator can make substantial gains on land acquired at low prices and sold after the city's infrastructure is complete.

The benefits of land speculation are likely to be inequitable. That is, benefits and costs are distributed among different groups of people. There is another disadvantage. Land speculation is destabilizing. Because land values are expected to continue to move upward, speculators will tend to hold land longer for maximum gain. The effect is to reduce the supply of land available in the market and to keep prices higher than they would be otherwise. Then, high land costs are built into the production costs of everything we buy, adding to price inflation. Furthermore, high land costs drive business and industry away from urban centers, contributing to urban sprawl. This adds to the costs of providing the community's infrastructure.

Communities have been unable to correct the problems created by land speculation. In part, the reason is the type of taxes levied on property. Property taxes increase when the owner makes capital improvements on the land. This type of tax penalizes those who make investments for increasing the land's productivity, but it rewards those who hold land idle in anticipation of an increase in its price. In this way, property taxes may encourage land speculation and a resulting misallocation of resources. Some communities have tried to solve this problem by placing a higher tax on unimproved land.

Other communities have tried to improve incentives by levying a tax based on the land's value in its most productive use. This has some unpleasant side effects, however. For instance, consider a farm located just outside the city limits of a growing city. If the land's best use is for an office building or a subway station, the use tax on the farm might exceed the annual output of the farm. For optimum resource allocation the farmer would have to move—a solution that may be politically unpopular. Moreover, the ultimate effect of such a tax might be a vast area of concrete and steel without trees and open spaces.

How can a community balance off the loss of income from buildings not built against the environmental gains from land left undeveloped? Is the economic concept of efficiency in use of resources broad enough to include goods and services which cannot be bought and sold? Discuss.

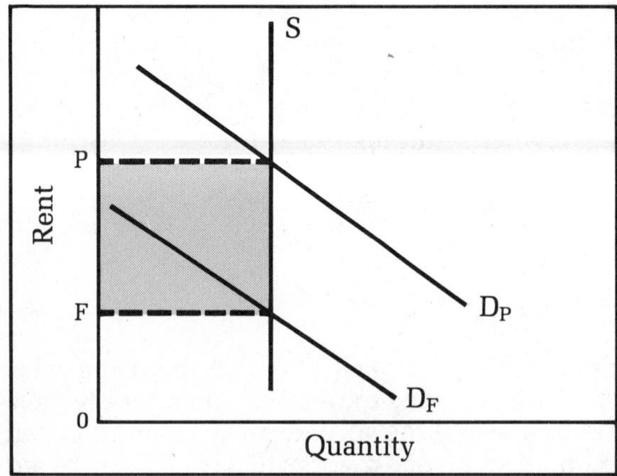

Figure 2 When land has alternative uses, a portion of the payment is an opportunity cost (OF). The excess payment over opportunity cost is the landlord's surplus (FP), or rent.

share of total output going to landowners would reduce the share going to owners of other resources. But the growing prosperity of landowners would provide no incentive toward greater production. Stagnation and economic decline would be the result.

Since rent provides no incentive, George believed it should be taxed away. Because the supply of land is inelastic, a tax on land would not reduce the quantity supplied in the market. George believed that the revenue from this source would be so great that no other tax would be necessary, so he called his proposed tax the **single tax.** Figure 3 illustrates the argument. The equilibrium rent is OR. If a tax OT is levied on rental income, owners will continue to supply the same quantity but for a return of only TR.

A practical difficulty with the single-tax idea is that most landowners have had to pay a high price to acquire the land that now earns a large

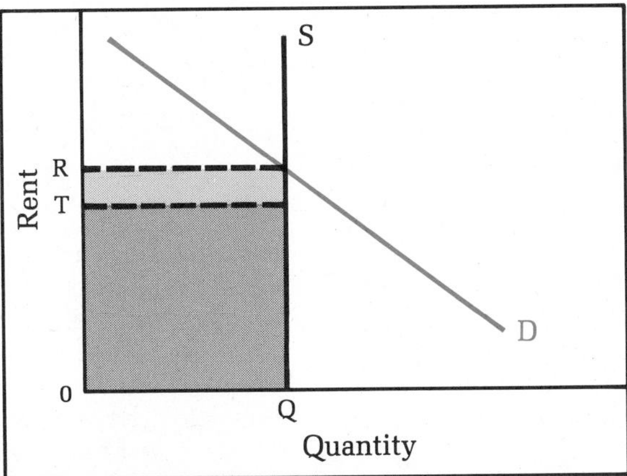

Figure 3 When supply is inelastic, it is possible to tax away the owner's surplus without reducing the quantity supplied in the market. If R is the rent, a tax of OT leaves only TR × OQ for the owner.

surplus. It would not be fair to impose a tax on the owner of a lot in Manhattan equal to the difference between its income and that of swamp land in Tennessee.

Our state and local governments depend on property taxes for a substantial proportion of their revenues. A number of urban economists have come to favor a tax on land rather than the prevalent property tax, as a way of raising revenue. They point out that property taxes fail to distinguish between land itself and the buildings or improvements on it. Taxes on buildings discourage investors from building and improving them. High property taxes have been one cause of the deterioration of some central city areas. American cities are dotted with rubble-strewn vacant lots. If the tax were imposed on land, the cost of keeping lots vacant would be high. There would be incentive to add income-earning buildings. A tax on land alone does not affect resource allocation: The most profitable use of land before the tax is imposed remains the most profitable use afterward.

The Rental Component of Wages

The word *rent* has more than one meaning. We commonly use the term for the monthly payment on an apartment or the cost of hiring a car from an "auto rental agency." These payments are not rent in the economist's sense because they include elements of wages, interest, insurance premiums, and other costs. **Economic rent** is something else: It is the surplus over and above the amount necessary to keep a resource (any resource) in its current employment. If a potato farmer leases land to a shopping center for a hundred thousand dollars a year, a portion of the payment is economic rent. It is economic rent because any payment above its value as a potato farm would be enough to persuade the farmer to give it up.

The same principle applies to prices paid for other resources, including labor. Economic rent paid to labor is any surplus over a worker's value in some other employment. For example, some workers have unique skills. The supply curve for their skills is perfectly inelastic (vertical), since their skills are rare and fixed in quantity. Star quarterbacks, pitchers, or goalies are examples. Others are concert musicians, popular lecturers, and skilled glassblowers. Such workers may earn high pay if the demand for their services is high.

The rental element in a pitcher's salary is shown in Figure 4. Total wage is OP. The pitcher's next most productive employment is bartending, for a wage of OB. The pitcher's opportunity cost is OB and economic rent is BP, the surplus over and above the wage necessary to keep him in his current employment.

There is a rental element in the wages of most ordinary workers. This can be seen in Figure 5, showing market supply and demand curves for bartenders. The wage rate OW is

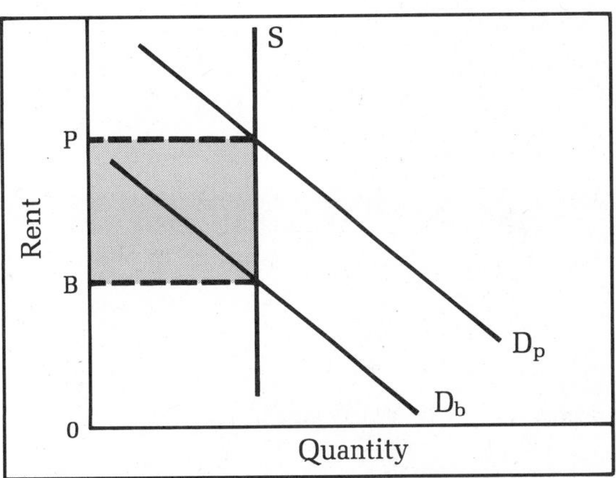

Figure 4 The demand for a baseball pitcher is D_p; the demand for the same person working as a bartender—his next most productive employment—is D_b. The wage OP breaks down into opportunity cost OB and rent BP. The total amount of rent paid is represented by the shaded area.

Extended Example
The Diminishing Supply of Farmland

Although land cannot be created or destroyed, it can be shifted around among various uses. Wilderness land becomes residential developments, aging residential land becomes shopping centers, and farmland becomes factories, resorts, and airports. This may be creating some problems.

The United States cultivates about 400 million acres of farmland and feeds about 300 million people. During the 1970s farmers sold about 3 million acres a year to nonagricultural users. Another 5 million acres a year was made unproductive by scattered development and by land erosion. Each year the lost agricultural land amounts to a strip four miles wide stretching from coast to coast.

As long as new technology was increasing the productivity of remaining acreage, the loss of agricultural land was not a serious problem. Lately, however, improvements in technology have come more slowly. Moreover, land lost each year tends to be some of the nation's best in terms of fertility and location. If these trends continue, analysts estimate that by the year 2000 the United States will produce only enough food to feed itself. After that, food exports will cease, and we will lose a valuable source of earnings for use in foreign trade.

It is ironic that policies of the federal government have worsened the problem. The government has financed highways and sewage and electrical systems that made rural land usable. By raising the return over costs for land, the government has increased its market price. Farmers increase their incomes by selling the land and investing the proceeds instead of selling their crops. Policymakers are looking for ways to encourage farmers to forgo this kind of opportunity for the sake of the nation's long-term health. But this is a difficult job.

How will the trend away from family farmers toward agribusiness affect this problem?

determined by the intersection of supply and demand. The slope of the supply curve shows that some bartenders would be willing to work for a wage less than OW. They are paid a wage higher than the wage they would be willing to accept because employers have to bid more to get all the bartenders they need, OQ. All bartenders to the left of Q are receiving more than enough to keep them from taking a different job. The difference between what they are actually paid and what they would accept is economic rent. The principle of rental surplus here is quite similar to the idea of consumer surplus.

CAPITAL: THE THEORY OF INTEREST

A favorite novel among economists is Daniel Defoe's *Robinson Crusoe*. You may remember the story. A sailor is shipwrecked on a deserted island in the South Seas and gradually builds up his own economic system from almost nothing. Crusoe made his own tools and built his own house. But in doing so he had to take time off from other activities, such as sleeping and gathering food. Eventually, he accumulated quite a lot of what we call capital.

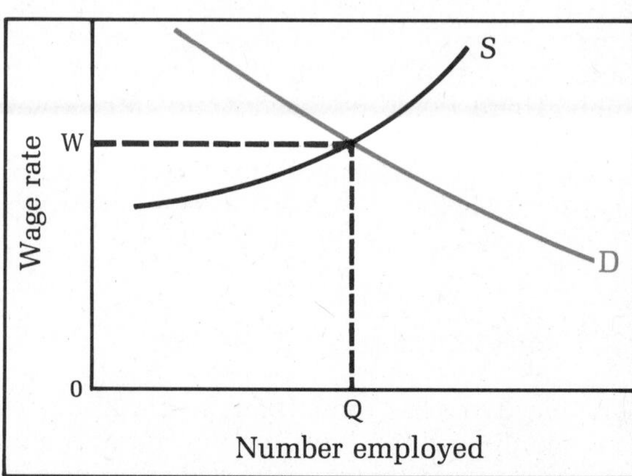

Figure 5 The labor market for bartenders. All the bartenders on the supply curve to the left of equilibrium would be willing to work for less than the market wage W; therefore, they are earning economic rent.

Saving and Investment

Capital includes all human-made resources. Capital is important in the economy because it magnifies the amount of work that can be done by a given amount of labor. But the process of creating capital is roundabout, since resources must be used first for producing tools before those tools can be used to produce the goods and services needed for consumption. In less developed countries this presents a problem: most of the available labor and resources are needed just to produce the necessities of life.

The earliest pieces of capital equipment were simple tools made of stone. Later, boats and sledges were built to make hunting and fishing easier. Eventually irrigation facilities, roads and bridges, and metal forges were constructed. More and more labor could be released from direct production of consumer goods and put to work in the roundabout process of making more capital goods—the means toward even greater production. Factories were built to make steel, the steel was made into rails, and the rails were used to build railroads to carry grain from the Kansas prairies to consumer markets in the East.

The process we have described is called *saving and investment.* To *save* is to refrain from consuming. Less consumption enables resources to move out of consumer-goods production into capital-goods production. Construction and installation of capital goods is called *investment.* Saving constitutes the supply of financial capital, and investment constitutes the demand for financial capital.

Compared to most of the world, the industrialized countries are rich in capital. They have been able to save and invest large amounts. But, like other resources, capital is limited even in the wealthiest countries. It should be allocated to its most efficient uses. In the United States and other countries where the market system predominates, prices are the mechanism through which financial capital is guided toward its best use. The price of investment capital, that is, the cost of borrowing it, is **interest.**

The Demand for Investment Funds: Capital Budgeting

A business firm must plan investment outlays just as a family must budget its income and spending. Both the business and the family try to get the most for their money. They set up priorities and allocate their resources first for those things that have the greatest priority. In a business, this means measuring the expected profitability of each investment path; it is called **capital budgeting.** Capital budgeting helps ensure the greatest benefit per dollar of investment expenditure.

Suppose a firm is considering the purchase of a fleet of delivery trucks. The initial outlay for the investment for one year is $100,000. At the end of the year the trucks can be sold for $75,000. Income from the use of the trucks during the year is estimated at $50,000. The cost of operating the trucks is expected to be $15,000, leaving a net income of $35,000. Thus, for an initial investment outlay of $100,000, the firm will realize $75,000 + $35,000 (the resale value of the trucks plus the net income from operations) = $110,000. This is a *benefit-cost relationship* of 110,000/100,000 = 110/100 = 1.10. The investment in the trucks returns an amount equal to the initial outlay plus 10 percent: 1 + 10%.

The company is also considering other investment projects. It could build a warehouse, instead of renting space in some other company's warehouse, and this would provide a return of 4 percent. And it could invest in a bookkeeping machine that would return 20 percent. In Table 1 we arranged these investment projects in descending order according to their *rates of return.*

The expected rate of return on investment projects is called the **marginal efficiency of investment** (MEI). Expected rate of return on all available investment projects, arranged from highest to lowest, combine to form a firm's marginal efficiency of investment schedule. The marginal efficiency of investment (MEI) schedule in Table 1 serves as the firm's demand schedule for investment funds. It resembles the demand schedules for other resources, which are based on the marginal revenue product (MRP) of those resources. The firm will demand the quantity of investment funds for which its

Table 1 **Hypothetical Investment Projects**

Project	Initial outlay	Rate of return over initial outlay
Bookkeeping machine	$ 10,000	20%
Fleet of trucks	100,000	10%
Warehouse	50,000	4%

marginal efficiency of investment is at least as great as the cost of borrowing those funds.

If the funds cost 16 percent a year, the firm will borrow only the $10,000 needed for purchasing the bookkeeping machine. Why? This is the only investment that will yield a return sufficient to cover the cost of borrowing at 16 percent. The bookkeeping machine, in fact, earns a 20 percent rate of return. If the interest rate is only 8 percent, the firm will demand investment funds totaling $10,000 + $100,000 = $110,000. The firm will invest not only in the bookkeeping machine but also in the fleet of trucks, since both projects will yield rates of return greater than the interest rate paid. In short, the firm will demand the quantity of funds for which the expected rate of return on investment is at least as great as the cost of borrowing. At 8 percent it will undertake the two most productive investment projects on its MEI schedule.

The firm's demand curve for investment funds is shown in Figure 6. The horizontal lines at 16 percent and 8 percent mark off possible costs of borrowing and show the quantity of funds that will be borrowed at each interest rate.

If the firm uses its own funds instead of borrowing, it will follow the same principle. In this case, the firm will consider the interest rate its cash could earn if loaned to another firm. It would make no sense to invest the firm's own cash for a return of 4 percent if the interest return on loans is 8 percent. The alternative interest income the firm could earn by lending its own cash is an opportunity cost to the firm

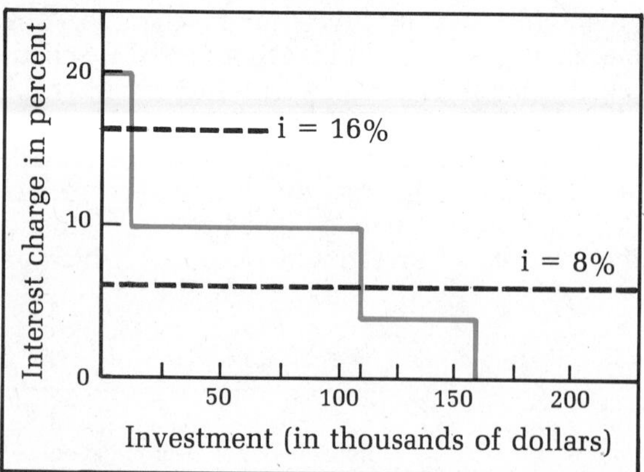

Figure 6 A firm's demand for investment funds is shown as the marginal efficiency of investment. The MEI for a single firm is a series of stair steps.

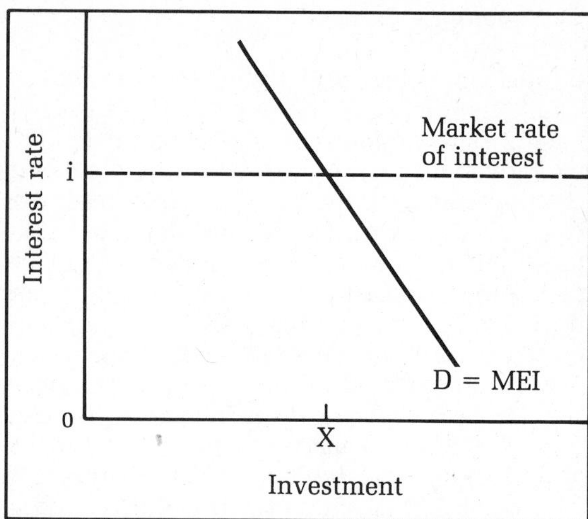

Figure 7 The market for investment funds. Market demand is equal to the sum of all individual MEI curves (D = MEI). At an interest rate of *i*, firms will undertake *X* amount of investment.

and must be considered in its budgeting process.

Business firms throughout the economy will calculate their investment priorities in this way. By combining their individual demand curves for funds we arrive at the market demand curve for investment capital. The market demand curve reflects the MEI for the entire economy. It resembles the demand curves for labor and other resources. Figure 7 shows a market demand curve for investment funds. All the individual curves of particular firms have been combined to make one smooth, downward-sloping curve. If the market interest rate is *i*, firms will invest the quantity shown at X, where MEI = *i*.

Investments Lasting More Than One Year

Our simple example involved investments lasting only one year. Most investments last much longer. To expand the preceding analysis to cover longer-term investments, economists use a procedure called **discounting.**

The equation for calculating the rate of return for one year is:

$$\frac{\text{Net benefits during the year}}{\text{Cost of one year's investment}}$$

$$= 1 + \text{rate of return over cost.}$$

Let us substitute in the equation as follows: net benefits for the year = R, the year's net income on the investment project; cost of one year's investment = P, the initial outlay for the investment; rate of return over cost = r, the marginal efficiency of investment.

The new equation reads $R/P = 1 + r$. Rearranging the terms, we get a more useful equation: $P = R/(1 + r)$. The term $(1 + r)$ is the quantity by which the income from the investment at year's end is *discounted*, or divided to equal its price. The income of the investment for one year discounted by one plus the rate of return is equal to its purchase price. Substituting the known value of P and estimates of R, the investor can determine the rate of return for one year.

If the investment project is expected to last two years, it must yield an acceptable rate of return in the second year as well as in the first. In fact, it must yield the acceptable rate of return not only on the initial outlay for the investment, but it must also yield the acceptable rate of return on the *return* that was earned in the first year. Otherwise, there would be no advantage in holding the investment after the first year.

To be profitable, the investment will earn some rate of return, r, on the initial outlay in year one. At the end of the year, the investment will be worth $P(1 + r)$. At the end of the second year the project must have earned the acceptable return on the total value of the investment after the first year. The investment should then be worth $P(1 + r)(1 + r)$. Multiplying the initial outlay by $(1 + r)^2$ gives the value of the investment at the end of the second year.

Earning a return on a return is known as **compounding.** Your return on your savings account is compounded. If you deposit \$100 in your account and the after-tax interest rate is 5 percent, your account will grow by \$5 the first year. During the second year it will grow by \$5 *plus* 5 percent of \$5, or a total of \$5.25. At the end of the second year your account will be worth $\$100(1 + r)^2 = \$100(1.05)^2 = \$100(1.1025) = \$110.25$. Each year your account grows by 5 percent times the original deposit plus 5 percent of 5 percent for each year the account is held. The formula for the value of your account after the second year is Final Value = Initial Deposit$(1 + r)^2$. The value after the third year is Initial Deposit$(1 + r)^3$.

An investment expenditure is similar to your bank deposit in that a certain amount is committed to it in the present. During the time the initial amount remains committed, it earns a return for the owner. The equation for an investment that yields a return over several years is

$$P = \frac{R_1}{(1 + r)^1} + \frac{R_2}{(1 + r)^2} + \ldots + \frac{R_n}{(1 + r)^n}$$

where R_1 is the net income for the first year, R_2 for the second, and so forth. Substituting values for P and R, the firm can calculate the MEI for an investment which produces income for several years. Then all investments should be combined in the firm's MEI schedule and the market demand curve for investment funds.

Nominal and Real Interest Rates

Just as we distinguished between money wages and real wages, we must distinguish between the *nominal* and the *real* rate of interest. It often happens that the rate of interest charged on a loan does not represent the real interest cost to the borrower. The difference results from changes in the price level.

The **nominal interest rate** is the amount the borrower pays, in terms of the cash payment made. The **real interest rate** is the cost in terms of actual purchasing power given up by the borrower. Suppose the interest rate is 12 percent, a rate high enough to discourage investors from borrowing under normal conditions. But if inflation is raising the price level at a rate of 9 percent annually, the real cost to the borrower is only 12 percent − 9 percent = 3 percent. The borrower will pay back the loan in dollars that have shrunk by 9 percent so that total repayment will be worth only 3 percent more in purchasing power than the loan.

The effect of moderate inflation is to *reduce* real borrowing costs and to encourage investment. Borrowers are able to pay back their loans with dollars that are worth less than the dollars they borrowed. Figure 8 illustrates the effect of this difference between the nominal and real rates of interest. Of course, inflation stimulates investment only as long as lenders take no action to protect themselves. If inflation is expected to continue, lenders will increase the nominal rate of interest sufficiently to make up for the loss in purchasing power during the period of the loan. By early 1980 high inflation had pushed interest rates as high as 20 percent. If inflation continues and worsens, it may create

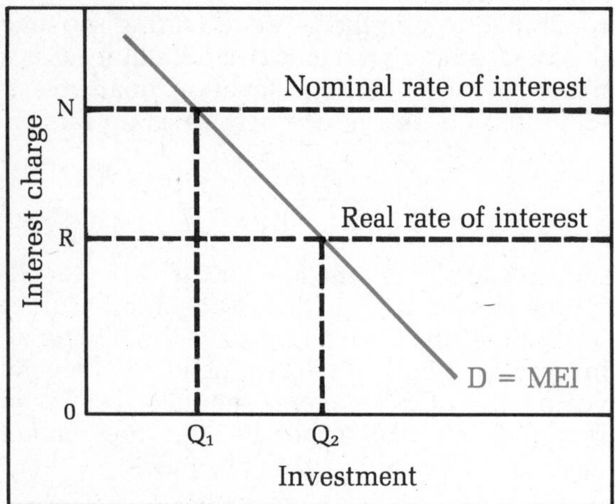

Figure 8 The effect of inflation on interest and borrowing. Inflation increases from OQ_1 to OQ_2.

such uncertainty among business firms that investment will finally be cut off, regardless of the rate of interest. This kind of uncertainty probably contributed to the low level of investment during the late 1970s. Business firms were unable to estimate with confidence the net income *(R)* from new projects, so they cut back their investment plans.

Tax Credits

In recent years the federal government has tried to stimulate capital construction by raising the marginal efficiency of investment. Under a tax law passed in 1964, business firms were allowed to deduct 7 percent of the price of an investment from their income taxes. In the 1970s, another tax credit, of 10 percent, was given in the hope of stimulating investment.

The effect of a tax credit is to reduce the initial outlay for an investment project. In our formula, this reduces *P* while *R* remains the same. When the capital budgeting equation is solved, the result is a higher value for *r*, the rate of return over cost. Since every investment project has a higher *r*, the MEI curve will shift upward. If the government's policy is successful, a larger quantity of investment demand will result at every interest rate. More new investment projects will be undertaken, and the nation's capital stock will increase.

There is another possible result. Lower taxes on business firms may mean higher taxes for consumers. If consumers reduce their purchases, net income *(R)* from new investment may fall. Then *r* would fall, too.

The Supply of Investment Funds: Savings

We have been analyzing the demand for investment funds. What about the supply side? Who supplies the funds available for business borrowing?

Much of the supply of loanable funds comes from the personal savings of households. Many families set aside a portion of their incomes to provide for their long-range security. They may keep their savings in the form of cash, deposit some of it in savings accounts, purchase insurance policies, or buy various kinds of securities. Little need be said at this point about holdings of cash, because these are not available for investment. But other forms of saving find their way into the supply of loanable funds and are used for investment purposes.

One way of supplying savings to business firms is through the purchase of corporate

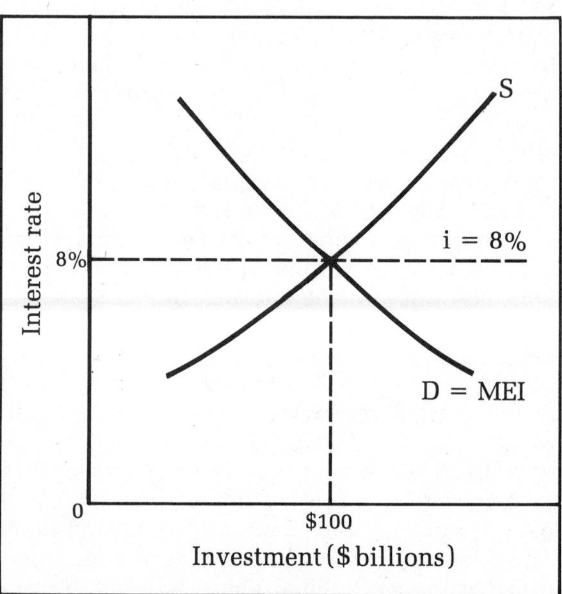

Figure 9 Equilibrium in the market for financial capital. When there is perfect competition in financial markets, supply and demand determine equilibrium price (i.e., interest rate) and quantity.

bonds. Households may buy corporate bonds through a broker. More often they buy bonds indirectly, through banks, savings and loan associations, and insurance companies. These institutions, called **financial intermediaries,** take savings that people have deposited with them and make them available for business loans.

There is some evidence that savers respond to high interest rates by increasing the quantity of funds available for lending. If this is true, supply curves will slope upward. Equilibrium is determined by the intersection of demand and supply. In Figure 9 the equilibrium price of financial capital (the interest rate) is 8 percent, and the equilibrium quantity is $100 billion.

Saving may also be affected by inflation. In general, expectations of new price increases stimulate "beat-the-price-rise" buying. Many consumers reduce their saving to negative amounts: they borrow to buy today what may be more costly tomorrow. The result is a lower level of savings supplied at every interest rate and a higher equilibrium interest rate. The net result is less funds available for investment projects.

Financial Markets

We have been speaking of the rate of interest as if there were only one interest rate at any time. In fact, there is a whole range of interest rates. For example, different kinds of bonds have different levels of risks and thus different interest rates. Government securities are the safest securities because they are backed by the taxing power of the U.S. government. However, because they are safe investments, they pay a low rate of interest. In May 1980 new issues of U.S. Treasury bills maturing in three months were paying 10 percent interest. U.S. three- to five-year bonds were paying 10.5 percent. Highly rated municipal bonds were paying about 7 percent. Interest earned on municipal bonds is exempt from federal incomes taxes, so an interest rate of 7 percent may be worth as much as 12 percent or more to lenders. Corporate bonds are not as safe as U.S. government securities, but they pay higher interest. The highest-graded corporate bonds were paying 11 percent, and bonds of lower grade, carrying more risk, were paying 13 percent in 1980.

Savers like to diversify their holdings. They supply their funds in various types of financial markets. They purchase not just one kind of bond but a variety so as to be sure of satisfying different financial needs. In doing so they take three things into account: the *yield* of a bond, time to *maturity,* and *risk.*

The **yield** of a bond is the percentage rate of return per dollar invested. Yield is sometimes the same as the interest rate on the bond, but often it differs because the price paid for the bond may be different from its face value. What counts is the percentage return received on the amount actually paid for the bond. Interest rates vary depending on the length of time until **maturity**—that is, the number of years and months before the investor receives face value of the bond. Long-term bonds generally pay higher interest rates than short-term ones. This is partly because a higher interest payment is necessary to induce lenders to wait longer for their money. Another reason for the higher interest on long-term bonds is the greater chance that the borrower might default, or fail to pay back on the investment. The probability of loss is what investors call **risk.**

Savers purchase a variety of securities to satisfy their need for the *highest possible yield* with the *lowest risk* and a *mix of maturities.* They will buy some short-term securities with low yields, some long-term securities with high yields, some risky securities with high yields, and some safe securities with low yields. They seek a *balanced portfolio* of securities rather than a specialized one. The result is different supply curves in different markets and different interest rates.

In summary, the demand for financial capital is based on the marginal efficiency of investment. A firm's MEI reflects the rates of return *(r)* on investment projects arranged from the highest to the lowest. The firm will continue to borrow for investment as long as the MEI of additional projects is greater than the interest on borrowed funds. Interest rates depend on the interaction of demand and supply in financial markets. The supply of financial capital is based on the actions of savers and the net change in the money supply. Savers supply their funds in a number of money markets so as to accumulate a diversified group of securities. Riskier and longer-term loans will normally be made only if interest income is higher.

When financial markets are operating efficiently, the result is to allocate investment funds to those projects which are expected to yield the greatest return. More funds flow to safe investments, and their interest cost is lower. Projects that involve risk are allocated fewer funds, and their interest cost is higher. New investment projects increase the nation's capital stock and help us produce more goods and services.

Efficiency in Financial Markets

We have discussed three important determinants of the interest rate on investment funds:

(1) Investment projects are expected to be profitable. The *rate of return* on an investment project provides funds to reward the lender for sacrificing current consumption.

(2) The nominal rate of interest paid should include an adjustment for inflation called *inflation premium;* otherwise the real rate of interest will not compensate lenders sufficiently for their sacrifice.

(3) There is a *risk component* to interest rates. Risky investment projects and those expected to be profitable only after a long time require additional interest earnings to compensate for the greater probability of loss.

All these interest-rate determinants can be illustrated graphically. Understanding the role of these factors in determining interest rates can help us understand how financial markets operate. Efficient financial markets allocate savings toward their most productive uses, ensuring growth in the nation's production possibilities.

The real return on investment capital has been fairly stable over the years. Figure 10 is a time series showing nominal and real interest rates on short-term business borrowing since 1950. Although the nominal rate has fluctuated widely, the real rate has remained fairly constant at between 1.5 and 2.0 percent. This was generally true until the exceptionally high inflation of the mid-1970s. These results suggest an average real return on business borrowing for investment of about 2 percent in normal years. Inflation and expectations of inflation can push the nominal rate up sharply. But in general, the real rate continues to reward savers at a fairly stable rate.

Figures 11 and 12 show the effect of risk on interest rates. Figure 11 illustrates the risk associated with time to maturity. It compares interest rates on U.S. Treasury securities having various maturities. Interest rate is measured on the vertical axis, and the time to maturity of newly

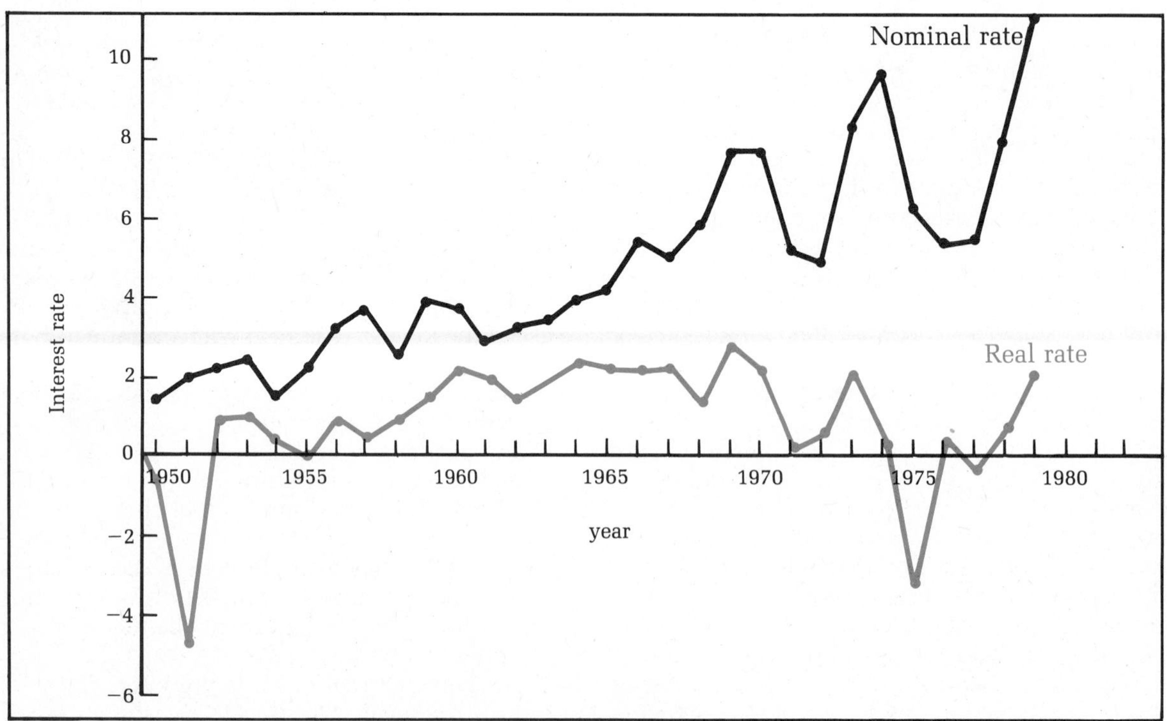

Figure 10 Interest rates 1950–1980 on prime commercial borrowing (4–6 months).

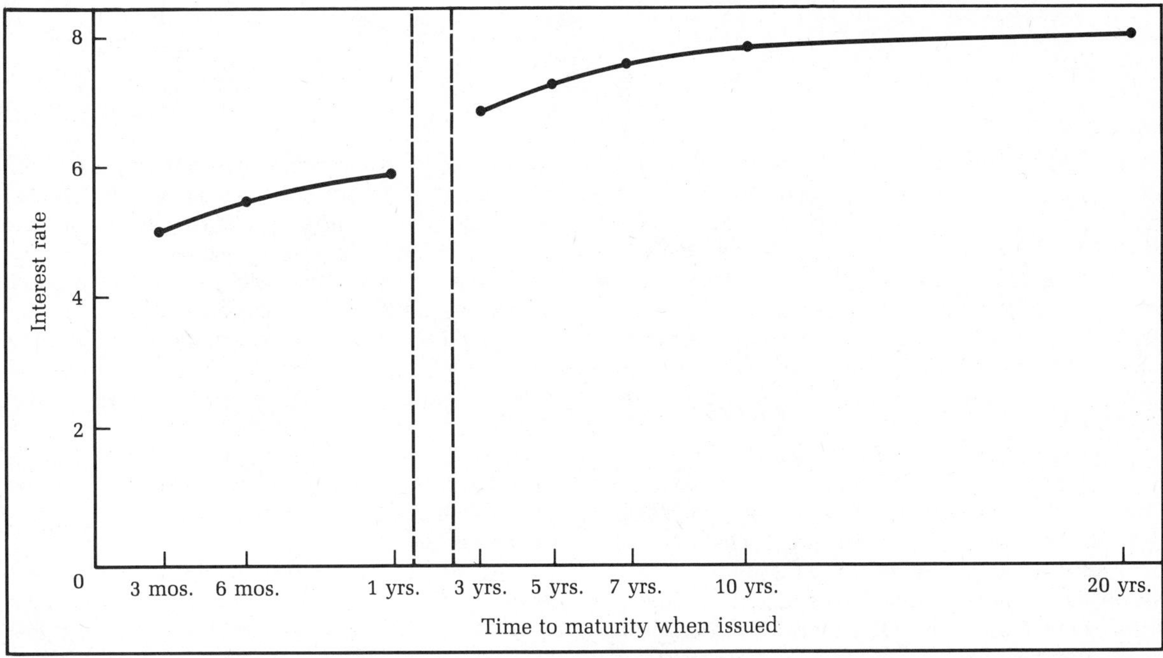

Figure 11 Yields on U.S. Treasury securities of varying maturities (1976).

issued securities is measured on the horizontal axis. The curve is called a *yield curve.* Since the yield on securities of longer duration includes a risk premium, the yield curve typically slopes upward.

The data used for drawing Figure 11 refer to 1976, the most recent year when the yield curve had the typical shape. For the remaining years of the 1970s and in 1980 the yield curve sloped downward, indicating higher interest rates on short-term loans. One reason was high inflation, which added a high inflation premium and made long-term rates so high that firms were forced to seek temporary funds in short-term markets. The expectation was that inflation and interest rates would eventually come down, enabling firms to convert their short-term loans to long-term at normal rates. In the meantime, the heavy demand for short-term funds kept their rates exceptionally high.

Finally, Figure 12 illustrates the effect of risk associated with the variability of return on some hypothetical securities. Risk is measured on the vertical axis. Risk is defined as the average *deviation* of return of a security from its average annual return. By this measure a security whose return fluctuates widely from year to year would have a high level of risk. To compensate for risk, the security would have to pay a high average return, measured on the horizontal axis. Securities with more stable returns are less risky and require a lower average return. Points *A* and *B* in Figure 12 represent, respectively, risky and safe securities. Other securities with varying risk and return are shown by points arranged in an upward-sloping pattern. The pattern suggests

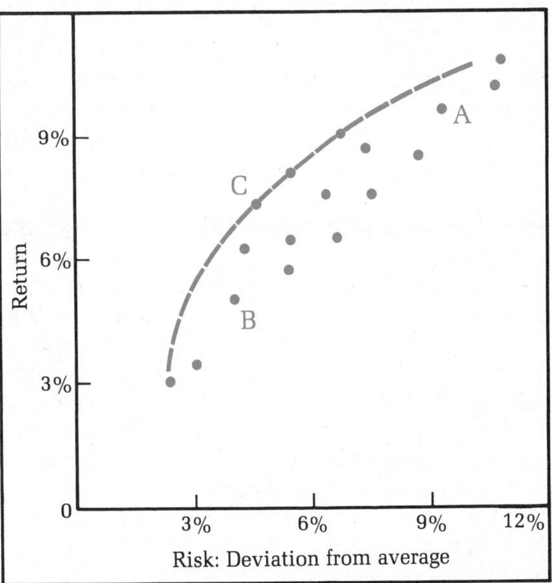

Figure 12 The relationship between risk and return for various securities.

Extended Example Capital and Growth

In 1976 the national wealth of the United States was estimated at $5.7 trillion. This amounts to $26,511 in land, buildings, and equipment for each of the nation's 214 million people. In 1776, per capita wealth was only about $1550; but wealth has grown faster than population so that workers today have substantially more capital to work with. To increase capital per worker is called "capital deepening"; increasing capital at the same rate as population increases is called "capital widening."

The rate of growth in national wealth has varied with changes in economic activity, war, and so forth. Changes have taken place also in the relationship between total productive wealth and annual national output: the capital/output ratio, K/O. As our wealth has grown, the quantity of capital (K) needed to produce a certain quantity of output (O) has fallen. The decline in the K/O ratio means a higher level of productivity for capital resources. For every dollar of new capital created, the potential output of goods and services has grown.

These favorable trends of recent decades may now be changing. Several factors are working together to reduce the productivity of our nation's capital stock. New capital requirements for environmental protection and occupational health and safety do not increase the nation's output of real goods and services. A relative decline in research and development outlays may mean fewer inventions and innovations. Uncertainties and wage-price controls during the 1970s may have distorted and misallocated investments.

Since World War II, growth of output in the United States has been slower than that of most Western European nations and Japan. Per capita output in the United States has fallen below that of several other nations. Many analysts blame our slow growth on a low rate of capital investment and thus they advocate policies designed to promote saving. Abundant savings for lending, they argue, would stimulate investment and enable the United States to resume fast growth in per capita living standards.

Edward F. Denison disagrees. Denison is one of America's foremost analysts of the sources of economic growth. His analysis suggests that factors other than new capital investment explain the different growth rates. In fact, Denison concludes that each 1 percent increase in saving would increase national output by less than 0.1 percent.

Beginning with the year 1960, Denison examined the differences between U.S. incomes and incomes abroad and analyzed the sources of the higher U.S. incomes. In general, between one sixth and one fourth of U.S. income advantage was attributable to our larger capital stock. Other advantages came from a

that higher risk requires higher interest payments to the lender.

Combining safe and risky securities in a single investment portfolio is called *diversification.* Diversification achieves a combination of risk and return that is preferred to the risk and return of either security taken separately. In Figure 12 the point labeled *C* represents risk and return for a portfolio composed half of *A* and half of *B*. Return on the portfolio is determined halfway between the return on *A* and *B*. Risk on the portfolio is less than half the distance between the risk of *B* and *A*. The reason is that two securities seldom move precisely the same distance or the same direction. While *A* may fluctuate widely, *B* may move in the opposite direction, cancelling out some of *A*'s variability and reducing total risk.

The dashed line on Figure 12 represents all the best combinations of the securities plotted in the space. Portfolios on the dashed line have returns which are a weighted average of returns on the securities included in the portfolio. Their risk positions lie to the left of points representing the average risks of individual securities. This makes portfolios on the dashed line preferred investment opportunities for savers. Savers who are willing to accept a high level of risk would select portfolios near the rightward end of the dashed line. Their returns might be high, but variable also. More cautious savers would select portfolios near the leftward end of the dashed line. Returns would be lower but more stable.

Financial markets are frequently described as "efficient." **Efficient markets** are those in which the four basic conditions of perfect competition are true: There are many small buyers

higher level of education among workers, a greater abundance of land, and fewer workers in farming and other types of small, inefficient establishments. The major sources of recent European growth have been the re-allocation of labor from farming and from self-employment in nonfarm establishments to more efficient production arrangements, increasing efficiency from economies of scale, applications of new knowledge to production, and changes in the composition of labor in terms of age and sex.

What causes an increase in capital stock? According to Denison, capital investment depends on the rate of return on investment projects. Capital and labor resources are subject to diminishing returns if combined with fixed quantities of the other. Thus, a high level of employment reduces the marginal productivity of labor and increases the marginal product of capital. The result is an incentive to invest. Moreover, whenever total output increases, both saving and investing are easier and the capital stock will grow.

What policy conclusions follow from Denison's analysis of the sources of economic growth?

Explain why environmental protection regulation increases the K/O ratio. Should this be an important consideration for making environmental policy? Why or why not?

and sellers, products are indistinguishable, buyers and sellers have complete information, and they react quickly to changing market conditions. Financial markets meet these conditions more completely than any others. The result is that market forces of supply and demand more completely determine price and quantity than may be true in other markets. Suppliers and demanders of savings understand their financial alternatives and make decisions designed to satisfy their financial objectives. They bargain and agree on a price that correctly reflects the circumstances above—the rate of return on investment, an inflation premium, and a premium for risk.

The results of these decisions are certain benefits for the economy as a whole. Recall the fundamental problem of all economies: the scarcity of resources. Financial resources are scarce, too, since saving requires a sacrifice of current consumption. Variability among interest rates helps ration scarce financial capital toward projects with the highest rate of return, toward long-term projects which increase productivity, and toward innovative projects whose return is uncertain. Expected returns on financial capital may also serve as an incentive for savers to provide more funds for enhancing the nation's growth.

ENTREPRENEURSHIP: THE THEORY OF PROFIT

We come now to the fourth kind of resource used in production, entrepreneurship. Just as other kinds of resources earn returns in the form of wages, rent, or interest, entrepreneurial resources earn a return in the form of profit. The term *profit* is probably the most controversial term in economics. Some people feel that collecting a profit isn't quite nice. According to public opinion polls, a large segment of the public thinks that business profits are too large. Many people in business, on the other hand, say that profits aren't large enough and that the federal income tax on corporations bites too heavily into them.

Whatever the truth may be, profit is in fact a *necessary* return to an important productive resource, entrepreneurial ability. The entrepreneur is the initiator, the creator, and the organizer of any productive enterprise. It is entrepreneurial talent that is responsible for combining other resources into a successful organization.

Functions of Profit

Profit is so important in our system that the system itself is sometimes called the "profit system." Profit serves two functions: It is a regular return for performing entrepreneurial duties; and it is a special return for exceptional services. In the first sense profit is similar to rent, wages, and interest incomes. It is the opportunity cost of hiring entrepreneurial ability. In this sense profit is what we have called *normal profit*. It must be paid if the entrepreneur is to continue in a particular employment.

In the second sense, profit provides the

incentive for new creative undertakings. Profit is the fuel by which the engine of capitalism operates. Without the hope of profit, entrepreneurs would not take the risks involved in starting new businesses or in moving existing firms along new paths. Profit has been the mainspring of modern capitalism, driving it along in its phenomenal growth and technological development. Without vigorous entrepreneurship, our resources might never have been developed to their full potential. In this sense the returns earned for exceptional service are *economic profits.*

In both of these functions profit is necessary because of *change.* If economic conditions were not constantly changing, entrepreneurs would not be needed for adapting to change. Production could continue year after year with no need for making new decisions. And if new creative undertakings were not forthcoming, there would be no need to reward their creators.

Fortunately, these characteristics are not true. Our economy does change, making entrepreneurship necessary and stimulating its development. Technology changes and business firms must adapt. Markets change and firms must respond. If the response is correct, there are profits. Whatever the response, however, there are risks of loss.

Risks are even greater when business firms act in advance of change. Instead of adapting to changes which have already occurred, firms may anticipate new markets and new technologies. To initiate change is called *innovation.* **Innovation** is the development and application of a new product or process. American entrepreneurs have been responsible for innovations in many areas: in *production,* the steam engine, computerized machine tools, mass production, and the assembly line; in *communication,* the telephone, telegraph, and transistors; in *transportation,* the internal-combustion engine, the airplane, and diesel and rocket engines. Successful innovators reaped great profits. Some innovations have been spectacular: the Polaroid camera, which made fortunes for its developers, and the new microcomputers that combine thousands of transistors on one silicon chip, enabling pocket calculators and digital watches to be produced inexpensively.

Other innovations were not as successful. Occasionally a new product or process may be technically a very good one and yet be unacceptable to consumers. When that happens, the whole investment may be lost. The Edsel automobile introduced by Ford in 1958 is the classic example of such a failure. Millions of dollars were spent developing and testing the Edsel, but it failed. Quadrophonic sound seems to be another example of an innovation that didn't catch on. Can you name others?

Frequently, economists distinguish between *risk* and *uncertainty.* Risk refers to predictable losses. Fire, theft, delays in shipments, and equipment failures occur with fairly predictable regularity, so that probabilities can be attached to their occurrence. Losses like these can be insured against, either by an outside insurer or by building an added cost into the firm's own production cost estimates. On the other hand, the *uncertainty* that goes along with completely new undertakings is an uninsurable risk. It is uncertainty, the danger of loss because of unpredictable changes in conditions, that is usually associated with profit. The innovating entrepreneur accepts the uncertainty that goes along with change and earns the profit—or the loss—that follows.

If profit serves such important functions, why is profit so often condemned? There are two related explanations. Most American workers are removed from the risk-taking aspects of business. Whereas small entrepreneurs of the past were very much aware of the risks of any new business undertaking, today's wage earners are less so. Second, today's workers often fail to see how their own jobs depend on profits, how profits provide the motivation and the funds for building a business and creating job opportunities.

Some economic profit is a result of monopoly. The successful innovator enjoys a monopoly, at least until imitators catch up and take over part of the market. That is one reason why dynamic firms keep trying to develop innovations, in order to enjoy the exceptional profits that go with them. But monopoly profits are generally temporary. They result from natural frictions in the marketplace, from a lack of complete and immediate response to market conditions. Eventually, rivals come in and monopoly profits disappear.

Only when these natural frictions become institutionalized can monopoly profits persist. If competitors are prevented from entering the industry an entreprenuer may continue to receive economic profit. A patent is one form of institutionalized monopoly. Inventors are en-

Extended Example Profits

An important difference between our free market economy and a command economy is the use of profits. In our system, profits are a necessary return to a vital resource. Profits perform two functions: They ration out scarce entrepreneurial resources to the industries where need is most urgent; and they provide the incentives to assume the risks that accompany change. In a communist system, scarce resources are allocated according to a central plan, and incentives take the form of awards, bonuses, and public recognition of service.

In 1979, American corporations earned pretax profits of $237.0 billion. This was 10 percent of the value of total sales for that year. Federal, state, and local governments collected $92.7 billion in corporate profit taxes, and corporations paid out $52.7 billion in dividends. The remaining $91.7 billion was retained in corporations for reinvestment.

Since 1929, after-tax profits have averaged about 7 percent of net domestic product, but the profit share has been declining in recent years. For manufacturing industries, the usual profit is about $.05 for each dollar of sales, and about $.12 for every dollar of common and preferred stock outstanding.

Is this too much? Are corporations collecting too great a share of output? The answer depends on the level of competition in U.S. industry. Where there is competition, it is not possible for a single firm to collect excess profits. Prices will be forced down to the competitive level and wages will be forced up to the going rate in the industry. This will leave firms with only normal profit for the entrepreneurial resources used in production.

Suppose you own stock in a profitable corporation. Would you prefer to receive dividends on your shares of stock or to have earnings retained by the corporation? What considerations would govern your decision? Suppose you are chairman of the Board of Directors. What considerations would govern your decision to pay dividends or retain earnings? How would both types of decisions affect others in the community?

sured protection from competition for seventeen years. The patent laws are intended to encourage innovation by giving inventors a chance to profit from their work. This kind of temporary restriction on competition is probably desirable. There are other means of guaranteeing control of the market for early comers. Certain property rights and leasing or franchising privileges are some examples. Not everyone can open a McDonald's or a Kentucky Fried Chicken restaurant.

Building Human Capital

Many of us make investments without going near financial markets. We invest in ourselves. We build up our entrepreneurial ability by going to school or taking special courses in business management. The decision to invest in human capital is similar to a decision to invest in any other kind of capital. In part, it rests on a comparison between what we hope to earn in alternative employments.

What is the price of an investment in human capital? Education requires expenditures for tuition, books, and extra living expenses. But the price also includes the opportunity cost of the student's time while in training—the income that could be earned by working instead of studying.

The expected return from an investment in human capital is higher income in the future. A prospective student might compare the average income for various occupations and calculate the flow of future earnings. Then, the student would compare the income flows with the cost of the training to acquire the necessary skills. Of course, the decision that follows isn't just a matter of dollars and cents. Not all the benefits from developing skills can be measured that way.

Some of the gains from having skills are what economists call *psychic benefits.* Thus, schoolteachers may draw certain satisfactions from their work over and above their paychecks—satisfactions they would not obtain from working as secretaries. Deep-sea divers and trail guides may value the thrills of their jobs above their actual incomes. On the other hand, some unpleasant jobs provide negative

Economic Thinker **Frank Knight**

Among economists, Frank Knight (1885–1972) is known more as the philosopher than the scientist. Born in rural McLean County, Illinois, Knight attended Cornell University, intending to pursue a Ph.D. in philosophy but switching his major interest to economics. Soon after receiving his doctorate in economics, he went to the University of Chicago as an instructor. There, in 1921, he published his most famous book, *Risk, Uncertainty, and Profit.* This study marked the beginning of his reputation as a proponent of the theory of pure economic competition. In it Knight distinguished between risk and uncertainty: risk is insurable, while uncertainty isn't. Profit is thus the reward to businesses for facing uncertainty in their decisions.

His writings and teaching at the University of Chicago, along with those of Henry Simons and Friedrich von Hayek, helped establish that institution's reputation as a citadel of neoclassical, libertarian economics. The "Chicago School of Economics," as it is known, is the foremost advocate of free enterprise and the greatest opponent of government "interference" in the market. That tradition is carried on today by Milton Friedman, George Stigler, and many others.

Knight recognized that the economic model of perfect competition is only an ideal. He was well aware that the marketplace is subject to the irrational application of power by individuals and groups and that this power distorts the free enterprise ideal. Nevertheless, to Knight, unbridled free enterprise was the only true economic wisdom. Economists, social scientists, and governments must not interfere with this ideal by trying to change social institutions through regulations and control. Such interference can only lead to revolution and dictatorship.

Knight's preoccupation with the virtues of free enterprise led him to the conclusion that the only economic models worth attention by economists were models based upon the ideal of perfect competition. Models and theories based upon the possibility of monopolistic interference with the marketplace were unproductive. If such monopolistic tendencies did exist, they would correct themselves in time. If there were imperfections in the free market system, such imperfections were caused by the ignorance of consumers, often influenced by advertising. Labor unions, with their great power to influence costs and prices, represented a dire threat to the free market system. On the other hand, corporate power, because it was subject to the uncertainty and risk of profit making, could not in the long run permanently disrupt the free market.

Despite his defense of the free enterprise system, Knight saw that the greatest enemies to the free market were some of those who argued for it. In *The Ethics of Competition,* a collection of his essays written between 1921 and 1935, he criticized free market arguments designed solely to defend the special interest of those who profited by the existing social and economic order. Knight argued that there was nothing ethical about competition that resulted in unfair distribution of productive resources and monopolistic ownership of property and productive capacities. A truly free economic system must not be corrupted and abused by power-seeking individuals and institutions.

Knight, however, did not consider this possibility an economic or even a social problem. The problem is a moral one. Science had destroyed religion as a moral force but had left nothing in its place. The danger existed that humanity would now turn to government to solve its problems. That road, Knight argued, could only lead to dictatorship and loss of freedom. The tendency of power to corrupt the free enterprise system must be checked by a common morality based on freedom to seek out the truth and on honesty and mutual respect.

Although firm in his insistence that the ideal of pure competition represented the best of all possible economic worlds, Frank Knight was equally insistent that all dogmas should be challenged. Generations of his students were taught to distrust all authority—even his. The quest for truth, he argued, in economics as in all else, must be an unending one if society is to remain free.

psychic income, which should be deducted from the worker's paycheck to arrive at net benefits from work. Air-traffic controllers and marriage counselors probably fall in this category.

Richard B. Freeman of Harvard University has estimated (1976) lifetime earnings for male college graduates as $821,909 and for male high-school graduates as $601,882. The difference in earnings appears to justify the investment in a college education. Nevertheless, the pattern of earnings may alter the results. Since the college graduate will receive the higher pay later in life, the earnings must be discounted to reflect their value in the present. The rate of discount depends on various factors: the interest rate on funds borrowed for schooling, the interest rate which could be earned on funds invested in some way other than schooling, and the particular preference of the individual for income now or in the future. When future income is discounted at a high rate, earnings of the average high-school graduate may exceed the deferred earnings of the average college graduate. This is probably true in the case of certain jobs where capable high-school graduates could quickly achieve high earnings.

Investment in human capital poses another problem involving the time required for learning new skills. Since college programs typically last four years, response to demand for college graduates lags four years. High demand at one point in time may raise wages and encourage investments in human capital. Four years later when the increased supply reaches the market, the equilibrium wage might drop sharply. Incentives would disappear and college enrollments would decline. The resulting shortage would finally push wages up again and the cycle would be repeated. (Fluctuating supply and wages for college graduates is similar to the "Cobweb" phenomenon in agriculture.)

RESOURCE PRICING AND INCOME DISTRIBUTION

We have described the institutions which influence resource markets and the economic analysis which underlies resource employment and prices. We may conclude that resource allocation tends in general to conform to marginal pro-

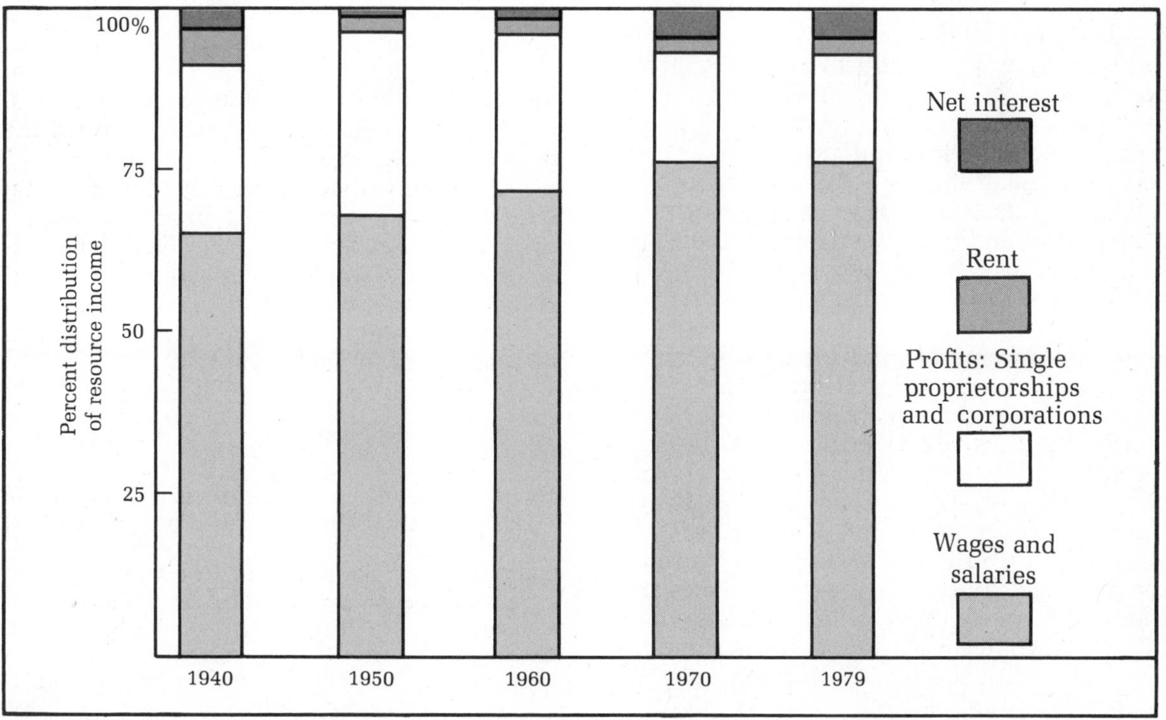

Figure 13 Trends in the distribution of resource income.

ductivity theory, but that certain institutions act to interfere with free market equilibrium.

The largest resource employed in the United States is labor. Labor's share of national income has increased in recent decades: from 65 percent in 1940 to 76 percent in 1979. Greater union strength may be partly responsible; but a more fundamental cause is probably a movement away from self-employment (where income is classified as profit) to wage employment in corporate industry. Profits declined from 27 percent to 16 percent over the same period. Rental incomes also declined, from 3 percent to 1 percent. Interest income has been increasing as a share of total income, in part because of higher nominal interest rates associated with high levels of inflation. Figure 13 shows income shares for selected years.

How do these trends compare with predictions from the past? The shift from profits to wages contradicts Marx's theory of the increasing misery of the working class. In fact, today's workers enjoy rising standards of living from wages, along with the opportunity to invest their savings in corporate stocks and bonds. Ricardo's predictions were mistaken, too. The scarcity of land has not yet caused such high rentals as to increase landlords' share of national income.

To the extent that income distribution conforms with marginal productivity theory, it may be described as equitable, or fair. It is fair if resources are rewarded proportionately with their contributions to output. Rewards may then serve a rationing and an incentive function: allocating the scarcest resources to their most productive uses and encouraging greater development of scarce, highly productive resources. Thus income distribution may also be described as efficient.

While income distribution may be fair, it may also be unequal. Inequality of incomes is necessary if resource markets are to give the proper price signals to owners and users of resources. Extreme income inequality is not acceptable in our society, however. A democratic nation cannot tolerate wide extremes of wealth and poverty. The next chapter examines the problem of poverty in the United States and the policies we use to deal with it. Policies which interfere with free market functions may reduce economic efficiency while achieving gains in social stability and justice.

SUMMARY

Demand for land depends on its marginal productivity. But unlike many resources the supply of land is fixed or inelastic. Rent is a surplus paid any resource in fixed supply. When supply is fixed, any payment is more than the amount necessary to keep the resource in production. Therefore, rent cannot serve an incentive function, but only an allocative or rationing function. Henry George proposed a single tax to collect the rental surplus from landlords, but it is important to tax only the land itself and not the *improvements* made on the land. Some types of labor may earn "economic rent" if their payment exceeds their opportunity cost in the next most productive employment.

Demand for financial capital depends on the marginal efficiency of investment, calculated as the rate of return above the initial outlay for investment projects. Capital budgeting is a means of comparing returns on alternative investments with the cost of borrowing. The capital budgeting decision can be influenced by inflation, which affects the real interest rate, and by tax credits, which affect the initial outlay for a project. The supply of financial capital flows from business and personal savings and from commercial bank lending. Savings are supplied in various financial markets according to yield, time to maturity, and risk. The result is different interest rates for different types of securities. Interest rates help allocate savings toward the most profitable uses.

Entrepreneurship earns profit for initiating, creating, and organizing a productive enterprise. Exceptional performance of entrepreneurial duties is rewarded with economic profit. Sometimes economic profit is the result of monopoly. Entrepreneurship may be developed by investment in human capital.

Key Words and Phrases

capital budgeting a process of establishing priorities in investment projects based on their expected profitability.

compounding earning a return on an investment plus a return on earlier returns from the investment.

discounting calculating the current value of an investment by dividing the future income payment by one plus the rate of return.

economic rent payment to any resource over and above its opportunity cost.
efficient markers financial markers are described as efficient because the four conditions of competitors are generally present; thus, market supply and demand determine price and quantity.
financial intermediaries institutions that collect the savings of households and make them available to business for investment.
innovation the development and application of a new product or process.
interest the annual return on capital; the cost of borrowed funds for investment.
marginal efficiency of investment the expected rate of return on investment projects.
maturity the time that must elapse before an investor receives face value of a bond.
nominal interest rate the stated amount of charge on a loan.
profit a financial return paid for entrepreneurial activity.
real interest rate the cost of borrowing in terms of actual purchasing power given up.
rent payment to households that supply land resources for use in production.
risk the probability of loss.
single tax a proposal to tax away the rent, or "unearned surplus" from land.
uncertainty the danger of loss because of unpredictable changes in conditions.
yield the rate of return from an investment per actual dollars paid.

Questions for Review

1. Explain why a growing share of output going to landowners might be a disadvantage to the economy.
2. How would you describe the elasticity of supply of urban land, farmland, recreational land? What is the effect of taxing land with these particular uses?
3. Suppose the interest rate is 8 percent. What is the most you would pay for an apartment building which would earn a net income of $50,000 over each of five years, after which you would sell it for $250,000?
4. State clearly the economic definition of rent, whether applied to land or any other resource. Show why rent can perform only a rationing function. How is this significant in levying taxes?
5. Use the data below to draw a firm's demand curve for financial capital:

Proposed investment	*Initial outlay*	*Expected rate of return*
Stamping machine	$200,000	8%
Crane	150,000	11%
Computer	30,000	7%

6. Distinguish between the real and nominal rates of interest. Show how a difference between the two can lead to a change in the level of investment in capital resources.
7. Explain why different bonds carry different rates of interest. How does a buyer determine which bonds to buy?
8. Complete the table below:

Year	*Rate of inflation*	*Interest rate on U.S. Treasury bills*	*Real rate of interest*
1960	1.7%	2.9%	_____
1970	5.4%	6.5%	_____
1975	9.7%	5.8%	_____
1979	8.7%	10.0%	_____

9. How does the payment of dividends to stockholders fulfill the two functions of profit?
10. Suppose there were perfect competition in all markets. How would you describe the level and type of profit? How would total income be divided among resources? What institutional factors distort these results? Are our lives made better or worse because of them? Explain.

CHAPTER 16

Poverty, Discrimination, and Public Assistance

Learning Objectives

Upon completion of this chapter, you should be able to:

1. Distinguish between relative and absolute poverty and explain, by each definition of poverty, who are the poor.
2. Discuss the many programs for aiding the poor.
3. Explain how negative income taxes work and how their work incentive factor compares with current aid programs.
4. Explain how dual markets work.
5. Discuss the way income is distributed in the United States.
6. Show the effect of urban poverty on cities.

In the previous two chapters we showed how resource owners receive their shares of national income. A free market rewards resources according to their contributions to production. Although income shares may be "fair," they may still be too small to provide a decent life. Some people are unable to earn any income at all: they may be disabled and unable to work or they may face educational or job discrimination. There are not always enough jobs for everyone who can work, and there are structural problems in matching available jobs with unemployed people. The single worst result of these market imperfections is the existence of poverty.

Most of us have seen poverty. We have contributed to food baskets for poor families, we have played with deprived children in public schools and playgrounds, or we have driven along country roads past tar-paper shacks or through the slums of large cities. We may have wondered about the differences among standards of living in a country as rich as ours.

In this chapter we will consider some important questions about poverty in the United States:

Who are the poor?

Why are they poor?

What, if anything, can be done about poverty?

How does poverty affect those of us who aren't poor?

DEFINING POVERTY

It is hard to say exactly what poverty is. We think of being poor as having to live in a shack, wear secondhand clothes, and eat cheap food. But this is not poverty of the sort suffered in much of the world. To a Pakistani or African

Hottentot, U.S. poverty would not be poverty at all. Many of the poor in the United States are only poor *relative* to the living standards the rest of us enjoy. We refer to this type of poverty as **relative poverty:** a condition of living substantially below the standards of others nearby.

By modern American standards, most of the human race has been poor throughout most of history. Our predecessors on this continent lived in huts made of birchbark or animal skins and survived on dried corn and the meat of wild animals. They were poor by our current standards—though they were not poor relative to those around them. Even the wealthiest lords and kings of medieval Europe lived in unheated fortresses, ate coarse black bread, and died of untreated illnesses.

To have no suitable home or food at all is **absolute poverty:** a condition of living below a level currently acceptable as necessary for human health and existence. In the United States, fewer people than in years past now face the problems of absolute poverty—of wondering where their next meal is coming from, or fearing exposure from the winter, or watching their brothers and sisters die in infancy.

People in much of the world are still poor, not only in a relative sense but also by absolute standards. One measure by which we can compare the poverty and wealth of nations is **output per capita:** the amount of annual production of goods and services per person. In 1978 in the United States, output per capita was about $9644. Switzerland ranked significantly higher (about $14,000). For Denmark, Sweden, and West Germany the figure was about $10,000; for Britain it was about $5500; for Greece, about $3300; for Peru, $850; for Thailand, $400.

Income figures may be misleading. Levels of living can't always be measured in dollars and cents. Many people in Asia, Africa, and Latin America live outside the market economy, where output is not recorded or exchanged for money. They have fairly well-organized systems of sharing in production and distribution, through which those in need are helped and sustained by other members of their society. Still, it is fair to say that masses of them are poor in terms of health, nutrition, and life expectancy, and poor also in being condemned to lives of unremitting struggle for survival. Table 1 lists other measures of levels of living for selected nations.

The industrialized nations have been able to eliminate most of the absolute poverty known by our ancestors. The Industrial Revolution brought tremendous growth in output and incomes, making it possible to invest in new capital, which led to still greater output.

Throughout most of the twentieth century in the United States both the number and proportion of families living in absolute poverty have declined significantly. Better educational and job opportunities have improved the earn-

Table 1 **Some International Comparisons of Levels of Living (Varying Dates 1975–77)**

	Life expectancy m.	Life expectancy f.	Illiterate population	Homes with running water	Number persons per physician
Argentina	65	71	8.4%	—	—
Bangladesh	36	36	78.0	—	—
China	60	63	—	—	—
France	69	77	3.6	97%	1.4
Greece	—	—	15.6	65	.5
Iran	51	51	63.1	13	2.8
Italy	69	75	6.1	—	.5
Japan	72	77	2.2	95	—
Mexico	63	67	25.8	39	—
Poland	67	75	2.2	47	.5
South Africa	50	53	43.0	—	—
Thailand	54	59	21.4	—	—
United Kingdom	68	74	—	—	.8
USSR	64	74	.3	—	.3
United States	69	77	1.0	98	.6

ing capacity of many workers. Furthermore, labor force participation has increased as more women have become wage earners. As a result, per capita incomes have increased. Today the number of people living in the United States who can be said to live in absolute poverty is quite low—though not as low as it might be.

The U.S. government has its own definition of absolute poverty. According to the Social Security Administration, an acceptable minimum level of income is three times what a family needs to buy essential food. This government definition is known as the **poverty line.** In 1979 a family of four living in a city needed about $6662 to meet this standard. Those earning below this minimum necessary for life were said to be living in absolute poverty (as well as poverty *relative* to the rest of us). In 1979 the federal government estimated 24.5 million Americans were poor. This means about 11.4 percent of the U.S. population was below the poverty line. The many forms of government assistance, however, help move about half of these families above the desperation of absolute poverty.

There are critics of this federally defined poverty line. Some feel it is arbitrary. For instance, a family of four with a total income of $6661 might be listed as poor, while another family earning $6663 would not be classified as poor. The poverty level changes each year to reflect price inflation. But since most price indexes are based on the cost of the average amount of food purchased by a *middle-class family*, the dollar level of the poverty line may be incorrect. Other critics maintain that the poverty line measures only absolute poverty, that is, those barely able to survive. To these critics, relative poverty should be emphasized more. To be cut off from a share of this country's wealth, they say, and from participation in this country's freedom of choice or to be locked into a pool of unskilled labor is a major injustice and deserves government attention.

Who Are the Poor?

The poor in America are not easy to categorize. They include all ages and races of people, and they are poor for a variety of reasons. Studies have been made to find out the most common characteristics of the poor.

Although most poor people are white, a larger percentage of the black population are poor. Blacks constitute only one eighth of our population but almost a third of all poor people. The poor are about equally divided among male- and female-headed families; but again, since there are fewer female-headed families, they are proportionately more likely to be poor. In past decades poor people tended to be scattered widely in rural areas; lately, however, the poor are increasingly concentrated in central cities. About one sixth of the nation's urban population is classified as poor. Many disabled persons are poor.

Many of the poor are elderly and past the earning age. Their only regular income is from Social Security. A word of caution is necessary here because the statistics may be misleading. Many elderly people own homes and other property. They may also be able to draw on savings or other assets, so they are not as poor as the level of their current incomes might suggest. But those who have nothing to fall back on

Table 2 **Characteristics of the Poor (March 1979)**

(1) Characteristic	(2) Number classified as poor	(3) Percent of characteristic classified as poor*
Total families	5.3 million	9.1%
Central-city families	3.3	15.4
White families	3.5	6.9
Over-65 persons	3.2	13.9
Female-headed families	2.7	31.4
Male-headed families	2.5	5.2
Nonwhite families	1.6	27.5

*Figures do not total because some persons are counted in more than one classification.
Source: "Current Population Reports: Consumer Income," Series P–60, No. 190, U.S. Department of Commerce, Bureau of the Census, November 1979.

except Social Security are in dire straits indeed.

Table 2 presents information about persons who have one or more of the four characteristics of poverty mentioned above. That is, they are nonwhite, live in central cities, belong to families headed by females, and/or are old. Column (3) shows that in 1979 some 27.5 percent of nonwhite families were classified as poor, compared with 6.9 percent of white families. Of urban families, 15.4 percent were classified as poor. Of female-headed families, 31.4 percent were poor compared with 5.2 percent of male-headed families. Finally, 13.9 percent of persons over sixty-five were poor.

Aiding the Poor

To say that almost 25 million Americans live in poverty is to make a pretty startling statement. After all, we are the world's richest country. We seldom see beggars in our streets. Most of the poor, of course, aren't to be seen unless we go where they live—down into the black ghettos of the inner city, into the cheap rooming houses of the elderly, or out to the depressed areas of the countryside. The poor may not look any different from other people. Many, if not most, have refrigerators and washing machines and television sets. After all, they live in a society where such things are standard equipment.

Programs for dealing with poverty take different forms, depending on the reasons why people are poor. We can distinguish several categories of poor people; those who are able to work but can't find employment; those who are employed but whose incomes are below the poverty level; and those who, for one reason or another, are mostly outside the labor market. The latter are sometimes called the "hard-core" poor because no matter how prosperous the national economy becomes, they will still be poor. **Hard-core poverty** includes some of the elderly, the disabled, the handicapped, and those who must stay home to care for dependent children. It also includes those lacking in human capital, that is, those who have received little education and are not prepared for work in available jobs.

Hard-core poverty. The hard-core group accounts for at least half of the poverty population. Their problems have to be handled on a case-by-case basis, usually through the welfare departments of their communities and states. Each poor family is assigned to a caseworker who is responsible for investigating their circumstances and determining what kind of aid is needed and how much. There are a number of separate **welfare programs** designed to help such families, using federal, state, and local funds.

The largest welfare program is called Aid to Families with Dependent Children (AFDC), which gave an average of $254 a month to more than 3.5 million families in 1978. Another program is the Supplemental Security Income program (SSI), which helps the aged, blind, and disabled. There were over 4.2 million SSI recipients in 1978. The federal Food Stamp Program enables about 15 million low income families to purchase food at reduced cost. Health care is provided to welfare families under the Medicaid program, which pays the cost of medical and hospital services.

Welfare programs have been widely criticized. They are complex and overlapping. Some people receive benefits under several programs, while others receive nothing at all. Benefit payments vary widely among states, usually being lower in the poorer states and higher in the richer states like New York and California. A class of "welfare cheaters" has grown up, consisting of people who would rather live on welfare than work. Cheaters may draw benefits under multiple names, or from two different counties, or even from two different states. To combat cheating, the welfare agencies must use administrative methods that are cumbersome, costly to the taxpayers, and humiliating to recipients. A bureaucracy is needed to handle the paperwork and to decide who is entitled to benefits and how large the benefits should be. In an effort to cut down on the number of "freeloaders," the system often denies aid to families with able-bodied men. One unfortunate result of this is that it may give fathers an incentive to desert their families, knowing that their wives and children will receive more aid without a man in the household. Many states now give benefits to families with able-bodied males and make efforts at the same time to guide recipients toward jobs.

There are two basic forms of public assistance for the elderly: Social Security and Medicare. Social Security is one of the oldest programs of public assistance, having been leg-

Extended Example
Lyndon Johnson's War on Poverty

When Lyndon Baines Johnson became President, conditions were ripe for beginning new initiatives to attack old problems. Economic advisers in the executive branch of government, Walter Heller and Kermit Gordon, had been conducting research into the extent of poverty in the nation. Their findings and recommendations formed the basis for a new poverty program.

There was a national commitment to act decisively, and Lyndon Johnson was uniquely prepared to lead the effort. He had been born in southern Texas and had grown up among poor blacks and Chicanos from across the Mexican border. As a public schoolteacher, he had seen how poverty and illiteracy stunted the lives of poor children. During the New Deal of the 1930s, he had served as state director of the National Youth Administration, providing training and jobs for disadvantaged young adults. As Congressman and Senator, he had come to understand the importance of government's role in setting policy to moderate the inequalities of the market system.

It was Johnson's aim not only to help the nation's 35 million poor people, but to strengthen the entire moral and economic fabric of the nation. While the economy was booming and jobs were plentiful, many poor people remained outside the system, trapped by circumstances that prevented them from participating in and contributing to a more productive economy. The President sought to focus government's creative efforts on preparing young people to move out of the poverty cycle so as to provide the benefits of a "Great Society" to all Americans.

On January 8, 1964, President Johnson declared War on Poverty. He allocated a billion dollars from the current budget and appointed Sargent Shriver to direct the effort. Congress passed the Economic Opportunity Act, establishing a wide array of programs to get at the causes and effects of poverty:

The Community Action Program set up local agencies to organize the poor for planning and carrying out programs involving neighborhood education, health, and legal services.

The Job Corps and the Neighborhood Youth Corps provided training and education for young adults and teenagers from poor families. Head Start and Upward Bound aimed at providing equal educational opportunities for preschool children and for potential college applicants. Operation Mainstream and New Careers were adult retraining programs, and the Work Incentive Program trained and placed welfare recipients. Other education programs provided special assistance to needy children, educationally deprived students, immigrant students, and handicapped students.

In 1965 Medicare and Medicaid were passed, providing health insurance for the aged and for the poor. As demand for health services increased, funds were provided for nurses' training, for aid to medical schools and medical students, and for hospital construction and modernization.

The Housing and Urban Development Act of 1965 provided subsidized loans for building low-rent housing and gave rent supplements to poor families.

The War on Poverty differed from earlier, more generalized approaches which depended on the "trickle-down" theory of aid for the poor. The old idea was that any federal spending would be spent over and over, gradually finding its way into the incomes of poor families. The new approach emphasized services and in-kind programs, providing specific goods and services to particular groups of the disadvantaged. Between 1965 and 1969 federal welfare spending grew from $53.5 to $86.5 billion (in real dollars, or constant purchasing power), an increase of 62 percent in four years.

During the Nixon administration, some changes were made in these programs, and many were finally phased out as the nation returned to general assistance programs. Between 1970 and 1974 welfare spending grew from $93.7 billion to $139.6 billion (again in constant, or real, dollars), a 49 percent increase in four years. As a percentage of total national output, federal social welfare expenditures were 5.8 percent in 1965, 9.1 percent in 1970, and 11.2 percent in 1975. The percentage in 1975 would have been smaller if it had not been for the severe recession.

When President Johnson left office, the nation's poverty population had been reduced to 24.1 million—a 31 percent reduction in four years. The War on Poverty and a growing economy had been moving people out of poverty two and a half times faster than at any other time in history. During the early 1970s, the poverty population stabilized at about 25 million, in part because of two recessions.

In the presidential election of 1964, the public had supported Lyndon Johnson's vision of the Great Society with the largest plurality in history—61 percent of the popular vote. But four years later distrust and fear had set in. Candidate Richard Nixon pointed to "an ugly harvest of frustration, violence, and failure" and gained a narrow victory over Johnson's Vice-President, Hubert Humphrey. The public seemed to renounce the philosophy of the Great Society.

Other factors were also sapping the nation's resolve to correct some of the inequalities of the market system. In the earlier period a growing economy had been providing the resources for new government programs, but by 1968 the Vietnam War was claiming more of the nation's resources and raising the cost of social welfare programs.

What were the net effects of the War on Poverty? Analysts have explored the benefits and costs of specific programs and found, in general, that results did not come up to expectations. This could mean that the programs themselves were failures, or it could mean that the original expectations were not realistic. The conclusion that a program has failed depends on the perspective of the examiner; the fact that change of any sort will benefit some groups more than others may label it a success in the eyes of one and a failure in the eyes of another. For blacks and many of the poor there was definite progress in education, employment, income, and civil rights in the 1960s.

The programs were costly, and some of the costs were the result of experimentation. Government operates in a fishbowl; its mistakes are widely labeled the result of inefficiency and waste. In the private sector, however, high costs are often associated with superior quality and with progress in research and development; high costs are regarded as a necessary price for quality and growth. Many War on Poverty programs were interrelated so that it was impossible to separate the costs and benefits of a single one. Unemployment, for instance, was attacked through education and vocational training, job counseling, fair-hiring standards, transportation and placement services, and child care. No single program can have much impact without coordination among all programs. And often no single program will achieve benefits equal to the cost of that particular program.

Discuss efforts to relieve poverty in terms of a production possibilities curve. What considerations influence the decision to embark on a War on Poverty, or a war against any social problem?

islated during the depths of the Great Depression in the 1930s. Benefits under the Social Security Act are paid by the federal government to retired workers and their dependents on the basis of their past contributions to the Social Security Trust Fund. Both workers and employers pay 6.13 percent (1980) of a worker's paycheck up to $25,900 (for a maximum worker contribution of $1587.67 a year). The fund makes transfer payments to retired workers and to dependent spouses and children of deceased workers. Payments average only about $250 a month, but they help stave off abject poverty for the 34 million people who receive them. Because the program applies only to formerly employed workers, many needy families are not eligible for benefits. For these families, welfare payments are financed primarily by federal funds, supplemented by state and local tax revenues.

The other important public assistance program for the elderly is Medicare, which was passed by Congress in 1965. Medicare helps pay medical bills for the aged. This program became necessary because old people, who become ill more frequently than any other age group, were no longer able to bear the increasing costs of medical care.

Cyclical poverty and jobs. The best remedy for poverty is a job. Most families with a working adult are above the poverty level. Those who aren't have wage earners in the very lowest-paid jobs, have unusually large families, or both. In 1979, a year of prosperity, only about 50 percent of poor families received any income from work. Many were headed by people who were working only part time. The remaining poor families had no one in the labor force. Thus many poor families have no working adults, either because they are unable to work at all or because they can't find jobs.

Finding and holding a job is difficult when business is bad. Our capitalist economy passes through cycles of recession, expansion, prosperity, and decline. Because of business cycles, the level of employment is constantly changing, sometimes expanding and sometimes contracting. Poverty associated with rises and falls in the nation's output is called **cyclical poverty.**

In the good years of the business cycle, employment opportunities are rising and many poor people are able to find jobs that require only a low level of skills. It follows that, in bad years, unemployment is hardest for workers who are just above the poverty level. Many of

Viewpoint Can Poverty Be Abolished?

How many poor people are there in the United States? According to the Bureau of the Census, there were 26 million poor people in September 1976, or 2.5 million more than the year before. Nonsense, responded some economists. "If poverty is a lack of basic needs, we have almost eliminated poverty in the United States," says Professor Sar A. Levitan of George Washington University.

The disagreement involves the definition of poverty. The Census Bureau defines poverty in terms of money income. In 1977 a nonfarm family of four was counted as poor if its money income was $6,190 or less. But those were the very people who benefited from *in-kind programs of aid* (i.e., nonmoney assistance) such as food stamps, subsidized housing, and Medicaid. According to Professor Edgar K. Browning, these and other types of income in-kind were enough to raise the average income of "poor" families well above the poverty line. Moreover, these forms of family assistance are not taxed as income and, therefore, provide poor families greater benefits than an equal amount of income.

A study by the U.S. Department of Health, Education and Welfare, cited by Browning, concluded that the federal government channeled $11.1 billion of goods and services to poor families in 1973. The total included benefits in the form of food, housing, education, health care, and job training programs. The value of these in-kind transfers amounted to $637 per poor person. "When in-kind transfers (exclusive of public education provided by state and local governments) are counted as income, the average poor family in 1973 had an income that was approximately 30 percent *above* the poverty line."*

This may be only a way of saying that the government's welfare programs are accomplishing what they were set up to do. The Census Bureau's figures are confusing because they count only the money benefits paid to people on welfare and not the nonmoney, or in-kind, benefits. Either the Bureau should count in-kind benefits, in which case there would have been almost no poor people in 1973, or it should leave out all welfare benefits, in cash as well as in kind, thus increasing the number of poor people in 1976 to more than 26 million.

An economist might prefer to define poverty to include all those who depend on welfare benefits for their support—that is, all those who are unable to earn their own way. A social worker or a nutritionist might prefer the other measurement, which shows that almost nobody in America has to go without food, clothing, and shelter. After all, there are many countries around the world where the living standards of U.S. welfare recipients must seem the height of luxury.

Why should we try to keep strict, separate measurements for income and in-kind payments?

*Edgar K. Browning, "How Much More Equality Can We Afford?" *The Public Interest*, No. 43, Spring 1976, p. 92.

them are thrust back down into the poverty from which they had risen. In 1975, a year of recession, the average rate of unemployment for the country as a whole stood at 8.9 percent. But as in previous recessions, it was much more serious among teenagers (20.7 percent), nonwhites (14.4 percent), and low-skilled workers in general (12.8 percent). Among inner-city teenagers, unemployment reached as high as 40 percent. At the other extreme, among married men in general, unemployment averaged only 5.1 percent.

Fortunately, many of the unemployed receive other income to help tide them over. Those whose unemployment is only temporary can be helped through **unemployment compensation,** money payments made for a given length of time. In most states, workers who lose their jobs can collect unemployment checks for a period of up to six months, and many states have extended the period by three or six months more. These payments are made to workers who have lost their jobs but who are still actively seeking work and are willing to accept a suitable job offer. The payments are financed through a tax on employers. The amount of the individual benefit depends on how much the person was earning and the length of experience on the job. Benefits vary across the country, being lowest in Mississippi and highest in Washington, D.C.

More than two thirds of the unemployed received unemployment compensation in 1975. Others who were not eligible for unemployment compensation received public assistance and food stamps. Programs that help the unemployed are of great value, not only in preventing hardship but also in helping counteract the business cycle by putting purchasing power in the hands of spenders. In 1975 unemployment compensation, public assistance, and food stamps provided eligible families with about 90 percent of their previous after-tax incomes. As a result of these programs, real per capita disposable income fell only slightly during the recession.

Islands of poverty. We have discussed two kinds of poverty: hard-core poverty, which afflicts those who are outside the labor market, and cyclical poverty, which results from business cycles. A third kind of poverty is caused by *structural* changes in the economy. When workers are unable or unwilling to respond to economic change, they may be left high and dry outside the mainstream of economic life. Such groups comprise islands of poverty.

Islands of poverty are the result of human immobility. If people were always able to move about or learn new skills in response to changes in the economy, this kind of poverty would not exist. If a coal mine in Kentucky closed down, miners would move somewhere else. If demand for welders dropped off, welders would switch to bricklaying or carpentry.

In actual life, of course, many people cannot or will not change their locations or their skills. They may be reluctant to leave a place where they have lived all their lives and where they have friends and relatives. They may not know of opportunities thousands of miles away. Parts of the southeastern United States and Appalachia have high levels of unemployment today because their traditional industries have declined while many workers have remained.

Not all workers stay rooted, of course. Some workers do migrate—especially the younger ones. One famous example of poverty and migration was the Oklahoma dust bowl of the 1930s, when drought forced thousands of farmers to abandon the land. John Steinbeck wrote of them in *Grapes of Wrath,* telling of one family's journey to California with all their belongings piled on an old truck.

Governments have tried to deal with this sort of poverty in a number of ways. One basic question is whether workers should be helped to move from a depressed area to locations where there are jobs, or whether new industry should be encouraged to move to the depressed area. There are difficulties in both approaches.

Extended Example
An Island in Kentucky

Martin County, Kentucky, was once an island of poverty. In 1964 unemployment was more than 21 percent and the county had one doctor, two lawyers, no dentists, no drugstore, no newspaper, and no radio station. By 1977 there were twelve lawyers, nine doctors, two dentists, three drugstores, better roads, and unemployment of 3 percent. Weekly paychecks were averaging $350 and annual salaries from $15,000 to $20,000.

What brought on this miraculous transformation?

The first helpful change was the decision to build a twenty-four-mile branch line of the Norfolk and Western Railway through the county. The railroad offered a means of moving the region's low sulfur coal to market, coal that was increasingly in demand as the nation's energy crisis worsened. Cheap transportation facilities encouraged five coal producers to move in and invest $200 million in new facilities. Today the expected annual production is 13 million tons. Three thousand of the region's work force are now employed in ninety coal mines.

The growth in economic activity stimulated development of financial intermediaries. Bank deposits have more than tripled, and a savings and loan association collects savings for local investment. Tax revenues have been increasing, too, providing the means for building a garbage collection system, water system, recreation park, and swimming pool.

The new prosperity has brought a few problems. One big problem is a lack of housing for the workers attracted to the area. Another is the strain on public services that normally result from heavy population inflows. Still, the county's residents are pleased with the turn their region has taken and are hopeful they can maintain a steady rate of growth in production and incomes.

Can you cite other examples of how a shift in technology or consumer demand has created or relieved poverty?

If workers are to be taken up by the roots and transplanted somewhere else, they must be assured of jobs, homes, and a welcome from their new neighbors. People in other communities may resent the arrival of poor groups, who compete with them for existing jobs and services. And it is difficult for any government agency to guarantee workers permanent jobs in private industry in a distant part of the country.

The usual approach is for governments to try to bring industry into areas where it is needed. This method has been tried in a number of counties with varying results. In theory, a region having surplus labor should be attractive to outside firms because wages will be lower there. But the very fact that industry is lacking in an area suggests that business opportunities may be limited. If profits were there for the taking, companies would already have moved in. There may be a mismatch between the area's resources and the needs of industry: lack of the necessary job skills, lack of industrial capital, or lack of transportation facilities. If government is to encourage the movement of industry, it must help train workers, give tax credits for investment, and enable firms to borrow cheaply.

Many state governments in the United States use these incentives to attract industry, and they are helped in this effort by the federal government. The Economic Development Act of 1965 and the Appalachian Regional Development Act of 1966 were passed by Congress in an effort to encourage area redevelopment. A danger is that government may be asking taxpayers to subsidize unprofitable enterprises in one part of the country that will compete with businesses elsewhere. Then, one region's gain might be another's loss. The hope, of course, is that the new enterprises will create jobs without taking them away from other workers, and that eventually government subsidies can be discontinued.

New Approaches

Welfare programs have become very expensive, amounting to about 10 percent of all government outlays (not counting Social Security). The high administrative costs and a growing belief that the present system of public aid has been a failure have led to a search for a new approach.

Direct grants. In 1979 federal and state governments spent more than $60 billion on public welfare and housing assistance. If this amount had been distributed directly to the nation's estimated 24.5 million poor, it would have amounted to more than $2450 for each of them, or about $9800 for a family of four. Much of it did not go directly to the poor, of course, since administrative costs had to be paid in the form of salaries for government employees, particularly the thousands of case workers engaged in deciding who is to get public assistance and how much.

It might be cheaper to support the poor through **direct grants** or outright payments of cash, rather than to channel funds through public welfare programs. One objection to this idea is that direct payments to the able-bodied poor might destroy their incentive to work. Low-skilled workers might receive more in welfare grants than they could earn on the job. Some people don't mind living off public funds rather than supporting themselves, and perhaps others would come to accept that way of life. Another objection is that direct payments would do nothing to correct the causes of poverty. (This assumes that current assistance programs help families deal with particular problems that make them poor in the first place.)

Negative income tax. A widely discussed proposal would channel funds directly to the poor while preserving work incentives. It would use the federal income tax system to set a **negative income tax** to make payments to poor families. Just as people above a certain level of income pay taxes to the government, those below a certain level of income would receive payments *from* the government. The amounts they would receive would depend on the size of their earned incomes.

Suppose the government set $6000 as the amount of income needed to enable a family of four to subsist in today's economy. A family with no income at all would receive a negative tax equal to the entire $6000. If the family began to have earned income, the negative tax payment would decrease—but not by as much as the earned income. The purpose of this provision is to give people an incentive to work at paying jobs rather than stay home and collect money from the government. There would obviously be no monetary advantage to the head of the family in accepting a part-time job paying, say, $1000 if government reduced the family's tax payments by the same amount.

Suppose that earnings from work cause the negative tax payment to be reduced by 50 percent of earnings. Then a family with earned income of $1000 would have its benefits reduced by .50($1000) = $500, giving it a total income of $5500 + $1000 = $6500. The family would be better off than if it had no earned income. Likewise, a family earning $3000 would have its benefits reduced by .50($3000) = $1500, giving it a net income of $4500 + $3000 = $7500. When its earned income reached $12,000, its benefits would be reduced by .50($12,000) = $6000, and the government would no longer be paying the family a direct subsidy. Income of $12,000 would be the cutoff point at which families stop receiving negative payments from government and begin paying a positive tax.

The chief disadvantage of the negative income tax idea is that it would cost more than direct grants, and probably more than the existing system of public welfare. The cost would be high for two reasons. First, the minimum income guarantee would have to be high enough to provide for families in which no one is able to work at all. Second, the percentage loss of benefits associated with level of earned income would have to be small enough to give able-bodied people an incentive to look for jobs. The smaller the benefit loss, the higher would be the cost of the program. That is because the payments would taper off at a higher level of family income. In the example above, reducing the benefit loss would increase work incentives. If the tax on earned income were reduced to 25 percent, the family with income of $12,000 would have benefits reduced by only .25($12,000) = $3000. Its benefits would not stop until earned income reached $24,000, since .25($24,000) = $6000. At such a high level of income, perhaps three quarters of the families in the country would be receiving negative income-tax payments. Of course, nobody is proposing such an extensive program as that.

The negative income tax would have the advantage of being simple to administer. Negative tax payments could be made through the existing Internal Revenue Service—instead of sending tax bills, government would mail checks to families who report income less than the cutoff level. This would probably require a larger Internal Revenue staff, but it would eliminate the need for social workers and the present public welfare bureaucracy.

Another advantage of the negative income tax proposal is that it might encourage individual initiative. Many of those benefiting from the negative tax would be given a sense of personal control over their family budgets and an incentive to look for a paying job.

Leaders of both the Democratic and Republican parties have at times given support to the negative income tax. President Nixon went farthest with it when, in 1969, he asked Congress to enact a modest "workfare" plan calling for a guaranteed minimum of $2320 a year (including about $850 in food stamps). Opposition in Congress held back the proposal and eventually the administration dropped it.

One of the chief arguments against it was that people would be able to get money without working. Even with the system of incentives, the critics argued, there would be many who would refuse to work. This objection was tested in an experiment begun in 1968. A group of 2700 families in seven states was given direct cash assistance over 3- or 5-year periods. Some of the families had been receiving public assistance under various welfare programs, and some were classified as "working poor." Another group of 2000 families was chosen to serve as a control group. This group continued under existing welfare programs or struggled along without any aid at all. Then comparisons were made of work effort in both groups.

Evidence of work disincentive in the group receiving direct cash assistance was stronger than some had hoped, but weaker than many feared. Although few workers actually quit their jobs, men who were receiving direct assistance worked 6 percent fewer total hours than men in the control group. Wives and female heads of households worked 17 percent and 12 percent fewer hours, respectively, than those in the control group. As expected, the disincentive appeared greatest when benefit loss associated with earnings was high. Also, the disincentive was twice as high among blacks and Hispanics as among whites.

Researchers were surprised to find a decline in family stability in the group receiving cash assistance: a 60 percent higher rate of separation and divorce. A possible reason for family breakups was that cash benefits provided opportunity for some to get out of an unpleasant marriage. Family instability was lower among Hispanics.

Researchers found some of the hoped-for results of direct assistance. Many families used their benefits to get training or to seek better jobs. One fourth of the group earned so much that they were no longer eligible for the program. Participants reported that the program had helped them to become self-sufficient, to budget their incomes, and to be more understanding of the problems of others.

Researchers recommended that this kind of program replace the current hodge-podge of public assistance programs, but that a mandatory work program be included. Adding job requirements would increase costs. The budget-conscious Congress of 1979 was cool to the proposal, but supporters hope eventually to revive it.

DISCRIMINATION

Racial and sexual discrimination continue to be a major cause of poverty. Poor jobs and low earnings for blacks and females are not necessarily a result of discrimination, of course. Some of the differences result from high job turnover, inadequate training, a lack of commitment to the work force, and personal limitations as to job hours or location. Still, researchers have found greater wage gaps than can be explained by these differences in worker quality. Where such gaps exist, the cause is probably discrimination.

Racial Discrimination

About a third of the poor are nonwhite. Nonwhites find it harder to get jobs than whites, and the jobs they do get tend to pay less. They are among the last to be hired and the first to be fired. They may have difficulty finding housing at a fair price or in a neighborhood of their choice. As a result, the poverty rate among nonwhites is three or four times as high as among whites.

Poverty among nonwhites has several causes. Many nonwhites come from rural farming backgrounds in the South; rapid mechanization in agriculture forced them to migrate to the cities at a time when demand for unskilled workers has been decreasing and when even semiskilled workers find it difficult to get jobs. Many unions have in the past set up direct and indirect barriers which discriminate against blacks—unions of construction workers such as electricians, carpenters, and bricklayers are examples. Relatively fewer nonwhites find office jobs, and relatively more are forced into service occupations that pay low wages. In 1979 half of all white workers were in professional, administrative, or selling jobs while only 36 percent of nonwhite workers were. Fewer than one eighth of white workers were in service occupations, while one fourth of nonwhite workers were. Average wages of nonwhites were 80 percent of those of whites. And, as we have already noted, unemployment is much higher among nonwhites.

Sex Discrimination

Sex discrimination may explain the incidence of poverty among female-headed families. Throughout most of history, women have generally been assigned different jobs or received lower pay for the same tasks as men. In Western society, the movement to a more industrialized economy increased the demand for unskilled labor and led previously unemployed women toward greater participation in the labor force. The trend toward ever increasing numbers of women working outside the home continues.

Economic discrimination against women is no longer legally or culturally acceptable. Income differentials based on sex still persist in many areas of employment, though they have narrowed over the last twenty-five years. In 1979 women were earning an average of only 60 percent of male earnings for full-time work. The earnings gap is not the result of present discrimination alone. Some of the difference is probably the result of lack of continuity or experience in the job market, a possible result of past discrimination. Still, there is evidence that among males and females of comparable experience, the wages of male workers tend to rise more steeply than those of females.

Dual Markets

Discrimination affects more than just the money incomes of the poor. To a great extent, families live and work and consume in two different economies, known as **dual markets.** Discrimination forces poor people to sell their labor within the occupations and industries that are opened to them. And what is opened to blacks and women is a labor market smaller and at times separate from that for white males. Because the

Extended Example Women in the Labor Market

Economics is the study of how a society uses its scarce resources to fulfill its unlimited wants. Labor is a scarce resource. In past years labor resources consisted chiefly of adult males, and production was limited as a result. But recently the United States is benefiting from use of another valuable labor resource: women.

Women are entering the labor force in greater numbers than ever before. Early in this century only one fifth of the female population worked outside the home, and these generally retired when they married. Following World War II, women's participation in the labor force rose to 46 percent of the female population. By 1979 women constituted 42 percent of total U.S. employment of 98 million workers, up from only 30 percent in 1950. The great surge in demand for female workers is partly a result of the growing volume of clerical work required by government agencies and partly a result of changing technical requirements in many industries. The growth in supply is a result of smaller families, the need for two paychecks in many households, and more female-headed families.

Female-headed families constitute 15 percent of all families or 8.5 million families, and their numbers are increasing at a rapid rate. They make up almost half the nation's poverty population.

Although their job opportunities have been improving, women continue to be employed principally in low-paying jobs. Only 19 percent of women workers are employed in professional or technical jobs, while 40 percent hold clerical jobs, and 13 percent are employed in service industries, including household workers. Women are still poorly represented in law, engineering, and medicine.

Their low job status helps explain the low relative wages of female workers. Another reason in many cases is the part-time or temporary nature of their employment. But discrimination in pay and hiring continues to play a major part in low female earnings. While the median earnings of full-time working women rose from $4134 in 1967 to $9641 in March 1979, their earnings relative to male workers remained only about 60 percent. The average full-time male employee earned about $5,000 more than the average full-time woman.

The gap between earnings of white and black women has been narrowing. The median earnings of black women in 1979 averaged 93 percent as much as those of white women: $9020 compared to $9732.

The problem of low female earnings is partly a result of the successful breakdown of social and economic barriers to employment. Because women have been seeking employment in greater numbers, more females are now in entry level jobs. More years are needed before women can build the job experience that brings rising productivity. Educational and skill development for the professions and for technical jobs will qualify females for higher earnings. Still, it is important to continue efforts toward elimination of job discrimination and other barriers to the use of this important resource.

Because of their low seniority women are often the first to be laid off in a recession. Some labor-market analysts contend that including females in the unemployment statistics overstates the actual problem of unemployment in the economy. They suggest that unemployed women should be left out of unemployment calculations—especially if they have working husbands. What is wrong with this proposal?

"It is ridiculous for upper-class wives to have jobs just so they can buy a fancy new car." Evaluate this statement.

How can investment in human and material capital help to relieve the problem of low female earnings? Illustrate graphically.

jobs they can get are limited and a large number of workers are competing for them, wage rates tend to be lower. Figure 1a illustrates price and quantity determination in labor markets for the general population; Figure 1b shows what happens to those who are forced to sell their labor in a more restricted market. In Figure 1b demand for labor is relatively low and supply is relatively large, resulting in a lower equilibrium price. The restricted workers are condemned to low wages or unemployment.

But that is not all. There are also dual markets for consumers. Nonwhites often pay more for housing, health services, and education than their white counterparts. This is true even when we take into account the lower rents in slum areas, because overcrowding and poor quality are likely to mean higher costs per unit of hous-

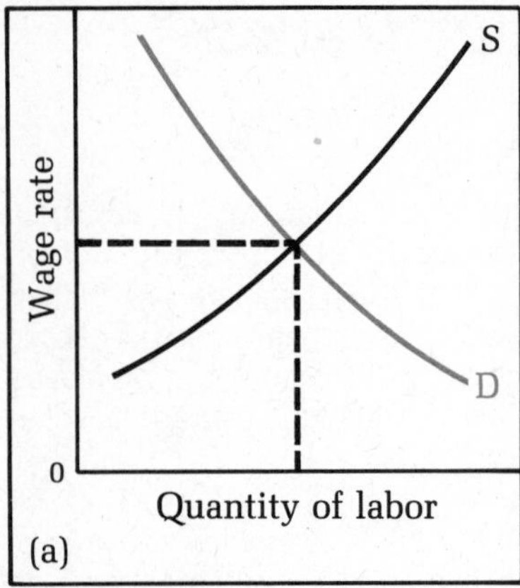

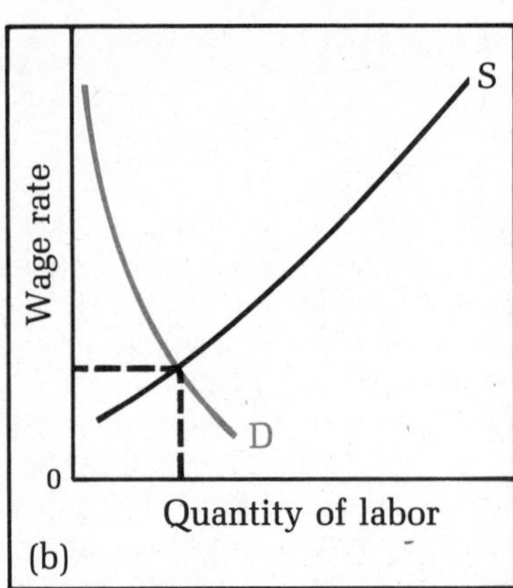

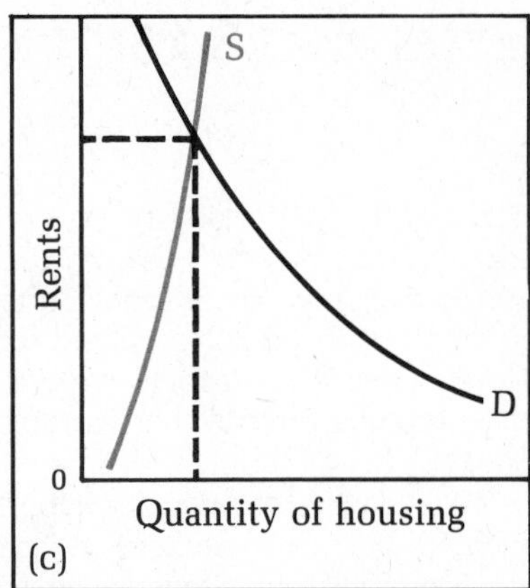

Figure 1 (a) General market for labor. (b) Dual or restricted market for labor. The quantity of labor demanded is smaller and the supply is greater; wages are therefore lower. (c) A dual market for housing available to the poor. As the supply is restricted, the supply curve moves to the left; rents increase.

ing service. The prices of groceries are often higher in ghetto areas, insurance rates are higher, and bank credit for business and real estate is often limited and costly. Figure 1c shows how a large demand for the limited housing available can keep housing costs high.

Government Policies Against Discrimination

A number of federal and state laws have been passed in recent years in an effort to end discrimination in the job sector. The Civil Rights Act of 1964 made it unlawful for an employer, labor union, or employment agency to discriminate against workers because of race, color, religion, or national origin. In 1969 discrimination on the basis of sex was outlawed. The new laws authorize the Equal Employment Opportunity Commission (EEOC) to enforce the law.

One problem facing the EEOC is how to define discrimination, since discrimination or bias may take many subtle forms. Under the law, persons who feel they are victims of discrimination can file complaints with the commission and even take legal action in the courts. The commission issued the following warning to employers:

> If a statistical survey shows that minorities and females are not participating in your work force at all levels in reasonable relation to their presence in the population and the labor force, the burden of proof is on you to show that this is not the result of discrimination, however inadvertent.

An example of the complex forms discrimination can take is a case involving the U.S. Steel Company. In its Birmingham, Alabama, mill it had a dual seniority system, under which some lines of work were reserved for whites and others for blacks. If a job became open in the white seniority line, it had to be filled by the white worker who had been there longest. The same was true for the black seniority line. A black could not be put in a white job no matter how long he or she had been employed or how qualified he or she might be. Likewise, white workers could not fill jobs that were in the black seniority line. A federal district court held that this was against the law and ordered the company to establish a single seniority system under which any worker could fill a job if he or she had the proper qualifications and had been there long enough.

Another way of overcoming job discrimination is through Affirmative Action programs. This approach requires employers to make a special effort to find nonwhite and female workers who are eligible for higher positions or who can be moved into departments where minorities are underrepresented. The federal government has applied the Affirmative Action approach to companies and other organizations above a certain size that have federal contracts, including universities.

Affirmative Action has its critics. They say that employers are often pressured to hire less productive workers than they otherwise would, resulting in a decline in work standards. The use of quotas has come under the heaviest fire. Quotas are said to involve "reverse discrimination"—that is, discrimination against nonminority groups like white males. These men grumble, "You have to be either black or female in order to get ahead." Much of the criticism has been over the issue of job security. Because blacks and women are often the last hired, they tend to be the first fired when production is cut back. But if an employer must maintain a quota, it may be necessary to fire white male workers with longer seniority instead. Minority leaders reply that even if reverse discrimination occurs, this doesn't make up for all the past injustices to minorities.

INEQUALITY

We are slowly wiping out absolute poverty in the United States. If we consider the food and housing aid given to people on welfare, fewer and fewer people in the United States live below an acceptable standard of living. Poverty as it was known throughout human history, and is still known in much of Asia and Africa, no longer exists in the United States. Many people, however, are relatively poor: Although they do not live below a standard consistent with physical well-being, they live at levels substantially below those of most of us.

This can be seen by comparing different family incomes with the median for the whole United States. The *median family income* is in the middle of all incomes—that is, half the families have incomes that are higher and half have incomes that are lower. In 1979 the median family income in the United States was $17,640. About one fifth of the families had incomes that were less than half the median—that is, about 12 million families, or about 40 million people, had family incomes less than $9000. This comparison shows that there is a fairly wide spread of incomes down the lower end of the income range; they are not bunched together near the median. Table 3 shows the numbers of families falling into various income categories.

Reading a complicated table of numbers may be difficult. That is why economists use the *Lorenz curve,* shown in Figure 2. A **Lorenz curve** is a graph that shows at a glance just how equally or unequally incomes are distributed. Here is how it works. On the horizontal axis we measure percentages of families in 20 percent intervals. On the vertical axis we measure percentages of total income from 0 percent to 100 percent. We plot points to show the percentages of total income received by families as we move up the income scale. If income distribution were perfectly equal—that is, if every family received exactly the same income—points would be plotted on the diagonal line connecting opposite corners of the square. This is because the first 20 percent of families would receive 20 percent of total income, the first 40 percent of families would receive 40 percent of total income, and so on up to 100 percent. We call this diagonal the *reference line.* By comparing actual curves of income distribution with the reference line we can see how unequally income is distributed.

The Lorenz curve in Figure 2 illustrates income distribution in the United States in 1950. It tells us that the lowest 20 percent of families received about 5 percent of income. The lowest 80 percent of families received almost 60 percent of income. This means that the top 20 percent of families received more than 40 percent of income. Putting it another way, the top 20 percent of families received more than eight times as much income as the bottom 20 percent of families. The space between the Lorenz curve and

Table 3 **Money Income of Families (March 1979)**

	Percent distribution							
	Under $3000	$3000–$4999	$5000–$6999	$7000–$9999	$10,000–$14,999	$15,000–$24,999	$25,000 and over	Median
White families	2.5	4.0	5.6	9.4	16.6	32.5	29.5	$18,368
Black families	8.3	12.2	9.5	13.3	17.4	23.4	16.0	$10,879
All families	3.3	4.9	6.1	9.8	16.7	31.4	27.9	$17,640

Source: "Current Population Reports: Consumer Income," Series P–60, No. 190, U.S. Department of Commerce, Bureau of the Census, November 1979.

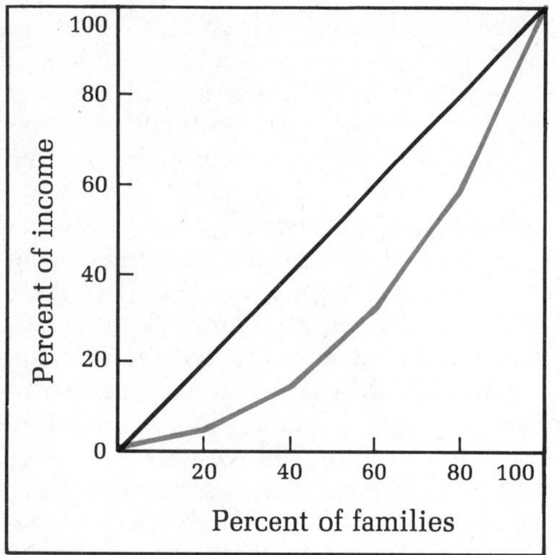

Figure 2 A Lorenz curve showing income distribution in the United States in 1950.

the reference line indicates substantial income inequality in 1950.

Changes since 1950 are shown in Figure 3, which gives Lorenz curves for the years 1960 and 1977. The curves have moved a little closer to the reference line over this period of time, but their basic shape has remained the same.

Table 4 provides the percentage data from which Lorenz curves are drawn. The Bureau of the Census makes the data available annually. The figures include all kinds of income: Social Security, public welfare, and other transfer payments. Without those transfer payments income distribution would have been even more unequal. The major shifts in income distribution actually occurred before 1948. Since then, the share of the lowest fifth has stabilized at about 5 percent, and the share of the highest fifth at 40 percent. The share of the top twentieth of the population declined slightly from 17.5 percent in 1947 to 15.6 percent in 1979. These are not great changes. We may conclude that although absolute levels of living have improved, there has been no significant gain in income equality in recent decades.

Most economists who have studied the facts of income distribution do not expect any great change to take place in the foreseeable future. This is because the forces making for more equal distribution are offset by forces that work for less equal distribution. Among those that tend toward less equality are the tendency of labor unions to win benefits for middle-income workers rather than lower-income workers; an increasing tendency for wives of middle- and higher-income men to enter the labor force, thus increasing their family incomes substantially; and the fact that low-income men are retiring at an earlier age.

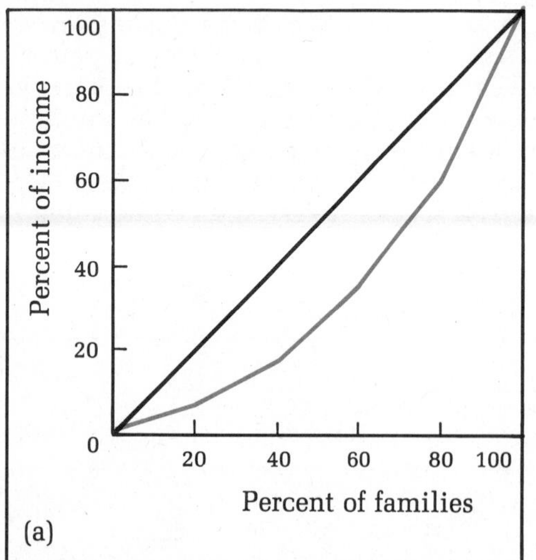

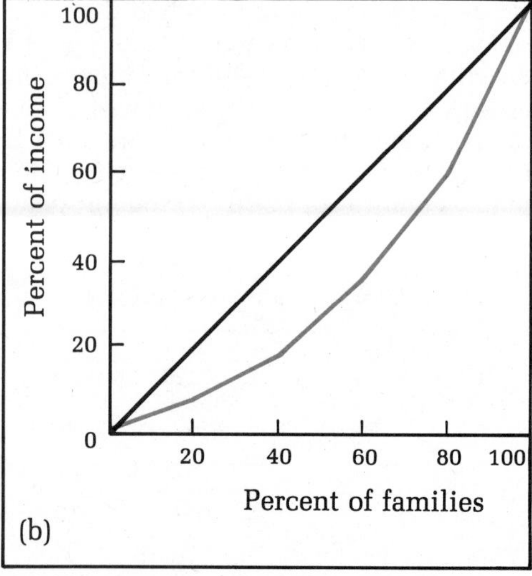

Figure 3 Lorenz curve for the United States in: (a) 1960; (b) 1977. Notice their similarity. This indicates income distribution has changed very little.

Table 4 **Share of Aggregate Income Before Taxes Received by Each Fifth of Families, Ranked by Income**

	1947	1950	1960	1966	1979
Lowest fifth	5.1%	4.5%	4.8%	5.6%	5.2%
Second fifth	11.8	11.9	12.2	12.4	11.6
Third fifth	16.7	17.4	17.8	17.8	17.5
Fourth fifth	23.2	23.6	24.0	23.8	24.1
Highest fifth	43.3	42.7	41.3	40.5	41.5
Top 5 percent	17.5	17.3	15.9	15.6	15.6

Source: *Economic Report of the President*, February 1974, and "Current Population Reports: Consumer Income," Series P–60, No. 190, U.S. Department of Commerce, Bureau of the Census, November 1979.

Among the forces working toward greater equality are some migration of farm workers to the city, where even low-paying jobs are better than rural unemployment; a reduction of income differences between whites and nonwhites; more equality for women; and further increases in welfare benefits for the poor.

Some people look to taxation as a way of reducing inequality. Politicians speak of "closing the tax loopholes" through which people with high incomes are able to reduce their federal income-tax bill. But as it stands, the present tax structure probably has little effect on income shares. Some taxes are progressive: They take a larger fraction of higher incomes, as the federal and state income taxes do; others, such as sales taxes and the Social Security tax, are regressive, weighing more heavily on lower incomes. Taken together, it appears that people at the lower end of the income distribution pay about the same proportion of their income in taxes as do people in the middle and upper-middle range. Only when we get to the $100,000-a-year level and above do we find people paying a significantly greater proportion of their income to the tax collector.

If we wished, Americans could choose to restructure the tax system to make it more progressive. But tax reform is politically very difficult to accomplish. There are literally hundreds of groups representing special interests that bring pressure to bear upon legislators to gain favorable treatment for themselves. The result of any change may be a tax law that is different but not much better than before. The tax-reform bill of 1976 was 1500 pages in length and so complex that even tax lawyers were not certain what some of the provisions meant.

Of course, an important part of any program to reduce poverty is a strong commitment to economic growth. A growing output of goods and services enables more families to enjoy rising living standards without reducing the living standards of others. A democracy like ours must be responsive to the needs of the people. If those needs remain unfulfilled and become intense and widespread, voters will demand redistribution from the haves to the have-nots. To avoid political disruption and social unrest, it is important to increase the size of the economic pie, encouraging all to contribute to production and allowing all to share in its distribution.

URBAN POVERTY AND CRISIS

In the past, we thought of poverty as primarily a rural problem. In 1930 nearly half the U.S. population was rural and many rural families lived lives of hardship. This was especially true of sharecroppers and hired farmhands. But since 1940, our rural population has been declining fairly steadily, while city population has been increasing by about 3 million a year. By 1950 the urban population had reached 64 percent, and by March 1979 the ratio was 96 percent.

Many new city dwellers came seeking the greater opportunities the city promised: escape from rural drudgery and relief from the uncertainties of nature and fluctuating agricultural prices. All too often they found that city life had its own drudgery and uncertainties. Many came to the city with serious employment disadvantages: low education, few skills, poor health, and little understanding of their new surroundings. Many cities could no longer absorb vast tides of unskilled migrants. The number of industrial jobs for such people had declined as

Economic Thinker Arthur Okun

When economists serve in government, they can influence policy in ways they believe will improve our economic system. This is a valuable opportunity, but it also implies an obligation to state clearly the basis for their policy recommendations.

Arthur M. Okun (1928–80) had wide experience in academic economics before becoming a part of policymaking. He was Professor of Economics at Yale University before becoming economic adviser and Chairman of the Council of Economic Advisers under President Lyndon Johnson. Later he served as economic consultant to private corporations and as senior fellow at Brookings Institution in Washington.

Dr. Okun's primary concern was the conflict between economic efficiency and equality of income distribution. (See his book *Equality or Efficiency: The Big Tradeoff.*) Under the market system, free competition in the marketplace will mean inequality of income distribution. We permit these inequalities to exist because we believe they help our system to operate efficiently. We believe increasing equality would involve a cost in terms of efficiency; that is, there is a tradeoff that prevents us from moving too far toward perfect equality.

Okun did not advocate absolute equality, because efficiency would decline so much that there would be fewer goods and services to redistribute. After some point, as the slices of our "economic pie" became more equal, the pie would decline in size, or at least fail to grow. Our system can be healthy and continue to have substantial differences in income. What is not healthy is the sharp "contrast in civilization" that exists between the very rich and the very poor. Socialist governments have chosen equality over efficiency and have suffered lower productivity as a result. Authoritarian systems have chosen efficiency but only at tremendous costs in terms of equality and human liberties.

Democratic capitalism has followed a third route, through an "uneasy compromise" between equality and efficiency. The United States has established what Okun calls a "split-level society." On the social and political level, our system grants equal rights to all citizens. Equality of rights guarantees our personal freedoms against any move by government to take them. It ensures that individuals are treated fairly—that human beings are treated with dignity simply because they are human beings.

The second level of our split-level society is our economic institutions. Our economic system is characterized by the free market where individuals must "succeed or suffer." Okun believed that these two levels are inconsistent: that personal freedom is not compatible with economic suffering, that starvation and dignity do not mix.

This is where the "uneasy compromise" in our system breaks down. Okun was surprised that the strains are not more disruptive. Despite the fact that the lowest half of income earners in the United States have only one-fourth of the nation's income and one-twentieth of its wealth, still there is little pressure for change. Apparently we fear government's power to achieve equality more than we would welcome greater equality.

Okun believed that movement toward greater equality could help to increase efficiency as well. To

technological progress put increasing emphasis on training and skill. Add to this the higher living costs in cities and it is not surprising that 10.7 percent of central-city whites and 31.2 percent of central-city blacks were reported in March 1978 as having incomes below the poverty line.

These circumstances combine to create a spreading cancer in our cities: Overcrowded and decaying housing, poor nutrition, low standards of health care, inadequate education and lack of industrial skills all work upon each other to produce still worse conditions for future generations of city dwellers. The cities are faced with increasing problems while their resources for solving them are dwindling.

Urban Finance: Tax Revenues

Cities get their money from taxes and from funds turned over to them by state and federal governments. The mayor of a large city has to make regular pilgrimages to the state capital to plead for help and to Washington to add another voice to the national chorus of mayors imploring Uncle Sam to be more generous.

provide greater opportunities for human resource development would tend to increase our nation's productive capacity and improve living standards for all of us. Progressive income taxes play a role in this objective, and federal outlays for the disadvantaged are also important. In-kind aid, like public education and health care, job counseling and training, and public housing, should be directed toward those in need. All these efforts would help narrow the disparities that now shut off some groups from participation in our economic system.

The ability of any city to raise money through its own taxes is limited. Taxpayers can usually move outside the city to avoid paying, while continuing to enjoy many city services. Thus the cities are caught between the need to collect more revenue and the fear that higher tax rates will drive away people and business. Cities must adjust tax rates to fit different elasticities of supply: They must set high tax rates on activities that must be located in cities (inelastic) and lower rates on activities that may be carried on elsewhere (elastic). This leads to a heavy dependence on property taxes. In 1977 taxes on property accounted for a quarter of all city revenues from cities' own sources.

The property tax has been with us since the days of ancient Rome. In the modern city, however, it is an unsatisfactory way of raising revenue. For one thing, the area of land within city limits is practically fixed and cannot be expected to grow. If the city tries to increase property tax revenues to meet increasing financial needs, it must tax owners of existing property more heavily. Unless their property has become more productive, owners will not be able to pay. The city's economy must first prosper if the revenues from property taxes are to grow significantly.

Second, while the supply of land is relatively inelastic, the supply of improvements that can be made on the land is relatively elastic. Owners can choose to make capital investments on their urban properties or to invest somewhere else. If improvements are taxed too heavily, investment funds are likely to flow elsewhere—taking people, business firms, and jobs along with them. The city can't prosper if its tax policies drive enterprises away or discourage new enterprises from coming in.

Third, property taxes are thought to fall more heavily on people with lower incomes than on those with higher incomes, at least where housing is concerned. The reason is that the cost of their dwellings is a larger portion of the incomes of poorer families; this is true whether the family buys or rents its housing. Heavy property taxes tend to reduce the purchasing power of the very families whom city services are intended to help.

For all these reasons, property taxes are an inadequate source of revenue for city governments. Since 1950 city expenditures in the United States have increased by eleven times while revenue from property taxes has increased only eight times. The gap has been filled largely by federal and state funds—about two thirds of the amount coming from the states.

Urban Finance: Expenditures

At the same time that their taxing capabilities are dwindling, cities are faced with increased demand for public services. Growing concentrations of poor people in the central cities has increased the need for welfare assistance, child-care facilities, low-cost housing, mass transportation, health services, schools, and public safety.

Welfare assistance. Cities depend heavily on federal help for their welfare programs. Federal grants finance from half to three quarters of the public assistance programs administered by state and local governments. Washington distributes its help on the basis of per capita income in the different states, with wealthy New York state receiving 50 percent of its welfare funds from the federal government and poorer Mississippi 78 percent. This still leaves some large cities with the problem of paying for part of their welfare costs; New York City, for example, pays 75 percent of its welfare burden. This is why the increase in urban poverty has worsened the financial problems of our large cities, particularly those in the industrial areas of the Northeast.

One possible solution would be to let the federal government pay the entire welfare bill, on the grounds that the problem of urban poverty is not really a local problem. A large proportion of those on welfare rolls in northern cities did not live there originally but moved there to escape even worse conditions somewhere else. Under this proposal, federal income-tax revenues would replace state and local taxes as a means of financing welfare. Then state and local governments could concentrate their efforts on other public services related to purely local needs. This would have the added advantage of making it easier to standardize welfare procedures and benefits nationally. If the negative income tax idea were adopted, most city and state welfare bureaucracies would close down.

Housing. Since World War II, the housing of the urban poor has deteriorated. Very little new housing has been built for low-income families. While metropolitan areas have grown tremendously, the new housing has been in the suburbs or in luxury high-rise apartments in the cities, leaving the poor to crowd together in older dwellings.

Some low-rent housing has been provided for poor families through public housing projects, housing built by local governments with the help of federal funds. This approach has not gone very far. One reason is that few neighborhoods want a public housing project built nearby, bringing in hundreds or thousands of poor people of different racial or ethnic backgrounds. Some public housing developments in central cities have become giant concrete slums, breeding crime and violence to such a degree that poor families have refused to move into them. One large development in St. Louis remained almost empty for years until it was finally torn down.

A better approach might be to give poor families direct payments to spend for housing. It would then be up to each family to decide where it wanted to live. The housing market might be expected to respond to the demand from low-income groups just as it would to any other group of buyers. Private builders would construct housing especially for this market. In one respect, this plan would place the poor on the same footing as other groups. Middle-income and upper-middle-income homeowners now receive indirect housing subsidies: the federal government permits them to deduct the interest payments on their mortgages from taxable income when figuring their income taxes. Low-income families aren't able to get mortgages and are deprived of this benefit. Giving them a housing subsidy would help offset the inequity.

Health, education, and public safety. Welfare and housing are not the only financial problems the cities have had to wrestle with. The costs of services such as police and fire protection, schools, and hospitals have shot up in recent years. Public-service costs tend to rise faster than costs in manufacturing because there is no way of increasing output per worker. The public still wants a police officer on the block and a fire station close at hand, small classes in the schools, and adequate medical facilities. Workers who provide these services are just as concerned with the rising cost of living as other workers are, and they are determined not to be treated as second-class citizens. Their unions have grown stronger and more militant in recent years. The steady rise in public-service costs has added greatly to the financial problems of the cities.

The Three E's

You will remember the three E's: efficiency, equity, and externalities. They will help gain perspective on the complex issues of urban poverty.

Efficiency. Economic decisions are made by many different individuals and groups. They make decisions after comparing benefits and costs. Consumers compare the benefits they expect to get from their purchases with the prices they will have to pay. Business firms compare the productivity of resources with their prices. Savers make benefit-cost comparisons when they decide where to put their investment funds. When all individuals and groups are maximizing their benefits and minimizing their costs, we say an economy is efficient. It is efficient because it is channeling resources into employments where they will produce the greatest benefits; it is obtaining maximum output at the least expenditure of scarce resources.

Equity. The principle of equity involves the fair distribution of benefits and costs among our population. A free market system by itself would distribute private benefits only to those willing to pay for them. The ability to pay would be measured by each person's contribution to the system through his or her own production. One can argue that the market system is "fair" if it rewards persons strictly according to their contribution to output. But most modern industrial societies feel this is not enough. For one thing, it takes no account of people's actual needs—which may have little to do with their earnings. Our system of taxes and transfer payments helps deal with these needs by taxing some groups more heavily than others and by paying income supplements to poor families.

A second point against the distribution of benefits that a free market system provides is one we have already touched on: Externalities may be distributed in a quite random fashion, giving benefits to some and imposing costs on others.

Externalities. Sometimes we receive benefits or costs that nobody intended. We call them externalities because they are outside the decision making process of the individual consumer, business firm, or investor. They represent added benefits or costs to the community as a whole. Some examples of external costs are the air pollution that results when a consumer drives a polluting automobile, the water pollution when business firms pour dangerous chemicals into rivers, and the visual pollution from strip-mining or unattractive factory construction. Some examples of external benefits are the increase in human capital when the labor force develops new skills, the improvement of our social environment when jobs are plentiful, and the larger tax revenues generated by greater economic activity.

If we are to judge the efficiency of an economy correctly, we should include the externalities the system produces along with the real goods and services. If the community enjoys external benefits from a particular activity, then it makes sense to channel more resources toward that activity. If an activity results in external costs, we may want to move fewer resources in that direction.

It is difficult to measure external benefits and costs precisely, since they are outside the market system. It is government's job to estimate them and to include them when making decisions about public services. In this way we may hope to achieve a more efficient allocation of resources toward those activities which yield the greatest total benefits at the lowest total cost.

The Three E's and Urban Problems

The problems of the cities are a reflection of the efficiency of our market system, the externalities that it sometimes creates, and the equity (or inequity) with which it distributes benefits and costs. The free market was allocating resources efficiently when it encouraged the great migration of workers to the cities. Often without knowing it, workers were responding to market signals: a long-term decline of jobs in agriculture and an increase of opportunities in industry. But the system didn't distribute the costs and benefits of this process equitably. The private benefits of industrial development went disproportionately to highly skilled workers, who eventually moved to more pleasant surroundings in the suburbs. The external costs fell disproportionately on low-skilled workers, members of minority groups, and others who were unable to escape the external costs of growth: the slums, traffic congestion, air and noise pollution, and crime.

The result was what now appears to have been excessive investment in goods and services that provide private benefits: urban high-rise buildings and luxury apartments, highway systems rather than mass transit, and sprawling suburbs. At the same time, too few resources have flowed into activities for which external benefits are high but private benefits are low. One can argue that public housing, health, and education have been neglected, although they could have brought external benefits far greater than their costs. Increasing income-support payments and welfare benefits might also bring external benefits in terms of greater social stability and human resource development.

In the last analysis, it is the general public that must decide these issues. Efforts to correct inequities depend on the support of voters. Cities and localities find it difficult to shoulder an additional tax burden for this purpose. If the nation as a whole is willing to undertake the commitment, it can do much to make our system more equitable. If efficiency is defined to mean the maximum output of *all* benefits relative to costs, then perhaps the final result will be to make our system operate more efficiently, too.

The Cost of Poverty

Probably the greatest cost of poverty is underdeveloped productive resources. Unhealthy, poorly trained, and badly motivated workers are unable to make much of a contribution to national output. Instead, they represent a drain on it. No modern nation can afford a large poor population.

Great inequality in incomes may have made some sense when our economic system was younger. Poverty at one end of the scale made wealth possible at the other end. A large class of rich people were able to save much of their income and thus make funds available for business to invest. The existence of poverty enabled capitalists to accumulate the resources through which they built up the means of production. A parallel to this can be seen in the recent history of the Soviet Union, where incomes are also very unequal and where the masses of the population have been held to a low standard of living so as to make resources available for industrial development.

In a modern, developed economy like ours, high rates of saving are less important. The necessary rate of new investment often declines as an economy develops, and it becomes important to ensure a high level of consumption instead. This requires a broad base of secure, middle-income families. Poor families do not purchase new automobiles, buy new homes, or take expensive trips to vacation resorts. They provide little market for the fruits of technological advance, and they pay few personal taxes.

Although poor people spend little to boost our economy, they add significantly to its costs. The costs include increased crime, ill health, and urban blight. These costs are borne by the rest of the population through higher taxes and the loss and deterioration of property.

SUMMARY

Poverty can be characterized as relative poverty, if living standards are below the levels of others in the community, or absolute poverty, if living standards are below what is considered necessary for human health. The productivity of the U.S. economy means that few families live in absolute poverty. The poverty line refers to a level of income three times the cost of a nutritional diet: $6662 for an urban family of four in March 1979.

The poverty population in the United States includes disproportional numbers of central-city families, nonwhites, and female-headed families. Elderly people also receive low incomes, but many are saved from poverty by past savings and investments.

Poverty programs aim at filling particular needs of certain poor groups. Hard-core poverty is treated through Aid to Families with Dependent Children, Supplemental Security Income, the Food Stamp Program, and Medicaid. The elderly are aided through Social Security and Medicare. Cyclical poverty is treated through unemployment compensation, welfare assistance, and food stamps. Islands of poverty are treated through inducements to industry to move into depressed areas.

Current proposals involve significant changes in the present welfare system. Direct grants would channel funds directly to the poor with less administrative waste. A negative income tax would have similar advantages, and it would provide incentives to find employment, but its cost would be high. Other positive programs aim at reducing racial and sexual discrimination in hiring. Since 1950, there has been little change toward greater equality of income distribution in the United States.

In recent years poverty has become more an urban problem than a rural problem. The movement to the cities by the poor and the departure of the affluent have left cities unable to finance their necessary services: welfare assistance, housing, health, education, and public safety. Proposals to deal with urban poverty should be based on the concepts of efficiency, equity, and externalities. When all external benefits and costs are considered, the principle of efficiency may justify allocating more resources toward solution of urban problems. Correcting the problem of poverty can help increase the prosperity of our entire economy.

Key Words and Phrases

absolute poverty a condition of living below standards currently considered necessary for human health.

Affirmative Action programs government-imposed guidelines or quotas that require employers to seek out and employ members of groups which may have suffered discrimination in hiring.

cyclical poverty poverty that results from a temporarily low level of total production and employment in the nation's economy.

direct grants outright money payments to poor people.

dual markets separate labor markets to which most blacks and women are restricted; for the poor in general, consumer markets are also dual.

hard-core poverty poverty that results from conditions which make an individual unsuited for work in the modern economy, including the elderly, the disabled, the handicapped, and the unmarried parent of dependent children.

islands of poverty poverty that results from structural changes, such as the decline or disappearance of an industry in a particular region.

Lorenz curve a graph that illustrates the degree of income inequality in the nation.

negative income tax transfer payments to poor people based on level of incomes below some particular level.

output per capita the nation's total amount of production divided by its population.

poverty line the Social Security Administration's definition of poverty based on three times the cost of a normal nutritional diet.

relative poverty a condition of living far below the level of others nearby.

unemployment compensation payments intended to relieve the harmful effects of temporary unemployment.

welfare programs government-administered systems designed to help the poor by giving them money, services, or other aid.

Questions for Review

1. Under what circumstances is the following statement correct: "There will always be relative poverty"?
2. Discuss the problem of islands of poverty and the difficulty of developing solutions. Cite specific examples from current affairs.
3. Discuss the pros and cons of Affirmative Action programs.
4. Outline the major causes for the problems facing American cities. What are the advantages and disadvantages of suggested solutions?
5. Use current statistical publications to draw up a table showing the proportions of various populations classified as poor: that is, urban, elderly, nonwhite, and female-headed families.
6. Distinguish between a negative income tax and direct grants to the poor.
7. Is poverty simply a matter of a lack of money? If all poor people were handed a large sum of money (by Santa Claus) would poverty disappear?
8. How is poverty a result of immobility? Cite examples.

PART 5

Market Failure: Problems and Responses

17 Market Failure and Public Choice

18 Market Failure: Health Care, Energy, and Environmental Protection

19 Alternative Economic Systems

CHAPTER 17

Market Failure and Public Choice

Learning Objectives

Upon completion of this chapter, you should be able to:

1. Explain why competitive markets are efficient.
2. Explain the causes of market failure.
3. Discuss why welfare economists see a need for government action.
4. Discuss the notion of "government failure" and the ideas of public choice economists.
5. Discuss the various costs and benefits of government regulation.

Much of the economics you have read in this text may be described as "theoretical," that is, based on an abstract view of reality in which simplifying assumptions are made about the behavior of economic variables. Building abstract models is necessary to understand the economic system and to evaluate alternative policies to change it. Nevertheless, we have tried always to show the relevance of theoretical models to real decision making. We have applied theoretical reasoning to ordinary problems and encouraged you to think in economic terms when making your own choices each day.

This chapter and the next will extend this process of theory and application to some of the most complicated economic decisions confronting us all. Dealing with today's complex problems involves questions of both economic efficiency and social equity. As a citizen of a democracy, you influence—and are influenced by—these decisions. Understanding the basis for such decisions can help you be a more effective participant in the political process.

DECISION MAKING IN PERFECT COMPETITION

We have described free, perfectly competitive markets as *efficient*. Efficient markets allocate resources so as to achieve maximum benefits per unit of resource cost.

Consumers allocate their budgets according to the equal marginal utility principle:

$$\frac{MU_a}{P_a} = \frac{MU_b}{P_b} = \ldots = \frac{MU_z}{P_z},$$

where MU stands for marginal utility, P for price, and *a*, *b*, . . . *z* stand for each possible good or service. No good or service will be bought unless it yields utility sufficient to offset its price.

Producers satisfy consumer demand by hiring resources according to the equal marginal productivity principle:

$$\frac{MRP_a}{P_a} = \frac{MRP_b}{P_b} = \ldots = \frac{MRP_z}{P_z} = 1,$$

where MRP stands for marginal revenue product, P for price, and *a*, *b*, . . . *z* stand for each possible resource input. Resources will be used only to the point where they produce benefits of sufficient value to offset their cost.

When all consumers and producers follow these rules, scarce resources will be used only for producing the things people want most. The economy is said to be efficient.

This result can be illustrated graphically. Figure 1 allows us to compare the marginal benefits and marginal costs of using our nation's scarce resources to produce goods and services. The graph is drawn with certain simplifying assumptions: technology is fixed, the quantity of resources is fixed, and benefits and costs can be given dollar values. Units of production are measured on the horizontal axis and the value of marginal benefits and marginal costs on the vertical axis.

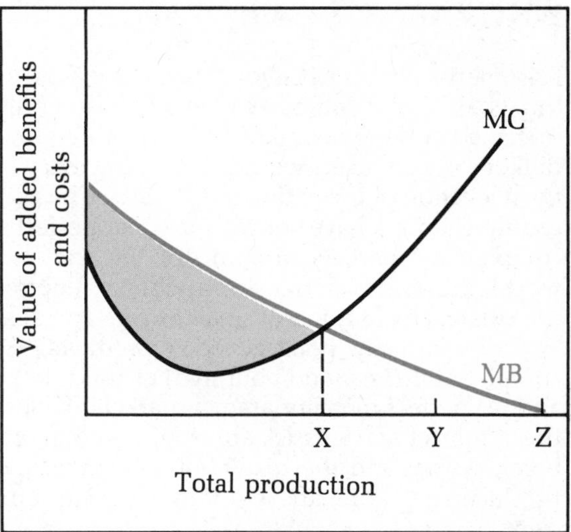

Figure 1 After some level of total production, costs of additional production (MB) tend to fall. At X, production yields marginal benefits equal to marginal costs. Beyond X, marginal costs exceed marginal benefits and production is inefficient. The shaded area between the MC and MB curves represents net benefits from production of X.

The curve representing marginal benefits from production *(MB)* slopes downward, since goods provide diminishing marginal utility. Total benefits from any level of production are represented by the area under the curve up to that quantity of goods and services. The curve representing marginal costs *(MC)* slopes upward because of the principle of diminishing marginal product. Since the productivity of variable resources falls, the resource costs to produce additional goods and services increase. Total costs from any level of production are represented by the area under the curve. In short, the curves have their shapes because each additional unit of resources used in production yields fewer goods and services and the additional goods and services themselves yield less consumer utility.

The curves cross at a point which we have labeled X. To the left of X, marginal benefits of additional production exceed marginal costs; to the right, marginal costs exceed marginal benefits. The relationship between MB and MC is a measure of efficiency. Where MB lies above MC, $MB/MC > 1$, increasing production would increase total benefits more than total resource cost. Where MB lies below MC, $MB/MC < 1$, additional resources are not producing benefits of sufficient value to offset their cost. It follows that the economy is most efficient if resources are used for producing goods and services up to the level where $MB/MC = 1$.

At *X*, the nation is achieving maximum **net benefit** from the use of available resources. Recall that total benefits received from production are represented by the area under the curve MB. Total costs are the area under the curve MC. Net benefit is the shaded area between the two curves. Net benefit is maximum at *X;* to expand the use of the resources beyond *X* would reduce net benefit.

WHY MARKETS FAIL

Free, perfectly competitive markets help achieve the goal of maximum net benefit. The fully informed decisions of millions of consumers and millions of producers would ensure efficiency in the allocation of the nation's resources. The preceding chapters have shown that free, perfectly competitive markets are unlikely in the real world, however, perfect competition requires the existence of (1) many small buyers and sellers, (2) perfectly homogeneous products, (3) complete information about market conditions, and (4) perfect mobility among markets. Unless these four characteristics are true, free markets break down, and the results of consumer and producer decisions are less than perfectly efficient.

Market failure occurs when one or more of the four conditions of perfect competition are not operating. (1) Without perfect competition, resource markets may be inefficient or inequitable. (2) Competition may not be capable of providing needed public goods and services. (3) Market power may disturb competition. (4) Externalities may occur.

In the last chapter we examined the problems of *inequities* in resource markets: poverty and the programs to contain it. The problem of providing *public goods* was discussed in Chapter 4.

Market power, whether on the side of consumers, business firms, or resource owners, frequently establishes production at a level of resource use where MB/MC$\neq$1. The development or exercise of market power is often prohibited through antitrust legislation, countervailing power (in the case of labor unions and consumer cooperatives), and regulation (in industries like communications, transportation, and electric power). The use of government regulation to correct market failure due to market power is one of the most controversial areas in economics. We will discuss this controversy in more detail later in this chapter.

Externalities are the costs and benefits that occur outside the market, removed from the free choice of consumers and producers. When external benefits are produced, the true value of the ratio MB/MC is increased over a broader range of production. The neighbor who landscapes the yard next door with attractive flower beds is yielding external benefits to you and the other neighbors. Activities which yield external benefits should be carried on beyond the point dictated by the market. When external costs are imposed, the true value of MB/MC is reduced. Activities such as pollution impose external costs that should be cut off before the point decided by market processes.

Full information on external benefits and costs is seldom available in the market, so the most efficient decision may not be reached through normal market processes. In the United States we have given government the power to overrule the market in these kinds of decisions. Figure 2 shows some of the agencies of government that deal with the problems of market power and externalities.

DEALING WITH MARKET FAILURE

When markets fail, our economy suffers a loss of efficiency and of equity: *efficiency* because resource allocation does not produce maximum total benefits at lowest total cost and *equity* because benefits are often received and costs paid by different groups of people. As we have seen before, economists disagree on the priorities of the goals of efficiency and equity. Some see market power and externalities as inevitable obstacles to equity. Others place greater priority on efficiency and recommend policies to improve private decision-making in free markets. Whereas the second group would allocate more resources toward private purposes, the first would provide more resources to government for use in promoting equity.

The goals of both groups can be illustrated through the use of the production-possibilities curve. The production-possibilities curve in Figure 3a shows all possible combinations of production for private purposes and for public purposes. A decision to allocate most of the community's scarce resources to production of private, market-oriented goods and services would be shown as a point on the curve near the vertical axis. Allocation of most resources toward production of public, government-mandated goods and services would be shown as a point on the curve near the horizontal axis.

The actual position chosen depends on the values and preferences of the community. Citizens must individually evaluate the expected benefits of private market activity relative to the expected benefits of public programs. Individual preferences may differ widely, but a consensus decision can be reached through a combination

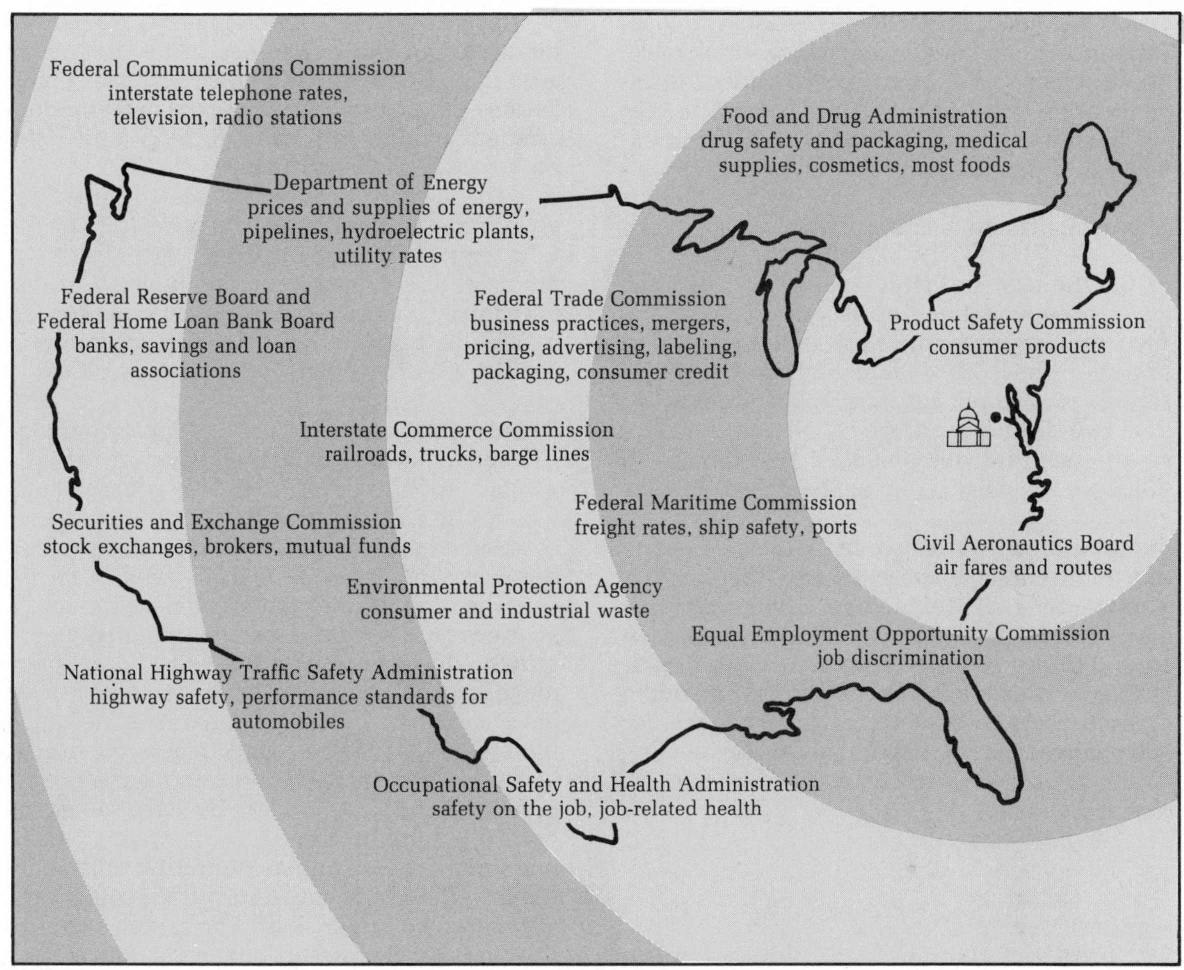

Figure 2 How government regulations affect many aspects of American life. (Based on a drawing from *U.S. News & World Report*.)

of market and political activities. The preferences of the community as a whole can be illustrated by the slope of a *preference line*, as shown by line *AB* in Figure 3b. The slope of *AB* reflects the relative value of private goods and public programs; it is the quantity of private goods citizens are willing to sacrifice to acquire public programs. Thus, a steep preference line reflects substantial willingness to sacrifice private, market-oriented activity for the sake of public, government-mandated programs. A flat preference line reflects an unwillingness to do so.

Once the slope of the community's preference line is determined, the appropriate position on the production-possibilities curve is simple to locate. It is the point at which the slope of *AB* is precisely equal to the slope of the production-possibilities curve. At that point the community's preference for private goods and public programs is equal to their relative costs. Thus, MB/MC = 1.

In Figure 3c a community's preference line has been drawn tangent to its production-possibilities curve at point X. At X the allocation of resources toward market activities and government programs satisfies the community's goals of efficiency and equity. To produce at any other point on the production-possibilities curve would reflect a priority of goals different from the actual preferences of the community.

Deciding on what government policies, if any, are appropriate for dealing with market failure is enormously complex, since many diverse situations must be evaluated separately and objectively before action can be taken. The frequent result has been a tangle of legislation and regulation that completely satisfies no one. Economists find such circumstances intolerable. So, in recent years, analysts have focused greater attention on these economic issues. The goal has been to evaluate the results of government policies, determine the areas of strengths and weaknesses, and propose new approaches for achieving maximum efficiency and equity in the future.

In the sections that follow, we will examine the recommendations of economists with respect to the appropriate slope of the preference line and the corresponding allocation of resources toward private and public purposes. At least two distinct positions on the proper role of government and the ability of government to influence private markets can be discerned. One group of economists sees substantial government intervention in private markets as necessary and workable and asks only that policies achieve desired results most efficiently. This group is often referred to as *welfare economists.* A second group sees government intervention as both contrary to maximum individual freedom and often less efficient than private markets for solving problems of market failure. The leading members of this approach are called *public choice economists.*

Welfare Economics

The branch of economics that studies government policies for handling market failure and allocating resources is called **welfare economics.** Welfare economics does not offer precise, foolproof guidelines for government policy, however, partly because costs and benefits are hard to measure and partly because value judgments are required in assessing efficiency and equity. Welfare economics recognizes the need for government action and tries to develop some criteria for assessing performance.

The welfare economists see the need for government intervention whenever one of the following four broad problems is present: (1) potential direct economic harm inflicted by one individual or group on others; (2) changing definitions of property rights leading to economic conflict; (3) "free-riders"; or (4) externalities.

Direct harm. America's revolutionary heritage has made us suspicious of government. We wanted to escape Old World governments, which often limited freedom arbitrarily, so we established a government whose major prohibition was "direct harm" to its citizens.

The direct harm prohibition has produced a strange result. Over the years, as population has grown and technology advanced, the opportunities for individuals to do harm to *each other* have increased. Often the harm is not fully understood; it may be indirect, far in the future, and subject to chance. Laws designed to protect groups harmed in this way may at the same time harm other groups directly, immediately, and in ways that are well understood. Air-quality standards, for example, are designed to protect large groups against the risk of lung cancer, but they impose heavy costs on certain manufacturing firms. Since reducing indirect harm to the first group causes direct harm to the second, government may be prevented from acting effectively.

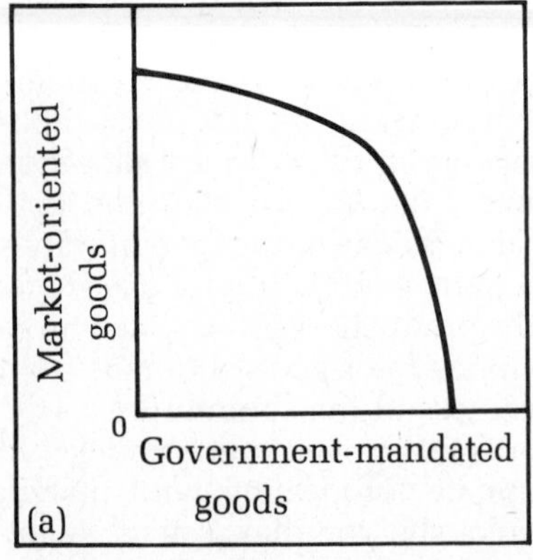

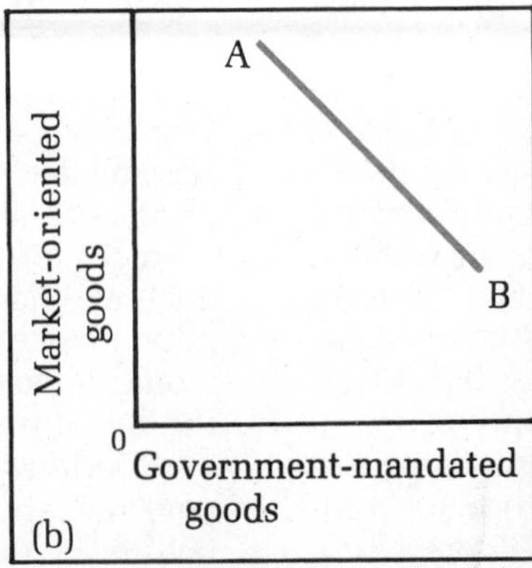

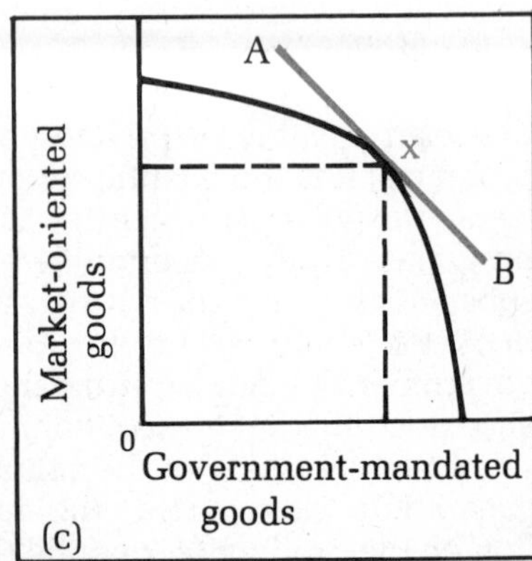

Figure 3 (a) Production-possibilities curve showing all efficient combinations of market-oriented vs. government-mandated goods that can be produced by the economy. (b) Preference line shows willingness of the community to trade off private goods for public programs. (c) Optimal production occurs at point X, where the community's preference line is tangent to the production-possibilities curve.

Economic Thinker Kenneth Arrow

The debate over government's role in the economy is not new. Adam Smith's theory of market economics was an argument against the oppressive power of eighteenth-century governments under mercantilism. The neoclassical economists of the nineteenth century glorified the role of free markets in allocating resources and distributing output for maximum efficiency. Under the market system, they said, an *optimum* level of material welfare would be reached: *optimum* in the sense that no change would improve any one person's position without causing greater losses to someone else. Government intervention was neither necessary nor desirable.

Toward the end of the nineteenth century, government began to intrude more forcefully into the market, changing the allocation of resources and the distribution of output. Many voters favored an increased role for government, so as to deal with the growing power of private monopolies and to provide needed public goods and services. Welfare economists supported this objective. They pointed out the existence of externalities and urged that some of the market's efficiency be set aside for the sake of greater equity. Some economists abandoned their role as positive economists to become normative economists: prescribing policy which they said would truly maximize welfare under their new definitions.

Probably the most significant critic of welfare economics is Kenneth Arrow. Arrow was born in 1921 and educated in New York and Chicago. He earned

degrees from Columbia, the Universities of New York and Chicago, Hebrew University, and the Universities of Vienna and Helsinki. He has been a member of the faculties of the University of Chicago, Stanford, Harvard, and Churchill College in Cambridge, England. He served in the U.S. Army during World War II and in 1962 was appointed to the President's Council of Eco-

Changing definitions of property rights. Another problem arises from the difficulty of defining property rights. As technology has advanced and our economy has become more closely interdependent, the nature of property has changed. We have grown concerned about rights to clean air and water, a healthy environment, and economic security. Existing property laws do not fully reflect the new realities of these rights and responsibilities.

When old laws fail to reflect the actual arrangement of property rights, the market system cannot function well. The simplest approach for dealing with new forms of property rights is for government to pass new laws identifying these rights and specifying how they are to be protected. Typically, the new laws prohibit behavior that contributes to pollution or establish regulatory limits on activity that endangers public health. Anti-burn laws and restrictions on industrial waste disposal are examples.

Such government coercion over private behavior may be appropriate in situations where costs and benefits are easily recognized and measured. But coercion is not appropriate when each situation requires a separate decision based on the particular characteristics of the problem. In cases like these, thousands of small, incremental decisions may be necessary, with separate benefit-cost calculations for each. A more suitable approach than coercion would be for government to provide healthy incentives for

nomic Advisers. Arrow was awarded the Nobel Prize for economic science in 1972 and today is on the Stanford faculty. His critique of activist positions for remedying market failure is well summarized in his book *Social Choice and Individual Values.*

Arrow's criticism of welfare economics has to do with the procedure for choosing production. Perfectly free, competitive markets allocate resources on the basis of individual tastes; goods and services are produced up to the point where marginal utility is proportional to price and price is equal to minimum average cost. In this way, production is sure to provide maximum total utility within the limits of existing resources and technology.

In contrast, welfare economics attempts to maximize *social welfare,* allocating resources according to society's ethical values. Under welfare economics, production is carried on up to the point where marginal *social* benefits equal marginal *social* costs. The goal is to include all external benefits and costs when resource allocation is decided. Needless to say, measuring social benefits and social costs is complex and subjective. Arrow doubts that policymakers can ever acquire the information needed to compare the utility schedules of all citizens and make these kinds of decisions. How can central planners know what kinds of production actually increase social benefits or reduce social costs?

Value judgments are complicated by another problem. Determining society's values through the electoral process may be impossible. The reason is the *paradox of voting.* Consider groups 1,2, and 3 and public projects A, B, and C. Suppose the groups prefer the projects according to the rankings below:

	Most preferred	*Second-most preferred*	*Least preferred*
1	A	B	C
2	B	C	A
3	C	A	B

Although their rankings differ, we can see that no project or policy can win a majority of support. For example, group 1 supports A; but groups 2 and 3 prefer C. Group 2 would support B; but then groups 1 and 3 would support A.

Arrow pointed out that any similar arrangement of preferences will produce contradictory results. It is impossible to identify a single project that correctly reflects the values of the community. However, since minorities strongly support each project separately, coalitions will form and it is likely that *all* projects will be undertaken. The result could be a total level of governmental activity far beyond that which would be justified by benefit-cost criteria. Moreover, note that while all projects can be supported by a large number of members of the community, all are also strongly *opposed* by a *majority.* This suggests that a majority suffers a *loss* of welfare through any decision made in this way.

private buyers and sellers to behave in the desired way.

Free riders. Some amount of government coercion and regulation will always be necessary in certain kinds of activities. One reason is the existence of *free riders.* A **free rider** is someone who enjoys the benefits of actions taken by others and who pays none of the costs. The free rider problem makes it difficult to achieve voluntary compliance with certain objectives favorable to the community as a whole.

Consider, for example, auto drivers. Most of us know that driving uses up costly imported oil and contributes to air pollution. Each of us would like others to cut back their driving and to install antipollution devices. But will most of us behave this way ourselves? Probably, suggest most observers, we will not. We realize our benefits (from energy independence and a clean environment) depend more on the combined efforts of other drivers to limit their driving than on our individual act of installing an antipollution device. So, we can reduce our own costs, and inconveniences, by waiting for others to act.

There are many other opportunities for individuals to be free riders. The result is that few individuals ever assume the responsibility for making the socially desirable investment.

When no individual is led to take action, government coercion may be needed to force compliance with certain standards.

Externalities. Another reason for government coercion is the existence of **spillover effects,** or externalities. Broad social benefits or social costs magnify the effects of certain individual actions so that government must prohibit or encourage them. Local and state governments are often unable to deal with externalities because of their limited jurisdictions. This places the problem in the hands of the federal government, whose broad reach can better identify and measure spillover effects and administer a coherent program.

Figure 4 illustrates an example of pollution spillover effects familiar to citizens of the New England states. Since several states experience spillover effects, no single state or local government has jurisdiction, and the federal government must become involved in the problem.

The problem of designing efficient policies. For all these reasons, welfare economists believe that the role of government must increase as our economy becomes more complex and more interdependent. But policies for intervention need to be designed carefully. Care should be taken not to lock the economy into rigid technological procedures that discourage a search for better methods. Policies should be designed for maximum possible efficiency, using market incentives as much as possible to encourage socially desirable results. For example, welfare economists suggest that:

Instead of prohibiting polluting activities, government *should* establish graduated fees which would encourage business firms to minimize pollution at lowest cost so as to maximize their own profits.

Instead of subsidizing particular approaches to environmental problems, government *should* subsidize or reward results, where efficient approaches to environmental problems are initiated by the firms involved.

Instead of prescribing safety procedures in industry, government *should* levy an "injury tax" or improve the workman's compensation system so as to encourage individual business firms to develop their own safety programs.

Instead of regulating energy prices and production, government *should* supplement the results of private decisions with sponsored research and development and with measures to increase competition.

Instead of providing free health care, government *should* draw up tax and subsidy programs that encourage development of efficient forms of private health care and provide health vouchers to accommodate the needs of low-income families.

In every case, the goals of government regulations should be adjusted for differences in costs and other local circumstances so as to achieve maximum flexibility. And, finally, the results of government programs should be evaluated by comparison not with the expected results of an ideal market system but with the results of a failed market.

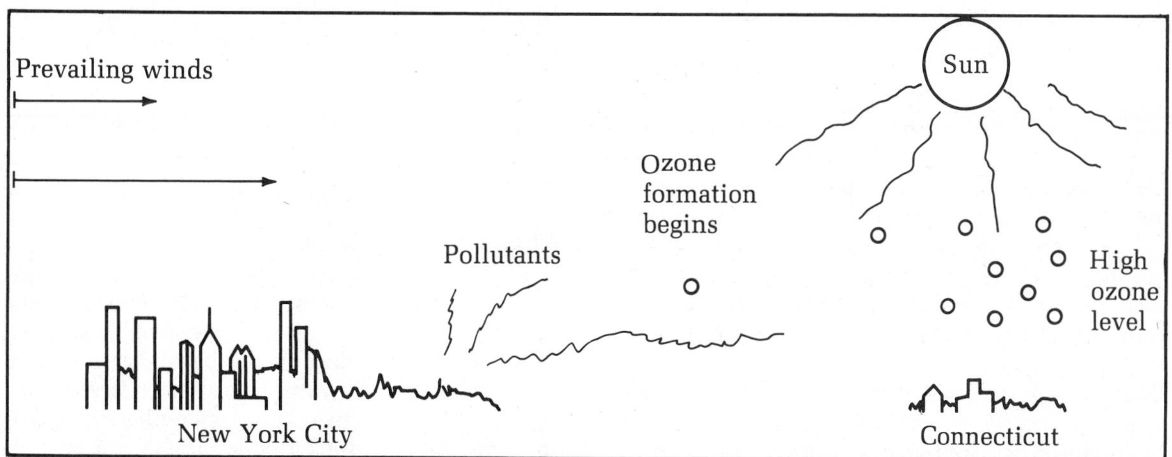

Figure 4 Spillover effects. New York City's auto and industrial pollutants are transformed into ozone (O_3) by the sun. Their most serious effect is felt in Connecticut and Massachusetts, 200 miles away.

Public Choice Economics

Has *government* failure worsened the problems created by *market* failure? Some economists think so. They worry about the continued erosion of individual liberties and about the loss in economic efficiency that they believe results from government's power to influence the economy. **Public choice economics** stresses government shortcomings in the economic arena and outright government failure. Public choice economists worry about the government's role in the economy because they see an imperfect political process leading to many unforeseen problems. The best intended political intentions go awry because the political process itself includes compromises and imperfect human actions. Additionally, every government action has many unforeseen side effects.

Problems in deciding current policy. We may summarize the role of modern government in two ways. As an *enforcer* of laws, it *protects* agreed-on property rights. As a *producer* of public programs, it *allocates* current resources according to the preferences of the majority.

Laws and public programs are the means of carrying out majority decisions regarding the proper distribution of the community's property rights and obligations. Government is charged with the responsibility of enforcing these decisions. Whenever current conditions change, a new majority may take steps to alter the system of laws and production of public goods.

Consider a majority decision to use general tax revenues to finance particular public goods or services. Some members of the community will be required to pay taxes to support the programs but will receive no benefits; they will suffer a net loss. To offset their loss, these citizens will propose other programs, beneficial to themselves and financed by the community at large. These programs impose a net loss on still other members of the community, who will react similarly to offset their own losses. The result is that additional programs will continue to be enacted, each favoring a specific minority but financed through general taxation.

Coalitions. Since public production decisions must be made currently, voters have some opportunity to influence decisions. Their influence declines, however, with the growing size and increasing centralization of government. When government is large and distant, there is an incentive to form **coalitions:** groups of minorities organized to support particular public programs. (This practice is sometimes called *logrolling*.) Coalitions loudly recommend the benefits of programs which enhance their interests while neglecting to mention the costs. Independent voters may not organize an effective resistance, since no single program increases their tax bill sufficiently to justify complaint. The result is to distort benefit-cost calculations with many programs benefiting a few at the expense of many and with increasing inefficiency in the allocation of community resources.

The larger government becomes, the greater is the tendency to form coalitions and to demand increases in the number of services provided by government. The result is still larger government, which, according to public choice economists, becomes a threat to individual liberty. The power of coalitions pushes individuals farther and farther away from decision making.

Politics. Politicians who guide and implement decisions may influence them in ways that favor their own personal preferences toward greater government—a result of their belief that government can improve the life of the community and of their tendency to want to make decisions for others. (If they did not have these preferences, they would probably not have been attracted to a political career.) Moreover, politicians gain more votes by approving individual projects popular with individual groups than by urging tax reductions that benefit all voters only slightly. Some politicians may even expect to profit financially through fraudulent administration of new government programs. Finally, the number of government employees increases with the size of government, producing a substantial voting bloc in support of continued growth in public programs.

Changing the political system. Citizens of a modern nation have less basis for overthrowing their government than citizens of revolutionary nations of the past. This is because most modern nations are governed by the people rather than by a dictator. According to public choice economists, correcting unwanted growth of government does not require that we look for and punish evil citizens, but that we begin to look instead at the institutions run by ordinary people. Ordinary people themselves must establish new rules to restrain the kind of behavior which increases the power of government. Public choice economists want citizens to demand rigid benefit-cost standards in all government programs. They want citizens to forgo some of their own individual benefits from public programs so as to restrain government growth.

MEASURING THE COSTS OF GOVERNMENT REGULATORY POLICIES

As we saw earlier in this chapter, the net benefit of production in our economy reaches a maximum when the marginal benefit of additional production is equal to the marginal cost. This same general rule holds true for government policies to regulate against market failure. Determining the benefits of government regulatory policies is difficult, however, since there are no suitable market processes for measuring the value citizens place on public goods and services. Moreover, many benefits extend for an indefinite time into the future and over unidentified populations. Some spillover benefits may not be counted at all. Most of these same difficulties arise in trying to measure costs.

When benefits are impossible to measure, benefit-cost ratios cannot be determined, and regulatory programs must be evaluated in other ways. One way is to make sure that programs are *cost-effective*. To be **cost-effective,** a program must accomplish a certain agreed-on objective at lowest cost. If the community can establish explicit goals of policy, the next step would be to measure the costs of various alternatives for achieving these goals. Then the lowest-cost alternative could be chosen.

The costs of government regulatory policies fall into three categories. *Direct* costs are government's costs of administering the regulatory agencies and are easiest to measure. *Indirect* costs are business costs of complying with government regulations and are a large and growing component of total regulatory costs. *Induced* costs are most difficult to measure and include the long-range effects of regulation on the nation's capital stock, innovative activity, and industry structure.

Direct Cost

During the 1970s the number of federal regulatory agencies grew by about 60 percent, and total regulatory budgets increased by more than 500 percent. Most of the new agencies were charged with regulating energy and environmental health and safety. The estimated regulatory budget for 1980 was $6 billion, or about 1 percent of total federal government expenditures for the year. Over the decade, the regulatory budget grew faster than the total federal budget, total population, or total national output.

Indirect Cost

The direct cost to taxpayers of regulatory agencies is rather small. A much greater indirect cost is paid by all consumers in the higher production costs of business firms. Figure 5 shows one example of indirect costs of federal regulation.

Washington University economist Murray Weidenbaum calls the indirect costs of regulation a "hidden tax" which makes our tax structure more regressive and contributes to inflation.* For example, federal safety regulations had added $666 to the retail price of automobiles by 1978. Business costs for meeting OSHA requirements are estimated at $3.5 billion a year. Over the decade of the 1980s an estimated $361 billion will be spent to meet new federal environmental standards.

In general, cost investigations have found about $20 in compliance costs for each $1 appropriated by Congress to meet regulatory objectives. The result was a total compliance cost of more than $100 billion in 1979, or almost $500 for every U.S. citizen.

Induced Cost

Perhaps the most dangerous results of government regulation are those that reduce our nation's productivity, contribute to slow growth, and subject consumers to the threat of growing industrial concentration. Induced costs of regulation take many forms. For instance, the long time required for getting government

*Murray L. Weidenbaum, "The High Cost of Government Regulation," *Challenge*, November–December, 1979, p. 32.

approval of new products and processes tends to discourage business innovation and reduce our competitiveness in world markets. Many firms must allocate scarce research and development funds toward regulatory compliance rather than toward innovative activity, retarding technological progress. Uncertainty about future regulations discourages new capital formation; funds which might otherwise be used for investment must be used to meet environmental standards instead. Regulations establishing minimum wage rates reduce employment; the costs fall most heavily on disadvantaged members of the work force. Heavy compliance costs force many small firms out of the market, changing the structure of the nation's industry toward larger, more powerful firms. Finally, concern about regulations diverts attention and energy away from creative economic activity toward minimizing a firm's exposure to regulatory prohibitions.

In the beginning, the goal of regulation was to protect consumers from powerful business interests who might attempt to increase their profits at the expense of consumers. Today, goals are often set by small groups who tend to identify their own narrow interests with the national interest. Now consumers pay the price.

For example, here is a list of federal regulations you pay for every time you buy a hot dog. Should any of these regulations be eliminated?

On-site federal inspection in plants if hot dog is shipped in interstate commerce;
Pure-food standards;
No more than 30 percent fat content;
Coloring dyes must be shown by the manufacturer to be not injurious to health;
Only the casing can be artificially colored;
Extender (flour, cereal, etc.) cannot exceed 3½ percent of weight and must be part of the name of the product;
Labels must be approved;
Labels must contain all ingredients in descending order of amount;
Labels must bear net weight, manufacturer's name and address, and federal inspection stamp.

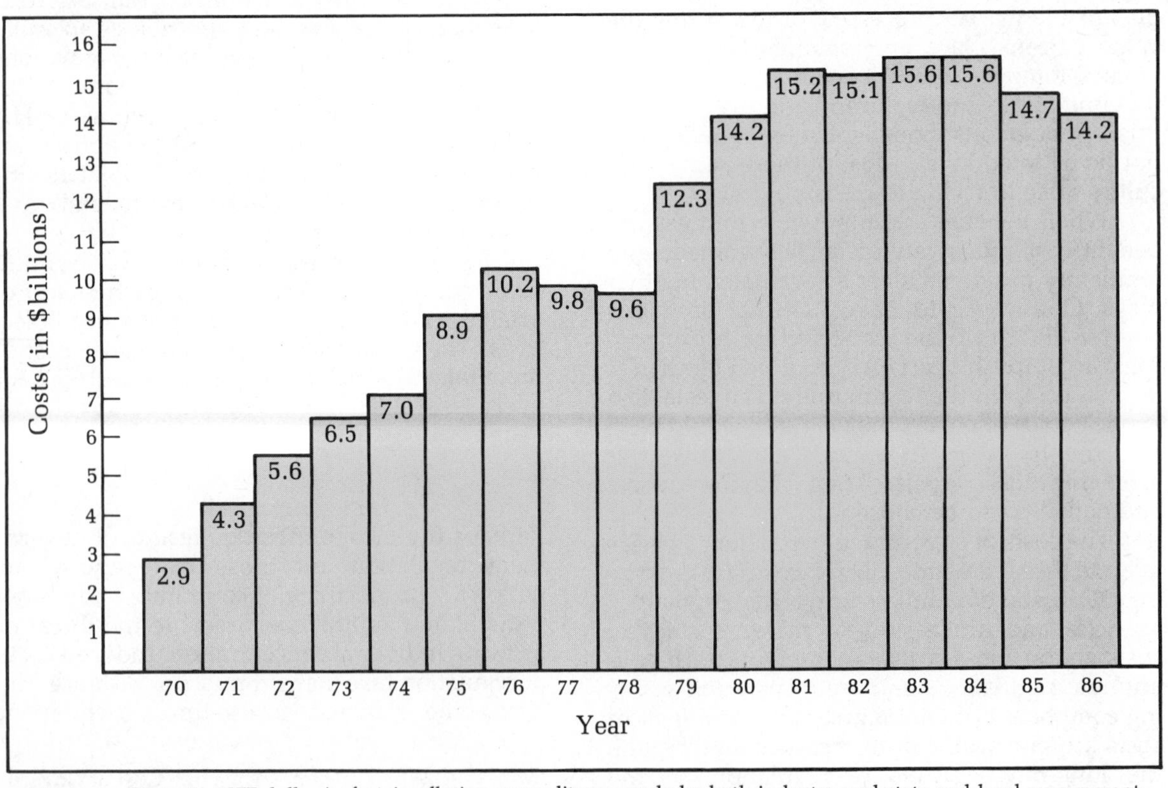

Figure 5 Costs (in 1977 dollars) of anti-pollution expenditures made by both industry and state and local government. (Source: Data Resources.)

Extended Example Regulation Benefits

In order to assess the value of regulation, we need a good measure of costs and benefits. Recently, studies on costs have captured the limelight, especially those efforts by Murray Weidenbaum of Washington University. We have not had any good measure of total benefits, since benefit studies tend to be narrowly focused on one agency and maybe one geographic region. But in 1980 an attempt was made to give an overview of regulation benefits by gathering together all previous studies on the subject. The Center for Policy Alternatives at MIT put together a report for the U.S. Senate.

Automobile safety is regulated by the National Highway Traffic Administration. The Department of Transportation, responsible for this agency, calculated that the loss of a life costs society $287,000. Using this figure and auto repair costs, a study concluded that annual costs of auto accidents and deaths ran more than $37 billion. The benefits of auto safety regulation have been calculated to have saved 28,230 lives in the period 1966–74.

The total benefits of air pollution controls by the Environmental Protection Agency are estimated to run as high as $58 billion each year. Auto pollution controls alone (valued in 1974 prices) yielded annual benefits worth $2.5 billion to $10 billion. Among these benefits, for example, are the rise in property values.

The Occupational Safety and Health Administration (OSHA) regulates the American workplace. OSHA standards have prevented accidents worth around 350 lives and $4.6 billion. It has been estimated that in 1975 the costs of all deaths and injuries from workplace accidents totalled $14.7 billion. OSHA views its job in part as eliminating these costs to society.

This is but a small list of the benefits from government regulation. What is needed is further study, not only of benefits but also of costs. If any regulation's cost exceeds its benefits, then that regulation may need to be dropped.

Careful measurement of costs and benefits should certainly be a part of any policy decision regarding regulation. Costs are often easy to see. They are immediate and painful, and those who must pay are loud in their complaints. The costs of regulation raise production costs, reduce productivity, aggravate inflation, and undermine our position in international trade.

On the other hand, for us to refuse to pay these costs may condemn certain members of our society to a steadily deteriorating quality of life. Future generations may find the clean-up costs even higher and the hazards of inaction even worse.

Is there currently a question in your community regarding the costs and benefits of environmental health and safety regulations? What interest groups are most active in the controversy? What are the expected results?

A FINAL WORD

The issues raised in this chapter and the next fall within the scope of *political economy*. Resolving them requires consideration of the values of the voting members of the community. Some voters follow the philosophy of the welfare economists, regarding social benefits as important enough to justify the costs of many public programs. Their preference would be for production near the horizontal axis in Figure 3a. Some follow the public choice economists, fearing a loss of individual liberties large enough to offset the benefits of many programs. Their preference would be for production near the vertical axis. And, finally, others believe that the high, induced costs of government programs impair the long-range health of our economic system. They would want to ensure that all the costs of government programs are considered when drawing the production-possibilities curve. An objective of our political system should be to ensure that each of these positions is fully heard and represented when important decisions are made.

Whatever the final decisions, policymakers are faced with the knowledge that their decisions may have enormous consequences for years to come. To erase the costs and reverse the damage of incorrect actions may be impossible. In the next chapter, we will examine in detail three issues on which important decisions are being made, with many wide-reaching consequences for your own well-being.

SUMMARY

Free competitive markets are efficient when individual consumers and producers evaluate the benefits and costs of market decisions. They are usually equitable, too, since persons who receive benefits must pay the costs. When there is market failure, however, results may not be efficient or equitable, and government must intervene in market decisions.

Attempts to deal with market failure have encountered difficulties arising from characteristics of our political system. Welfare economists point out that the prohibition against direct harm tends to paralyze government and that vague forms of property rights lead to coercive laws. Free riders and spillover effects make some federal government programs necessary, but programs should make greater use of market incentives to encourage efficient decisions in the private sector.

Public choice economists believe the coercive power of the state should be limited. Minority coalitions may combine to support public programs which are financed by general taxation. To correct the loss of individual rights requires that ordinary people decide to do without costly new programs, to support efficiency and equity in distribution of property, and to limit the size of government.

Government programs involve three kinds of costs. Direct costs of administering programs consume about one percent of federal government expenditures. Indirect costs of business compliance amount to about $20 for each $1 appropriated by Congress and raise prices paid by consumers. Induced costs are the incalculable costs in terms of reduced innovation, investment, and growth.

Key Words and Phrases

coalitions combinations of minority groups that join in support of certain government programs.
cost-effective a condition in which certain goals are accomplished at minimum total cost.
"free riders" persons who receive benefits from production for which they do not have to pay.
market failure the inefficiency or inequity that results when one or more of the four conditions of perfect competition are not operating.
market power ability of a market participant to influence the market in which it operates.
net benefit the difference between total benefits from any level of production and total costs.
public choice economics a body of economic thought that questions the ability of government to protect property rights and to allocate resources.
spillover effects the broad externalities that magnify the effects of individual actions.
welfare economics a body of economic thought that studies government policies for handling market failure and allocating resources.

Questions for Review

1. Explain how the "no direct harm" provision may have hampered the growth of government. Explain how the free rider problem may have encouraged its growth.
2. What changes in property laws have become increasingly necessary as our economy has developed?
3. What are the difficulties of decision making through political processes? How are the difficulties related to the level of government?
4. Distinguish among the direct, indirect, and induced costs of government programs.
5. How would welfare economists and public choice economists respond to issues raised by production of nuclear energy? Consider each of the following concepts in your answer: the prohibition against direct harm, free riders, coalitions, induced costs of regulation.
6. Describe the coalitions which might emerge in the public debate over construction of a dam.
7. Have you ever been a free rider? Explain and give examples of other free riders.
8. Describe the cost-effectiveness approach to decisions on energy production.
9. What are the advantages of taxing or rewarding the results of private antipollution actions as opposed to subsidizing particular methods?

CHAPTER 18

Market Failure: Health Care, Energy, and Environmental Protection

Learning Objectives

Upon completion of this chapter, you should be able to:

1. Explain why market failure has occurred in the health-care industry.
2. Discuss the various government programs and market incentive programs to ensure health care for all and to reduce costs.
3. Discuss various energy price controls and what effects decontrol would have.
4. Discuss alternative sources of energy supplies.
5. Explain the various types of pollution.
6. Discuss the various methods for reducing pollution.

This chapter continues our discussion of the breakdown of markets. We will look closely at three current issues involving a failure of markets to operate with maximum efficiency and equity: the health-care industry, energy, and environmental health and safety. In these cases, market failure is a result of market power, externalities, or of other factors that interfere with the free operation of competitive markets. In each case, we will examine the advantages and disadvantages of various policy alternatives, including legislation, countervailing power, and regulation.

We will reach no clear conclusions on "correct" policies. Circumstances inherent in each of these issues make clear-cut policy choices impossible. This means that decisions must often be made in the political arena, using data and devices supplied by positive economics and weighing nonmaterial considerations according to the preferences of the community. You should keep in mind, as we examine the following problems, the various approaches to remedying market failure that were discussed in the last chapter. How active a role should government play?

THE HEALTH-CARE INDUSTRY

Market failure in the health-care industry is due mainly to the fact that benefit-cost comparisons are made by persons other than consumers and producers of the service itself. Instead of individual consumers balancing the marginal utility per dollar (MU/P) of additional units of health care and choosing accordingly, physicians make the choices. Physicians have knowledge of the benefits of health services that consumers lack, and they want to ensure the maximum quantity and quality of benefits for their patients. Frequently, however, physicians are unaware of service costs, making it difficult for them to choose the precise quantity at which MU/P is equal to that of other consumer purchases.

Not only are consumers uninformed about benefits, they are largely uninterested in costs as well. For many consumers, costs are *hidden*, so health care appears to be a "free good." This is because most health costs are paid by **third-party health plans:** medical insurance. In 1979, public and private insurance plans paid 95 percent of total hospital costs. With apparent zero prices for health services, quantity demanded can expand infinitely (MU/O = ∞), and there is no assurance that resources will be allocated efficiently. Physicians are likely to overprescribe, and consumers are likely to pass the costs to insurance plans. So both parties tend to do very little about rising costs. The costs of insurance are, of course, quite high, but most of this cost is borne in the fringe benefits paid by employers.

The result is a situation where the use of resources is excessive, such that MB/MC < 1, as at point Y in Figure 1. In fact, if the costs of health services are perceived as zero and if some positive benefits are associated with all services, production of health-care services will be carried out to the maximum, at Z. Services will continue

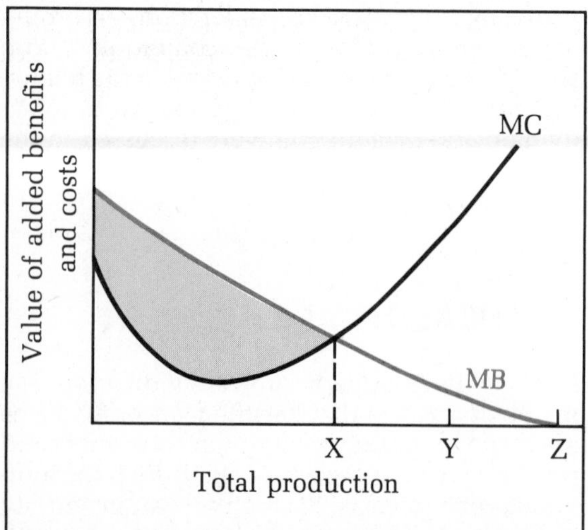

Figure 1 The effects of market failure can be analyzed in terms of marginal benefits and marginal costs.

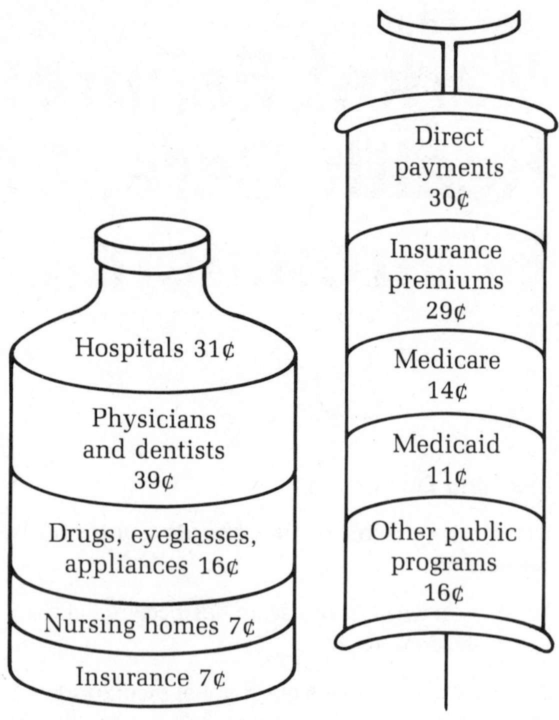

(a) Who receives each dollar? (b) Who pays each dollar?

Figure 2 The distribution of (a) benefits and (b) costs for health care, 1978.

to be provided to persons who gain little in terms of added life or quality of life.

The excessive costs of health care must finally be paid, of course. Private insurance companies finance their high costs by raising premium rates, and public insurance companies by raising taxes. When employers pay these costs, they have less money for increasing wages, or they must pass their higher input costs on to the consumer by raising prices. Thus, consumers must eventually pay the high cost. Still, since costs are not directly connected with benefits, consumers are not able to choose quantity *efficiently*. The result is not *equitable* either, since many insurance owners and taxpayers must pay the costs of excess health-care services provided to others.

The problem can be illustrated by an analogy.* Imagine a dining party that enters a restaurant and agrees to share the dinner check equally. Every member of the group will find it to his

*Laurence S. Seidman, "Hospital Inflation: A Diagnosis and Prescription," *Challenge*, July/August, 1979, p. 17.

Table 1 **Index of Medical Care Prices***

	1960	1965	1970	1977	1979
Consumer Price Index	88.7	94.5	116.3	181.5	217.4
Medical Care Services	74.9	87.3	124.2	216.7	254.4
Physicians' Services	77.0	88.3	121.4	206.0	240.7
Dental Services	82.1	92.2	119.4	185.1	212.4
Hospital Room	57.3	75.9	145.4	299.5	363.9
Drugs and Prescriptions	104.5	100.2	103.6	134.1	152.4

*1967 = 100.
Source: *Statistical Abstract of the U.S.*

Table 2 **Measuring Improved Health Care: Life Expectancy at Birth**

	All Americans		White		Black	
Year	Male	Female	Male	Female	Male	Female
1920	53.6	54.6	54.4	55.6	45.5	45.2
1940	60.8	65.2	62.1	66.6	51.5	54.9
1960	66.6	73.1	67.4	74.1	61.1	66.3
1977	69.3	77.1	70.0	77.7	64.6	73.1

or her advantage to order the largest and most expensive items on the menu. To order differently would not reduce a single individual's share of the bill very much, but would only raise the share he or she pays for someone else's meal. As a result, all the diners tend to overorder. (They become "free riders.") When all members of the group behave this way, the total bill increases substantially, without providing any incentive for individuals to allocate their resources efficiently.

In the case of health care, the incentives may actually be to increase facilities in order to stimulate consumer demand. Since physicians make the consumption decision, producers of health care compete to attract the largest possible number of physicians. To do this, hospitals tend to install the most advanced technology. This costly equipment must then be put to use—whether or not patients actually need the service—so as to pay the cost.

Duplication of hospital technology has been a major factor in the rising cost of health care. (Other contributing factors have been stronger unions of health-care workers and greater costs for bad debts and malpractice insurance.) Over the thirty years 1950–79, hospital costs increased twice as fast as other items in the consumer price index. The index of medical costs has quadrupled since 1957. In 1980, total health costs were almost 10 percent of GNP, up from 6 percent in 1965. Table 1 compares rising medical costs with the consumer price index.

Employer-financed insurance programs are costly, too. Ford Motor Company has estimated the cost of regular insurance at $2700 per worker in 1979, up from $350 in 1965. The cost of employee health care in the automobile industry is ultimately added to the cost of automobiles.

The federal government's share of health-care costs is almost 13 percent of the federal budget and is rising. Health care is the nation's third largest industry—after agriculture and construction. In spite of these heavy expenditures the United States does not rank highest in terms of the quality of health. For example, the United States ranks seventeenth, behind most other industrialized nations, in *infant mortality* (infant deaths as a percent of births). Some other health statistics for the United States are shown in Figure 2 and Tables 2 and 3.

Table 3 **Infant Death Rates (per 1000 live births)**

Year	White	Black and Other
1960	22.9	43.2
1970	17.8	30.9
1977	12.3	21.7

Extended Example
The American Medical Association*

The American Medical Association (AMA) was organized in 1846 to represent the interests of the medical profession in the passage of health legislation. More than half the nation's 300,000 practicing physicians belong to the AMA and to the 2000 county medical societies across the country.

One of the goals of the AMA has been to avoid government scrutiny of private medical care and fees charged. Placing a third party—the insurance company—between the physician and government has helped minimize the direct role of government. The AMA successfully resisted most attempts to increase government involvement, until the 1960s when Congress passed laws creating Medicare and Medicaid. Medicare provides grants to the states to pay medical benefits to nearly all persons over sixty-five years of age. Medicaid uses federal and state funds to pay health assistance to low-income families. Most Medicaid recipients are aged, disabled, or children. Medicare and Medicaid currently provide medical benefits, respectively, to more than 26 million and 9 million persons annually. Annual costs are about $24 billion and $2 billion, respectively.

Most of the physicians' share of payments made under Medicare are administered by Blue Shield. Blue Shield was established in 1939 to provide medical insurance to low-income families. The program was made available to all families in 1946. Although Blue Shield is strongly influenced by the interests of physicians, there have been recent moves to set maximum allowable charges for certain services.

In 1972 Congress passed a law requiring establishment of Professional Standard Review Organizations (PSROs). The purpose of PSROs was to determine, first, whether care and services provided to patients under federal health programs were necessary and, second, whether care met certain professional standards. Many local medical societies qualify as PSROs, which places physician review in the hands of local physicians.

The AMA regards advertising by physicians as unethical and contradictory to professionalism. The Federal Trade Commission, however, charges that to prohibit advertising is an illegal restraint of trade. The result is to deny consumers information needed to select a physician. A recent study found that the prices of eyeglasses are lower in states which permit advertising. The AMA also opposes prepaid group medical programs and Health Maintenance Organizations (HMOs) because of their effect on physicians' fees.

Since 1970 the greatest potential for change in medical practice has involved the increasing use of physician assistants. State medical boards may certify a physician assistant to work along with a physician, handling about 75 percent of common medical problems and substantially improving productivity. The AMA has attempted to ensure that allied health personnel may not function independently of the licensed physician.

The supply of physicians depends on the licensing policies of state medical boards. Applicants must be graduates of accredited medical schools, whose enrollments are carefully controlled. The AMA has resisted federal support for health education, but in 1963 the Health Professions Educational Assistance Act was passed, providing federal funds for medical schools and loans to medical students.

In what ways is the AMA like a labor union? Illustrate graphically the effect of the AMA's supply policies on the market for medical care. Aside from increasing supply, what are other effects of federal loans to medical students?

*For further information see Paul J. Feldstein, *Health Associations and the Demand for Legislation: The Political Economy of Health.* Cambridge, Mass.: Ballinger Publishing Co., 1977.

Medicare and Medicaid

Rising health-care costs have denied many of the nation's low- and middle-income families adequate health care. Catastrophic illness is reported to be the number one cause of personal bankruptcy in the United States today. Forty percent of Americans have no insurance against catastrophic illness, and twenty percent of Americans have inadequate insurance or no medical insurance at all. In 1965, Medicare and Medicaid were established to provide low-cost care to the elderly and the poor. Still, 26 million Americans have neither health insurance nor access to free care.

Outlays under the Medicare and Medicaid programs have increased from less than $10 billion at the start to almost $50 billion in 1980. One reason for the high cost of Medicaid is the common practice before Medicaid of price discrimination among physicians. As discriminating monopolists, physicians often set fees according to ability to pay. By charging high fees to high-income families and low fees to low-income families, physicians as a group could collect revenue equal to almost the entire area under the health-care demand curve in Figure 3. In effect, high revenues from affluent patients were used to subsidize care for needy patients. The passage of Medicaid removed the need for this kind of subsidy and enabled physicians to set all fees in the high range of the demand curve. Figure 4 shows the result when the fee for a certain service is set at price P_3 and the service is provided to all consumers. Income to physicians now becomes the shaded rectangle.

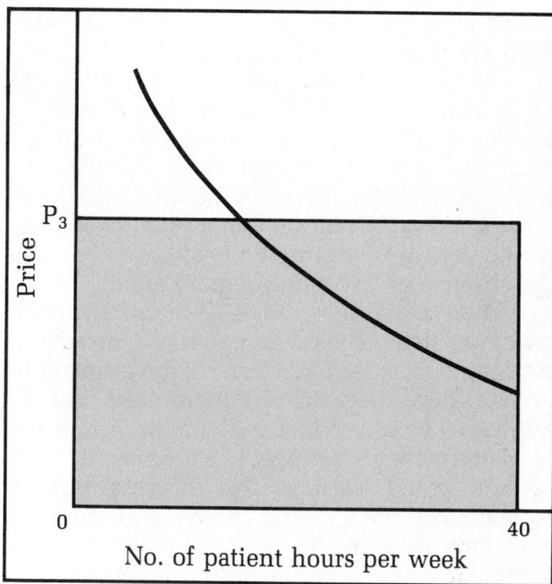

Figure 4 Fixed pricing by a physician. Total income is the shaded area.

Market Supply

High incomes for physicians may have had another effect on the costs of health care. High incomes provide incentives for persons to move into the profession. In a free, competitive market this should push equilibrium price down. This has not happened in the market for physicians. Entries to the health-care industry have moved into the highest paid specialties rather than into general practice. The result is an excess of, say, surgeons—maintaining high prices and perhaps performing unnecessary surgery. At the same time there is a shortage of general practitioners. This means that patients must visit costly specialists for even minor ailments.

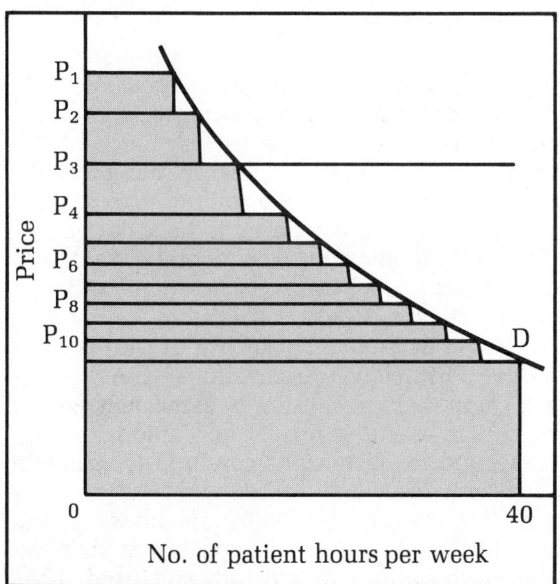

Figure 3 Price discrimination by a physician. Total income is the shaded area.

Proposed Government Programs

Most proposals to deal with the problems of the health-care industry include regulation to control price increases and government insurance programs to ensure equity in the allocation of health resources. To restrain health-care inflation, President Carter in 1979 proposed a hospital cost containment bill that would have limited hospital cost increases to 9.7 percent annually. Congress passed a weaker bill that encouraged voluntary cost containment. Congress also requires states to enact certificate-of-need laws to reduce duplication of hospital services and to slow hospital construction.

Proposals for additional government insurance programs are also under consideration. The programs differ in the portion of a patient's health costs each would pay and in the ways they are financed—by consumers, employers, or taxes. The various programs could be handled either by private insurance companies or by a government agency, and most would include a price ceiling on health-care costs. All the proposed health-care plans would cost billions of dollars a year, but it is not clear how these costs would compare with rising health-care costs in the absence of any new program at all.

There are disadvantages associated with all programs being considered. A major disadvantage is the increased influence of government in private decision-making. Guaranteed health-care plans would reduce individuals' incentives to plan for their own needs; government intervention could weaken the intimate doctor-patient relationship and perhaps discourage new entrants to the medical profession. Finally, the paperwork required in any government program would add substantially to costs and reduce efficiency.

Market Incentive Programs

One new proposal would allow consumers to select quantity of health care purchased according to MU/P and would thus improve efficiency in the allocation of health resources. It would be more equitable, too, in that most consumers of health care would pay only for the services they alone use. This proposal would set some percentage of income—say 5 percent—up to which consumers would pay the entire cost of health care. Since consumers would pay their own service costs, they would be less likely to purchase a larger amount than they actually need. Above this minimum amount, a percentage of health-care costs could be subtracted from income-tax payments; this would enable consumers to purchase additional care with a subsidy for more costly needs. Finally, beyond some percentage of income, say 20 percent, all further health costs would be subtracted from taxes due. For these patients alone, health care would be a "free good."

There are several advantages to this proposal. Under a tax-credit plan, consumers would seek to purchase needed care at minimum costs. They would exert pressure on physicians, who, in turn, would select hospitals and other health resources according to the quality of service relative to cost, according to their efficiency or MRP/P. The result could be greater competition in the health-service industry, with innovative approaches to filling patient needs.

For this proposal to be effective, it would be necessary to eliminate job-sponsored health-insurance programs. Currently, an employer's contribution to a worker's health-insurance plan is not taxed as income.

Another market incentive program involves the growth of **Health Maintenance Organizations** (HMOs). HMOs are groups of medical specialists with offices in a single location. Residents of the community may join the HMO by paying regular monthly dues of about $100, part of which may be paid by their employers. Under a federal law passed in 1973, a firm employing at least twenty-five people in an area with an HMO must give workers a choice of membership in an HMO or regular health insurance. In 1979, there were 203 HMOs operating in the United States, providing health services to 7.4 million members.

HMO members may consult physicans at the HMO for all needed health services, but the emphasis is on preventing major health problems through regular check-ups. HMOs perform eye examinations, immunizations, cholesterol checks and labwork, allergy treatments, prenatal and maternity care, physical examinations, and electrocardiograms. They encourage healthful habits by providing clinics for physical therapy and for members who need help to stop smoking or drinking.

Physicians in the HMO receive salaries and are relieved of the costs of private practice: overhead, rent, malpractice insurance premiums, and the costs of office personnel. Since HMOs perform only necessary labwork and prescribe substantially less hospitalization than private physicans, they are believed to have cut health-care costs significantly. The federal government provides funds for technical assistance and loan guarantees for HMOs.

Another innovation in health care is **Individual Physicians' Associations** (IPAs). IPAs are composed of physicians associated with a particular business firm, labor union, or consumer group. Physicians continue to maintain their own individual offices and medical practices. Members of the group can choose among the physicians, with the cost paid from their regular contributions to a health-care fund. IPAs have an advantage over HMOs in the greater degree of consumer choice of physician.

ENERGY

Since World War II, much of the prosperity of the Western world has been the result of cheap oil. We have enjoyed travel, and we have consumed goods from faraway places. We have developed new consumer technologies: food processors, styrofoam containers, polyester clothing, and a dazzling variety of goods for improving the quality of life. Our high living standards were based on energy from oil—energy which made work easier and play more fun. Year after year, total production grew, and goods were shared among more segments of our population.

Until 1964 the United States was the world's largest producer of oil. The low marginal cost of producing oil blinded American consumers to the long-range costs of replacing oil when current supplies finally run out. Consumers pushed production beyond X (in Figure 1) to a level where marginal benefits were probably less than the long-range marginal costs of producing alternative energy sources. American oil companies realized well before 1964 that this would happen and began to expand their investments in other parts of the world, the Middle East, Nigeria, and Venezuela in particular. The concentration of oil investments in small parts of the world finally raised the possibility of the use of organized power to control supply and raise prices. The Organization of Petroleum Exporting Countries (OPEC) was born in 1960. Initially, OPEC didn't seem to be much of a problem to oil consumers. The 1960s saw oil surpluses, and the major international and American oil companies still dominated the terms of oil production and ownership in the host countries. But, in 1970, U.S. oil production peaked and oil imports rose dramatically thereafter. This gave OPEC the opportunity to exert its power to control supply and raise prices. OPEC began to use its market power to push production to the left in Figure 1 so as to maximize monopoly profits.

For OPEC members, eventual depletion of oil stocks would mean a return to the poverty of years past. To avoid this, they determined to use oil profits to develop other industrial sources of income for the future. Since 1970, OPEC has demanded a larger and larger share of the world's output of goods and services in return for their oil. The rising price for OPEC oil raised living costs for American consumers and production costs for American business firms. Higher oil prices would normally have reduced consumers' remaining purchasing power for spending on other goods; lower sales would have reduced the return on other resources used by business firms. The resulting lower real incomes in the United States would have been the incentive for distributing more U.S. goods and services to oil producers abroad. To a certain extent this has happened, but we have all resisted it.

American consumers and producers have resisted a decline in real incomes. We have demanded additional compensation—higher wages, salaries, and profits—to offset the higher prices we have to pay for energy and energy-related goods. The result has been higher nominal incomes and higher prices. We have paid OPEC more dollars for oil, but we have inflated domestic prices so as to minimize OPEC ability to buy substantially more goods and services. We have refused to distribute a much larger share of U.S. output in return for our oil purchases.

The result of this kind of conflict is not necessarily equitable. Groups in the United States that lack power to obtain wage or profit increases must, in fact, submit to a redistribution of real income to oil producers. Other groups which own oil resources may benefit from OPEC-enforced redistribution. Even more important, to the extent that U.S. consumers are dependent on OPEC oil supplies, our nation becomes more vulnerable to greater exercise of political pressure from abroad.

For a democracy like the United States, dealing with a long-range problem is difficult. Since elections come every two years, and business firms evaluate profits every year, we tend to think in terms of the short run. There is no clear, consistent mechanism for putting programs in place which are painful today but necessary if we are to avoid even worse problems in the future. Furthermore, the restaurant analogy from the previous section applies here as well. Even though many American consumers recognize they are wasteful and must eventually change their habits, there is little incentive for any individual to do so. Anyone who reduces energy consumption sacrifices a part of the "good life" for himself or herself and enables others to enjoy the good life even longer. In the meantime, American consumers enjoy the benefits of energy consumption while avoiding paying the costs.

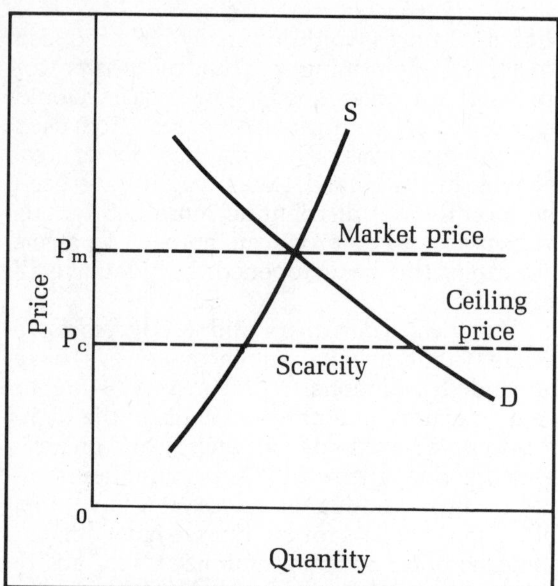

Figure 5 Price controls discourage production and conservation. The result is a scarcity at the ceiling price.

Present Policies: Price Controls

With the exception of medical care, no other consumer prices have increased as fast as energy.* In the last twenty years, energy prices have almost tripled, and the use of high-cost energy has raised other production costs substantially.

American oil and natural gas prices have been subject to various types of price controls. Figure 5 illustrates the effects of price controls. Recall that a price ceiling places a legal limit on price increases. When price is held below equilibrium, quantity demanded exceeds quantity supplied. The low price encourages wasteful consumption and discourages production, leading to a shortage. Table 4 shows estimated energy waste in 1978.

Hoping to reduce the shortage resulting from price ceilings, government price regulators established a system of **two-tier pricing for oil.** The lower tier included "old oil" from wells already in operation, using equipment already in place. The price of old oil was controlled at about $6 a barrel; government felt that the low price would not discourage additional production since these wells were already in place and marginal costs were low. The upper tier included new oil, for which exploration and recovery was more costly; a price of about $13 a barrel was allowed for new oil. *Stripper wells,* very old wells that require costly procedures if they are to produce additional oil, were not covered by the two-tier pricing system. Oil from stripper wells could be sold at the unregulated world price, about $23 a barrel (1979).

Price to American consumers became an average of controlled U.S. prices and the price of imported oil, which by 1980 constituted about half our total consumption. Since this average was below world equilibrium prices, U.S. consumers continued the wasteful use of oil products, in effect subsidizing OPEC revenues and maintaining our dependence on foreign suppliers. Chairman of the Council of Economic Advisers Charles L. Schultze pointed out that "we pay OPEC more for oil than we are willing to pay Americans who produce oil substitutes." In terms of Figure 1, we are operating in the range around *Y*. The artificially low price excludes the cost of replacing depleting energy supplies and enables us to avoid the painful adjustments in energy consumption that will ultimately be necessary.

Continuing U.S. inflation has led OPEC repeatedly to increase the dollar price of oil, worsening the distortions caused by price ceilings in the United States. Many economists urge that oil price controls be removed so that domestic oil prices can move toward an equilibrium, market-clearing level. They argue that a higher price would encourage domestic producers to seek new sources of oil and consumers to conserve existing supplies.

Table 4 **Energy Consumed and Wasted Each Day**

Source	Consumed*	Lost*
Utilities	10.9	7.4
Industrial production	10.3	4.6
Use of autos	4.9	4.2
Use of all other transportation	4.8	4.2
Commercial buildings	3.2	1.9
Private residences	5.4	3.1
Other	.7	—

*In millions of barrels of oil equivalent per day.
Source: Brookhaven National Laboratory

*Rising energy prices include the costs of piped gas and electricity; fuel oil, coal, and bottled gas; and gasoline, motor oil, coolant, etc.

Should We Decontrol Prices?

When we talk about *decontrol of prices,* we mean removing all price controls. Since we are actually talking of price ceilings, the short-run effect of decontrol is for oil prices to rise. The forces of supply and demand come into play again, and oil prices will move upward toward equilibrium. Whether decontrol of oil prices would actually relieve microeconomic and macroeconomic problems originating with oil depends on elasticities.

Let us consider demand elasticity first. As consumers move up their demand curves, the substitution and income effects should work to reduce quantity demanded. For this to happen, there must be acceptable substitutes available at lower prices, and there must be an effective decline in consumers' real income. Neither of these conditions has been true. In the first place, prices of available substitutes (natural gas, coal, nuclear power, etc.) have risen almost as fast as oil; in the second place, consumers have demanded increases in incomes to compensate for higher living costs. Thus, demand curves have been relatively inelastic. Initially, oil consumption responded only slightly to higher prices.

Although demand curves are relatively inelastic in the short run, they may become more elastic over the long run. Over time, lower-cost substitutes may be developed to fill many of our energy needs: improved mass transit, improved home insulation, and conversion of oil-fired power plants to coal. The time for adjustment may be lengthy, however. Replacing much of our energy-using capital will require substantial new investment over the coming decades. Buildings with sealed windows requiring continuous use of air conditioning must eventually be replaced; energy-guzzling autos will finally wear out; even living patterns will change as some commuters move from suburban neighborhoods to areas nearer their places of employment. Thus higher oil prices will eventually encourage consumers to adjust their spending to the new price ratios.

With respect to supply elasticity, response to higher prices requires that additional resources be applied to oil production, that new technologies be installed, and that efficiency of recovery be improved. Again, substantial time is required for these measures to be implemented. To the extent that they are successful—and if undiscovered sources of oil actually exist—oil production may be a **decreasing cost industry** or a **constant cost industry.** Long-run supply curves may be relatively elastic. But if new recovery techniques fail and if new oil sources are limited, oil production will be an **increasing cost industry.** Long-run supply curves will be highly inelastic. Substantially higher prices will be necessary to bring on additional supplies. No one knows how much additional oil is actually available or how much it will cost to produce, so it is impossible to say with certainty how supply will respond to price increases.

Backward-Bending Supply

Higher prices for oil could actually lead to smaller quantities. Producers may decide that producing for maximum short-run profits will endanger long-run profits. Maximum long-run profits depend on maintaining a share of industry output over time. Thus, there may be infor-

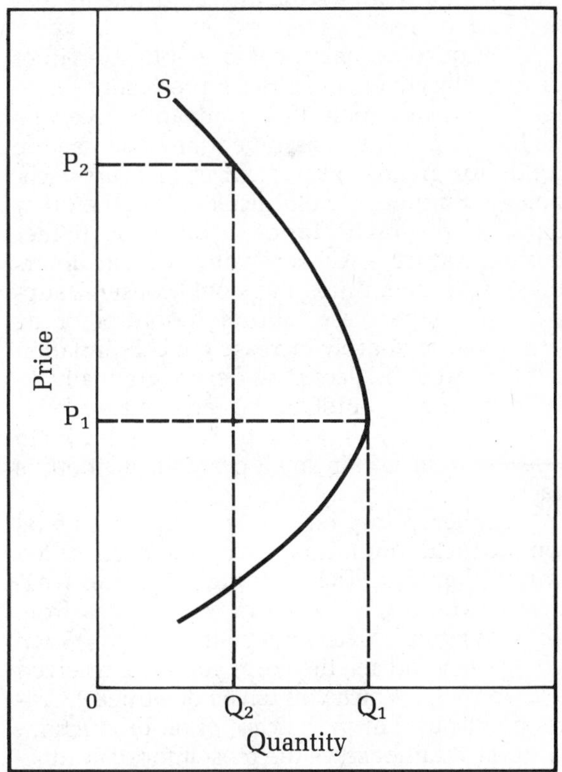

Figure 6 A backward-bending supply curve. A rise in price enables suppliers to reduce quantity supplied and still collect the same revenues.

mal agreement among producers to limit sales in the short run. Instead of setting a level of output that would maximize profits, they may set a target level of revenue from current production. The target revenue would be set at an amount sufficient for paying operating costs and adequate dividends to stockholders. Note that higher prices would enable producers to achieve the target revenue with fewer barrels of oil.

In our chapter on labor economics, we illustrated this situation with a **backward-bending supply** curve like the one in Figure 6. In Figure 6, producers' target revenue can be achieved by selling OQ_1 barrels of oil at price OP_1 or only OQ_2 barrels at price OP_2.

Windfall-Profits Taxes

In spite of uncertainty about elasticities, economists generally favor removing price controls so that demand and supply adjustments can begin to take place. They feel that the longer controls remain in effect, the more serious the distortions and the more extreme the final adjustments that will be required.

Oil price decontrol could emphasize either of two objectives: to increase production or to reduce consumption. If oil companies receive a higher oil price, it is assumed they will use the funds for greater investment in recovery technology. Supplies should increase. On the other hand, if the higher price is offset by higher taxes, producers will not gain. But consumers must pay higher prices and would conserve supplies. In either case, abrupt decontrol of oil prices would sharply increase the U.S. inflation rate. Therefore, decontrol began gradually in 1979, with all controls to be removed by 1981. The procedure was to change "old oil" (at \$6) to "new oil" (at \$13) in small percentage amounts each year.

Higher prices on existing supplies of oil would yield producers what has been called **windfall profits.** (The term originated from a situation where a wind blows, say, apples from your neighbor's trees onto your property; when you gather and sell the crop, you have received a "windfall," which you have not earned.) Critics point out that in the case of oil production, windfalls cannot serve the most important function of profits: the incentive to expand output. They represent only a substantial transfer of income from consumers to owners of oil facilities, income which may or may not be spent in ways that increase energy production.

Windfall profits act as a kind of tax on consumption. This "tax" may be used for additional investment or paid as dividends to company stockholders. But such short-run purposes may offer no real, long-term benefits for U.S. consumers in general. Furthermore, as we have seen, higher prices may not encourage additional oil production, since oil left in the ground may be increasing in value faster than any other investment oil companies might make.

The actual amount of windfall profits is difficult to measure. Profits will depend on prices, which depend on the actions of OPEC, and on costs, which depend on the accessibility of new oil supplies. Using reasonable assumptions about the probable behavior of prices and costs over the twelve years 1979–90, Congressional staff analysts have predicted U.S. oil revenues of about \$1 trillion, of which more than \$900 billion will be profits.

Oil companies insist that these windfall profits are necessary if they are to invest in new productive facilities. The argument sounds reasonable but is false. Investment decisions depend not on past profits but on the expectation of future profits. Any firm would be wise to invest its financial capital in industries where expected returns are greatest, whether that turns out to be shale-oil fields, mail-order companies, or whatever. If the private benefits and costs of additional oil investments are such that $MB/MC < 1$ (or less than the MB/MC of other projects) the investments will not be made, regardless of the amount of windfall profits available for use.

In 1980 Congress enacted a 50 percent tax on windfall profits. With no windfall-profits tax, state, local, and federal taxes would take about \$500 billion of oil companies' \$900 billion profit. This would leave oil companies with after-tax profits amounting to $400/1000 = 40$ percent of sales revenue. The windfall tax legislation will take about \$225 billion in additional revenue, cutting profits to about 27 percent of sales.

Revenue from the windfall-profits tax is to be used in three ways: for distribution to poor families to shield against the higher cost of necessary energy, for construction of mass transit systems, and for research and development of alternative energy supplies.

Alternative Energy Supplies

According to the U.S. Energy Research and Development Administration (now the Department of Energy), "no technological challenge the nation has ever faced in its history has been as critical as these new tasks. We face the prospect of ever diminishing energy supplies while our demand continues to increase."* There are some possibilities developing for alternative energy supplies, however. Researchers are at work exploring new technologies for filling our energy needs and reducing the threat of international political pressure. As you read each of the following descriptions, make a list of the benefits and costs you think would follow from the use of the various technologies.

Coal. Except for wood, coal is nearly our oldest active source of energy. It came into wide use in the sixteenth century and now satisfies 20 percent of total U.S. energy requirements. Coal has many defenders now who maintain it can solve the present energy crisis.

There have always been problems associated with the use of coal. Coal mining has cost the lives of 100,000 miners in accidents in the United States during this century. Many thousands more suffer from black lung, a disease that causes suffering and death. Coal is a heavy polluter, and strip-mining of coal also damages the environment. The costs of increasing safety and protecting miners are considerable. So too is the cost of paying for pollution-control equipment. Facing these problems in the 1960s, many utilities changed from coal-fired plants to cleaner oil-burning plants.

However, rising prices of OPEC oil have caught up with coal. In early 1980, it cost $35 for a ton of delivered coal and another $25 per ton burned for pollution control. This contrasted with $165 for the energy-equivalent amount of delivered oil. Still, utilities are reluctant to pay the high cost for reconversion to coal.

A key advantage of coal is that the United States possesses vast amounts of it—in fact, the world's largest amounts of recoverable coal. In 1980, the World Coal Study Organization, based at MIT, issued a report called *Coal—Bridge to the Future.* It called for a threefold increase in the production of coal by the year 2000. The report indicated that coal could meet pollution guidelines and solve our energy crisis.

*Henry Simmons, "The Economics of America's Energy Future," U.S. Energy Research and Development Administration, Washington, D.C., 1975.

Synthetic fuels. For decades scientists have had the technology for breaking apart the carbon and hydrogen composition of coal and recombining it to build synthetic fuels, known for short as *synfuel.* Synfuel can substitute for natural gas, gasoline, and petroleum; it is particularly well suited for producing electricity. The process is costly, however, and would require that government guarantee a profitable price for producers. Of course, as world energy prices rise, profits would increase naturally, and the need for government guarantees would disappear. On the other hand, increasing scarcity of other energy sources would ultimately raise the price of coal, and environmental health and safety regulations may limit its use. Producing synfuels may itself cause environmental problems. All these factors would reduce the profitability of synthetic fuel production.

Oil shale. Shale deposits in the western United States contain about six times as much oil as our proven reserves of petroleum.* Shale rock in Colorado, Wyoming, and Utah contains twenty or more gallons of oil per ton. One process for removing the oil requires that the rock be mined, crushed, and heated to high temperatures. Large amounts of scarce water would be needed to dispose of waste, and environmental damage in shale rock states would be immense. Another process has been proposed to overcome some of these disadvantages. Under this process, heat is applied to underground rock so that the oil flows out and can be pumped to the surface. Although the mining and disposal costs involved in processing oil shale would be high, price would be less than that of synthetic fuel.

Nuclear power. Most nuclear energy produced in the United States today uses uranium enriched with the isotope uranium-235. In seventy-seven plants around the nation, heat from a nuclear reaction is used to produce steam for running turbines to generate electricity.

This process has some disadvantages aside from the risks of nuclear accident and the problems of nuclear waste disposal. Nuclear reactors

*Proven reserves consist of the petroleum available at current prices with existing technology.

Extended Example Health Hazards from Electric Power Generation

About 15 percent of the energy used in the United States is electricity. Consumers pay the immediate costs of their electricity, but there are environmental and health costs that do not appear on any consumer's electric bill. William Ramsay of Resources for the Future in Washington, D.C., estimates the following unpaid costs of electric power from coal and nuclear fuel.

From coal used annually to generate electricity

0–6000 deaths from air pollution
0–1250 deaths from occupational accidents and disease
10,000–1 million cases of respiratory disease in children
60,000–6 million cases of chronic respiratory disease
600,000–60 million days of heart-lung symptoms among the elderly
100,000–10 million asthma attacks
100,000–200,000 acres of land to be reclaimed
1.6 billion metric tons of carbon dioxide in the atmosphere causing a .001°C warming of the environment

From the same power generated by nuclear fuels

20–200 deaths from occupational radiation exposures
.3–1 death from radioactive atmospheric emissions
4000–7000 nonfatal accidents and illnesses
20,000 acres for mining and processing fuel
2000 acres for storing wastes
In the event of a major accident: 3000 deaths from radiation poisoning and 45,000 cancer deaths.

Many of us fear large-scale use of nuclear energy for generating electricity. The dangers are new and poorly understood. However, as Ramsay's research demonstrates, even the alternative sources of energy have their costs. Whatever our decision on energy sources, we must accept the existence of trade-offs and try to select the alternatives for which the costs are lowest.

discharge about 30 percent more heat to the environment than coal-fired generators; thus a substantial portion of uranium's potential energy is lost. Inefficiency in the use of fuel means that larger amounts will be needed, leading to shortages and substantially higher fuel costs in the future. Lower-yielding uranium ores will have to be mined and billions of tons of earth moved every year to feed the reactors.

A possible solution to the fuel problem in nuclear reactors would be to recycle plutonium. The isotope plutonium-239 is produced in the normal course of reactor operations and can be recovered by reprocessing nuclear fuel. The Energy Department has recommended building reactors which would use a core of plutonium surrounded by uranium-238. These reactors would produce plutonium-239 faster than they use plutonium in the core. Such reactors are called "breeder reactors"; it is estimated that breeder reactors would double their original fuel in as few as ten years.

Lead times for planning and building nuclear plants are currently about twelve years, during which time construction costs for some plants have tripled. Electric utilities have had difficulty raising funds for nuclear investments. The possibility of fuel shortage and environmental risks have discouraged investors and delayed development of nuclear energy. Since plutonium can be used for making bombs, the U.S. government has imposed a moratorium on construction of breeder reactors.

In the very long run, the nation may turn to nuclear fusion for its electric power. Fusion has several advantages: There is no possibility of a nuclear accident; there is less radioactive material to transport, handle, and store; there is less risk of radiation. The process requires heating a special mixture of deuterium and tritium to a temperature of 100 million degrees, four times hotter than the center of the sun. Heat from the resulting reaction is converted to steam for generating power. If conditions are precisely correct, the process can produce hundreds of times more energy than it uses. Deuterium can be derived from sea water; tritium can be produced within the reactor itself, but it is radioactive. However, tritium is an input to be used, not an output that has disposal problems.

The Soviet Union has had some success in developing this process, but nuclear fusion has not yet been found to be economical for U.S. use. Still, its eventual development could finally enable the nation to become energy self-sufficient. In fact, in addition to producing electricity, nuclear fusion could be used to manufacture hydrogen for running aircraft, trucks, and buses.

Geothermal power. Hundreds of hot springs, *fumaroles* (openings in volcanic areas from which smoke and gases arise), and volcanic areas in the American west may hold the answer to part of our energy problem. Underground steam and pressurized hot water could be used to drive turbines for generating electricity. It is estimated that within the United States the upper six miles of the earth's crust holds heat equivalent to one hundred times the earth's petroleum reserves. Already, near San Francisco, geothermal energy is being used to produce seven hundred megawatts of electricity a year. The cost of the steam has been estimated at about $.35 a ton, substantially less than steam produced by burning fuel oil.

There are some problems with geothermal power. Few existing sites are precisely suited for power generation. Moreover, some of the underground steam contains mineral impurities which must be removed to avoid damaging pipes and equipment. Probably the best use of underground steam would be for direct heating.

Solar energy. Fundamentally, all energy comes from the sun: fossil fuels, geothermal, and even wind and wave energy. Using the sun's rays directly has the advantage that solar energy is clean and abundant. Analysts estimate that a solar collector the size of Massachusetts would receive enough solar energy to provide the entire nation's consumption of electricity. Such a facility would not be practical, of course. The sun's rays are scattered widely over the earth's surface, so collectors would have to be built in many locations. Furthermore, the sun's rays are not continuous, so energy would have to be stored for use when the sun is not shining. All this would raise costs substantially.

Development of solar energy has been slow. Although operating costs are relatively low for solar power, initial capital requirements are high. Home builders, business firms, and banks are less impressed with the long-range savings from solar installations than with the short-range costs. Government-guaranteed loans and property tax exemptions might be needed to encourage construction of solar energy devices. Currently, most solar energy is used for heating and cooling, which together account for about one fourth of U.S. energy consumption each year.

Other possible sources of future energy include conversion of waste materials to energy, solar cells to produce electricity in space, turbines driven by temperature differences at various ocean depths, and wind energy machines.

The Department of Energy spent $60 million on wind turbine technology in 1979 and estimates that wind could generate between 3 and 5 percent of the nation's electricity by the year 2000. The largest wind turbine now in use is in Boone, North Carolina. Built at a cost of $4 million, it has rotor blades measuring two hundred feet in diameter. It generates 20 million watts of electricity, enough to supply five hundred average-sized homes. Costs are now $.08 per kilowatt hour and must fall to $.03 to be competitive with other energy sources.

Wind turbines are most effective for the western and Plains states and for islands. However, analysts believe that small turbines could generate power for individual homeowners in rural areas or for small-town utilities.

Some Energy Recommendations

Using tax revenues for energy research and development has some opposition. Unless investments are based on market criteria, they are likely to be inefficient. Private producers may be more able than government to calculate the benefits and costs of specific energy projects. If government programs result in inefficient resource allocation, the result would be a lower rate of return for U.S. investment as a whole and a lower rate of economic growth for the nation. On the other hand, government may be better able to measure broader benefits and costs. Since private firms must focus on their immediate profits or losses, they may ignore the long-range consequences of their actions.

Some compromise between government and private decision-making may be the answer to this problem. Rather than selecting particular alternative energy projects for investments, government might offer incentives to producers to seek the most efficient processes. Energy production could be encouraged through tax credits or specific dollar payments per unit of energy produced. Manufacturing firms could be urged to establish a compressed workweek with special accommodations for worker carpooling. Subsidies for home insulation and storm windows and for more fuel-efficient autos would encourage conservation among consumers. Drivers could be encouraged to forgo use of their autos one day a week. In general, the objective should be to use government subsidies to develop new energy procedures with the greatest economic potential, flexible enough to respond quickly and efficiently to technical and economic developments.

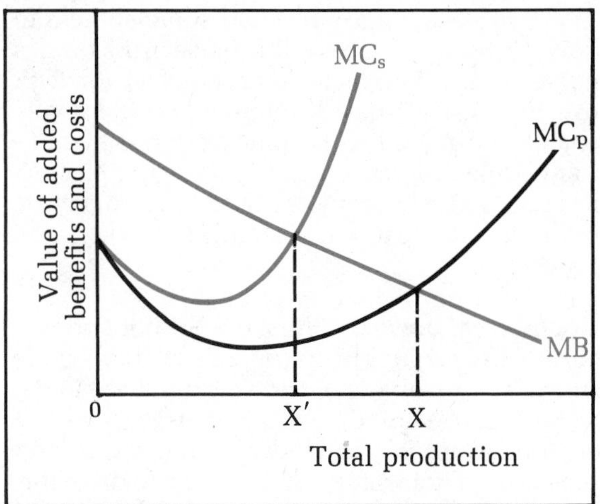

Figure 7 Adding externalities raises the costs of production and may reduce the efficient level of output from X to X′.

ENVIRONMENTAL HEALTH AND SAFETY

Perhaps the most complex example of market failure in the United States today is the problem of environmental health and safety. As we have become a more industrialized and a more urban society, our individual actions have come to affect strongly the health, safety, and environmental quality of others around us. This is true of our actions as individual consumers, private business firms, and government. Moreover, scientists are discovering that actions once believed to be harmless may, in fact, cause serious health damage ten, twenty, or even more years in the future. The unwanted and unintended spillover effects of our actions are called *negative externalities* or *external costs*. They are external costs because they are paid by all members of society whether or not they receive compensating benefits. The combination of the private costs and the external costs of an action is called its social cost.

We have illustrated the relationship between private costs and individual benefits by the ratio MB/MC. When externalities exist, marginal external costs (MC_e) must be added to marginal private costs (MC_p) to compute the denominator of the ratio, marginal social cost (MC_s). Thus

$$\frac{MB}{MC} = \frac{MB}{MC_p + MC_e} = \frac{MB}{MC_s}.$$

In Figure 7 marginal external costs have been added to marginal private costs to form a marginal social cost curve. Notice that the addition of external costs shifts the efficient level of production from X to X′. In theory, members of any family, business firm, or community would evaluate the ratio associated with additional productive activity and carry on that activity only as long as $MB/MC_s > 1$. This would ensure efficiency in the use of resources: Marginal benefits to the group would be at least sufficient to offset all the marginal costs, both short and long term, private and external.

In practice, computing the ratio MB/MC_s is difficult. This is because many external costs are not measurable and some are not presently understood. Some must be weighted by a factor that estimates the probability (from 0% to 100%) of their occurrence at all. Moreover, benefits and costs which occur in the future must be *discounted,* marked down by a factor which depends on the distance in the future and the preference of the community for experiences in the present. Whatever the value of MB/MC_s, there are likely to be complex feedbacks within and among activities which make clear conclusions impossible. In short, the market depends on individual consumers and producers to evaluate benefits and costs and to allocate resources efficiently. But when externalities are involved in production, the market breaks down.

Let's look at the various environmental external costs that pose problems to our health.

Atmospheric Pollution

We used to consider the air around us a "free good." We expelled wastes into the earth's atmosphere with no thought of the potential harm to life. Only critical levels of particles and chemicals in the air have finally awakened the public to the need for environmental protection.

For decades the burning of fossil fuels (coal, oil, and natural gas) has added sulfur fumes to the air, creating suffocating smog and causing respiratory and vision problems. Illness and death from respiratory disease are major problems in many American cities. Sulfur in the air falls back to earth in the form of sulfuric and nitric *acid rain.* The acids kill fish and damage agricultural crops hundreds of miles from the polluting source. Other chemical and nuclear wastes in the air can poison our bodies and create genetic or neurological problems far into the future. Scientists are only beginning to discover the health implications of many of today's manufacturing processes.

Aerosol sprays using fluorocarbons were ordered phased out in the United States in 1977, but they continue to be used in other parts of the world. Aerosol chemicals destroy the atmosphere's ozone, which screens out the sun's harmful ultraviolet rays. Scientists fear that depletion of the ozone shield will cause thousands of cases of skin cancer and damage plant life as well. A reduced ozone layer may even alter the world's climate patterns.

Another climatic problem is the result of what scientists call the *greenhouse effect*. Around the globe, the increasing use of fossil fuels has been increasing the carbon dioxide (CO_2) content of the atmosphere faster than nature can recycle it. A change of this magnitude can lead to substantial changes in our way of life. Air-conditioning costs will rise, movement of population away from urban areas will accelerate, and entire regions will experience massive population shifts. Coastal flooding may occur as polar icecaps melt. Drought and extremes of temperature will raise agricultural costs and require additional irrigation and improved transportation facilities. Fish populations will be affected by changing ocean currents and temperatures.

Trees absorb carbon dioxide and help slow down the greenhouse effect; excessive cutting of trees for industrial use and residential development worsens the problem of excess carbon dioxide. Moreover, as oil and gas become scarcer, the greater use of coal will put even more CO_2 into the atmosphere. For every ton of coal burned, it is estimated that three tons of CO_2 are released into the atmosphere.

To estimate the social costs of changes in our weather is an impossible task, making efficient resource allocation especially difficult. The problem of carbon dioxide emissions also complicates the energy decisions we discussed in the previous section.

Water Pollution

An estimated twelve thousand potentially toxic chemicals are used by American industry, with five hundred new chemicals introduced each year. When these chemicals are discharged into our water supply by industrial firms, we may be subject to cancer or genetic abnormalities some thirty or forty years in the future. The Environmental Protection Agency (EPA) estimates that four thousand illnesses each year occur as a result of unhealthy drinking water.

Analyzing and regulating chemical pollution is difficult since many chemicals used by business firms are trade secrets. Moreover, chemicals are costly to remove from water and to dispose of. They are an important part of many consumer goods and provide jobs to thousands of workers. Many important items, from decaffeinated coffee to plastic seat covers, are made with chemicals that are suspected of causing cancer. The value of these products and the jobs they provide must be compared with all these long-range costs—a difficult exercise.

Land Reclamation

About two thirds of the nation's coal is produced by strip mining, more efficient and less costly than underground mining. But costs are sure to rise as state and federal strip mining regulations begin to be fully enforced. Under new laws, strip miners will be required to restore the land to its original shape and use: filling holes, contouring land, removing wastes, and replanting trees and grass. Land reclamation will add from \$.85 to \$1.30 per ton to the cost of strip-mined coal and put as much as 141 million tons of coal a year off limits for mining, primarily because it lies beneath prime agricultural land.

Mine owners are resisting the new regulations, and the courts have ruled that closing mines for environmental violations amounts to taking private property without due process or compensation. The costs of complying with federal regulations could have the effect that EPA rules had on the copper industry. High reclamation costs made many small asset-rich but cash-poor copper firms more vulnerable to takeover by large firms. The effect was to increase concentration in the industry and to worsen a tendency toward inflation—again an impossible cost to measure.

Consumer Product Safety

Agencies of the federal government have imposed bans on the sale of various consumer products that have been shown to be dangerous to health or safety. Often a ban itself has created additional dangers that cannot be measured. For example, the ban on certain diet sweeteners was expected to reduce the risk of cancer. But without diet foods, certain consumers may face increased tendency toward obesity and even diabetes.

A temporary ban on cranberries because of the use of a cancer-causing pesticide on cranberry fields left many farmers and entire communities without income during their important seasonal sales peak. Their loss of income should also be considered when evaluating the benefits and cost of product safety regulations.

These regulations also raise a more serious potential problem. If American business firms are frequently subject to consumer protection regulation, will they hesitate to put in place new procedures for improving productivity and quality of goods? Fear of new regulations may thus stifle industrial innovation, with costs far beyond our capacity to measure.

Employee Health and Safety

Employee health and safety comes under the jurisdiction of the Occupational Health and Safety Administration (OSHA), established in 1970. OSHA regulations fill volumes and cover everything from location of coathooks to safety guards for heavy equipment operators. But OSHA has only 2500 investigators to cover five million workplaces. For OSHA investigators, enforcing trivial rules is easier than fighting major violations. As a result, investigators may require business firms to pay thousands of dollars to correct minor work problems while neglecting major health hazards. Stepladders may be redesigned while dangerous chemicals continue to be used. Moreover, because OSHA sets forth particular solutions to particular health and safety problems, firms are not encouraged to seek cheaper and more effective solutions. Thus, the costs of OSHA's regulations may be higher than necessary. OSHA is presently trying to correct the policies that brought these kinds of criticism and is encouraging the development of consulting services to help business eliminate hazardous conditions.

Environmental Policies

Through our elected representatives, we help determine government's policies toward environmental externalities. The objective of policy should be to improve efficiency of decision making, to allocate resources according to MB/MC_s so that our society achieves maximum net benefits from available resources. To do this we must add external costs to private costs, shifting the marginal cost curve in our graph upward and moving point X to the left, as shown on Figure 7. Thus, including external costs may reduce the appropriate level of resource use for maximum efficiency.

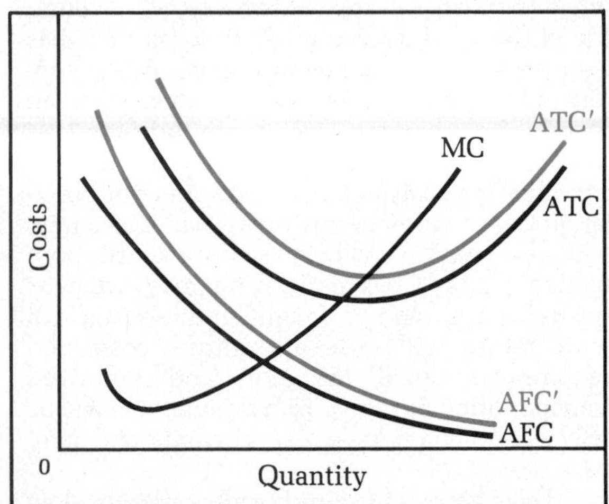

Figure 8 Internalizing externalities through investment in anti-pollution equipment. The cost of the equipment raises ATC, reducing profit or increasing loss.

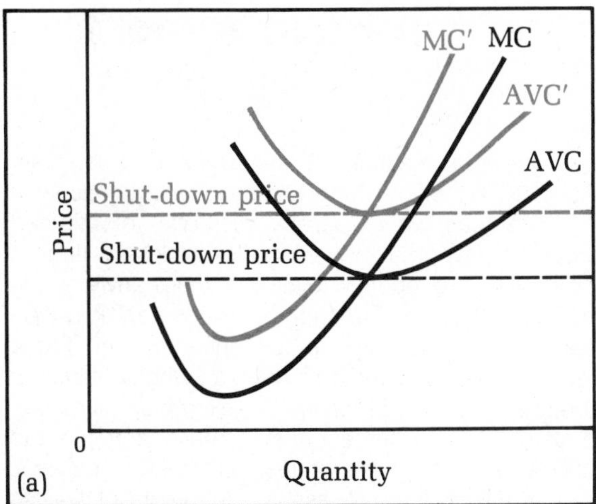

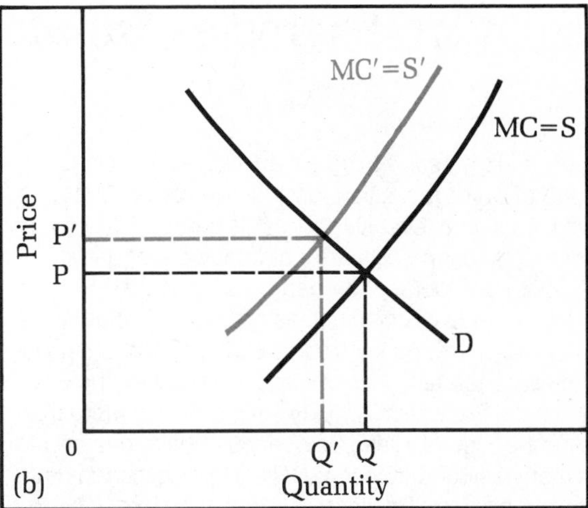

Figure 9 Internalizing externalities through unit taxes changes production procedures. (a) Higher unit variable costs require higher prices to stay in business. (b) Higher marginal costs increase price and reduce quantity.

As we have shown, determining the full costs of resource use and the appropriate value of X' may be difficult. Several different policies have been attempted for this purpose, with varying levels of success.

Legislation. Laws have been passed forbidding certain activities that endanger the health, safety, and environment of the community. Consumer goods have been taken off the market; polluting activities have been forbidden; health and safety standards have been enforced on business firms. Laws like these attempt to reduce social costs by curtailing resource use. Other legislation provides subsidies for carrying on particular kinds of activities. The objective is to encourage activities that are believed to yield external benefits.

Most economists oppose policies which mandate a particular kind and level of resource use. According to economic theory, the objective of the community should not be to eliminate costs or increase benefits but to maximize *net benefit*. Legislation forbidding certain activities—strip mining, for example—eliminates the benefits of these activities as well as their costs. Similarly, subsidies can have the effect of promoting certain activities far beyond the level at which additional benefits justify their cost.

Regulation. In general, the regulatory approach to environmental problems is to require an industry to install certain devices and use certain procedures to reduce its contribution to pollution. The aim is to "internalize externalities": to force the firm which produces a problem to pay the cost of correcting it. Electric generating plants are required to install costly *scrubbers*, paper producers to install water purification systems, and so forth. Another way to internalize costs is to levy a tax on activities with health, safety, or environmental hazards and to use the tax revenues to restore the environment or to compensate victims of industrial pollution.

Both these approaches raise costs of producing the good or service and raise its price. In Figure 8, the cost of mandated antipollution equipment raises average fixed costs (AFC) and reduces profits (or increases losses). In Figure 9 (a), new antipollution procedures and unit taxes raise average variable costs (AVC) and marginal costs (MC). A rise in AVC raises the shut-down price, such that grossly inefficient firms may be forced out of business. The rise in MC shifts supply curves to the left in Figure 9(b), raising equilibrium price and reducing industry sales (if demand is elastic). In either case, production from the offending industry is reduced.

Regulation may nonetheless be more equitable and more efficient than prohibitive legislation. The higher production costs mean higher equilibrium prices, such that consumers of offending products must bear the cost. There are no free riders. At the higher price, only those consumers whose expected benefits exceed full costs will buy the good. In this way, there is some assurance that resource use is pushed only to the level at which $MB/MC_s = 1$.

Extended Example Tanstaafl and the Environment

There ain't no such thing as a free lunch. This is the motto of an organization formed several years ago to remind us that everything has its price. The day of reckoning, when costs are paid, may be long in coming, but it will come. You can be sure of that!

Residents of communities around the country are now paying the costs of improper disposal of chemical wastes generated decades ago. A report for the Environmental Protection Agency estimates that more than a hundred lethal sites pose serious health hazards to as many as 600,000 people. Clean-up costs could run into the billions of dollars.

The problem of disposal of hazardous wastes continues even today. Roughly 57 million tons are generated every year by 750,000 industrial plants. Wastes include lead, asbestos, arsenic, beryllium, and mercury, all of which can poison and some of which may cause cancer. New chemicals with strange names like PCBs, TCE, and TCDD can cause a variety of serious health problems. If chemicals are sealed in drums and buried carefully in pits lined with clay or plastic, they may never cause problems. But the EPA estimates that 90 percent of current disposal methods are unsafe. "Midnight dumpers" have even been caught spilling poisonous chemicals on lonely country roads at night. The most familar recent example of improper disposal is Love Canal in Niagara Falls, New York. Proper disposal would have cost less than $1 million, whereas the damages have already cost $36 million.

Under the Resource Conservation and Recovery Act of 1976 the EPA has authority to regulate disposal of hazardous wastes. Many members of affected industries favor the new regulations. Unless all firms in an industry are required to assume these environmental costs, they say, irresponsible firms can hold their costs down and capture the entire market. Some industries will be affected more than others. Manufacturers of sodium dichromate, for example, will experience about a 40 percent cost increase, compared to only 3 percent for most industries. The EPA believes that requiring firms to assume full costs of wastes would provide the incentive to develop effective new solutions to the problem.

Who should pay the costs of damage done in the past? This is a difficult question, since some of the offending firms are unknown, out of business, or without the means to pay. Assigning responsibility for actions taken long ago is difficult, particularly when such acts were not illegal at the time. The Carter Administration asked for creation of a sort of insurance fund, with contributions from the chemical companies, to be used to compensate victims of improper disposal.

Suppose new EPA regulations put firms out of business. Is this an efficient result? Explain.

Show how the costs of proper waste disposal are passed on to users of the product.

A market approach. Legislation and regulation to correct environmental problems have some disadvantages. Both involve substantial government decision-making. Government must decide what kinds of production to prohibit altogether and what level of taxation or specific technical procedures are appropriate over a wide range of complex circumstances. For government to make such decisions correctly requires costly expertise and a vigilant bureaucracy. The result is what public choice economists see as a substantial loss of individual freedoms and what welfare economists criticize as inefficient.

Although it is difficult for government to make these production decisions efficiently, the market can be helped to do so. For firms to decide efficiently, however, they must first have complete information. All the external costs—both short and long term—must be known and included in their calculations. Also, whatever costs are involved must be charged to the firm itself, not shifted to others.

To help firms measure and allocate costs, the community may establish quality standards for use in choosing production techniques. Standards should differ among industries, according to the relationship MB/MC_S in each, and among geographic regions, according to the added levels of environmental damage each could sustain. In fact, a total level of allowed annual pollution might be established for the community as a whole.

Once quality standards are set, there are

alternate ways for encouraging firms to comply. One possibility would be to impose fines for violating the standards. Another would be to sell licenses representing a permitted share of allowed annual pollution. An advantage of both is that firms would seek improved methods of production in order to avoid paying the fine or purchasing additional licenses. They would develop technologies for reducing environmental hazards at lowest cost. In industries lacking low-cost remedies, firms could pay fines or purchase licenses entitling them to a greater share of the community's total annual pollution. But these payments would raise their costs. This type of approach would help achieve a level of total production where $MB/MC_s = 1$. Consumers would continue to enjoy the benefits of production, and net benefit would be at a maximum.

Results of Environmental Policies

Progress toward solving many of our environmental problems has been slow. Although our air is cleaner, smog is still a problem in one-fourth of the nation's counties. The shift from coal to cleaner fuels helped reduce sulfur fumes in the air, but scarcities are now forcing many industries back to coal. Water quality has also improved little. Sewer overflows, industrial wastes, and land runoff continue to pollute drinking water reserves, coastal fisheries, and wetlands. Bans on the use of DDT and other dangerous chemicals have reduced the level of poisons in the food chain, however.

Chemical contamination remains a problem in the Great Lakes. Harmful DDT, PCB, and asbestos continue to threaten health, although there has been some improvement. Phosphorus levels have declined, bringing some formerly "dead" areas of the lakes back to life. Industrial wastes are being recycled and sewage disposal has been modernized along the lakes. Many beaches have been reopened for swimming.

Land resources have continued to deteriorate. During the 1970s the United States lost 17 million rural acres to highways, subdivisions, shopping centers, and parking lots. Forests continue to suffer from increased lumbering and recreation. Noise pollution has probably worsened; twenty million Americans may suffer some hearing loss from noise in city neighborhoods.

Extended Example
The Economics of Georges Bank

One hundred miles off the shores of Cape Cod lies one of the richest fishing grounds in all the world. Georges Bank was probably dry land twelve thousand years ago. Today, the Gulf Stream and the Labrador Current converge in its shallow waters, circulating nutrients consumed by plankton, which, in turn, are consumed by fish. The area produces two hundred species of seafood, amounting to $168 million a year and providing 17 percent of the nation's saltwater catch.

Beneath Georges Bank there is oil, probably 123 million barrels—enough to satisfy the U.S. market for only a week. There is natural gas, too, but again in amounts too small to affect U.S. stocks significantly. In December of 1979 the U.S. Department of the Interior auctioned off drilling rights to oil companies for a total of $828 million.

The area's fishers strongly resisted the move. They worry about oil spills and destruction of the fish. Analysts estimate that at least one major spill would occur during the twenty years covered by the lease. Everyday operations would also release some pollution, causing serious harm to the fish. The result could be the collapse of a 350-year-old industry.

The Northeast needs a dependable source of energy, and twenty years of drilling could earn about $7 billion. The oil companies have agreed to use the safest available technology and to compensate fishers and coastline industries if a spill occurs. Policymakers in the Department of the Interior appear to believe that exploiting a nonrenewable resource is worth the potential risks to a renewable one.

In what sense is this decision an efficient one? Is it equitable?

While environmental policies have not yet succeeded in their environmental goals, they have caused a loss of jobs in some areas. Rather than make the costly investments required by new environmental standards, hundreds of firms have gone out of business. The cost of the jobs lost must be added to the social costs of a healthy environment. Coal miners in the Appalachian states know well the effect of increased air quality standards on mining of the region's high-sulfur coal: The demand for cleaner air forced power plants to use western coal and put many miners into unemployment.

The National Economic Research Association reports that a 1 microgram increase in sulfates in the air means a 0.01 percent increase in infant mortality. But the same study reports that a 1 percentage point increase in the percentage of the population in poverty raises infant mortality by the same amount. Thus, an environmental policy that improves air quality but significantly reduces job opportunities might leave human health unchanged.

Over the long run, higher environmental standards may well have the effect of increasing the number of jobs. Jobs will be created in the industries producing antipollution equipment, measuring levels of pollution, and designing new technologies. During the 1970s it is estimated that sixteen jobs were created for every job lost through new environmental legislation. Productivity should increase, too, as improved health reduces absenteeism and industrial accidents.

SOME FINAL REMARKS ON TRADE-OFFS

Perhaps you have noticed the interrelationships among the issues discussed in this chapter: Industrial development requires energy; but production of energy depletes resources, pollutes the environment, and creates health problems. Health problems call for expanded medical services, putting pressure on health-care resources, increasing inflation, and threatening equity. Environmental regulation reduces productivity in the short run and aggravates inflation. Inflation leads to further OPEC price demands, increased use of coal, and additional pollution. Demands for equity call for increased production, which accelerates environmental deterioration. The list goes on and on.

The aim of this chapter has been to establish a framework within which complex problems like these can be studied. We end with no clear recommendations for the proper policies for dealing with these major issues. The positive economist is hindered in evaluating alternative policies because of the difficulty of measuring benefits and costs. Measuring benefits requires subjective judgment, so decision making cannot be based on purely scientific analysis. Measuring costs requires the use of probabilities, which might be estimated differently by different economists. The measurement problem makes a perfectly efficient policy decision unlikely.

At the very least, however, increased concern for efficiency is a healthy result of the discussion in this chapter. Increased concern for equity should be another result. We must ask: Who pays the costs and who receives the benefits of policy? Our fundamental concept of fairness should raise awareness of the distribution of our nation's costs and benefits.

SUMMARY

The free market has suffered market failure in at least three important areas: health care, energy, and environmental protection.

Market failure occurs in health care because sellers (physicians) often decide what buyers (patients) should consume and because costs are often borne by third parties (insurance plans). Thus rising costs are a problem in health care.

The government's role in health care has been to provide Medicaid and Medicare to those who can't afford health care. The government has tried unsuccessfully to implement a cost-containment program for rising hospital costs. It has been proposed that government bear the cost of a national health insurance plan for all.

Several market incentive programs have been proposed as alternatives to a heavy government role. One is a tax-credit plan. Another program, now in use, is the Health Maintenance Organization (HMO), a group of health practitioners in one location administering to a large subscriber group. A variant of HMOs, also in use, is Individual Physicians' Associations (IPAs), where independent physicians are associated with a particular group, such as a business firm. The employees then subscribe by monthly payments.

Market failure in energy is due to the fact that the Western world's reliance on cheap oil left it prey to the monopoly power of OPEC. So now we find we must develop alternative energy sources.

Presently, domestic prices for oil and natural gas are subject to price ceilings. While keeping prices lower to the consumer, there is less incentive for firms to develop further supplies. Decontrol of oil prices has gone into effect gradually. In order to prevent the oil companies from receiving windfall profits from decontrol, Congress enacted a windfall profits tax of 50 percent. The United States is subsidizing the development of synthetic fuels and encouraging the further use of coal. Government funds have also been invested in developing solar and geothermal power.

Market failure in the environment is generally due to (negative) externalities, usually pollution. Pollution has occurred in the atmosphere with various fumes and particles that can cause health problems; acid rain, destruction of the ozone cover, and the greenhouse effect are also serious problems. Water pollution due to chemicals and land despoliation due to strip mining are other burdens. Another problem is unsafe consumer products, particularly processed foods, and worker safety on the job.

Various government policies have been undertaken to improve the environment. Most of these policies are either legislation to forbid an activity, or, more likely, regulation to set some sort of quality standards. Some market-oriented approaches to pollution have been proposed, such as fines and licenses.

Key Words and Phrases

backward-bending supply a condition in which producers reduce production in response to higher prices.

decreasing, constant, and increasing cost industries industries that experience falling, constant, or increasing costs as a result of industry expansion.

HMOs Health Maintenance Organizations; medical teams that provide regular, prepaid health services to members.

IPAs Individual Physicians' Associations; independent physicians available to a particular group by a prepaid contribution to the group's health plan.

third-party health plans insurance plans for medical costs.

two-tier pricing for oil lower price ceilings for "old oil" from existing wells and higher price ceilings for newly discovered oil.

windfall profits a term used to describe petroleum profits from higher world prices on existing supplies.

Questions for Review

1. What are some of the problems with comparing a price index for health-care costs with consumer prices in general?
2. Dick Martz of Dartmouth Medical School has proposed a government program to make medical education free. What are the costs and benefits of such a program?
3. Studies have shown that areas with the largest supply of physicians also tend to have the highest health-care costs. Does this fact violate the laws of economics? Explain.
4. How would changing all hospitals and insurance programs to profit-making enterprises affect health care?
5. Co-insurance refers to the portion of medical costs paid by the patient, currently about 18 percent. What would be the benefits and costs of raising the co-insurance rate to, say, 25 percent?
6. What are the benefits and costs of a law limiting hospital cost increases to 9.7 percent annually?
7. Brazil plans to convert all its automobiles to alcohol fuel within the next eight years. Currently it costs about twice as much to distill a gallon of alcohol as to refine a gallon of gasoline. What are the benefits and costs of such a plan?
8. A Himalayan country cut down half its forests during the last ten years and used 90 percent of the wood for fuel. What does this suggest about the problems of less developed countries in the decade ahead? What impact will this have on our own prospects for rising living standards?
9. What are the disadvantages of government subsidies to reduce the costs of synthetic fuels and of financing the subsidies through taxation?
10. Michael K. Evans, president of Evans Economics, opposes government investments in energy research and development on the grounds that investments would not be based on market criteria. If he is correct, how would such government investments affect prospects for economic growth of the nation?
11. Some opponents of national oil policy blame high prices on monopolization in the petroleum industry. They would solve the problem of high fuel prices by forcing the major oil companies to sell off divisions engaged in various stages of petroleum processing. This process is called *vertical dis-integration.*

How would such a policy be likely to affect oil prices? Discuss.

12. Robert S. Pindyck of the Massachusetts Institute of Technology has proposed that instead of subsidizing energy research and development, government should provide subsidies for home insulation and storm windows, more efficient autos, and enhanced recovery of oil and gas. What are the advantages and disadvantages of this plan?

13. Concern about chemical pollution has produced an entirely new industry: disposal of toxic chemicals. What are the advantages and disadvantages of leaving this problem to private entrepreneurs?

14. Robert H. Haveman of the University of Wisconsin claims that two thirds of Corps of Engineers water projects would fail a rigid benefit-cost analysis. Yet Congress has willingly appropriated funds. Why?

15. An important industry in Nicaragua has been the capture of sea turtles for their meat, oil, and shells. Following a revolution in 1979 the government imposed a ban on further capture of sea turtles and established a sanctuary where they would be protected. What are the costs and benefits of this decision? Can you suggest more efficient policies?

16. The goal of OSHA should be to eliminate occupational disease and deaths. Discuss.

CHAPTER 19

Alternative Economic Systems

Learning Objectives

Upon completion of this chapter, you should be able to:

1. Explain Marx's labor theory of value and the stages in the decline of capitalism.
2. Discuss the five basic characteristics for judging all economic systems.
3. Explain how economic planning works.
4. Discuss the workings of the Soviet economy and compare the system to ours.
5. Explain how the economy of Yugoslavia is similar to and different from that of the Soviet Union.

Most people have dreamed at one time or another of a world where life would be easy and all could live in harmony. Some visions are fanciful: The song "Big Rock Candy Mountain" tells of a world where people played for many a day, there were no cops, lemonade flowed from springs, and, of course, the mountain itself was edible. For many people, an island in the South Pacific would be enough, as long as the weather was warm, life's comforts were at hand, and little or no work was required.

In either of the above worlds, there would be no need for economists. The common theme of each vision is that scarcity has been overcome. Without scarcity, there is no need for economic decisions or economic analysis.

The search for a better world has often been tied to a basically religious vision. In nineteenth-century America, Shakers formed numerous communities in which all members lived together and shared the products of their labor. Colonies formed in Pennsylvania and later at New Harmony, Indiana, were based on the writings of Scotsman Robert Morse, whose work combined religious thought with social and political philosophy.

In this chapter, we will examine several possible alternatives to the market system described in earlier chapters. The main emphasis will be to show the principles that determine how the various systems operate and how we may decide which is "better" in some ways. Few pure systems actually exist, be they pure communism or pure capitalism. Perhaps, after making some comparisons, you will be able to decide which variation you would like to see in your world.

THE ROLE OF KARL MARX

There can be little doubt that Karl Marx (1818–83) has had more impact on the recent history of world economics than almost any other economist or economic thinker. Marx's economic philosophy is built around the **labor theory of value** which states, in its simplest form, that goods which require the same amount of labor input should all be worth the same. For example, suppose it takes three hours to get a barrel of crude oil out of the ground, and suppose it takes three hours for a cobbler to produce a pair of shoes. Then, since each contains three hours of labor, the barrel of crude oil should exchange for exactly one pair of shoes.

Direct and Indirect Labor

The simple labor value idea clearly has some shortcomings. Let us complicate the model just a little. Three hours of **direct labor** was used for both products. But now add the idea that making a pair of shoes also requires a barrel of crude oil as a raw material. Some of the oil might be used for energy to run the cobbler's machines; some for plastic materials; the rest for glue, dye, wax, etc. The shoes now contain three hours of direct labor—but what about the labor required for producing the crude oil? The answer, according to Marx, is that shoes also include three hours of **indirect** (sometimes called "dead") **labor.** We would now expect the shoes to be worth twice what a barrel of crude oil was worth. A pair of shoes would be worth two barrels of oil because there are six total labor hours in the shoes and only three in the barrel of oil.

If nothing else was required, then the exchange value of goods would be determined by the socially necessary labor contained in the goods. **Socially necessary labor** is both direct (the three hours of the cobbler's time) and indirect labor (the three hours required for the oil inputs used).

Constant and Variable Capital

Marx renamed direct and indirect labor. He did so to explain the role of the capitalist, who owned the *means of production* (factories, machinery, etc.). Direct labor became **variable capital.** In modern accounting and finance terms we might call it the *working capital*. The capitalist had to be able to meet a payroll while the work was in progress, before the final product was sold. Thus the capitalist was advancing funds to pay direct labor from the savings the capitalist had in control.

Constant capital, in Marx's scheme, refers to dead labor or indirect labor. In modern terms, it is *inventory investment*. In some cases it might include fixed capital, but in Marx's time, production machinery was not very important. Constant capital was an expenditure of the capitalist to purchase the inputs to the production process so the workers would have needed raw materials. If you add constant capital and variable capital you get the same result as if you added direct and indirect labor. Thus, exchange of the finished product depends on the amount of *either* capital or labor used but not both.

Surplus Value

Today, we expect anyone who owns a factor of production to be rewarded for the use of that input. Marx did not see it that way. In particular, Marx did not see that capital or land needed to be rewarded, though he was aware that capitalists indeed were able to earn a profit. As he looked around him, Marx felt it was seldom possible for ordinary people to be thrifty and save enough to become a capitalist. It was seldom possible to become a landowner unless one was born to a family of landowners. Inheritance seemed the only source of wealth. In short, a worker could never become a capitalist, and those who were capitalists had probably become so by luck, not by thrift or hard work.

Starting from that point, Marx saw that workers were dependent on the capitalist to supply raw materials and to advance wages until the production process was complete. While not earned in the same sense that wages are earned, the capitalist would be able to extract a profit, an interest rate, or rent as a constant percentage of direct labor. Marx called the capitalist's earnings the **surplus value,** since no work was performed by the capitalist.

Alienation and Exploitation

Marx explained **alienation** as follows. Because the capitalist's surplus value is added to the price of goods, a worker must pay more for the goods produced than the amount the worker received for producing the goods: The worker is *alienated* from the fruits of labor. The cobbler does not receive enough for making the shoes to buy them.

Exploitation refers to the process that determines the surplus value which the capitalist receives. The price at which a product sells in the market is determined by the same competitive forces which affect markets everywhere. Demand sets an upper limit on what can be charged. Thus the capitalist cannot increase the markup by raising prices beyond what the market will bear. The only way to increase profit is to reduce wages. However, in both the short run and the long run, workers' actions place a floor under wages.

According to Marx, there exists at all times a reserve army of the unemployed. If the wage rate is too low, many workers would prefer to become or remain unemployed. In the short run, the number of unemployed and their willingness to work determines the wage that will be paid.

Over the longer run, labor would require that amount which would enable the labor force to maintain itself. That is, workers need just enough food, clothing, and shelter to stay alive and to raise enough children to replace older workers. This is *subsistence,* and Marx argued that the real wage paid must be close to the subsistence level. Productivity of labor had nothing to do with the wage; it was life itself that mattered. The capitalist would hire workers for subsistence wages and sell products for what the market would bear. Marx called this **exploitation** of the workers.

The Eventual Decline of Capitalism

Marx did not stop with the above ideas. He went further and developed a model whereby capitalism would eventually perish.

Capital accumulation. Marx thought that capitalists would not be able to use all their exploited surplus value and would save a large part of it. As their wealth grew, they would want more wealth, in ever increasing amounts. The drive to accumulate wealth (or financial capital) would lead to large-scale production, which in turn would result in monopolies.

Declining profit and labor-saving inventions. Marx recognized that as more capital was accumulated, it would be harder to find equally profitable ways to use it. Thus marginal profits would fall. Also, labor would become relatively scarce so wages would rise. The capitalists would have to fight back by developing labor-saving machinery. As a result, more workers would become unemployed. The reserve army of the unemployed would grow, wages would fall, and workers would be forced below the subsistence level.

Economic instability. As monopoly became the general form of business organization, mistakes in decisions by capitalists would create economic instability. Business cycles would become increasingly severe. Inflation would be general as capitalists raised prices to recover lost profits. Capitalists would become richer, but not as fast as they might like. Workers would certainly become poorer and much worse off because of the alternate periods of boom and bust.

Class struggle and revolution. In Marx's day few democracies existed in Europe; monarchies still ruled. Marx believed that monarchies and the aristocrats would fall to the capitalist bourgeoisie. The capitalists, in turn, would lose out when the business community finally became one big monopoly. At that time, things would become so bad economically that the impoverished worker class, the **proletariat,** would rise up and, in a violent revolution, take control. The revolution would have to be violent because the capitalists would not give up their position without a fight. After the revolution was won by the workers, there would be common ownership of capital so no capitalist class would exist. Without capitalists, there would be no need for government, so a communal form of both economic and political organization would prevail.

Marxism Updated

Marx had observed the colonial policies of Europe, yet in his model of capitalism he did not give a great deal of attention to the process of colonization. Some of his followers, however, have claimed that advanced capitalistic countries have survived a while longer by economically exploiting other countries. When investment opportunities at home dry up, there are still other areas to exploit, especially in those nations rich in raw materials and in a large, unskilled labor force.

Most people who consider themselves Marxists still feel that a revolution must happen. Modern-day Marxists also feel that capitalism can be replaced sooner with military conquest or peaceful political action. The revolution will always follow the advanced capitalistic stage unless military or political action come first. Then, a socialist state may be needed to transform the economy to the final worker's communistic form of economy. The bourgeois period may be skipped. Today, as in the Soviet Union, China, and Cuba, it may not be the workers but the peasants who make up the proletariat. In the poorer nations of the world, capitalism may never develop, since incomes are so low that no saving is possible. Thus a state socialism is necessary to bring the nation into the economic mainstream. The nation as a whole becomes a proletariat revolting against the economic imperialism of the advanced nations.

BASIC CHARACTERISTICS OF ECONOMIC SYSTEMS

We have spent a lot of time learning a small part of the economic contribution of Karl Marx. We must not decide, however, that there are only two possibilities: the economy as we know it in the United States and the Marxian economy. There are many varieties of capitalism and there are many varieties of economies which are supposedly based on Marx. Not all Marxists agree as to what Marx said, so the various attempts at putting his ideas into practice have produced very different results. We need to look at the variety of economic systems which are in existence in the world today.

We sketched an overview of different "isms" or systems at the end of Chapter 2. Let's review a few of the definitions before we start comparing economic systems. **Capitalism** (pure capitalism) is an economic system characterized by the following: (1) private ownership of capital; (2) free enterprise, which is the ability to start or dissolve a business; (3) free markets; and (4) freedom of choice for consumers and workers. No system exists that can be described as pure capitalism. However, many countries, including the United States, can be described as **mixed capitalism,** in which the characteristics of capitalism are modified by government action.

Marx's definition of communism is also a hypothetical or ideal system that no country matches. **Communism** is a system of communal ownership of all property and of centralized economic and political power. **Socialism** is a system in which government owns all major capital goods and means of production. The Soviet Union, China, Vietnam, and the Eastern European countries are socialist. They also have either centralized economic decision-making or economic planning and are political dictatorships.

There are also countries, like Sweden, that can be described as socialistic but where the decentralized market economy has an important role and political democracy flourishes. We refer to this variant of socialism as **market socialism.** See Figure 1 for a summary of basic types of economic systems.

If we tried to classify most of the world's 150 countries, we would find that many don't fit comfortably into a category of some "ism." It is often difficult to separate the economic system from the rest of a society. What is economic and what is social and political are very closely related. For some societies, the economy is essentially the same as the society itself. Some nations may be part of an economic system that extends beyond their borders. A few nations may be so large as to have separate economies in various sections. In most cases, though, the economy and the society are the same, and a study of the economy will go a long way toward understanding the entire society.

In order to compare economic systems, we need to identify basic characteristics that are common to all systems. Let's look at five charac-

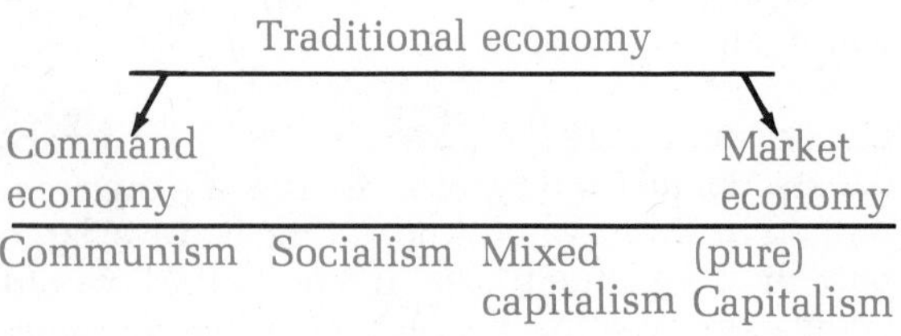

Figure 1 Summary of the types of economic systems.

teristics that will prove useful: (1) property rights and ownership; (2) the role of labor and the nature of labor contracts; (3) the degree of centralization in economic decision-making; (4) market allocation vs. economic planning; and (5) incentives.

Ownership and Property Rights

For most of us, ownership is a relatively simple concept. Either we own something or we do not. It is either ours or it belongs to someone else. The "someone else" may literally be a person, or it may be a group, such as a corporation, a church, or even a state. Some things, such as parks or highways, belong to everyone; that is, they belong to government.

In one sense, ownership is a legal matter. For some things, we issue a piece of paper called a *title*. This is done for larger items, such as real estate, cars, and shares of corporations. For other things, we are expected to keep track of our purchases without the formality of a title, though we are the nominal owners by virtue of purchase and possession. Legal ownership is what we usually think of when we hear the term *ownership*, but it is not automatic. We exercise ownership first, and then we formalize that ownership in the law.

What we are really interested in is called **substantive ownership,** which is the *exercise* of ownership. It is a right conferred by society. There are several property rights that are part of substantive ownership:

Possession—the right to use it;
Usufruct—the right to any income (interest, rent, or profit) the property may generate, as well as to any new assets created—such as offspring of breeding livestock or new shares created by a stock split;
Alienation—the right to sell or give it away;
Destruction—the right to destroy or discard it.

Legal ownership does not necessarily permit full use of these rights. Any of these rights may be restricted or even taken away. Income may be subject to taxes. You may have the use and income from your wealth and goods during your lifetime but not the right to give it all away or bequeath it without being taxed. If your home is a national historical site, you may not be able to tear it down. If you own a few shares of, say, General Motors or IBM, you do not have possession of the firm. In short, ownership is a complicated idea.

Substantive ownership can be divided into three basic categories: government, private, and collective or cooperative. Government ownership may be federal or some form of local ownership (for example, what we have called state or local government). Private ownership can be by individuals or partners or corporations. Collective or cooperative ownership grants limited control to individuals. The collective or cooperative is usually a large group.

As we examine the different economic systems, we will be especially concerned with ownership of two important inputs: land and capital. Economic systems are often distinguished by whether land and capital goods, such as factories and stores, are owned and controlled privately or by government. (See Figure 2 for a comparison of state ownership of key industries in selected Western countries.)

Role of Labor

Economic systems can be distinguished by the role assigned to labor and by the rights of the worker. What kind of job mobility does a worker have? Can he or she change jobs and professions freely? What geographical mobility does a worker have? What rights, if any, does a worker have in deciding his or her compensation or income? What are the terms of compensation?

We can distinguish several forms of labor arrangements or institutions: (1) slavery; (2) forced labor camps; (3) indentured servitude; (4) labor with some limitations; and (5) basically free labor.

Slavery. The owner of labor is in turn owned by another individual. The laborer has nothing to say about the labor services to be performed and does not have any social or political rights either. The slave is often attached to one or more physical assets, usually land, but sometimes a factory or other asset. Ownership of the slave and the other assets of production is most often by individuals rather than by government. Most nations throughout history practiced some form of slavery. The nineteenth century saw the elimination of slavery in most parts of the world.

Forced labor camps. This labor institution is basically a prison and thus has limited use in

○ Privately owned ◔ 25% ◑ 50% ◕ 75% ● All or nearly all publicly owned

	Postal Service	Tele-communications	Electricity	Gas	Coal	Railroads	Airlines	Autos	Steel	Shipbuilding	Government spending (as a % of G.N.P.) 1962	1978
United States	●	○	◔	○	○	○	○	○	○	○	28.4	32.2
Australia	●	●	●	●	○	●	◕	○	○	*	19.3	24.5
Brazil	●	●	●	◕	◕	●	◔	○	◕	○	12.0	35.0
Britain	●	●	●	●	●	●	◕	◑	◕	●	40.5	43.9
Canada	●	◔	●	○	○	◕	◑	○	○	○	34.4	46.0
France	●	●	●	●	●	●	◕	◑	◕	○	36.3	43.0
Italy	●	●	◕	●	*	●	●	◔	◑	◕	32.4	47.3
Japan	●	●	○	○	○	◕	◔	○	○	○	12.3	16.5
Sweden	●	●	◑	●	*	●	◑	○	◔	◕	36.0	61.6
W. Germany	●	●	◕	◑	◑	●	◕	◔	○	◔	35.6	46.5

Rounded to nearest quarter
*Industry is negligible

Figure 2 Government ownership of key industries in selected Western nations. (Source: *Time,* April 21, 1980, p. 54.)

many parts of the world. Usually the laborers are under the indirect control of the government, and those in charge of the camp actually direct the use of labor. Labor has only the rights of a prisoner. Of course, some governments treat prisoners better than others. Obviously, mobility is limited or the inmates would soon leave. Confinement in labor camps is punishment for a crime. In most cases, labor is confined to the camp for a limited period of time and then returns to ordinary life. In the United States, use of such camps has been mainly confined to rural areas and the South. In some countries, political crimes will result in confinement in labor camps. For example, in the Soviet Union slandering the state is a crime that can land an individual in a forced labor camp.

Indentured labor. The main difference between slavery and indenture is that indenture is usually for a set term rather than for life. Also, the indentured worker may have some rights. In the colonial era of the United States, many immigrants secured passage here by entering indentured servitude, usually for a period of seven years. In the nineteenth-century Western world, some young people were indentured by their parents in exchange for room, board, education, and a suit of clothes when the agreement was completed. There may be indirect control of the laborer when there is an absentee owner. Both slavery and indentured service are illegal in the United States today.

Labor with some limitations. This form of labor, where the worker has only limited freedom of choice, is one of the most common arrangements in the world today. Typically the worker has little or no geographical mobility. In Vietnam and China, for example, workers are usually assigned or limited to certain regions of the country; migration to cities is strictly controlled. Also, workers cannot generally leave their country. Workers may or may not be able to choose their profession, and they often don't need to look for a job because the government will assign them an employer. In the Soviet Union an individual can usually choose a profession but generally can't pick his or her employer. Workers may or may not get vacations and, when they do, are usually assigned vacation times. Workers can't form unions. There are limited opportunities for self-employment. Workers can't generally choose not to work (i.e., choose leisure) or, as in the Soviet Union, they are deemed parasites, which is a criminal offense.

Free labor. This form of labor, allows the worker to choose professions, choose employers, bargain for wages, and have a good deal of mobility. The worker also has a wide range of professions to choose for self-employment; unions are allowed. This form of labor is not totally free, however. Individuals have limits to skills. We can't all become mathematicians; most of us don't have the ability. Likewise, mobility is a relative possibility, not unlimited or costless.

Degree of Centralization

Economic systems can be distinguished in part by the degree of centralization in economic decision-making. A centralized economic system has few people making decisions on production and consumption. The two extremes are one person making every economic decision or every individual making many decisions. No system exists that is close to either of these extremes. Americans would probably prefer the second alternative, but, even in our system, many larger groups, such as corporations, make production and consumption decisions.

Every decision maker has both inputs and outputs. The outputs are the decisions and the inputs are information. Without useful information, "correct" decisions can't be made. So the first problem confronting a centralized decision maker is the gathering and processing of large amounts of information.

The decentralized economic system has as many people as possible making their own production and consumption decisions. Such a system is designed to gratify consumers, that is, individual decision makers. A decentralized economy may choose—because many people are willing to pay—to produce pornography, punk rock, fuzz-busters, and the *Gong Show*.

A highly centralized economy can and often does produce goods and services that the consumer "ought to like" because those items "are good for the people." Maoist China produced ballets and movies with only revolutionary themes; most of the movies played to generally empty theaters. Russian decision makers decided to produce military equipment and capital goods and have generally ignored the consumer sector, where consumers scramble in line for many basic goods. Cuba decided to emphasize health care and education for everyone and has done a good job of providing them, but at the expense of many consumer goods, including food.

A centralized economy will generally also have a centralized political authority; politics usually follows economics in the realm of power. Few highly centralized economies have a free press. A free press supports itself with ads, which are paid for by many (usually competing) small decision makers—either firms or individuals. Additionally, a free press criticizes both political and economic decision makers. A central economic decision maker usually tolerates as little criticism as possible.

Market Allocation or Economic Planning?

How does an economy allocate its resources and attain economic growth? Answers to this question help shape an economic system.

We have just spent many chapters examining how a market economy makes resource allocation decisions: Many producers and consumers determine the use of resources. There is an alternative to market decision-making: economic planning. We define *economic planning* (or *planned economy*) as the use of national planning boards to determine overall production goals. Goals are usually set for each industry and directives passed down to plant managers.

Market allocation and economic planning are two diametrically opposed schemes of allocation. In our real world, no economy is a model of either. All countries mix elements of both together. If we broaden our definition of economic planning to mean *government allocation,* we can quickly see that all governments make some allocation decisions.

Consider the difference between transfer of goods and exchange for goods. *Exchange* of goods and services implies trading or bartering. A market economy is an economy of many exchanges. *Transfer* of goods and services is a one-way allocation of resources—from one group to another. Transfer payments in the United States are an example of a one-way allocation of resources. All income-earners (both individuals and firms) are taxed to provide welfare and in-kind payments to the poor; taxes are a transfer. Unemployment insurance and GI Bill payments are likewise transfers undertaken by the government. So transfers as well as economic planning are a form of resource allocation.

There are economies that mix planning and decentralized decision-making. As we shall see shortly, countries as diverse as France and Yugoslavia utilize both economic planning and decentralized decision-making.

Incentives

How does an economic system motivate economic production? Why should an individual work hard? The answers to questions like these also determine the nature of an economic system.

You probably don't think about this as a criterion. After all, most of us are used to a system that fosters competition and material rewards. But what if we lived in a society where all people received the same share of goods and income? We call such a society *egalitarian.* How do you motivate people in such a society? Why wouldn't they spend most of the time reading or talking to friends instead of working? One answer is to motivate people by offering moral incentives. Another is to offer hard workers status.

Nearly all economic systems offer both material and moral incentives.* Systems differ in the *degree* to which and *method* by which material incentives are used. The market economy promotes efficiency by rewarding some firms and workers with higher incomes. Followers of Marx try to emphasize moral incentives. Marx did recognize the need for income differentials but he assumed that when a communist society was established, moral incentives would predominate.

In our real world, moral incentives do not fuel an economy over extended periods of time. No system that seeks growth—let alone rapid growth—can avoid using material incentives. The Soviet Union motivates workers with a system of bonuses; in addition, many consumer goods are available only to certain important workers, usually bureaucrats belonging to the Communist Party. Also, the Soviet Union rewards the hard work and good behavior of intellectuals and athletes by offering travel abroad; such travel enables them to purchase consumer goods not available at home.

*Individuals also work for *psychic income:* They enjoy certain types of work. However, it is assumed that we can't readily distinguish psychic income since we can't easily discern it and people in *all* systems labor for it.

ECONOMIC PLANNING

Before examining the economic systems of individual countries, we need to look in greater depth at economic planning. Many countries that offer a real alternative to the U.S. system rely either partially or extensively on economic planning. What is an economic plan, how is it formulated, how does it work, and how effective has planning proved to be in reaching its goals? Let's try to answer these questions by examining the planning process used in the Soviet Union.

The Task of Planning

Consider the problem faced by economic planners. Imagine a Sears mail-order catalog that runs about 1000 pages with dozens of items per page. Now suppose you are the economic planner in charge of producing all these items. As an economic planner, you would not only have to give the orders for each of the thousands of items in the catalog, but would have to give very detailed orders. It would not do just to say you wanted to produce men's shirts or fuel pumps or pairs of shoes. You would have to specify sport shirts or dress shirts, various colors, pin stripes, patterns, various collar sizes and sleeve lengths. For fuel pumps, you would have to order those which fit currently produced cars and also some to fit old lead-fuel autos. It would even be necessary to order the same number of left and right shoes of each size or they might not all match.

Beyond that, you would have to give detailed orders to ensure that the necessary transportation facilities were available to move the raw materials into the factories and to deliver the goods to consumers. You would have to arrange to build roads and railroads, trains, trucks, and planes. You might have to order a postal service into being. You would have to give detailed instructions for all the services needed to install the goods you sold. You would have to arrange for all the service people to keep the goods functioning. Finally, you would have to order the appropriate amount of trash collection to haul off the wrappings and other trash generated by all the other activities.

Just making a list of all the things which must be produced is not enough, of course. You must detail all the materials to be used, in the right quantities and in the right places. Your plans would also have to include timing of delivery. Snow tires in April and swim gear in November would be of little use to anybody.

In addition to listing all the products and materials, you would also have to set all the prices. Remember, the economy still works with a series of money transactions just like a market economy. The difference would be that the prices do not reflect the scarcity of the items in the market place. The prices would tend to reflect official thinking about the value of certain items. If carpenters were "in" and lawyers were not, then the price of carpenters would be set high as a reward and lawyers fees would be set low. Artists, ballerinas, and star hockey players would be well rewarded, but factory workers may not receive any reward at all. The same applies to commodities. Steel and tractors may be favored and highly priced. On the other hand, vodka, potatoes, and beets may have very low prices. The prices would only determine the amount of money needed to buy the commodity. As planner, you would determine how much would be produced.

One thing is clear: You would need a lot of help. The result would be a large bureaucracy to do the planning and to transmit the official thinking about how the economy should operate. This bureaucracy would need a great deal of power. After all, the work required to generate a plan must not be upset because people want cars in some color other than black. Anyone who wants a blue car with a racing stripe must be ignored, or that individual would complicate the plan. Not only would it be powerful, but the bureaucracy would be very conservative. Once a plan had been devised, with all the work it took, any attempt at change would be resisted, and any attempt by firms to innovate on their own would be punished.

Such a system has operated in the Soviet Union for nearly fifty years; in some ways, it has worked fairly well. The above paragraphs have pointed out the problems of economic planning in a tongue-in-cheek style. Now let us see how a serious attempt has been made to deal with these problems.

Setting Goals with the Material Balance Approach

There are several planning horizons considered at any particular time. There is the very long-term plan to move toward a better, stronger society; there are medium-range plans, usually five years in length. These *five-year plans* deal with strategy. Goals are stated in terms of growth rates, investment projects, and the relative emphasis to be placed on broad areas such as agriculture, consumption, or regional development. Within the five-year plans, there are a series of annual plans. These plans deal with the details of logistics and set forth the tactics required to achieve the five-year planned goals. **Logistics** is the science of planning for the movement of resources and goods so that everything arrives in the right amounts at the right time and place.

The targets of the one-year plans are varied. Naturally, high priority projects get first attention. These might include investment projects, outer-space research, and military goods. From there, the targets are set in terms of gross output of a number of highly important commodities. There are also some goals set in terms of the aggregate output of some industries which produce a variety of products. The plans serve to ensure full employment as well as a mix of products, although consumer goods may not get much attention and what is produced sometimes seems more a way of using up available raw materials than of fulfilling important goals.

Once the major goals are established, input requirements needed to meet those goals are determined. These include inputs for further production, for final sales, for export, for inventories, and for *reserves.* The last item is essentially a fudge factor so the planners can make up for mistakes as the planning period unfolds.

After the requirements are known, sources of the inputs can be determined. As in any economy, inputs can come from domestic production, from imports, and from inventories. The planner must do the allocating or rationing that the market would do in a capitalistic society. This balancing of inputs to reach certain output goals is known as the **material balance** approach to planning.

It is at this point that *counterplanning* comes into play. Remember, firms are not allowed to interact as firms in market economies might. But firms can tell the central planners what they expect to produce and what inputs they will need to produce it. This is the heart of **counterplanning.**

To avoid problems, managers of the various firms naturally set their output objectives low enough that they will have no trouble reaching them. Still, they must show growth in output, so they set their output higher than the year before—but not by much.

Since there is a great deal of uncertainty as to whether their input will arrive, there is a natural tendency to request as much as possible. Also, managers do not depend entirely upon the planners. Though they are not allowed to do so officially, most good managers have a network of people available to help obtain needed supplies if the official supplies do not arrive. Through a series of exchanges, most shortages can be overcome.

The planners, are aware of the games the managers play. Naturally, the planners have to make sure the plans are consistent. When the responses from the firms are in, they adjust the plan somewhat to account for reality. The output of some items may be reduced, while the availability of some inputs to some industries may be increased. Sometimes the plans must be adjusted for past failures. After crop failures for several years in a row in the late 1970s, Soviet grain output plans were decreased while purchases from the United States were increased. Other emergencies must also be considered.

In addition, the planners engage in what is called **pressure planning.** They know the managers have been conservative. So they plan for somewhat more output than the managers said would be produced, and requests for inputs are never fully granted. In this way, a bargain is struck, and the plan for each commodity is eventually set forth.

Once the allocation of resources is decided on, the next step is to plan the operation of each firm. The **enterprise operation plan** is a detailed set of orders for running the firm. The outputs of each product are specified, as are all the inputs to be used. The management of the plant is responsible for implementing the plan. Failure to do so will result in a loss of bonuses and other incentives to perform. Once the plan is complete, the firm enters the market to obtain the necessary supplies. This is done by a contract with the supplying firm specified in the plan and at the prices set by the planners.

Economic Accounting and Financial Planning

The plans we have seen so far should appear a little strange to us. They have been entirely in terms of physical units. We are much more accustomed to seeing accounting statements in money terms. Costs and revenues are in dollars, as are profits or losses. The planned economies also have a money accounting statement. If nothing else, there is the need for a standard unit of measurement. Further, the transactions take place using money, so there is the need to account for the money flows in the overall plan.

The financial plan duplicates the operations plan, except that it is in money terms, and it is a binding plan for the firm to follow. It would look very much like an accounting statement in our own system, except it is prepared before the fact rather than after. The revenues come from the sale of the output of the firm. The expenditures are the cost of inputs, the payments to labor (including the managers), the earnings (normal profit) of the firm, and the various fees and taxes which must be paid.

It is at this point that the somewhat arbitrary price structure causes a problem. The revenues are simply the output valued at the official price. The costs depend on the resources used valued at the official prices. There is nothing which can guarantee that the revenues will cover the cost. Indeed, the financial plan may not even balance. That does not bother the planners, however. They simply refer to the planned losses as a necessary part of achieving their overall plan.

In recent years, the financial plan has taken on a larger role. Many firms produce a variety of products, and it is only in money terms that the performance of the firm can be measured. Not all commodities are planned under the material balance approach. For these commodities, the financial plan is the only guideline available. Thus, the firms have more room for maneuvering within the plan. Further, there have been some attempts to actually make prices more realistic in reflecting the cost of production. Economic studies in both the planned economies and in the West have shown that relative prices alone are enough to guide an economy, but the planners want to continue with detailed plans. Thus, the reform of the pricing structure is not complete. However, with more realistic prices, the financial plan can be used not only as a guide to production but as a means of evaluating the managers. The planned losses disappear and actual losses mean bad management.

Planning Problems

Many of the difficulties faced by central economic planners have already been mentioned. Some result from the complexity of a modern economy. Others are the result of the planners themselves: Both their methods and their beliefs interfere with the process. For example, because planners have pushed for high economic growth, there is an unwritten rule that the manager of a firm will less likely be punished if consumer goods fail to appear than if the desired growth is missing. Thus, managers often treat consumers as a "slack variable." Consumer products are available only if everything else has been taken care of.

Some problems, such as the timing of output, seem to have no good solution under a planned system. The oversight is too great for even an army of central planners to handle.

Other problems have been partially solved. One is the problem of measuring output. In the material balance and operating plans, the output goals are stated in physical units. In some cases, that makes good sense; in others, it has led to bad results. One way to overcome the problem is to use the financial plan. But there are still some difficulties. We have mentioned that the prices are set more on belief than on the workings of supply and demand. Managers naturally produce those items which are most advantageous to themselves: the ones with the high prices. Just because the planners favor these items does not mean the consumers also do. Some odd mixes of output may thus result.

Another problem is that firms are judged on the value of output, not on efficiency or profit. As a result, firms try to use as much material and as little labor and processing as possible. This has led to the gigantic nature of machinery and buildings in the planned economies. Even the aircraft are huge. At the same time, they are poorly constructed and often use the highest priced raw materials. Spare parts are often missing since spare parts take more labor to produce. Designs are relatively fixed since it is easier to keep producing the old and known products than to try new ones. The main idea is to keep output high with as little effort as possible.

Judging Economic Planning

With all the problems just listed, why do some people still look to centrally planned economies as a desirable way to run an economy? There are a wide variety of answers. We must remember that there have been some mild reforms in recent times which make the Soviet-style planned economy work a little better. We should also remember that there are other versions of planned economies. We will look at some of these more closely later. The variations make it clear that there is not just one way to plan an economy.

First, many arguments in favor of a planned economy boil down to the statement that planning works. That is hard to deny. How well is another matter. Of course, the same may be said for the capitalist economy with a market system. Failures of the market system are matched by failures in planning. Disagreement with the results of a market system leads to use of a planned economy, but some of the same problems may remain.

Second, most Western economies look for efficiency in the use of resources. In the planned economies, growth is the key variable. That is not surprising, since many had relatively low-level incomes before becoming planned economies. And most have achieved rapid growth—at the price of choice and freedom. In capitalist economies, if consumers want skateboards, hula hoops, and discos instead of oil refineries, that is what they get. The planned economies have restricted consumer spending in ways that would not be possible in the United States and have instead produced steel mills, housing, railroads, and space programs—not to mention military might. In fulfilling the planner's, and the state's, desires for growth, the planned economies have done very well. With respect to fulfilling the desires of consumers, they seemingly have not fared as well.

Third, the less developed countries (LDCs) still envy the rapid development that some planned economies have achieved. LDCs often have ownership of resources and decision-making power tied to an outdated colonial system. Some suffer from repressive political organizations. Many citizens in less developed countries feel they cannot wait until the market directs the needed economic development; they see a planned economy as the only way to break out of economic prison and achieve rapid development and modernization.

Indicative Planning

Some economies attempt to allocate goods with planning while retaining the basic market structure of the economy. Such an economic system is called **indicative planning.**

One element of indicative planning is that there is a public statement that some activities are favored and others are not. Such public pronouncements would not be very effective if they were not backed up by some form of stimulus. In some cases, prices are allowed or even compelled to rise as a stimulus to favored economic activities. Thus we might have an announcement that the economy needs a 20 percent increase in steel production along with an increase in the price of steel. In some cases, taxes rather than prices are used. The profit rates of some industries may be increased or decreased by use of taxes. Sometimes plans of this type are even used to reduce unemployment or control inflation.

In France, indicative planning came into use after World War II. Long a country with a tradition of heavy state involvement in economic affairs, France has government ownership of many large industries, such as transportation (rail, air, and auto) and energy (nuclear power, coal, and gas). The key to French indicative planning is the **General Planning Commissariat,** which coordinates both state and private firms along with unions and civil service workers. All these groups have some say in determining the plan. The French plan is not coercive as in the Soviet Union—hence the name "indicative." Rather, the Commissariat dangles various financial "carrots"—favorable tax rates or subsidies, for example—in front of private firms. The French plan usually indicates broad aggregate goals for industry, not goals for individual firms.

Another version of indicative planning is the Swedish model. Here, the emphasis is on the production side. Incentives play a major role in changing patterns of production. Capital is given incentives to go to areas where labor is abundant and not fully employed. Workers are trained or retrained for skills which are most needed and are assisted in moving to areas where jobs may be found. In this way, the allocation of resources is directed and full employment assisted.

THE SOVIET ECONOMY

The modern planned economy of the Soviet Union developed after the end of the Russian Revolution in the 1920s. The starting point was very low indeed. Not only had the country suffered the rages of World War I and the civil war, but 80 percent of the labor force was in agriculture. Planning was effected as a means compatible with the ideas of Marxism-Leninism and with the goals of rapid growth. The national planning board known as **GOSPLAN** came into existence. The Communist Party of the Soviet Union sets broad goals or directions and GOSPLAN is in charge of developing specific details and determining the material balance.

The first five-year plan came about in 1928. Its initial emphasis was on rapid industrialization, and the consumer was allocated little more than subsistence wages. It was not until the five-year plan covering 1971 to 1975 that consumer goods were given any important emphasis in the Soviet planning process. Soviet consumers are much better off today than in the earlier periods, though their living conditions are not good by comparison with most of the rest of the industrialized world. Still, they are ahead of enough of the rest of the world to be viewed with a certain amount of envy.

Labor

Marx thought that, eventually, a communist economy would evolve into pure socialism, with the workers in harmony with each other and no need for a state. In the Soviet Union, this notion was translated to a dictatorship of the proletariat. As it worked out, they got the dictatorship,

Extended Example **Work in the Factory***

The life of workers in Soviet factories has a monthly routine almost unique, as it is derived from the features of a planned economy. Each factory has a monthly quota to fulfill. The first ten days of the month are very slow—little work is done. Partly this is due to workers recovering from the excesses of spending their paycheck, which is paid on or about the first and fifteenth of the month. However, the slow pace is due more to the fact that all the components haven't been delivered yet; many won't make it until the tenth of the month.

The second ten days of the month are rather hectic, as workers try to make up for the shortfall of the first ten days. Actually, around the fifteenth of the month (payday again) things tail off as workers are more interested in spending their paycheck.

The work pace in the last ten days is really feverish, as workers race to fulfill the monthly plan. More than half the work is accomplished in this timespan. Workers will generally work the Saturday and sometimes the Sunday in this period. Also, overtime (not paid for directly) is often required. During this frenzied ten-day period, workers are concerned only about quantity, not quality. Since Soviet goods generally carry a tag with the production date, consumers will often try to avoid buying any goods dated after the twentieth of the month. When the month is over, the workers are in a state of exhaustion and once again start the next month very slowly. This cycle of activity is repeated each month!

Another interesting aspect of Soviet industrial production is that all goods are targeted into one of three categories: (1) military; (2) export; and (3) domestic consumption. The military always gets the best goods. Sometimes this is done on a separate assembly line manned by the best workers. Other times the military has its own representatives in a factory who make first pick of the goods.

The next group of goods based on quality go for export. The poorest quality goods are for domestic consumption.

The Soviet Union has been called a worker's paradise. Would you like to work in the Russian factory described? How is the Russian worker better off than the American worker?

*See Hendrick Smith, *The Russians* (Quadrangle Publishers, 1976) for many more fascinating stories on this subject.

but the party elite became a fairly exclusive group. The workers participated in ways that had little real effect.

Soviet workers do have some freedom to offer their services. Within local labor markets, workers may work at professions of their choosing, at the set wage rate. There is little geographic movement allowed, however, unless the worker volunteers for the high-pay, hardship zones like Siberia.

Because of planning, all labor offered is used; something like full employment is always at hand. Early in the history of the GOSPLAN, women were encouraged to enter the labor force, since Soviet growth was very labor intensive. In fact, all adults were expected to work in order to achieve the economic growth desired by the planners.

Wages for most jobs are still relatively low—compared to what they will buy. Common labor, even most skilled labor, receives little. That has helped hold down consumption and the labor costs of production. However, some persons are very well paid. Athletes of Olympic caliber and dancers for the Bolshoi Ballet have been well rewarded, receiving not only high wages but other "perks," such as housing, better health care, and even very scarce autos. These things are allocated to the favored, which also includes engineers, cosmonauts, and scientists.

All Soviet workers and their families receive free health care and free education. Public transportation and housing costs are very low. It appears that the Soviet poor receive at least as good health care and education as their U.S. counterparts. However, the average Soviet citizen does not have access to the quality health care available in this country. While education is free, not all citizens are permitted to pursue a higher education. A strict educational elite does result. The plan has not put housing in a high priority role; thus young married couples may live for some time with parents, and divorced people may live together separated by a blanket on a clothes line.

Agriculture

The bulk of farm output in the Soviet Union comes from state and collective farms. State farms are owned and run by the state with labor hired to work the farm. **Collective farms** are also owned by the state, but, in theory, workers themselves operate the farm as a cooperative. In fact, control of the collective farms is so tight that there is little difference between the two. Some farms are privately owned, and farmers on the collectives are allowed to till small plots for their own benefit. Though the total output from these private ventures is relatively small, the private farm plots are much more productive than the state or collective farms.

Farm wages are low, since official policy requires low food prices. As a result, many people would like to head for the bright lights of the cities. But such movements of labor are not allowed. Americans see this as a restriction of freedom not to be tolerated. The planners simply argue that it is an example of the superior nature of a planned economy. Workers are permitted to move when jobs are available in the industrial cities; in the meantime, they are on the farms where food, housing, and clothing are available. By contrast, similar workers in the United States often end up unemployed and living in slums in the cities.

The Soviet Union leads the world in production of steel and some other raw industrial products, but Soviet agriculture can only be judged a failure. It has never been able to provide a varied diet for its people. Black bread and potatoes are still a cornerstone of the diet. Because grain is so often in short supply, animals grown for slaughter are not found in large numbers, and meat is a rarity in many diets. Additionally, the severe Soviet winter means that fruit and vegetables are in short supply for a large portion of the year.

Growth

We have said several times that growth was highly desired by the planners of GOSPLAN and the leaders of the Soviet state. Certainly the Soviet economy has been transformed from a rural to an industrial economy. But how about the goal of economic growth?

The answer is not easy to obtain. In part, the necessary data has not been available to Western economists. Much about the Soviet Union has been kept secret by its leaders. In some cases, data has been available but has been deliberately falsified. It is also hard to get estimates of total national production when markets do not determine prices. To compare the Soviet Union to the United States, we need to be able to either value U.S. production in rubles or Soviet production in dollars. However, there is no market that allows us to determine the relative value of the two currencies, and the ruble is artificially valued.

Some estimates are possible, however. As the decade of the 1980s opened, Soviet production was still smaller than that of the United States. Most estimates place it at three fifths to three quarters of our own. The Soviet population is much larger, so the average Soviet citizen has only about half as much output to consume as the average American.

In general, however, growth has been very rapid. Since World War II, the Soviet Union has grown at close to 6 percent per year. During the 1960s, its economic growth may have been twice as fast as that of the United States. In the 1970s, the growth rate slowed some. As the result of a crop failure and an increasing energy problem, the Soviet economy grew about 2 percent in 1979, while the United States managed 2.3 percent. The plan for 1980 was 4.5 percent growth.

Prices and Taxes

There are actually two sets of prices in the Soviet Union. As we have seen, prices are set as a matter of policy, and that policy depends upon the analysis of the planners, not the market. Food prices, for example, are kept low so that low-income workers can eat inexpensively. However, there is another device used by the planners to keep consumer prices much above industrial—what we would call wholesale—prices.

On all consumer sales, there is a *turnover tax*. It is much like the value added tax used in much of Europe, but in the Soviet Union it is applied only at the retail level. The average level of the tax is about one third the price of a product. However, the planners use the tax to specify the pattern of production and consumption. On items that are necessities for low-income workers, the tax is very low. Thus, food, which

Extended Example Consuming and Selling in the Soviet Union

Beginning in 1965, Soviet economic planners tried to deliver more goods to consumers. But, even today, the typical Soviet consumer is well behind the typical U.S. consumer. Roughly half the total national production of the Soviet Union is for consumer goods, while in the United States the figure is close to 70 percent. Of course, the lower levels of consumption lead to higher investment and growth in the Soviet Union: Only about 15 percent of total U.S. national production goes for investment; about 30 percent is used in the Soviet Union. If you do some quick arithmetic, you will see that the Soviet Union also has a larger share of output available for government purchase, particularly military needs. The Soviet Union still must import most of the more sophisticated machinery it needs, but great strides have been made in producing heavy machinery and arms.

The consumer sector is an entirely different matter. Shortages of consumer goods are the main, but not the only, reason that Soviet consumers purchase less than their counterparts in the United States and elsewhere. The activities we call selling or merchandising have been absent from the Soviet scene. Advertising is limited and other attempts to increase consumer's purchases are viewed as exploitive. In many stores, piling whatever goods are available on a table is about the extent of retailing activity allowed.

Consumer income has risen faster than the output of consumer goods, and shortage of some items is a problem. The problem is aggravated by hoarding. When a hard-to-get good becomes available, consumers buy more than they need; the surplus can be used later or used as barter for other scarce goods.

Yet even in a world of constant consumer shortages of many goods, there are some goods that simply will not move at the prices set. The stores cannot change prices because the prices have been determined in the central plan. But the planners can be called in with the request that they review the prices in the plan. Usually, the planners will lower the prices to move the goods. While the planners would not call this action a sale, that clearly is what it is.

Advertising may also come into play with the use of a central advertising bureau. If the store wants consumers to buy a product, they will send the notice to the bureau. If the bureaucrats find the notice socially useful, the bureau will send it on to the media. There it will be used as sort of a cross between a news item and a want-ad: A simple statement that the store has a certain product for sale at a certain price.

is already low priced, also has a low tax. Items considered luxuries, such as automobiles, have a very high tax. This discourages consumption of these items. The tax revenues are used for investment projects to expand output. Thus, Soviet consumers are forced to invest every time they consume. If they consume items that reflect "capitalistic decadence," they invest even more in the nation's productive capacity.

Inflation

With officially set prices, we might think that inflation would be impossible. Yet, the Soviet economy has suffered inflation. There are some prices that are not set by the planners; also, when the price cannot rise, inflation shows up as shortages of almost everything. This has occurred in the past and is evident today.

After World War II, the Soviet Union suffered inflationary pressure along with most other economies. The Soviet central bank discovered what most central banks have known for a long time. It is easy to finance a war by increasing the money supply. The central bank bought government debt and in other ways made more rubles available. After the war, the Soviet people were ready to spend that money. When consumer goods remained in short supply, inflation resulted.

A planned economy is more effective than market economies at fighting such monetary inflation. Commerical banks are not allowed. Instead, the central bank itself has hundreds of branches all over the Soviet Union. Workers are allowed to maintain accounts in the banks. When the money supply became too large, after the war, the bank simply reduced it. Rubles were removed from circulation, bank deposits simply disappeared, and Soviet workers found their savings gone. The move was effective, but brutal. Russian economists would point out that inflation itself removes bank balances, but with less predictability than the central bank. For a time, inflation was controlled, but today, energy costs and lower economic growth produce the same inflationary pressure for the Soviet economy that is apparent in Western economies.

The Role of the Free Market

We have been describing the Soviet Union as basically a highly centralized, bureaucratic monolith. To a certain degree, this is true. But because such a system can't satisfy consumer demand, a black-market economy has sprung into existence. This *countereconomy* is basically the Soviet Union's free market economy, and it is widespread.

The countereconomy is fueled in different ways. There is theft by workers of virtually all types of consumer goods. These goods enter a "free" market, either in black markets around town or underneath the counter at the state stores. Impromptu markets spring up where buyers and sellers of used cars can meet and haggle over price.

Workers offer their services after work hours; plumbers, electricians, tutors, and many others in similar professions can earn a large amount of outside income by working in this countereconomy after their official work for the state is over. These workers may even deliberately do a poor job during the day so they can come back at night and charge high rates for repairs.

International Trade

The Soviet Union trades most frequently within a group of Eastern European nations known as **COMECON.** These nations all have planned economies and similar political philosophies. There remains a serious problem for this group: They have failed to develop a common currency or some other means of paying each other for the items traded. As a result, they have had to make payments to each other using their own currencies—the Bulgarian lev, Czechoslovak crown, East German mark, Hungarian florint, Polish zloty, Rumanian leu, or Soviet ruble. The rates of exchange of one currency for another are set as arbitrarily as are prices. Thus, much of the trade is on a barter basis. Barter is usually between two countries; efficient trades among three or more countries simply are too complicated to arrange.

Payment in currencies is complicated by inflation and energy shortages. Rumania recently refused to accept currencies from tourists from other COMECON nations; they wanted money only from Western nations. That was not such a problem for Poles, who may keep dollars if they can get them. However, holding any currency other than rubles is a criminal offense in the Soviet Union, and Soviet tourists in Rumania were often stranded.

The Soviet Union also trades with the West. When it needs to make large purchases—such as grain purchases from the United States—it uses gold. Fortunately, the Soviet Union is a major gold producer. The Soviets claim their ruble is backed by gold, and they criticize Western nations for not backing their currencies with gold. However, the rate of exchange for the ruble is still artificial. The price set by the central bank places the ruble at $1.50 or more. (It changes once a month.) But Americans or other tourists with dollars can buy two to three times as many rubles on the street with dollars as they could if they went to the Soviet central bank. The money markets in cities such as London and Zurich place the value at about $.25. Thus the actual purchasing power of the ruble in trade is much below the official value given it by the central bank.

The Future

In November of 1979, President Brezhnev told the Communist Central Party Committee that there were shortages of medicine, soap, needles and thread, and diapers. There are probably many more. Lines formed at a Moscow store which had a stock of imported detergent.

The goals stated in the five-year plan beginning in 1981 have been scaled down. However, delivery on consumer goods remains poor, and incentives given by the planners seem not to be enough to get Soviet workers to do their best.

The old appeals to party loyalty and love of fatherland are being revised, but speeches by supervisors are seldom more effective in the Soviet Union than they are in the United States.

The major challenges facing the Soviet Union in the 1980s are threefold: (1) The high growth rates of the past were achieved through labor-intensive methods. In order to maintain high growth, the Soviet Union must increase productivity through a more capital-intensive approach. Buying sophisticated technology from the West is not enough; soon the Soviet Union must adapt its very conservative industrial system to the production of sophisticated capital goods, such as computers. (2) The Soviet Union has been an exporter of oil to the COMECON countries, but the 1980s will see the loss of energy independence and the beginning of Soviet import of oil. High energy costs will act as a barrier to growth, as it has in the West for the last several years. (3) The Soviet Union must satisfy rising aspirations on the part of consumers. If consumers receive a greater share of output, less will be available for investing in the capital goods that lead to higher growth rates.

YUGOSLAVIA

Before World War II, Yugoslavia was basically capitalistic. World War II ended with Yugoslavia under Soviet control and under a communist government. However, at that time, Yugoslavia was far behind Russia in economic development. Education levels were low in general and skilled workers almost nonexistent. There was little industry and agriculture was very backward. Faced with the need to develop rapidly, Yugoslavia turned to the Russian model. The farms were collectivized and planning instituted. The Yugoslav economy was to develop in the traditional communist mold.

However, that plan did not work out. Marshal Tito, the leader of Yugoslavia until 1980, broke with Russia and developed his own form of socialism. When collective farms were not productive, peasants were ready to leave them. Unwilling to use the Soviet methods to keep them there, the Yugoslav planners decollectivized the farms in 1953. Since then, the state-owned land has gone back to the farmers. About half the land is still owned by the state, but the farmers operate the land as true cooperative farms. Farmers' earnings depend on productivity, so there is incentive for efficiency and hard work.

Industrial Organization

The state owns most of the capital goods and all the large firms. In 1950, however, Yugoslavia set up a system of syndicalism, in which firms are managed by labor. The workers at a firm elect a workers' council, which in turn selects a management committee. The committee selects a manager from among the workers, usually with the consent of the local Communist Party. However, the manager may be selected from outside the plant, as the workers try to find persons with greater managerial skill.

The workers have only a small guaranteed annual income. The rest comes from the profits of the plant. Thus, they have every incentive to run it well and to produce products that will sell at as high a price as possible. Firms buy inputs on the market and may even import materials. Capital comes from the government, though the firm may have to pay for it. Machinery may also be imported. The profits of the firm may be distributed to the workers or reinvested in the firm. Taxes must also be paid.

The workers' self-managed firm operates much like a market-directed capitalist firm. Decision making is thus somewhat decentralized. Firms will fire surplus labor to hold down costs. As a result, Yugoslavia does not have full employment, as Russia does. The managers also understand that the ability to raise prices is important to the success of the firm. As a result, the tendency to form monopolies has been a problem in Yugoslavia. However, as with monopoly firms in the Western countries, prices are regulated by government. Up until around 1970, the marketplace set prices for almost 60 percent of the goods produced. However, the 1970s saw high inflation rates—both in Western countries and in Yugoslavia. The Yugoslav response has been to subject more prices to control. Now nearly 80 percent of all prices are controlled.

Planning still exists in the Yugoslav economy. However, it comes closer to the indicative planning used in France and other countries than to the centralized planning of the Soviet Union. The plans set targets for the output of strategic raw materials and capital goods. There are also plans for areas where economic development can occur. Because the state owns land and factories, the plans are more effective than the plans in France, which are carried out mostly by private firms. In Yugoslavia, most investment comes from the government, which raises investment funds with taxes. The government controls the banking industry and foreign exchange.

What happens if a firm can't earn a profit? Will it go out of business if it continues to run deficits? Yes and no. There is limited free enterprise, and thus several firms have gone out of business. However, many more are bailed out through either subsidies or preferential taxes.

Labor

Not only are workers' wages dependent upon the performance of the firm, but wage differentials exist among the workers at almost any given firm. Wage differentials depend on the experience, ability, and contribution of each worker. Furthermore, a more successful firm will pay higher wages for a given job than a less successful firm. Overall, however, wage differentials in Yugoslavia are still less than in most Western countries.

Strikes, though very limited, do occur occasionally. Worker mobility is generally limited to regions, since the country is composed of several regionally based ethnic clusters. However, workers can emigrate. Yugoslavia could have an explosive unemployment problem, but many workers are employed elsewhere in Europe, especially in Germany. These workers usually return (most host countries are reluctant to grant citizenship), and their earnings also return home.

The Future

The future of the Yugoslav economy is an open question. Inflation has been running at 23 percent to 30 percent. The central bank was able to restrain inflation in 1971 and again in 1975; however, the monetary controls used then are not as effective now. Yugoslavia, along with many other economies, is finding that inflation is caused by increases in energy costs, much of which comes from outside the local economy. Also, the Yugoslav people have been experiencing an increase in living standards they are reluctant to give up. A cooling off of the economy will result in a lowering of living conditions. Both the European Common Market and the United States are trying to assist Yugoslavia in improving trade balance. Unless the Yugoslav economy can be restored, the death of President Tito may have profound economic as well as political effects.

SUMMARY

There have been many attempts to devise an economic system that would be superior to the market system. Abuses of political power and market failure have often been the reason people sought other systems. Rapid transformation of a colonial economy to a modern one has become another reason for seeking alternative economic organization.

Karl Marx has had a great impact on economics and on the philosophy of alternative economic systems. Marx used labor input as his absolute measure of value. Value was created by both direct and indirect labor. Marx's labor theory of value stated that the amount of labor should determine the rate at which two goods would exchange.

Marx recognized the role of the capitalist and the fact that the capitalist could earn profit. The capitalist could do this by advancing wages, or variable capital, to enable the worker to keep working and by providing the raw materials, or constant capital, that the worker used. The capitalist was then able to obtain a surplus value, or markup, based upon the amount of direct labor or variable capital used.

Because of the surplus value, the price of a good was greater than the wages required to produce it: Workers could not buy their own product and were thus alienated from it. Since there was an army of unemployed, wages in the short run could be kept as low as possible, depending upon how anxious workers were to obtain jobs. In the long run, wages would have to be no more than the subsistence level, which would allow the work force to reproduce itself but have no chance to advance economically.

Marx thought capitalism would eventually be replaced by worker communism because of endless accumulation by capitalists; declining profits, leading to the use of labor-saving inventions and increased unemployment; growing economic instability through business cycles; and class struggle and violent revolution.

All economic systems fall between the extremes of pure capitalism and communism. Countries are more accurately described as either socialistic or mixed capitalistic. A better method to identify and distinguish economic systems is to examine the following characteristics: (1) private property and ownership; (2) the nature of the labor contract; (3) the degree of centralization in decision making; (4) allocation by market or plan; and (5) the nature of incentives.

Economic planning is the most noteworthy achievement of socialist countries. Some countries, like France, utilize indicative planning.

The Soviet Union has a centrally planned economy. The Soviet central planning agency (GOSPLAN) develops a five-year plan for general goals and annual plans that are more detailed. For the planned commodities a material balance is worked out. Counterplanning allows the firms to respond to the inputs and outputs planned. After some bargaining, the output of the commodity is planned in physical units. Detailed plans for the operation of each enterprise are then developed. Goals are set for the firm in terms of physical output, and the compensation of the manager depends upon meeting the goals. Parallel with the operation plan is an accounting or financial plan that may have a planned loss built in. There are problems with planning. It is a very complex process with chances for many errors.

Growth in the Soviet Union has been greater than economic growth in the United States since World War II. Part of the success was the result of suppressing consumer demand. Various reforms were made in the process of planning in the mid-1960s which improved the lot of the consumer. However, with the slowdown in growth in the 1970s, some of the old methods were revived. Inflation and business cycles have not been eliminated as predicted by Marx. The Soviet Union trades within COMECON; most of the trade is on a barter basis. There is also trade with the West, both on a barter basis and for gold.

Yugoslavia followed the Soviet planning process closely after World War II. But the economy of Yugoslavia was less developed, so Yugoslavia moved to its own form of socialism. As a result, since 1950, Yugoslavia has decentralized the planning process while retaining state ownership of most land and capital. Some land has been returned to farmers. Worker syndicalism has been used in industry; workers manage the firms through an elected management committee with hired managers. Salaries are low, but since the workers share in the profits they have an incentive to keep the firm efficient.

Key Words and Phrases

alienation theory that a worker is alienated from his or her production because he or she receives only wages yet must pay both wages and the markup for surplus value to buy the goods produced.

capitalism an economic system characterized by private ownership of capital, free enterprise, free markets, and free choice for consumers and workers.

collective farm a farm in the Soviet Union where the land is owned by the state and controlled by the state but operated by the workers as a cooperative.

COMECON a group of Eastern European countries with planned economies that trade with each other.

communism a system of communal ownership of all property and a centralized economic and political power.

constant capital purchases by the capitalist of the necessary raw materials for workers to use; in recent times, it has come to include physical capital of all types, such as machinery and buildings.

counterplanning feedback from firms to a central planning agency as to expected output and necessary inputs.

direct labor the amount of labor used to produce a product.

enterprise operation plan a detailed plan for the operation of each firm, setting the output goals for the firm and determining the compensation of the manager.

exchange a reallocation of goods or resources with a return flow of goods, resources, or money.

exploitation determination of the capitalist's markup by reducing wages: In the short run, the capitalist can keep wages low because of the reserve of unemployed; in the long run, wages are low, since there is no reason to pay more than subsistence, the wage at which the labor force will just reproduce itself.

General Planning Commissariat French government body that coordinates indicative planning.

GOSPLAN the central economic planning agency for the Soviet Union.

indicative planning an economic system that uses planning to allocate goods while retaining the basic market structure.

indirect labor the labor embodied in a product from earlier stages of the production process; *dead labor*.

labor theory of value Marx's notion that goods requiring the same amount of labor input for production should be worth the same.

logistics the science of planning for the movement of resources and goods by the most efficient method(s) so that everything arrives in the right amounts at the right place and time.

market socialism a socialistic economic system in which the decentralized market economy plays an important role and political democracy flourishes.

material balance in a planned economy, the first step of the annual plan, in which the inputs needed to produce the desired output of a commodity are planned.

mixed capitalism an economic system in which the characteristics of pure capitalism are modified by government action.

pressure planning the tendency of planners to require managers to get along with fewer inputs than requested and/or to produce more output than the manager expected to produce, in order to overcome the tendency of managers to overstate their needs and understate their abilities to produce.

proletariat the formerly impoverished and powerless class that would come to control the communist economy after the revolution.

socialism an economic system in which government owns all major capital goods and means of production.

socially necessary labor the labor required to bring a product to market, including both direct and indirect labor.

substantive ownership the exercise of ownership, including one or more of possession, usufruct, alienation, or destruction.

surplus value the profit, interest rate, or rent the capitalist gets as a constant percentage of variable capital or direct labor.

syndicalism an economic system in which firms are managed by the workers, through an elected management committee and employed managers, and in which capital is owned by the state but profits are shared with the workers.

transfer a one-way reallocation of resources

usufruct a right of ownership which includes the claim to all income generated by a property and the claim to any increase in physical or financial value of the asset.

variable capital payments by capitalists to workers (wages) before the goods produced are sold.

Questions for Review

1. Professor Milton Friedman likes to point out that everyone is familiar with the common yellow wood pencil, but nobody knows how to make one. Suppose you are a central planner in charge of pencil manufacture. Plan production of the pencils. Start with the rubber trees for the eraser, cypress trees for the wood, graphite for the core (we usually call it lead), metal for the band to hold the eraser on, glue to hold the whole thing together, and, of course, the yellow paint. Make sure you package them and at least get them to a distributor.
2. Can you think of something to which you have complete rights of ownership? Do you have possession of anything for which you do not have claim to the income generated?
3. If you could design an ideal economy, what would it be like? Have you designed a system where everyone else does the work and you get all the "goodies"?
4. Would you be willing to sacrifice personal freedom for an economic system that was more productive? For a system that was more equitable? Why or why not?
5. What reasons might the leaders of less developed nations give for being interested in planned economies? What would be the hidden assumptions in their reasoning? Which of their reasons would likely be accurate? Why?

PART 6

International Economics

20 International Trade

21 International Commercial Policies and Institutions

CHAPTER 20

International Trade

Learning Objectives

Upon completion of this chapter, you should be able to:

1. Show how trade affects the price and quantity produced of a good.
2. List the benefits of free trade.
3. Show how trade affects the aggregate demand of a country.
4. Explain how absolute advantage affects trade.
5. Explain the principle of comparative advantage and show how it affects trade.

Sometimes very old words are useful for describing very new phenomena. ***Synergism*** is an old word used to describe a process which produces more output than the sum of its inputs. Medical science uses the word to describe how two drugs interact to produce a greater total effect than the sum of the two used separately. Managers of enterprises use it to describe how cooperative effort can yield greater output than individuals working alone. In both cases, synergism is the process by which the whole becomes greater than the sum of its parts.

The concept of synergism is especially useful for describing economic phenomena. In this chapter we will explore the synergistic effects of trade. Trade is synergistic because its total benefits are greater than the sum of the individual benefits enjoyed without trade. When individuals trade, the total utility of all goods and services received is greater than the utility or satisfaction given up. Synergism has taken place.

Trade between nations is especially synergistic. The people of a trading nation receive more additional utility per dollar from consuming goods produced in another country than they give up in the goods they exchange.

As trade grows to include many nations, the synergistic effect increases. Trade permits each nation to **specialize**—that is, to do what it does best. Each nation uses the **division of labor** that allows its workers to develop greater skills for making the products in which it specializes. Specialization and division of labor result in improved technology and greater productivity throughout the world. When nations trade freely, all peoples enjoy higher standards of living and a greater variety of social and cultural opportunities. And the total improvement is greater than the sum of improvements each country would have achieved without trade.

Trade, then, bestows benefits on trading nations. It also bestows power. The United States, because of its climate and land mass, has been able to develop a highly efficient agricultural technology. Through trade, we are able to feed one fourth of the world's population. Our high productivity in agriculture also frees other resources for the production of manufactured goods and for research and development of new technology. We can produce many more of such goods and services than we need for our own use, but other nations need and want them. The United States thus has great power—leverage, you might call it—to influence economic and political decisions.

The oil-producing nations of the Middle East enjoy the power associated with their wealth of energy resources. As global requirements for fuel increase and as alternative sources are gradually depleted, their power to withhold supplies and raise prices lends much weight to their political and economic demands.

Other nations and blocs of nations exercise the power of trade. Some have strong trading capabilities and hence much power. Some have relatively less. Some third world nations, for example, have little or no influence in world decision-making. They lack materials and goods for trade. Therefore, they lack the power to command goods and services to expand their production and raise their standards of living. Trade is power.

BEGINNINGS OF TRADE

Early primitive tribes understood the benefits of trade. Without trade, each extended family group within the tribe had to produce its own requirements of food, shelter, and decorative ornaments. Eventually, family groups began to specialize—some in food gathering, some in weapons production. Some even specialized in performing rituals to placate tribal gods. Such goods and services came to be traded within a single tribe.

Later, some isolated groups expanded their trade to include other tribes. They were cautious at first. In remote areas of Africa, northern Russia, and the southern Pacific, a form of silent barter developed. A member of one tribe would approach a familiar trail crossing and deposit items for trade: beads, clay pots, and dried fruits, for example. Then the primitive merchant would retreat to a nearby sheltering bush to watch.

Soon a trader from another tribe would approach and deposit other goods believed to be acceptable in exchange: cloth, a tool, and perhaps a goat. The second trader likewise would disappear into the bushes.

The first trader would return and, if the offering was acceptable, take what the second had brought and leave. If the offering was too small, the trader might remove one item from the first pile. If the second trader found the exchange agreeable, the trade would be complete. The fine art of haggling has a long history!

THE PURE THEORY OF INTERNATIONAL TRADE

The pure theory of international trade has microeconomic and macroeconomic implications. Its microeconomic aspects refer to the interaction of demand and supply in individual markets. As in domestic markets, trade establishes an *equilibrium* price and quantity for traded goods and services. When markets are linked through trade, equilibrium occurs at the intersection of *global demand* and *global supply*.

The macroeconomic aspects of international trade refer to the effects of trade on a nation's total output, income, and employment. Growth in aggregate global demand can stimulate greater production and help relieve problems of domestic unemployment. Excessive global demand can push a nation beyond its normal productive capacity and lead to inflation. An even more important macroeconomic aspect of international trade is the growth in production possibilities that results from specialization and international division of labor.

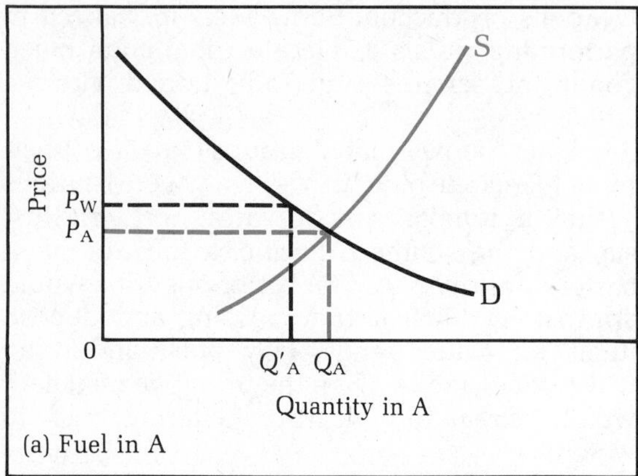

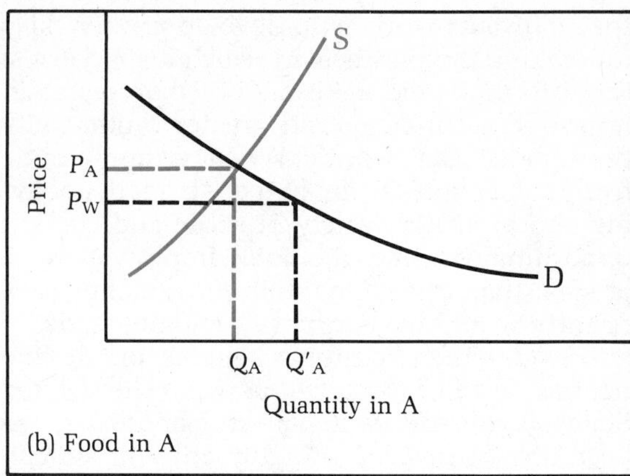

Figure 1 The supply and demand within country *A:* (a) for fuel; (b) for food. Notice that fuel is more plentiful. The equilibrium price and quantity in both markets are P_A and Q_A. P_W is the world market price and Q_A' is the quantity demanded in *A* at the world price.

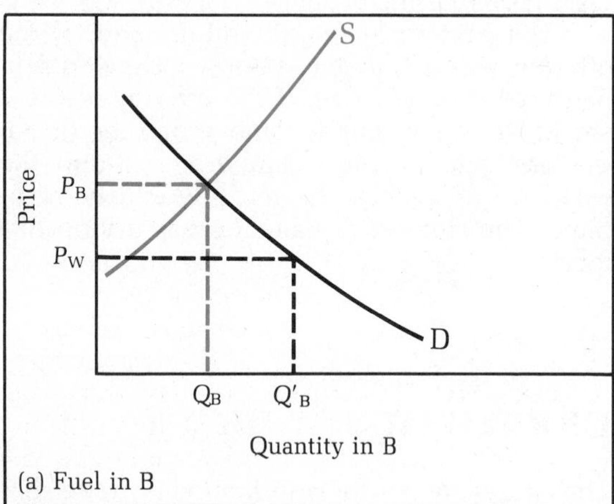

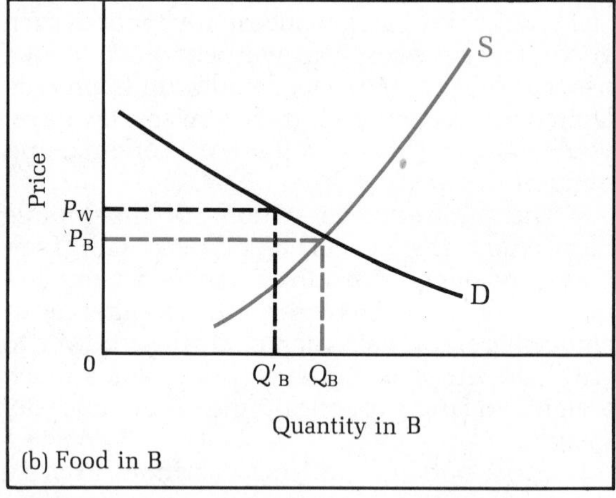

Figure 2 The supply and demand within country *B:* (a) for fuel; (b) for food. Notice that food is more plentiful. The equilibrium price and quantity in both markets are P_B and Q_B. P_W is the world market price and Q_B' is the quantity demanded in *B* at the world price.

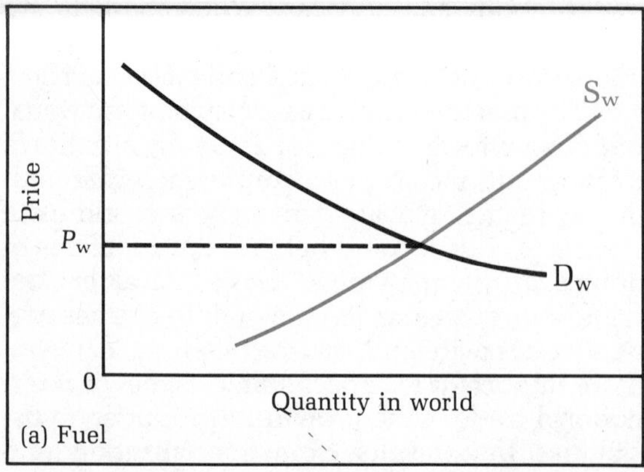

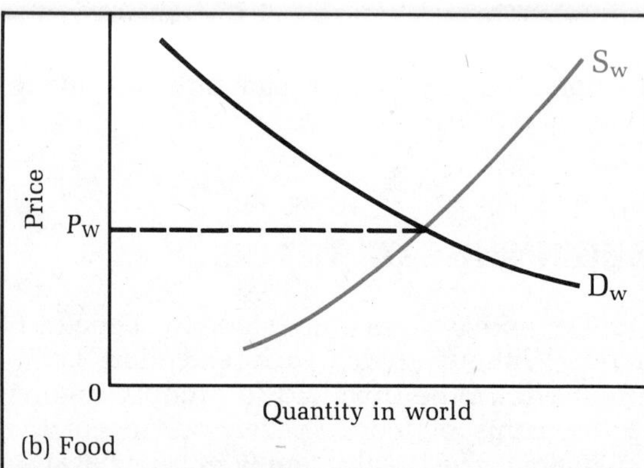

Figure 3 World markets for: (a) fuel and (b) food. Specialization and trade enable consumers to change consumption patterns so that prices and marginal utilities are equal worldwide.

MICRO ASPECTS OF INTERNATIONAL TRADE

Imagine a world composed of only two nations. Citizens of both nations must consume certain quantities of food and burn certain quantities of fuel. Their demand curves for food and fuel are shown in Figures 1 and 2. Demand curves are downward-sloping. This shows that some quantity must be used regardless of price (everyone has to eat) and that larger quantities will be consumed at lower prices. The curves are drawn identically to simplify the explanation.

Now suppose that country *A* is uniquely situated to produce fuel and country *B* to produce food. *A*'s resource capabilities make its costs of producing fuel very low and its costs of producing food high. This means that *A*'s short-run supply curve for fuel will lie low and to the right, suggesting low unit costs for fuel production. *A*'s supply curve for food will lie high and to the left, suggesting high unit costs for food production. Conversely, *B*'s short-run supply curve for fuel will lie high and to the left and its supply curve for food will lie low and to the right.

Without international trade, domestic demand and supply alone will determine the equilibrium price and quantity for both commodities in both markets. Fuel will be abundant and cheap in *A* and food scarce and expensive. In *B*, fuel will be expensive and food cheap.

Citizens in both countries will expand consumption of both food and fuel as long as they feel the use of each adds more to their total well-being, or total utility, than they must give up to purchase the food or fuel. The additional well-being or utility contributed by the last unit consumed is its marginal utility.

Because of the low price of fuel in *A*, fuel consumption is expanded to a large quantity, $0Q_A$. So much fuel is used that the last unit provides little additional utility, by the principle of diminishing marginal utility. In *B*, the higher price restricts the quantity of fuel consumed to $0Q_B$. Consumption is limited to this small quantity by the high price. As a result, the additional utility of the last unit consumed will be very high.

Differences in marginal utility of consumption between nations open the possibility for trade to enhance global welfare. Total world utility will be increased if fuel is transferred from regions where its marginal utility is low to regions where its marginal utility is high. To transfer a unit of fuel from country *A* would cause only a small loss in total utility. The gain in utility to *B* would be comparatively much greater.

The same generalization applies to the marginal utility of food in the two countries. Trade permits citizens of *A* to trade fuel, for which their marginal utility is low, for food, for which their marginal utility is high.

How Will International Trade Affect Price and Quantity?

Let us suppose free trade is opened between countries *A* and *B* so that their goods are traded in a single combined market. For simplicity, we will assume there are no transport costs. The combined world markets for fuel and food are shown in Figure 3. Global demand for fuel is the sum of demand of *A* and *B*. Similarly, global demand for food is the combined demand of *A* and *B*.

With trade, *A* may now specialize in the production for which its resources are best suited—fuel. *A*'s short-run supply curve then becomes the world supply for fuel. With total specialization, *A* can avoid wasting resources on food production. As a result, its supply curve for fuel will lie farther to the right than before trade. *B* will use its resources only in food production. Its short-run supply curve becomes the world supply of food. Total specialization will also move *B*'s supply curve farther to the right than before trade.

Compare $0P_A$ and $0P_B$ in Figures 1 and 2 with $0P_w$ in Figure 3a. The new equilibrium price for fuel is now greater in *A* and lower in *B* than before trade. Citizens of *A* move up their demand curves for fuel until marginal utility is sufficient to justify the new higher price. Citizens of *B* move down their demand curves for fuel until marginal utility is consistent with the new lower price. Citizens of *B* gain utility which is greater than the utility given up by citizens of *A*. Verify that this is true by comparing purchases in each country at the new world price (P_W in Figures 1 and 2). Show that the utility gained in the importing nation is greater than the loss to the exporter. At equilibrium, the utility of the last unit of fuel used is the same in both countries. There can be no further benefit through shipment of fuel from one nation to the other. Fuel consumption is now greater in *B* than before trade and lower in *A*.

Similar results occur in the world market for

food. The new equilibrium price equates marginal utilities worldwide so that no further benefit can be made from trade in food. At equilibrium, food consumption is greater in *A* than before trade and lower in *B*.

Note that *total* consumption of fuel and food worldwide may actually be greater than before trade. With specialization, producers of the two commodities may achieve cost savings allowing them to produce a larger total supply.

What Are the Benefits of Specialization?

As nations specialize, resources move into particular kinds of production and short-run supply curves shift to the right. Greater specialization may involve lower unit costs, the same unit costs, or rising unit costs. The effect of specialization on unit costs depends on the availability of particular resources needed for production.

Rising unit costs occur when an industry uses a particular resource which is in short supply. If many firms begin production, they will bid up the price of the scarce resource. Even the United States cannot fulfill *all* the world's food needs. To do so would require plowing up city streets, marshes, and mountains, and costs would rise prohibitively. Even plentiful Arab oil resources are not unlimited. At some point oil deposits will become depleted and recovery costs of petroleum will rise.

When particular resources are limited, unit costs will eventually rise with expanded production. At first, specialization will cause short-run supply curves to shift rightward, but resource scarcity may finally prevent further increases at the same cost. The result of specialization may be an increase in world prices.

You may recognize this result as an example of the principle of diminishing marginal product (see Chapter 2). Diminishing marginal product results from the application of additional variable resources to a resource which is fixed in supply. As the proportion of variable to fixed resources reaches and exceeds the optimum, productivity declines and costs rise.

Falling unit costs occur when the increase in production brings on technological progress. For instance, labor skills may grow with specialization. The entry of many new firms into an industry may make specialized transport or power facilities practical. Large industry requirements for raw materials or component parts may lead to economies of scale in their production. Specialization in coffee production has enabled Brazil to develop technological aids which reduce unit costs. Specialization in electronics has permitted Japan to focus its research and development energies toward this industry. Other examples come to mind: meat from Argentina, aircraft from the United States, precision instruments from West Germany. Specialization and large-scale production of these goods for export have permitted technical cost advantages.

Whenever technological progress accompanies specialization, unit costs will fall. Short-run supply curves will shift rightward by larger and larger amounts so that more units can be produced with fewer resources. World prices will fall with specialization and trade.

Constant unit costs are the result of offsetting changes in resource costs and technological advances. Specialization will cause short-run supply curves to shift rightward moderately as more units are produced at the same unit costs.

To the extent that unit costs are constant or falling, the world will enjoy the greatest gains from trade. When unit costs increase, specialization and trade may result in rising world prices. But still costs will generally be lower than without specialization.

How Will International Trade Affect Incomes?

Changing price patterns have further effects that benefit the citizens of trading nations. In our hypothetical example, we assumed that different resource advantages brought on the cost advantages that stimulated trade: an abundance of fuel-producing resources in *A* and an abundance of food-producing resources in *B*. Without trade, *A*'s plentiful fuel-producing resources would command a low price. This is because a plentiful supply relative to domestic demand means a low equilibrium price. Without trade, Japan's skilled labor force would command low wages; Japanese consumers could not possibly purchase all the cameras and electronic equipment they produce. Without trade, Kansas wheat fields would be worth much less, and farmers' incomes would be lower.

When particular resources—land, labor, capital, and entrepreneurship—are plentiful relative to the domestic *derived demand* for their services, incomes will generally be low. (Recall that derived demand is the demand for a resource that results because of the demand for the goods the resource can produce.) The reverse is true when resources are scarce relative to domestic demand. In our hypothetical example, scarce food-producing resources command high incomes in country *A*: Supply is low relative to the demand for output. Wheat-producing lands in Canada and mineral deposits in Japan are real-world examples of resources that are in short supply relative to domestic derived demand. Without trade, their incomes would be very high.

Trade narrows the gap between earnings paid to a region's various productive resources. Trade raises the derived demand for the fuel-producing resources of *A*. The rise is reflected in higher returns for oil fields, drilling and refining equipment, and pipelines. In *B*, trade increases the derived demand for food-producing resources. Wage rates rise for farm laborers and rents rise on farmlands. Entrepreneurs receive higher profits for production of agricultural equipment. The United States resembles country *B* with regard to the benefits of trade to farmers. Sales of grain to Russia in the mid-1970s enabled American farmers to enjoy higher incomes. The benefits of this trade also provided the extra income needed to buy new farm equipment.

With free trade, resources in both nations are employed in industries for which they are best suited. Resources receive incomes according to the value of their output in *total* world markets. Higher return to resources encourages greater productivity and provides funds for new capital investment. Research and development efforts can focus on technological progress in the region's specialty. As a result, production may take place at even lower unit costs, further enhancing the basic benefits from international trade.

Trade reduces the derived demand for high-priced resources and products that are not a nation's specialty. Resource owners complain that cheap foreign imports cut into their domestic market and reduce their incomes. Workers complain about the loss of job security and the need to learn a new trade. The fact that over all and in the long run *everyone* will be better off will not comfort them. As we shall see later, powerful voices have been raised throughout modern history to restrict international trade. They are still being raised, and they are still powerful.

Table 1 **Trade as a Percentage of GNP for Selected Countries, 1977**

Country	GNP (in billions of dollars)	% Imports	% Exports
Argentina	89.5*	4.3	8.2
Australia	93.8	18.3	30.7
Belgium	81.7	17.1	38.2
Brazil	105.6*	21.3	23.5
Japan	418.5*	21.9	12.4
Mexico	57.1*	8.2	8.4
Netherlands	105.8	14.0	45.3
Nigeria	17.2*	35.4	55.7
Norway	35.7	21.1	15.2
South Africa	29.2	43.5	36.1
Spain	116.3	8.3	16.1
Switzerland	63.1	17.2	21.5
Turkey	45.5	3.19	9.3
United Kingdom	246.4	20.6	21.8
United States	1887.2	9.9	9.3

*Estimated

MACRO ASPECTS OF INTERNATIONAL TRADE

The macroeconomic aspects of international trade include the broad national and world aggregates in economic activity: the levels of output, income, and employment; resource allocation and income distribution; and growth in production possibilities.

National Income and Trade

For some nations, international trade represents a major part of total production. Production for export has long been significant in Belgium and the Netherlands, where exports represent more than one half the total national output, or gross national product (GNP). Other European nations export large percentages of their national output to pay for necessary imports of food and raw materials. Table 1 shows the relationship between imports and exports and total output for selected countries.

In the United States, our large and varied land mass provides most of the food and materials we need, and a large domestic consumer market provides outlets for our manufactured goods. Therefore, imports and exports represent only about 10 percent of the United

States GNP. However, the United States is the world's largest trader. In 1978, imports amounted to nearly $217 billion and exports $205 billion.

The strength of trade in a nation's total output is reflected in *aggregate demand*, the sum of consumption expenditures, business investment, government purchases, and net exports. In mathematical terms,

$$\text{aggregate demand} = C + I + G + X_n.$$

Net exports are the excess of foreign sales over purchases from foreign sources:

$$X_n = \text{value of exports} - \text{value of imports}.$$

X_n can be a positive or a negative number. What nations in Table 1 enjoyed a positive value for net exports in 1977? What nations had a negative value?

If the value of imports exceeds the value of exports, X_n becomes a negative number. The result is a decrease in aggregate demand and a fall in national output, income, and employment. Spending for imports is a "leakage" from aggregate demand. For an economy at full employment, a fall in aggregate demand may mean the loss of jobs and a drop in efficiency. Our slow growth in recent years may be partly a result of our high level of imports while exports have remained relatively stagnant.

If the value of exports exceeds the value of imports, X_n will be a positive number. The result is an addition to aggregate demand. This means an expansion of output, income, and employment. For an underemployed economy, a rise in aggregate demand can give a welcome boost to output. But for an economy already at full employment a rise in aggregate demand can produce inflation and distortion in the use of scarce resources. Some oil-producing nations are facing this problem, along with resulting social unrest and revolutionary politics.

Table 2 shows the components of U.S. exports and imports for selected recent years. What has been the trend in these values? What commodities seem responsible for changes in the flow of trade?

Figure 4 shows how shifts in X_n affect an economy. An increase in X_n is shown in Figure 4a. An increase in X_n may be caused by an increase in exports or a decrease in imports. The diagram is drawn with a parallel upward shift in the aggregate demand curve. At less than full employment the increase in X_n may be welcome; at full employment the increase may be inflationary.

A decrease in X_n is shown in Figure 4b. The decrease may be the result of a decrease in exports or an increase in imports. At full employment or below the decline in X_n will mean a disturbing loss of jobs. But if the economy is suffering from inflation, the decline may help control inflation.

Table 2a **U.S. Exports--Each Given as Percent of Total Exports**

Item exported	1960	1971	1977
Food and live animals	13.2%	10.0%	12.0%
Beverage and tobacco	2.4	1.6	1.6
Crude materials, except food and fuel	13.7	10.0	10.9
Petroleum and products	2.3	1.1	1.1
Other mineral fuels and related materials	1.8	2.3	4.7
Chemicals	8.7	8.8	9.2
Machinery and transportation equipment	34.3	44.7	43.3
Other manufactured goods	18.7	16.4	15.8
Total value of exports*	$20,408	$43,493	$117,963

*Value in millions.

Table 2b **U.S. Imports--Each Given as Percent of Total Imports**

Item imported	1960	1971	1977
Food and live animals	19.9%	12.1%	8.5%
Beverage and tobacco	2.6	1.9	1.1
Crude materials, except food and fuel	18.3	7.4	5.4
Petroleum and products	10.3	7.3	28.3
Other mineral fuels and related materials	.2	.9	1.7
Chemicals	5.3	3.5	3.7
Machinery and transportation equipment	9.7	30.4	24.2
Other manufactured goods	30.3	32.8	24.7
Total value of imports*	$15,073	$45,563	$146,817

*Value in millions.

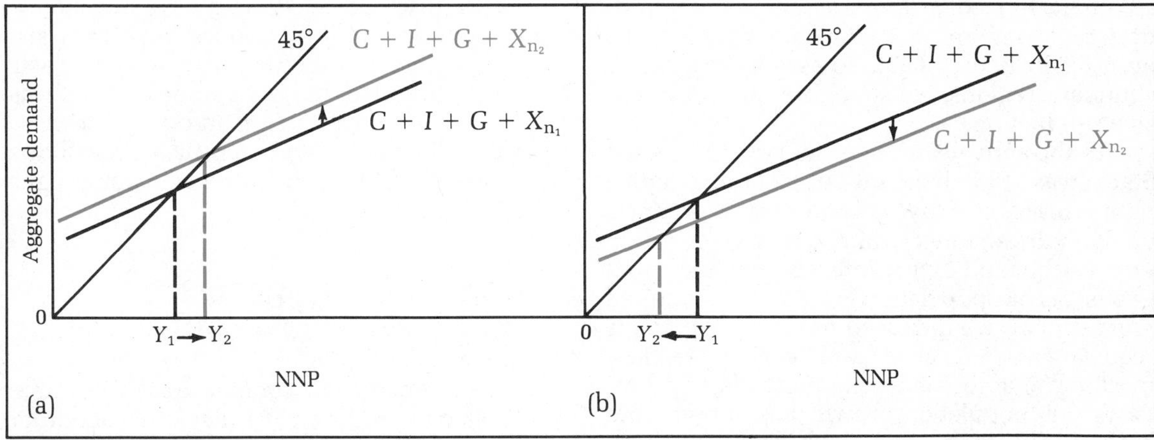

Figure 4 (a) An increase in net exports (from X_{n1} to X_{n2}) causes an increase in aggregate demand, which leads to an increase in NNP (unless Y_1 is at full employment). (b) A decrease in net exports reverses the process. Aggregate demand falls and so does output (NNP) and employment.

The Foreign Trade Multiplier

Changes in consumption, investment, and government purchases (C + I + G) are known to have a multiple effect on national output, income, and employment. Changes in these components of total spending produce multiple changes as incomes are spent and respent throughout the economy—much like ripples in a pond. The total change in income is a result of this *multiplier effect*.

Changes in net exports (X_n) produce similar results. The **foreign trade multiplier** is a measure of the change in output, income, and employment that results from a change in net exports. The size of the foreign trade multiplier depends on the response of a nation's economy to a change in the level of foreign spending. Compare the vertical shift of X_n in Figure 4 with the greater horizontal change in national income and output. The greater change is a result of the foreign trade multiplier.

The foreign trade multiplier can be stated simply:

The foreign trade multiplier reflects the tendency for an increase (decrease) in net exports to produce a larger increase (decrease) in total production and income.

The foreign trade multiplier in action. World War I brought economic dislocation to the warring nations and a collapse of world trade. When peace came, nations tried to rebuild domestic industry by discouraging imports. Every import was seen as a threat to jobs at home. Trade was blocked by tariffs in order to protect local industry from international competition. But a restriction on one nation's imports is necessarily a restriction on another's exports, and if country *A* will not buy food from country *B*, then *B* cannot buy fuel from *A*. International trade collapses. The X_n component of aggregate demand fell to zero or below in many nations when world trade collapsed after World War II.

With the drop in export sales, Western nations experienced sharp declines in output, income, and employment. The drop in aggregate demand culminated in the Great Depression of the 1930s. Other factors contributed to this great decline in economic activity, of course, but the loss of foreign markets was a serious problem in many nations. Recognition of the bad effects of tariffs led to more enthusiastic support for free trade in later years. By the 1970s there was renewed support for tariffs to protect local jobs during periods of high unemployment. Economists feared new legislation that would restrict trade.

Resource Allocation

Regions differ in their resource endowments, and products differ in their resource requirements. A region with plentiful labor and little capital may be characterized as labor abundant and capital poor. Products requiring much labor are characterized as *labor intensive,* while products requiring much capital are called *capital intensive.* It is reasonable to assume that labor-abundant regions will specialize in labor-intensive production.

In the early years of our history, the United States was land abundant but labor and capital poor. This allowed us to export the raw products of our mines, forests, and farms. We had to import labor and capital-intensive manufactured goods. As our population grew and we acquired more capital, we increased production of goods requiring more labor and capital: textiles, machinery, automobiles, and aircraft. In recent years our population growth has slowed. But high productivity and high incomes have enabled us to save and invest in larger quantities of capital. We have been able to continue to increase specialization in capital-intensive goods for export—aircraft, for example, and power plants.

Our growing stock of capital has enabled us to produce some goods generally associated with other countries. For generations the abundance of labor in certain Oriental countries enabled them to export fine carpets to the United States. In recent years, however, we have developed computerized looms for duplicating Oriental rugs at much lower unit costs. The carpet industry has become more capital-intensive, giving our carpet exports an advantage over labor-intensive carpets produced abroad.

Not all capital is material. In addition to machinery and equipment, we have invested in *human* capital. Investment in labor skills enables us to produce goods that are labor saving, land saving, and *material* (capital) saving. Many U.S. exports should be characterized as human-capital intensive.

A high level of human capital is required in the production of chemicals, data processing equipment, and precision instruments. Even agricultural products are human-capital intensive insofar as specialized education and scientific research have enabled the American farmer to outproduce other farmers. For example, American rice producers use advanced knowledge and scientific techniques to plant, wash, and process rice. Productivity is thus vastly superior to that of the rice paddies of Southeast Asia. We also export human-capital–intensive *services.* Business and technical consulting, insurance, and financial services require highly trained human capital.

PRODUCTION POSSIBILITIES AND ABSOLUTE ADVANTAGE

A nation's particular combination of resources enables it to produce particular kinds of output. To demonstrate the relationship between resources and output, we will construct models of production possibilities for two nations with different resource endowments. As in our previous model, we will assume that all possible output for each country can be classified as either fuel or food. We will also assume that each nation owns one hundred labor hours to use in production.

Comparing Productivity

Table 3 shows the quantities of food and fuel that can be produced per labor hour in the two countries. Each labor hour in country *A* can produce either 10 units of fuel or 5 units of food. In country *B* each labor hour can produce 2 units of fuel or 6 units of food. *A*'s resources are more suited for the production of fuel and *B*'s for the production of food. This can be seen by comparing productivity in the two countries or by comparing costs for the two commodities.

To compare productivity, read the columns vertically. You can see that *A* outproduces *B* ten to two in fuel and that *B* outproduces *A* six to five in food.

With each labor hour, country *A* can produce five times as much fuel as country *B*. Stating this relationship differently, country *B* produces only 1/5 as much fuel per unit of resource as country *A*. However, country *A* can

Table 3 **Production per Labor Hour of Resource**

	Units of fuel	Units of food
Country A	10	5
Country B	2	6

Table 4 **Production Costs in Labor Hours**

	Fuel	Food
Country A	1/10	1/5
Country B	1/2	1/6

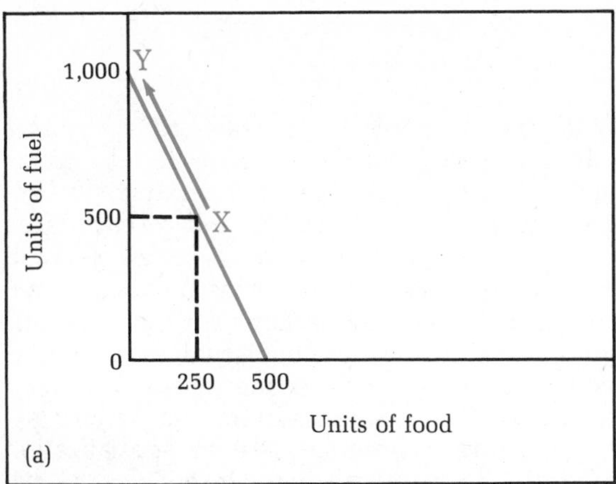

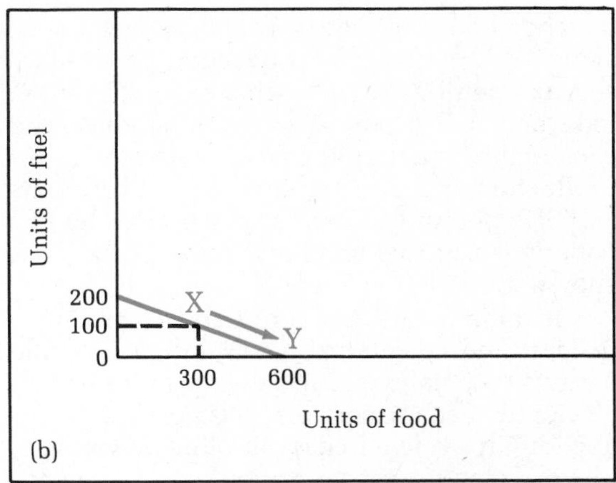

Figure 5 Production possibilities for: (a) country *A* and (b) country *B*. Notice that country *A* is able to produce more fuel than food, while *B* can produce more food than fuel. Before trade, each nation must be self-sufficient; production and consumption are shown at point X. With trade, nations specialize according to absolute advantage; production is shown at point *Y*.

produce only 5/6 as much food as country *B* per labor hour; country *B* produces 1 1/5 as much food as country *A* per unit of resource.

The *absolute costs of production* are the quantities of resources given up in the two countries. Since one labor hour will produce 10 units of fuel in country *A*, one unit of fuel costs 1/10 labor hour in *A*. Since one labor hour will produce only 2 units of fuel in *B*, one unit of fuel costs 1/2 labor hour in *B*. Clearly, fuel production is less costly in *A*. Each unit of food costs 1/5 labor hour in *A* and 1/6 labor hour in *B*; food production is less costly in *B*. Table 4 shows production costs in *A* and *B* for fuel and food.

The Principle of Absolute Advantage

Refer again to Table 3 showing production in countries *A* and *B*. In *A*, the use of a single labor hour will be more productive in fuel production. Producing a unit of fuel requires fewer productive resources in *A* than it does in *B*. We say that *A*'s resources have *absolute advantage* in the production of fuel. *B*'s resources are more productive in food production. Producing a unit of food requires fewer productive resources in *B* than it does in *A*. *B* has absolute advantage in the production of food.

The principle of **absolute advantage** can be stated simply:

Whenever a nation can produce a particular good or service more cheaply, in terms of resources used, than another nation, it is said to have absolute advantage in production of that good.

For example, the character of Spain's natural resource endowment gives it absolute advantage in cork production. Sweden has absolute advantage in lumber, Norway in seafood, Denmark in ham, and the Netherlands in cheese. In addition, specialized capital resources in these nations have enhanced their absolute advantage as they concentrated their energies on developing these particular industries.

To see how absolute advantage can enhance the benefits of trade, let us look at *A*'s and *B*'s total production possibilities. Assume that each nation has one hundred labor hours for use in production. Total production possibilities are shown in Figure 5.* *A*'s resources and technology enable it to produce more fuel; *B*'s enable it to produce more food. Using all its resources, *A* could produce either 1,000 units of fuel, 500 units of food, or any combination shown on its production-possibilities curve. Using all its resources, *B* could produce either 200 units of fuel or 600 units of food. Without trade, *A* and *B* must produce their entire requirements of both goods.

Suppose each nation decides to allocate half

*For simplicity, the production-possibilities curves have been drawn with a constant slope. The constant slope implies constant opportunity costs in the production of food and fuel. As *A* moves resources from production of fuel into food production, each additional unit of food requires the same opportunity cost in fuel not produced. The constant opportunity cost for producing a unit of food in *A* is 2 units of fuel. Similarly, to move resources from food production to fuel production in *B* requires a constant opportunity cost of 3 units of food.

its labor hours to food and half to fuel. Move along each nation's production-possibilities curve to point *X*, where each is self-sufficient in food and fuel production: *A* can produce and consume 500 fuel units and 250 food units; *B*'s production and consumption are 100 fuel units and 300 food units. Total production in the two nations is 600 fuel units and 550 food units as shown at the left in Table 5.

If trade opens between *A* and *B*, total production and consumption will increase. Trade permits both nations to use their resources more efficiently. Each nation can specialize in the production in which it has absolute advantage. Move along each nation's production-possibilities curve to point *Y*, where each specializes according to absolute advantage: In *A*, specialization in fuel will yield total production of 1000 units; in *B*, specialization in food will yield 600 units.

Dividing output in half and trading will provide both nations more total units than without trade. Check Table 5 to see that this is true. When countries *A* and *B* were not trading, each consumed what it produced; total consumption was 600 units of food and 550 units of fuel. When they decided to trade, they specialized and increased production. In our example, they decided to trade one half of food output—500 units—for one half of fuel output—300 units. They could have decided a different ratio of trade—perhaps a unit of food for a unit of fuel. As Table 5 shows, the final result is that each country is able to consume more after trading. Total consumption becomes 1,000 fuel units and 600 food units.

At the beginning of this chapter we used the term *synergism* to describe the gains from trade. From the discussion above, you can see that, in economic terms, the whole can indeed become greater than the sum of its parts.

Absolute Advantage of Individuals and Among Nations

Like nations, some individuals enjoy absolute advantage in the production of certain goods and services. Their superior productivity encourages them to specialize and to earn large returns from their specialty. Reggie Jackson earns substantial returns for his skill as a home-run hitter, Joan Sutherland for her operatic voice, and Dr. Christiaan Barnard for his surgeon's skills. The world economy would suffer if they used their resources in mining, weaving—or teaching economics. Their specialization according to absolute advantage enables the rest of us to enjoy the benefits of their talents.

It is generally assumed that modern, industrialized nations have absolute advantage in manufactured goods and that less developed nations have absolute advantage in basic materials. The assumption is that costs of producing basic materials are lower in less developed countries. In actual fact, industrialized countries rather than developing countries have absolute advantage in production of most raw materials.

Less developed countries produce only 28 percent of world mineral products; free market economies produce 45 percent and command economies 27 percent. Less developed countries do produce as much as 90 percent of a limited list of commodities: coffee, cocoa, tea, jute, hard fibers, and natural rubber, for example. Specific geographical features give them absolute advantage in the production of these commodities. Such commodities, however, are few. Moreover, the actual marketing and transporting of these commodities often depend on the resources of the industrialized countries. Among less developed countries, resource endowment and absolute advantage are unevenly

Table 5 **The Benefits of Specialization According to Absolute Advantage**

	Without trade, production and consumption		With trade			
			Production		Consumption	
	Fuel	Food	Fuel	Food	Fuel	Food
Country A	500	250	1,000	0	500	300
Country B	100	300	0	600	500	300
Total	600	550	1,000	600	1,000	600

Table 6 **Production per Labor Hour**

	Fuel	Food
Country A	10	5
Country B	10	2

Table 7 **Opportunity Costs**

	Fuel	Food
Country A	1/2 food unit	2 fuel units
Country B	1/5 food unit	5 fuel units

distributed. Only a few have the capacity to produce and export large quantities of minerals.

What can we conclude with respect to absolute advantage among nations? We must acknowledge that some nations—the industrialized nations—may possess absolute advantage both in the production of basic materials and in manufacturing. If this is true, does this contradict the pure theory of international trade? Will only favored nations benefit from trade? The answer is no. The benefits of trade do not depend on the existence of absolute advantage. Even nations without absolute advantage in any production at all may still gain from world trade. The world economy will benefit and their producers will benefit when such nations specialize according to *comparative advantage.*

COMPARATIVE ADVANTAGE

Thus far, our trading model has been unrealistic. There may be some commodities in which neither country *A* nor country *B* enjoys absolute advantage. Still, specialization and trade will permit more effective use of resources and greater total production of most goods.

In Table 6, output figures have been changed so that *A* and *B* are equally efficient in the production of fuel. However, *A* outproduces B five to two in the production of food, giving *A* absolute advantage in food production.

Opportunity Costs

This time, specialization will depend on the principle of comparative advantage. The principle of **comparative advantage** is somewhat more complex than the principle of absolute advantage: Whenever a nation can produce a particular good or service at lower cost in terms of *other goods,* it is said to have comparative advantage in producing that good.

Comparative advantage is based on a comparison of production costs in terms of other goods. *Comparative cost ratios* express the *opportunity cost* of producing one good instead of another and are read horizontally in Table 6.

Reading horizontally shows the costs of producing food and fuel in the two nations. The opportunity cost to *A* of producing 10 units of fuel is the 5 food units a labor hour could have produced. The cost per fuel unit is 5/10 or 1/2 food unit. Similarly, the opportunity cost to *A* of producing 5 units of food is 10 fuel units or 2 fuel units for each food unit. In *B*, the cost of producing 10 fuel units is the 2 food units a labor hour could have produced, or 1/5 food unit per fuel unit. *B*'s cost of producing 2 food units is 10 fuel units or 5 fuel units for each food unit. Opportunity costs are shown in Table 7.

A's opportunity cost is lower for food production and *B*'s is lower for fuel production. Each unit of fuel requires a smaller opportunity cost in *B*. We say that *B* has comparative advantage in the production of fuel. Similarly, *A* has comparative advantage in food production.

Again, specialization and trade will increase total production. Without trade and using half their resources in food and half in fuel, the two countries produce the quantities shown at the left in Table 8. With specialization and trade based on comparative advantage, total production is as shown at the right. Total world output is increased when nations specialize according to the principle of comparative advantage.

Table 8 **The Benefits of Specialization According to Comparative Advantage**

	Production without trade		Production with trade	
	Fuel	Food	Fuel	Food
Country A	500	250	0	500
Country B	500	100	1,000	0
Total	1,000	350	1,000	500

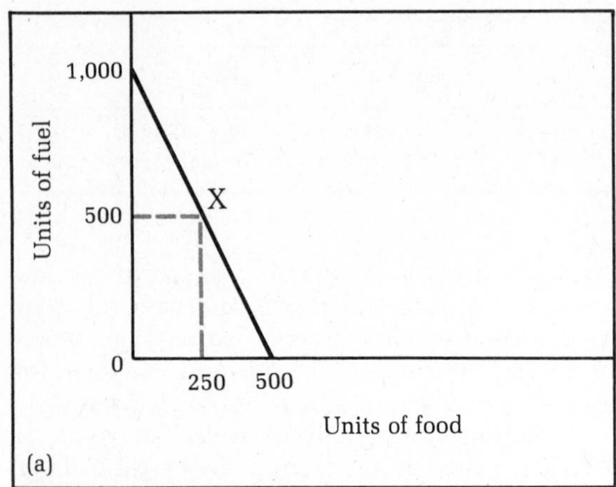

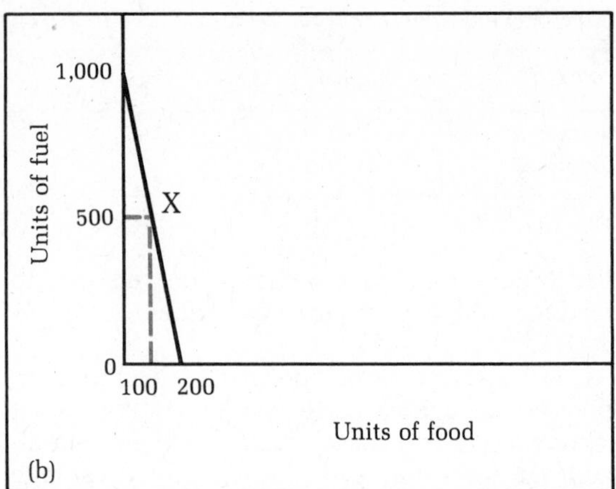

Figure 6 Production possibilities for: (a) country *A* and (b) country *B*. Country *A* has absolute advantage for producing food, while *B* has comparative advantage for producing fuel. If they do not trade, each must be self-sufficient—at point X. Total output without trade is 250 + 100 = 350 units of food and 500 + 500 = 1000 units of fuel.

Combined Production Possibilities

Production-possibilities curves show the benefits of specialization according to comparative advantage. Without trade the two nations must be self-sufficient, allocating half their resources to the production of each commodity. Consumers are limited to the combination of goods available on their nation's production-possibilities curve. The curves for *A* and *B* are shown in Figure 6.

Using one hundred labor hours, *A* can produce 1,000 units of fuel or 500 of food. *B* can produce 1,000 units of fuel or 200 units of food.

The production-possibilities curves are drawn as straight lines for simplicity. Movement from total specialization in fuel to 500 units of food requires an opportunity cost of 2 fuel units in *A* and 5 fuel units in *B* for each food unit produced. Each curve has been drawn with a constant slope, but the steeper slope for *B* indicates *B*'s higher opportunity cost for food. Without trade and with national self-sufficiency, the nations produce and consume at the level designated by point *X*.

Now suppose the economies combine production possibilities through trade. Total production possibilities are shown in Figure 7. Global specialization in fuel would yield 1,000 + 1,000 = 2,000 fuel units, as shown on the vertical axis. Global specialization in food would yield 500 + 200 = 700 food units.

However, if *A* specializes in the production of food and *B* in fuel, total yield is 1,000 fuel units and 500 food units. Movement from global specialization in fuel requires an opportunity cost of only two units of fuel per unit of food. This is because of *A*'s comparative advantage in the production of food. Movement of *A*'s resources into food production requires a sacrifice of only two units of fuel until *A* is finally fully specializing in food. (To move beyond this point would require the use of *B*'s resources in food production at an opportunity cost of five units for each unit of food.)

The Rate of Exchange on Traded Goods

With combined production possibilities, *A* and *B* can produce and consume a larger total. Again compare production after trade with production before trade in Table 8. Specialization and trade yield an additional 150 units of food. How will the larger total output be distributed between the two nations?

The answer depends on exchange rates. **Exchange rates** measure the relative value each nation places on the goods exchanged in international trade. The relative value is based on the strength of demand in each country and on the supply costs of production.

First, let us assume that consumer demand for the two goods is identical in both nations. This allows us to compare their production costs alone. Refer back to Table 7 for opportunity costs in the two countries. Assume that *A* specializes in the production of food, where its opportunity cost is lower. *A*'s food is exchanged

Table 9 **Consumption after Trade**

	Fuel	Food
Country A	500	375
Country B	500	125
Total	1000	500

for *B*'s fuel. *A* will be willing to exchange food for at least 2 units of fuel, its costs of production. *A* will not accept fewer than 2 units. *B* will be willing to pay up to 5 units of fuel, the opportunity cost of producing food domestically. *B* will not pay more than 5 units. Thus the *exchange rate* for a unit of food must fall between 2 and 5 units of fuel:

1 unit of food = 2 units of fuel to 5 units of fuel.

At the same time, *B* is specializing in the production of fuel. *B* will be willing to exchange its fuel for at least 1/5 unit of food, its costs of production. *B* will not accept less than 1/5 unit. *A* will be willing to pay up to 1/2 unit of food, the opportunity cost of producing fuel domestically. *A* will not pay more than 1/2 unit of food:

1 unit of fuel = 1/5 unit of food to 1/2 unit of food.

The exact value of the exchange rate is determined by the strength of demand in the two nations. If food is the more essential good, its price, or exchange rate, will be higher. The exchange rate will lie near the upper limit of the acceptable range:

1 unit of food = 4 units of fuel.

The high value of food implies a correspondingly low value for fuel near the lower limit of the acceptable range:

1 unit of fuel = 1/4 unit of food.

When food is the more highly valued good, the nation producing food will enjoy a larger share of total production. *A*'s producers will receive four units of fuel for each unit of food they export. When fuel is less highly valued, producers of fuel in *B* will receive a smaller share of total output. Producers of fuel in *B* must give up more units of fuel for each unit of food they import.

Even so, consumers in both nations will benefit from trade. Refer again to Table 8, showing production before and after specialization. Assume that *B*'s fuel is to be exchanged for food at an exchange rate of 1 fuel unit = 1/4 food units. In order that *B*'s consumers might enjoy the same level of fuel as before trade, we will allow them to keep 500 units and trade the remaining 500 units. Exchanging four fuel units for one food unit yields a total of 125 food units, 25 more units than *B* consumed before trade.

A must pay only 1/4 food unit for each fuel unit received. To receive 500 fuel units, *A* pays a total of 125 food units. This leaves *A* with 375 food units, 125 more than *A* consumed before trade. Table 9 summarizes these results and shows consumption by each nation after trading. Compare this with Table 8, which shows consumption without the benefit of trade.

Specialization increased total production by 150 food units. Of the greater output, 125 additional units were consumed in *A* and 25 additional units were consumed in *B*. Both nations gained. *A*'s gain was greater because *A*'s resources are more productive in the more highly valued commodity. *A*'s gains from trade will enable it to expand production, focusing research and development efforts on technical progress in food production.

B's gains are not as great, but any gain is a

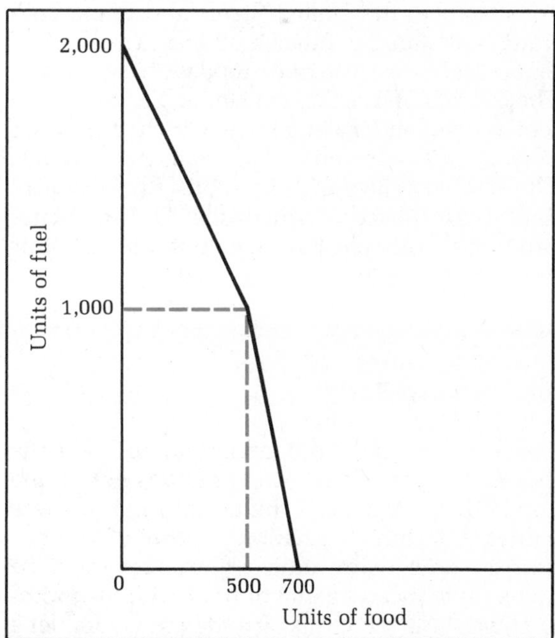

Figure 7 If country *A* specializes in food, *B* in fuel, and both trade, the world is better off because 1000 units of fuel and 500 units of food are produced. The world has 150 more units of food with specialization.

plus. Furthermore, world economic conditions are constantly changing, altering the structure of gains from trade among nations. Cost relationships change as natural resource endowments are depleted. A nation's comparative advantage may shift as certain types of production become more costly. Or a nation may increase its resource capabilities through capital investment. Comparative advantage may then shift toward the production of goods requiring heavy use of capital.

World demand may change also. Industrial development may increase the value of fuel relative to food. Or the spread of scientific agriculture may reduce a particular nation's cost advantage in food production.

Changing world conditions may gradually alter trading relationships, shifting the benefits of trade from one nation to another. New conditions may provide nations with incentives for industrial development that were previously lacking. So the benefits from trade need not be equally divided, but the world will still be better off with trade than without it.

In the real world, there are more than two trading partners and more than two products traded. Clearly, this makes the results more complicated than in our simple example. But the principle of comparative advantage still applies. For instance, the United States and Brazil both trade with many other nations. The United States and Brazil also trade food with each other. The exports of Brazil to the United States are coffee, cocoa, and bananas, in which Brazil has both an absolute and a comparative advantage. The United States in turn sends Brazil wheat, rice, and tobacco, which the United States produces with comparative, but not absolute advantage.

Changing Terms of Trade and National Power

As we have pointed out, an exchange rate is the measure of the relative value nations put on the goods they exchange. The actual ratio of these values determines a nation's **terms of trade**—that is, how many units of product must be given up to receive a unit of product from another country. If the terms of trade are favorable, a nation gives up fewer units of product than it receives. Favorable terms of trade depend on the market value of the goods traded. Put simply, if there were more demand for apples to keep the world from starving than for gasoline to keep it on wheels, nations with apple trees would enjoy more favorable terms of trade than nations with oil wells.

Favorable terms of trade enhance national power. Unfavorable terms of trade may condemn a nation to prolonged backwardness. Many less developed nations need capital equipment to build an industrialized economy. They complain that the cost of such equipment has increased. Manufacturing nations, they say, have the power to force them to pay high prices because their need is so desperate. Manufacturing nations demand more and more units of their raw materials in exchange for fewer and fewer units of machines as the needs of the less developed nations grow.

Manufacturing nations say this is untrue. A thorough analysis of price trends, they say, shows that the terms of trade have not shifted in this manner. Improved technology and vigorous competition in the manufacturing nations may have actually reduced prices of capital equipment relative to prices of raw materials.

Be that as it may, the argument goes on. And there can be no doubt that many of the commodity-producing nations are among the most backward in the world. What can such nations do to prevent deterioration of their terms of trade? Or to change the terms in their favor? They can band together to form a *cartel* to increase their economic power in the world.

A **cartel** is an international monopoly that sets prices and allocates output. The Organization of Petroleum Exporting Countries (OPEC) is an outstanding example. The economic power of OPEC is evident to drivers of cars and users of other petroleum products throughout the world. Coffee-producing nations of Latin America have entered into similar agreements to restrict output and raise prices—though they are not as effective as the OPEC cartel. Third World producers of bauxite have also combined their interests for economic advantage. They produce half the world's supply of this commodity. Banded together, they can exert considerable economic power.

Still, for many nations of the Third World, specialization in commodities has great risks. If world demand changes suddenly, a nation may not be able to sell its specialty. Moreover, advanced nations may develop a cheap synthetic to compete with its natural resources and undercut its entire market. Or the raw commodity itself may gradually disappear from the

Extended Example Changing Terms of Trade

Nations gain power through their capacity to cheaply produce goods and services in demand in world markets. Production of highly valued items gives a nation favorable terms of trade: Export of its specialty enables it to import larger amounts of goods and services produced abroad. Market conditions change, however, on both the demand side and the supply side. Terms of trade shift and change the pattern of benefits from world trade.

In 1941 U.S. markets were cut off from supplies of natural rubber grown on the plantations of Southeast Asia. Malaysia, Indonesia, and Thailand were unable to ship rubber because of invasion and war at sea. Research into the production of synthetic rubber had only just begun, but the U.S. government invested $700 million in about fifty private firms for the production of synthetic rubber. By war's end, we were producing about a million tons a year.

The development costs for producing synthetic rubber were high—too high for private industry to manage alone, particularly when natural rubber was cheap. But once the technology was available and capital in place, the synthetic product gained a hold on the market at about half the price of natural rubber. Plants have since been built in Eastern Europe, South Korea, India, Brazil, and Argentina. In the United States, research is proceeding into cultivation of guayule, a desert plant that produces rubber. The high cost of natural rubber and the availability of a substitute have changed the terms of trade sharply against Southeast Asian producers.

The story of synthetic rubber may have a parallel today. Rising world demand for Arab oil has produced strongly favorable terms of trade for oil-producing nations. Every year their oil exports earn more in terms of imports of goods and services produced in Europe, Japan, and the United States. At one time, war prevented shipments of any oil at all, and the threat of further restraints on oil supplies hangs over the industrialized world.

Can we follow the pattern of World War II—develop substitutes for oil, and shift the terms of trade in favor of the United States? In 1977, the Carter Administration proposed an Energy Security Corporation, which would provide direct loans, guaranteed loans, and price guarantees for firms engaged in energy research. The expected total expenditure of $88 billion would dwarf the spending on synthetic rubber, and the goal is production of 130 million tons a year. The Energy Mobilization Board would cut through red tape to guide development of alternative energy sources and to deal with environmental costs. Private firms are given encouragement to exchange information and coordinate efforts in the direction of energy self-sufficiency.

How did the changes described above affect the economic development of the Southeast Asian countries involved? How is this situation similar to that of other less developed countries today? How are oil-producing nations attempting to avoid these same results?

nation through continued exploitation. The east African nation of Kenya has been threatened by this very result. For many years, a major export was animal products: wild animal skins, tusks, and carcasses. Little by little, trade was depleting Kenya of an important resource that attracted tourists to the country. Finally, in 1977, the government imposed a ban on further shipments of animal products. In the future, Kenya would like to specialize in providing services to tourists, rather than in exporting its valuable animal resources.

Diversification may be one answer to the risks involved in specialization. Third World nations might divert more of their export earnings toward building an industrial economy. They might increase government spending for public health and education. This, in turn, could lead to increased work skills and technological progress within their borders. A diversity of exportable products is a good hedge against unfavorable changes in terms of trade.

The United States is not immune to the ups and downs of changing terms of trade. Production of many of the products we once made for our own use and for export has slowed. Changing world conditions have altered our areas of specialization. You have only to look at the brand names of your TV set, your phonograph, and your tape recorder to know this is true. Changing terms of trade have led us to import many of these products from West Germany

Viewpoint The North-South Dilemma

Rising energy costs and the worldwide recessions of the 1970s were especially damaging to less developed countries, or LDCs. While import bills were rising, demand for their commodity exports fell off. The result was increasing indebtedness, falling standards of living, and a reduced capacity for economic development.

Something had to be done.

Most of the LDCs fall in the Southern hemisphere. The widening gap between their incomes and those of Northern industrialized nations led to demands for new trade policies. The problem was brought before the United Nations Conference on Trade and Development (UNSTAD) in 1979 with the goal of easing North-South tensions through new international agreements.

The debate centers on the terms of trade between LDCs and industrialized nations. Representatives of commodity-exporting nations point to the wide fluctuations in prices of raw materials they sell in world markets. In the case of many raw commodities, price changes have little effect on the quantity supplied; supplies of sugar, rubber, and sisal hemp, for instance, are not very responsive to changes in price. The result is widely fluctuating prices. In years of high demand relative to supply, prices rise sharply, raising production costs in the manufacturing industries of importing nations. Because prices of manufactured goods seldom fall, the effect is a permanent inflationary trend in the prices of manufactured goods traded. On the other hand, years of low demand relative to supply mean falling commodity prices and reduced purchasing power for the LDCs. Widely fluctuating incomes produce other harmful effects.

The risks associated with resource development slow capital investment in the LDCs and keep resource costs higher than they might otherwise be. LDC representatives argue that price stability in commodity exports would help smooth out this worldwide "stop-go" cycle in trade. Furthermore, greater stability would help moderate inflation, and it would encourage investment in LDCs. These nations want agreements that would help smooth the flow of their commodity exports and keep their revenues more stable.

Some commodity agreements have been in effect for years. They involve mainly food and fiber exports and basic industrial materials. The oldest formal agreement is the International Tin Agreement, established in 1956. Members are the seven leading tin producers, which include Malaysia and Bolivia (the largest producers) and some importing nations. Exporting nations contribute to a fund that is used to purchase tin in years when supply is greater than private demand at current prices. Without the fund, prices would fall and revenues of exporting nations would suffer. The fund gradually accumulates a buffer stock of tin to be sold in years when supply is less than private demand at current prices. Without the buffer stock, prices would rise and contribute to world inflation.

The buffer stock of tin is now about one tenth of world annual sales. The fund is used to buy tin when price falls below an established floor; sales are made when price rises above an established ceiling. The result of purchases and sales is a profit for the fund. Average earnings for exporters have not changed, but cyclical fluctuations have levelled off.

Other agreements in coffee and cocoa have been less effective in recent years because of poor harvests. There are proposals to buy buffer stocks for sugar, copper, cotton, rubber, tea, jute, and sisal.

Many economists doubt the wisdom of any such restrictions on free trade. Price guarantees could lead to inefficiency in resource allocation and higher production costs throughout industry. There is the suspi-

and Japan. Brazil, with cheap hides available from herds of the pampas, sells the United States millions of shoes a year. And the sneakers you wear more likely came from Taiwan than from Massachusetts (which, at one time, produced nearly all the shoes sold in this country).

This does not mean that the United States has become a have-not nation. Our resource capacity is vast. We are able to alter our areas of specialization to meet changing trends. Our technology and our investment in human capital allow us to export sophisticated computer equipment, aircraft, nuclear power plants, and other goods and services. Progress in agricultural technology—complex planting and harvesting devices, techniques for fast freezing of perishable meat and poultry—enable us to help feed the world.

cion that poor nations are more interested in price *increases* than in price *stabilization;* if that is the case, any future attempt to hold prices down would lead to resistance. Furthermore, the cost of storing buffer stocks adds to the final price of all goods using the stored commodity.

There is another element which bears on this question. In many LDCs pressure is building to establish more complete control of supplies—following the example of the OPEC petroleum cartel. Commodity agreements could be a first step in that direction. On the other hand, they could be a means of forestalling that kind of pressure and for redistributing some of the world's income in favor of poor nations.

Probably the best hope for the LDCs lies in fundamental changes in production processes around the world. Developed nations are beginning to experience serious shortages of energy and other materials, and they are becoming more concerned about industrial pollution. Many LDCs have vast potential for clean hydroelectric power and are hungry for industrial development. They have the labor and the energy for manufacture. Moreover, processing and manufacturing near the source of raw materials may turn out to be more economically efficient, producing gains for the LDCs.

Regrettably, development of manufacturing industries is often limited by restraints on import sales into industrialized nations. LDCs would like these restraints removed, and they would like special aid programs to speed their development.

Demonstrate graphically (1) the microeconomic and (2) the macroeconomic aspects of commodity agreements in the LDCs. What are the effects in importing countries? How could a commodity agreement become a cartel?

The United States will continue to trade on favorable terms if we maintain our ability to react constructively to changing trends. Our technical superiority and our material and human resources can give us the power to export our products on favorable terms. They can also enable us to import the foreign commodities and consumer goods we need and enjoy.

SUMMARY

The growth in benefits that nations enjoy from specialization and exchange are synergistic effects of world trade. The microeconomic aspects of trade involve supply and demand in domestic markets. Without trade, equilibrium price and quantity depend on production costs in separate national markets. In any single nation, scarce, high-priced goods will be consumed in small quantities and their marginal utility will be high. Plentiful, low-priced goods will be consumed in larger quantities and their marginal utility will be low. Trade among several nations enables exchange of goods providing low marginal utility for other goods which provide higher marginal utility. Total world utility is increased.

Specialization yields further benefits when improved methods of production lead to falling unit costs. Moreover, specialization and trade help adjust incomes worldwide, raising incomes for resources used in a nation's specialty and reducing incomes for others. The total benefits of added production are greater than the loss of income to those displaced.

The macroeconomic aspects of trade involve the relative value of total exports and imports. Net exports are included in aggregate demand and help determine the level of output, income, and employment: $C + I + G + X_n = GNP$. Changes in X_n produce multiple effects on output in both an upward and a downward direction. A decline in trade after World War I contributed to the severity of the Great Depression among Western industrialized nations.

A nation's resource allocation helps determine its specialization. The United States has changed from a land-abundant nation exporting raw materials to a capital-abundant nation specializing in capital-intensive products for export. Some important exports are characterized as human-capital intensive.

When a nation produces a particular good or service more cheaply than another in terms of resources used, it is said to have absolute advantage in production. When two nations specialize according to absolute advantage and engage in trade, total production possibilities are increased. Modern industrialized nations often enjoy absolute advantage in production of both manufactured goods and raw materials. Developing nations have absolute advantage in only a narrow range of commodities for export.

Lacking absolute advantage in production, a nation will still enjoy comparative advantage. Comparative advantage exists when production costs are lower in terms of other goods which could have been produced instead: the familiar opportunity costs. Again, specialization according to comparative advantage increases total world output.

Comparative costs of production and the strength of demand worldwide determine exchange rates on traded goods. In turn, the exchange rate determines the units of exports a nation must give up in order to receive a unit of imports; its terms of trade. Favorable terms of trade enhance a nation's wealth and power and enable it to accumulate productive capital.

Key Words and Phrases

absolute advantage a condition in which a nation produces some good or service using fewer resources per unit of output than other nations.

cartel an international monopoly that allocates output and sets prices for some good (usually a raw material).

comparative advantage a condition in which a nation produces some good or service at a lower cost in terms of the opportunity cost of other goods which could have been produced.

exchange rate the relative value placed on units of goods traded for units of other goods.

foreign trade multiplier a measure of the multiple effects on output, income, and employment in a nation when it is able to sell goods abroad.

specialization and division of labor concentrating efforts on the production of certain goods and services.

synergism a condition in which the total result of some activity is greater than the sum of the results of individual activities taken separately.

terms of trade the relative quantities of imported goods received compared to quantities of exports.

Questions for Review

1. In our discussion of the microeconomic aspects of trade, we assumed no transportation costs. How would including transportation costs affect the conclusions we reached? How does this help explain why food is more expensive in the Bahama Islands than it is in Florida?
2. Explain how specialization may cause unit production costs to fall. What circumstances would cause unit production costs to rise with specialization?
3. How can specialization and trade reduce incomes for some groups? In what way is this an advantage to the world economy?
4. Are there other disadvantages of specialization and division of labor? Cite current examples.
5. How would you explain Brazil's absolute advantage in the production of coffee? What are the resource costs of coffee production? Does Brazil also have comparative advantage in coffee production? How would you describe the cost of coffee production in terms of computers not produced?
6. Explain how comparative advantage is related to opportunity costs. How are opportunity costs reflected on a nation's production-possibilities curve?
7. Explain what happens when the foreign trade multiplier takes effect. Use an example from current news: increased oil imports from OPEC nations, reduced coffee exports from Brazil, increased television sales from Japan, revival of tourism in Cuba.
8. The hypothetical data below show the quantities of fuel and food that can be produced in country *A* or country *B* per unit of resource. Which nation has absolute advantage in fuel production? in food production? Which nation has comparative advantage in fuel production? in food production? What is the opportunity cost of fuel in terms of food in *A*? in *B*? Assume each nation has one hundred resource units. What is the change in output following specialization if we assume resources were formerly equally divided between the two goods? How does this example differ from the example given in the text? Why?

Output per Unit of Resource

	Fuel	Food
Country A	5	8
Country B	4	6

9. There's an island off the Florida coast named Cedar Key because of the great cedar trees that once grew there. There was also a flourishing pencil factory, and the natives grew prosperous from the sale of the island's product. Today there is very little industry and the inhabitants are no longer prosperous. Can you speculate as to what went wrong?
10. American aluminum companies buy bauxite from Jamaica for $25 a ton (1974). The cost to produce aluminum from low-grade clay in the United States is $40 a ton. How does this information help determine the exchange rate for bauxite? What other circumstances are involved in determining a nation's terms of trade?

CHAPTER 21

International Commercial Policies and Institutions

Learning Objectives

Upon completion of this chapter, you should be able to:

1. Explain with graphs how tariffs affect a good's price and quantity sold.
2. Give four arguments in favor of tariffs.
3. Explain both verbally and with graphs how quotas, export duties, export subsidies, and foreign exchange controls affect trade.
4. Discuss the highlights of international trade agreements and U.S. tariff actions since World War I.
5. Explain how the International Monetary Fund works.
6. Explain how customs unions and free trade areas work, citing actual examples.
7. Discuss current international financial problems.

We have described the theory of trade and the benefits that flow from trade. In this chapter, we will discuss the policies and institutions that nations use to regulate trade, to increase the benefits and reduce the problems. A single nation's policy may enhance the benefits for all nations or cause added problems for others. In a world of interdependent nations, cooperative policies and institutions are becoming increasingly necessary to ensure maximum trade opportunities for all.

POLICIES TO PROTECT DOMESTIC INDUSTRIES

When nations trade, consumers may choose high-quality, low-cost items from producers the world over. International competition brings benefits for consumers and efficiency in the use of world resources. But it may create problems for domestic producers of lower-quality, higher-cost items. When this is true, producers may demand protection from imports through tariffs, quotas on some imported products, and even outright prohibition of certain imports. Protectionist sentiment is especially strong in periods of reduced economic activity, with unemployment and low incomes in domestic industries. Policies of trade restriction aimed at protecting domestic producers, **protectionism,** may be effected or strengthened.

Tariffs

The most common protectionist device is a tariff—a tax on imported goods. Tariffs may be *revenue tariffs* or *protective tariffs*. **Revenue tariffs** are not designed to hamper free trade; they are designed only to secure revenue for the importing nation. Therefore, the tariff rate must be low enough not to discourage imports. In the United States, revenue tariffs (custom duties) accounted for most of the government's revenue until introduction of the income tax in 1913. (Long before that, a revenue tariff on tea led to a party in Boston Harbor that helped change world history.)

Protective tariffs are designed to raise the selling price of imported products. The nation's consumers will consequently buy fewer of these goods and more goods produced by domestic industries. Sometimes the tariffs are set so high that they become *prohibitive:* no purchases of foreign-made goods can be made at all. Protective tariffs may also be *preferential*. That is, they impose a lower rate on the products of one nation than on those of another. Blocs of nations often use such tariffs to favor members of the group.

Figure 1 illustrates the effect of a tariff in domestic markets. The model shows domestic demand for a foreign good, in this case Japanese motorcycles. Before the imposition of a tariff, the supply curve is as shown by *S*. At equilibrium, buyers will purchase 1000 units per month at a unit price of $2000.

But cycle imports reduce the X_n component of aggregate demand and threaten unemployment in domestic industries. (Remember that X_n equals the value of exports minus the value of imports.) Consequently, the importing nation may decide to levy a tariff to reduce cycle imports and raise domestic production.

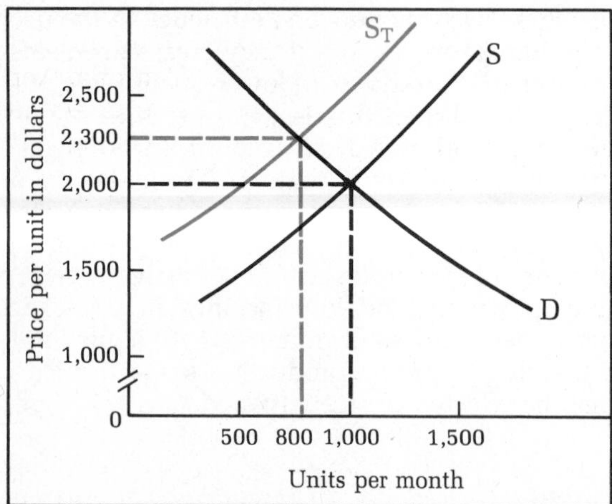

Figure 1 The effect of a tariff on an imported good like Japanese motorcycles. A $500 tariff adds $500 to the supply cost of each motorcycle. Supply shifts up from S to S_T. The equilibrium price rises $300, from $2000 to $2300. Quantity sold falls from 1000 to 800.

A tariff of $500 per unit shifts the supply curve upward by $500 at each quantity, as shown by the curve S_T. Equilibrium price and quantity after a tariff is imposed are shown at the intersection of demand (*D*) and S_T. Only 800 units will be bought at a price of $2300. Of this unit price, $500 is collected by customs officials and $1800 is paid to the Japanese manufacturer.

American consumers must pay a higher unit price and will also enjoy fewer units of the imported item. But the X_n component of aggregate demand will rise with the fall in imports. Furthermore, many buyers will shift their purchases to American-made cycles, raising income and employment in the domestic economy.

Final results are not always as planned, however. Restrictions on U.S. imports also restrict the export sales of foreign producers. Workers in foreign nations will lose jobs. To avoid loss of jobs and a general decline in economic activity, other nations may retaliate by imposing tariffs of their own.

Retaliatory tariffs will restrict U.S. sales to foreign consumers. A drop in U.S. export sales will cause a decline in net exports. The X_n component of aggregate demand shifts downward, with multiple contractionary effects on domestic output and employment. The only real beneficiaries of the tariff may be U.S. motorcycle manufacturers.

It is easy to see why protectionism is called a "beggar thy neighbor" policy. It is also clear that thy neighbor can just as easily beggar thee. If tariffs are likely to produce these unfavorable results, why are they ever used? There are some fairly persuasive arguments in favor of tariffs.

The infant-industry argument. One argument in favor of tariffs is that they protect new domestic industry. Without a tariff, established competitors in other countries would undersell a beginning industry and prevent it from ever reaching efficient operation. Supporters of **infant-industry tariffs** want to exclude import competition until the new industry gets on its feet.

Such tariffs were useful during our own early years as a nation, when our industries were just beginning to develop. Even today, many developing nations employ tariffs to protect their young industries. Successful industrial growth will help these nations diversify their economies.

A disadvantage of infant-industry tariffs is the industry's unwillingness ever to see the tariff removed. After years of a protected domestic market, producers are often reluctant to move out into the real world of free competition. Infant-industry protection may have other unhealthy effects on productive efficiency. The exclusion of competition may discourage technical development and reduce incentives to cut production costs. The "infant" may never grow up. The end result of infant-industry tariffs may thus be slower economic growth, a lessened ability to compete in world markets, and higher domestic prices.

The strategic-industry argument. The objective of some tariffs is to protect an industry that produces goods vital to a nation's defense. In the case of a *strategic industry*, productive efficiency relative to that of other nations may not be an important consideration. The domestic industry—oil, natural gas, shipping, or steel, for example—may require protection because of its importance to national defense. Without protection, such industries might be weakened by foreign competition. Then, in an international crisis, the nation might find itself in short supply of products essential to national defense.

The argument for a **strategic-industry tariff** seems reasonable on first hearing. However, it is difficult, if not impossible, to determine precisely which industries are essential to a nation's defense. Almost all industries would be able to cite good reasons why their products are "essential" to the defense effort.

In any case, economists generally recommend policies other than tariffs to protect domestic producers of strategic goods or materials. A tax-supported subsidy may accomplish the desired results. A subsidy is a direct payment for a specific objective. It can be made subject to strict control and quick termination. It is also subject to periodic review by Congress. Consequently, it is a more flexible form of industrial support than a tariff.

In the United States, subsidies are awarded to the merchant marine industry to overcome its cost disadvantage relative to foreign shippers. Tariffs and quotas have been used to protect domestic producers of essential energy supplies. As a result, prices are higher for some products than they otherwise might be, but producers are expected to use some portion of their profits for industry expansion. In this way, the nation will have a ready supply in case of national emergency.

The production-costs argument. A common complaint of U.S. producers, especially in the 1950s and 1960s, has been that the wage rates of American workers are too high. The resulting high production costs, it is argued, call for a **production-costs tariff** to raise the price of foreign products and prevent a drop in sales of domestic goods. Proponents of the production-costs argument classify this as a "scientific" tariff. Supposedly, it is calculated to bring production costs in line worldwide.

An obvious criticism of this argument involves the fundamental basis for trade. Trade is possible and beneficial because of different production costs in different countries. Different production costs are the basis for comparative advantage. To equalize costs throughout the world would eliminate the need for trade altogether.

High wage rates for U.S. workers generally reflect our comparative advantage. In free markets, workers are paid according to their productivity. Well-paid U.S. workers receive high rewards because their productivity is high. Our unique combination of resources and technology permits us to produce a larger output per labor hour. As a result, labor costs *per unit of output* may actually be lower for the American worker. If this is so, no tariff on imported goods is necessary to protect the American producer.

This does not mean that all U.S. industries and jobs are secure against competition from low-cost foreign-made products. It is true only in industries where U.S. resources possess comparative advantage. Where productivity of *foreign* workers is greater and unit costs lower, the principle of comparative advantage dictates a shift of U.S. resources away from that industry.

U.S. textile manufacturers have been experiencing such a shift. Foreign producers have undercut markets for certain types of textiles. Jobs have been lost, factories have closed, and return on capital investment has dropped in the United States. The adjustment has been painful for many individuals and communities.

Fortunately, long-range benefits can accrue to the economy as a whole. The movement of

U.S. resources away from this industry (and others like it) frees resources for employment in industries in which we enjoy comparative advantage. In another industry—electronics, chemicals, or transportation equipment, for example—workers might well produce relatively greater output per unit of resource. U.S. incomes and total world output would be increased if resources shifted from industries in which their productivity is low to industries in which their productivity is high.

The terms-of-trade argument. The terms-of-trade argument for tariffs is often voiced by developing nations producing low-value commodities for export. Their export earnings on raw commodities may be insufficient to finance imports necessary for economic growth. They must solve their balance of payments problems, and to do so, they say, they must impose tariffs to improve their **terms of trade.**

Figure 2 illustrates how a tariff can improve a nation's terms of trade. A tariff on imported manufactures will shift supply curve S up by the amount of the tariff. Equilibrium price before the tariff is imposed is 0P and quantity is 0Q. The tariff *ac* shifts supply up to S_T. Equilibrium price rises to $0P_T$ and quantity falls to $0Q_T$. At the lower equilibrium quantity, unit cost to the foreign producer is measured along the supply curve S at Q_Ta. The importing nation pays out a smaller price for each unit of manufactured goods imported and the remainder is collected as tariff.

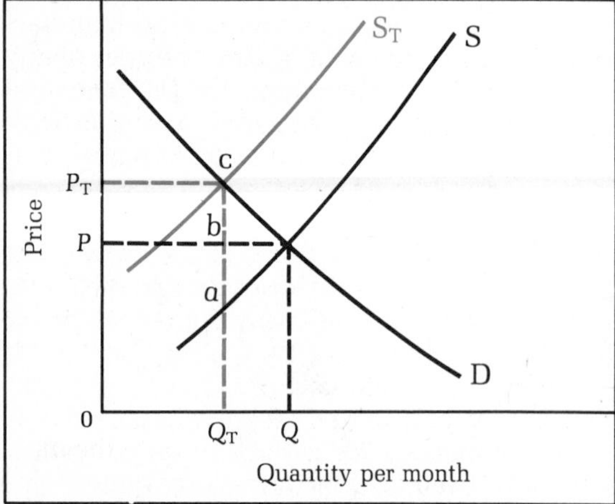

Figure 2 Use of a tariff to improve terms of trade. Tariff *ac* moves supply from S to S_T. The new equilibrium price is P_T and the new equilibrium quantity is Q_T. Producers receive Q_Ta of the higher price. The tariff *ac* is shared by consumers and producers; consumers pay *bc* and producers pay *ab*.

With the tariff, the amount foreign producers receive for their product is lower by the distance *ab*. In effect, foreign producers pay *ab* of the tariff to customs officials. The remainder of the tariff *bc*, is paid by local buyers in the form of the higher total price they pay for imported goods. The terms of trade are said to be more favorable for the commodity-exporting nation because a smaller quantity of raw commodity exports must be paid out for each unit of manufactured imports.

As noted above, the terms-of-trade argument for tariffs is often made by developing countries. Yet tariffs can be particularly damaging to a developing nation. Its imports are often necessary to aid industrial development and to satisfy the material needs of its people. With the tariff, the domestic price of imports will increase, raising the cost of economic development. Furthermore, a retaliatory tariff on the developing nation's commodity exports would aggravate the problem.

Actually, a tariff may not improve a nation's terms of trade at all. If domestic demand for imports is inelastic, purchases will remain the same despite the higher price.* In this case, the entire burden of the tariff is shifted to local buyers. Outpayments remain high, and the domestic economy pays higher prices for necessary imports.

Each of the arguments favoring tariffs is plausible. But each has the effect of encouraging and prolonging inefficiency in the allocation of scarce resources. Because of the long-range harmful effects of tariffs, most economists recommend monetary and fiscal policies to correct short-run problems of domestic unemployment. Appropriate expansionary policies can produce healthy changes in output, income, and employment. They need not produce the economic distortions and the retaliatory measures likely with a tariff.

Other Barriers to Trade

Quotas Tariffs are the most common form of trade restriction, but there are others. An especially damaging trade barrier is the quota. **Quo-**

*To say that demand is inelastic means that buyers will purchase roughly the same quantity regardless of price. If this is true, price will rise by the full amount of the tariff and the portion paid to the foreign producer will remain the same.

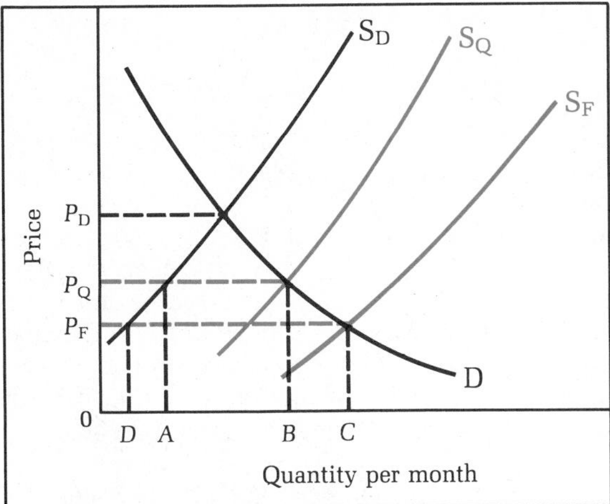

Figure 3 A quota affects supply. S_D is domestic supply; S_Q is the sum of domestic supply and the amount supplied by the quota; S_F is what the supply would be without a quota. The quota permits an imported quantity of only AB. Without a quota, quantity imported would be larger—DC—and price would be lower—P_F. Notice the effect of the quota on domestic production: With the quota, domestic production is 0A; without it, production falls to 0D.

tas set limits on the quantity of imported goods. In the United States, quotas have been used to limit imports of certain kinds of steel, petroleum, textile products, and other goods. In 1959, for example, quotas were placed on Arab petroleum imports into the United States to protect U.S. producers and keep prices from falling!

Figure 3 illustrates the effect of a quota on the domestic market for specialty steel. Demand, D, is the sum of the U.S. industrial demand for steel, whether produced domestically or imported. Supply, S_D, is the sum of supplies offered for sale by domestic producers alone. Total supply, S_Q, is equal to domestic supply plus the import quota. Without a quota, foreign producers would supply a larger quantity, making total supply S_F.

At an equilibrium price of $0P_Q$, the quantity 0A is supplied by foreign producers. Steel prices are lower (at $0P_Q$) than they would be without trade, at $0P_D$. But without a quota, foreign supply would be larger and price even lower, at $0P_F$. Moreover, the quota places limits on the increase in supply if demand should increase. As industrial needs grow, additional supply must come from local sources alone, at higher prices; foreign firms are unable to increase their sales in the protected market.

In spite of the damaging effects of a tariff, at least it enables imports to increase. Buyers who are willing to pay the tariff are able to increase their purchases without restrictions. For this reason, a tariff, while objectionable, is still preferable to a quota.

Export duties and subsidies. **Export duties** are taxes paid by exporters on goods shipped abroad. The objective is to reduce the profitability of export sales in order to retain goods for domestic markets. Governments occasionally impose export duties to reduce exports of valuable commodities. **Export subsidies** have the opposite effect. They are payments to exporters for goods sold abroad. A portion of the production cost of an exported good is returned, in effect, by government to the producer.* This allows exporters to reduce their prices in foreign markets and undersell domestic competitors. Some nations subsidize their national airlines—Air France, for example, or British Airways. In the United States, privately owned airlines complain that this gives foreign airlines an unfair advantage in international transport competition.

Governments of importing nations are usually aware of the use of subsidies to reduce import prices below domestic competitors. When possible, these governments impose **countervailing duties** on the import. Countervailing duties add a tariff to bring the final selling price in line with domestic prices. The result is to capture the subsidy for the importing nation.

Some nations impose **quality standards on imports.** The effect is to protect local manufacturers without imposing quotas or duties of any kind. In the United States, for instance, imported automobiles are required to have antipollution equipment and to meet other design and safety specifications. Florida tomato farmers once attempted to block imports of Mexican tomatoes by establishing size requirements, but the regulation was not allowed. Quality standards like these may be difficult or impossible for foreign producers to meet. They may effectively limit a nation's imports.

Foreign exchange controls. Perhaps the most serious interference with free trade comes from **foreign exchange controls.** Such policies are

*In Europe this is accomplished by refunding to exporters the Value Added Tax (VAT) paid on goods, enabling them to be sold abroad at lower prices. In the United States the chief taxes charged in the production costs of goods are corporate income taxes, which are much more difficult to measure and refund.

Extended Example Pressure for Protection

The 1950s and 1960s were prosperous decades for industrialized nations. Broad, worldwide reductions in tariff barriers played a large part in stimulating production and employment and in increasing real incomes. Regrettably, the 1970s brought a whole new set of economic circumstances. Rising OPEC oil prices shoved many nations into international payments deficits. Recessions with persistent unemployment and staggering inflation led to calls for new trade policies.

National political leaders tend to seek policies that will improve their own nation's economic position. Interest groups at home apply pressure for policies that favor their particular industries. Labor unions lobby for policies to preserve jobs. Some of the loudest calls for protectionist barriers have been occurring here in the United States. The greatest pressure for protection has been in steel, electronics, sugar, shoes, and textiles.

U.S. trade policy is proposed by the International Trade Commission and the U.S. Treasury under the Trade Act of 1974 and within broad guidelines set through membership in the General Agreement on Tariffs and Trade (GATT). The President must approve recommendations for tariffs or quotas, subject to Congressional overrule. He must balance industry and union arguments for protection against the higher consumer prices which result from restrictions on trade. He must consider the long-range resource costs of protecting a domestic industry which may be less efficient than foreign producers. Even more importantly, he must consider the dangers of foreign retaliation against U.S. exports.

Steel Domestic steel producers have been experiencing rising competition from foreigners who, by 1976, had captured about one fifth of the market for basic steel; on the West Coast, Japanese manufacturers were supplying one third of the market. In 1976 voluntary quotas on certain steel imports were arranged with Japan and were enforced also on the Common Market, Canada, and Sweden. But imports are increasing from Poland, South Africa, and Spain, where the quotas aren't applied. Quotas are permitted by U.S. trade law under its "escape clause," if imports can be shown to have injured domestic producers. The clause has been used only in the case of stainless or specialty steel. Although quotas are illegal under GATT, they can often be agreed to voluntarily among nations.

Imports of low-priced steel have forced reductions for domestic steel and cut profits, already low because of recessions. U.S. steel producers contend that low import prices are actually a result of tax rebates paid foreign producers by their governments; that is, the low prices result from a form of export subsidy. They accuse other governments of attempting to export their unemployment—increasing their own sales at the expense of American workers. The steel producers have asked our government to impose countervailing duties whenever foreign prices fall below established "trigger prices." But action is slow.

Electronics Until recently, the United States has hesitated to regard rebated taxes as export subsidies, but pressure is building to do so in electronics as well as steel. Imposition of countervailing duties will have particular impact on Japanese and Common Market sales of electronics in the United States: More than 60 percent of radios and 70 percent of televisions are imported. During the 1970s, probably 100,000 U.S. jobs in this industry alone were lost through imports. In April 1977, a New York Customs Court ruled that Japanese tax rebates were in fact export subsidies and clamped duties of roughly 15 percent on imports. The ruling was appealed and overturned, but in the meantime Japan agreed to cut its shipments of television sets to the United States by almost one half.

Sugar One of the first acts of the U.S. Congress in 1789 was to impose a tariff on sugar. Sugar producers continue to have substantial influence on trade policy. U.S. cane and beet sugar producers have been supplying more than half the domestic market. But during the 1970s low wage costs abroad reduced the world price of raw sugar below U.S. costs of production. To allow collapse of domestic production would severely damage the economies of agricultural regions in the United States and leave us open to unreasonable foreign price demands in the future. But to protect inefficiency would be costly and would invite competition from corn-based sweeteners, produced largely in Japan. In this case President Carter decided on a subsidy to local growers, raising the price of sugar by about one half. A quota was placed on sugar imports to keep prices high. As a result, Americans must spend over $1 billion more every year for soft drinks, cookies, and other sugar products.

Shoes A classic problem in trade and tariff policy is the one facing U.S. shoe manufacturers. The shoe industry began in New England more than a century ago. Because production used minimal capital and cheap labor, it was ideal for a primitive stage of industrial development. Today these same qualities make shoe manufacture attractive for nations like Italy, Spain, Taiwan, Brazil, and South Korea. Their cheap labor has enabled these nations to undersell U.S. producers. During the first half of the 1970s, more than one half of the remaining American shoe manufacturers went out of business. By 1975, almost half of U.S. sales were imports; domestic production and employment had fallen by one third. The U.S International Trade Commission recommended quotas and high tariffs on imports greater than the quota, but President Carter rejected the request. Instead he proposed some voluntary quotas and increased aid for workers displaced by foreign competition.

Under present laws, workers displaced by foreign competition may receive up to 70 percent of earnings for as much as a year, plus training in new job skills, allowances to search for work in other cities, and partial payment of moving expenses. Technical assistance and low-interest loans are also available to companies threatened by foreign competition.

Textiles Opening diplomatic ties with China in the late 1970s has aggravated the problems of the U.S. textile industry. Until recently, much trade with China was boycotted under the U.S. "trading with the enemy" act. But since trade has resumed, hundreds of millions of yards of fabric have been imported from China. China's large population is a real threat for such a labor-intensive industry in the United States.

American textile firms have been suffering for years under increasing foreign competition. In spite of voluntary quotas with fifty textile exporting countries, domestic firms' share of the U.S. market is dwindling. Part of the problem is inefficiency: Most U.S. firms are small, employing fewer than a hundred employees. Many are being forced out of business or are merging with other, larger firms for improved efficiency. Massive capital investment is needed to change the industry from labor-intensive to capital-intensive. Much of the added investment must go toward meeting new health and environmental regulations, adding to the industry's costs and reducing productivity. Recognizing the long-range peril for U.S. textile manufacture, many U.S. firms are diversifying.

Evaluate overall U.S. trade policy. What are the important arguments for and against present policy? Evaluate specific solutions in the problem industries discussed. Consider other industries facing foreign competition: autos, for example. What solutions would you suggest to their problems?

possible only if the national government has control of all currencies used in foreign exchange. Foreign trade dealings must be conducted through a nation's central bank or some other government agency. In effect, the nation controls its traders' purse strings. For example, a trader in a country with such a managed economy may wish to import American cement. The government may feel that the nation's own cement-makers need protection from foreign competition. It does not have to use tariffs or other such devices to limit imports. It merely denies the trader the currency necessary to make the trade. For cement purchases, the foreign exchange window is closed. A developing nation may close its foreign exchange window for imports of luxury items such as jewelry or automobiles and open it for items such as industrial machinery or food needed for economic development.

This type of control is sometimes an advantage to a developing country. It enables government to exercise control over international trade as a means toward economic growth. But it has the same disadvantages as other barriers to free trade: It may inhibit the operation of comparative advantage; it may limit the long-run benefits derived from free international trade; and it may easily result in collusion between government officials and business interests. Bribes may open the foreign exchange window to favored traders, so the nation's long-range plans for economic development may be frustrated.

In some nations, exchange controls lead to a system of **multiple exchange rates.** Exchange rates may be set very low for imports of capital equipment and high for luxury imports. This helps conserve foreign exchange for purchases that contribute to economic growth.

Strict control of foreign exchange is practiced by the Soviet Union. The Soviet government controls all trade and is able to manipulate all exports and imports according to national goals.

Boycotts and embargoes Boycotts and embargoes are used to halt trade altogether. A boycott is a refusal to deal with particular nations, and an embargo is a refusal to ship certain goods. Such devices are normally used in wartime, since a nation at war does not trade with its enemy. But they are also used in peacetime, for both political and economic reasons. The United States, for example, has invoked "trading-with-the-enemy" laws to boycott trade with

Cuba and North Korea. Export licenses are required on two hundred categories of products that might be used by Communist nations for strategic purposes.

In 1973, Arab oil-producing countries placed an embargo on oil shipments to the United States. These countries were not at war with America. The embargo was placed to protest against and perhaps reduce U.S. support for Israel against Egypt and Syria. For many years Arab nations have boycotted the goods of foreign companies who trade with Israel. Arab trade prohibitions may be regarded as *secondary boycotts* since the restrictions are aimed at one nation as a result of a dispute with another.

Occasionally, nations use such devices, rather than less-restrictive import and export quotas, to protect their domestic economies. In 1973, domestic shortages forced the United States to place embargoes on the export of soybeans and forty other commodities. It was felt that U.S. domestic needs at the time were simply too great to allow free trade in these products.

In 1975, an embargo was placed on shipment of U.S. grain to the Soviet Union. Russia had recently bought huge amounts, leading consumer and other interest groups to fear that depletion of our grain stock would push grain prices too high. This would cause unacceptable increases in the cost of food at home. The embargo was soon lifted, but the government persuaded U.S. grain companies to accept a moratorium—a temporary embargo—on grain shipments to world markets. It also entered into an agreement with the Soviet Union whereby Russia agreed to limit its 1976 purchases of American grain to 17 million tons. The Soviet Union also agreed to buy at least 6 million, but not more than 8 million, tons each year until 1982.* In 1980 the Soviet invasion of Afghanistan led President Carter to ban further grain sales to the U.S.S.R.

Devices such as boycotts and embargoes may be temporarily justifiable to protect a nation's vital political interests. They may be necessary to prevent domestic shortages and harmful distortions of a nation's internal economy. Nevertheless, they are barriers to the full benefits of international trade.

*Crop failures in the Soviet Union raised this issue again in 1979. Arrangements were made to increase permissible sales to perhaps 15 million tons.

Efforts to Eliminate Trade Restrictions

As we have shown, free international trade can provide benefits to the economies of all nations. Why, then, do nations put up barriers to free trade? Governments are subject to many pressure groups, who clamor for protection of their immediate interests. Organized business groups may want special advantages for their products in order to increase profits. Organized labor may support tariffs in order to keep wages high or to prevent layoffs in affected industries. Politicians are influenced by the people whose votes and financial support help keep them in office.

From enactment of the so-called *Tariff of Abominations* in 1828 until 1934, the overall trend in the United States was toward higher tariffs. In 1930, the *Smoot-Hawley Tariff* (named for the men who sponsored the bill in Congress) brought the highest rates ever imposed. Average duties amounted to 60 percent of the value of the imports covered by the legislation.

In 1930, the United States was sinking into the depths of the Great Depression. By 1934, Americans saw that high tariffs were no real answer to the great economic decline, which by then had spread throughout the world. In that year, Congress began the long process of dismantling our high-tariff structure by passing the *Reciprocal Trade Agreements Act*. The act called for reduction of U.S. tariffs as foreign nations reduced their own. The reductions could be as high as 50 percent of existing rates for cooperating nations.

Reciprocal trade agreements are two-nation agreements. A broader approach is needed if trade barriers are to be reduced worldwide. In 1947, the *General Agreement on Tariffs and Trade (GATT)* came into being. It was signed by twenty-three countries, the United States included, and now has more than eighty member nations, including some communist countries. Members of GATT participate in regular negotiations to resolve trading conflicts and to plan freer trade policies. Negotiations have led to percentage reductions of tariffs in broad product categories. Moreover, all tariff reductions are applied according to the **most-favored-nation principle.** That is, any tariff reduction is extended on nondiscriminatory terms to all members of GATT. The agreement also prohibits most import quotas.

Negotiating tariff reductions is not a simple

Extended Example Exporting Technology

One of our most valuable exports is ideas. We sell foreigners the rights to use U.S. ideas, and in return we receive royalty payments and license fees from abroad. These payments constitute an important part of our income from foreign sales.

The result is not all gravy, however. With the right to use our technology, foreign producers can make the goods we want to sell in world markets. Many can undersell us, causing us to lose comparative advantage and producing multiple effects on domestic output, income, and employment. What can be done? To forbid the export of technology would not be tolerable in our free economy and would probably lead other countries to establish similar trade barriers against the materials we need to buy. A better solution would be to increase the pace of technological development so that the United States maintains its competitive edge.

It used to be that technology traveled from nation to nation through the life cycle of a product. The innovating nation would design a product and enjoy a monopoly in its production. Gradually, production would begin in other countries, however, and the initial producer would turn to other, entirely new products. All this is happening much faster now, making it increasingly necessary to develop new products for export.

Regrettably, technical development appears to be slowing in the U.S. Expenditures for research and development are now only 2.2 percent of total national production, down from 3 percent during the 1950s and 1960s. Some critics attribute the decline in new product development to U.S. tax policies that are less favorable to research and development expenditures than the policies of other countries. High interest rates and the scarcity of risk capital are also cited. Other critics blame government regulations involving pollution control and worker safety. The effect of regulation may have been to stifle innovation and freeze production processes at obsolete levels. Probably the major reason for the decline in R & D, however, has been a lack of national commitment to capitalize on technological advances for commercial purposes.

How might you argue against critics of environmental regulation and its effects on U.S. trade? How might U.S. antitrust policy contribute to a decline in innovation?

job, particularly when nations are experiencing high domestic unemployment. This was true of the almost continuous tariff negotiations in the 1970s. Agreements in 1975 produced tariff reductions but also included clauses calling for financial aid to industries hurt by lower tariffs. The aid would be used to retrain and relocate workers in other industries. The 1975 agreements also included *escape clauses*. One such clause called for imposition of higher tariffs whenever an import reached a certain percentage of its total domestic sales—its "peril point." Some analysts regarded such provisions as a step backward toward more protectionism. The clauses could conceivably be used to postpone necessary—though painful—adjustments required by the principle of comparative advantage.

More than five years of new tariff negotiations ended in 1979. The "Tokyo Round" provided for average cuts of about one third in U.S. tariffs over the following eight years. Even more important than tariff cuts was the removal of many nontariff barriers that had kept U.S. goods out of foreign markets. The new rules permit governments to purchase aircraft and other supplies from foreign manufacturers and discourage discrimination in setting quality standards on imports. Importing nations are authorized to impose countervailing duties if exporting nations subsidize their manufactures to gain a trade advantage.

In general, U.S. industries have welcomed the results of the Tokyo Round. They feel that the small loss of tariff protection is offset by the greater freedom of world trade. Industries significantly injured by foreign competition may receive government aid for modernization to improve productivity.

Trade and Long-Run Economic Growth

If a nation is to continue to enjoy the benefits of trade, it must maintain comparative advantage in production of certain goods demanded in the

Extended Example
Responding to Import Competition

The clothing industry has a fundamental characteristic that makes it vulnerable to international competition: Fashions change quickly, so complete automation is not practical. This makes the product highly labor intensive and suitable for low-wage countries. Workers in Taiwan and Korea earn $.50 per hour compared to $4 per hour for U.S apparel workers. Even after paying tariffs of 16 percent to 32 percent, foreign manufacturers can underprice U.S. producers. This is particularly true in the markets for sweaters, woven garments, and tailored suits, which require much labor. Fifteen thousand U.S. firms employing 1.3 million workers are threatened by foreign competition.

The federal government has responded to industry cries for help by negotiating voluntary quotas with some countries, but these are difficult to enforce. Some U.S. firms are developing strategies to profit from the advantages of off-shore production. Under one arrangement a U.S. manufacturer designs and cuts fabrics in the United States and ships it to a low-wage country to be finished. A tariff is charged only on the value added abroad, helping reduce the selling price of the finished garment. Another firm provides marketing and technical advice to foreign firms and receives foreign-made goods in exchange. Other firms are increasing mechanization to increase the productivity and reduce the costs of U.S. manufacturers. Many are diversifying into brand name clothing items, which are less sensitive to import competition; such a strategy requires heavy advertising expenditures, however. Some firms are even beginning to promote exports, participating in exhibitions abroad and looking into establishing a U.S. trading company patterned after the large trading institutions in Japan.

What arguments can be made in favor of tariff protection for this industry? opposed? Discuss in terms of comparative advantage.

world economy. A favorable trading position depends on production of high-quality goods and services at low cost, so as to attract consumer spending in a foreign market. Nations strive to develop resources and expand technology in order to improve their productivity and reduce costs. Success in these efforts determines a nation's area of specialization and affects its terms of trade. Governments, therefore, are very active in such endeavors.

Government-subsidized research, for example, has contributed to technical advance in U.S. industry. Although most research funds have focused on military development, the results have often been applicable to industrial processes and consumer products. Tax credits to businesses for investment in expansion have also been used to spur productivity increases.

In 1971, a device was set up to help U.S. manufacturers increase their competitiveness abroad. Business firms were encouraged to establish **Domestic International Sales Corporations, (DISCs)** as subsidiaries to handle their export business. As a DISC, a company producing at least 90 percent of its output for foreign markets is allowed certain tax advantages. It is allowed to deduct any taxes paid to foreign governments from its U.S. tax bill. It is also excused from all U.S. income taxes until its profits are returned to this country. In effect, this amounts to an interest-free loan to the exporting firm.

The United States **Export-Import Bank** is another device to encourage foreign trade. It finances a variety of trade between the United States and the rest of the world. The goal is to increase world—especially U.S.—trade by providing low-cost credit to countries buying our exports. Eventually, the foreign country makes payment, to the U.S. supplier through the Bank, plus interest charge, to the Bank.

Some nations have attempted to spur industrial growth by establishing **free trade zones,** into which imported materials and components can be shipped duty-free. These goods are then processed or assembled and exported without having to pay any kind of local tax. One result of free trade zones has been more efficient utilization of a nation's labor resources.

INSTITUTIONS FOR INTERNATIONAL COOPERATION

As the world becomes increasingly interdependent, nations are faced with an increasing number of trade problems. Just as no man is an island, no nation is insulated from the effects of the policies of its trading partners. Frequently, multinational conferences are held to seek compromise solutions to common problems. Compromise sometimes reduces a nation's freedom of action, but trading nations have generally been willing to accept minor loss of national sovereignty because of the long-range benefits of cooperation. International institutions have been established to deal with some common problems: to provide short-term credit to satisfy balance of payments deficits and long-term credit to accommodate development needs and to encourage freer intraregional trade.

International Credit Organizations

As part of its efforts to stabilize exchange rates, the Bretton Woods conference held at the end of World War II established an international body to provide short-term loans to nations experiencing balance of payments deficits. This organization is known as the **International Monetary Fund (IMF)** and now includes 135 member nations. Its representatives meet yearly to plan international credit and exchange policy.

Members of the IMF contribute gold and national currencies to the Fund in amounts which depend on their national income and their participation in international trade. In years of payments deficits, member nations are permitted to borrow those funds to settle their international accounts. Frequent borrowing is discouraged, however. A continuing need for loans suggests a fundamental disequilibrium that needs to be corrected.

The borrowing nation may be required to make certain fiscal and monetary arrangements as a condition for receiving a new loan. For example, continuing deficits in its balance of payments may imply rampant inflation in the borrowing nation. Consumers may be using their inflated incomes to purchase too many low-priced imports from producers abroad. Domestic producers may be unable to sell their high-priced goods abroad, thus aggravating the currency outflow. Before an IMF loan is made in this instance, the borrowing nation may have to agree to impose contractionary fiscal and monetary policies to correct its inflated economy.

The IMF may also influence the policies of nations with a surplus trade balance. Such nations accumulate currency reserves as their exports rise relative to their purchases from abroad. When reserves pile up, a nation may be urged to adopt expansionary monetary and fiscal policies. Expansionary policies raise domestic incomes and stimulate purchase of imports from other nations. For example, as the recession of 1973–75 drew to a close, deficit nations were urging the United States, Japan, and Germany—the three largest economies of the free world—to expand their economies and speed global recovery. It was hoped that higher incomes would stimulate import demand and contribute to economic expansion in the deficit nations of the trading world.

The IMF is also involved in preventing or relieving shortages of currencies used in trade. Severe shortages may cause a **liquidity** crisis, stifling trade throughout the world. To meet such a shortage, the IMF created a new form of currency: **Special Drawing Rights (SDR).** SDRs (sometimes called "paper gold") are guaranteed rights to borrow. They are issued by the IMF according to a nation's reserve holdings in the Fund. (The value of an SDR unit is a weighted average of sixteen trading currencies. In 1980, it was about $1.30.)

When a member nation needs funds to finance a deficit, it can exchange its holdings of SDRs for equivalent amounts of the foreign currencies it needs for trade. Then these currencies can be used to settle its accounts. There are some restrictions on the use of SDRs. The restrictions are intended to prevent nations from becoming too dependent on credit and to encourage them to establish the proper internal policies to correct their payments problems.

It has been suggested that the allocation of SDRs among member nations should be based on need rather than on the amount a nation contributes to the Fund. The original plan, in effect, rewards nations that have already achieved success in production and trade. The richer they are, the easier it is for them to borrow through SDRs. The new proposal would link borrowing privileges to the *lack* of success. It would provide international credits to nations in greatest need of imported machinery and equipment for developing their economies. It would thus

Extended Example Aid for Developing Nations

The International Monetary Fund provides special loan programs for nations suffering serious economic problems. But a necessary condition of lending is that the borrowing nation agree to establish monetary and fiscal policies to cut inflation, eliminate unnecessary spending, and increase investment in productive facilities. It is expected that such policies would bring on healthy economic development, encourage balance of payments surpluses, and enable loans to be repaid.

Mexico, Egypt, Sri Lanka, Haiti, and the Philippines have participated in these loan programs, but without much success. One problem is their extreme poverty, which makes contractionary policies especially painful. Another is worldwide oil price increases, which raise the cost of development programs. Moreover, within each of these capital nations there is intense competition among industries for the scarce capital for investment.

National governments hesitate to impose harsh economic conditions on their people. This is particularly true where living conditions are already poor and social unrest could lead to revolution. To ease the process, the United States has contributed aid to developing nations through the Agency for International Development (AID). Recessions in the United States and calls for a balanced federal budget have reduced this form of aid in recent years to about $6 billion in 1980. This is only 0.25 percent of total U.S. national production, a smaller share than that contributed by most other developed nations.

Foreign aid has helped South Korea, Singapore, Taiwan, Malaysia, and Thailand begin to develop their economies and has lifted others out of desperate poverty. As conditions improve, they begin to buy U.S. goods, often spending substantially more in the United States than we contributed to their development.

Aid programs redistribute wealth from industrialized nations to poorer, less developed nations. Can you think of similar programs within a single nation? What are the expected results in both cases? Explain in terms of production possibilities. What are the consequences of continued backwardness?

enhance world trade and development. Developing nations support this proposal enthusiastically. They would like to receive SDRs in amounts based on the GNPs of the nations contributing to the Fund's reserves. That is, the higher a nation's GNP, the greater its contribution of SDR loans to developing nations.

In 1975, the IMF agreed to begin to sell a portion of its gold holdings (totaling 17.5 million ounces) and distribute half the proceeds of the sale to poor nations. The profit on gold sales was about $1.6 billion in 1979. Half of the gain was allocated to nations with per capita incomes of less than $400. Unfortunately this amount is small relative to the total debt in these countries. In 1979, accumulated deficits totaled around $258 billion.

The IMF also created a special "Oil Facility" and an "Extended Fund Facility": $20 billion to help developing nations pay for their necessary imports of high-priced oil.

Developing nations have another source of long-term credit. The **International Bank for Reconstruction and Development (IBRD)**—often called the *World Bank*—was established in 1945 as a companion organization to the International Monetary Fund. The purpose of the World Bank is to provide long-term loans for construction of industrial capital in developing nations. Transportation and communication facilities, power plants and irrigation facilities, steel mills, and furniture factories have been built in developing nations through low-interest IBRD loans.

Intraregional Trading Organizations

Much of the phenomenal growth of the U.S. economy may be attributed to our large internal free trade area. An important part of our Constitution was the prohibition against barriers to trade between the states. This encouraged movement of resources and products throughout the nation. As a result, regions were able to specialize according to comparative advantage. The South, for example, could take advantage of its favorable land and climate for cotton production. It could ship cotton to the North, where factories were waiting to process it into clothing and other products. Similarly, the North's industrial capacity enabled it to sell machinery and other industrial products to consumers in the South.

Today most of us tend to take our internal free trade for granted. But imagine what our lives as consumers would be like if this trade were severely restricted. What if Detroit could not easily sell cars to consumers in Kansas City or St. Paul? What if Florida's oranges were not allowed easy entrance into New Jersey or Illinois? What if California's food products were forbidden to consumers in New York City or in Baltimore? Our lives and the economic life of our nation would be quite different.

Customs unions. Following World War II, a momentous step was taken toward achieving some of the same benefits for the nations of Western Europe. Belgium, the Netherlands, and Luxembourg joined together in a customs union known as *Benelux.* A **customs union** is an agreement to eliminate tariff among the member countries and to impose common tariffs on trade with nonmember nations. Elimination of tariffs enabled the three small nations of Benelux to exchange freely the materials and components needed for developing their industries.

The success of Benelux led to its expansion. West Germany, France, and Italy joined the bloc. It became known as the **European Economic Community (EEC).** In 1973, Great Britain, Ireland, and Denmark were admitted to the EEC. The EEC is now generally called the *Common Market.*

The coordination of trade policies within the common market suggests future coordination of other policies as well: domestic fiscal and monetary policies to maintain similar growth rates and similar levels of inflation or unemployment; external political strategies to enhance their strength as a bargaining unit; and possibly a common currency to give further stimulus to the free movement of resources and goods. There is even consideration of a common passport for EEC citizens.

Free trade area. Some other European, Latin American, and communist nations have also formed trade blocs. A typical form of such cooperation is a **free trade area.** Members of a free trade area remove most internal tariffs within the trade bloc, but there is no common external tariff. This may create problems when foreign producers export to the lowest tariff member and then reship freely within the free trade area. It is difficult if not impossible for the importing countries within the bloc to collect the actual tariff rate they have imposed on trade from outside the bloc.

Free trade areas of the world include the Latin American Free Trade Area (LAFTA), the European Free Trade Area (EFTA), and the Eastern European Council for Mutual Economic Assistance (Comecon). In the mid-1960s, Bolivia, Chile (which withdrew in 1976), Colombia, Ecuador, Peru, and Venezuela formed a Latin American common market generally known as the Andean Pact nations.

Commodity agreements. Commodity-producing nations of the Third World have also formed trading organizations to stabilize prices for their exports. These blocs often take the form of marketing organizations, which purchase and sell commodities for the group as a whole. Coffee producers, for example, suffer a sharp decline in export earnings when world coffee prices fall. Under a **commodity agreement,** coffee-producing nations contribute to a fund to buy coffee when excess supply threatens to drive prices down. The marketing organization holds the coffee until market conditions are more favorable for selling. Commodity purchases and sales by marketing boards can stabilize prices and incomes for commodity producers. Other developing nations have entered into similar arrangements for the sale of commodities such as cocoa, tin, wheat, and sugar.

INTERNATIONAL CAPITAL MOVEMENTS

Freer trade relationships have increased the flows of capital among nations. The United States, for example, sends billions of dollars abroad to pay for our purchases from foreign nations. These flows increased during the late 1960s because of the boom in economic activity in Europe and many other parts of the world.

Eurodollars

One result of the burst in international capital flows from the United States has been the appearance of so-called *Eurodollars.* Eurodollars are dollar balances owned outside the United

States, mostly in Europe (hence the name). They may be deposits in European banks, U.S. banks, or European branches of U.S. banks. Eurodollars are the result of payment for U.S. imports, U.S. investment abroad, and other transfers of U.S. dollars. Holders of U.S. dollars deposit them in bank accounts where they earn interest income. In turn, banks lend Eurodollars to credit-worthy borrowers. Total Eurodollar holdings were estimated at $600 billion in 1979.

Depositors typically seek the highest interest income on Eurodollar balances, and banks seek the highest interest on loans. As a result, Eurodollar balances are subject to frequent shifts among banks and even among nations as holders seek investments that will pay them high incomes. Sudden shifts in dollar holdings can lead to drastic changes in a nation's money supply and uncontrolled disruption of a nation's economy.

By the mid-1970s exports of high-priced oil had caused a shift in Eurodollars to the bank accounts of Arab oil producers. Eurodollars in the hands of Arab nations became known as *petrodollars*. The situation grew more complex as Eurodollars were joined by Euroyen, Euromarks, and any number of other currencies. The term **Eurocurrency** has been coined to include all national currencies on deposit outside the home country.

A nation's central bank can regulate the nation's currency supply. A central bank cannot, however, control its currency outside its borders. Central bankers around the world are working together to devise instruments for regulating Eurocurrency. However, the problem is not yet sufficiently understood to permit clear-cut solutions.

Multinational Corporations

Another result of plentiful international capital has been the phenomenal growth of multinational corporations.

Multinational corporations are large firms having extensive production or distribution facilities in more than one nation. Most large U.S. corporations are multinationals.

Direct investment in a foreign country allows a company to avoid tariff charges. Multinational corporations have other advantages. Firms engaging in many operations can plan production on the basis of different resource costs in their several locations. Labor-intensive processes can be performed in nations where wages are low. Investment capital can be borrowed in nations where interest charges are low. It is even possible to shift profits to countries with low income taxes. This is done by setting the prices of components produced for use within the company according to the various tax rates.

For example, suppose a corporate division in England produces electronic circuits to be used for communications equipment ultimately assembled and sold by another division in Switzerland. Charging a low price for the circuits would shift taxable income to Switzerland; a high price would retain income in England. The choice of strategy would depend on which country had lower tax rates.

At first, multinational firms were welcomed in the host nations. They brought capital investment, provided jobs, paid taxes, and contributed to rising incomes and output. Eventually, the climate of acceptance began to change. Host nations came to resent the profits accumulated by foreign firms, profits which were often sent back to the country of ownership. They came to resent the avoidance of full tax payments. And they were fearful of the alien political power that might result from heavy foreign financial involvement in their economies. For example, the interference by ITT in Chilean politics in the early 1970s frightened many nations where multinational corporations were active. They began to wonder if multinational companies in their midst might someday contribute to the overthrow of *their* governments.

Some multinational investments have been nationalized by host countries. Owners are usually paid a portion of the value of the investment. In other nations, foreign governments have insisted on 51 percent of share ownership. Saudi Arabia, for example, took ownership of 25 percent of Anglo-American oil concessions in 1970. It also stipulated that its share was to rise year by year until it reached 51 percent in 1981.

The great size and potential economic and political power of many multinational firms raise serious questions about their proper international control. In fact, multinational corporations may operate outside the control of any government at all. Coherent policies for dealing with this kind of international power are still to be developed. Such policies may entail some form of supranational organization on the order of regional or world government—not a likely prospect in the near future.

SUMMARY

Nations do not always enjoy the full benefits of international trade. Free trade may create problems involving domestic output, income, employment, and growth. Or free trade may create payments problems for importing nations.

Problems of domestic unemployment are often dealt with by imposing tariffs on foreign imports. Supporters of tariffs claim they are necessary to protect infant industries, to encourage development of strategic industries, to offset lower wage costs in other nations, or to improve the terms of trade between raw commodity exports and manufactured imports. Opponents of tariffs point out the higher prices and smaller quantity of goods traded under protectionist policies; they advocate subsidies and monetary and fiscal policies to increase domestic employment without interfering with efficient resource allocation.

Quotas limit the quantity of certain imports and protect domestic producers. But they also keep prices above the lowest free trade price and prevent quantity from increasing fully when demand curves shift.

Export duties make exported goods more expensive to foreign buyers and reduce sales abroad. Export subsidies make exported goods cheaper and more competitive in world markets; however, importing nations may impose countervailing duties to offset this advantage to exporting nations. Another means of protecting local production is through quality standards on imports. Control of foreign exchange and multiple exchange rates help limit imports to only essential items. Boycotts and embargoes are more restrictive barriers to trade, set up for political or economic reasons.

The highest U.S. tariff rates were levied under the Smoot-Hawley Act of 1930. Since 1934, the United States has engaged in reciprocal tariff reductions with our trading partners. The recession of 1973–75 led to changes in American tariff laws, calling for special aid to domestic industries harmed by imports. The Toyko Round of tariff negotiations ended in 1979 called for tariff reductions and reductions in nontariff barriers to trade. The General Agreement on Tariffs and Trade (GATT) is a multinational organization for extending tariff reductions according to the most-favored-nation principle. Governments have encouraged productivity growth and trade through subsidized research tax credits, Domestic International Sales Corporations, the Export-Import Bank, and free trade zones.

To help finance deficits, the International Monetary Fund (IMF) was set up to provide short-term loans to members. The IMF adds to total world liquidity by issuing Special Drawing Rights (SDRs). The International Bank for Reconstruction and Development, or World Bank, provides long-term loans at low interest, primarily for development projects in less developed countries.

Some neighboring nations have formed customs unions or free trade areas to liberalize trade among members. Other commodity-producing nations have formed marketing organizations to raise and stabilize prices of their commodity exports. Freer trade has increased international capital flows; large holdings of Eurocurrencies threaten to disrupt monetary policy in some nations. Also the size and power of multinational corporations may present some problems in the future.

Key Words and Phrases

boycotts refusal to deal with certain nations or businesses.

commodity agreement organization for purchasing and selling commodity exports at stable prices.

countervailing duties taxes placed on certain imports to offset export subsidies paid foreign sellers by their government.

customs union a group of nations having no internal tariffs and a common external tariff.

embargoes refusal to ship certain goods.

Eurocurrency currencies owned by persons or institutions outside the issuing nation.

European Economic Community the customs union consisting of most Western European nations and known as the Common Market.

export duties taxes on exports designed to discourage sale abroad of certain domestically produced goods.

Export-Import Bank primarily a U.S. credit facility set up to provide trade credits for foreign purchases of American goods.

export subsidies payments to domestic producers that enable them to sell abroad at lower prices.
foreign exchange controls government control of foreign currency markets for the purpose of determining how foreign exchange is spent.
free trade area a group of nations having no internal tariffs and various external tariffs.
free trade zones areas where foreign materials may be processed and exported without payment of domestic tariffs.
infant-industry tariffs tariffs to protect young industries from more established foreign competitors.
International Bank for Reconstruction and Development the World Bank for extending long-term loans for economic development.
International Monetary Fund (IMF) international organization for helping nations with payments and liquidity problems.
liquidity availability of sufficient currencies for trade.
most-favored-nation principle an agreement to extend any trade advantage equally to all parties to the agreement.
multinational corporation a business firm with subsidiaries in more than one nation.
multiple exchange rates prices for foreign exchange that differ according to the proposed use of foreign exchange.
production-costs tariff a tariff to equalize low costs of production abroad with higher domestic costs of production.
protectionism policies of trade restriction aimed at protecting domestic producers.
protective tariffs import duties designed to restrict imports
quality standards on imports legal standards on goods that often exclude foreign-made products from domestic markets.
quotas legal restrictions on the quantity of a foreign good that can be imported.
revenue tariffs import duties designed to collect revenue.
Special Drawing Rights (SDR) guaranteed rights to borrow currencies from IMF for use in trade.
strategic-industry tariff a tariff to protect domestic producers of products essential to a nation's security.
terms of trade quantity of domestic goods that must be exported per unit of goods imported.

Questions for Review

1. Outline the most persuasive arguments in favor of protectionist tariff policies. Point out the weaknesses of each argument. Suggest other approaches to minimize the internal problems associated with trade. In what way are quotas even more damaging than tariffs?
2. Distinguish between export duties and export subsidies. What are the objectives of each?
3. What are the usual justifications for foreign exchange controls? For multiple exchange rates?
4. List significant legislative events in U.S. tariff history, together with the approximate dates of each. What have been the recent trends in trading relationships?
5. Explain how a nation can "export" inflation. How can it "export" unemployment?
6. What are the chief objectives of Domestic International Sales Corporations? of free trade zones? Distinguish between free trade zones and free trade areas.
7. How would a "liquidity crisis" affect trading nations? What has the International Monetary Fund done to help forestall such a crisis? How do the credit policies of the World Bank differ from those of the IMF?
8. Describe the origin and historical development of the European Common Market. What future developments are possible?
9. What are the major problems associated with the growth in Eurocurrencies?
10. What are some advantages and disadvantages of multinational corporations?
11. Zaire produces more than half the world's cobalt, with Zambia and Morocco supplying most of the rest. Suppose the three countries combined to control supply and raise price. What circumstances would determine the benefits to producing nations?
12. Japan has resisted international pressures to reduce its import tariffs and quotas on agricultural products. What circumstances of Japanese agriculture make movement to free trade especially difficult?

Index

Abrams, Martin B., 209
Absolute advantage, 423–25
Absolute poverty, 335
Accountant, measuring production costs, 155
Accounting, business. *See* Business accounting
Acreage allotment program, 144
Adair, Red, 206
Ad valorem subsidy, 131–32
Ad valorem tax, 128–29
Advertising
as a factor of production, 242
false, 60
in nonprice competition, 241–42
and product differentiation, 232
in professions, 261–62
Affirmative Action, 13, 346. *See also* Discrimination
The Affluent Society, 19, 267
Africa, 303, 335, 347, 415
Aged, and poverty, 336–37, 339
Agency for International Development, 444
Aggregate, 3, 5
concentration ratio, 265
demand, 420
Agribusiness, 146
Agricultural Adjustment Act (1938), 143, 144
Agriculture
cobweb theorem of prices, 201–3
dealing with price instability, 145
and demand curves, 135–36
excess capacity in, 143–44
in the 1980s, 146
policy toward, 143–45
problems in, 141–43
revenue problems in, 110–11
and supply elasticity, 135–38
Agriculture and Consumer Protection Act (1973), 145
Aid to Families with Dependent Children (AFDC), 337
Albania, 34
Ali, Muhammad, 209
Alienation, 394–95
of property rights, 397
Allocation, 399–400. *See also* Resource allocation
Alternative economic systems. *See* Economic systems, alternatives
Aluminum Company of America (Alcoa), 259
Aluminum industry, concentration in, 238–39
American Agricultural Movement, 145
American Brands, 264
American Federation of Labor (AFL), 10, 294
American Federation of Labor and Congress of Industrial Organizations (AFL-CIO), 298
American Federation of State, County, and Municipal Employees (AFSCME), 297, 298
American Medical Association (AMA), 374
American Stock Exchange, 151
American Telegraph & Telephone Company (AT&T), 149, 208
American Tobacco Company, 254, 258, 260
Amtrak, 223, 262, 264
Andean Pact, 445
Antitrust, philosophy of, 258–61
Antitrust Division, Department of Justice, 253
Antitrust laws, 62, 251–54, 255–56. *See also specific acts*
Antitrust policy, 266, 268
Appalachian Regional Development Act (1966), 342
Applied research, 29
Applied sciences, 4
Arbitrator, 296
Archimedes, 5–6
Argentina, 418
Armour, 257
Arrow, Kenneth, 363–64
Artificial monopolies, 206, 209
Asia, 303, 335, 347
Assets, 173–74
Atlantic Richfield, 259
Automatic stabilizers, 67
Average fixed cost, 162–63
Average product, 160–61
Average revenue, 166–67
Average total cost, 163
Average variable cost, 163
Backward-bending supply curve, 379–80
Bacon, Francis, 5
Bakke case, 13
Balance sheet, 173–74
Banks for Cooperatives, 288
Baran, Paul, 218
Basic research, 28
Basing-point system, pricing, 239–40
Belgium, 445
Bell, Alexander Graham, 209
Benefit-cost relationship, 319
Benelux, 445
Big business, attitudes toward, 248
Bigness
coping with, 266–68
defined, 265–66
opposition to, 268–70
Binding arbitration, 296
Black Americans, 239
and Affirmative Action, 13
and poverty, 336
Black market, 135–36
economy, 408
Board of directors, 150
Bolivia, 428, 430, 439
Borlung, Norman, 126
Bottom line, 155
Boycott, 295, 439–40
Brazil, 428, 430, 439
Break-even point, 166
Breeder reactors, 382
Bretton Woods, 443
Brezhnev, Leonid, 408
Britain. *See* Great Britain
Brown Shoe Manufacturing Company, 259
Brown & Williamson, 264
Browning, Edgar K., 340
Budget
and capital, 319–20
consumer's, 95–96, 98, 127, 359
and isocost curve, 180–81
line, 95
Bureau of the Census, 340, 348
Bureau of Land Management, 24
Business accounting
balance sheets, 173–74
depreciation, 172–73
hierarchy in, 148–49

income and expense statements, 172–73
organization of, 149–51

Cable TV, 154
California, rent control, 135
Canada, 150, 419, 438
Capital, 275
Capital, 313
accumulation, 395
budgeting, 319–20
defined, 21, 319
as factor of production, 21
financial aspects of, 323–27
gain, 72, 151
and growth, 326–27
and interest rates, 321–22
savings and investment of, 319, 322–23
subsidies, 288
tax credits, 322
and theory of interest, 318–27
types of, 394 *See also* Labor; Land
Capital goods, 21, 27–28
Capital-intensive production, 32, 422
Capitalism
cycles of, 339–41
decline of, 395
defined, 36–37, 396
and economic concentration, 266–68
Marx's criticism of, 275–76
mixed, 37, 396
Capitalist's surplus, 275
Carnegie, Andrew, 251, 252–53
Cartel, 239–40, 428
Carter, James Earl (Jimmy), 223, 288, 295, 375
Cash-balances theory, 171
Celler-Kefauver Amendment, 256
Center for Policy Alternatives (MIT), 369
Centralized economic system, 399
Ceteris paribus, 7, 9
Change, 328
in demand, 42–43, 44, 48–49
in quantity demanded, 44
in supply, 45–46, 48–49
Characteristics, of goods and services, 79–80
"Chicago School of Economics," 330
Chile, 445, 446
China, 31, 34, 396, 398, 399, 439
Chrysler, 37
government aid to, 63
Cities
and tax revenues, 350–51
and three E's, 352–54
urban poverty and crisis, 349–54
Civil Aeronautics Board (CAB), 219, 223
Civil Rights Act (1964, Title VII), 13, 346
Civil War, 249
Civilian goods, 26
Clark, John Bates, 276
Class
and capitalism, 275–76
struggle, 395
Clayton Antitrust Act (1914), 116, 254, 255, 256
Closed shops, 295
Coal, 381
Coal—Bridge to the Future, 381
Coalitions, 366
Cobweb theorem of agricultural prices, 201–3
Collective farms, 406
Collusion, 235
Colombia, 445
Columbia Broadcasting System (CBS), 257
COMECON, 408, 445
Command economic system, 34–35
Commodities, 50
Commodity agreement, 445
Common Market. *See* European Economic Community
"Common situs," 295
Common stock, 150
Commoner, Barry, 84
Communal property, 59
Communism, 34, 396
Communist Central Party Committee, 408
Communist Party, 400, 409
Community Action Programs, 338
Comparative advantage
and changing terms of trade, 428–31
combined production possibilities, 426
opportunity costs of, 425
and rates of exchange, 426–28
Comparative cost ratio, 425
Competition
government regulation of, 62
import, 442
monopolistic, 206, 228–34
Competition, imperfect
defined, 227
and demand, 281–83
and monopolistic competition, 228–34
nonprice competition, 234, 241–45
oligopoly, 234–41
See also Oligopoly
Competition
perfect conditions for, 362
decision making in, 358–59
resource demand in, 276–77
and wage determination, 305–7
Competition, perfect, long run
equilibrium in, 183–84
industry growth/changing costs in, 194, 196–99
and plant size, 185–89
profit maximization in, 190–94
Competition, perfect, short run
businesses, 148–51
costs, 161–65
defined, 152
demand curve in, 153–54
economic profit in, 169–72
four basic conditions of, 152–53
isoquants and isocosts, 177–81
measuring costs of production in, 154–57
production decisions in, 157–61, 169–72
profit maximization in, 165–69
resources in, 157
Competitive equilibrium, 191–92
Competitive model, wage determination, 305–7
Complementary goods, 43, 98, 114
Compounding, 321
Concentration
in industry, 239, 263–65
and market system, 268
in military-industrial complex, 269–70
of power, 219
ratio, 264
trends in, 265
Conduct, of firms, 258
Conglomerate mergers, 257
Congress
and agriculture, 143, 145
and antimerger legislation, 251, 254
and antitrust laws, 256, 257–58, 259
and capital subsidies, 288
and farm price supports, 111
and foreign competition, 217
and health care, 274
and industry regulation, 222–23
and labor legislation, 294–95
and poverty programs, 336–39
regulation of market power, 261–63
and revenue sharing, 64–65
See also Government
Consolidated Rail Corporation (Conrail), 262, 263, 264
Conspicuous consumption, 207
Constant average costs, 185
Constant capital, 394
Constant cost industry, 198, 379
Consumer
budget, 95–96, 98, 127, 359
choice of characteristics, 79–80
defined, 41
demand, 279–80
and energy, 377
expectations, 43–44
goods, 21
income, 97
and law of demand, 41
price index, 299
product safety, 386
surplus, 88–89
tastes, 42–43
Consumer demand
and changes in income, 97
and consumer's budget, 95–96, 98, 127, 359
curve, 96–97
and elasticity, 104
for goods and services, 79–80
indifference curves, 93–94
indifference schedules, 92–93

and utility, 80–91
See also Utility
Consumer Products Safety Commission, 60
Consumption
exclusivity, 60–61
nonexclusivity, 60–61
Contracts
defense, 270
exclusionary, 213
sanctity of, 59
tying, 254
union, 50, 295–96
Corporate bonds, 322–23
Corporation,
behavior, 150–51
government, 263
multinational, 446–47
Corporation Accountability Research Group, 151
Cost
accounting, 155
changing, industry growth, 194, 196–99
economic, 61–62, 155
explicit, 155
external, 384
fixed, 162
of health care, 371–73, 374–76
indirect, 367
induced, 367–68
in monopolistic competition, 231
opportunity, 425
of poverty, 354
and production decisions, long run, 182–99
and production decisions, short run, 161–65
of regulation, 369
in short run, perfect competition, 148–74
social, 53–55, 61–62, 198–99
Cost-effective program, 367
Cost-of-living adjustments (COLAs), 299
Cost-push inflation, 245
Council of Economic Advisers, 350, 363–64, 378
Council on Wage and Price Stability, 256, 262
Countereconomy, 408
Counterplanning, 402
Countervailing duties, 437
Countervailing power, 223, 245, 268
Craft unions, 294, 308–9. *See also* Unions
Creative destruction, 268
Crosland, R. A. S., 224
Cross-elasticity of demand, 113–14
and the law, 116
Cross subsidy, 224
Cuba, 396, 399, 440
Custom duties, 70
Customs union, 445
Cyclical poverty, 339–41
Czechoslovakia, 139
Davis-Bacon Act, 294
Decentralized economic system, 399
Decision making, in perfect competition, 358–60
Decontrol of prices, 260, 379
Decreasing cost industry, 196, 379
Defoe, Daniel, 318
Demand, 41–44
aggregate, 420
and buyers, 43
changes in, 42–44
consumer, 80–104
derived, 276, 418–19
elasticity of, 100–116
global, 415
graphing, 42
under imperfect competition, 281–83
inelastic, 105
for investment funds, 319–20
for labor, 303–11
law of, 41
and market equilibrium, 47–51
schedule of, 41
Demand curve, 42, 85–86, 96–97, 102–3
horizontal, 106
kinked, 236–37, 245
in monopolistic competition, 230–31
in perfect competition, 153–54
for resources, 277–79
and time, 113
Demand, elasticity of
and decontrolling prices, 379
and demand curve, 102–3
determining elasticity, 111–13
elasticity, 103–11
example of, 112
final product, 281
and firm's revenue, 107–11
interpretation of, 105
in monopoly, 214–15
for resources, 281
special features of, 111–15
Democracy, economic, 40
Democratic socialism, 34
Denison, Edward F., 326–27
Denmark, 29–30, 34, 335, 423, 445
Department of Agriculture, 111, 135, 137
Department of Commerce, 264
Department of Energy, 381, 382
Department of Health, Education, and Welfare, 340
Department of the Interior, 389
Department of Justice, 62, 255, 256, 257, 258, 259
Department of Transportation, 262, 369
Dependent variables, 17–18
Depreciation, 172–73
Depressions, periodic, 229. *See also* Great Depression
Deregulation, 223
Derived demand, 276, 418–19
Destruction, of property, 397
Development, 28
Deviation, 325
Differentiated oligopoly, 244. *See also* Oligopoly
Diminishing marginal product of labor, 304
Diminishing marginal utility, 80, 81, 89–90, 102, 207
Direct costs, 367
Direct grants, 342
Direct harm, 362–63
Discounting, 320–21
Discrimination, 12–13, 344–49
economic, 64, 344
and government policies against, 63–64, 346–47
job, 346–47
racial, 64, 344–46
reverse, 13
sex, 344
See also Inequality; Poverty; Welfare; Women
Discriminatory price cutting, 254
Diseconomies of large scale, 185, 187
Disequilibrium, 50
Disincentives, 130–31
Distribution, of income resources, 53
Diversification, 326, 429
Dividends, 72, 150
Domestic International Sales Corporation (DISC), 442
Dual markets, 344–46
Dumping, 217
Duopoly, 235–36

Eastern Europe, 28, 31, 34, 133, 139, 396, 408
Eastern European Council for Mutual Economic Assistance (COMECON), 408, 445
Eckstein, Otto, 9
Econometric models, 8
Economic
costs, 61–62, 155
democracy, 40
Development Act, 342
models, 6–7, 8–9
Opportunity Act, 338
profit, 156–57, 212–14, 215, 328
stability and security, defined, 12
surplus, 34
table, 8
See also Profit
Economic problem
choosing production, 29–33
defined, 19–20
and kinds of resources, 20–21
managing in world of scarcity, 20
and production possibilities, 22–29
and types of economic systems, 33–37
Economics
defined, 2–5
and distribution, 12–13
and factors of production, 20–21
and fallacy of composition, 11

and four questions of production, 32–33
goals of system, 12–13, 204–5
and monopoly, 217–19
and performance criteria, 12–13
and personal bias toward, 11
and politics, 10, 366
positive and normative sciences, 7, 9–11
and public choice, 366–67
and role of government, 58–75
and scarcity, 20
and social science, 5–12
and welfare, 365–67
Economics, international. *See* International trade
The Economics of Imperfect Competition, 229
Economics, Peace, and Laughter, 267
Economics and the Public Posture, 267
Economic systems, alternatives
allocation in, 399–400
basic characteristics of, 396–400
degrees of centralization in, 399
economic planning in, 400–404
incentives in, 400
and Karl Marx, 394–96
ownership and property rights in, 397
and role of labor, 397–99
in Soviet economy, 404–9
in Yugoslavia, 409–10
Economies of large scale, 185–87
Economists
measuring costs of production, 155
methods of, 5–12
monetary, 3
neoclassical, 276, 363
as normative scientists, 10–11, 363
and political economy, 11
role of, 2–3
welfare, 363, 365
Ecuador, 445
Edison, Thomas, 28
Edsel, 328
Efficiency, 217, 352–53, 362
defined, 12, 203–5
in financial markets, 324–27
in military, 309
in monopolistic competition, 232
and oligopoly, 245
Efficient markets, 326–27
Egalitarian society, 400
Egypt, 440, 444
Eisenhower, Dwight D., 269
Elastic and inelastic supply curves, 124
Elasticity
calculating, 104–5
defined, 104
and indifference curves, 118–39
infinite, 106, 124
interpretation of, 105
in monopolies, 214–15
politics of, 291
unit, 105
See also Demand, elasticity of; Supply, elasticity of
Elderly. *See* Aged
Embargoes, 439–40
Employees, in government, 64
Employing resources. *See* Resource allocation
Employment Act (1946), 62
Energy
alternative sources of, 381–83
and backward-bending supply curve, 379–80
crisis, 27
decontrol of prices, 260, 379
and price controls, 378–79
recommendations, 383–84
and windfall profits tax, 380
Energy Mobilization Board, 429
Energy Security Corporation, 429
Engel curves, 103
England. *See* Great Britain
Enterprise operation plan, 402
Entrepreneur, 21
Entrepreneurial talent, 313–14
Entrepreneurship, 21
building human capital, 329–31
functions of profit, 327–29
theory of profit, 327–31
Envelope curve, 188
Environmental health and safety
air, water pollution, 385
consumer product safety, 386
employee health and safety, 386
land reclamation, 385–86
policies regarding, 384–90
Environmental Protection Agency (EPA), 60, 369, 386, 388
Equal Employment Opportunity Commission (EEOC), 346
Equal marginal productivity principle, 180, 276
Equal marginal utility principle, 84–85, 359
Equality, defined, 205
Equality or Efficiency: The Big Tradeoff, 350
Equilibrium
competitive, 191–92
isocosts, 180
in labor market, 303–11
in long-run competition, 183–84
price, 47–48, 127, 286–87, 415
in the short run, 170–72
Equity, 217, 353, 362
defined, 13, 204–5
and monopolistic competition, 234
and oligopoly, 245
Estate taxes, 70
The Ethics of Competition, 330
Eurocurrency, 446
Eurodollars, 445–46
Europe, 395
European Economic Community (EEC), 111, 253, 410, 438, 445
European Free Trade Area, 445
Evans, Michael, 9
Exchange rates, 426–28
Excise taxes, 70
Exclusionary contracts, 213
Exemptions, 71
Expectations, 127
Explicit costs, 155
Exploitation, 395
Export duties, 437
Export subsidies, 437
External diseconomies, 197–98
External economies, 196–97
Externalities, 198–99, 221, 223, 225, 353, 365
negative, 384
Exxon, 259

Factors of production, 20–21
Fair Labor Standards Act, 304
Fair trade laws, 256
Fallacy of composition, 11
False cause fallacy, 12
Farm Act (1977), 145
Farmers Home Administration, 288
Federal agencies, 222–23. *See specific agencies.*
Federal Energy Administration, 260
Federal income tax, 71–74
advantages and disadvantages of, 72–73
and Social Security, 73–74
See also Tax
Federal Land Banks, 288
Federal National Mortgage Association, 288
Federal Power Commission, 51, 219
Federal Trade Commission (FTC), 60, 213, 219, 222, 243, 254, 255, 256, 259, 274
Field, Marshall, 315
Final-product demand elasticity, 281
Financial capital, 21
Financial intermediaries, 323
Financial markets, 323–27
Financial planning, in Soviet Union, 402–3
Firms
defined, 149
determining number of, 192, 194
performance and conduct of, 205
First Amendment, 262
Fitzsimmons, Frank, 295
Five-year plan, 28, 32, 404
Fixed costs, 162
Fixed productive resources, 157
Flows, income and expense, 172–74
Food and Drug Administration (FDA), 59–60, 235
Food industry, 164
Food Stamp Program, 337
Forced labor camps, 397–98
Ford, Gerald, 10, 270, 288, 295
Ford Motor Company, 300, 373
Foreign exchange controls, 437, 439
Foreign trade multiplier, 421
Formal pricing agreements, 239
Four questions of production, 32–33
Fragmented industry, 233
France, 8, 400, 404, 445
Franchisees, 195
Franchises, 195–96

Franklin, Benjamin, 224
Free enterprise system, 330. *See also* Free market
Free goods, 20, 62, 372, 376, 385
Free labor, 399
Free market, 54
  and Adam Smith, 40–41
  and commodities, 50
  defined, 40
  dimensions of, 39–40
  and functions of price system, 51–53
  and government role in, 63
  market equilibrium in, 47–51
  pros and cons of, 53–55
  role of, 408
  supply and demand in, 39–55
Free press, 399
Free riders, 364–65, 373
Free trade area, 445
Free trade zones, 442
Freeman, Richard F., 331
Friedman, Milton, 54, 330
Fringe benefits, 299–300
Function, 17–18
Functional graph, 17–18

Galbraith, John Kenneth, 19, 222, 243, 245, 267, 268, 270, 293–94
Gary, Elbert, 239, 253
Gasoline tax, 70
General Agreement on Tariffs and Trade (GATT), 438, 440
General Dynamics, 270
General Foods, 255
General Mills, 255
General Motors, 206, 248
General Planning Commissariat, France, 404
General strike, 297
George, Henry, 315–16
Geothermal power, 383
Germany, 30, 40, 279, 304, 410
GI Bill, 400
Giffin goods, 103
Giffin, Sir Robert, 103
Gift tax, 70
Gilbreth, Frank and Lillian, 283–84
Goldwater, Barry, 10
Gompers, Samuel, 294
Goods
  capital, 21, 27–28
  civilian, 26
  free, 20, 62, 372, 376, 385
  Giffin, 103
  inferior, 43, 97, 103
  luxury, 112
  military, 26
  necessary, 112
  private and public, 30–31, 60–61
  substitute, 43, 111–12, 114–15, 229
  superior, 43, 97, 103
Gordon, Kermit, 338
GOSPLAN, 404, 405, 406
Government
  and agricultural price supports, 136–38, 141–46
  allocation, 399
  antitrust laws, 62, 251, 254, 255–56, 258–61
  corporation, 263
  economic functions of, 59–64
  evaluating tax structure of, 74–75
  levels of, 64–65
  and market, 51, 63, 128–32, 261–63, 372–77
  monopolies, 219–25
  outlays of, 65–67
  role of, 3–4, 366
  securities, 323
  setting prices, 133–36
  subsidies for resource development, 288
  taxation policies of, 68–71
  use of economists, 3
Government, federal
  cost of market regulation, 367–68
  defining poverty, 334–36
  environmental policies of, 384–90
  and health care, 375–78
  health-care costs, 373
  levels of spending, 64–65
  policies against discrimination, 346–47
  progressive tax of, 71–74
  purchases and transfer payments of, 66–67
  and state and local government, 64–65
  taxation, 69–74
Government, state and local, 64, 65–66
  subsidies of, 132
  taxation, 68–69, 129
Government National Mortgage Association, 288
Grapes of Wrath, 341
Graphs, 16–18
  consumer's indifference schedule, 93
Great Britain, 29–30, 31, 150, 224, 335, 345
Great Crash, 62
Great Depression, 26, 62, 143, 145, 218, 255, 339, 440
Great Society, 338
Greece, 335
Green revolution, 126–27
Greenhouse effect, 385
Greyhound Company, 257
Grievance committee, 296
Grievances, 296
Gross National Product (GNP), 419
Gulf, 259
"Guns versus butter," 26, 30

Haiti, 444
Hard-core poverty, 337
Head Start, 338
Health-care industry, 371–76
Health Maintenance Organizations (HMOs), 373, 376
Health Professions Educational Assistance Act (1963), 374
Heller, Walter, 338
Hertz Corporation, 98, 257
"Hidden" tax, 367
Higher Learning in America, 208
Hill, James J., 249
Hispanics, 343
Holmes, Oliver Wendell, 66
Horizontal demand curves, 106
Horizontal merger, 249–51, 256
Housing, 352
  economics of, 3–4
Housing and Urban Development Act (1965), 338
Human capital, 21, 329–31, 422
Humphrey, Hubert, 10–11, 339
Hungary, 34, 53, 139
Huntington, Collis P., 249
Hypothesis, 6

Immediate-period supply curve, 127
Immediate time period, 125
Imperfect competition. *See* Competition, imperfect
Implicit costs, 155
Imports, 132
Incentive function, 52, 400
Income
  consumer's, 97
  consumption line, 119–22
  and demand, 43
  determining, 288–89
  distribution, 9–10, 331–32
  effect, 102, 112
  elasticity of demand, 113
  and energy problems, 377
  and expense statement, 172–73
  inequality of, 347–49
  and marginal revenue productivity, 290
  proportion spent, 112
  and trade, 418–20
Income-support payments. *See* Transfer payments
Increasing cost industry, 198, 379
Indentured labor, 398
Independent variable, 17–18
India, 28
Indicative planning, 404
Indifference curve, 93–94, 98
  analysis, 98–100
Indirect cost, 367
Indirect labor, 394
Individual Physicians' Associations (IPAs), 376
Induced cost, 367–68
Industrial Revolution, 27, 35, 274–75, 294, 335
Industrial union, 294. *See also* Unions
Industries, 149
Industry, structure of, 205
Industry demand curve, 211
Industry planning curve, 188
Inelastic demand, 105
Inequality, 347–49. *See also* Discrimination; Poverty; Welfare
Infant industry tariff, 434–35
Inferior goods, 43, 97, 103
Infinity elasticity, 106, 124

Inflation, 12, 390
  and COLAs, 399
  and commodities, 50
  cost-push, 245
  and oil prices, 378
  and overemployment, 26
  premium, 324
  in Soviet economy, 407
Infrastructure, 315
Injunction, 295
In-kind programs of aid, 340
Innovation, 29, 268, 328
An Inquiry into the Nature and Causes of the Wealth of Nations, 40, 275
Insolvent, 174
Interest, 319
  theory of, 318–27.
  See also Capital
Interlocking directorate, 254
Internal Revenue Code, 72
Internal Revenue Service, 343
International Bank for Reconstruction and Development (IBRD), 444
International commercial policies, institutions
  barriers to trade, 437–40
  efforts to eliminate trade restrictions, 440–41
  institutions for cooperation, 443–45
  international capital movements, 445–47
  protection of domestic industries, 433–41
  tariffs, 433–36
  trade and long-run economic growth, 441–42
International credit organizations, 443–44
International Monetary Fund (IMF), 443, 444
International Telephone & Telegraph Corporation (ITT), 257, 258, 446
International Tin Agreement, 430
International trade, 408, 414–31
  beginnings of, 415
  changing terms of, 428–31
  comparative advantage in, 425–31
  and institutions of cooperation, 443–45
  and international capital movements, 445–47
  and long-run economic growth, 441–45
  macroeconomic aspects of, 419–22
  microeconomic aspects of, 417–19
  North-South dilemma in, 430–31
  and policies for domestic industries, 433–42
  and production possibilities, absolute advantage, 422–25
  pure theory of, 415
  specialization in, 414–15, 418
International Trade Commission, 438, 439
Interstate Commerce Act (1887), 251
Interstate Commerce Commission (ICC), 219, 222, 223, 251, 261–62
Intuition, use of, 8
Investment
  demand for funds, 319–20
  in human capital, 329, 331
  inventory, 394
  more than one year, 320–21
  supply of funds for, 322–23
Investment bank, 150
"Invisible hand," 40, 53, 55
Ireland, 445
Islands of poverty, 341–42
Isocosts, 179–81
Isoquants, 177–79
Israel, 440
Italy, 439, 445

Japan, 30, 31, 32, 40, 253, 258, 279, 326, 419, 430, 438, 443
Jaroszewicz, Piotr, 139
Jevons, William Stanley, 90
Job Corps, 338
Job discrimination, 346–47
Job opportunities, 300
Johnson, Lyndon B., 13, 26, 63, 338–39, 350
Justice Department. *See* Department of Justice

Kellogg Company, 255
Kennedy, Edward, 10
Kennedy, John F., 270
Kenya, 429
Keynes, John Maynard, 5
Kinked demand curve, 236–37, 245
Kinney Shoes, 260
Klein, Lawrence, 8–9
Knight, Frank, 330
Knights of Labor, 294
Korea, 442
Korean War, 269
Kroc, Ray, 195–96

Labor, 293–311
  demand and equilibrium, 303–11
  as factor of production, 21
  and income distribution, 332
  management cooperation, 296
  role of, 397–99
  in Soviet economy, 404–5
  subsidies, 288
  supply, 301–3
  theory of value, 275, 289, 394
  types of, 394
  unions, 294–301
  and wage determination, 305–11
  in Yugoslavian economy, 410
  See also Capital; Land; Production; Resource allocation; Unions
Labor-intensive, 422
  production, 32
LaMothe, William E., 255
Land, 20–21, 313
  alternative uses for, 314–15
  subsidies for, 288
  tax on, 315–17
  theory of rent, 314–18
  urban speculation in, 315–16
  See also Capital; Labor; Production; Resource allocation
Land-intensive farming, 32
Landrum-Griffin Act (1959), 295
Latin America, 335
Latin American Free Trade Area, 445
Law or principle, 6
Law of demand, 41. *See also* Demand
Law of diminishing returns, 158–59
Law of increasing costs, 24–25
Law of supply, 44–45. *See also* Supply
Less developed countries (LDCs), 404, 430–31
Levitan, Sar A., 340
Lewis, John L., 291, 295
Ligget & Myers, 260
Limited liability, 150
Ling, James L., 257
Ling-Temco-Vought (LTV), 257
Liquidation, 174
Litton Industries, 257
Lockheed, 270
Logistics, 401
Long run, 125
Long-run average cost curve, 186
Long-run competitive equilibrium, 184
Long-run equilibrium, in monopolistic competition, 231–32
Long-run planning curve, 188–89
Long-run supply curve, 128
Lorenz curve, 347
Losses, in short run, 169–70
Love Canal, 388
Luxembourg, 445
Luxury goods, 112

Macroeconomics, defined, 5, 419–22
Malaysia, 430, 444
Malthus, Thomas, 11
Marginal
  analysis, 158–59
  costs, 163–64
  efficiency of investment, 319
  product, 158–59, 160–61, 276–77
  productivity, 276–79
  rate of production, decline, 281
  rate of substitution, 94
  rate of technical substitution, 178
  resource cost, 307
  revenue, 109, 167–69
  revenue product, 277, 290
  tax rate, 71–72
Marginal utility, 80–81
  applications of, 89–91
  and consumer demand, 83–88
  and consumer surplus, 88–89
  schedule, 85
Market
  allocation, 399
  defined, 40
  economy, 35–36, 40–41

efficiency, 376–77
power, 214–15, 248–70, 362
socialism, 53, 396
Market demand
determinants of, 279–81
and economic system, 35–36, 40, 53–55
in international trade, 417–18
for labor, 301–11
and monopoly, 214–15
positioning, 244–45
for resources, 279–83
and socialism, 53, 396
Market equilibrium, 127–28
changes in supply and demand, 42–43, 44, 45–46, 48–49
defined, 47
and expectations, 49
and price, 47–48
search for, 49–51
Market failure
cost of government regulation, 367–68
dealing with, 362–67
and decision making, in perfect competition, 358–59
defined, 362
and energy, 377–84
and environmental health and safety, 384–90
and health care, 371–76
and public choice, 358–59
reasons for, 362
See also Energy; Environmental health and safety
Market power, public policy
antimerger legislation, 251, 254
contradictory attitudes toward, 248–49
curbing market power, 261–63
defined, 249
first great merger movement, 249–51
horizontal and vertical mergers, 249–51
and issue of bigness, 263–70
second great merger movement, 254–56
third great merger movement, 257–61
See also Monopoly; Oligopoly
Mark-up pricing, 238–39
Marshall, Alfred, 40, 171, 276
Marx, Karl, 11, 35–36, 218, 229, 275, 276, 289, 293, 297, 313, 332, 394–96, 400, 404
Marxism, 34, 395–96
-Leninism, 404
Marxist theory, 218
Material saving, 422
Maturity, 323
McDonald's, 195–96
Meany, George, 298
Median family income, 347
Mediator, 296
Medicaid, 10, 67, 338, 374–75
Medicare, 67, 337, 339, 374–75
Mercantilism, 40
Mercantilistic system, 40
Mergers, 249–61. *See also* Market power, public policy
Mexico, 306, 444
Microeconomics, defined, 5
Middle East, 377
Military expenditures, 270
Military goods, 26
Military-industrial complex, 269–70
Mill, John Stuart, 11
Miller-Tydings Act (1937), 256
Minimum wage laws, 50, 304
Minorities, 13, 64
Misallocation of resources, 219
Mitsubishi, 258
Mitsui, 258
Mixed capitalism, 37, 396. *See also* Capitalism
Mixed economy, 37, 54–55. *See also* Economics
Mobil, 259
Models, economic, 6–7, 8–9
Money, 267
government regulation of, 60
marginal utility of, 86–88
wages, 303, 310
Monopolies, 62
Monopolistic competition, 206, 228–34
Monopolist's cost curve, 211–12
Monopolist's demand curve, 210–11
Monopoly, 116
artificial, 206, 209
capitalism, 218
characteristics and methods of, 206–9
and competition, 227–34
decision making in, 210–17
defined, 205–9
and economic profits, 212–14, 215, 328–29
efficiency and equity in, 104–5
government regulation of, 219–24, 225
inefficiency and inequities in, 219
and innovation, 268
natural, 194
power, 50
and price discrimination, 215–17, 220
in professions, 262
shared, 255–56, 261
shortcomings of, 217–19
See also Oligopoly
Monopoly Capitalism, 218
Monopsony, 307–8
Morgan, J. P., 251, 252
Morse, Robert, 393
Most-favored-nation principle, 440
Multinational corporations, 446–47
Multiple exchange rate, 439

Nader, Ralph, 151
National Association of Manufacturers, 10
National Broadcasting Company (NBC), 244
National Defense Education Loans, 288
National Economic Research Association, 390
National Highway Traffic Administration, 369
National Labor Relations Act (Wagner Act), 294
National Recovery Act, 255–56
National Youth Administration, 338
Nationalization, 268
Natural monopolies, 194, 206, 208–9, 219
Necessary goods, 112
Negative economic profit, 166, 167
Negative income tax, 342–44
Negative tax, 75
Neighborhood Youth Corps, 338
Neoclassical economists, 276
Net benefits, 359–60, 387
Net tax, 75
Netherlands, 8, 419, 423, 445
New Careers, 338
New Deal, 255, 338
New York City, 130–31, 134–35
New York Stock Exchange, 151
Newland, Kathleen, 306
Nigeria, 377
Nixon, Richard M., 263, 338–39, 343
Nobel Peace Prize, 126, 364
Nobel Prize for Economics, 8–9, 215, 363–64
Nominal interest rate, 321, 324
Nonprice competition, 234, 241–45
Normal profit, 156, 327. *See also* Profit
Normative science, 7, 9–11
Norris-LaGuardia Act, 294
North Korea, 440
Nuclear power, 381–82

Occupational Safety and Health Administration (OSHA), 60, 222, 369, 386
Oil industry
and antitrust laws, 259–60
producers in, 132
production, 377
and shale, 381
tax on, 132
Oil Producing and Exporting Countries (OPEC), 50, 111, 240, 377, 378, 380, 381, 390, 428, 431, 438
Okun, Arthur, 350–51
Oligopoly, 234–41
defined, 228
differentiated/undifferentiated, 244
pros and cons of, 245
See also Monopoly
Open shop, 295
Operation Mainstream, 338
Opportunity cost, 23–24, 155
of research and development, 28–29
Optimum scale, 187–88
Output per capita, 335
per worker, 304

Overemployment, 26
Ownership, 397

Paradox of value, 171
Paradox of voting, 364
Parallel performance, 260
Parity prices, 143
Partnership, 149–50
Patent, 209, 328–29
Payoff matrix, 241
Percentage costs, 281
Perfect competition. *See* Competition, perfect
Perfect inelasticity, 124
Perfectly inelastic curve, 106
Performance criteria, economic system, 12–13
Personal freedom, and equality, 12–13, 59
Peru, 335, 445
Philippines, 444
Phillip Morris, 264
Physical sciences, 5
Physiocrats, 8–9
Picketing, 295
Planned economy, 399
Planning, economic, 399–400, 400–404
Plants, defined, 148–49, 185–89
Poland, 34, 139, 217, 438
Policies
 agricultural, 143–45
 antitrust, 266, 268
 against discrimination, 346–47
 environmental, 384–90
 and market power, 248–70
 against poverty, 63–64, 346–47
 to protect domestic industries, 433–42
 taxation, 68–74
Political economy, 4, 11, 369
Politics, and economics, 10–11, 366–67
 of elasticity, 291
Pollution, 54–55, 288, 366
 cost of controlling, 369
 social cost of, 62
 See also Environmental health and safety
Poor, and market system, 53–55
Population, and labor force, 299
Portfolio, 323, 326
Positioning, 244–45
Positive science, 7, 9–11
Possession, 397
Post Office, 224–25
Poverty
 aiding the poor, 337–42
 cost of, 354
 cyclical, 339
 defined, 334–36
 and government programs, 63
 hard core, 337
 and inequality, 347–49
 islands of, 341–42
 line, 336
 new approaches to welfare, 342–44
 and number of poor, 340
 and racial discrimination, 344
 relative, 335
 urban, and crisis, 349–54
 war on, 338–39
 See also Discrimination; Inequality; Welfare
Predatory price cutting, 206–7
Preference line, 361
Preferred stock, 150
Pressure planning, 402
Price
 basing-point system, 239
 ceilings, 133–34
 changes in resource, 290–91
 -consumption line, 118–19
 controls, 378–79
 decontrol of, 379
 and demand, 43
 elasticity, 118–19
 equilibrium, 47–48, 127, 286–87, 415
 fixing and elasticity, 136
 floors and surpluses, 133, 135–36
 and government, 133–36
 and incentive function, 52
 inflation, 26
 and international trade, 417–18
 and isocost curve, 180–81
 leadership, 237–38
 and output in oligopoly, 234–35
 and production questions, 52–53
 rationing function of, 52
 regulated by government, 219–20
 of related goods, 43
 of resources, 280–81
 rigidity, 50, 236–37
 in Soviet economy, 406–7
 and supply, 46
 supports, 111
 system, 48, 51–53
 takers, 154
 war, 238
Price discrimination, 220
 in horizontal mergers, 250–51
 in monopoly, 215–17
Pricing
 agreements, 239
 approaches to, 241
 and income distribution, 331–32
 resources, 331–32
 two-tier, 378
Principle of diminishing marginal product, 157–59, 276
Principles of Economics, 171
Private goods, 30–31
 and services, 60–61
Private property, 59–60
Private sector, 149
Procter & Gamble, 235
Product differentiation, 228
Product safety, 59–60
Production
 advertising as factor in, 242
 changes in cost of, 46
 choosing, 29–33
 costs and decisions in, 157–74, 182–99
 four questions of, 32–33
 and labor resources, 290–311
 and leisure, 31
 in market system, 40–41
 measuring costs of, 154–57
 military, 30
 plant size and long run, 185–89
 possibilities, 22–29
 and price system, 51–53
 private versus public consumption, 30–31
 pros and cons of market system, 53–55
 and specialization, 29–30
Production-costs tariff, 435–36
Production-possibilities curve, 23, 26–29, 43–44, 362, 426
Productivity
 comparing, 422–23
 defined, 12
 of labor, 303–5
 resource, 279
 theory of marginal, 276–91
 trends in, 280
 See also Resource allocation
Professional Standards Review Organizations (PSROs), 374
Profit, 155, 207–8, 303
 defined, 156–57
 economic, 169–72
 functions of, 327–29
 theory of, 327–31
Profit maximization
 in the long run, 190–94
 in monopoly, 212–14, 215
 in the short run, 165–69
Progressive taxes, 71–74
Proletariat, 275–76, 295
Property rights, 363–64, 397
Property tax, 68
Protective tariff, 434
Psychic benefits, 329
Public choice economics, 366
Public goods, 30–31
 and services, 60–61
Public policy. *See* Congress; Government; Market power; Policies
Public sector, 149
Public utilities, 219
Pure sciences, 4
Pure theory of international trade, 415

Quaker Oats, 255
Quality standards on imports, 487
Quesnay, François, 8
Quotas, 436–37

Racial discrimination, 304, 344
Radio Corporation of America (RCA), 257
Railroads, 223, 250, 261–62, 263–64
Rate bureaus, 223
Rates of return, 319, 324

Rationing, 133
  function, 52
Reagan, Ronald, 10
Real interest rate, 321
Real wages, 303, 310
Reciprocal Trade Agreements Act, 440
Regional Rail Reorganization Act (1973), 263
Regional Transit Authority, 224
Regressive tax, 68–69
Regulation, weakness of, 262–63
Relative poverty, 335
Rent, theory of, 314–18
Rent control, 134–35
Research and development (R and D), 28–29
Resource allocation, 155, 274–91
  background, 274–76
  capital, theory of interest, 21, 313, 318–27
  earnings of resource suppliers, 288–91
  entrepreneurship, theory of profit, 21, 313, 327–31
  and income distribution, 331–32
  in international trade, 421–22
  and labor, 21, 293–311
  land, theory of rent, 20–21, 313, 314–18
  and market demand, 279–83
  for maximum profit, 283–86
  in perfect competition, short run, 155, 157
  pricing and income, 331–32
  and resource supply, 27–28, 286–88
  and theory of marginal productivity, 276–79
  See also Capital; Labor; Land
Resource Conservation and Recovery Act (1976), 388
Resource productivity, 279
Retail Clerks International Association, 297
Retail stores, elasticity of demand in, 114–15
Retailers, 158–59
Reuther, Walter, 298
Revenue, of state and local governments, 68
Revenue sharing, 68
Revenue tariffs, 433–34
Reverse discrimination, 13
Reynolds, R. J., 260, 264
Ricardo, David, 11, 275, 332
Right-to-work laws, 295
Risk, 323, 325, 328
  component, 324
Risk, Uncertainty, and Profit, 330
Robinson, Joan, 229
Robinson-Patman Act (1936), 256
Rockefeller, John D., 249, 251
Roosevelt, Franklin D., 255
Roosevelt, Theodore, 253, 254
Rule of reason, 258
Russia. *See* Union of Soviet Socialist Republics
Russian Revolution, 404
Salary, 303
Sales tax, 68
SALT treaty, 270
Satisficing, 215
Saudi Arabia, 446
Savings, 322–23
  and investment, 319
Scanlon, Joseph, 296
Scarce resources, 19
Scarcity, problem of, 20
Schedule of demand, 41
Schultze, Charles L., 378
Schumpeter, Joseph A., 268
Scientific method, 5–6
Secondary boycott, 295, 440
Sectors, 149
Securities and Exchange Commission (SEC), 62, 222
Service Employees International Union, 297
Seven Sisters, 149, 259, 260
Sex discrimination, 344. *See also* Women
Shakers, 393
Shared monopoly, 255–56, 261
Shaw, George Bernard, 33, 262
Shell Oil, 259
Sherman Antitrust Act (1890), 251, 254, 257, 259, 261, 268
Shop steward, 296
Shopping malls, and monopoly, 213
Short run, 125
Short-run supply curve, 128
Shortage, 47, 51, 133–34
Shriver, Sargent, 338
Shut-down point, 170
Simon, Herbert, 215
Simons, Henry, 330
Singapore, 444
Single proprietorship, 149
Single tax, 316–17
Slavery, 397
Small Business Administration, 249, 288
Smith, Adam, 11, 40–41, 52, 152, 266, 276, 293, 363
Smoot-Hawley Tariff, 440
Social benefits, 198–99
Social Choice and Individual Values, 364
Social costs, 198–99
  assessment of, 61–62
  of market system, 53–55
Social economies and diseconomies, 198–99
Social responsibility, 59
Social sciences, 5
Social Security, 10, 66–67, 69, 70
  Act, 339
  Administration, 336
  taxes, 73–74, 337–39, 348, 349
  Trust Fund, 73–74, 339
Socialism, 34–35
  defined, 34, 396
  market, 53, 396
Socially necessary labor, 394
Solar energy, 383
South Africa, 438
South Korea, 438, 444
Soviet Union. *See* Union of Soviet Socialist Republics
Soyuztorgreklama (National Trade Advertising, USSR), 243
Spain, 423, 438, 439
Special Drawing Rights (SDR), 443
Specialization, 29–30, 414–15, 417–18
Specific subsidy, 131
Specific tax, 128–29
Spillover effects, 365
Split-level society, 350
Squeeze operation, 207–8
Sri Lanka, 444
Stalin, Joseph, 33
Standard Oil
  of California, 259
  of New Jersey, 254, 258
  of Ohio, 249, 251
Stanford, Leland, 249
Steinbeck, John, 341
Stigler, George J., 268, 330
Stocks, 150–51
Strategic-industry tariff, 435
Strike, 296–97
Stripper wells, 378
Structure, of industry, 268
Subsidies, 128, 131–32, 221, 223, 288
Substantive ownership, 397
Substitutability, 281
Substitute goods, 42, 111–12, 114–15, 229
Substitution effect, 102, 103
Sumitomo, 258
"Sunset Amendment," 222
Superior goods, 43, 97, 103
Supplementary Security Income (SSI), 337
Suppliers, expectations of, 46
Supply
  change in, 45–46
  curve, 45, 121–24, 302–3, 379–80
  global, 415
  law of, 44–45
  and market equilibrium, 47–51
  schedules, 45
Supply, elasticity of
  calculating, 123
  and decontrolling prices, 379
  defined, 122–24
  determination of, 124–27
  and government policy, 121–39
  in the market, 128–32
  and price setting, 133–36
Supreme Court
  and antitrust laws, 116, 253, 254, 255, 258, 260–61
  and cross-elasticity of demand, 116
  and professional advertising, 262
Surplus, 47, 51, 135–36
  consumer, 88–89
  value, 394
Sweden, 34, 279, 335, 396, 404, 423, 438
Sweezy, Paul, 218

Switzerland, 335
Syndicalists, 294
Synergism, 414, 424
Synthetic fuels, 381
Syria, 440

Taft-Hartley Act (1948), 295
Taiwan, 439, 442, 444
Tariffs, 70, 433–36
Tariff of Abominations (1928), 440
Tax
  ad valorem, 128–29
  advantages to investors, 32
  city, 68
  code loopholes, 72
  credits, 322
  and demand elasticity/inelasticity, 128, 129–30
  to discourage resource use, 288
  and disincentives, 130–31
  estate, 70
  excise, 70
  gasoline, 70
  gift, 70
  "hidden," 367
  on imports, 132
  incidence, 74, 130
  income, and marginal utility, 86–87
  inequalities, 349
  inequities, 54
  on land, 315–17
  negative, 75
  negative income, 342–44
  net, 75
  oil-depletion allowance, 260
  personal and income, 68
  and pollution, 62
  progressive, 68, 71–74, 86–87
  property, 68
  proportional, 68
  and public benefits, 54–55
  regressive, 68–69
  sales, 68
  single, 316–17
  in Soviet economy, 406–7
  structures, evaluation of, 74–75
  transfer, 131
  turnover, 406
  user, 70
  Value-Added, 73, 437*fn*
  and Vietnam war, 26
  on windfall profits, 380
Teamsters Union, 223, 295, 298
Technology, 28–29, 328, 363
  and farming, 142–43
  and monopoly, 219
  and supply curves, 137
  and supply elasticity, 126–27
  and trade, 441
Technostructure, 294
Terms of trade, 428–31, 436
Texaco, 259
Textron, 257
Thailand, 335, 444
Theory
  of consumer choice, 78, 80
  of interest, 318–27
  of marginal productivity, 276–79
  Marxist, 218, 275–76, 293, 394–96
  of profit, 327–31
  of rent, 314–18
The Theory of Capitalist Development, 218
The Theory of the Leisure Class, 207
Theory of Political Economy, 90
Therbligs, 283
Third-party health plans, 372
Third World, 428–29, 445
Time
  and elasticity, 113
  and elasticity of supply, 125
Time and motion studies, 283–84
Time series graph, 17
Tinbergen, Jan, 8
Title, 397
Tito, Marshal, 409, 410
Total costs, 162
Total product, 159–61
Total revenue, 108–9, 110, 165–66
Total utility, 81–82
Tokyo Round, 441
Trade. *See* International trade
Trade Act (1974), 438
Trademarks, 243–44
Traditional economic systems, 33–34
Transfer payments, 66–67, 399–400
Transfer tax, 131
"Trickle-down" theory, 328
Trusts, 249
Turnover tax, 406
Two-tier pricing, for oil, 378
Tying contracts, 254

Uncertainty, 328, 330
Undifferentiated oligopoly, 244
Unemployment, 12, 300–301, 339–41, 346–47
  compensation, 340
  rates of, 64
  of resources, 25–26
Union of Soviet Socialist Republics, 31, 32, 34, 133, 193, 383, 396, 398, 399, 419, 440
  advertising in, 243
  black market in, 134–35
  consuming and selling in, 407
  and defense, 270
  economic planning process of, 400–404
  economic system of, 400, 404–9
  five-year plans, 28, 33, 404
  and international trade, 408
  production possibilities of, 28
  sale of grain to, 144
Unions
  activity of, 295–97
  brief history of, 294–95
  collective bargaining, 295–96
  contracts, 50, 295–96
  craft, 308–9
  industrial, 294
  labor issues for 1980s, 298–301
  and labor market, 308–11
  public employee, 298
  shop, 295
  trends in membership of, 297–98
  and wages, 308–11
  See also Labor
Unit elasticity, 105
United Auto Workers, 294, 298, 300
United Mine Workers, 291
United Nations Conference on Trade and Development (UNCTAD), 430
United States
  agriculture in, 141–46
  barriers to trade, 438–39
  economic system of, 40–41
  estimated wealth (1976), 326
  farmland of, 318
  and foreign competition, 217
  and government expenditures, 66–67
  growth compared to Soviet Union, 406
  labor force of, 301
  poverty in, 334–44
  power through trade, 415
  private versus public consumption, 31
  production possibilities of, 28
  structure of government, 64–65
  trade and GNP, 419–21
United States Energy Research and Development Administration. *See* Department of Energy
United States Export-Import Bank, 442
United States International Trade Commission. *See* International Trade Commission
United States Postal Service, 224–25
United States Steel Company, 239, 251, 253, 255, 346
United States Treasury, 438
United Steel Workers, 296
Unlimited liability, 149
Unlimited wants, 19
Upward Bound, 338
Urban finance, 350–52. *See also* Cities
User tax, 70
Usufruct, 397
Utility
  analysis, 84–85
  defined, 80
  graphing, 82
  marginal, 80–81, 83–91
  total, 81–82
Utils, 80

Value
  added, 264
  -Added Tax (VAT), 73, 437*fn*
  determining, 171
  labor theory of, 275, 289, 394
  and market choices, 364

Vanderbilt, Cornelius, 249, 250
Variable capital, 394
Variable costs, 162
Variable resources, 157
Veblen, Thorstein, 207–8, 293
Venezuela, 377, 445
Vertical demand curves, 106
Vertical merger, 249, 251, 256
Vietnam, 396, 398
Vietnam war, 26, 270
Villard, Henry, 249
von Hayek, Friedrich, 330

Wage, 298–99
  defined, 303
  determination, 305–11
  effect of international trade on, 419
  and leisure, 301–2
  in military, 309
  minimum, 304
  and price controls, 326
  real, 303, 310
  rental component of, 317–18
  for Soviet Workers, 405
  subsistence, 395
  and union activity, 308–11
War on poverty, 63, 338–39
Weber case, 13
Weidenbaum, Murray, 369
Welfare
  cheating, 337
  economics, 362–67
  economists, 337
  See also Discrimination; Inequality; Poverty
West Germany, 32, 296, 335, 418, 429, 443, 445
Western Europe, 34, 223, 306, 445
Wheeler-Lea Amendment (1938), 243, 254
Wildcat strike, 297
Wilson, Woodrow, 254
Windfall profits, 380
Women
  in the labor market, 345
  sex discrimination against, 344
  and unemployment, 64
  See also Discrimination
Work versus leisure, 301–2
Work Incentive Program, 338
Worker mobility, 306
Workfare plan, 343
World Bank, 444
World Coal Study Organization, 381
World War I, 404
World War II, 133, 134, 191, 195, 223, 238, 253, 256, 258, 262, 269, 291, 326, 345, 352, 363, 377, 404, 407, 409, 421, 429, 443, 445
Worldwatch Institute, 306
Wurf, Jerry, 298

Yasuda, 258
Yield, 323
Yield curve, 325
Yugoslavia, 53, 400, 409–10

Zero population growth, 3